explorer

GW01458262

Qatar
Residents' Guide

ther**e**'s more to life...
ask**explorer**.com

www.education.gov.qa

e-Education

المجلس الأعلى للتعليم

SUPREME
EDUCATION
COUNCIL

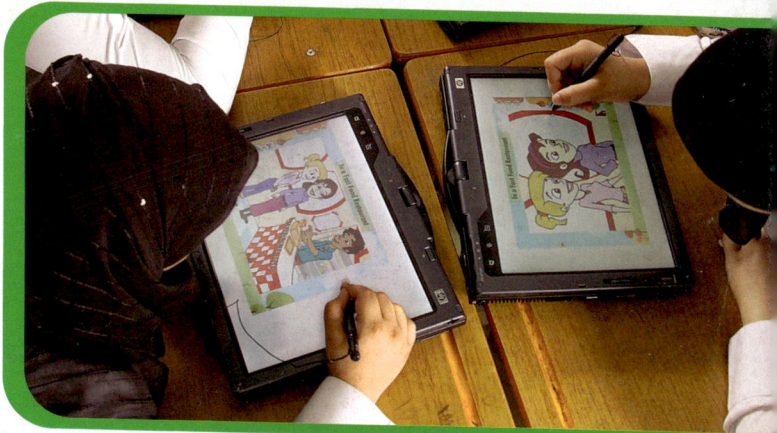

 twitter  facebook

شاورما البيسانة
Shawarma Albisana

Shawarma Albisana...
you'll taste the difference

An Everlasting Tradition
Succulent, thinly sliced chicken and beef stripes grilled to perfection on charcoal, wrapped in wholesome fresh pita bread.

Sunday to Wednesday : 3 PM to 12 PM
Thursday to Saturday   : 1 PM to 1 AM

Katara Valley of Cultures - Doha, Qatar
Tel. +974 44081400 | Fax. +974 44082086

كنافة البيسانة
Albisana Kunafa

Come, discover delightful Kunafa treats

An Everlasting Tradition
Crisp, delicate shredded strands of homemade fresh kunafa, fragrant Nabulsi cheese, drizzled with delightful sugar syrup and sprinkled with crushed pistachios.

Sunday to Wednesday : 3 PM to 12 PM
Thursday to Saturday   : 1 PM to 1 AM

Katara Valley of Cultures - Doha, Qatar
Tel. +974 44081200 | Fax. +974 44082086

CELEBRATING
40 YEARS

Reputation built
on trust for
over 40 years.

• AL MUFTAH SERVICES • AL MUFTAH REAL ESTATE
• AL MUFTAH GARAGE • AL MUFTAH TRANSPORT

AL MUFTAH
RENT A CAR SINCE 1971
Comfort on wheels

PO Box 1316, Doha, Qatar. Main Office,
D-Ring Road Tel: (+974) 44634444/44328100
Fax: (+974) 44414339
E-mail: rac@qatar.net.qa

Grand Hamad Avenue Tel: (+974) 44426649/4432840 Fax: (+974) 44312899
Airport Tel: (+974) 44634433 (Open 24 Hours), Mob: (+974) 55525639
C-Ring Road Tel: (+974) 44442003 Fax: (+974) 44441003
Ras Laffan Industrial City (RLC Complex) Tel: (+974) 44748840
Al Khor Tel: (+974) 44113344
Bahrain Office: P.O. Box 75287 Tel / Fax: (+973) 17179190 Mob: (+973) 66331234
Email: rac@rentacarbahrain.com

w w w . r e n t a c a r d o h a . c o m

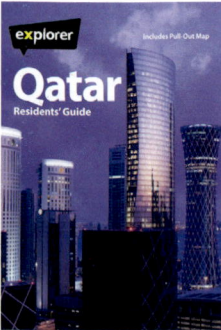

Qatar Explorer 2012/5th Edition
First Published 2006
1st Edition (Revised) 2007
2nd Edition 2008
3rd Edition 2010
4th Edition 2011
5th Edition 2012 ISBN 978-9948-450-84-9

Copyright © Explorer Group Ltd, 2006, 2007, 2008, 2010, 2011, 2012.
All rights reserved.

Front Cover Photograph – Qatar Skyline – Victor Romero

Printed and bound by Emirates Printing Press, Dubai, United Arab Emirates.

Explorer Publishing & Distribution
PO Box 34275, Dubai
United Arab Emirates

Phone	+971 (0)4 340 8805
Fax	+971 (0)4 340 8806
Email	info@askexplorer.com
Web	askexplorer.com

While every effort and care has been made to ensure the accuracy of the
information contained in this publication, the publisher cannot accept
responsibility for any errors or omissions it may contain.
No part of this publication may be reproduced, stored in a retrieval system, or
transmitted, in any form or by any means, electronic, mechanical, photocopying,
recording or otherwise, without the prior permission in writing of the publisher.

Welcome...

...to the 5th edition of the **Qatar Residents' Guide**, the ultimate insider's guide to living in and loving this fascinating country. From red-tape procedures to hotels and restaurants, we've got everything covered to help you make the most of your time in Qatar.

If you're still at home and thinking about making the move, **A Country Profile** (p.1) will give you an overview of Qatar's history, geography, culture and economics, while **Becoming A Resident** (p.29) will give you a sense of what it's like actually living here, plus directions to navigate the paperwork.

Work (p.99) and **Housing** (p.67) are jam packed with the essential info you'll need to set yourself up with that all important job and a place to live.

Once you've found your feet, **Discover Doha** (p.187) will be your personal tour guide for the capital, and **Out Of The City** (p.231) gives you insight into exploring the rest of Qatar and beyond.

To fill up your time off, get involved with your favourite **Activities & Hobbies** (p.263). Whether you're looking to furnish your new pad or find a killer outfit, **Shopping** (p.285) will guide you through Qatar's stores, souks, malls and markets. When it comes to hitting the town, **Going Out** (p.339) provides comprehensive reviews for the best restaurants, bars and clubs.

So now it's over to you. Get out there, explore and enjoy all that Qatar has to offer. If you think something has been missed out then log onto **askexplorer.com/qatar**, and share the knowledge with your fellow explorers. And don't forget – whether it's dining out or driving off-road, working in the gulf or whizzing off for a weekend break, Explorer has a guide for you. Check out all our guides, photography books, calendars and maps online.

There's more to life...
The Explorer Team

ask**explorer**.com

Mike Crosby

Mike arrived in Qatar on a four month work contract and much to his surprise, discovered a strong affinity with the culture. Twenty plus years later and he is still happy here. When he is not sailing, diving or motor boating he likes nothing better than a weekend desert camping.
Favourite Restaurant: The Grill Restaurant (p.360).
Best thing about living in Qatar: Floating around in the warm blue sea at one of the offshore islands (p.243) on a Friday afternoon.

Christine Gerber Rutt

Christine is a freelance writer and blogger. Since she moved to Qatar a few years ago, she's dedicated herself to uncovering the secrets of Doha, especially those outside the realm of five-star hotels.
Top-tip for a new Qatar resident: Exercise makes you less susceptible to illness and works out frustrations; good humour even more so, of course (p.177).
Best Qatar memory: Lying in a tent just metres from the Arabian Sea and watching the sun rise out from the blue ocean.

Shabina S. Khatri

Shabina is an American journalist who has lived in Qatar for several years. She teaches journalism at Northwestern University in Qatar and blogs for various websites. She is also the founder of DohaNews.com.
Favourite spot in Doha: Rumailah Park, across from the Corniche. The food stand there sells the best hot chocolate! (p.214).
Best Qatar memory: Picking up a roasted chicken and eating it with my husband on the Corniche while looking out at out the water.

Thanks...

There are many people who have dedicated their time and effort to the production of this book. Thanks in particular to our wonderful contributors and researchers who work tirelessly, pounding the streets, knocking on doors, tracking down leads and following rumours to bring you exciting hole in the wall restaurants, elusive organisations, and tucked away shops, museums and galleries; thanks to Frances Gillespe, Joe Chua Agdeppa, Katy Gillett and our whole team of reviewers who have chomped their way through dinners and been scrubbed, rubbed, wrapped and kneaded in the name of research. Thanks also go to everyone who has helped us explore Qatar and contributed suggestions and leads, particularly Abdallah Bibi, Dania Khaled, Fatima Ali Abdullha and Sarie Botes. Of course, our sincerest thanks goes to you, our fabulous readers and fellow Explorers, without whose comments, updates and passion for exploring, you would not be holding this marvellous guide book.

We've got Qatar covered

explorer

askexplorer.com

askexplorer

Contents

THE BOX IS OPEN.

THE COOLEST GIFTS AND TOYS IN TOWN.
RED BOX SECTION AT VIRGIN MEGASTORE.

ReD Box

Virgin MEGASTORE

Villaggio Mall Tel. 44135823 - Landmark Mall Tel. 44182245
www.virginmegastore.qa - facebook/virginmena

Qatar: A Country Profile

QATAR

Progressive and ambitious, Qatar is a Gulf nation that proudly retains its Arab heritage while also striving for modernity. The country is an international business and leisure hub, home to a multi-ethnic, global population, and is also a treasure trove of Arabic and Islamic cultural and historical heritage. Welcome to a nation which is rapidly opening up to the world, with spectacular mega-projects like the Pearl Qatar, the critically acclaimed Museum of Islamic Arts, mystical old souks full of hidden surprises, grandiose, bustling supermalls, beguiling deserts and endless charming beaches. Qatar also boasts a furiously developing sports scene which has led to the successful staging of the Asian Games in 2006 and the 2011 AFC Asian Cup. At the end of 2010, the world watched Qatar win the bid to host the 2022 FIFA Football World Cup and, looking ahead, the country is gearing up its efforts to bid for the 2024 Summer Olympics. Whether you're relocating here or just visiting, you can expect your time in Qatar to be a unique experience in a fascinating culture.

Location

The Gulf state of Qatar is a peninsula surrounded by the waters of the Arabian Gulf and anchored to the mainland at its border with Saudi Arabia. The country is about 11,437 square kilometres, running roughly 85km wide and 180km long, and located in the centre of the Gulf Cooperation Council (GCC) countries. Mud flats and sandy beaches make up a large portion of the shoreline, which is dotted with inlets and coves. The interior terrain is mostly flat, varying from just 6m above sea level in places to 103m at Qurayn Abu Al Bawl. Some rocky limestone outcrops are found in the most southern parts of the country, as well as spectacular sand dunes.

Qatar also encompasses several islands such as Sheraouh, Al Aliyah, Al Bushayriyah, Al Safiliyah and, about 80km north-east of the capital, Halul. This island, operated by Qatar Petroleum, is of particular importance as it serves as the export terminal for marine crude oil produced from Qatar's offshore oilfields.

The majority of the population of Qatar resides in the capital city, Doha, which is located on the east coast. Other major towns in the country include Mesaieed, Dukhan, Al Khor, Al Shamal and Al Wakra.

Qatar Fact Box

Coordinates: 25° 16' 55.59" N, 51° 31' 03.82" E
Bordering countries: Saudi Arabia
Total land borders: 60km
Total land area: 11,437 sq km
Bordering seas: Arabian Gulf
Total coastline: 563km

Climate

Qatar's subtropical desert climate is characterised by mild winters and very hot summers, with highs reaching over 40°C (104°F). The weather is highly agreeable between September and May, with warm temperatures and blue skies a feature of the majority of days. It becomes very hot and humid from June to August, when many residents join the summer exodus to their home countries to escape the oppressive and sometimes unbearable heat. Average rainfall is 81mm per year with an average high temperature of 31°C and lows of 22°C. Maximum temperatures average at 41°C in July, but fall to around 22°C in January, with average minimum temperatures ranging from 29°C in July to 13°C in January. There is also quite a large variance between daytime and night time temperatures.

Qatar Adds Digit To Phone Numbers

In July 2010, Qatar added an eighth digit to all mobile and landline phone numbers in the country. Officials said the move is an effort to create more phone numbers in a country that has seen its population double in a short period of time.

Under the plan, the first digit of both the fixed and mobile numbers gets repeated. Thus, if the old number started with 3, 4, 5, 6 or 7 all you need to do is to repeat the first digit such as 33, 44, 55, 66 and 77. All emergency telephone numbers within Qatar, including 999 and 112, remain unaffected by the change, and the country code is, as before, +974. Numbers beginning with 1, 2, 8 and 9 were not changed.

Generally, Qatar is humid, with average highs of 75%, although there is a slight dip in the evenings. With limited amounts of fresh water from ground wells, rain offers the only respite. Rainfall is rare, though not as unheard of as some locals might suggest. Due to its sporadic occurrence, there are no gutters on the roads so they can become flooded with standing water when the skies do finally open. Rural wadis (usually dry riverbeds) fill during the infrequent rainfall, satisfying the scarce vegetation. The lack of rainfall means only about 1% of the country is arable, with permanent crops registering barely a blip in the yearly agricultural output.

For updated weather reports, the local newspapers offer good daily versions in print and online (see gulf-times.com and thepeninsulaqatar.com), while the Qatar Civil Aviation Authority Meteorological Department website (qweather.net) is another local source of climate information. Additionally, bbc.co.uk has a reputable worldwide weather service, including a five-day forecast option.

HISTORY

Archaeologists uncovered evidence of human habitation in Qatar possibly dating back to the fourth and fifth millennia BC. In the fifth century BC the Greek historian Herodotus referenced the Canaanites as Qatar's first inhabitants, while the country also features on old maps of the region, suggesting that Qatar has been known to seafarers and traders since ancient times. As Islam swept the region in the seventh century AD, the inhabitants of Qatar are said to have aided the formation of the first Islamic naval fleet, a supposition aided by Qatar's maritime traditions like pearl fishing. The country also became well known for the quality of its textile manufacturing (especially cloaks) and for the making of arrow heads.

Around the 13th and 14th centuries, Qatar enjoyed a favourable relationship with the Caliphates (successors of the Prophet Mohammed) in Baghdad and it became an important centre for pearl trading. Evidence from this Abbasid era (Caliphate rule) can be seen in the architecture of Murwab Fort on Qatar's west coast. In the 16th and 17th centuries the Portuguese were a powerful force throughout the Gulf region. To protect itself from occupation and aggression, Qatar aligned with the Turks. This saw the start of over three centuries of rule by the Ottoman Empire, although throughout this period the real power in Qatar remained with local sheikhs.

The ancestors of today's ruling family, the Al Thanis, arrived in Qatar in the early 18th century. Originating from a branch of the Bani Tamim tribe from Najd in modern-day Saudi Arabia, they first settled in southern Qatar before moving to the north of the peninsula in the mid 1700s. Qatar, and especially the northern town of Zubarah, continued to be a key centre for the pearl trade.

Sandstorms

During winter, spring or even summer, the country can be dusty and occasional sandstorms can cause irritation to eyes if unprotected. The best option during a severe sandstorm is to remain indoors, and close all windows to avoid the dust finding its way into your home.

In the mid 19th century Sheikh Mohammed Bin Thani established Al Bidda, the modern city of Doha, as the capital and seat of power. Soon after, in 1868, a treaty negotiated with the British recognised him as the first official Emir of Qatar. This treaty signed with the British also recognised Qatar's independence. Three years later, Sheikh Mohammed signed another

Skyscrapers along Doha Corniche

History

treaty with the Turks, accepting protection against external attack. A Turkish garrison was established in Doha, but the relationship was an uneasy one and the Ottomans were forced to abandon Doha in 1915. In 1916, Sheikh Abdullah Al Thani signed a further treaty with the British promising not to enter into relations with any other power without prior consent. In return, Britain guaranteed the protection of Qatar 'from all aggression by sea'.

A number of factors, including worldwide economic depression and the introduction of cultured Japanese pearls, led to an almost complete collapse of the Gulf's pearling industry in the 1930s. Pearling had been the mainstay of Qatar's economy for generations, and while life for the country's inhabitants had never been easy, this development was a desperate blow. The region was plunged into dire poverty, and disease was rife among the undernourished people.

A glimmer of hope was provided by the discovery of oil. Bahrain had become the first Gulf state to discover oil earlier in the decade and, in 1935, Sheikh Abdullah signed the first Oil Concession Agreement with the Anglo-Persian Oil Company. Drilling began and oil was discovered in Dukhan in 1939. The onset

of the Second World War halted production almost immediately, and the first oil wasn't exported from Qatar until 10 years later. This new-found wealth transformed the lives of the population beyond recognition, as the rulers set about modernising the country's infrastructure and creating healthcare and education facilities. The wealth generated from oil exports, and the discovery and exploitation of the world's largest single reservoir of natural gas, means that Qatar today enjoys one of the highest levels of per capita income in the world.

In 1968, Britain announced its intention to withdraw from the Gulf region. Qatar entered into talks with Bahrain and the Trucial States (now the United Arab Emirates) with the intention of forming a federation, but agreement could not be reached and after Bahrain withdrew from the discussions, Qatar followed suit. When the British left in September 1971, Qatar became officially independent. The ruler at the time was Sheikh Ahmed bin Ali Al Thani, but he was succeeded the following year by his cousin Sheikh Khalifa bin Hamad Al Thani, with the full support of the ruling family, the Qatari people and the armed forces. Sheikh Khalifa led Qatar into a period of

QATAR TIMELINE

7th century AD	Islam sweeps the Arabian peninsula. Inhabitants of Qatar help form the first naval fleet
13th century	Qatar becomes established as a key pearling centre
16th century	Qatar aligns with the Ottomans as protection against the Portuguese
Early 18th century	Ancestors of the Al Thani arrive in Qatar
Mid 18th century	Mohammed Al Thani establishes Al Bidda (Doha) as capital
1868	Treaty signed with the British, recognising Qatar's independence, and Mohammed Al Thani as the first Emir
1871	Treaty signed with the Turks, accepting protection against external attack
1915	The Ottomans abandon Doha
1916	A further protection treaty signed with the British
1930s	Pearl industry collapses
1939	Oil found in Dukhan
1949	First oil exported from Qatar
1971	Discovery of the world's largest single concentration of natural gas
1971	Qatar declares independence on 3 September
1995	Sheikh Hamad Al Thani succeeds his father Sheikh Khalifa as Emir of Qatar
1995	The Qatar Foundation for Education, Science and Community Development is established
2006	The 15th Asian Games are held in Doha
2008	Northwestern University becomes latest varsity to join the Education City complex featuring top universities from around the world
2009	Qatar Science & Technology Park, the country's first free zone, opens its doors and the first residents move into their homes on the country's manmade island, The Pearl Qatar
2010	FIFA awards Qatar the World Cup 2022 bid. Since the announcement, the country is pouring billions into developing the infrastructure to support the Cup
2011	The AFC Asian Cup is held in Doha

continued prosperity, especially thanks to the huge rises in oil and gas prices during the 1970s. He also went some way to diversifying Qatar's economy by establishing facilities for producing goods such as steel and fertiliser.

In June 1995, Sheikh Khalifa was succeeded as Emir by his son and heir, the Crown Prince and Minister of Defence, Sheikh Hamad bin Khalifa Al Thani. Sheikh Hamad continued with the modernisation and liberalisation programmes he had started as Crown Prince. Press freedom was extended and, in 1997, the state-funded satellite TV news channel Al Jazeera was launched, quickly gaining a reputation for its outspoken coverage of sensitive topics. In 1999 the country took its first steps towards democracy, when free elections for the Central Municipal Council were held. Women were allowed to stand for office as well as to vote. Sheikh Hamad is seen as a progressive ruler and is widely respected by Qatar's citizens, who benefit from the country's wealth in the form of free or subsidised healthcare, education and housing. His wife, Sheikha Mozah bint Nasser Al Missned, is a popular public figure (see Sheikha Mozah: A Profile (p.5).

In April 2003, Qataris voted to approve a new constitution, which established a 45-member parliament. Thirty members of parliament were directly elected and the remainder were to be appointed, with the new constitution overwhelmingly accepted with 96% of the votes. The new constitution came into effect in 2005, and in early 2007 the first legislative elections in the history of Qatar took place to choose a new consultative assembly. In 2008, Qatar made a significant mark on the diplomatic stage by hosting several European leaders, and also by playing a leading role in mediating in regional conflicts, such as helping to resolve the internal political crisis in Lebanon – the settlement reached is commonly known as the Doha Agreement. In December of 2010, Qatar, which had already hosted the biggest Asian Games in history in 2006, won its bid to host the FIFA Football World Cup in 2022. In the ensuing decade, the government plans to pour billions of dollars into developing transportation, stadia, housing and other infrastructure to support the tournament.

GOVERNMENT & RULING FAMILY

Qatar is governed by hereditary rule. The head of state is the Emir, His Highness Sheikh Hamad bin Khalifa Al Thani, who came to power in 1995. He has introduced many reforms and steered the country towards a more open and democratic system of government. The Emir's son, His Highness Sheikh Tamim bin Hamad Al Thani, is the crown prince and heir apparent.

SHEIKHA MOZAH: A PROFILE

Sheikha Mozah bint Nasser Al Missned is the wife of His Highness Sheikh Hamad bin Khalifa Al Thani, the Emir of the State of Qatar. As Qatar's 'first lady' she has won international recognition for her wide-ranging work in education development and other social programmes. As the chairperson of the Qatar Foundation (see p.146), she has become an icon of progressive change and educational activism in countries throughout the region and the world. She is also the vice chair of the Supreme Education Council, the president of the Supreme Council for Family Affairs, and has initiated programmes for the under-privileged, people with disabilities and children with special needs through these various positions. On an international level she has worked to raise education standards around the world as part of her role as Unesco special envoy for basic and higher education, and in 2003 established the International Fund for Iraqi Higher Education to help with the rehabilitation of Iraqi schools. In 2007 she was named as one of *Forbes* magazine's 100 most powerful women in the world. Her website, mozahbintnasser.qa, gives details of her many projects and causes.

A 2003 referendum saw a permanent constitution overwhelmingly approved by the local people. The Emir holds legislative and executive powers and he appoints a Council of Ministers by an emiri decree. The head of this council is the prime minister and foreign minister Sheikh Hamad bin Jassem bin Jabr Al Thani (elected in 2007). The role of the Council of Ministers is threefold: to draft, discuss and vote on proposed laws, after consultation with the Advisory (or Consultative) Council, the Majlis Al Shura; to approve the national budget; and to monitor the performance of ministers.

The constitution promises freedom and equality, and provides for a 45 member Majlis Al Shura, two thirds of which are elected by the public with the remaining members appointed by the emir. The first Shura Council elections were held on 1 April 2007. Qatar held historic democratic elections in 1999 (subsequently held every four years) for the Central Municipal Council (CMC), made up of 29 councillors representing the country's municipalities.

Women were eligible to vote and stand for election, and in 2003 Sheikha Al Jefairia was the first woman to be elected, and received a record highest number of votes in that election.

The CMC has consultative (but no executive) powers and is aimed at improving services in the municipalities.

Qatar
In Figures

World Cup 2022

Qatar emerged victorious from the bidding campaign in 2010 and will become the first Middle Eastern nation to host the FIFA World Cup, in 2022. To combat the conditions of the extreme summer heat (which can rise above 45°C), Qatar has proposed nine state-of-the-art, low-carbon, climate-controlled stadia to silence critics.

Qatar GDP By Sector

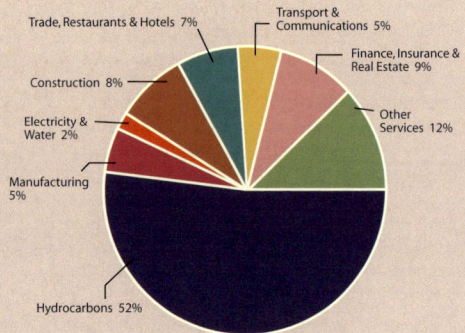

Trade, Restaurants & Hotels 7%
Transport & Communications 5%
Construction 8%
Finance, Insurance & Real Estate 9%
Electricity & Water 2%
Other Services 12%
Manufacturing 5%
Hydrocarbons 52%

Source: IMF Article IV consultations, 2009

Temperature & Humidity

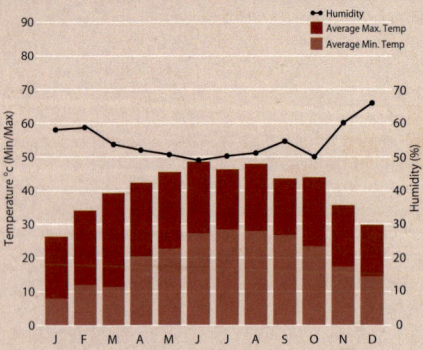

- Humidity
- Average Max. Temp
- Average Min. Temp

Source: State of Qatar, The Planning Council

Rainfall

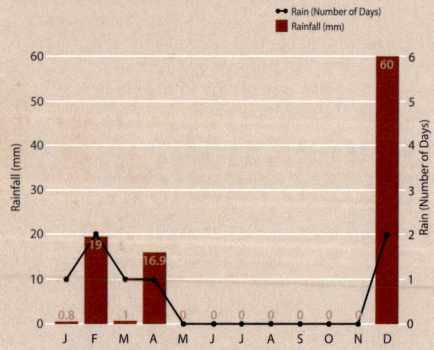

- Rain (Number of Days)
- Rainfall (mm)

Source: State of Qatar, The Planning Council

High Earners

Salaries in Qatar are officially the highest in the Middle East, as revealed by jobsite Bayt.com in 2011. Research showed that 39% of professionals in Qatar earned between $3,000-$8,000 per month, while only 37% of their UAE counterparts fell into this bracket. Over 10% earned above $8,000 in Qatar.

Live Long

The CIA World Factbook estimates that the average life expectancy in Qatar is 75.7 years – that's just over 74 years for men and over 77 for women.

Education Levels

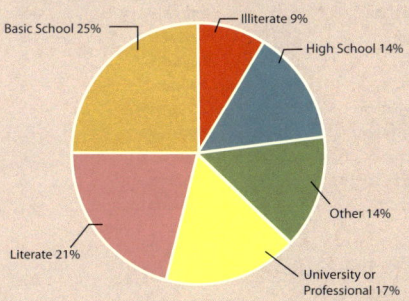

Basic School 25%
Illiterate 9%
High School 14%
Other 14%
University or Professional 17%
Literate 21%

Source: State of Qatar, The Planning Council

Qatar's Ethnic Make-Up

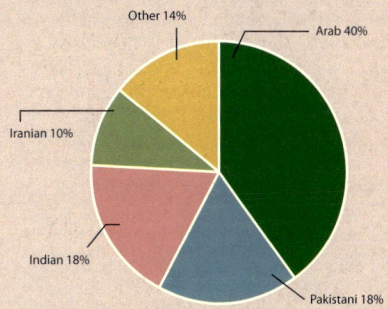

Other 14%
Arab 40%
Iranian 10%
Indian 18%
Pakistani 18%

Source: CIA World Factbook

Qatar Population Age Breakdown

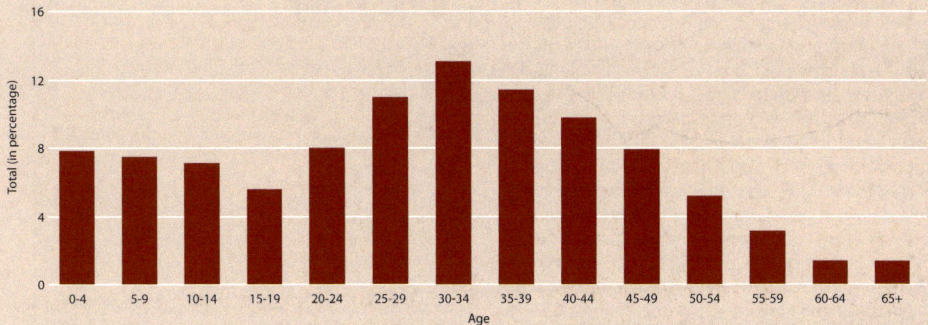

Source: State of Qatar, The Planning Council

INTERNATIONAL RELATIONS

Qatar is gaining a reputation as a successful mediator in both regional and international politics. The country stepped in and successfully mediated negotiations in the 2008 Lebanon political conflict, which resulted in celebrated peace accords; it has also mediated in other conflicts, including in the Darfur region. Overall, Qatar plays a key role in regional politics. In 2009, the country chaired the Arab League and hosted the Arab League Summit. In 2011, Qatar gained worldwide attention during the popular revolutions also known as the Arab Spring that took place across the Middle East; the only Gulf country that did not see protests, Qatar publicly backed revolutions in Egypt, Yemen and Libya.

Qatar is committed to the support of Arab unity, and enjoys strong international relations, but in the 1990s upset its Arab neighbours when discussions took place with Israel regarding the possible supply of natural gas. Qatar is a founding member of the Gulf Cooperation Council (GCC), which includes Saudi Arabia, Kuwait, Oman, UAE and Bahrain. The objective of the GCC is to encourage integration and coordination between member states. Presidency of the GCC rotates annually between its members. All major embassies and consulates are represented in Qatar and the country is a member of the International Monetary Fund (IMF), the Organisation of Petroleum Exporting Countries (Opec), the United Nations (UN), the World Health Organisation (WHO) and the World Trade Organisation (WTO).

FACTS & FIGURES

Population

There are varying estimates of Qatar's population, with projections for 2009 varying from around 1.2 million (World Bank sources) to 1.4 million (UN), to 1.69 million from the Qatar Statistics Authority. Whatever the exact total is, no one can dispute the fact that Qatar's population has grown exponentially in recent years. With the total population having stood at around half a million some 10 years ago, the rapid rise is expected to continue despite the economic crisis which has seen population levels fall in other Gulf countries. Officials in the country had expected a slowdown in population growth or even a reverse trend as a result of the global financial catastrophe, but numbers reportedly continued to rise and the sizable number of expatriates in the country is still on the increase. The majority of the population, possibly as much as 80%, live in Doha. Only around 20% of the population is estimated to be Qatari nationals, while

around 75% of the total number of people living in the country is male.

Local Time

Qatar local time is three hours ahead of UTC (Coordinated Universal Time, also known as GMT). It is fixed across the country and there is no summertime daylight saving. So when it is 12:00 in Doha, it is 13:00 in the UAE, 09:00 in London, 04:00 in New York, 18:00 in Tokyo, and 14:30 in New Delhi (not allowing for any daylight saving in those countries).

Time Zones

		Los Angeles	-11
Amman	-1	Manama	0
Athens	-1	Mexico City/Dallas	-9
Auckland	+9	Moscow	0
Bangkok	+4	Mumbai	+2.5
Beijing	+5	Munich	-2
Beirut	-1	Muscat	+1
Canberra	+7	New York	-8
Colombo	+2.5	Paris	-2
Damascus	-1	Perth	+5
Denver	-10	Prague	-2
Dubai	+1	Riyadh	0
Dublin	-3	Rome	-2
Hong Kong	+5	Singapore	+5
Johannesburg	-1	Sydney	+7
Karachi	+2	Tokyo	+6
Kuwait City	0	Toronto	-8
London	-3	Wellington	+9

Social & Business Hours, Weekends

The working week in Qatar runs from Sunday to Thursday, with Friday (the holy day for Muslims) and Saturday off. Some business offices choose to take only Friday off, or give an additional half day on Thursday. Government office hours are 07:00 to 14:00,

National Flag

The Qatari flag is maroon with a white serrated band that has nine points on the hoist side. The flag was adopted in 1971, the year that Qatar declared its independence. Officially, the white represents peace, the maroon is a tribute to the blood spilled during the several wars Qatar has undergone, while the nine points on the serrated line acknowledges Qatar's position as the ninth member of the 'reconciled emirates' of the Arabian Gulf following the Qatari-British treaty in 1916.

The flags of Bahrain and Qatar are very similar, with only a slight difference in colour, depicting the two countries' historical links.

matching those of Qatar Petroleum and most of the oil, gas and petrochemicals companies.

Banks open from 07:30 until 13:00, although some branches, especially those located in shopping malls, also open in the evenings.

Commercial offices have two shifts – the first from 07:30 to 12:00 and then from 15:30 to 19:30, though this may vary. As a result, siesta (or Qaylūlah in Arabic) is a common practice among locals and residents who tend to stay up late and then have to wake early for their first shift, making an afternoon nap a necessity. Major shopping malls are usually open from 10:00 until midnight, but shops within the malls may close by 22:00. The majority of malls close on Friday mornings. Timings for independent shops vary but are generally from 08:30 to 12:30 and 16:00 to 21:00. Many are closed all day Friday, although some do open in the afternoon.

Ramadan Hours

Timings change during the holy month of Ramadan, with government offices working two or three hours less and commercial shops usually closing during Iftar (the breaking of the fast just after sunset) and re-opening later in the evening. Shopping malls that remain open during the day (without serving any food or beverage between dawn and dusk) usually close later than normal – sometimes as late as 02:00. Late shopping and hanging out in malls for evening coffee during Ramadan is very common, so don't be surprised if you can't find a place to park at midnight.

Public Holidays

The two major public holidays in Qatar are religious ones: Eid Al Fitr and Eid Al Adha. Eid Al Fitr marks the end of the fasting month of Ramadan, which is the ninth month of the Islamic calendar (Hijri calendar). During this month, Muslims are required to abstain from food, drink, cigarettes, sexual acts and unclean thoughts from dawn until dusk.

The Islamic calendar is based on the lunar months, thus the beginning and the ending of Ramadan is not fixed but instead is decided on the sighting of the moon. As a result, religious holidays are only confirmed 24 hours in advance.

Eid Al Fitr is usually marked by a three day celebration where almost every business in the country shuts down for the occasion. Eid Al Adha, the festival of the sacrifice, commemorates Ibrahim's willingness to sacrifice his son to God. It follows Eid Al Fitr by around 70 days and is marked by a four-day celebration. On the occasion of this Eid, some Muslims slaughter sheep and distribute the meat to the poor. Besides these two religious celebrations, National Day was introduced in 2007 and has a fixed date of 18 December.

Non-Muslim holidays such as Christmas or Easter will be given in expatriate schools and also foreign businesses in Qatar, although this is discretionary.

The Islamic New Year is celebrated on the first day of Muharram in the Islamic calendar, although it is not officially a public holiday.

Public Holidays 2012-13

2012
Eid Al Fitr (3)	19 Aug (Moon)
Eid Al Adha (4)	26 Oct (Moon)
National Day (1)	18 Dec (Fixed)

2013
Eid Al Fitr (3)	08 Aug (Moon)
Eid Al Adha (4)	15 Oct (Moon)
National Day (1)	18 Dec (Fixed)

Lunar Calendar

The Hijri calendar is lunar-based; there are 354 or 355 days in the Hijri year, which is divided into 12 lunar months, and is thus 11 days shorter than the Gregorian year. There are plenty of websites with conversion tools, so you can find the equivalent Hijri date for any Gregorian date, and vice versa. Try rabiah.com/convert.

Currency

The monetary unit of Qatar is the Qatari riyal (QR). It is divided into 100 dirhams (not to be confused with the UAE dirham, which has almost the same value as the Qatari riyal). Banknote denominations include QR 1 (grey-green), QR 5 (green), QR 10 (orange), QR 50 (pink), QR 100 (purple-grey), and QR 500 (blue). The coins that are most commonly found are 25 and 50 dirhams. One, five and ten dirham coins are still legal tender but are rarely seen. The riyal is pegged to the US dollar at a rate of QR 3.64. Exchange rates of all major currencies are published daily in the local newspapers and exchange centres are found in most malls.

Exchange Rates

Foreign Currency	1 Unit FC = QR x	QR1 = xFC
Australia Dollars	3.83	0.26
Bahrain Dinars	9.65	0.10
Bangladesh Taka	0.04	22.43
Canada Dollars	3.64	0.28
China Yuan Renminbi	0.57	1.75
Czech Republic Koruny	0.18	5.64
Egypt Pounds	0.60	1.66
Euro	4.47	0.22
India Rupees	0.08	15.26
Iran Rials	0.0003	3366.49
Japan Yen	0.05	21.49
Jordan Dinars	5.15	0.19
Kuwait Dinars	12.93	0.08
Lebanon Pounds	0.002	413.05
Malaysia Ringgits	1.16	0.86

New Zealand Dollars	2.95	0.34
Oman Rials	9.46	0.11
Pakistan Rupees	0.04	26.02
Philippines Pesos	0.09	11.51
Russia Rubles	0.11	8.85
Saudi Arabia Riyals	0.97	1.03
Singapore Dollars	2.92	0.34
South Africa Rand	0.44	2.25
South Korea Won	0.003	311.36
Sri Lanka Rupees	0.03	36.19
Switzerland Francs	3.72	0.27
UAE Dirhams	0.99	1.01
United Kingdom Pounds	5.72	0.17
United States Dollars	3.64	0.27

Rates correct as of July 2012
Source: xe.com

Exchange Centres

Al Jazeera Exchange 4436 2822
Al Zaman Exchange 4444 1448,
alzamanexchange.com
Alfardan Exchange 4440 8408,
alfardan.com.qa
Almana Exchange 4462 1450,
almanagroup.com
City Exchange Company 4441 4638,
cityexco.com
Habib Qatar International Exchange 4442 4373
Lari Exchange Company 4441 9010,
lariexdoha.name.qa

ENVIRONMENT

Flora & Fauna

As you might expect in a country with such an arid climate, the variety of flora and fauna in Qatar is limited, although still interesting. Much of the country consists of sand dunes, rocky hills, and expanses of sabkha (salt flats) with little vegetation. However, directly after the winter rains it is fascinating to take a trip to one of the country's many deserts and watch as the desert blooms with green plants and bushes brought about by the much awaited watering from above. Qatar has no rivers, although there are coastal wetland areas with extensive mangrove woodlands, such as in the Al Wakra area just south of Doha (p.86), and after heavy rainfall, water may gather in wadis.

Creatures that may be encountered in the wild include the Ethiopian hedgehog, the Arabian red fox, jirds, jerboas, and various species of reptiles including snakes, geckos, and the spiny-tailed lizard (or dhab). Qatar also has a number of resident and migratory bird species, including gulls, cormorants, herons, flamingos (which form part of the landscape of the Inland Sea, p.243), egrets and terns. A number of uninhabited offshore islands act as important breeding grounds for birds. If you'd like to discover more about the country's flora and fauna, try joining the Qatar Natural History Group (p.270).

Fishy Business

The warm waters of the Arabian Gulf are home to a rich variety of marine life. Studies have recorded around 150 species of fish, in addition to dolphins, whales and porpoises. The region is home to green and hawksbill turtles and a significant population of the endangered dugong (sea cow).

Environmental Issues

The Supreme Council for the Environment & Natural Reserves (SCENR, qatarenv.org) was set up in 2000 with the purpose of protecting the environment, conserving endangered species, and protecting their natural habitats. With the continuing population growth and the country's massive investment in hydrocarbon industries, Qatar's environment is clearly under threat. These threats include spillages of oil, gas and hazardous chemicals, and production facilities damaging the marine environment. However, Qatar has been working in this regard and has established protected areas officially designated for nature conservation (see Environmental Initiatives & Organisations, p.10). Additionally, the SCENR and the gas and oil companies have programmes in place to monitor the local environment and minimise their impact on it.

Qatargas (qatargas.com.qa) achieved ISO 14001 certification (for environmental protection and management) in 2000, and Qatar Petroleum (qp.com.qa) has initiated schemes to conserve Qatar's mangroves and protect the sea turtle population. Qatar is a signatory to a number of environmental conventions, including the Bio-diversity Convention and the 1969 Kuwait and 1971 Brussels conventions. In addition, Qatar's Vision 2030 National Policy programme (gsdp.gov.qa) has set out clear environmental sustainability standards.

Environmental Initiatives & Organisations

The protection of the environment in Qatar is taking on an increasing importance, as can be seen from a variety of new initiatives and protected areas which aim to preserve Qatar's natural environment and protect it from destructive influences. Recently established protected areas are: Al Thakhera, Khor Al Udeid Fish Sanctuary, Plants Protected Area, Ras Hicharige Protected Area, Umm Al Hawaya Gazelle Conservation Farm and Umm Alhol. The Supreme Council for the Environment & Natural Reserves (SCENR) undertakes all environmental protection

explorer

there's more to life...

Breathtaking views of Qatar's majestic beauty

askexplorer.com/shop

askexplorer

responsibilities, and drafts laws and protection policies for environmental issues. Other conservation groups and initiatives in Qatar include: the Emirates Wildlife Society-WWF's coral reef conservation project (uae.panda.org), marine turtle conservation initiatives at Ras Laffan Industrial City, and environmental awareness-raising, beach cleaning, recycling drives and tree planting organised by groups like Green Qatar Green Center (p.270) and Sustainable Qatar (p.270). The Qatar Animal Welfare Society works to protect animals in Qatar, rescuing and sheltering abandoned animals of all kinds. The organisation is always looking for volunteers, and offers adoption of pets for animal lovers (qaws.org). The Qatar Natural History Group is a good organisation for anyone interested in learning more about the country's environment. See Environmental Groups, p.270, for more details of these and other associations.

Water Usage & Desalination

High water consumption is a concern around the world, and for Qatar, an arid country, the issue is a serious one. In 2008 the government began a drive to help save the country's water resources. New laws were introduced that penalise the wasting of tap water for activities such as gardening and washing cars, and a public campaign was launched to educate the public on easy methods of saving water. Examples included simple measures such as turning off the tap when brushing your teeth, washing fruits or vegetables in a bowl, or taking a shower rather than a bath. Fines for wasting water can reach up to QR 1,000, although it is assumed that sensible water consumption will be adopted by residents as part of their individual environmental responsibility.

A large proportion of Qatar's water is used in the agricultural industry, but with the rapidly expanding urban population comes increasing domestic demand. Most of Qatar's drinking water comes from desalination, and this is another area where improved efficiency is being pursued; in 2010 the Texas A&M University in Education City launched an initiative to bring about improved technologies for water desalination, efficient reuse and zero-liquid discharge systems.

BUSINESS & COMMERCE

Overview

The Qatari statistic that most often captures the global headlines is the country's GDP per capita, which the International Monetary Fund (IMF) estimates will sit at $106,000 in 2012. This puts Qatar in pole position in international comparisons – yet the top-ranking purchasing power reading is just one part of the emirate's astonishing growth story: since the mid-1990s, when Emir Sheikh Hamad bin Khalifa Al Thani committed to a development strategy that based his country's future on developing gas reserves, Qatar has gone from strength to strength.

Qatar has one of the strongest economies in the Mena (Middle East and North Africa) region and, with the possible exception of Dubai, no other regional economy experienced the 2003-08 global boom as strongly, with gross domestic product increasing rapidly over the six year period. After initially borrowing billions of dollars to pay for its expensive energy infrastructure, Qatar has become the world's leading exporter of liquefied natural gas (LNG) and with some 15% of the world's LNG reserves, the prospects for further growth in this field remain bright.

Buoyed by the strong petrochemical sector, Qatar's GDP expanded to $195bn in 2011. On a year-by-year basis, this represented growth of 18%, which put Qatar among the strongest-performing economies in the world. Looking ahead, Qatar's economic performance is expected to remain robust, with the IMF forecasting that the GDP will grow by a further 6% in 2012 to hit $207bn.

Industry

Qatar has not been too heavily hit by the global economic downturn. The economy's current reliance on gas exports has helped – some 75% of its LNG exports are sold under long-term contracts, meaning fixed revenue streams in comparison to neighbours who have to rely on global spot markets for their oil. Indeed, some see the global slowdown as welcome, allowing Doha's property boom to cool off. The overheated property sector in recent years meant soaring rents, which were off-putting to businesses thinking of moving to Doha. Infrastructure bottlenecks and manpower issues have also improved as the region took a breather. In the boom years leading to 2008, Qatar had one of the GCC's highest inflation rates (15% in 2008), but by the end of 2011, the rate stood at much more manageable 2.5%, according to the IMF.

Qatar has run one of the largest energy investment programmes ever seen, but is now nearing the end of its LNG master plan. The last 'mega train' – Train 7 – was completed in 2010 as part of the Qatargas 4 initiative, and has opened up four new markets for LNG, predominantly in the Asia Pacific area.

In the middle of the last decade, Doha announced a moratorium on further development of its North Field gas reserves, effectively locking international firms out until further studies were done. The moratorium was recently extended until 2014 – Qatar is understandably anxious not to damage the reservoir and while there is more global gas supply than demand, this makes economic sense.

Doha's burgeoning skyline

Going Green

According to the WWF, Qatar is putting severe stress on local water resources by using over 100% more water than its natural reserves regenerate each year. Water conservation is just one area in which residents can make a positive impact on the environment.

Responsibility

Perhaps as a result of living in a nation inhabited by a vast majority of expatriates, or perhaps because of the low cost and ready availability of power and water, the average Qatar resident feels limited responsibility towards the country's environment. Expats from countries where 'green' initiatives such as household recycling are commonplace may be surprised by the lack of awareness and facilities for similar schemes in Qatar. While government efforts are starting to head in the right direction, there is a pressing need for all residents to start making a personal contribution to reduce the impact of their presence.

The Three Rs

The first step towards a greener way of life in Qatar is simply to consider the three Rs – Reduce, Reuse and Recycle. Look for a positive and practical change that you can make to a routine – like switching off the lights when you leave a room – and make it a habit. Once you've done that, don't rest on your laurels – find the next change that you can make, and the next. You'll soon find that looking for ways to use the three Rs becomes habit in itself, influencing your buying decisions, your product consumption and usage levels.

Getting Started

It's easy to start making positive environmental changes in your own home which contribute to a greener Qatar. Here are a few suggestions to get you on your way:

- Cut down on wasted produce in your own household by planning your meals for the week ahead, before you head to the supermarket. Write a shopping list and only buy items which are on the list so that you know you'll be able to use them up before they go bad.
- Simple actions such as turning your air conditioning up by a few degrees or replacing traditional light bulbs with energy efficient ones can have a big impact on your energy usage. Plus, the less energy you use, the lower your electricity bills will be!
- Opt for water coolers rather than buying bottled water – a 5 gallon bottle contains nearly 19 litres, meaning you will only use a fraction of the number of plastic bottles over the course of a year. Most water companies recycle or reuse water cooler bottles, so ask your water bottle company (p.90) when you phone for your next order.
- Do you really need that litre of milk right now, or can you pick one up on your way to somewhere else later? Think twice before jumping in the car for small errands, and try to combine trips to cut car usage and emissions.

Green Qatar

> *Cover your pool in the summer. An uncovered pool loses up to 3,785 litres of water per month through evaporation.*

- Freshening up your look? Recycle your used clothes by dropping them off in charity bins located around town in places like Villaggio and Landmark Mall. Keep your eyes peeled for clothing appeals around Christmas or Ramadan and donate new and used men's clothing for distribution to low-paid labourers.
- Give your used towels, sheets, blankets to QAWS (p.109) to help them look after the shelter animals in their care.
- Set up separate bins in your utility room or kitchen to collect paper, glass, plastic and aluminium waste and then drop it off at the recycling bins dotted around Doha – but don't run up your carbon emissions by making a special journey in the car; plan your route so you can drop your recycling off when you're on your way to run another errand.
- Switch off appliances at the wall, rather than switching them to standby, and unplug your phone charger. Between 65% and 95% of the energy used by mobile phone chargers is wasted by leaving them plugged in when not in use.
- Create your own desert oasis and choose native plants for your back yard to cut down on the volumes needed for daily watering. Speak to the gardeners at your local nursery for advice (see Gardens, p.96).
- Make the most of Doha's arid climate and dry your laundry in the open air rather than using the tumble dryer.
- Freshening up your home? If there's still life in your old furniture and appliances, extend their useful life and prevent them from ending up in landfill by selling them on. Post your classified ads on one of Qatar's community websites (p.23). You know what they say – one's man's junk is another man's treasure!
- Invest in reusable carriers or trendy jute bags for your weekly shop and save on the millions of plastic bags which go into landfill every year.
- If you've got some time on your hands why not get involved with an environmental volunteer programme? See p.270 for more details of groups that you can join.
- All aboard! Doha's bus network is efficient, reliable and costs next to nothing to travel on. Before you jump in the car next time, log on to mowasalat.com and find out if there's a Karwa bus heading your way. Not only will you be doing your bit for the environment, but you'll arrive more relaxed after letting someone else tackle the Doha traffic. Find out more about travelling by bus on p.57.

R e c y c l e & S u s t a i n Katrin Scholtz-Barth, president, Sustainable Qatar

Since moving to Doha in August 2008, I have taken all of my recyclables (paper, glass, plastic, aluminium) to the various recycling stations around town. There are recycling containers in many family parks (such as around Landmark Mall and the Corniche), plus at Doha Zoo, Qatar Green Centre and other places. These containers are provided and managed by Q-Kleen, a Division of the Ministry of Municipal Affairs & Agriculture and the Urban Planning General Cleaning Project, who are also responsible for composting organic matter. You can request compost for gardening for a minimal fee from the Municipality's Organic Fertilizer Factory (see gov.qa).

Growth & Diversification

Qatar's main challenge for the next decade is economic diversification. With most of the emirate's energy industry investment shortly to be completed, the government is currently drawing up a long-term strategy that will satisfy a young and booming population and provide long-term employment for its nationals. The non-oil and gas sector has witnessed good growth in recent years, averaging 32.9% in the 2004-08 period, and officials want the non-energy sector to account for 90% of the economy by 2015.

In 2008 the country's national master plan, the Qatar National Vision 2030, was announced – this will integrate human, social, environmental and economic development. Much investment has already been made in the education sector; the RAND Corporation was introduced in the early 2000s to draw up a new national curriculum in an effort to place Qatar students on a level with those in western economies. In 2011, Qatar also introduced the National Development Strategy, a five-year plan that addresses its goals for tourism, culture (a large museums package is underway), healthcare, information and communication technology, higher education, manufacturing (aluminium, steel, power, water and petrochemicals projects), transport (Qatar Airways continues to grow), construction (including mega-projects such as Lusail and the Pearl) and infrastructure ($20 billion is to be spent on new roads in the next five years and a new airport is expected to complete its first phase in late 2012).

Business & Leisure Tourism

With year-round sunshine, golden beaches, exciting outdoor activities and a fascinating culture and history, Qatar is a prime tourist destination that remains relatively undiscovered. Qatar doesn't necessarily want to attract mass tourism, but aims to become known as a high-quality destination that appeals to high-income sectors such as the MICE market (Meetings, Incentives, Conferences and Exhibitions).

The state-owned Qatar Tourism Authority promotes the emirate as a business, upscale leisure and cultural destination. Hotel capacity is increasing at a rapid rate to an estimated 29,000 by 2012. Open since December 2011, the Qatar National Convention Centre has brought another growth avenue. Providing a 40,000m2 exhibition space and a conference hall for 4,000 delegates, the new centre has got off to a flying start by hosting a number of big-ticket events, such as the 2011 World Petroleum Congress, in its first year of operation. Qatar's expansion into this sector is also being pushed by the Qatar MICE Development Institute (QMDI), a joint venture launched two years ago between the Qatar Foundation and the more experienced Singaporean company Singex Global. In

the years ahead, QMDI will host a growing number of events, ranging from conferences to various sports happenings and commercial exhibitions.

CULTURE & LIFESTYLE

Culture

Qatar's culture is a fascinating synergy of ancient Arabian heritage and Islamic tradition. Islam influences day-to-day living, from the clothes Muslims wear to what they eat and drink. While Islamic fundamentalism has unfortunately shrouded the Muslim religion in negative stereotypes in parts of the world, Qatar is a largely tolerant and welcoming country, with few restrictions placed on foreigners living or visiting here. Women are able to drive and walk around unescorted, and alcohol is available in licensed hotels. Among the most highly prized virtues of Islam are courtesy and hospitality, and visitors are sure to be charmed by the genuine warmth and friendliness of the local people. Women are not obliged to cover up completely in public (see What To Wear, p.20), but they are expected to dress conservatively, especially during the fasting month of Ramadan. Public displays of affection are considered immoral and not permitted, although in recent years holding hands in public has become more acceptable.

Cultural Understanding

If you'd like to learn more about the religion and culture of the region, the Qatar Center for The Presentation of Islam (islamweb.net.qa) offers a variety of workshops and courses on the subjects, including introductory sessions on understanding the principals of Islam, and beginners' courses on classic and cultural Arabic. Fanar, the Qatar Islamic Cultural Centre, also runs language and cultural programmes (fanar.gov.qa).

Language

The official language in Qatar is Arabic. It is used by locals and the relatively large Arab community residing here. The Arabic dialect used in Qatar is commonly dubbed 'Khaleeji', in reference to the Gulf or Al Khaleej.

English is widely spoken in Qatar, and most road signs are written in both English and Arabic. English is also used in the workplace, especially at private or international companies, and it is widely used in tourist areas, hotels and malls.

You might get by using English in governmental buildings, although taking along an interpreter will help in situations where details are important. All official documents such as visa and resident permits should be translated into Arabic. Urdu and Hindi are

Cultural Dos & Don'ts

You'll find that, in general, people in Qatar are patient when it comes to cultural etiquette and are keen to explain their customs to you. However, there are a few cultural dos and don'ts that you should be aware of to avoid causing offence to others.

PDAs

Not a reference to the handheld gadget but to public displays of affection: these are not looked on favourably in the region, and anything more than an innocent peck on the cheek will at best earn you disapproving looks from passersby.

Appropriate Attire

While beachwear is fine on the beach, you should dress more conservatively when out and about in public places. If in doubt, ensuring that your shoulders and knees are covered is a safe bet. A pashmina is always useful for the journey home or in case the air conditioning is set to 'deep freeze'.

Photography

Normal tourist photography is fine, but like anywhere in the Arab world, it is courteous to ask permission before photographing people, particularly women. In general, photographs of government and military buildings should not be taken.

Arabian Coffee

It's likely that you'll be served traditional Arabian coffee (gahwa) during formal business meetings. This is an important social ritual in the Middle East so be polite and drink some when offered. Cups should be taken in the right hand and if there is a waiter standing by, replenishing your cup, the signal to say that you have had enough is to gently shake the cup from side to side.

Meeting People

Long handshakes, kisses and warm greetings are common when meeting people in the Middle East. It's normal to shake hands with people when you are introduced to them, although if you are meeting someone of the opposite sex, be aware that a handshake may not always be welcome. It's best to take your cue from the other person and not offer your hand unless they first offer theirs. It's polite to send greetings to a person's family, but can be considered rude to enquire directly about someone's wife, sister or daughter. You may see men greeting each other with a nose kiss; this is a customary greeting in the Gulf region but is only used between close friends and associates and you should not attempt to greet someone in this way.

Out On The Town

Alcohol is available in hotel bars, pubs and clubs (see Going Out, p.339), but remember, however, that you're in a Muslim country and drunken or lewd behaviour is not only disrespectful but can lead to arrest and detention.

Business Etiquette

Business meetings in the region will usually start with introductions and small talk before you get down to business. Business cards will be exchanged – you should treat them with respect as an extension of the person who gave them. Punctuality to meetings is important and arriving late is considered to be very bad mannered. Do not assume, however, that your meeting will start at the appointed time or that once started it will not be interrupted.

Home Values

When visiting a local home it is customary to remove your shoes, however, it's best to take your cue from your host. Traditionally, men and women dine separately and meals are eaten while seated on floor cushions. When you sit, be careful not to point your feet at anyone or to show the soles of your feet. Mealtimes are long and leisurely and as a guest your plate will be heaped high. Try everything offered but if you're not sure you'll like something, take a small amount that you can finish. If you invite a Muslim to your home, you should not offer alcohol, as this may cause offence.

also commonly used languages in Qatar due to the huge community of south Asian workers. For a list of language classes, see p.154.

Religion

For most Qataris, Islam is more than just a religion, it is a way of life. Qataris in general are conservative and most practise their religion. The basis of Islam is that there is only one God (the same God as Christians and Jews) and that Prophet Muhammad is the messenger of God. Islam is based on five pillars: profession of faith or Al Shahada; praying; fasting; pilgrimage to Mecca (or Makkah) in Saudi Arabia; and giving charity or Zakat. The holy book of Islam is the Quran. There are two main forms of Islam: Sunni and Shia. Almost 90% of Qataris are Sunni Muslims, but there is no real tension between Sunni and Shia Muslim communities in the country, with both practising their beliefs in peaceful co-existence. Islam requires believers to pray (facing Mecca) five times a day: fajr (at sunrise), dhuhr (at noon), asr (at mid-afternoon), maghrib (at sunset) and isha (at nightfall). Locals and residents pray at home, at work or at a mosque. The call to prayer, which are reminders of the prayer times, are broadcast from loudspeakers installed on the minarets of the many mosques. Praying must be preceded by ritual cleansing, so washing facilities can be found in buildings and public places.

BASIC ARABIC

General
Yes	na'am
No	la
Please	min fadlak (m)
	min fadliki (f)
Thank you	shukran
Please (in offering)	tafaddal (m)
	tafaddali (f)
Praise be to God	al-hamdu l-illah
God willing	in shaa'a l-laah

Greetings
Greeting (peace be upon you)	
	as-salaamu alaykom
Greeting (in reply)	
	wa alaykom is salaam
Good morning	sabah il-khayr
Good morning (in reply)	
	sabah in-nuwr
Good evening	masa il-khayr
Good evening (in reply)	
	masa in-nuwr
Hello	marhaba
Hello (in reply)	marhabtayn
How are you?	
	kayf haalak (m) / kayf haalik (f)
Fine, thank you	
	zayn, shukran (m)
	zayna, shukran (f)
Welcome	ahlan wa sahlan
Welcome (in reply)	
	ahlan fiyk (m) / ahlan fiyki (f)
Goodbye	ma is-salaama

Introductions
My name is...	ismiy...
What is your name?	
	shuw ismak (m) / shuw ismik (f)

Where are you from?
	min wayn inta (m) /
	min wayn inti (f)
I am from...	anaa min...
America	ameriki
Britain	braitani
Europe	oropi
India	al hindi

Questions
How many / much?	kam?
Where?	wayn?
When?	mataa?
Which?	ayy?
How?	kayf?
What?	shuw?
Why?	laysh?
Who?	miyn?
To/for	ila
In/at	fee
From	min
And	wa
Also	kamaan
There isn't	maa fee

Taxi Or Car Related
Is this the road to...	hadaa al
	tariyq ila...
Stop	kuf
Right	yamiyn
Left	yassar
Straight ahead	siydaa
North	shamaal
South	januwb
East	sharq
West	garb
Turning	mafraq
First	awwal

Second	thaaniy
Road	tariyq
Street	shaaria
Roundabout	duwwaar
Signals	ishaara
Close to	qarib min
Petrol station	mahattat betrol
Sea/beach	il bahar
Mountain/s	jabal/jibaal
Desert	al sahraa
Airport	mataar
Hotel	funduq
Restaurant	mata'am
Slow Down	schway schway

Accidents & Emergencies
Police	al shurtaa
Permit/licence	rukhsaa
Accident	haadith
Papers	waraq
Insurance	ta'miyn
Sorry	aasif (m) /
	aasifa (f)

Numbers
Zero	sifr
One	waahad
Two	ithnayn
Three	thalatha
Four	arba'a
Five	khamsa
Six	sitta
Seven	saba'a
Eight	thamaanya
Nine	tiss'a
Ten	ashara
Hundred	miya
Thousand	alf

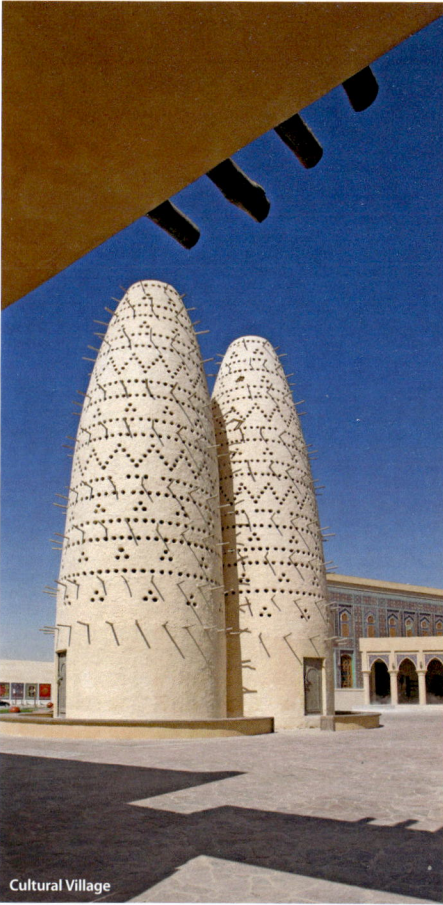
Cultural Village

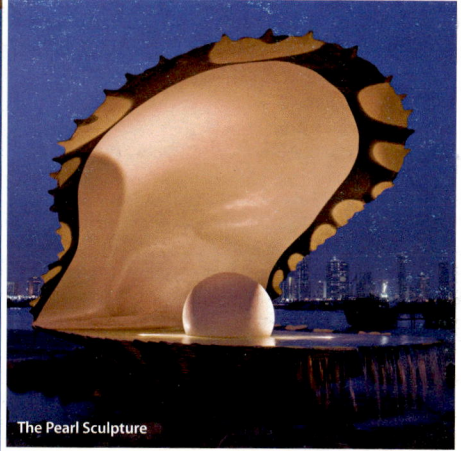
The Pearl Sculpture

Falconry

Museum of Islamic Art

Culture & Lifestyle

Friday is the holy day of the week. Mosques are usually packed with mostly male worshippers on a Friday, when they get to listen to a sermon, or khutbah, given by a preacher or imam. Some mosques have separate spaces for women. Two mosques in Doha currently conduct sermons in English – Aspire Mosque across from Vilaggio Mall and the Fanar Cultural Centre, the spiral-shaped building near Souq Waqif.

Demonstrating a tolerant attitude to other religions, His Highness Sheikh Hamad bin Khalifa Al Thani has granted land for churches to be built (see p.49). The first church, which caters to Qatar's Catholic residents, opened three years ago and is located several kilometres outside of Doha. Other churches for people of other Christian denominations are popping up in the same area.

Family Names

Arabic names have a formal structure that traditionally indicates the person's family and tribe. Names are usually taken from an important person in the Quran or someone from the tribe. This is followed by the word bin (son of) for a boy or bint (daughter of) for a girl, and then the name of the child's father. The last name indicates the person's tribe or family. For prominent families, this has Al, the Arabic word for 'the', immediately before it. For instance, the Emir of Qatar is His Highness Sheikh Hamad bin Khalifa Al Thani. When women get married, they do not change their name.

Ramadan

Fasting is observed for a whole month during Ramadan, which is the ninth month of the Islamic lunar calendar and determined by the cycles of the moon. Believers are required to fast from dawn until dusk, as well as giving up other bad habits. The fast is broken by Iftar, a meal usually enjoyed with family or friends. Eating or drinking in public is prohibited during the fasting period, even for non-Muslims. Restaurants are closed during the day, except for some in major hotels, but Doha seems to be awake all night once the sun sets (expect a lot of traffic in the evening!). Alcohol is never served or sold during the holy month. A religious celebration, Eid Al Fitr, follows the month of fasting. Around 70 days after Eid Al Fitr, Muslims celebrate Eid Al Adha, which translates as the festivity of sacrifice, in which Muslims slaughter sheep and distribute part of the meat to the poor.

National Dress

Generally, the local population wears traditional dress in public. For men this is the dishdasha (or khandura, or thobe) – a white full-length shirt dress, which is worn with a white, or red and white checked, headdress called a gutra, secured with a black cord (agal). Sheikhs, emirs and important businessmen may also wear a further robe with fine embroidery called a bisht, or mishlah, over their dishdasha at important events or celebrations such as weddings. Qatar has a tradition of producing quality embroidered textiles and clothing.

In public, Qatari women wear the black abaya – a long, loose black robe that covers their normal clothes – plus a headscarf called the sheyla. The abaya is often made of a sheer, flowing fabric and may be open at the front. Some women also wear a thin black veil covering their face, and/or gloves, and older women sometimes still wear a leather mask, known as a himaar, which covers the nose, brow and cheekbones. Underneath the abaya, women traditionally wear a long tunic over loose, flowing trousers (sirwall), which are often heavily embroidered and fitted at the wrists and ankles. However, these are used more by the older generation and younger women will often wear the latest fashions from international stores underneath.

What To Wear

Qatar is not as strict as some of its neighbours in the region, but visitors and residents should still show respect for the local customs and sensibilities. Women are not required to cover their hair, but should avoid tight or revealing clothing. When out in public, men and women should wear garments that cover the shoulders and knees.

Skirts or shorts above the knee should be avoided, as should sleeveless tops that expose the shoulders or upper arms. You'll encounter some unwelcome attention and remarks if you do go out underdressed, and there have even been some reports of women being fined for having their shoulders uncovered in public. Respecting these customs is particularly important during Ramadan. It's fine to wear shorts at a sports club, and swimming costumes are acceptable at swimming pools and beaches.

You should certainly cover up in the strong summer sun, however. Hats and sunscreen are a must and it is not uncommon to see people carrying umbrellas to act as parasols.

Shopping malls, restaurants and cinemas can be a little cold due to the air conditioning, so it's worth taking along a sweater or cardigan.

Food & Drink

Culinary styles from all around the world have made their way to Qatar to cater to the tastes of the cosmopolitan society. The most sophisticated restaurants are all located in hotels (and therefore able to sell alcohol), but there are also some really good (and cheap) meals to be had from the many street cafes around town. Most western fastfood brands have found a home in Qatar and many

Eating Arabian Style

Arabian food is tasty, healthy, cheap and generally comes in sharing-sized portions. Get to know the local dishes and tuck in.

Spending time in Qatar is the ideal opportunity to familiarise yourself with Arabian cuisine. Street restaurants selling shawarma, falafel, tabbouleh, hummus and fresh fruit cocktails are a good place to start, and there are plenty of other, more exotic tastes waiting to be explored. Early traders introduced new spices and flavours that subsequently have become essential ingredients in Arabian cooking. Cinnamon, saffron, turmeric, nuts (especially almonds and pistachios), limes and dried fruits all add interesting flavours to many well-known Arabian dishes.

Qatari Cuisine

Local food is often served with a steaming portion of spicy, delicious rice and a healthy portion of delightfully soft meat, mostly lamb – a local favourite. But the various dishes listed below all offer culinary delights for the unknowing tastebuds.

Harees: Soaked split wheat and meat, cooked for several hours

Margooga: Meat cooked with vegetables and bread

Madhrooba: Rice, vegetables and chicken stew

Mashboos: A meal of mutton cooked until it is very tender, and served with spices and rice

Eating in the Middle East is traditionally a social affair. Whether eating at home with extended families, or out with large groups, the custom is for everybody to share a feast of various dishes, served in communal bowls. A combination of starters, known as mezze, is usually enjoyed with flat bread, and main courses are often eaten with the fingers. Here are some classic dishes to try:

Baba ghanoush: A dip comprising of a coarse mixture of grilled aubergines, garlic, tahina (sesame seed paste), lemon juice and olive oil. It is often garnished with cumin, parsley, tomatoes and olives, and is delicious with the addition of pomegranate syrup.

Fatayer: Hot pastries with various combinations of fillings and toppings, including cheese, spinach, labneh (yogurt), zaatar (a mixture of dried thyme, sesame seeds and olive oil), minced meat and tomatoes.

Fattoush: A Lebanese salad combining an assortment of salad greens and tomatoes with pieces of either toasted or fried Arabian bread in a mint, lemon and olive oil dressing.

Hummus: A smooth dip made from pureed chickpeas, lemon juice, tahina, garlic and olive oil. Hummus awerma, with the addition of grilled lamb and pine nuts, is more substantial, while hummus beiruti has added garlic, parsley and a sprinkle of chilli.

Kibbe: Hot, crispy, coated balls of burghul (cracked wheat) stuffed with minced meat and pine nuts.

Labneh: Thick, creamy yoghurt that is often served by itself, garnished with olive oil, or as jaajeek, slightly thinned and mixed with diced cucumber, crushed garlic and mint.

Manakeesh: Flatbread topped with zaatar.

Moutabel: Similar to baba ghanoush but smoother.

Tabbouleh: A salad usually made with burghul, parsley, mint, onions, green shallots and tomatoes, all finely chopped and mixed with olive oil, lemon juice, salt and black pepper.

Warak enab: Vine leaves stuffed with rice, meat and onions, mixed with spices and cooked with olive oil and lemon juice. Cold vine leaves usually contain no meat.

Grills – kebab and shish ta'ooq: Two popular hot grills are plates or sandwiches of shish ta'ooq (marinated, boneless chicken or fish cubes) and kebabs. The latter is made from minced chicken or lamb mixed with parsley and spices, wrapped around a broad flat skewer and grilled.

Arabian Coffee & Dates

Coffee and dates are an important ritual of hospitality in this part of the world. Traditional Arabian-style coffee (gahwa) is mild with a distinctive taste of cardamom and saffron. It is served black without sugar, but dates are presented at the same time to sweeten the palate. The cups are very small, so it's similar to drinking a shot of espresso.

Dates are one of the few crops that naturally thrive in the Middle East and have been cultivated for around 5,000 years. High in energy, fibre, potassium, vitamins, magnesium and iron, with next to no fat, salt or cholesterol, dates are a cheap and healthy snack.

supermarkets stock items to give you a little slice of home – wherever you're from. See Going Out, p.339 for a comprehensive directory of restaurants, and Supermarkets & Hypermarkets (p.324) for all your grocery shopping needs.

Don't Drink & Drive

There is zero tolerance on drinking and driving practises; there are no excuses, and the offence is punished with a jail term, even if you've just had one drink. If you've been out enjoying Doha's hospitality, always take a taxi home or get a lift with someone who hasn't been drinking.

Pork

Muslims do not consume pork and you won't see it used at all in local cooking. Pork is outlawed in Qatar, so cannot be bought anywhere, and it is illegal to bring it into the country. Pork aside, Muslims are forbidden to eat the meat of an animal that has not been slaughtered in the correct manner. The meat of animals killed in accordance with the Islamic code is known as halal.

Alcohol

You won't be able to get a beer in a shopping mall or street cafe, or anywhere that is not attached to or inside a hotel or sports club. Residents can get a licence to buy alcohol for home consumption but don't expect to find a dedicated aisle in your local supermarket. Instead you will have to visit the special liquor store. See Liquor Licence on p.44 and Purchasing Alcohol on p.294.

Shisha

Shisha

Smoking a shisha pipe is an important part of socialising for locals. It is often savoured in local cafes while chatting with friends. Shishas are filled with water, and the tobacco, which has a texture similar to molasses, is available in different flavours such as apple, strawberry, grape and mint. Even if you don't smoke cigarettes or cigars, you should try shisha at least once; the smoke is 'smoothed' by the water, creating a much milder effect. However, it should be noted that the negative health effects of smoking shisha are said to be more powerful than those of cigarettes so caution should be taken not to smoke too many of these scented wonders.

Tipping

Tipping in Qatar is not yet as rigid a customary practise as it is in North America and Europe. Tips are most commonly given in restaurants, averaging 10%, although some establishments automatically add a 10% service charge (this was outlawed in 2010 but still continues). Taxi fares are generally minimal so tips that round out riyals are quite common, although there is no hard and fast rule. Normally, tips are given according to the feeling of the individual in relation to the situation. Tipping for tour guides is subjective, but is good practise. In hotels and other luxury places tips can be well looked upon, and another area where tips are common with expats is at petrol stations, where a few extra riyals are often handed to the petrol station workers for their efforts in re-fuelling your car. Porters at the airport will request QR 20 for helping with your luggage. This is a flat fee, and they will even provide you with a receipt.

LOCAL MEDIA

Newspapers & Magazines

The three main English newspapers published in Qatar are *Gulf Times*, *Qatar Tribune* and *The Peninsula*. They are published every day of the week (with Friday editions being added in recent years) and cover a range of international and local issues, with a focus on local news, regional issues of importance, and the activities of the south Asian community in Qatar.

Each newspaper costs QR 2 and is widely available in supermarkets, shops, hotels, bookshops, offices, cafes and other public places. They were also once sold by street vendors located at most traffic lights, although this has recently been outlawed. Alternatively, you can purchase yearly subscriptions, and the paper will be delivered straight to your home or office address.

Some UAE-based English publications like *Khaleej Times* and *Gulf News* are also available on the day of publication. Foreign newspapers like the *International*

Herald Tribune and others, mostly British, American and Asian, are also available, but they may arrive 24 hours after the publication date. They can be found in supermarkets, hotels, and some shops, but are more expensive than in their places of publication.

There are three local Arabic dailies issued from Qatar: *Al Raya*, *Al Sharq* and *Al Watan*, which all cost QR 2. English language magazines published in Qatar include *Qatar Today*, which focuses mainly on business issues but also covers news, motoring, travel, and technology. *T Qatar* is the Qatar edition of the *New York Times Style Magazine* and offers interesting features that focus on culture, travel, design and lifestyle.

Other publications include *Woman Today*, which has articles and features aimed at all the working women in Qatar, while *Glam* features women's fashion, beauty treatments and make-up and tips. *Abode* is a locally published lifestyle magazine that prints local event information and also features fine photography. The high-end magazine *Isola* has luxurious travel reports and attractive photo shoots filling up its pages. There are several entertainment and lifestyle listings on offer too, including *Time Out Doha*, *Qatar Happening* and the quarterly *Marhaba*.

Imported English language magazines are also available in Doha, but be warned that they are usually more expensive than their standard retail price.

Radio

There are only a few Qatar-based radio stations available. Qatar Radio (QBS) is the main station, which operates in both English and French on 97.5 FM and 102.6 FM. In January 2011, Qatar introduced Oryx FM Radio Station, a new French radio service that broadcasts all day. Arabic-speaking listeners can tune into Voice of the Gulf on 100.8 FM. Online radio, such as is offered by the BBC, is a good option for expats looking to keep up with their home favourites.

Television

A recently introduced service called Mozaic TV+ offers Qatar residents a big range of digital television channels, plus telephone and internet, delivered through one Qtel ADSL line. The price is QR 250 per month, and installation is now free. It has over 160 digital TV channels (including channels from the Orbit Showtime Network, ART, STAR, Turner, MBC and Al Jazeera). An electronic programme guide and pay-per-view service are included. Services such as Caller

USEFUL WEBSITES

Qatar Information
expatwoman.com > *p.28*	Popular expat forum with a specific Doha section
gov.qa	Qatar government online
iloveqatar.net	Listings and community forum
mofa.gov.qa	Ministry of Foreign Affairs
moi.gov.qa	Ministry of Interior
qatarhappening.com	Event listings
qatarliving.com	What's on and community forum
qatartourism.gov.qa	Qatar Tourism Authority
qsa.gov.qa	Qatar Statistics Authority
qatarvisitor.com	Tips on the basics

News & Media
ameinfo.com	Middle East business resource
dohanews.co	News and current events site in an interactive format
aljazeera.com	Qatar and world news in English
gulf-times.com	Biggest and oldest newspaper in English
qatar-tribune.com	Newest addition to English news
thepeninsulaqatar.com	News, economic information, photos

Culture
education.gov.qa > *p.ii-iii*	Supreme Education Council
heritageofqatar.org	Heritage info compiled by Carnegie Mellon University Qatar
cnc.com.qa	National Council for Culture, Arts & Heritage
ndqatar.com	Information about National Day events
qatar-info.com	Background, cultural and religious information
qf.edu.qa	Qatar Foundation
qma.com.qa	Qatar Museums Authority

ID are available on the telephone facility and speed upgrades on the internet service are planned.

There are two television channels operated by Qatar Television – Channel One, which is in Arabic, and Channel Two, which is mostly in English.

Al Jazeera is a Qatar-based television network which offers a whole array of news, sports and entertainment options in Arabic and English. The launch of its Al Jazeera English channel in 2006 has created an alternative to the top duo of CNN and BBC, with regular news bulletins, top features stories, documentaries and debates forming part of this young but ambitious channel, which has nabbed top news anchors from around the world.

As well as Mozaic, Qtel continues to offer cable television (Qatar Cablevision), which supplies all available networks through one decoder. You can get a range of programmes suitable for both English and Arabic speaking viewers. This system has many channels, including STAR, Orbit Showtime Network and ART. Qatar Cablevision also offers the 'combo' receiver, which enables you to watch all the free-to-air satellite channels, together with the cable channels, on one decoder. Most expats subscribe to one of these networks, which is possible to do through a number of companies. See Housing, p.67, for installation details.

Internet

Qatar residents are able to get connected to high-speed broadband and cheaper dial-up services through Qtel. Prices vary according to the speed of connection – see Internet, p.92. Qtel Wi-Fi HotSpots are all over the city, mainly in hotels and cafes, and free Wi-Fi is offered in parks, Souq Waqif and along the Corniche. Customers with a wireless-enabled laptop or mobile can buy HotSpot cards.

QATAR CALENDAR

Major events take place in and around Doha throughout the year to keep residents entertained. Sports fans can get close to some of the world's top tennis and golf players and music fans have a jazz festival to look forward to.

Al Khor Fly In   January
Al Khor Airfield Al Khor **4472 3490**
alkhorflyin.net
Map **Qatar Country Map C2**
The annual Al Khor Fly-In brings together a group of pilots from around the Middle East who will perform stunts for the general public to view. The event aims to promote aviation as a new sport or hobby for people to participate in.

Qatar ExxonMobil Open   January
Khalifa International Tennis & Squash Complex
Lekhwair qatartennis.org
Map **2 N4**
Attracting top players each year in January, the ExxonMobil Open is Doha's ATP men's tennis tournament. Among the recent winners are tennis ace Roger Federer, who won the title in 2011, and France's Jo-Wilfried Tsonga, who won in 2012.

Qatar International Rally   January
Various Locations **4437 9884**
qmmf.com
A three-day event which takes place across Qatar's varied terrain, starting and finishing on Doha Corniche. Spectate from points along the route or volunteer for marshalling duties for a closer view of the action.

Camel training

Qatar Motor Show
January
Doha Exhibition Centre Al Gassar **4428 2828**
qatarmotorshow.gov.qa
Map **1 K3**
This event is an annual draw for the motoring trade and consumers alike; in addition to showcasing the latest models by international automakers, the latest auto and performance trends are on display.

Commercial Bank Qatar Masters
February
Doha Golf Club Al Egla **4496 0712**
qatar-masters.com
Map **1 H1**
The Qatar Masters is an annual event on the PGA European tour. The event attracts some of the world's best players who compete for a share of the $2.5 million prize money.

Qatar International Equestrian Festival
February
Al Rayyan Racetrack New Al Rayan
qrec.gov.qa
Map **1 B9**
Some of the fastest horses in the world visit Doha for this annual festival that is held at Rayyan, in the north of Doha.

Qatar International Regatta (Sail The Gulf)
February
Doha Sailing Club Al Khulaifat **4442 0305**
qatarsailing.org
Map **2 V8**
An extremely popular sailing event with both the locals and expatriates, the Doha Sailing Club plays host to this interesting celebration of all things nautical every February.

Qatar International Sailing Championship
February
Doha Sailing Club Al Khulaifat qatarsailing.org
Map **2 V8**
A competition that attracts sailing enthusiasts of different ages to compete in various categories.

National Day
Held on 18 December, this national celebration was established as recently as 2007 to commemorate the assumption of power of Sheikh Jassem bin Mohamed bin Thani in the late 19th century. Most government offices will be closed, and a number of celebrations are held to mark the occasion. Past festivities include parades along the Corniche, poetry recitals, horse racing, camel dressing, and culinary feasts. Keep an eye on local press for details of events.

Qatar Ladies Open
February
Khalifa International Tennis & Squash Complex Lekhwair
qatartennis.org
Map **2 N4**
The best international tennis players on the global circuit make their way to the Middle East to compete for the QTF cup.

Traditional Sports
As well as the major annual events listed, there are also plenty of opportunities to spectate at traditional Qatari leisure pursuits. Camel racing is particularly popular in the region, with race meetings held at Sheehaniyah (p.237). It's a fascinating spectacle that's worth experiencing. Dhow races are held off the Corniche in the cooler months, where these admirably crafted vessels with their brilliant white sails glide majestically through the blue waters.

Qatar Open Chess Championship
February
Bu Hamour **4494 4292**
qatarchess.com
Map **2 G13**
Expat and Qatari chess enthusiasts, from all over Qatar and beyond, come together for this annual chess tournament.

Terry Fox Run
February
College of the North Atlantic Al Tarfa
terryfox.org
Map **1 F3**
This annual charity run sees hundreds of participants turn out to run the route at the College of the North Atlantic, raising money and awareness for cancer research and the Terry Fox Foundation.

Halal Qatar Festival
March
Katara Cultural Village Al Gassar **4408 0000**
katara.net
Map **1 K3**
Launched in 2012, the week-and-a-half long event gives an insight into all things Halal, including the breeding of animals, animal trade and opportunities to sample Qatar's traditional foods.

Powerboat Racing
March
The Corniche Al Dafna
f1h2o.com
Map **2 P4**
Class 1 offshore powerboat racing is the fastest and most exhilarating of all watersports, and each year Qatar hosts two rounds of the world championship.

Qatar Calendar 2012-13

Spectators can enjoy the action along Doha's Corniche and cheer on the local Qatar team, which – despite being a relatively new entrant to the sport – has already posted some impressive results.

Commercialbank Grand Prix Of Qatar
April

Losail International Circuit Jabal Thuaileb
motogp.com
Map **Qatar Country Map C2**

The impressive Losail motor racing circuit outside Doha is the venue for the Qatar Commercialbank Grand Prix, a round of the MotoGP World Championship.

Capital Of Arab Culture

Doha was the Arab Capital of Culture for 2010, a mark of honour awarded by the Arab League in conjunction with Unesco. The city continues to stage a variety of activities to celebrate Arab culture throughout the year, including musical performances, traditional Arabic displays of falconry, hunting and camel traditions, and many other events. Keep an eye on the local papers for announcements of upcoming events throughout 2012-13.

International Wedding Exhibition Doha (IWED)
April

Doha Exhibition Center Al Gassar
qatar-expo.com
Map **1 K3**

The perfect place for brides-to-be (and grooms) to get inspiration, expert advice and useful contacts for organising their big day.

Doha Tribeca Film Festival
October

Various locations
dohafilminstitute.com

A top international movie festival originally pioneered by Robert De Niro in New York. The Doha event brings together the top names in world cinema and is a must for film fans.

Doha International Book Fair
December

Doha Exhibition Center Al Gassar
4442 9955
qatartourism.gov.qa
Map **1 K3**

In its 23rd year in 2012, the biggest international book fair in the country celebrates the art of reading and offers a host of books in Arabic, with an increasing array of books in English.

Powerboat racing

World Cup 2022

In December 2010, FIFA amazed the world when it awarded the bid to host the 2022 football World Cup to Qatar. The tiny Gulf state is the first Arab country to receive the bid, and it is taking its role as host seriously, pouring billions into building the infrastructure needed to sustain the World Cup.

Controversy

The Qatar bid is not without its fair share of controversy and, in the aftermath, some were quick to point the finger and suggest foul play. But questions also include issues about how players will be able to withstand the desert nation's searing summer heat, as well as concerns over the lack of alcohol in the region. Qatar has confidently addressed all of these issues, starting with how it will handle an influx of 400,000 fans – roughly 25 percent of its current population.

Plans & Developments

Over the next decade, the country will spend an estimated $70 to $100 billion on new housing, public transportation and stadia for the games. That includes shoring up the number of available hotel rooms, from 12,000 in 2010 to 90,000 by 2022 and building housing and schools for expats who move to the country to work on the projects. Qatar will also construct nine air-conditioned stadiums to counter the inevitable and searing summer heat, which reaches as high as 50°C in June and July, when the games will take place. Three existing stadia will undergo major renovations. The first five proposed stadia for the World Cup were unveiled at the beginning of March 2010. The stadia will employ cooling technology that can reduce temperatures within the stadium by up to 20 degrees Celsius. There is even talk of constructing remote-controlled 'clouds', or helium-filled airships, to hover above the stadiums to provide shade. Other major construction projects include a national rail system and metro lines, further development of the airport, a deep water port and a causeway connecting Qatar with Bahrain.

Environmentally Friendly

Qatar has promised that all stadiums will be zero carbon emitting and has established an environmental working group to study the environmental impact and develop a green plan for 2022. Once the games are over, the country has said it will dismantle the upper tiers of the stadia and donate them to countries with less developed sports infrastructure.

Infrastructure aside, Qatar has less than a decade to adjust to the cultural realities of the World Cup. Though most locals are largely supportive of the bid, many are concerned about the rowdy crowds the games will attract. Alcohol is currently available in Qatar in a limited number of venues, and public drunkenness – common during the World Cup – is illegal. World Cup organisers in this conservative Muslim country have promised the availability of 'fan zones' during the games, where alcohol will be sold and consumed.

Even though the Cup is still a decade away, excitement continues to build in Qatar. Posters of the Emir and his family celebrating, dating back to that fateful decision day in December, hang in many storefront windows, and 2022 has given the country a renewed sense of urgency in completing its to-do list. And with so much to do, organisers expect the years to pass in a flash. When 2022 finally does roll around, the bid team intends to fulfill its grand campaign promise –'Expect Amazing' indeed.

ExpatWoman.com

1 FORUM
in the UAE

by traffic
(by miles)

...answers to ALL your questions

www.ExpatWoman.com

Qatar: Becoming A Resident

CITY PROFILE

Being a resident in one of the wealthiest countries in the world naturally has its fair share of benefits: the standard of living is high and the wages are better than average; as an added bonus, the weather is always warm. Shopping and dining choices are varied and excellent, and there is no shortage of things to do, especially if you live in the capital, Doha. High standards of healthcare and schooling and a low crime rate make Qatar a safe, pleasant environment to live in. About 75% of Qatar's population are non-nationals, which produces an eclectic mix of cultures, people, activities and recreational choices. Clubs and associations provide a wide variety of pastimes and the climate offers plenty of freedom to pursue outdoor interests for much of the year. Shops retailing the world's finest luxury brands can be found alongside dirt-cheap bargain stores, while eating options range from inelegant fastfood joints to five-star gourmet experiences.

With its low crime rate and its handy access to enviable travel destinations, life in Qatar is indeed good, but, as a new resident, you will have to deal with a sometimes overwhelming amount of paperwork before it feels that way. This chapter is here to help you, whether you are making the decision to move or not, you've just arrived and don't know where to start, or if you find yourself drowning in red tape. Just remember, procedures and laws do change regularly, often in quite major ways. While these changes are generally announced in newspapers, they are often implemented quickly so it's a good idea to be prepared for the unexpected.

QATAR'S ECONOMY & TRADE

GDP

Qatar's gross domestic product (GDP) reached nearly QR 633bn in 2011, having rebounded largely due to a global increase in oil prices and registering a solid economic growth rate of 18%.

The sector officially referred to as mining and quarrying (which covers the extraction and production of oil and gas) accounted for more than half of the GDP, proving that Qatar's economy is very much reliant on hydrocarbons. The other significant contributors to GDP were government services, manufacturing, finance, insurance, real estate and business services, and building and construction. ›

Industry

Qatar's main exports are liquefied natural gas, petroleum products, fertilisers and steel to mostly Japan, South Korea, Singapore and India. Qatar's

main import partners are the US, Italy, South Korea and Japan.

Proven oil reserves currently stand at 25 billion barrels, which is an approximately 40 year supply. In an effort to boost oil production, significant sums have been invested to locate additional oil fields and to prolong the productive life of existing ones.

Expat League Tables

Qatar is ranked as the sixth highest country for financial well-being in HSBC International's Expat Explorer Survey 2010, which takes into account aspects including earnings, disposable income, the cost of living, the ability to save and the affordability of luxury items.

In non-financial categories it scores average ratings for friendliness, but is the lowest scorer in terms of making friends with the local population. Source: offshore.hsbc.com.

Economic Diversification

Qatar has recognised the dwindling future of the oil industry, hence is diversifying its economic future with heavy investment in liquefied natural gas (LNG). The country's gas reserves are the third-largest in the world (behind Russia and Iran), exceeding 25 trillion cubic metres – about 14% of the world's total. Qatargas is one of the world's leading LNG companies and with orders from new markets in countries that include China, Canada, US, UK and India, its annual exports had reached 77 million tonnes per annum by 2011 – making Qatar the world's largest producer and exporter of LNG.

Qatalum, the world's largest aluminium smelter opened in 2010, with the capacity to produce 585,000 tonnes of aluminium per year.

The international exhibitions and events sector is set to explode following the completion of the Qatar National Convention Centre (qatarconvention.com) at the end 2011 and the Doha Exhibition Centre and Tower in 2012. With investments of some $1.2bn in both facilities, Qatar is looking to emerge as a major player on the international exhibition circuit.

Looking ahead, Qatar is investing some $17bn on tourism infrastructure in preparation for the FIFA World Cup. Currently, the plans stand at a 400% increase in hotel capacity with 29,000 luxury rooms and furnished apartments to be completed in the next few years.

Initiatives such as Qatar Foundation's Education City, Qatar Science & Technology Park and the Qatar Financial Centre reflect a dedication to education, technology and multinational investment, and a recent $25bn agreement with Deutsche Bank to build a domestic rail network, pledges vital improvement to internal transport infrastructure. The New Doha International Airport (scheduled for full completion in 2015) will be 12 times larger than the existing airport while the Qatar-Bahrain Friendship Bridge will make transfers between the two Gulf states easier. Overall, the investments in improved transportation infrastructure are geared towards to boosting Qatar's profile as a leading destination for sporting events, business and leisure tourism.

Employment

With its continued growth and strictly controlled residency policies, it is not surprising that Qatar has one of the lowest unemployment rates in the world. In 2010, only 0.5% of the population were unemployed in the country (second only to Monaco) with almost 45% of workers employed in construction. The remaining workforce is predominately engaged in the mining, manufacturing and trade sectors. Despite a thriving economy and low unemployment rates, jobs in the country were not fully immune to the effects of the global recession around 2009. However, the situation never got as grave as in some countries thanks to Qatar's booming economy, and by 2011, salaries were already on the steady rise following an improved outlook. Looking ahead, Qatar's successful FIFA World Cup bid should ensure a huge surge in

demand for skilled workers in the lead-up to the 2022 tournament, with a reported U$S 57 million already set aside for the world cup projects.

The National Vision

The government has set an ambitious objective to transform the country by 2030 into an advanced society capable of sustaining its own development – human, social, economic and environmental – and providing a high standard of living for its entire population. Initiatives like the Qatarisation programmes are fundamentally working to reach this goal.

Qatarisation Programmes

Qatarisation is a government initiative launched in 2000 to encourage Qatari nationals into the labour force. Companies have been directed to fill 50% of their job quota with Qataris; however, few firms have managed more than 20%, mostly due to skills shortage, but also due to lack of interest. Private firms have an apparently negative perception of Qatari workers in terms of productivity rate, lack of expertise and incumbent costs, while the nationals themselves are reportedly finding the choice of jobs

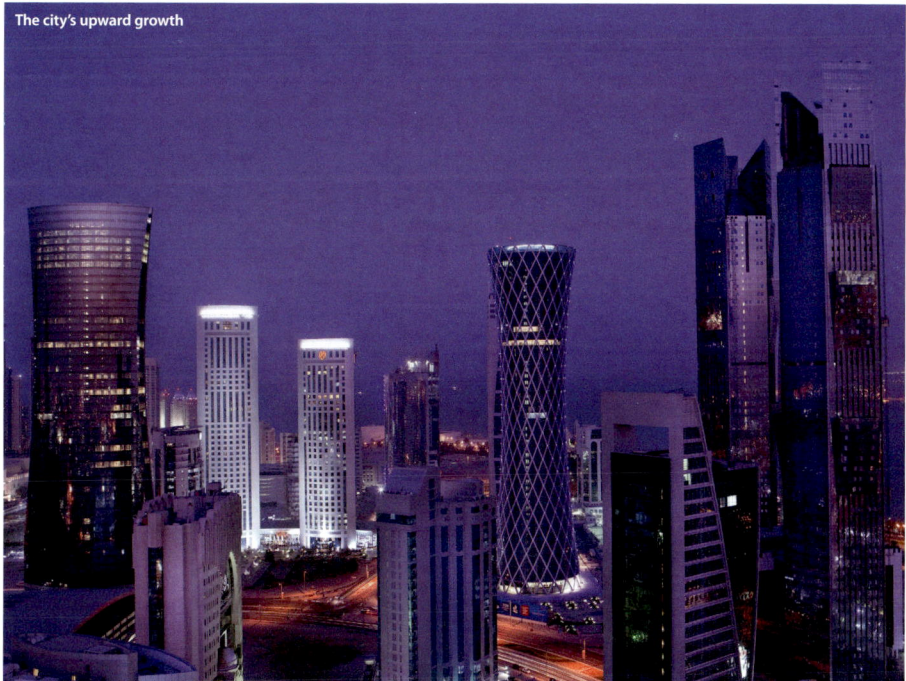

The city's upward growth

Qatar: Becoming A Resident

unappealing – especially those requiring lengthy educational training, long working hours or offering an unsatisfactory wage. Companies who fail to implement the Qatarisation scheme will face a fine of up to QR 100,000.

KEY DEVELOPMENTS

As part of Qatar's massive investment in its infrastructure, many new and exciting projects are under construction, or planned over the next few years. A selection of these is featured below. Some projects have fallen behind their original construction schedule following the global recession, but most seem to be going ahead, albeit at a slower pace than planned.

The Arab & Islamic Heritage Library
Old Al Rayyan qf.org.qa
Map **2 A3**
Once open in its new home at the Central Library in Education City, the Heritage Library will house the works currently on display at the National Heritage Library near the Corniche, which includes rare Arabic manuscripts and European Orientalist maps and documents. The completion date for this project is expected to be sometime in 2013.

Doha Exhibition Centre & Tower
Doha Corniche Al Dafna Map **2 Q2**
This tower, designed by architect Helmut Jahn, will be the tallest building in Doha when it is completed in 2012. It will have an anticipated 100 storeys, with retail space and an exhibition centre.

Education City
Al Luqta St Al Shagub **4454 0400**
myeducationcity.com Map **2 A3**
Developed by the Qatar Foundation, Education City is already home to a number of institutions and international university campuses, and still its growth continues. Projects currently at the planning stage or under construction include a 350 bed teaching hospital, a conference and convention centre, and the Al Shaqab riding academy.

Hamad Medical City
Al Rayyan Rd Hamad Medical City
hmc.org.qa
Map **2 L6**
This is a QR 1.5 billion development on Al Rayyan Road. Hamad General Hospital and the Women's Hospital are already open on the site, which will eventually have three new hospitals, including an orthopaedic hospital and a paediatric facility in partnership with Toronto's Hospital for Sick Children.

The Pearl Qatar

Heart Of Doha

Musheireb dohaland.com.qa
Map **2 Q8**

The Dohaland project, otherwise known as the Heart of Doha, involves the regeneration of the entire Musheireb area. The aim of the project is to recreate a modern community based on traditional Qatari principles; it will be a community-centred district designed to foster interaction between the people who live and work there, with amenities within walking distance. The first phase of the project is scheduled to be completed by the end of 2012.

Katara Cultural Village

Off Lusail St Al Gassar **4408 0000**
katara.net
Map **1 K3**

Since its opening in mid 2010, the Katara Cultural Village has become a favourite night time hub, encompassing an open-air amphitheatre, opera house, drama theatre and a handicraft souq, as well as international restaurants and cafes. During the day, the public beach – one of the few in town – is a main attraction with plenty of activities and play zones in the water for children, and watersports activities are avaliable for the young at heart. The public beach entry is QR 100.

Lusail City

Al Istiqlal St, 15km north of Doha
Jabal Thuaileb **4497 4444**
lusail.com
Map **1 K1**

Launched at the end of 2005, this mixed-use development will eventually cover 35 square kilometres and be able to accommodate about 200,000 people. Occupying a strip of coastline 15km north of Doha, the project will have 10 districts featuring marinas, hotels, entertainment and leisure, office towers, lots of shopping, two golf courses, apartment blocks and exclusive gated communities, plus an Energy City, Entertainment City and Media City.

New Doha International Airport

Ras Abu Abboud **4467 9888**
ndiaproject.com
Map **2 V10**

Construction is well under way on Doha's new airport, located a few kilometres east of the existing airport and partly on reclaimed land. With two runways, and designed to cater to the growing number of visitors expected over the coming years, the airport is being built in phases. The first phase is scheduled for completion by the end of 2012. The final completion date is scheduled for 2015 when the airport will be equipped to handle 50 million passengers a year.

The Pearl

North of West Bay The Pearl Qatar **4446 3444**
thepearlqatar.com
Map **1 M2**

Perhaps the best-known of Qatar's latest development projects, The Pearl is the new island complex built on reclaimed land off the shore of the West Bay Lagoon. Designed to become the Riviera of the Middle East, it features apartments, town houses and villas, plus retail outlets, excellent restaurants, entertainment venues, and luxurious five-star hotels. The Porto Arabia sector is already open and is home to designer shopping boutiques and trendy eateries; for more on the restaurants, see the Going Out chapter on p.339. The design of The Pearl means it will have four separate marinas with berths for 700 boats. It will eventually be home to 35,000 residents and, significantly, it was the first development in Qatar to offer freehold property to non-locals; all owners are issued with a residency visa.

Qatar National Convention Centre

Al Luqta St Gharrafat Al Rayyan **4454 6008**
qatarconvention.com
Map **2 A2**

Open since late 2011, the Qatar National Convention Centre is located opposite Education City. It is a vast building with a giant, steel sidra tree holding up the roof. Apart from its striking appearance, the sidra tree symbolises the centre's green credentials. The building incorporates water and energy efficiency in its design and one eighth of its power will come from solar energy. It will have vast exhibition space, auditoriums and meeting rooms.

Qatar State Mosque

Cnr of Khalifa & Al Istiqlal St Al Jebailat
Map **2 L3**

A vast state mosque is under construction on the corner of Khalifa Street and Al Istiqlal Street. When complete it will feature no fewer than 99 domes; inside, the impressive mosque will have space for 20,000 worshippers, making it one of the largest places of worship in the region. Estimates put the total project spend at somewhere around the $110 million mark.

Qatar-Bahrain Causeway

Nr Al Zubara, Ras Ashairij Doha
Map **Qatar Country Map A1**

The 'Friendship Causeway' will be a 40 kilometre road link between Qatar and Bahrain, consisting of a series of bridges and highways built on reclaimed land, some sections of which may have to be 40 metres above the sea to allow shipping to pass beneath. Estimates for the cost of the project vary from $2 billion to $4.7 billion.

Doha's Striking Skyline

Writer and long-term expat Frances Gillespe comments on the remarkable changes to Doha's urban horizon witnessed over the last decade.

Over the last few years the skyline of Doha, especially along its elegant Corniche, has seen a dramatic transformation. Multi-storey towers, each higher than the next and outlandishly designed by world-renowned architects, jostle for skyline space in a city which a decade ago boasted nothing much taller than the Sheraton Doha.

Sheraton Doha, West Bay

For years after its construction in 1982 this iconic building stood alone at the northern end of the bay, a ziggurat-shaped landmark visible from far out at sea. Designed by the American architect William Pereira, it came to be regarded as the symbol of Doha and continues to command the affection of its citizens. Many other 5-star hotels have been built and the Sheraton is now dwarfed by the forest of multi-storey towers around it, but the airy pyramidal interior, with its jewelled lifts, still holds a unique atmosphere of luxury and sophistication.

Office Tower, Doha Corniche

Architect-designed by Ateliers Jean Nouvel, which claims that this 231 metre slim, bullet-shaped tower owes its inspiration to a medieval spiked helmet. It's also reminiscent of the small minarets on some of the country's older mosques. The sleek, glass-clad building is surrounded by a lacework of aluminium featuring the traditional Islamic designs of light grilles, known in Arabic as mashrabiya. Each floor commands panoramic views of the sea, Doha port and the city, and looking northwards the desert, fast being swallowed up by development, can be glimpsed. The internal glass atrium rises an impressive 112m to the 26th of the 45 floors.

QIPCO Office Tower, Doha Corniche

Near Nouvel's tower stands the QIPCO Office Tower, named the 'Tornado Tower' for its distinctive shape. Recently it won the best tall building award in the Middle East and North Africa. Designed by the architects CICO/SIAT, the 200m hyperboloid-shaped tower features a spectacular lighting system by Thomas Emde. 35,000 light fittings on the junction points of the steel girders are selectively controlled to highlight the structure of the supporting framework. Besides office space and parking the tower features 16 high-speed lifts and a helipad on the 51st floor.

Fanar, Grand Hamad Avenue, Near The Corniche

The Islamic Cultural Centre (p.206), opened in 2006, is known as Fanar (The Lighthouse) for the distinctive external pink stone spiral minaret of its mosque, the only one of its kind in the country, which was inspired by the Al Mutawwakil Mosque in Samarra, Iraq and the Ahmad Ibn Tolon Mosque in Cairo, Egypt. At night the building is illuminated and glows with golden light. It was designed by an Egyptian architect and built with the support of the Islamic Affairs Ministry.

The Aspire Tower, Sports City, Al Waab Street

This 300m tower is currently the tallest structure in the country (although it will soon be overtaken). Designed by architect Hadi Simaan, it served as the focal point for the Asian Games held in Doha in 2006 and was completed the following year. During the Games, the flame atop lit up the night sky. The tower will eventually house a five-star hotel and conference/business centre, a restaurant, gymnasium, a sports museum and an observation deck providing panoramic views. It features a swimming pool cantilevered 80 metres above ground.

Zig Zag Towers, West Bay Lagoon

These 141m high twin towers, said to be the tallest zig-zag-shaped towers in the world, are a talking point, either admired or derided by Doha's residents. Each is a 34 storey residential block. Designed by MZ and Partners, the towers overlook the sea and, when complete, a large mall complex with a public plaza, food court, shops and a cinema will connect the two.

Doha Corniche skyline

CONSIDERING QATAR

Expats have traditionally been tempted to Qatar by great employment opportunities, offering generous tax-free wages and benefits such as company-provided housing, schooling and free flights home. However, job packages, while still attractive, are not on the whole as bounteous as they once may have been, nor have they enjoyed an increase relative to the cost of living.

A UBS poll on prices and earnings in 2010 found that while Doha is cheaper than Dubai, price levels are on a par with Moscow, Johannesburg and Shanghai. On the other hand, petrol prices are still extremely cheap and the cost of a new vehicle is very reasonable.

School fees are sometimes provided as an employment benefit, but families who do not receive assistance toward schooling may find the move less worthwhile financially. Availability of places in schools is also something to investigate before arriving.

Doha is the capital city, and it is here where most expats live and work. Some companies are starting to house families in nearby satellite towns though; these areas are consequently experiencing their own rapid growth in order to keep up with the high quality of living enjoyed by Doha residents, and are all within reasonable proximity of the capital with decent roads providing convenient access to the capital for amenities that aren't yet available on your doorstep.

Locations out of Doha include: Dukhan, 84km (50 minutes) west of the capital and heavily associated with the oil and gas industries; Al Khor (40 minutes away), which houses employees of Qatargas and RasGas and is situated 50 kilometres to the north of the capital; and Al Wakra on the south coast (a 15 minute drive) is undergoing a re-emergence as 'the radiant south', and offers a cheap alternative to Doha's housing prices.

The speed of progress in Qatar means there is generally a strong job market; refer to p.102 for advice on finding work and a list of recruitment companies.

QATAR FACTS

- There are 10 provinces in Qatar. Ad Dawhah (or Doha) is the largest by population, while Jariyan al Batnah in the south is the largest geographically
- Just 2% of Qatar's land is arable
- Qatar successfully won the bid for the 2022 FIFA World Cup
- At the 18th annual World Travel Awards in 2011, Qatar was named as Middle East's Leading Emerging Business Destination
- The total workforce was estimated as 1.254 million at end of 2010

Part-time and freelance opportunities are on the rise too, but ensure that you obtain the correct visa if you are pursuing this option (see Work, p.99).

Most companies recruit from outside the country so it is most likely that you will arrive following an offer of employment. Your company will effectively 'sponsor' you as their employee, and make all the necessary arrangements for you to legally enter and live in the country (see Sponsorship, p.40). If you wish to set up a business here, you must find a Qatari national to officially represent you and your enterprise.

Liquor Licences

While drinking is forbidden for Muslims, it is served in many hotel clubs, bars and restaurants. To purchase alcohol for home use you must first obtain a liquor licence (p.44) by visiting Qatar Distribution Centre. You may only buy alcohol for your strict personal use and your purchase must be concealed from view and transported directly to your home.

BEFORE YOU ARRIVE

The red tape in Qatar can seem endless and you will be required to present personal documents whenever you apply for a visa, licence, telephone line, health card, or school admission. Essential documents include your passport, birth certificate, marriage certificate, children's birth certificates and any relevant education or training certificates. Once you have gathered all of your important documents you should make copies and have them certified while still in your home country. Your government's foreign affairs office will be able to instruct on the process. Documents must be in English or Arabic – translated copies should also be attested.

Ensure you have your financial affairs in order before you leave, closing any unnecessary bank accounts or standing orders. If you plan to transfer money home from Qatar, research fees and charges imposed by your bank and register for online banking. Your bank or loan provider should be informed of your departure if you have any outstanding debts, including student loans. Inform your tax office that you are leaving the country – you may be eligible for non-resident concessions plus you need to be aware of any regulations concerning earnings accrued while living overseas. Your superannuation/pension provider should also be advised of your departure as it may affect your contributions (see Work, Finance & The Law, p.99).

If you own a property then you might consider renting it out while you are abroad, especially if you plan to only move temporarily, or if you need to survive a probation period with your new employer.

Cafe culture in Souk Waqif

If your company will be providing accommodation for you check whether it is furnished or not – this could determine whether you need to ship your whole household or only your personal belongings (see Housing, p.67). Families should research suitable schooling as early as possible as most have extensive waiting lists (see Education, p.137).

Customs

Qatar maintains a zero-tolerance policy on recreational drug use – even the smallest amounts will get you arrested. Codeine, tranquilisers and some anti-depressants and sleeping pills are banned so carry your prescription and a verifying letter from your doctor if you are dependent on these medicines. Your bags will be scanned on arrival (likewise your shipping container) and any prohibited items (pornography, alcohol, narcotics, pork) will be confiscated. Each passenger is allowed a reasonable amount of tobacco and perfume for personal use. There is no restriction on currency.

You do not require any special immunisations or medical certificates prior to entry into Qatar, but you will be expected to undertake a medical test before residency can be granted, including screening for HIV and TB.

Finally, familiarise yourself with local laws and regulations before you arrive. Qatar is an Islamic nation and heavy penalties are administered for disregard of its customs. Strict dress codes apply (particularly on the public beaches), and there is zero tolerance towards drinking or being drunk in public. Never drink and drive as you will wind up in jail or being deported, or both.

Cohabiting is illegal so you may need to take the plunge before you leave home. Some people do live together as unmarried couples, but the penalties – including deportation – are severe so it is a risky

practice. Some employers offer greater benefits to married personnel (better housing, for example) and it is easier for a woman to leave and enter the country if she is sponsored by her husband, as opposed to an employer. It is against the law for an unmarried woman to have a baby in Qatar. For more detailed information, see Culture p.16 and Legal Issues, p.117.

WHEN YOU ARRIVE

Relocating to a foreign country can be daunting, and that's before you've encountered the mountain of legal paperwork that awaits you. It helps to prepare your original documents and certified copies in order to process your Residence Permit, without which very little can be achieved. Most companies will sort this out for you but if not then consider hiring a PRO, or mandoub, to act on your behalf (see p.40).

Unless your housing has been pre-arranged, refer to p.68 for information on seeking accommodation, as well as connecting your utilities and furnishing your new home.

As for transport, you are likely to need to hire a car (p.61) for the first month or two of your stay as you cannot buy a vehicle until your Residence Permit has been issued. You are permitted to drive (but not own a vehicle) on your foreign licence for a period of one week, after which you must obtain a temporary licence from the traffic department (p.59). You can apply for a full Qatari driving licence when you have your residence permit. Be aware that you can't apply for a temporary driving licence once your residency is underway, so this is one of the first things that will need your attention when you arrive.

If driving isn't an option, taxis and private limousines are available and are cheap to hire. Alternatively, you could catch one of the new air-conditioned buses that have recently arrived in the city. Travelling by bus is cheap, but it is rarely utilised by westerners. (see Public Transport, p.54).

Advice From A PRO Ann Thomas, Indian expat & personnel relations officer

When moving to Qatar you need to be very patient, purely because of the amount of red tape that you go through here. It can be trying, so be prepared for a struggle at times, but it's important not to panic or get too flustered – these things take time here, it's just the way it is. When you move, bring all of your original certificates with you and lots of copies, and get them attested first if you can. Bring evidence of all of your qualifications, especially those that are relevant to the type of job you will be doing, plus your marriage certificate, and birth certificates of any children, as well as their leaving certificates from their current school and their latest report cards. Bring your medical records with you too; this can be helpful if your medical test comes back inconclusive, so they can check to see what the problem might be. Bring lots of passport photos, some with white backgrounds and some with blue. Most importantly, bring a sackful of patience. Different places ask for different things, and there really isn't that much you can do apart from bring your essential documents. Everything here revolves around your residence permit, and for that all you really need is your passport and photos, which you can get here.

Coping With Culture Shock

Doing some basic preparation and having an open attitude will help you adjust to your new home in no time at all.

Moving to a new place can be a daunting prospect regardless of whether you're heading to the next neighbourhood or the opposite hemisphere. Different customs and cultural traditions can make moving seem even more intimidating, but often the reality is far less scary than anticipated. Patience and an open mind are indispensable when adjusting to life in a new country, but researching the key cultural differences can help prepare you in advance.

Clarifying your motivations for moving is an important step in your decision making and helps to keep things in perspective. Think about the reasons for your move – are you pursuing a better career? A richer cultural experience for your children? Higher earnings with an improved quality of life? Whatever the answer, make sure that you understand your reasons for stepping into the unknown before you commit.

But if you don't expect your new country to be a different life from the one you are now living, then you might be in for a struggle. The food, the language and the culture is probably going to be like nothing you have experienced before, so it is important to ready yourself for some adjustment. It will take some time but it will happen, especially if your move is for the right reasons.

One of the inevitable hurdles of moving to Qatar is the mass of paperwork that needs to be processed when you first arrive. It can be frustrating, but if you accept that's how it is going to be then it will be much easier to bear. Think of it as the 'Three Times Rule' – nothing ever seems to be as easy as it should be and you will probably need to return at least three times for the correct, copied, certified, translated, forgotten paperwork to be successfully submitted. Bring your sense of humour.

The driving is equally overwhelming and will at first seem chaotic and ruthless. However, it really isn't as bad as it looks; you'll just need to adopt a change in attitude and road sense. You might need to concentrate a bit harder and be more alert than you would be in your home country, but after a while you will get a feeling for how it all works. The roads are good and well-maintained in populated areas and travel distances are usually reasonable.

The Qatari people are warm, friendly and accommodating with impeccable taste, manners and etiquette. As hosts they express extraordinary generosity and are extremely hospitable. Be courteous and respectful and you will have no trouble fitting in.

If you do begin to feel a little culture shock, overcome it by accepting that Qatar is your home, and not a temporary posting. Live your life as you would elsewhere – decorate and furnish your environment to your taste and get involved with all your favourite hobbies and pursuits. Being an expat community, there is a wealth of lively activities on offer and some valuable groups ready to provide their support and assistance. Get out there, meet new friends and enjoy the benefits that make Qatar such a desirable place to live.

Thanks to video calling, internet shopping, international post and good flight connections, home is never really that far away, so if you are feeling homesick, then there are plenty of ways to bring home a little closer to you. It is not just a cliche that life is what you make it, in this expat community it is the golden rule.

Top Tips On Settling In

- Check out Social Groups on p.48 and set up your social sphere.
- Be open to new experiences: decide to accept every invitation that comes your way for the first three months of your stay.
- Peruse Activities & Hobbies on p.263 and find the people in Qatar who share your interests.
- Get online and find out what Qatar's like from the people who live there. Join Qatar's active online community and meet expat residents who are only too keen to share their experiences. See Useful Websites, p.23.

Making new friends will help you to settle in quickly; take some time to investigate local clubs and societies that you might like to join, and get out and socialise.

Visas On Arrival

Citizens of the following countries can get a visit visa on arrival: Andorra, Australia, Austria, Belgium, Brunei, Canada, Denmark, Finland, France, Germany, Greece, Hong Kong, Iceland, Ireland, Italy, Japan, Liechtenstein, Luxembourg, Malaysia, Monaco, Netherlands, New Zealand, Norway, Portugal, San Marino, Singapore, South Korea, Spain, Sweden, Switzerland, United Kingdom, USA and Vatican City.

GETTING STARTED

Entry Visa

Visa requirements for entering Qatar vary depending on your nationality and purpose of visit. Always check current regulations before travelling as details can change unexpectedly. Your passport must be valid for at least six months and have at least one blank page. GCC nationals (Bahrain, Kuwait, Oman, Saudi Arabia and UAE) do not need a visa prior to visiting Qatar.

Citizens of 33 countries are eligible for automatic visas on arrival (see Visas On Arrival, above). When you arrive, head to customs and your passport will be stamped with a 30 day renewable visit visa. It costs QR 100 and is payable by credit card only. If you wish, you may opt for a joint tourist visa which also allows you entry into the Sultanate of Oman. You can visit the government website (gov.qa/wps/portal), and pre-order your visa online for QR 55 (tourist visa) or QR 100 (joint tourist visa). You can extend your visit visa in person at the Department of Immigration (opposite the airport car park, open 24 hours). Just present your passport prior to the visa's expiration period and pay a QR 100 fee. A fine of QR 200 per day is applicable if you overstay your visa.

In early 2010, the Qatari government announced the end to visas on arrival for all nationalities, effective from 1 May; however, shortly after this announcement, these new regulations were put on indefinite hold. At the time of writing, the old ruling remained and citizens of all 33 countries could still receive visas on arrival, but you are advised to check with your local Qatari embassy prior to travelling, to find out the latest regulations.

All other nationalities can get a 30 day tourist visa, costing QR 200, from either a Qatar-based sponsor or by arrangement with one of the hotels. Most hotels can arrange a tourist visa with relatively short notice but it is best to allow at least 3-5 working days. Check the finer points of your entry conditions with the hotel before confirming, as some require that you book your entire stay at their establishment, which could turn out to be costly. The visa can be extended by one month and incurs penalties for overstaying. A requirement of this visa is that you arrive on a Qatar Airways flight.

PROs & NOCs

In Qatar, a PRO or mandoub is your company's 'man who can' – he liaises with various government departments and carries out admin procedures. The PRO will take care of all visa, residency, health card and labour card applications. An NOC is a no objection certificate, and is essentially a letter stating that the person in question permits you to carry out a certain procedure. You will need one of these in a variety of situations whether it's from your employer allowing you to switch jobs or your own NOC permitting a family member to work.

If you are entering Qatar with a confirmed job offer, your employer should send you a copy of your approved entry visa. This is usually a single page document that must be presented at passport control. If you fail to enter the country on the correct visa, the passport control department will ask you to leave Qatar (probably at your own expense), then re-enter the country and start the residency process all over again.

Visa runs for potential residents are largely a thing of the past, as the one month renewal process offers plenty of time for your residence permit to be issued. However, if you are unable to extend your visa, it is possible to fly to a neighbouring country and then return to Qatar (the same day is fine) to receive a brand new 30 day visa.

Sponsorship

Residence Permit

In order to live in Qatar you need to have a residence permit. There are three types of permit, two of which require the individual to be sponsored: one is for those sponsored for employment and the other for residence only (for example when you are sponsored by a family member who is already sponsored by an employer). Both types of permit are normally issued for a maximum period of two years, and can be renewed an unlimited number of times.

The third entitlement to residency was introduced in 2004 when Qatar announced the provision of residence visas for foreigners who purchase approved freehold properties – such as those offered in The Pearl – of at least 80 square metres in area. Conditions

"Mommy, Daddy, will I make new friends?"

The most important thing to me?
Is to make sure my child has the easiest time settling in to the new surroundings

"The intercultural and school search program have helped our daughter find the right school and settle in very quickly. She is happy and we are. Thanks Crown for making this part of my move easy."
~Turkey to Dubai

Crown service offerings include:
- Home Search
- Visa & Immigration Services
- Family Assistance & School Search
- Household Goods Shipment & Warehousing
- Intercultural Training
- Spouse Career Support
- Pet Relocations

Tel: +974 4 4621115
doha@crownrelo.com
crownrelo.com

YOUR HAPPINESS IS THE MOST IMPORTANT THING TO US

Well Connected. Worldwide.™

CROWN
RELOCATIONS

Getting Started

Qatar: Becoming A Resident

of the visa are subject to the same medical and character requirements of a regular residence permit and are valid for a renewable period of five years.

Applications for renewing residency must be submitted prior to the expiry date, otherwise you will have to undergo the whole process again (including medical testing). If you plan to be out of Qatar for six months or more, you should apply for a visa extension (QR 500) to avoid losing your residency status. This is particularly relevant to women returning to their home country to give birth, or children studying abroad.

Employer Sponsorship

If you have moved to Qatar to take up a job offer, your employer is obliged to sponsor you. Your new company's PRO will handle the paperwork on your behalf and apply for your residency permit, but it's up to you to ensure that your personal documents are in order when you arrive. Any certificates need to be attested or legalised, including marriage, educational and qualification certificates and your children's birth certificates. This can be a lengthy process as it involves obtaining stamps from both your country of origin's office of foreign affairs and the Qatari embassy, and so is best carried out before you leave your country of origin. The process is slightly different for each country, so check with the foreign office in your home country for the procedure you need to follow (see p.390 for a list of embassies in Qatar).

Your employer is also responsible for all costs associated with your sponsorship and residency permit application, including the cost of your medical testing (p.43).

Working Wives

It is possible for a working wife to sponsor her husband and children, providing she meets the minimum wage criteria set by the government. If her husband finds employment, he must then transfer to his new employer's sponsorship. Qatari women have only recently won the entitlement to sponsor foreign husbands and children.

It is important to remember that sponsors will ensure that their employees abide by local laws and regulations. If an employee is found in violation of any local policies, including zero tolerance for drink driving, then they are generally on their own and can face legal repercussions such as imprisonment or deportation.

If a company sponsors the employee and their spouse is not working, then the working spouse can sponsor their partner and children. If both partners are working then they may have two different sponsoring organisations, depending on the rules of the company.

Family Sponsorship

Providing you are earning over QR 7,000 per month, you may sponsor your spouse and children to live with you. Sons up to the age of 25 can be sponsored, as can unmarried daughters of any age. Again, your employer is most likely to handle your application for you, or you can undertake the application process yourself. You will need passport copies for all applicants, a copy of your employment contract stating your wage, and attested copies of your marriage certificate (if sponsoring your spouse) and/or birth certificates (if sponsoring children). Your family members will also need to successfully complete the medical testing and fingerprinting (see p.43).

If you have a family residence visa and decide to start work, you can remain under family sponsorship, unless the original sponsor (your spouse or parent) changes jobs. In this case you will be required to move under your new employer's sponsorship, and you will have to re-do all of the paperwork and tests required for sponsorship.

Sponsoring A Maid

Many expat families enjoy the luxury of domestic help in Qatar. By law, you are required to offer sponsorship to a domestic helper in your employment, and they are supposed to live in your home.

It is illegal for a single man to hire a live-in maid. A married man looking to hire a maid for his family must first get an NOC from his sponsor, but this is only once his wife has her residency.

It is possible to hire a maid locally by obtaining an NOC from her current employer and taking over her sponsorship, or you can hire a new maid from abroad. There are a few agencies that can assist you with the process, the advantage being that you can effectively return your maid and request a new one if she doesn't work out. Agencies will also sort out the visas and paperwork for you, but at a cost. Once your maid arrives, she will need to undergo the usual residency procedure including the medical testing and fingerprinting. Her residence permit will cost you QR 300 per year and approval for her initial sponsorship will cost you QR 1,500.

Only women from certain countries are allowed to work as maids in Qatar, and her salary will depend on her nationality, as per agreement between the Qatari government and the relevant embassy. Filipinos are usually paid between QR 1,500 and QR 1,800 per month, while Sri Lankan and Indian ladies tend to earn between QR 800 and QR 1,200 per month. Besides providing housing, you will be expected to subsidise your housemaid's pay with additional food, clothing and optional extras. You are also required to obtain a health card for her. Contracts are usually for a renewable period of two years, after which you must pay for a return flight for your maid to her home

42

Qatar Explorer

country. Bear in mind that as her sponsor, you are responsible for the behaviour and welfare of your maid.

Exit Visa

All expats residing under a work sponsorship must obtain an exit visa from their employer whenever they wish to leave Qatar. Husbands who have been sponsored by their wives must acquire an exit visa if travelling alone, but wives and children of employer-sponsored husbands are exempt.

You can apply for an exit visa up to seven days in advance of travel by downloading the application form at moi.gov.qa and selecting either a single exit visa (QR 10) or multiple exit visa (QR 500, valid for one year). After your sponsor has signed the completed form, you may take it to the Department of Immigration (across from the airport car park, open 24 hours) along with payment, your passport and your sponsor ID (if necessary). The exit visa will be stamped in your passport and is valid immediately.

It is worth noting that employers have the right to refuse a request for an exit visa and there have been instances where people with outstanding loans have been barred from leaving at the border.

Medical Test

As part of the residency process you will need to undergo a medical test within the first week of arriving in the country. This involves verification of your blood type and screening for tuberculosis and HIV. Your blood-type certificate can be acquired from any clinic at a cost of QR 15 (most employers will recommend somewhere to you). It involves a simple finger-prick, followed by a few minutes' wait, and needs to be performed by all new arrivals who wish to become residents, regardless of age.

For the medical test, you will need your blood-type certificate, an application form (typed in Arabic), a copy of your passport, two passport photos and QR 100. Take everything to the Medical Commission on Al Muntazah Street near the Industrial Area – it will be helpful if you have a company representative with you for assistance. Male and female sections are in separate areas of the building.

Enter the building and follow the signs to counter one – you may need to take a ticket if there is a queue. Here you will have your documents checked and your payment received. Keep the receipt as you will later need it to collect your results. Go to room three to have your blood drawn for HIV testing, then to room four where an x-ray will be performed to check for TB. Women who are pregnant do not need to have the x-ray done. Check with reception to confirm that you have completed all necessary tests before leaving – you don't want to have to return a second time.

After about a week, the commission informs your company of the results of your tests. If all is clear, you

will then be asked to proceed to CID for fingerprinting (see below). If there are any discrepancies in the results, you may be asked to return for re-testing or to provide further information regarding your medical history. If your HIV test returns a positive result then you will be deported from Qatar.

Fingerprinting

About a week after your medical, you will be invited for compulsory fingerprinting at the CID building (off Sports City Street, map 2 E13). Children under 12 do not need to be fingerprinted. The process is straightforward enough and your company will supply you with the necessary paperwork. These documents are also available on site, but you will need QR 5 for your personal details to be typed in Arabic.

Once you have registered your arrival (men and women have separate registration windows) you will be issued with a queue number and directed to the fingerprinting room to wait your turn. There you will have your finger and hand prints electronically scanned, which takes about five minutes. You then collect your form which will be typed in Arabic (QR 10) and return it to your employer. Your company should then submit this along with your medical test results and original passport to the Immigration Department for your residency application. Your permit will be ready after approximately six weeks.

Health Card

Even if you have private medical insurance it is recommended that you obtain a health card for you and your family members – you will need it to receive treatment at the government health clinics and hospitals. Your employer may arrange for your card or you can easily obtain it yourself from your local clinic. Complete the necessary forms and submit with two passport photos, a copy of your Qatari ID, proof of your address and the QR 100 fee. The card should be ready after two or three weeks, during which time you may use your receipt when seeking medical attention. The card is valid for the same period as your residency and can be renewed in person at the post office, at any government health clinic or online at gov.qa/wps/portal using your credit card.

ID Card

A Qatari ID card is compulsory for all residents over the age of 18 and must be carried with you at all times. It is issued with your residence permit and costs QR 100 to renew or QR 200 to replace if lost, stolen or damaged. You will be asked to produce the card for official purposes (such as opening a bank account or requesting a telephone line), when visiting secure areas (like offices, schools and compounds) and to enter licensed establishments such as pubs or nightclubs.

Getting Started

Qatar: Becoming A Resident

Qatari nationals have welcomed the introduction of the electronically readable Smart Card in place of the ID. It is capable of holding biometric data and bank account information, and can be used for various online transactions including the renewal of health cards and driving licences. Plans are currently under way to offer the Smart Card to expats, but your company PRO should keep you up to date on any changes.

Driving Licence

You are permitted to drive a rental car for six months on an international driving licence. To continue to drive beyond this period you must obtain a temporary licence from Madinat Khalifa Traffic Department (Map 2 G2), but this cannot be issued while your residency is being processed. You either need to apply for a licence before your residency visa process starts or wait until you have your residency letter in your passport and then apply for a full licence. For further details and information about driving licences see Driving p.57.

All drivers who have a residence permit must carry a Qatari driving licence (valid for five years or 10 years for Qatari nationals) – failure to do so can result in severe penalties, which include hefty fines and the potential impoundment of your vehicle (see Getting Around, p.51, for more details).

A GCC licence can automatically be exchanged for a Qatari licence and so can holders of driving licences from 33 other countries (see Visas on Arrival, p.40). However, as visa regulations and legislation concerning such issues in general is subject to change, it's best to check for the latest information and advice at the Madinat Khalifa Traffic Department office.

If you are not eligible for automatic licence transfer, you must first sit and pass a driving test before a full Qatari licence can be issued (see Applying For a Full Driving Licence, see below). Anyone who does not hold a driving licence but wishes to learn may undertake lessons at any one of the authorised driving school (see p.59). You should ensure that you always carry your driving licence as failure to produce one when stopped can result in a fine of upwards of QR 500, or more serious punishment.

Traffic Department Offices

Madinat Khalifa is the primary traffic department and the only office where you can obtain a new licence. At all other locations you can perform tasks such as licence renewal and payment of traffic fines.
Airport: 4465 3444
Al Rayyan: 4480 7722
Al Maamoura: 4469 5555
City Center Doha, Al Dafna: 4493 4101
Madinat Khalifa: 4489 0666

Applying For A Temporary Driving Licence

To obtain a temporary licence, you will need to apply in person at the Madinat Khalifa Traffic Department, where you will be required to fill in an application form. This will have to be completed in Arabic (there are a number of typing shops within the confines of the traffic department which will assist, for a small fee). If you have entered the country on a business visa, your sponsor will need to sign the form. You'll need to bring your original licence from your country of origin, your passport (and copies) and your Qatar ID card, and three passport photographs (if you normally wear glasses for driving, you should be wearing them in the photo). You will need all of these things to apply for a full licence too, plus an NOC from your sponsor, your sponsor's ID and a copy of your trade licence (if necessary), and you will need to pass an eye test (which is performed on site on the day of application and is included in the fee). The fee is QR 150 for a temporary licence, payable by credit card only.

Applying For A Full Driving Licence

Holders of GCC driving licences can obtain a permanent Qatar driving licence automatically, regardless of their country of origin. The majority of European and western licences can also be automatically exchanged, however, due to the constantly changing regulations, it is worth checking with the traffic department at the time of applying.

If you do have an exchangeable licence, you will need to apply in person at the Madinat Khalifa Traffic Department (4489 0666) and complete an application form that then needs to be typed in Arabic and signed by your sponsor. The process is similar to applying for a temporary licence (p.44). You'll need to take your original licence from your country of origin, a no objection letter from your sponsor (in Arabic), a copy of the trade licence (if you are sponsored by a company), a copy of your sponsor's ID, your original passport or your Qatar ID card, passport copies and three passport photographs. You'll then need to undergo an eye test, which is performed immediately on the premises. Pay the cashier a fee of QR 250 (no cash payments are accepted so take your credit card). You should be able to collect the licence within the next couple of days.

The vehicle-type validity of your Qatari licence will be the same as your overseas licence, including motorcycle qualification if you have one on your foreign licence, but entitlement to drive heavy goods and public service vehicles licences requires a separate test.

Liquor Licence

Only bars and restaurants in certain hotels, sports and leisure clubs are licensed to sell alcohol, with an added tax of 17.5%, to patrons 21 years and over.

You will not be able to find alcohol at independent restaurants or supermarkets. It is possible to purchase alcohol for home use but you must be a non-Muslim, a resident and earn over QR 4,000 per month – and you can only purchase these goods from the Qatar Distribution Company, the sole importer of alcoholic beverages in Qatar.

Nightclub & Bar Entry

As it is illegal for Qataris to consume alcohol, the Government law in Qatar states that to enter any nightclub or bar, you should have membership for that establishment. Most hotels charge QR100 per membership per year and you will need to show your original passport as a form of ID. Most memberships are completed on the spot and you must be over 21 years old to obtain one.

To apply for a liquor licence, you need an application form together with a QR 1,000 returnable deposit, an NOC from your employer stating your basic salary, a passport copy, a copy of your residence permit and a passport photo. You will also need a passport photo of your spouse if you want them to share your licence. Submit your application in person at Qatar Distribution Company (for store location, see Alcohol, p.294). The licence takes around 10 days to be processed, and if approved will state the maximum amount you can spend at QDC per month (usually 10% of your wage). To renew your licence, you can scan and email an application form, copy of your ID and a recent letter from your employer stating your salary to permit@qdc.com.qa. You will be informed by SMS when your renewed licence is available for collection.

Under The Influence

Think before you drink! If you are caught drinking and driving, you will be arrested immediately and your licence confiscated. You will not be able to leave Qatar until your court case is heard, which may take up to six months, and you will likely lose your job and housing. If convicted, you could face a fine of between QR 10,000 to QR 50,000 and up to three years imprisonment.

Only permit holders are allowed inside the QDC shop (no children) and you may not buy alcohol on behalf of anyone else. You must conceal your purchases during your journey, which should be directly to your home (severe penalties apply).

You do not need a liquor licence to purchase duty free alcohol from the airport, and you are permitted to take alcohol purchased in Qatar through customs, providing it is carried in your luggage and not on your person.

Busy traffic

BEFORE YOU LEAVE

Whether you've been here for months, years or decades, it is important that when the time comes to move on from Qatar you tie up all loose ends before you leave. Stories of ex-residents trying to depart without correctly closing bank accounts or loans only to be stopped from departing at the border have become more common over the last 18 months. Your company should help you with most formalities, but it is recommended that you follow a checklist to ensure you don't get accused of 'doing a runner'.

If applicable, give your landlord plenty of notice that you are leaving, allowing enough time for a final inspection and return of your deposit. Tenants are usually responsible for restoring the premises to its original state so you may need to repaint walls and arrange a thorough clean. Cleaning companies (p.94) are inexpensive and offer a good service.

It is wise to get your utilities fully disconnected, especially if the bill is in your name. Contact your local Kahramaa service centre (listed on km.com.qa) to request a final bill. A representative will visit your premises and read the meter in order to calculate the outstanding amount. You then proceed to your local office to pay your bill and retrieve your security deposit (you will need to show your deposit receipt).

Before You Leave

Inform your bank well in advance of your move to settle credit card bills and any outstanding loans. A few days before you leave, check again that everything has been correctly closed – an overlooked banking fee can result in fraud or debt-related theft charges. In this case, you could face severe penalties including jail and you will not be allowed to re-enter Qatar. A tarred international credit rating may also result in denied travel to other countries, such as the USA.

Cancelling Your Visa

If you are under company sponsorship, you will need to hand your passport and Qatari ID, as well as the passports and ID cards of any individuals that you have subsequently sponsored, over to your employer a week before your departure. Your employer can then arrange for your visa to be cancelled, after which you have seven days to leave Qatar. An individual under family sponsorship who wishes to leave permanently may present their passport and ID card in person at the Department of Immigration building opposite the airport car park. It will cost QR 20 to cancel their residence permit, and they will have seven days to leave the country. A fine of QR 10 per day applies to anyone who overstays this grace period and, if caught, they will be deported immediately.

Pets need to be vaccinated against rabies between 30 and 360 days before departure and should be able to meet any other health and welfare requirements of the country you are travelling to, noting that Qatar does not participate in the EU pet passport scheme. Airlines will not allow your pet to travel without a certificate of health, attainable from the veterinary department of the Ministry of Municipal Affairs & Agriculture office near the airport (4456 0444). The certificate is valid for seven days and is issued once your pet has been examined and vaccination records have been checked. Present the health certificate at the QNT office in the cargo section of Doha airport at least five days before you travel to arrange a flight booking and airway bill. You will be expected to pay all fees and handling charges at this time. Qatar Pet Relocators (5528 6335, qatarpetrelocators.com) can assist you with any problems related to exporting your pet.

If you do need to ship your goods, it's best to obtain quotes and make a booking with your preferred company well ahead of time. A full list of relocation companies is available on p.88, some of which offer packing services. Second-hand items are always popular with new arrivals so you shouldn't have trouble selling anything that you don't intend to take with you, including your car. Websites, such as Qatar Living and ExpatWoman (see p.23) have classifieds sections, or you can advertise in the newspaper or on noticeboards in supermarkets – which has proved very successful in the past. Some charities, such as QAWS accept donations of used bed linen and towels (p.15). There are a number of used car dealerships that might be interested in buying your vehicle (see p.62) if you have trouble selling privately or are short on time. Be sure to pay any traffic fines relating to the vehicle before the registration is cancelled or transferred to a new owner.

Finally, be sure to collect any other refundable deposits (such as for your liquor licence) and don't forget to cancel your visa.

Moving On   Kavitha Sri, 34 Indian expat

We moved from Doha to Kuwait 18 months ago. We didn't have any difficulty moving from Doha – everything was well organised by our company – but after eight fantastic years I was sad to leave Qatar.

As an Indian, it was a great place to live. Lots of Indian families live in Qatar – there is a population of 200,000, parties are held on a big scale, there are many religious activities and cultural classes that kids can participate in, and plenty of opportunities to make some really good friends.

In terms of practicalities when we left Qatar, we did not face any issues when closing our bank accounts as the procedure was very simple – we just had to fill out a few forms stating the reason (moving to another country) and provide some other simple information. Qataris are very friendly people and very down to earth, communicating with them is easy and we got everything done in plenty of time. Packing and shipping, again, was arranged by my company staff. Our things were neatly organised and it took only four days for our goods to travel from Doha to Kuwait. It was exactly on time as promised, but more importantly, all the goods were intact without any damage to any of our expensive pieces, including the fragile items.

I would say that any place is better to live in if you have good friends around you, and this is one of the reasons why we still miss Doha.

explorer

there's more to life...

Maximise your holiday, minimise your hand luggage

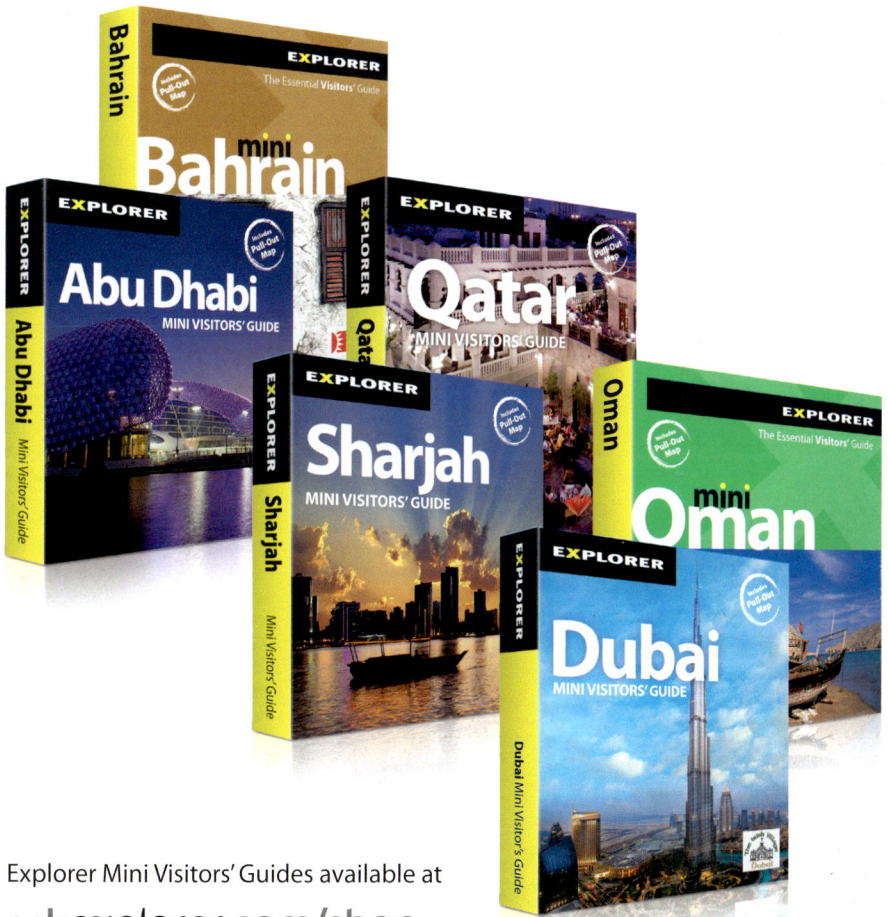

Explorer Mini Visitors' Guides available at

ask**explorer**.com/shop

askexplorer

Meeting New People

Getting to know new people is one of the most important things you can do to settle in – here are some ways to get connected.

The thought of moving away from home and leaving your circle of family and friends can be a daunting prospect, but the good news is that expat communities are made up of people in exactly the same boat, all looking to make new friends and have new experiences. If you don't know anyone in your new home town, it's important to get out and about as soon as you can to meet people. Not only will these acquaintances be able to offer you loads of help in terms of cutting through red tape and getting word-of-mouth recommendations for a good school, doctor or hairdresser, some of them may also end up becoming life-long friends. Expats come and go regularly in Doha, with friendships tending to develop quickly as a result, and you're likely to find yourself mixing with a broader circle of people than you did in your home country. Finding things to do in Doha is not difficult – it's a simple matter of deciding how you want to get out there and when you want to start.

Social Groups

Meeting people early on is essential for deflecting the onset of culture shock by helping you to get your bearings and settle in. Work colleagues, neighbours and associates are your best sources of local information and advice, for everything from dealing with visas to finding the right school or hairdresser. The first people you come into contact with will usually become your first set of friends, some of whom will end up being your friends for life.

There are plenty of ways to locate people who share a similar hobby, interest or nationality, in order to broaden your social network. For the ladies, recreational women's groups such as the American Women's Association (awaqatar.com) and the Tuesday Ladies' Group (tlgdoha.com) provide terrific opportunities to meet people through a variety of exclusive classes, events and catch-ups. Web-based group ExpatWoman (expatwoman.com/qatar) connects people online, helping you to find friends and ask questions about all aspects of Qatar life. See Websites p.23 for other online communities.

Professional networking groups can also expand your social horizons. See Business Councils, p.104.

If you have small children or are pregnant, it is definitely worth joining one of the mum and toddler groups, such as Doha Mums (dohamums.com) or Mums in Doha (mumsindoha.com). See the Family section (p.126) for more information on parenting groups.

Getting in touch with other nationals from your homeland is a nice way to settle in initially and will establish that all-important link to home.

American Women's Association
In addition to regular gatherings that provide opportunities to socialise and network, the association sponsors activities to raise funds for local charities. awaqatar.com

Mingling with the locals

> *Finding things to do in Doha is not difficult – it's a simple matter of deciding how you want to get out there and when you want to start.*

ANZIQ (Australians & New Zealanders In Qatar)
An email service and group for antipodeans in Qatar offering event information, job ads and classifieds auziq@yahoo.com.au.

Canadians In Qatar
A group aimed at connecting Canucks through events, activities and information canadiansinqatar.com.

Dutch Speaking Association Of Qatar
With over 550 members, this group welcomes all Dutch speakers. It has an active social calendar and celebrates Dutch feast days dsaqatar.org.

French-Speaking Women's Committee
A well-established group celebrating Gallic culture with meetings, coffee mornings and scheduled outings vivreauqatar.com.

German Ladies Coffee Group
Pop along for breakfast in The Ritz-Carlton's Lagoon Restaurant on the second Wednesday of every month.

The Qatar Caledonians
Holding a number of annual Scottish celebrations, this group has been running for over 35 years scotsinqatar.com.

Qatar Irish Society
A group connecting the Irish contingent. It has strong ties with Qatar's Gaelic football team (p.272) irishinqatar.com.

South Africans In Qatar
This group run regular activities where you can meet fellow Safas southafricansinqatar.netfirms.com

Swedish Association Of Qatar
A great way to meet Swedish nationals, with regular outings and special events saq.nu.

Leisure Groups

Whatever your hobby, from salsa dancing to scrabble, chances are there are other people in Qatar who are also into it, and many sports and activity groups have busy social calendars for their members. Associations such as the Doha Rugby Club (p.278) are just as popular with sports enthusiasts as with those just looking to enjoy the social scene. For something a little less physical, Doha Players (p.269) is the place for thespians, while nature enthusiasts should check out the Qatar Natural History Group (p.270). The Qatar Scientific Club (p.270) boasts over 4,000 members whose interests include model aircraft, scuba diving and astronomy. Check out the Activity Finder (p.264) to locate other people who share your interests.

Churches

His Highness Sheikh Hamad bin Khalifa Al Thani has recently designated areas of land for the building of new churches, demonstrating a welcoming attitude to various religions outside Islam. A new Catholic chapel now stands near the Industrial Area, while Anglican and Orthodox churches are currently in the planning stages. Even if you're not a regular church-goer, these places also act as good community hubs.

Church Of The Epiphany (Anglican/Episcopal) 4416 5726, epiphany-qatar.org

Malankara Orthodox Church 5589 2711, mocdoha.org

Catholic Church Of Our Lady Of The Rosary 4416 5550, rosarychurchqatar.com

Greek Orthodox Church Of Qatar qorthodox.org

St Thomas Syro – Malabar Church 4416 5060, syromalabarqatar.org

ASCOTT

DOHA

Elegant Living in the Heart of Doha

Step into luxury. Tailored for discerning international travellers, expect state-of-the-art recreation and business facilities along with elegantly designed residences and personalised services at the new Ascott Doha. Located at the north end of Corniche Bay, Ascott Doha offers stunning views of the Arabian Gulf and is within walking distance to Qatar's best known retail and entertainment destinations. Make yourself at home at the prestigious Ascott Doha. **Because life is about living.**

For further information and global reservations, please visit www.the-ascott.com or call (974) 4497 1234

Managed by

THE ASCOTT
LIMITED

A Member of CapitaLand

Ascott Doha is managed by The Ascott Limited, a member of CapitaLand. It is the largest global serviced residence owner-operator in Asia Pacific, Europe and the Gulf region, managing the *Ascott, Citadines* and *Somerset* brands in over 70 cities across more than 20 countries.

Getting Around

GETTING AROUND IN DOHA

The car is both the saviour and the curse of Qatar. Doha has recently gone from being a quiet backwater with negligible public transport to a city of highways crowded with cars, with a fleet of highly efficient and economical new buses, and a squad of rather more expensive taxis.

However, the private car is still king. With public transport largely overlooked until now, Qataris and expats alike have become accustomed to driving around in large cars, despite the volume of traffic and lack of parking spaces in the city centre. With the high temperatures and humidity experienced during the summer, most people still prefer an air conditioned four-wheel drive over sweltering at a bus stop or standing at the side of the road waiting for a taxi.

Lost?

If you're struggling to find your way around the city, turn to the fold-out map at the back of this book. For something a little more portable, Explorer's *Doha Mini Map* is small enough to fit in your pocket. Buy online at askexplorer.com/shop.

The roads are good, but the problem is the quantity of cars on them, and the driving standards are fairly unpredictable to say the least.

Major changes are on the way though. A metro system is on the drawing board and initial contracts have been signed to connect the country to the proposed GCC high speed rail network, with a provisional completion date of 2016.

Traffic Police

Qatar's Road Network

Doha can be a confusing city to navigate for the simple reason that it is built around a large bay. The inner thoroughfare, the attractive Doha Corniche, is semi circular, as are the A, B, C and D Ring Roads. By the time you get to the E Ring Road the curve starts to diminish. When going from north to south you never travel in a straight line.

Travelling inland is a less confusing prospect as the main Salwa Road and Rayyan Road, along with a few minor thoroughfares, radiate out like the spokes on a wheel.

While Doha's main thoroughfares are wide, when not obstructed by the continual infrastructure improvement roadworks, congestion is a problem at most times of the day. Almost all Qatar's commerce, trade and shopping is done in Doha, making it a busy place. There are also a large number of roundabouts in the city, which can be both daunting and confusing.

Heading south out of Doha there is only one major highway, the Mesaieed Road (Route Q7), which takes you to Al Wakra and then on to Mesaieed.

Two roads run north from Doha. One is the Shamal Road (Route Q1), often known as the North Road, which is best avoided at the moment – it is being reconstructed as the eight-lane Doha Expressway and will eventually join the new Qatar-Bahrain Causeway, once the causeway is completed. The Al Khor Road (Route Q1A) is a better option for travelling north.

From Doha, the south-west corner of Qatar and the Saudi border are reached by the newly reconstructed Salwa Road (Route Q5).

Road Rage

If you are a victim of road rage never make rude gestures to the other driver, and don't let your passengers do so either. This is a particularly strong insult in local culture, and is likely to get you in serious trouble, regardless of the driving offence committed by the other party. If the other driver reports you to the police, you will be arrested and taken to the police station. You will not be released until you have apologised, and you could also be fined and spend a night or more in the cells.

There is one more major road, running in a westerly direction from Doha. Rayyan Road turns into Dukhan Road (Route Q3) at Wajbah and goes via the camel racing town of Sheehaniyah to Dukhan. From Sheehaniyah it is a newly reconstructed, under-used, eight-lane highway.

There are no toll roads, bridges or tunnels in Qatar; all roads are free to use and the only vehicle tax is a nominal administration fee of QR 100 each time you re-register your car (see Registering A Vehicle, p.63).

Traffic Regulations

Driving is on the right hand side of the road and the maximum speed limit out of town is 120km/h. Limits in town are variable, but are usually between 80km/h and 100km/h, depending on the area.

Traffic regulations are similar to anywhere else in the world, with a few odd local provisos (see Traffic Fines & Offences, p.59).

Tailgating is a huge problem; the concept of safe stopping distances is not generally respected, and lane discipline is poor. There is zero tolerance to drinking and driving in Qatar, so even if you're having one drink you are taking a big risk by driving home.

Petrol stations can be found throughout Doha and along the main roads in Qatar, and most visitors will be pleasantly surprised to find the price of fuel is a lot lower than elsewhere in the world.

Roundabout Wrongs

Your first encounter with Doha's roundabouts may leave your head spinning. Other drivers' lane choices seem to have little bearing on where they exit and the correlation between indicator use and the direction of travel can be baffling. Pay attention to the road markings when you approach a roundabout, make sure you're in the correct lane and indicate to let other drivers know where you're heading. Be aware that in Qatar the left lane is also used for going straight on. Keep your wits about you at all times and use particular caution when sharing the roundabout with a large or long vehicle.

Parking

Before Qatar's recent development, parking used to be easy – you arrived where you wanted to be, stopped and got out. This may still be true in the rural areas, but things have become less casual in Doha as the city has grown. Parking is more difficult, there is a trend towards charging for it, and parking fines are now commonplace.

Higher priced apartments will usually have a space dedicated for one car; lower priced apartments often have none at all. In the West Bay area most of the big office developments only have parking in their underground car parks for about one third of their staff. Some companies located in this area rent spaces in a nearby multi-storey car park and operate shuttle buses for their staff, but this takes up spaces for other users.

The best legal on-road car parking is along the Corniche where there are dedicated areas, but it fills up quickly at peak periods. Alternatively, waste ground is the best bet, but this is rapidly disappearing under urban development.

Yellow lines at the side of the road are not used, so look for no parking signs and do not park on busy roads. If the Traffic Police decide that you are an obstruction, regardless of where you've parked, you will receive a ticket. The Traffic Police enforce parking rules even in private areas such as mall car parks. A parking ticket will cost you QR 300.

Road Signs

In recent years there has been a concerted street naming and sign posting effort, and consequently road signs are now up to world standards, and are all in Arabic and English. On main routes signs are blue, minor routes are indicated with green signs and places of interest are indicated with brown coloured signs. Speed limits are well signed, and are given in kilometres per hour.

Address System

Because of the confusion caused by the semi circular roads, and despite the now excellent naming of roads, the best way to navigate Doha is by roundabouts and landmarks. Doha residents tend to refer to their location by the nearest roundabout or road junction, and all roundabouts have names, such as Rainbow Roundabout, Slopey Roundabout and Green Steps Roundabout. (There used to be one called, for valid reasons, Crazy Roundabout – when it was replaced by traffic lights the name lived on as Crazy Signal.)

For navigating, apart from the obvious Corniche, the tower built to show the Asian Games Flame (Aspire Tower) at Khalifa Stadium can be seen from everywhere in Doha and is a very useful reference point.

Changing Names

With the reconstruction of many highways, some names and English spellings of places have changed, following a survey carried out by the government to establish the traditional names of villages and towns.

One example is Mesaieed, which used to be called Umm Said and is sometimes still referred to as such. A village called Owaina became Leowaina; Shahaniyah, the camel racing centre of Qatar, has become Sheehaniyah; and the village that was known as Jemaliya became Lujmiliya. Be aware that the name of the place you are looking for may appear as a variation of that name on the road signs.

People With Disabilities

Progress towards catering for people with disabilities in Qatar is slow but improving. Particularly bad are street furniture, signs, construction activities, advertising materials and other assorted pavement debris, which can make life difficult, particularly for those with sight problems. Such street furniture can also be problematic to wheelchair users and parents with pushchairs.

Public Transport

Getting Around

The major hotels have rooms and facilities for disabled guests, while most of the shopping malls have dedicated parking for those with disabilities, as well as lifts where appropriate.

E For Easy

Residents are able to get an e-gate card which allows them to skip the queues at arrivals and departures at the airport. Take your Qatar ID card, or passport showing your Residency Visa, to the Departures area of Doha International Airport. As you enter the terminal turn immediately to the right and go to the office ahead of you. Here you'll have your fingerprints scanned and pay a fee of either QR 150 for one year's validity, QR 250 for two years or QR 350 for three years, payable by credit card. The office is open during normal government working hours.

Doha International Airport has ramps and chair lifts available. For a fee, Al Maha Services (4465 6672, al-mahaservices.com) operates a meet and greet service at the airport, which can provide assistance for disabled visitors (see opposite). Taxis specifically adapted for people with disabilities are not available. However, many of the airport taxis are of the people carrier type and consequently have a little more space and legroom than standard taxis.

Cycling

Aggressive driving styles and the general lack of awareness of other vehicles on the road mean that cycling is a hazardous means of getting around the city. In the cooler months, recreational cycling on the Corniche is popular (although not officially permitted). If you prefer cycling on the right side of the law, there are facilities around the Khalifa Stadium and the Aspire Park (p.212) in the Al Azizia area. It is a legal requirement to wear a helmet while cycling.

For keen racing cyclists, the Doha to Al Khor Road, with its lack of heavy trucks and new surface, is extremely popular. Qatar Cycling Federation organises professional races, including the arduous Tour of Qatar, in the winter months. See Activities, p.263 and Qatar Annual Calendar, p.24, for details.

Walking

Perhaps because of the summer heat, or maybe because many people can afford luxury cars, walking is not really a common mode of transport in Doha. However, there are plenty of areas suitable for walking for those who do it for pleasure. The Corniche (p.190) and Aspire Park (p.212) are very pleasant places to walk and jog in the cooler winter months. Those who like to combine exercise with some culture can take a stroll around the newly reconstructed Souk Waqif in

the evening or late afternoon (p.189). Out of town, Al Khor also has a corniche (p.234) and Al Wakra (p.86) has a pleasant harbour area with a long pier. Simaisma has good sea frontage and a long jetty (p.234).

PUBLIC TRANSPORT

In preparation for the Asian Games held in Doha in 2006, the public transport system in Qatar was given a complete facelift. A new bus company was established which provides a viable way of getting around the city, and the previously independent taxi companies had their licences terminated in preparation for a national taxi company being formed. However, while the new taxi operation is improving, it is struggling to provide the same level of service as the old taxis.

Al Maha

If you have elderly, infirm visitors or guests who have a number of small children, Al Maha is a useful service which will fast track both inbound and outbound passengers travelling on any airline, and assist with visas, luggage collection and immigration processing. The costs are dependant on number of people in the party and whether the passengers are met off the aircraft or as they arrive at the terminal. Call 4465 6672 for full details. Advance booking is essential.

Air Travel

Doha International Airport is located at the southern end of the Corniche and, traffic permitting, is readily accessible from anywhere in Doha in a maximum of 30 minutes. The airport is home to the constantly expanding national airline, Qatar Airways. With one of the youngest fleets of Airbus and Boeing aircraft in the word, Qatar Airways currently flies to over 90 destinations, with new ones continually being added. To cope with this expansion, a new airport is under construction that will allow over 50 million passengers to pass through the airport, which will open in phases with the first phase scheduled for 2011 (see Key Developments, p.32).

There are Duty Free shops in both departures and arrivals, although the one in arrivals is relatively small. Apart from Qatar Airways, a large number of other airlines use Doha Airport, including the newly introduced low-cost services such as Flydubai, Air Arabia and Jazeera Airways. These airlines are mostly UAE companies and currently none are Qatar-based. There are also low-cost airlines operating from Bahrain, which is just a 30 minute hop from Doha. These include Air India Express and Jet Airways.

At certain times of the day, the queues to get through immigration can be lengthy. Residents can

Qatar Explorer

Old and new forms of transport in Doha

buy an e-gate card (see box, p.54) which allows them to use automated immigration gates, where they are identified by means of an electronic finger print and can skip the long queues.

Five and four-star hotels operate their own airport transfer services for their guests; you will see their desks as you leave the departures hall. Turn left outside the departures hall to find both Karwa Taxis and limousines. The airport taxi base charge is QR 18. You are also likely to be accosted by individuals offering private taxi services, but these are unofficial, unlicensed, and best avoided. Public bus services from the airport are limited, with only the number 49 circular route heading towards town.

Prohibited Goods

As a Muslim country, aside from the standard internationally prohibited items such as weapons, drugs, pirated goods and pornography, restrictions are placed on the import of pork, alcohol and certain medications that may be legal in other countries (see p.162). Personal religious material is permitted, but not material that could be used for proselytising. If in doubt, don't bring it. See customs.gov.qa for more details.

Air Arabia 4407 3434, *airarabia.com*
Air India 4441 6253, *airindia.com*
Alitalia 4444 1161, *alitalia.com*
Azerbaijan Airlines 4443 2233, *azal.az*
Bahrain Air 4442 1807, *bahrainair.net*
Biman Airlines 4441 3054, *biman-airlines.com*
British Airways 4432 1434, *ba.com*
Cathay Pacific 4432 8450, *cathaypacific.com*
China Southern Airlines 4431 4040, *flychinasouthern.com*
Cyprus Airways 4441 8666, *cyprusair.com*
Delta Airlines 4483 0725, *delta.com*
Djibouti Airlines 4431 4040
EgyptAir 4435 6020, *egyptair.com*
Emirates 4438 4477, *emirates.com*
Eritrean Airlines 4431 3030, *ertra.com/eal*
Ethiopian Airlines 4431 3030, *ethiopianairlines.com*
Etihad Airways 4436 6658, *etihadairways.com*
flydubai +971 4 231 1000, *flydubai.com*
Gulf Air 4499 8000, *gulfair.com*
IranAir 4432 3666, *iranair.com*
Jazeera Airways 4431 5050, *jazeeraairways.com*
KLM Royal Dutch Airlines 4432 1210, *klm.com*
Kuwait Airways 4442 2392, *kuwait-airways.com*
Lufthansa 4431 0623, *lufthansa.com*
Middle East Airlines 4434 2976, *mea.com.lb*
Nepal Airlines 4431 7070, *nepalairlines.com.np*
Oman Air 4431 7067, *omanair.com*
Pakistan International Airlines 4442 6290, *piac.com.pk*

Qatar Airways 4449 6666, *qatarairways.com*
Royal Brunei Airlines 4499 5739, *bruneiair.com*
Royal Jordanian 4443 1431, *rj.com*
Saudi Arabian Airlines 4444 0121, *saudiairlines.com*
Shaheen Air 4444 4440, *shaheenair.com*
Singapore Airlines 4499 5700, *singaporeair.com*
SriLankan Airlines 4444 1217, *srilankan.lk*
Sudan Airways 4444 1161, *sudanair.com*
Syrian Air 4441 2911, *syriaair.com*
Turkish Airlines 4443 3027, *turkishairlines.com*
Virgin Atlantic 4434 4445, *virgin-atlantic.com*

Out Of Town Express Route Pickup

If you are out of town on one of the main express routes the bus drivers will kindly pick you up and drop you off anywhere on the route – just wave them down.

Boat

Unless a slow boat to Iran takes your fancy, there really are no public ferry services from Qatar that will take you anywhere. There are however, dhows at the northern end of Doha Corniche (close to the famous Oryx statue) that will take you for a trip around the bay, which can often be a perfect cultural experience for any visiting family or friends. No booking is necessary and the cost will be about QR 15 per person for a 30 minute cruise. From the Dhow Harbour on Doha Corniche, pleasure dhows, that are most suitable for parties, can be rented out and are avaliable for hire by the day or half day. Prices, however, are by negotiation and it is recommended that you haggle hard. The phone numbers to call for a reservation are shown on the vessels. See Boat Tours, p.227.

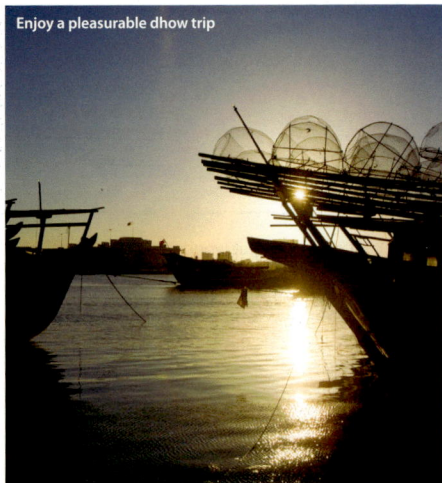
Enjoy a pleasurable dhow trip

Bus

Qatar's bus services offer an efficient and economical means of getting around. The route network covers most of Qatar with the exception of a few smaller villages. The fleet is modern and comfortable, but a couple of routes to the Industrial Areas tend to get a bit overcrowded. Services commence at 04:00 with the last buses terminating about midnight. All buses are in constant radio contact with their control centre, which increases safety. There are dedicated areas at the front of each bus for ladies and family groups.

The main bus station, Al Ghanim, is off Grand Hamad Street in the centre of Doha and although it tends to be busy, it is being developed with full facilities.

Fares within the city range from about QR 3 to QR 9 depending on the distance travelled, and fares outside of town are very good value. Unlimited daily, weekly and monthly passes are available from the bus operator, Mowasalat, at the bus station. Otherwise pay the driver when you board (it is advisable to have the correct change). Further details on passes, saver cards and routes can be found on the Mowasalat website (mowasalat.com) or by calling 4458 8888.

Taxi

Getting around by taxi can be difficult, mainly due to a lack of available vehicles during peak times. Unless one has just dropped a passenger off in your locality you are unlikely to be able to hail a cab from the roadside. The national taxi company, Karwa, runs the entire taxi fleet, and while it plans to reduce waiting times to a maximum of 20 minutes during peak times, introduce more taxis and construct more taxi ranks around Doha, for now the number of cabs on the street remains inadequate.

Illegal Pick Ups

Because of the shortage of genuine taxis, a number of people operate unauthorised services. Their usual method is to toot the horn and stop. It is inadvisable to use these cars, especially if you are female. In the event of an accident they are not insured to carry fare-paying passengers.

The best option to grab yourself a cab is to go to where they congregate, which is at most of the malls and five star hotels. You can also order a taxi by phone on 4458 8888 or from one of the taxi ranks around Doha, but the response time is a minimum of 45 minutes, and sometimes it may not arrive at all.

The current standing charge is QR 4, with a day rate charge of QR 1.20 per kilometre and a night charge of QR 1.80 per kilometre. Charges for travelling outside of town are QR 1.80. The standing charge from the airport is QR 18.

Metered Taxis

There are signs in all taxis telling you that if there is no meter reading you do not pay. If a taxi driver claims that the meter is broken, you can refuse to pay when you arrive at your destination. Should this happen, take the taxi number and report the incident to Karwa on 4458 8888 and they will take appropriate action.

Although Karwa is a monopoly there is another option: limousines. These tend to cost even more than taxis, but if you need to use one on a regular basis, arrangements can usually be made with the limousine companies. The vehicles vary from genuine luxury cars to ordinary family saloons. Most five and four star hotels operate their own fleets of genuine limousines, which are expensive but, if you have just enjoyed a nice night out, probably worth it.

Limousine Operators

Al Watan Limousine 4447 7999
Doha Limousine 4483 9999
Elite Limo 4442 6184
Fox Limousine 4462 2777, *foxtransport.net*
Mustafawi Rent A Car 4462 1542
Qatar Limousine 4486 8688, *qatarlimousine.com*

DRIVING

Getting A Driving Licence

Until recently, if you had a valid driving licence from your country of origin, you were permitted to drive a rental car or a privately-owned car for a period of seven days and if you had an international driving licence the time limit was six months. Before the seven-day period was up, you were required to obtain a temporary driving licence valid for the period of your visa; once your residency was approved, you were required to switch your temporary licence for a full Qatari licence. The laws regarding driving licences change almost on a yearly basis. At the time of writing, visitors to Qatar can drive a car using an international driving licence; however those arriving in the country with a residence permit (or in the process of obtaining one) must sit a driving test to ascertain their ability. Until things become clear however, the best course of action is to apply for a temporary driving licence as soon as possible after arriving in Qatar (see Getting A Temporary Licence, p.44) as driving on the wrong licence can incur heavy penalties.

All nationalities may exchange their country of origin's licence for a temporary Qatari licence; however, you may not do so if you have already started the residence visa process. If this has been started, you will have to wait for your residence visa

Driving

to be approved before applying for a full driving licence, so again the best course of action is to get a temporary licence as early as possible.

If you have relatives or friends visiting who are going to drive your cars, it is advisable for them to acquire temporary licences (see Getting A Temporary Driving Licence, p.44).

Passing A Driving Test

You must be a minimum of 18 years old before you can apply to take a test, and if you are a new driver there are several driving schools offering courses (see p.44). The driving school will advise you when you are ready to apply for the test. The cost of a course of 25 lessons is about QR 2,000, and this usually includes the price of the test. The tests are conducted in manual transmission cars, so driving school cars are manuals too. Female instructors are available to teach female candidates if required, and a traffic policewoman carries out the road test for ladies (women are not permitted to take the test during Ramadan).

If the test is not included in the price of your driving lessons, or you don't require lessons, the charge is QR 200, payable to the traffic police. On the test day, you will need to present some form of ID (preferably your Qatar ID card, although a passport with a residence visa will suffice), and a letter of no objection from your sponsor allowing you to take the test. In the case of a

husband or wife sponsoring their spouse, the husband or wife can write the sponsor's letter.

The driving test itself can be completed in one day. Your driving instructor will tell you whether you are ready to take the test and what your chances of passing are; the failure rate is high. The driving test usually starts before 06:00 with the road sign identification test. If you successfully pass this stage you will be taken out to a test track to carry out the manoeuvring part of the test. This consists of driving through a long S-shaped course with plastic posts either side – if you touch a post at any time during the test you will automatically fail – followed by reversing round a corner, uphill and then into a fairly tight parking space.

Finally there is the road test, which you only get to take if you pass the first two stages. Four students and an examiner set off from the test centre and the candidates take it in turns to drive. If you are lucky and the tester feels confident in you, your turn can be as short as a couple of hundred metres. It is important to exaggerate actions during the test, so that the tester can be sure you know what you are doing; for example, even if the mirrors are fine when it is your turn in the driving seat, adjust them to prevent any ambiguity over whether you checked them.

If you pass, you will be issued with a document allowing you to drive, and your licence will normally

Buying your dream car

be ready at the traffic police one week later. If you do not pass, you simply have to reapply and take the test again, usually within a month.

Traffic Department

The operating hours for the Traffic Department (4489 0666) are 07:00 to 11:00 and 16:00 to 19:00. At closing time, you will be asked to return either in the evening or the next day, regardless of where you are in the queue. The service at the Traffic Department is now fairly efficient though, so you are unlikely to have to wait very long to be seen.

Driving Schools
Al Khebra Driving School 4451 6353, *alkhebradriving.com*
Al Rayah Driving School 5555 1682
Doha Driving Centre 4479 2263
Gulf Driving School 4465 2822
Karwa Transportation Training & Development Centre 4458 8935
United Driving Company 4468 1003

Renewing A Driving Licence
Driving licences for non-Qataris are valid for five years. Renewing a driving licence in Qatar is a relatively simple process. Go to Madinat Khalifa Traffic Department with your expiring licence, your ID card or passport, a letter from your sponsor authorising you to renew your licence, and two passport photos. If you normally drive wearing glasses it is a legal requirement that you wear them in the photos. The cost of renewing the licence is QR 100, which has to be paid with a personal credit card. You'll also be requested to re-take the eye test, and pay a typing fee of QR 10.

There is no grace period at all when your current licence runs out, and it's likely that your insurance may be invalid if your licence has expired, so it's vitally important to renew your licence quickly. The procedure is relatively straightforward and usually takes no more than 20 minutes to complete. Be aware that the expiry date is written in Arabic, on the driving licence, so when you collect it, make sure you keep a record of the date it was issued and the date it's due for renewal.

Traffic Fines & Offences
A penalty point system was recently introduced in Qatar, and certain fines were increased in a bid to cut the levels of dangerous driving. If you accrue 14 points or more in one year your licence may be suspended for a short period; if you offend again after you get your licence back the suspension period is longer. After one year the points are cleared and you start from scratch.

There are fines and sometimes points for the standard international driving offences. One of the biggest fines – QR 5,000 plus seven black points – is for jumping a red light; most traffic lights have automatic sensors to detect this. They can be particularly sensitive, and for this reason you will often see drivers stopping their vehicles a full car's length from any white line.

Most speed radars are easily visible at the side of the road, and it is common to see vehicles suddenly slow down when they approach one. Average speed radar is beginning to make an appearance on some roads, which may help alleviate this problem. Speeding fines are dependent on the amount a driver exceeds the limit by, and can range from QR 300 to QR 700 plus four black points.

To pay outstanding fines you should visit the Madinat Khalifa Traffic Department (4489 0644) or one of the Ministry of Interior kiosks that are being placed in some of the shopping malls. You can also pay online at moi.gov.qa.

This website is the place to look to see if you have any fines, as you won't otherwise be notified. You can register with the Ministry of Interior's handy Metrash service on the website. It's free, and will inform you of any traffic infringements in your name within a short time of them occurring. It will also notify you of any other government transactions applicable to you, including a warning that your annual vehicle registration is due to expire.

BLOOD MONEY

If you have an accident and someone dies, you will probably be liable to pay 'blood money'. This might be covered by your insurance, but check your policy carefully. It is not unusual for a court to instruct the insurance company and the offending driver to share the cost of blood money, particularly where there is major fault on the part of the driver, such as negligence or speeding.

If you don't keep track of potential fines, you may only find out about them when you have an encounter with the Traffic Police, such as when transferring vehicle ownership, renewing annual registration, acquiring an accident report or renewing a driving licence. In this instance they will automatically check for any traffic infringements and you will have to pay them before the transaction takes place. It's also worth checking if you have outstanding fines before you try to leave the country; as there is no way to pay at the airport, you could end up being refused exit.

It is normal for any infringement to be registered against the vehicle owner rather than the driver.

Driving

There is zero tolerance on drink driving, and although random breath testing is not normally carried out, if you have been drinking and someone drives into the back of you, you are likely to be found to be at fault – this even applies if you still have alcohol in your system from the night before. Apart from a substantial fine and the possibility of a one to six month prison sentence, expats are regularly deported for drinking and driving offences once they have served the prison sentence.

In the event of minor infringements of traffic regulations, the Traffic Police decide who is at fault. If you think you have been unfairly treated the only way to appeal is to go to the Traffic Police and talk to them; if you are calm and respectful you will find them quite reasonable to deal with. If an incident is more serious, particularly anything involving injury or a fatality, the matter will be referred to a court. In the case of death, the suspect will automatically be arrested. If it happens to you, you will need to contact your sponsor and your embassy representative immediately. See Legal Issues, p.117.

Breakdowns

In the event of a breakdown, companies provide roadside assistance, and you can take out membership to cover you for such an event. Contact one directly to establish protection tailored to your requirements. If you break down on a busy road you should try to move your vehicle out of the way of the traffic. If you can't do it yourself then call a towing service. Towing using another vehicle and a rope is illegal; you must use a trailer or a truck. Your garage can arrange this; alternatively, most of the tow trucks position themselves very visibly near busy roundabouts. The phone numbers are always on the vehicles and the drivers are never very far away. Prices vary with distance and negotiation, but as a guide, Al Khor to Doha will probably cost QR 100 to QR 200. The police may assist you if the car is blocking a main road or causing congestion. In summer, due to the heat, Qatar is not a good place to have a breakdown, particularly in remote areas. Always carry your mobile phone and make sure that there is drinking water in your car.

Roadside Recovery Companies
Al Maqased Transport 4460 0229
Arabian Allied Association 4413 0970, *aaa-qa.com*

Traffic Accidents

Should you be unfortunate enough to have a serious road accident you must call the police. It is now acceptable in the case of minor accidents for the parties to agree to go to the Traffic Police to report the incident, but if you are in any doubt call the police anyway.

Safety First

If you are involved in any accident or stop to help at a crash scene and have children or passengers with you, always ensure that they are either secure in the vehicle or under supervision away from the road. Secondary accidents are commonplace.

The number to call in an emergency is 999 and the operators speak both English and Arabic.

The old ruling in the event of an accident was that vehicles must never be moved until the police had attended the scene. This has now changed and it is actually an offence to block a road with a crashed vehicle if it can be moved.

Make sure that you have noted all the details of the incident before you move any vehicles, and have agreed who is to blame. If you're in doubt, phone the police and ask the operator what you should do.

If your vehicle is damaged you will not be able to repair it or register it again until you receive an accident report from the Traffic Police (see Vehicle Repairs & Maintenance, p.64). These are issued when the Traffic Police complete their investigations.

Road rage is a common cause of accidents. You can find yourself accosted in queues of traffic by speeding vehicles coming up behind you aggressively flashing their headlights; this sometimes develops into more serious incidents. The safest option is to let them pass and not get involved, however obnoxious the behaviour. Under no circumstances should make a rude hand gesture, as this could land you in trouble regardless of who is at fault of bad driving.

It is a legal requirement to carry your registration document in your car and to have your driving licence with you.

Your Phone Can Be Your Friend

Before you actually move any vehicles after an accident, don't forget your mobile phone can be your best friend. Take as many pictures as possible so that you have evidence of the incident. If you don't have a pen and paper, enter the registration numbers of any vehicles involved into your phone, just as you would with a phone number, then press call. The registration numbers will be stored in your phone's call memory.

Petrol Stations

Petrol stations can be found throughout Doha and are open 24 hours a day. The fuel is always dispensed by attendants. There are two grades and all payments must be made in cash. Woqod, the company with the fuel distribution monopoly, is currently building a modern network of western style service stations, complete with shops and car cleaning bays.

GETTING A CAR

Hiring A Car

Until your residence visa process is complete, your only option is to lease a vehicle. Bank loans and car finance cannot be finalised until your visa is stamped in your passport, so you won't be able to buy a car. In order to lease a car, you will need a credit card, a copy of your passport and a valid driving licence. You may only drive on a foreign licence for one week, after which time you must have a temporary Qatar licence (see p.44). People holding GCC licences can drive leased cars for three months.

There are a number of reputable leasing companies in Doha, many of which are internationally recognised. Some companies have branches at the airport, making it convenient if you frequently fly in and out of Doha and require a vehicle. In addition, there are a lot of small rental companies, mainly located in the Salwa Road area, who undercut the big players by providing older vehicles. The downside here is that these cars may not be as reliable or come with much support in an emergency.

You can lease by the day, week, month or year. The longer the leasing period, the better the discount you will be given on the price. Ball park prices start from about QR 1,700 a month for a Honda City or similar. Whenever you collect a vehicle from a rental company always thoroughly check it for previous damage.

With leasing you don't have to worry about the car breaking down or being without a vehicle if you have an accident, as the leasing company will provide you with a replacement car. You also don't have to pay additional fees for insurance or maintenance. Some expats feel that it is cheaper to lease long term than it is to buy their own car, particularly if they are away for long periods in the summer. If you rent a car with the intention of going off road, remember that it will not be insured once you leave the highway.

Car Hire Companies

AAB Rent A Car 4443 7000, aabqatar.com/rent
Acon Rent A Car 4441 0955
Al Muftah Rent A Car > p.v 5552 5639, rentacardoha.com
Al Rayah Transport 4444 2111, alrayalimo.com
Al Saad Rent A Car 4444 9300, alsaadrentacar.yellowbulletin.com
Al Sulaiman Rent A Car 4491 1711, alsulaimancar.com
Almana Rent A Car – Hertz 4448 9944, almanagroup.com
Avis Qatar 4462 2180, avisqatar.com
Budget Rent A Car 4431 0411, budgetqatar.com
Euro Dollar Rent A Car 4432 1313, eurodollarrentacar.com
Europcar 4466 0677, europcar.com
Mannai Autorent 4455 8636, mannaiautorent.com

Mustafawi Rent A Car > p.v 4462 1542
National Car Rental 4487 8068, national-me.com
Oasis Rent A Car 4413 0011, oasiscars.net
Payless Car Rental 4437 3267
Petra Rent A Car 4413 0404, petrarentacar.com
Prestige Cars Co. 4420 9102, prestigecarsco.com
Thrifty Car Rental 4462 1180, thrifty.com

Importing A Car

Importing a car into Doha is possible, but there are a couple of rules that must be complied with. Firstly, the car must be less than 5 years old, and secondly a tax of about 4% will be levied, based on its estimated value, if you have no documented proof of its value. To import a car from another GCC country you will have to obtain export registration plates in the original country. There is then a procedure to be followed with the Traffic Police (p.59) involving inspection and paperwork checks before you can obtain Qatari plates. You won't be able to use the car until you are officially a Qatar resident. Importing by sea is expensive, there will be delays with customs at Doha Port and you will have to appoint a clearance agent, but importing across a land border is simpler and a little cheaper.

If you are bringing a car from further afield, ensure that it is a model and specification sold in Qatar, and be aware that some models built for the Gulf have additional engine cooling capacities to help them cope with the hot summer weather.

Cars are relatively cheap in Qatar so unless you have a very specific reason for importing one, you may find that it is easier to sell it and buy another one when you arrive. If you are really set on importing, talk to Madinat Khalifa Traffic Police first.

Buying A Car

If you decide to buy a vehicle, you will need to wait until your residence visa is issued until you are allowed to make a purchase, but you can begin looking as early as you like. Many expats are pleasantly surprised to find that the cost of running a vehicle is significantly less than in their home country, which allows people to purchase cars that they wouldn't be able to afford at home. There is generally no age limit on insurance of certain cars as there is in many other countries, so people find that they can have the car of their dreams before they reach 40 (the cost varies with the type of car). If you want to buy a new car you should have no trouble finding something suitable, as there are a number of new vehicle dealerships in and around Doha.

The only problem you may face is that many dealers only import a few of each model, so you may have to wait for the next shipment if they don't have the one you want in stock. This can take anything from two weeks to two months, so patience is key here. Big 4WD vehicles are very popular and recommended if

Getting A Car

you have children – not only for more space, but for safety as well. Most families in Qatar have at own least one SUV, and brands like Toyota, Mitsubishi, BMW, Mercedes and Nissan are among the more popular makes. Toyotas dominate the market and always fetch a premium. SUVs are popular because they allow excursion options into the dunes at the weekend, and also because there are so many large cars on the road that from a safety perspective it can give you more presence while driving. With the low cost of fuel in the region, environmental concerns do seem to take a back seat to large sizes and glamorous, expensive style and quality.

Good quality used vehicles can be a little bit more difficult to find because sales are often not accompanied by maintenance records. There are lots of second-hand car showrooms in Doha, but the quality isn't always particularly good. High speed crashes are prevalent and many written-off vehicles make it back onto the road. This is fine if you are aware of it and have paid a commensurately low price, but not if it is being sold as an undamaged vehicle. It is best to go to a reputable dealer so you don't regret your purchase.

Expats come and go from Doha continually throughout the year, so it's highly possible for you to pick up an impressive bargain second-hand car from someone who is leaving. People wanting to sell cars will advertise on noticeboards in supermarkets, school car parks, and within several expat-heavy villa compounds. You may also find adverts in the local newspapers. Many people email their friends and club members about selling their vehicles so it's also a good idea to put up your own wanted notices in the different sports clubs and expat hang-outs around town. If you are unsure of the state of the vehicle, you can always ask to have it checked over by a professional or request taking it yourself.

If you do end up buying a second hand vehicle it is a relatively straightforward procedure to transfer the ownership from one person to another. Go to the Traffic Police department (p.59) with the current owner of the vehicle and complete the necessary paperwork together. You will need to bring passport sized photos, a form of ID and your pre-purchased insurance for the year. There must be visible proof that the car is insured and it will continue to be insured under the new owner. The new owner must renew the insurance when it expires. See Registering A Vehicle p.63.

New Car Dealers

Al Boraq Automobiles Porsche, 4459 9666, *porsche.com*
Alfardan Automobiles BMW, Mini, 4447 7577, *bmw-qatar.com*
Alfardan Premier Motors Jaguar, 4440 8490, *alfardan.com.qa*

Alfardan Premier Motors Land Rover, 4447 7566, *alfardan.com.qa*
Almana Auto Trade Infiniti, Nissan, Renault, 4488 8618, *shalmana.com*
Almana Motors Company Chrysler, Dodge, Jeep, 4448 9922, *almanagroup.com*
Doha Marketing Services Company (Domasco) Honda, Volvo, 4447 7800, *domasco.com*
El Naael Ssangtong, Citroen, 4443 2662, *elnaael.com*
Jaidah Automotive Chevrolet, 4401 6061, *jaidah.com.qa*
Lexus Qatar Lexus, 4462 9257, *lexusqatar.com*
Mannai Automotive Corporation Cadillac, GMC, Subaru, 4455 8888, *mannaiautos.com*
Nasser Bin Khaled Automobiles Mercedes-Benz, 4462 4444, *mercedes-benz.com.qa*
New Trade Engineering Alfa Romeo, Fiat, 4444 4622
Porsche Porsche, 4459 9666, *porsche.com*
Qatar Automobiles Company Mitsubishi, 4469 9665, *mitsubishi-motors.com.qa*
Rolls-Royce Motor Cars Doha Rolls-Royce, 4420 8887, *rolls-roycemotorcars-dealer.com/doha*
Saad Buzwair Automotive Volkswagen, 4462 6260, *volkswagen-qatar.com*
Saleh Al Hamad Al Mana Company Infiniti, Nissan, Renault, 4428 3333, *shalmana.com*
Toyota Qatar Toyota, 4462 9222, *toyotaqatar.com*
United Cars Almana Chrysler, 4448 9933, *mideast.chrysler.com*

Used Car Dealers

Abdullah Abdulghani & Bros Co. 4462 9222, *aabqatar.com*
Alfardan Automobiles 4447 7577, *bmw-qatar.com*
Alfardan Premier Motors 4447 7366, *alfardan.com.qa*
Alfardan Sports Motors Co. 4432 2577, *alfardan.com.qa*
Almana Used Cars 4448 9060, *almanagroup.com*
Doha Marketing Services Company (Domasco) 4447 7800, *domasco.com*
Jaidah Automotive Pre-Owned Vehicles 4446 6877, *jaidah.com.qa*
Mannai Trading Co 5564 9779, *mannaiautos.com*
Oasis Used Car Showroom 4431 1909, *oasiscars.com*
Qatar Automobiles Company 4469 9665, *mitsubishi-motors.com.qa*

Vehicle Finance

If you are lucky enough to be employed by one of the major companies in Doha, they often provide interest free loans to their staff. If this is not available to you, provided that you have a minimum salary commensurate with the amount of money you want to borrow, banks have no qualms about providing loans. Some car dealers can also arrange finance. See Financial Affairs, p.112.

Vehicle Insurance

You must have insurance valid for a period of 12 months before you can register a car; as in the rest of the world it is illegal to drive a car that is not at a minimum third party insured. Unusually, it is also illegal for insurance companies to refuse to insure a vehicle, regardless of the owner's driving record. If you need to reinsure a car, take it to the insurer before the old insurance expires, otherwise you may not get as good a rate as you might have done if you continued the policy.

In Qatar, the vehicle is insured and not the driver, and anyone you allow can drive your car. There is no culture of 'no claims bonuses' either. Insurance is based on the value of the vehicle; rates are generally about 6% of the value of the car for saloon cars. If you buy a high-performance vehicle, then the rates will be much higher. The insurance is valid for 12 months and you have a one-month grace period to renew your policy, during which time any comprehensive policy reverts to third party.

Qatar Insurance Company (QIC) has a network of offices throughout the Gulf, and is highly regarded by many expats. Other companies that will be able to assist you include Libano Suisse Insurance Company, Arabia Insurance Company and Doha Insurance Company.

Vehicle Testing Tips

If your vehicle has headlights that can be adjusted from the dashboard to compensate for load in the back, tell the tester. They do not look for this and will automatically fail the car if the headlights are adjusted low or high. Wash your car before you present it to the test station. Dirty bodywork (often referred to as dangerous paint) will be registered as a major fault. You will then be required to go through the whole queuing system again to have it retested and demonstrate that if you wash it, it comes clean.

Invariably, if you decide to use your car off road your insurance will be most likely become invalid, as companies tend not to underwrite vehicles for this purpose. There can also be exclusions on policies, in particular relating to lack of driving licences, which is something to be aware of if you have visitors as the driving licences of their country of origin are only valid for no longer than one week after arrival. Most companies also have exclusions relating to drinking and driving, although paradoxically, considering this practice is highly illegal, you can actually pay extra to obtain alcohol cover.

If you are looking to cross the country's border in your own vehicle, you can obtain an orange card to prove that you do have insurance cover for the vehicle in most GCC countries, with the exception of Saudi

Arabia and Oman. Insurance cover that is valid in these two countries is available but can only be bought at the borders.

For a list of companies providing vehicle insurance, see Insurance Companies, p.114.

Registering a Vehicle

When you buy a new car, the dealer will arrange registration for you. Likewise, if you buy a second hand car from a dealer, they will normally attend to all of the transfer details, but you will have to sign a transfer form (written in Arabic) and provide a sponsor's letter, a copy of your residency and a copy of your driving licence. An insurance certificate is also needed, but this normally comes with the car.

If you are buying privately, you will need to go to the Madinat Khalifa Traffic Police with the seller. There, both of you will give your driving licences and residency details to one of the scribes, who will produce the necessary form in Arabic for a fee of QR 10 to QR 15. Then go to the counter, take a ticket and wait your turn. Once you are served the first thing the official will do is check any traffic infringements against the registration number, and the vendor will have to pay these there and then. Following this, hand over all of your bits of paper and the transfer will be completed. The transfer charge is QR 100,

Cars are relatively affordable in Qatar

which has to be paid by credit card. Cars older than three years have to pass a test before registration can be transferred.

Annual Vehicle Registration & Test

All vehicles have to be registered annually; if they are more than three years old they also have to be tested. If your vehicle is less than three years old, simply take your old registration card (Istamara), and an insurance certificate valid for at least 11 months, to either the Traffic Police or to one of the Ministry of Interior kiosks in one of the malls (the malls are less crowded), pay QR 100 by credit card and the transaction will be complete.

Look After Your Spare

If you own a car that has its spare wheel mounted on the back door, as many four wheel drive vehicles do, use a tyre cover. If you try to use a tyre that has been sitting in the sun for a couple of years it will probably burst as soon as you fit it to the car.

If your vehicle is three years old or more it will have to be tested before it can be registered. The state authorised body for vehicle testing is called Fahas. The main testing station is in the Doha Industrial Area, but the vicinity suffers from traffic congestion and poor road surfaces, so you may be better off using one of the permanent or portable stations located in Doha and its surrounding area. These are prone to changing locations so it is best to ring Fahas on 4460 4029 to obtain current information. The test stations are normally open from 07:00 to 17:15 Sunday to Thursday and from 07:00 to 12:00 on Saturday. The test charge is QR 75. Queues can be lengthy at these stations, so take a good book, a flask of coffee and something to eat, and plan on being there for up to three hours. There are long term plans to open testing stations at Woqod petrol stations, which may ease the waiting times.

Once you have obtained your pass certificate the registration procedure is as for a car of less than 3 years old. The free Metrash system will efficiently advise you that your registration is about to expire (see Traffic Fines & Offences, p.59, for details) and if you are having trouble getting the car through its test the Traffic Police normally allow a one month grace period when you can still use the vehicle. Make sure that the insurance did not expire at the same time as the test.

Vehicle Repairs & Maintenance

Conditions in Qatar are harsh and any vehicle used here must be well maintained if you are to rely on it. In particular, batteries rarely last much longer than

Proceed with caution

a year, and if you go away on extended leave over the summer months, it is fairly commonplace for the battery to fail while you are away. Tyres should be regularly checked, especially for cuts if you have been driving off road in stony desert. The temperatures make tyres deteriorate very quickly, so always check their expiry date and change them even if they appear to be roadworthy.

Problems with older cars are often down to faulty air conditioning compressors and overheating engines. New air conditioning compressors usually start at about QR 6,000 dependant on the make of your vehicle. There are plenty of back street repair shops that will offer to fit one that they have reconditioned for around half the price of a new one, but as the parts will not be guaranteed you may find that this is a false economy.

Overheating engines can be a problem in the dense traffic of Doha. A car may run perfectly well on an open highway with air flowing freely over its radiator keeping it cool, but may not cope so well in slow traffic. With maximum air temperatures of over 50°C the last thing you want is a car that is going to overheat. If necessary change that old radiator and water pump.

Towing Trailers

Unusually, recreational trailers that you would use for carrying quad bikes, boat trailers and camping trailers are not normally fitted with rear lights or registration plates in Qatar. If you are towing at night, you should consider securing some form of red light to it for your own safety, and the safety of others. Towing with a rope is illegal and this law is enforced.

Traffic Accidents Repairs

Unfortunately, Qatar is home to a number of traffic accidents and it's not uncommon to spot at least one on your way to and from work. Despite the best due care and attention you may find yourself caught up in the middle of bad driving. If you meet with an accident, take note of the following steps on how to make a claim and organise a repairman to fix any damages made to your car.

Should you need to take a vehicle into a garage for accident repairs you will need to provide an original police report and hand it over at the counter. No garage will be able to accept your car, or even take a look at it without this report, as this is against the law.

With any luck your insurance company will already have several approved repairers for vehicles (this is mainly the case for vehicles over two years old) and will point you in the right direction towards the best repairman. However, be prepared that your insurance company may ask you to do the hard work and trail around the garages to obtain at least three competitive quotations on your own. In order to have repairs paid for by your insurance policy, you will have to make a copy of the police report and also provide evidence of the damaged vehicle. In addition, the insurance company may want to take a few photographs of the damage to file along with the necessary paperwork.

Non-Dealer Repair Workshops

Qatar is peppered with a handful of bad repair workshops and the only way to avoid one is by seeking the advice of others. Reputable repair shops (apart from a main dealer) are best found by word of mouth. and many of these businesses are located on Salwa Road and the Industrial Area of Doha, although others are in innumerable garage souk areas of Doha and throughout Qatar. Many cover specialist items, such as tyres, bodywork, exhausts, springs, radiators, A/C, auto electrics and the like. Research into a few workshops before settling on a company.

Once you have received approval from your particular insurance company they will either give you authorisation to take your vehicle to a particular repair facility or to one of your choice. It is possible to pay an additional premium on new vehicles if you want your car to go to the dealer for repairs. This can be arranged for three years if the car is new (depending on the terms and conditions of your insurance company). There may be a deductible for claims, depending on each individual policy, which will cost approximately QR 500 – QR 600.

All cars require good maintenance

IDdesign Qatar
1st. floor The Mall Shopping Complex
Tel: (+974) 44678777
                 (+974) 44669490
Fax: (+974) 44678555
Email: iddesign@qatar.net.qa
Website: www.IDdesignQatar.com

OPENING HOURS
Saturday - Thursday
10am - 10pm

Friday
4pm - 10pm

IDdesign

MORE LIVING   MORE STYLES   MORE TRENDS

Housing

HOUSING

Along with getting that all-important job, finding suitable accommodation is the other essential element in making your move to Qatar a success.

If you are fortunate enough to be employed by one of the major oil and gas companies, the national airline or educational organisations associated with Education City you may be provided furnished accommodation on compounds specifically rented or constructed for the purpose as part of your employment package. Some of the oil and gas companies even own and operate their own compounds in company towns, complete with clubs, restaurants, schools, medical centres and often free utilities. Qatar Petroleum's Dukhan Township and the RasGas/Qatar Gas AlKhor Community are examples of these. Unfortunately, those not employed by these key companies will have to look elsewhere for their housing requirements.

Residents who live in company allocated compounds get to enjoy many advantages – not least the built-in amenities which will come in very handy, but also the fact that the accommodation is provided furnished; there is no rent to pay, and, should things not turn out as you had hoped, you just hand the keys back and leave hassle-free.

Newcomers should be aware that there are also disadvantages to these types of residences. Being company controlled you will not be able to socially avoid people you work with, which may mean that work politics can, and often will, intrude into your family life. Also, you will come under the constant surveillance of your company's security personnel, which can feel disconcerting.

For those who have to find their own accommodation, and those employed by the major employers who have opted for an accommodation allowance in lieu of company accommodation, the first thing to decide is what sort of place you want (and can afford) to live in, and in what area. For the single person who likes the feel of urban living, an apartment in a high rise near Doha Corniche may be ideal, while compound life may be more suitable for those with young families. Even residing outside of Doha can be an attractive option, although consideration must be given to the fact that, with the exception of Al Khor City, all of the expatriate schools are located in Doha. If you have children, schooling arrangements must be a major factor in your choice of living location.

This chapter provides a detailed run down on the different residential areas in Doha and beyond (p.78), focusing on what kind of property is available, the amenities, and the general pros and cons. There are sections on the processes involved in both the rental (p.70) and owning (p.73) markets too, discussing what you need to do to secure your dream pad. Once you've found somewhere to live, this chapter also tells you how to get settled in, covering everything from getting your TV and electricity connected to sprucing up the garden. Happy house hunting.

ACCOMMODATION OPTIONS

Hotel & Serviced Apartments

Furnished hotel apartments can be a convenient option for single people, short-term stays or those whose job requires lots of travel. They provide many door-to-door services unavailable in villas or compounds, such as dry cleaning, mini-markets, or onsite hair salons. Furnished apartments can be more economical than villa leases too as they will often include items such as kitchenware and decorative artwork. Many of Doha's serviced apartments are new and are located in the West Bay area, within walking distance of the Corniche and City Center (p.331). Residents of serviced apartments usually also benefit from daily housekeeping and facilities including gyms and swimming pools.

Advertising Private Villas

A common method of advertising that a villa is for rent is for the owner to take an aerosol paint spray can and spray a telephone number on the outside wall, usually in Arabic numerals. It helps to be able to read the Arabic numbers, but if you can't and you are interested in contacting the property owner, copy the Arabic numbers on to a piece of paper and then go and look at car registration plates in the locality. Vehicle number plates have the numbers in both Arabic and European style and it is a simple matter to translate the Arabic number you wrote down into one you can actually read and understand.

Al Liwan Suites Umm Ghuwailina, 4424 2888, *alliwansuites.com*
Al Muntazah Plaza Hotel Al Mansoura, 4435 5677, *almuntazahplaza.com*
Al Siraaj Wakra Inn Al Wakrah, 4463 3737, *alsiraaj-group.com*
Ascott Doha > *p.71* Al Dafna, 4497 1111, *somerset.com*
Beverly Hills Tower Al Dafna, 4412 2222, *regencygroupq.com*
Ezdan Hotel & Suites Onaiza, 4496 9111, *ezdanhotels.com*
Gulf Paradise Musheireb, 4432 2212, *gulfparadisehotel.com*
Kempinski Residences & Suites > *p.81* Al Dafna, 4405 3333, *kempinski-residences.com*

Apartment living in Ad Dawhah

prices down – good news for potential buyers, not so great for those who bought at the peak.

If you are interested in buying and living in a property while you are in Qatar, then it's recommended that you do your research thoroughly. If you own a property in your home country, you may want to hold onto it until you've tested the water here first. For more detailed information, see Buying A Home on p.73.

Standard Apartments

Apartments in Qatar can range from the brand new units in high rises along Doha Corniche to the well-established three-storey buildings found near the urban centres. The advantages of apartment life include access to the shared facilities provided, which in the more upmarket ones include a gym and pool. Apartments come in various sizes, from studio to four-bedroom, with widely varying rents to match. Newer apartments usually have central air conditioning (C A/C) and older ones have noisier air conditioner units built into the wall. C A/C is usually more expensive, although in some apartment buildings your air-conditioning costs are built into the rent. Top of the range apartments often come semi-furnished (with a cooker, fridge and washing machine), and have 24 hour security, covered parking, private gym and swimming pool.

One downside to apartment living is that to some extent, you're at the mercy of your neighbours, especially those upstairs. Because most apartment parking is underground or on the street in front of the building, finding a space can be challenging if you have two cars or have visitors.

Le Mirage Executive Residence Musheireb, 4444 0111, *lemiragehospitality.com*
Le Mirage Suites Fereej Abdel Aziz, 4444 7111, *lemiragehospitality.com*
Liberty Suites Hotel Fereej Bin Mahmoud, 4441 1212, *liberty-suites.com*
Marriott Executive Apartments Doha, City Center Al Dafna, 4419 6000, *marriott.com*
Retaj Residence – Al Sadd Sports R/A, Fereej Bin Omran, 4489 5555, *retajhotels.net*
Somerset West Bay > p.197 Al Dafna, 4420 3333, *somerset.com*
W Doha Hotel & Residences Al Dafna, 4453 5000, *whoteldoha.com*

Villa Sharing

Villa sharing is a cost-effective option for single people moving to Qatar and, as long as you get on with the other people in the villa, comes with the added benefit of a ready-made social group. Bear in mind though that mixed cohabitation is illegal. While many young singles do share villas or apartments, the practise can be risky if you are in employer-sponsored accommodation and are effectively sub-letting to a roommate. The best way to find out if there are rooms for let or if people are interested in sharing a villa is to ask friends and neighbours for referrals.

Owning A Property

For non-Qatari nationals, property ownership in certain designated areas became a possibility in 2004 with the advent of large-scale real estate developments such as The Pearl project. Expats are technically sold contracts to lease the property for 99 years, after which the ownership can transfer back to the property developer.

At the height of the building boom in the GCC, around 2005-08, property prices were fairly high because of the anticipated resale value. Construction delays and the global recession have somewhat slowed the potential in the market for these properties as second homes or holiday rentals, bringing the

Villas

For families, villas are the most common accommodation option; many of them are spacious with three or more bedrooms and private garden areas. Across the city there are a large number of villas in compounds – walled neighbourhoods managed by property agents with 24 hour security– as well as stand-alone villas that are rented directly from a landlord.

In many new compounds, construction work is ongoing and it can take some time to straighten out maintenance issues. The more established compounds, although older, are more popular because they are completed and consequently the management processes run more smoothly. Also, they are usually, Riyal for Riyal, larger than modern compounds, with each villa built on a larger plot of land. If you are newly arrived, compound life may have advantages because it provides an immediate network of people and families to help you adjust to your new life.

If you prefer privacy over enforced community spirit, an independent villa may be the option to consider. However, if you don't speak Arabic, this can be a challenge as you'll have much more day-to-day interaction with the landlord who, unless you are renting in an area in which expats can own property, is likely to be Qatari. The other minus point about standalone rentals is that you don't have the same protection against rent rises as you do in a compound managed by an agent. Although it's technically against the law for landlords to increase the rent more than a fixed amount when the lease is due for renewal, the law is not heavily enforced so you may find yourself facing a rent rise or scrambling to find new accommodation at short notice.

RENTING A HOME

Most expats receive a contribution towards their housing as part of their employment contract. Many employers will lease a property on behalf of the employee, but some prefer to give a monthly housing allowance, leaving it up to the individual to find a suitable property. Since 2004 expats have been allowed to purchase property in Qatar, but the majority still choose to rent because contracts are for a fixed period of time, often a year, making it the more practical option. The cost of renting in Qatar can be very expensive, and prices are comparable to those of other international capitals. As Doha developed, the cost of living and in particular renting rose rapidly, peaking in late 2008. The global recession saw rental price falls in 2009 by as much as 16% according to Qatar Statistics Authority, bringing a welcome relief for renters. The market bottomed out in late 2009, after which the rents started to increase, albeit marginally, in 2010. After some further increases in early 2012, the average rent for a two bedroom apartment stood at QR 4,250 to QR 14,000, according to an Asteco report.

Finding A Rental Home

Many newcomers tend to use real estate agents to help them find a place to live. While it saves time, the downside is that it can raise your rent by anywhere from 5% -10% because of the agency's cut. If you want to rent directly from a landlord, look in the classifieds for private lettings, or pick an area that you want to live in and drive around looking for properties for rent. The risk with private lettings is that you are at the mercy of the landlord for things such as maintenance. If you are seeking shared accommodation, check out local websites (see p.23) and ads in the newspapers.

HOUSING ABBREVIATIONS

The following abbreviations are used in property adverts in Qatar's local press:

D/S	Double storey
F/F	Fully furnished
Majlis	Reception room
S/F	Semi-furnished – with a/c and/or kitchen appliances
S/P	Swimming pool
Split a/c	Air-con units on wall
U/F	Unfurnished

Adam Import Export & Real Estate Co Al Sadd, 4436 6930, *adamqatar.com*

Ahmed Hassan Bilal Trading & Contracting Co Al Doha Al Jadeeda, 4442 8877, *ahbqatar.com*

Almana Real Estate Al Hilal, 4448 9900, *almanagroup.com*

Apollo Real Estate Bu Hamour, 4468 9522, *apollopropertiesonline.com*

Asteco Al Dafna, 4411 3818, *asteco.com*

Better Homes Fereej Bin Mahmoud, 4444 5499, *bhomes.com*

Coreo Salwa Rd, 4469 9950, *mycoreo.com*

Direct Real Estate Rawdat Al Khail, 4442 1472, *directqatar.com*

Homes 2 Rent Al Aziziya, 4413 4839, *homes2rent.biz*

LS: Keep Moving Al Dafna, 4491 3222, *lskeepmoving.com*

Manazil Real Estate Rawdat Al Khail, 6650 1333, *manazil.com*

Mirage International Property Consultants New Al Mirqab, 4444 4431, *mirageproperty.com*

Qatar Real Property Al Gharrafa, 5509 8695, *qatarrealproperty.com*

Zukhrof Real Estate Fereej Abdel Aziz, 4442 2223, *zukhrof.com*

House Hunting Victoria Acquah, British expat and new Doha resident

There are several ways to try to find a property. My husband and I drove around various areas stopping and asking at nice looking compounds to see if any villas were vacant. The security guards will often let you view vacant properties. The ads in the classifieds section of the local newspapers were helpful too.

ASCOTT

DOHA

Elegant Living in the Heart of Doha

Step into luxury. Tailored for discerning international travellers, expect state-of-the-art recreation and business facilities along with elegantly designed residences and personalised services at the new Ascott Doha. Located at the north end of Corniche Bay, Ascott Doha offers stunning views of the Arabian Gulf and is within walking distance to Qatar's best known retail and entertainment destinations. Make yourself at home at the prestigious Ascott Doha. **Because life is about living.**

For further information and global reservations, please visit www.the-ascott.com or call (974) 4497 1234

Managed by

THE
ASCOTT
LIMITED

A Member of CapitaLand

Ascott Doha is managed by The Ascott Limited, a member of CapitaLand. It is the largest global serviced residence owner-operator in Asia Pacific, Europe and the Gulf region, managing the *Ascott*, *Citadines* and *Somerset* brands in over 70 cities across more than 20 countries.

Renting A Home

The Lease

Most lease agreements will be signed directly between the employing company and the property owner, unless you are expected to arrange your own accommodation. The lease should be in English, so insist on an English translation. Unless you are fluent in Arabic don't sign anything which is only in Arabic. If your company signs the lease it will attach a copy of its commercial registration and a copy of the sponsor's ID. If you sign your own contract, then you will need to attach a copy of your ID and your sponsor's ID.

If you are dealing with the accommodation yourself, remember that your lease is an important document and, in addition to the financial terms, will state what you are liable for in terms of maintenance as well as what your landlord's responsibilities are. Some rents might be fully inclusive of all maintenance and repairs, while you could negotiate a much cheaper rent (particularly on older properties) if you agree to carry out any maintenance work. While not common, some landlords will also include utility expenses in the rent. Therefore it is important that you read the contract and discuss any points of contention before you sign on the dotted line.

The normal notice period is two months prior to the expiry date on the contract. To renew your lease, the landlord will issue a new contract to be signed,

and then payment will be made as agreed between both parties, the tenant and the landlord.

As a result of the rising prices in recent years, the government introduced a rent cap in 2008 to prevent landlords from unfairly raising rental prices for existing tenants. This was a temporary measure to stabilise the market and effective for only a two year period. It was withdrawn in February 2010, leaving rental prices up to the negotiation of landlords and tenants. In April 2011 the Government announced that the committee on settling rental disputes was to be reinstated, and at the time of writing the mechanism for its operation has not been announced, but the previous method when in dispute with a landlord was for the renter to contact the courts, register a case and then pay the existing rent to the court until such time as an arbitration decision had been made.

Be sure to clearly understand the terms of your lease as there can be expensive clauses in the fine print that the landlord may gloss over. Terms for the return of security deposits and early termination can come as costly surprises. The reasons for moving can often determine the reaction to an early termination – if you are leaving the country for example, because of your employer, then you may not have to pay the remainder but if you are moving to another part of the city, unless you have a clause saying you can break

Urban sprawl in the capital

your lease, you may be obligated to pay the remainder or stay until it expires.

It is the landlord's responsibility to register the rental lease at the Office for Registration of Lease Contracts at the Ministry of Municipal Affairs & Agriculture; the fee to register a lease is 1% of the annual rent stated on the lease, and contracts must be registered within one month of signing.

Other Rental Costs

Most companies pay for accommodation, which means they usually cover the deposits required for various utilities. The deposit for electricity and water is QR 2,000. Security deposits for rented accommodation are usually one month's rent. Qtel charges a monthly line rental of QR 33 for landlines, which it bills three months in advance. In some cases, employers will pay the rental fees for accommodation, but employees are responsible for utilities such as water and electricity. It's best to check about this when you receive your job offer to ensure your expectations are met.

Commissions for real estate agents usually need to be paid by the tenant. The current rate is around two weeks' rent, although some agents may charge up to 4 weeks'. Maintenance is usually taken care of by the landlord, but again this should be agreed in advance and written into your contract. If you live in an apartment or on a compound it is easier to get maintenance work done as the development will usually have a contracted maintenance company which you can contact directly with any issues; if you live in an individual villa, it may be more difficult. If you rent directly from the landlord, you are more likely to have to wait a considerable time for maintenance work to be carried out, if it ever gets done. Try to ensure that the landlord commits to a company that can carry out routine maintenance work. This way, if the landlord is unavailable for any reason, you have a contact number for someone to help.

The garden, if the property has one, is the tenant's responsibility. Water charges are not that expensive in Qatar, so it doesn't cost a fortune to keep your garden in bloom, although the majority of properties have either interlocking bricks or tiles instead of grass. Most landlords will allow you to lift the tiles and plant greenery if you wish, but this can work out to be rather pricey, especially if you have a large outside area.

Finding A Home Online

Finding and contacting each developer or agent separately can be quite time-consuming. Propertyfinder.qa has listings for both commercial and residential properties from various sources; you'll also find useful information, buyers' guides and real estate news.

BUYING A HOME

It is only since 2004 that expats have been allowed to buy property in selected areas, so the foreign-ownership market here is still in its infancy. Buying a property in a foreign country always carries an element of risk, and even more so when it has only just become permissible to do so. If you are serious about buying a property in Qatar, it is important to do your research. It is also advisable to consult an independent lawyer, not the developer's lawyer, with regard to a contract before signing anything. Only Qatari nationals are permitted to buy undeveloped land to build on. Buying a property entitles the owner and their dependents, to a five-year residence visa, but not necessarily a work visa. It is also advisable to be aware that residency visas can be withdrawn without reason or right of appeal given.

The Pearl Qatar is the largest project that offers freehold properties to non-Qataris, and its first residents have already moved into their properties. If you're interested in buying a unit here, visit thepearlqatar.com. There are a variety of other real estate projects now available for purchase, including the ZigZag Towers in Lagoon Plaza, West Bay, which are ready for occupation. Property can also be bought in Lusail City (see p.33, 233), and Al Waab City (alwaabcity.com), near the heart of residential Doha, but both of these projects are running behind schedule. If you are buying off-plan, or before a building has been completed, be aware that the developers can – and frequently do – miss completion deadlines, and even change the scope of the project, and there's little cause for recompense. It is not unknown for purchasers to be paying off a mortgage whilst being unable to move into their property because it has not been completed.

The same methods as finding a rental property apply to looking for somewhere to buy. Newspaper property sections, and notice boards at shopping areas such as Mega Mart can give you leads. Real estate agents are invariably the most knowledgeable point of contact, but as there is currently no official regulator of the industry in Qatar, you should be careful to choose an agent that you can trust. Ask friends for recommendations, or seek advice from posters in online forums. If you want to buy off-plan, find out which developers are leading the projects you are interested in, and contact them directly.

Be sure to check for other (hidden) costs when purchasing a property in Qatar, particularly an apartment. There is often a maintenance fee, which is around QR 65 per square metre and is paid on an annual basis. Fees usually cover routine repairs; if you have a water leak that causes damage to personal property, however, you may find it better to reclaim those damages through property insurance. If you are buying off-plan, the best thing to do is ask before signing what type of services are covered under the agreement as these can vary across providers, and in some cases can be subject to increases at the whim of the developers. It is crucially important that you read all the small print and ask all the right questions before you commit.

Expat property sales and purchases are recorded in the Doha Municipality office, on the first floor of their building in the Al Sadd area, with the Department for Non-Qataris (4434 7476). You'll need copies of your passport and contract which will be issued in the buyer's name. Non-resident expats are allowed to purchase property, and will receive a renewable five year visa for themselves and family members; buyers must appear in person to finalise all paperwork.

Doha's Property Market
Along with most of the world in the wake of the 2009 financial crisis, Qatar's property market has seen its fare share of turbulence in the past few years. In the lead-up to 2008, the prices had been spiralling upwards, especially following Qatar's announcement that it was to host the 2006 Asian Games. However, after the global financial crisis hit at the tail end of 2008, house prices began to fall, according to some estimates by up to 20% at the depths of the international downturn. A modest recovery began to take place from late 2010 onwards, and the December 2010 announcement that Qatar had been awarded the 2022 FIFA World Cup undoubtedly helped to breathe life back into the market. By mid-2012, the market had returned to levels last seen in 2009: according to an Asteco report, apartment prices stood between QR 9,000 and QR 16,000 per square metre in the second quarter of 2012. For the time being, however, most real estate developers are proceeding more cautiously with many planned and under-construction developments, leading to a more stable balance of supply and demand than in the pre-crisis boom years. This being said, the prices still have the ability to shock and are often only affordable if employer housing allowances are received.

Mortgages
Mortgages for non-Qatari nationals are a fairly new concept due to the fact that it's only seven years since the market was opened up. The properties that allow expat ownership have generally negotiated their own deals with specific banks, so you may be limited in who you can borrow from.

If you do need to arrange your own mortgage, the most convenient way to do so is through a personal loan via a bank, preferably one you have already established a relationship with (such as through a car loan) because it will already have much of the paperwork related to your salary history, proof of

New residential developments at The Pearl

employment, and other required documents on file. While non-Muslim expats can be eligible for loans from Islamic banks, which are Sharia compliant and interest free, these have a shorter repayment period than those offered by the commercial banks.

Most banks will ask for at least a 10% down payment for a one bedroom apartment, 30% for three bedrooms, and so on. Recently though, mortgage lenders have become more cautious in the wake of the global economic downturn, so you almost certainly need to put down a higher deposit than previously.

Once the deposit has been paid to the developer, the buyer's interest payments begin immediately. Currently, interest rates are, on average, about 8.5%, with a slight discount on the rate if the buyer's wages are paid directly to the bank (some loans may require this salary transfer as a pre-condition to approval). Mortgages are typically for between 18 and 25 years, and interest rates are written into the term of the loan for the specified period. When assessing your eligibility for a mortgage, banks will often give you a price range within which you could look at prospective homes, but the exact final mortgage figure will be assessed on the specific property you opt for. Take a long-term view of the deal before you sign up as transferring a loan from one bank to another can be a complicated affair. Also, be sure to check your bank's policy on early repayments and default penalties as these can vary.

Other Purchase Costs
Before signing any contract, buyers should contact a law firm or lawyer to advise on any unfavourable aspects of the contract – especially if buying overseas

or in the Middle East for the first time. Hidden fees can often take the shape of maintenance costs or condo fees which are charged on a yearly basis as part of services used by the tenant and provided by the developer, such as landscaping, that are not covered in the mortgage payments. There are many online forums, including qatarliving.com where expats discuss the pros and cons of different strategies and suppliers at length. If you are seriously considering purchasing a property it would be wise to spend some time reading through the various discussion threads as the situations tend to vary, and sometimes nothing beats some insider tips and information.

Land Registry

All property purchases must be registered with the Ministry of Justice's Real Estate Registration Department because this is the governing body for purchasing real estate in Qatar. If you do purchase a property in Qatar, then having an estate agent to explain the process of registering your purchase can be very helpful as it involves lengthy procedures at the Ministry of Justice (4484 2222, moj.gov.qa). Note that the registry is not online yet in Qatar and that most of the business will be conducted in Arabic. The good news is that if you are buying directly from the developer, they will most likely take care of the entire process for you.

Selling A Home

If you're a homeowner in Qatar and have decided to move on, you have two options to choose from: you can have the bank turn your mortgage into a non-residential mortgage and continue making payments, or you can sell your property. If you decide to sell, you can market it through an estate agent (which will cost you a fee), see if the developer would like to re-purchase it, or try to sell it privately. Policies concerning resale vary across developers and this is something to investigate and take very seriously into consideration when purchasing. Word of mouth is also one of the fastest ways of circulating information in Qatar. Once you have identified a buyer, it's important that they go through the process with the bank of being authorised to take over your mortgage so that you are no longer held responsible for your housing lease.

Real Estate Law

The difference between a freehold and leasehold property can seem confusing at first since they both seem to span a buyer's lifetime. In Qatar there are currently only two areas where expatriates can buy freehold property – that is property that they own outright – The Pearl and West Bay Lagoon. In all other cases, purchasing a property as leasehold means the buyer has an initial lease for up to 99 years which can be renewable, and which could be sold to his or her heirs. Soon to be on offer are spaces in Al Waab City, Lusail and others, but these are all currently under construction and not ready for occupation.

Buying property for expats is a brand new venture for both the developer and the investor, and real estate law is still under development and is likely to take quite some time until it is set in stone. United Development Company is one of the first firms to deal with this new option as the developer of The Pearl project, and is planning to open a division to deal with all queries regarding legal proceedings; other developers are likely to follow suit. Because the rules are nascent and subject to change it is worth hiring a lawyer who is familiar with Qatari real estate to help you through the procedures and act on your behalf (see Law Firms, p.117).

It is also advisable to have a will written, if you haven't already got one, when you purchase a property. A valid will would ensure that, should anything happen to you, your freehold property will be allocated according to your wishes. For legal advice on this, see Wills & Estate Law, p.119.

All disputes will be settled in the civil courts so it is very important to engage an Arabic speaking lawyer who understands the Qatari legal system, if you need to file a grievance.

Aspire Tower

Residential Areas Map

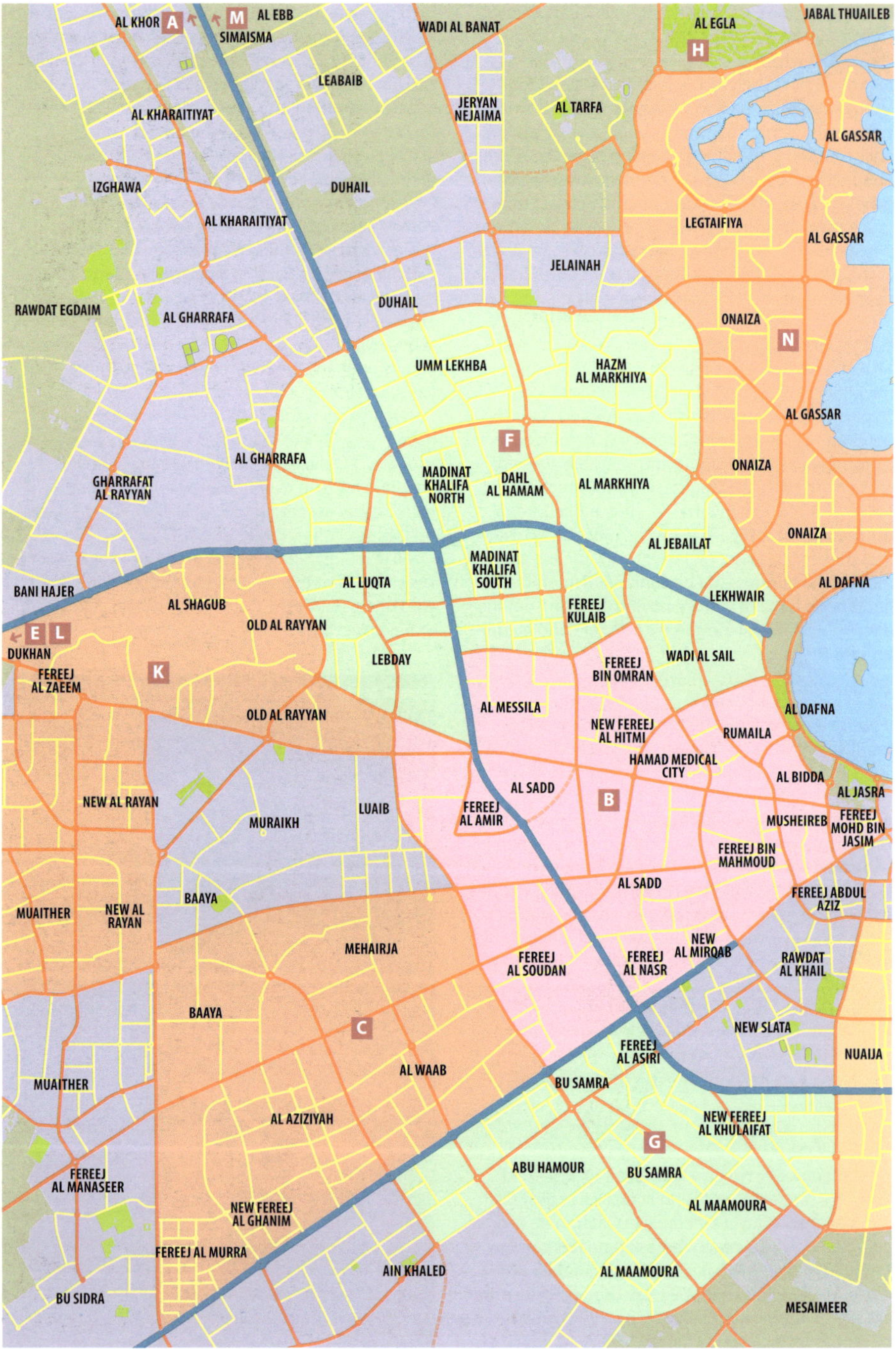

AL KHOR A ← M AL EBB
SIMAISMA

WADI AL BANAT

AL EGLA

JABAL THUAILEB

H

LEABAIB

JERYAN NEJAIMA

AL TARFA

AL KHARAITIYAT

AL GASSAR

IZGHAWA

DUHAIL

LEGTAIFIYA

AL GASSAR

AL KHARAITIYAT

JELAINAH

ONAIZA

RAWDAT EGDAIM

AL GHARRAFA

DUHAIL

AL GASSAR

N

UMM LEKHBA

HAZM AL MARKHIYA

ONAIZA

AL GHARRAFA

F

GHARRAFAT AL RAYYAN

AL GHARRAFA

MADINAT KHALIFA NORTH

DAHL AL HAMAM

AL MARKHIYA

ONAIZA

AL JEBAILAT

ONAIZA

BANI HAJER

MADINAT KHALIFA SOUTH

AL LUQTA

FEREEJ KULAIB

LEKHWAIR

AL DAFNA

AL SHAGUB

OLD AL RAYYAN

E L
DUKHAN

LEBDAY

WADI AL SAIL

FEREEJ AL ZAEEM

K

FEREEJ BIN OMRAN

OLD AL RAYYAN

AL MESSILA

NEW FEREEJ AL HITMI

RUMAILA

AL DAFNA

NEW AL RAYAN

AL SADD

HAMAD MEDICAL CITY

B

AL BIDDA

AL JASRA

MURAIKH

LUAIB

FEREEJ AL AMIR

MUSHEIREB

FEREEJ MOHD BIN JASIM

MUAITHER

NEW AL RAYAN

BAAYA

FEREEJ BIN MAHMOUD

AL SADD

FEREEJ ABDUL AZIZ

MEHAIRJA

FEREEJ AL SOUDAN

FEREEJ AL NASR

NEW AL MIRQAB

RAWDAT AL KHAIL

BAAYA

C

NEW SLATA

MUAITHER

AL WAAB

FEREEJ AL ASIRI

NUAIJA

BU SAMRA

AL AZIZIYAH

NEW FEREEJ AL KHULAIFAT

FEREEJ AL MANASEER

NEW FEREEJ AL GHANIM

ABU HAMOUR

BU SAMRA

G

AL MAAMOURA

FEREEJ AL MURRA

AL MAAMOURA

BU SIDRA

AIN KHALED

AL MAAMOURA

MESAIMEER

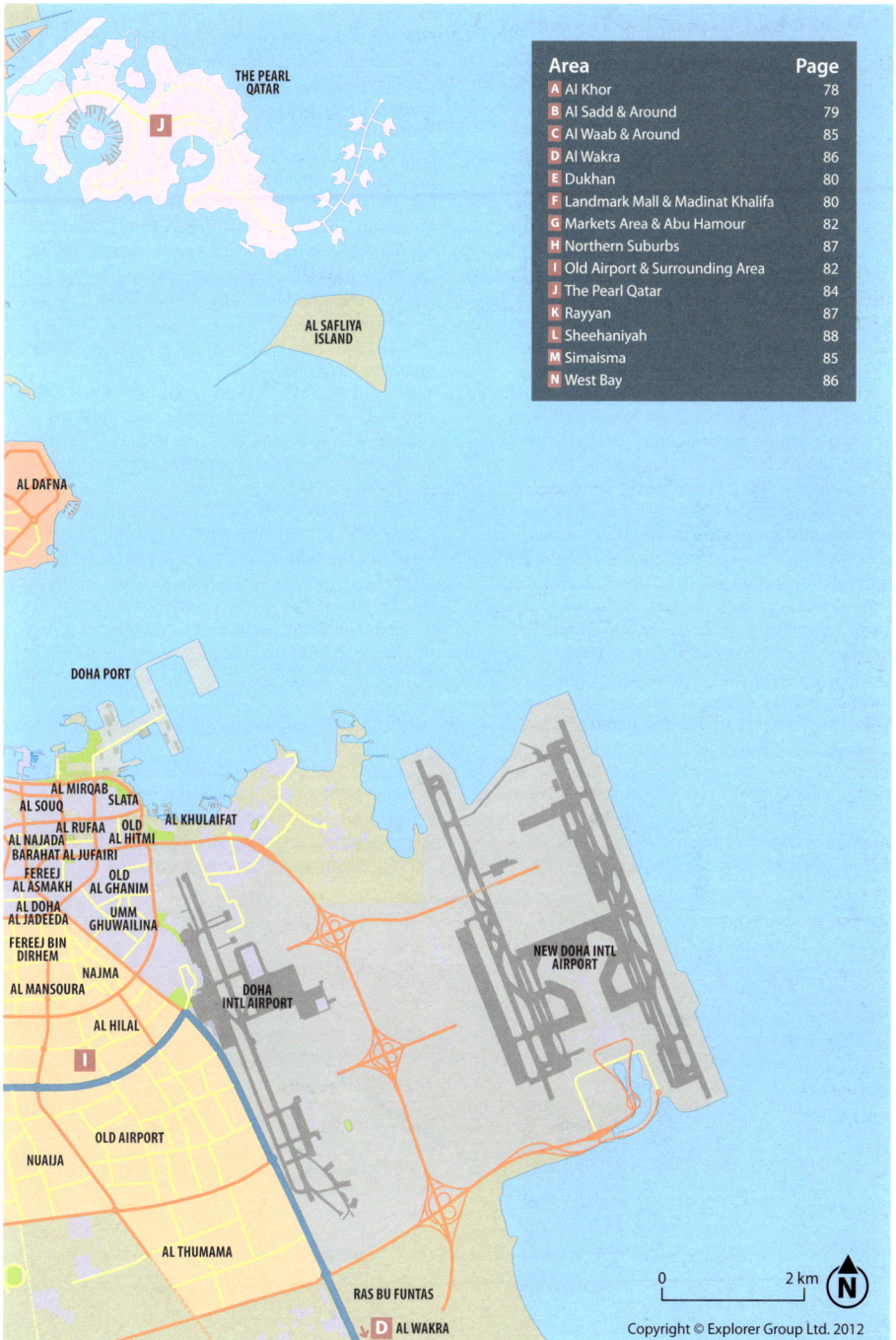

THE PEARL QATAR

J

Area	Page
A Al Khor	78
B Al Sadd & Around	79
C Al Waab & Around	85
D Al Wakra	86
E Dukhan	80
F Landmark Mall & Madinat Khalifa	80
G Markets Area & Abu Hamour	82
H Northern Suburbs	87
I Old Airport & Surrounding Area	82
J The Pearl Qatar	84
K Rayyan	87
L Sheehaniyah	88
M Simaisma	85
N West Bay	86

AL SAFLIYA ISLAND

AL DAFNA

DOHA PORT

AL MIRQAB
AL SOUQ   SLATA
AL RUFAA   OLD   AL KHULAIFAT
AL NAJADA   AL HITMI
BARAHAT AL JUFAIRI
FEREEJ   OLD
AL ASMAKH   AL GHANIM
AL DOHA   UMM
AL JADEEDA   GHUWAILINA
FEREEJ BIN
DIRHEM
NAJMA
AL MANSOURA

AL HILAL

I

NEW DOHA INTL AIRPORT

DOHA INTL AIRPORT

OLD AIRPORT

NUAIJA

AL THUMAMA

RAS BU FUNTAS

D AL WAKRA

0   2 km

N

Copyright © Explorer Group Ltd. 2012

RESIDENTIAL AREAS

For many cities the geographical map serves as a guide to its residents' wealth and status – it's usually safe to assume that anyone living in places like Manhattan's Upper East Side or London's Knightsbridge is not particularly short of money. Doha operates differently. There really is no 'wrong side of the tracks' and the majority of areas (with the exception of The Pearl, p.84 and West Bay, p.86) have a cross-section of houses, including low cost labourer housing.

Getting a handle on the layout of Doha is a bit tricky because people refer to few areas by their actual name. Instead, you'll hear someone say, for example, that they live near Lagoona Mall or Ramada Junction. Despite the continual road construction in the country, traffic in Doha can be a miserable experience. A journey that took 35 minutes a couple of years ago can now take nearly an hour. Public transport is relatively new, and while it's improving, the general population has still to embrace the concept. The fleets of Karwa buses generally service a small percentage of the population, although they are clean and comfortable and, with the exception of the crowded routes to the Industrial Area, there is no reason for others not to use their services. Taxi services are still often intermittent and so unless you wish to spend much of your time stressfully commuting, your choice of housing location must take into account your work location and any of your children's school locations. This however is not as straightforward as it seems. Because of congestion in Doha, time rather than distance is the main criterion to consider. For a person working in the City Center area it can be quicker and less stressful to travel the 50km from Al Khor in the northern part of the country, than for another person to travel the 10km from the Al Waab area within Doha.

Al Khor

A small seaside town about 30 to 40 minutes' drive from Doha, situated on a very pleasant sea inlet. The town is currently undergoing a great deal of additional housing construction and infrastructure building work including a major new shopping mall. Al Khor is the closest town to Ras Laffan, the enormous gas processing facility that is the source of Qatar's wealth. As a result of this, many employees of companies operating from Ras Laffan live in Al Khor and in the nearby seaside village of Dhakira. In general, prices for housing, and the cost of general commodities and services, are noticeably cheaper than Doha.

Between Al Khor and Dhakira is Al Khor Community (AKC). This is a walled-off company owned community, built specifically for the sole use of employees of RasGas, Qatar Gas and, more recently, Dolphin Energy and Shell, AKC is beautifully landscaped and very popular with families; children have a lot of freedom and there are plenty of organised events and activities.

Accommodation

Apart from AKC, where you can only live if you work for one of the owner companies, Al Khor and Dhakira offer a large choice of small flats, compound villas and stand alone villas, with more under construction. A major new housing project is being undertaken by a developer to build waterfront housing on Al Khor Bay.

Shopping & Amenities

The Al Khor Community has its own supermarket in the compound as well as health centre facilities, swimming pools, play areas, a gym, conference facilities, a library, bank and post office. Lots of activities are run for children, from playgroups to sports coaching, organised by the residents. AKC is also the only place in Qatar with on-street recycling

The quiet life

bins, although these are starting to appear in public places in and around Doha. Al Khor town itself has its own, currently rather run down Corniche but few facilities. There are useful shops such as tailors, supermarkets and stationers and many Doha based businesses have recently opened branches in the town. A Lulu Hypermarket and cinema are under construction. There are a number of restaurants for both eating in and take away. Apart from Al Khor Medical Centre in the centre of town, a major branch of The Hamad Hospital, with full facilities, is located on the road between Al Khor and Dhakira.

The surrounding areas have some particularly attractive beaches and Dhakira has a pleasant fishing harbour with boat launching facilities.

Education
There are limited education options for families with children in Al Khor. Al Khor International School (p.144) is a primary and secondary school with both English and Indian curriculum streams. It is situated within AKC and caters mainly for children of employees of the major oil and gas companies. Children are bussed to school, or can walk in cooler months. Qatar Academy Al Khor (p.148) is an affiliate of Qatar Academy, Qatar Foundation's main campus in Doha, offering private education for children from kindergarten to grade four with plans to add grades in succession.

Transport
Regular buses run from Al Khor Town and AKC to schools and shopping malls in Doha. The frequency of taxis is somewhat limited at various times of day, so most people rely on their own of transport. If you need a taxi, either call in advance to avoid standing on the side of the road for a long period of time or, in Al-Khor Town, walk to the Al Khor Medical Centre where there is a taxi rank.

Al Sadd & Around
This is a lively and busy commercial area with plenty of shops, local businesses, cafes, juice bars and restaurants. It's ideal for single people or couples with no children. There is a bustling street life and its central location means it's handy for almost everything; however it desperately lacks greenery, including a park, and traffic can be a real nightmare, with Al Mirqab Street often jammed up on weekend evenings. It's always busy and noisy with the traffic going past, even continuing late into the night, but amid all the hustle and bustle it feels very safe and secure. A few of the older malls such as Royal Plaza (p.336) and Centrepoint (p.336) provide shopping outlets, but again street parking can be difficult to find. New openings, such as La Cigale hotel, have added to the volume of traffic in the area and it can become quite congested at any time.

Accommodation
There are lots of new apartment blocks on Jawaan Street near Sports Roundabout, as well as some older villas and a few small compounds dotted around. Apartments are usually furnished. For a two bedroom expect to pay around QR 7,000 to QR 9,000 per month in a good location.

Shopping & Amenities
Royal Plaza on Al Sadd Street is a rather overlooked shopping mall which has a lot of good shops for clothes, and Articles (p.306) for cool house stuff. Nearby on Jawaan Street, before Sports Roundabout, is Centrepoint – also known as Al Asmakh Mall (p.336) – which features branches of Gulf chain stores selling well-priced furniture, electronics and fashion items. Al Mirqab (often referred to as Family Food Road), which runs parallel to Al Sadd Street, is one of Doha's most useful streets with loads of small shops selling everything from wooden toys to sports gear, mobile phones and glitzy evening dresses. Family Food Centre supermarket (p.325) is also on Al Mirqab Street; though relatively small when compared to the major malls, it has almost everything you could want, including a butchery counter, bakery, and a very good fruit and vegetable section. However, Al Miqab street is changing rapidly; recently many of the older shops have been demolished to make way for commercial office developments.

The Al Sadd area in general desperately lacks green space, so kids have to make do with indoor play places. Ray's Reef (p.133) at Royal Plaza and Fun City (p.132) at Centrepoint are worth checking out.

Entertainment & Leisure
It's very lively at night with lots of cheap (and good) restaurants around. Al Mirqab Street has some of the best, with Doha institution Thai Snack (p.370), which has a lovely garden and Turkey Central (4443 2927) for cafeteria-style grilled meats and pies. The nearest big hotels – The Millennium Hotel Doha (p.200) and the Grand Regency, just up from Centrepoint – are dry, but the latter has a popular Chinese restaurant, Chopsticks (p.357). One of Doha's newest and smartest hotels, La Cigale (p.200) on Hamad Street, has one of the best bars in the city, Sky View Bar (p.373), a couple of good restaurants, Le Central (p.364) and Le Cigalon (p.364), and an impressive but pricey food hall where foodies can indulge in lots of goodies.

Education
There are quite a few schools within very easy reach of Al Sadd, with the American School of Doha (p.144) and Doha College (p.146) right on the doorstep. The Central English Speaking Kindergarten (p.138) and Sunbeam Kindergarten (p.141) are also close by. The unusual-looking castle building just up from Sports

Residential Areas

Roundabout is a branch of the Dutch run Stenden University Qatar (p.150).

Dukhan

Out to the west of Doha lies Dukhan; home to several thousand employees of Qatar Petroleum. Residents live within a walled community, which means living alongside the same people which they work with. Whilst this suits many people and newcomers' social lives can be established very quickly, with the added bonus of a secure environment for families, it is not ideal for everyone. Living in this area can cause a feeling of isolation, particularly for non working wives. On the plus side a new eight lane highway connecting Dukhan to Doha has now been completed, and has reduced the travelling time to Qatar's main centres of population. If your preference is for peace and quiet you may appreciate the low-key atmosphere. You're near some great scenery on the west coast, so if you enjoy a bit of wildlife, the chance to see wild oryx and dodge camels on the road should provide plenty of diversion. Because all of the villas and apartments are provided by QP to employees and their families at no cost, you can save a lot of money living here. It's also great for small children who thrive on the freedom of the safe, enclosed compound.

Shopping, Amenities & Leisure

Some 'beautification' is underway to improve the look of the area and big expansion plans have recently been carried out. Within the walled community, and for QP employees only, are two recreation clubs with swimming pools, sports facilities, a large cinema, a state of the art gym and an 18 hole golf course made of compacted sand – lots of activities are organised for children and families. Just outside the compound are a branch of Doha Bank and a new mall encompassing a major supermarket, complete with a couple of fastfood outlets.

A couple of kilometres away on the shoreline is Dukhan Water Sports Beach Club, again exclusively for the use of QP employees. Either side of the Beach Club are public beaches, where sun shades have been installed. For more info on exploring the area around Dukhan, including the rest of the west coast and the Ras Abruk peninsula, see West Of Doha, p.237.

Education & Healthcare

Dukhan English Speaking School (4471 6147) is the oldest British curriculum school in Qatar and has a good reputation. It accepts QP employees' children from nursery (at 3 years old) right through to A-levels at 18. QP has provided a well-regarded medical centre with dental and emergency care. Since 2011, residents also have access to a new medical facility, the Dukhan Hospital.

Transport

Historically, the road to Doha was an atrocious route which had seen some appalling accidents. However, maybe as a reaction to this previously poor road, it has now been replaced by a magnificent eight-lane highway with hardly any traffic on it.

Karwabus services now provide a link with Doha, but taxi services are almost non existent, unless you are fortunate enough to capture one returning empty to Doha.

Landmark Mall & Madinat Khalifa

Accommodation

There are a mix of stand-alone villas and compounds. Big compounds include the pink-hued Riviera Gardens (one of the few types with an indoor pool – which is good for escaping both the heat and cold). Expect to pay QR 20,000 for a three-bed villa on or QR 11,000 off a compound.

Shopping & Amenities

The Landmark Mall (p.334) is one of the nicest malls in Doha – it is very light and airy and has a Marks & Spencer (p.324) and Bhs (4487 4271), as well as numerous fashion stores and a cinema. For food shopping there's a new Carrefour (p.334) attached to Landmark Mall. Local smaller shops like stationers, dry cleaners and bike repairers are on Khalifa Street between Burger King and TV Roundabout. And, for when it gets too hot, Landmark has a large indoor mini theme park, Circusland (p.131), with roundabouts, dodgems, arcade games and a soft play area.

Entertainment & Leisure

Landmark's food court offers most of the standard fast food options such as KFC, McDonald's and Dairy Queen, but there are an increasing number of fashionable cafes such as Maison de Paul, Maya, and the Chocolate Cafe. THE One (p.306) furniture store has a trendy cafe upstairs with a rather funky menu. There are a lot of options for eating out in this area too, with several restaurants and fastfood places on Khalifa Street. Yellow Cab Pizza (4488 8310) is particularly good and Star of India (p.369) is one of the better curry houses in Doha. Dahl Al Hammam Family Park (p.212) is on the corner of Arab League Street and Al Markhiya Street.

Education

This area is very well placed for schools, with Qatar Academy (p.148), Compass International School (p.144), Gulf English School (p.146) and Doha English Speaking School (p.146) all pretty close. The new Qatar Canadian School (p.148) is very handy too, as is the International School of London (p.146). There are a few

Kempinski Residences & Suites • Doha

At *home* in Doha...

Kempinski's *luxury* serviced residence is designed for hassle-free living. Simply move in with your suitcase, and we take care of the rest. All details, including utilities, furnishings and amenities, will be in place so that you have all the luxuries, comforts and conveniences you need to be *successful* from day one.

www.kempinski.com/doha · sales.doha@kempinski.com · T +974 4405 3333

Kempinski

RESIDENCES & SUITES

DOHA

nurseries; Starfish Lane (p.82) is particularly popular. This area is also convenient for Education City, which is home to branches of several American and Canadian universities: Carnegie Mellon, Georgetown, Texas A&M, University of Calgary, Virginia Commonwealth and Weill Cornell, plus Qatar Science & Technology Park (see University & Higher Education, p.148).

Markets Area & Abu Hamour

This is growing in popularity as a residential area due to the number of new compounds and villas being built and it's slightly cheaper than other parts of town. It's close to several schools and nurseries – which in the rising tide of traffic jams is worth a lot. However, there are no green spaces at all and it hasn't yet got much to offer in the way of other amenities. Salwa Road is one of the main thoroughfares into Doha so gets very busy, but there are short cuts and alternatives. There's currently loads of construction going on so it is dusty and noisy, and the lack of amenities means it feels a bit soulless.

Accommodation

New compounds and stand-alone villas are the main accommodation options. As it's a newly developing area the prices are slightly cheaper than other parts of Doha, and you can get a three-bedroom villa on a compound for around QR 15,000.

Shopping & Amenities

There are a few local shops next to nearby Abu Hamour petrol station on Mesaimeer Road, but no large supermarket. It is very handy for the busy fish (p.327) and fruit and veg (p.327) markets, just behind Salwa Road between Market and Decoration roundabouts.

The shaded Omani market (p.328) nearby, on the other side of Al Reehab Street, between Salwa Road and Haloul Street, has fantastic plants and baskets, and running alongside it are several garden nurseries. Further away from Salwa Road is the camel market, which is one for the visitors. The animal souk (p.327) and adjoining pet market are fascinating, but animal lovers might be upset by puppies and kittens in cages. Garvey's (p.358) has a gym and pool for members.

Entertainment & Leisure

There's not much in the area itself apart from a Pizza Inn (by Abu Hammour petrol station on Mesaimeer Road, 4469 2824), but you are a short drive from Salwa Road, which has lots of restaurants as you move nearer to town. Neo (p.366) does excellent sushi, and Layali (p.364) is a popular Lebanese restaurant. A little further out of town, off Salwa Road past the Tata Roundabout, is Garvey's which used to function as a pub, but is now home to the European Club, a

family recreational club with a yoga studio, Yama Yoga (p.179). Garvey's now exists as the club's unlicensed restaurant (p.358).

Education

Two big schools are right in the heart of this area – Park House (p.148) and Al Jazeera Academy (p.144); Doha College (p.146) is a short drive away. There are several nurseries including Tots Corner (p.141) and Little Angels (p.140).

Old Airport & Surrounding Area

This is one of the older areas of Doha, with busy main roads, but once you get off the main drag it is very peaceful. Despite its proximity to the airport you're not actually under the flight path. Some of the area's benefits are that it is slightly cheaper than other areas and that the local amenities are good, including The Mall. It's also handy for the airport. On the downside, there is very little green space and almost no leisure facilities. The main route through this area is the busy D Ring Road, which now offers better access to other parts of the city, via a new underpass.

Accommodation

There are a lot of stand-alone villas and some compounds, including what some consider the nicest in Doha – Al Fardan 1, which has great facilities and nice gardens. The compound managers have a good reputation and the properties have well-chosen furnishings and good finish so expect to pay top dollar – around QR 25,000 per month for a three bedroom, and be warned that empty villas are snapped up fast. Other compounds and villas in this area are cheaper, particularly some of the older ones, beginning at around QR 17,000.

Shopping & Amenities

The Mall (p.336) is one of the older malls, but it's a good one. It's got Q-Mart (4467 8822) supermarket, which has a lot of western products, including the nicest sausages in town, and ID Design (p.306), which has stylish albeit somewhat pricey Scandinavian furniture. Up on Airport Road (Al Matar Street), opposite the airport, are the super cheap Al Rawnaq (p.295) and Dream Shopping (4465 3211), which are a bargain (or tat) hunter's paradise. Just before them is a branch of the Family Food Centre (p.325). Another Doha institution is the massive Lulu Hypermarket (p.325) on the D Ring Road between The Mall roundabout and the airport lights; it has a good range and is competitively priced. For men's barbers (or saloons as they are called here) and various handy shops visit Al Matar Al Qadeem Street. The International Centre for Music (p.276) is behind Lulu and offers music and dance lessons.

Residential Areas

Entertainment & Leisure

Once again a shopping mall comes up trumps, with the Italian Biella and the upmarket Indian Garden Royal (4466 6876) in The Mall. There are various cafes too, including Opera Café (4467 8885), which is famed for its cakes. There are no parks, but there's an indoor play place at The Mall. However, Wakra Beach is only 10 minutes' drive away. The Gulf Cinema (p.343) is on C Ring Road, but it's not the smartest cinema in town.

Education

Nearby is the new Cedars Tutoring Centre (p.144). Also close by are Park House (p.148), Al Jazeera Academy (p.144) and Newton Secondary School (p.148). There are a few nurseries in the area too, including Elder Tree Nursery (p.138).

The Pearl Qatar

One of the most talked about developments in Doha, The Pearl covers 985 acres of reclaimed land to the north of the Corniche. While developers expect The Pearl to become the Riviera of the Middle East, Doha residents are simply delighted to have a refreshing change from the bustle of Doha. Residents can enjoy a selection of premium brand retailers and excellent restaurants, now open in Porto Arabia. In keeping with the high-end amenities, residential prices are quite expensive and there are a few more years of building work to go before this manmade masterpiece is completed. A one bedroom townhouse will set you back around QR 12,000 to 15,000 a month, with four-bedrooms advertised for QR 20,000. There is an eight-lane motorway planned to connect the island with the mainland, but construction has yet to begin. There are plans for several nurseries, three primary schools and a secondary school, but at present the closest schools are in the West Bay area.

Shopping & Amenities

High-end fashion names such as Jimmy Choo, Alexander McQueen and Ferrari keep retail lovers happy and more prestigious outlets are popping up all the time as the construction finishes in phases. Created with the designer shopper in mind, The Pearl's offerings are all pretty exclusive; for more mundane products, like bread and milk, you will need to leave your luxury surroundings to find supermarkets and petrol stations elsewhere.

Just outside of The Pearl development, The Lagoona Mall, being constructed under the ZigZag Towers at the entrance to the general area, will also have a few more exclusive shops and some high-end cuisine restaurants once it opens, but more importantly there are also plans for a large supermarket which will be welcome news to The Pearl's residents.

Entertainment & Leisure

The Pearl was the first place in Qatar to have independent, licensed restaurants and cafes, leading to many high-class restaurants deciding to set up shop here. Although its status remains unclear at the time of writing, the Pearl remains an area where you are sure to find a number of classy dining options. Eventually, a total of three five-star hotels will be located within the premises of The Pearl. Already, the development is shaping up to become a very beautiful part of Doha, with parks, canals, lakes and coves. There will also be three marinas, one of which is already complete. Just a short hop across the water to West Bay Lagoon, the Grand Hyatt, Ritz Carlton and the Diplomatic Club offer an array of entertainment and leisure facilities, including excellent bars and restaurants, plus health club memberships and private beach access. Ronautica Middle East

Life under the sun

(ronauticame.com) also offers water sports activities for those adventurous enough to try, with wake boarding, waterskiing and other family fun trips that depart directly from Porto Arabia Marina.

Simaisma

Exit Al Khor Road around 20km north of the Doha Golf Club, and you'll find the old pearling village of Simaisma, built and populated by fishermen and pearl divers in the mid 20th century. A local beach with traditional fishing traps and a mosque with adjacent traditional madrassa, or religious school, are some of the attractions in this area and the sleepy, laid back atmosphere is starting to draw expats, as well as day trippers, away from the urban bustle of Qatar.

New compounds are beginning to pop up in Simaisma, with five bedroom villas for rent starting at QR 8,000 a month. New shops are gradually opening, but residents should be prepared to drive the 25 minute commute to Doha for shopping and all other necessities. There are no expatriate school facilities in or near Simaisma although strangely the village is very popular with teachers working in Doha, who presumably take their children to the same schools that they work in. For more info on Simaisma's attractions, see Out of Doha, p.232.

Al Waab & Around

This area used to be considered outside the main part of the city, but the opening of Villaggio Mall immediately increased its popularity. Its proximity to several good schools and nurseries, as well as the green space of the sports grounds at Aspire Academy (p.144) and Aspire Park (p.212), make it particularly popular with young families. The big Al Waab City development, which is planned to be a city within a city with a plaza the size of St Peter's square in Italy, will gradually bring more shops, restaurants, parks and homes to the area when it opens. For those looking for nightlife, the nearest licensed restaurants are in the hotels on the Corniche, so going out generally involves a cab ride (albeit not a prohibitively long one). The traffic on Al Waab Street and Salwa Road can be at a standstill at the weekend, at school pick up times and during major sporting events.

Accommodation

This is a very popular area for expat living, probably due to the close proximity of good schooling, and there are lots of compounds, including some older ones like Beverly Hills Gardens 1, which have a bit more outside space. There are some stand-alone homes, but very few apartments. Expect to pay QR 14,000 to QR 18,000 for a four-bedroom villa on a compound, or QR 11,000 for a three-bed independent villa.

Villa living

Shopping & Amenities

Hyatt Plaza mall (p.336) has a wide selection of shops ranging from fashion and jewellery to homeware stores and souvenir shops. There's also a Geant supermarket and several eating options. Nearby, the Villaggio became a major draw following its opening in 2006: thanks to a huge number of shops with familiar names to western expats (Boots, Virgin Megastore and H&M), as well as an ice rink, amusement park, karting track and an IMAX cinema, the mall quickly established itself as the leading lifestyle destination in this part of town. In early 2012, a fire forced the temporary closure of the mall – see p.335 for additional information.

Aspire Park (p.212) is next door to Villaggio, with a track for running and walking. The Aspire Active (p.131) public fitness classes are popular because of their low fees and ladies-only sessions. Aspire Play Park (p.212) is nearby with a paved area perfect for kids to cycle and rollerblade on. Doha Zoo (p.216) and the Racing & Equestrian Club (p.225) are also nearby. The tower at Aspire, which held the flame during the Asian Games, is the major landmark in Qatar; it can be seen from almost anywhere. There are a number of private dental centres and medical clinics of various specialities in the villas lining Al Waab Street.

Entertainment & Leisure

After opening its doors in 2006, Villagio quickly established itself as a popular dining destination here, proving anyone with prejudices about eating in shopping centres wrong with a selection of eateries such as patisserie cafes Paul (4413 5508) and Le Pain Quotidien (4413 5245), as well as full-blown restaurants ranging from Thai, Italian and Persian to Indian cuisine. Qatar's first IMAX screen added another draw, as did an ice skating rink, Fun City amusement centre (p.132) and the Karting Track (p.274). In 2012, a fire forced the temporary closure of the mall; see p.335 for more.

Education

This area is near most of the big schools including Park House (p.148), Al Jazeera Academy (p.144) and Doha College (p.146). The American School of Doha (p.144) and Doha Montessori British School (p.146) are also close by. For younger ones, Tiny Town (p.141) is a short drive away, as is Apple Tree (p.138), near Aspire.

Al Wakra

Located on the coast, about ten minutes from Doha International airport, Al Wakra is a municipality with historical significance as a site for the early pearl diving and fishing industries. A small community with undeveloped beaches and an interesting dhow harbour, it has a relaxed feel and, while there is not much going on in terms of entertainment, it is a pleasant place to live. The development of Doha has spread to such an extent that Al Wakra is almost a suburb of the capital, and while in the past it wasn't a popular place for expats to live, the lower rents and slower pace of life are starting to attract interest. Particularly from the innumerable people working on the construction of the New Doha International Airport project.

Much of the housing is rented by single, lower-income men, as the rental rates are much cheaper here than inside the city. A two-bedroom apartment in the Ezdan compound costs around QR 3,200 but reviews of the maintenance are mixed. Elsewhere you can find a three-bedroom apartment for as little as QR 4,000. However, recently, modern compounds have begun to spring up and a development plan for the town has been created.

Airport Road is not far from Al Wakra and fulfils most needs in terms of amenities (see Old Airport & Surrounding Area, p.82). Schools in Al Wakra are mostly independent schools, segregated by gender, so those wanting an international experience will have to place their children in schools located within Doha city. The town boasts a stadium which hosts sporting matches and occasionally holds concerts.

West Bay

Reaching from the Corniche to West Bay Lagoon, the area known as West Bay has a variety of accommodation and lifestyle options. The area is smart and rather impressive, with massive villas on one side and sky-scraping high rises on the other, but it's also rather sprawling and lacking in atmosphere. The villas around Onaiza and Legtaifiya are popular with families who like a bit of peace and quiet, and the towers in Al Dafna, with its high concentration of high-end international restaurants and bars, are more suited to young professionals and singles. Traffic is normally quite light (by Doha standards), but can be bad with traffic entering and leaving The Pearl during rush hours.

Accommodation

There are plenty of huge stand-alone villas and some compounds; the biggest is West Bay Lagoon, which isn't like a typical compound. Houses are really stand-alone, but facilities like tennis courts and playgrounds are shared, and there are mini compounds within the site too. Residents also have access to private beaches.

Many of the stand-alone villas in Onaiza and Al Gassar have private pools, and a five-bed villa begins at around QR 25,000 a month, with three-beds costing around QR 18,000. Apartments are also available to rent and buy at the striking ZigZag Towers. Here a fully furnished, two-bed will cost upwards of QR 9,000. Serviced apartments are also an option in Al Dafna, with a two-bedroom apartment with full facilities starting at around QR 17,000 per month (see Hotel & Serviced Apartments, p.68).

Shopping & Amenities

The shopping facilities have improved dramatically following the opening of Lagoona Mall. This new leading retail haven has a wide selection of stores guaranteed to satisfy any shopper's wishes; for more, see p.332. Other nearby options include the vast City Center Doha (p.331) which has a big Carrefour (p.325) and countless other shops, as well as a cinema, kids' play areas, an ice rink and bowling alley. Neighbourhood convenience stores found all around the area complete the retail offering.

The Edge Of Town   Dawn Ali, 30, single professional

People think Al Wakra is a sleepy town, but it's so close to the edge of Doha and Airport Road with all of its shops, so it isn't as far away as many imagine – especially without the traffic. If you pick the right time of day you are only about 15 minutes away from the Corniche and the rest of the city. Al Wakrah itself has its own charm because of its historic nature as, unlike much of reconstructed Doha city, many of the old buildings are still intact. The traditional homes and the local stories – such as the haunted house in one of the neighbourhoods – are something everyone living in this area knows. If you want the city, it's just a few minutes by car. Meanwhile you can enjoy your peace and quiet and spacious garden that most city residents never experience.

Entertainment & Leisure

The Pearl is close by for restaurants, but now that Lagoona Mall is open, you won't even have to trek there – in addition to a good selection of shops, Lagoona Mall is home to over a dozen eateries to keep you well-fuelled while browsing the stores. For even more variety, The Pearl's many restaurants are within easy reach; for more, see p.348. Also nearby, City Center Doha adds to the options with its countless cafes and restaurants, including recent arrivals such as The Noodle House (p.366) and popular chains like Nando's, Biella, and Chili's.

Katara, the newly opened Cultural Village (p.362) is in West Bay too. This lifestyle destination has established itself as one of the city's most popular dining hubs as well. The options range from cafes and patisseries to restaurants serving a wide range of cuisines. Food aside, Katara's draws include theatres, art galleries, a heritage centre and a public beach. Surprisingly for a city sandwiched between the desert and the Arabian Gulf, there are few public beaches, so the opening of Katara's well-maintained stretch of seafront has been met with delight by local residents. Remember to dress conservatively when heading here; avoid very skimpy dressing and bikinis.

Hotels in the area also offer bathing facilities. The InterContinental (p.198), Four Seasons (p.198) and Sheraton (p.204) all have beaches accessible to health club members and paying day visitors. The Ritz Carlton does not have a beach, but the hotel's pontoon with deck chairs on it comes as a close second. Bikinis are acceptable at all of these facilities. Just beyond West Bay, The Golf Club (p.273) offers good food, sun shades and refreshingly green vistas. The Diplomatic Club (p.178), which has a large local membership, has a great beach and is good for water sports.

Education

There are a few schools around West Bay, with more planned. Newton International School (p.148), the French School (4496 0300), and Qatar International School (4483 3456) are based there. More nurseries are springing up too, with Fun First nursery (p.138) and Starfish Lane's second branch (p.141) already open. Qatar University (p.150) and the College of the North Atlantic (p.150) are close by. Also for kids in West Bay is My Gym (p.133), a franchise with play classes to help children develop. It's located opposite the International Exhibitions Centre on Lusail Street.

Northern Suburbs – Gharrafa, Kharatiyat, Umm Salal Mohammed, Khissa & Duhail

These areas are on the northern edge of Doha and stretch in a ribbon from Gharrafa Roundabout through Kharatiyat to Umm Salal Mohammed along the western side of the Doha Expressway (Shamal Road) and from Gharrafa Roundabout through Duhail and on to Khissa Village on the eastern side of the Doha Expressway. These suburbs mostly tend to be quite pleasant dormitory areas on the edge of town containing a mix of accommodation types to make the area an viable option for many.

Accommodation

Similar in nature they contain mostly a mixture of compounds and individual villas. The areas of each of these suburbs where they are closest to the Doha Expressway have suffered major blight in the last few years due to heavy construction activities on the Expressway; this is now slowly easing off as the project nears completion.

Shopping & Amenities

There are adequate shops in each area for day to day requirements and for that big weekly shop Landmark and Lulu Malls are within 6 km.

Entertainment & Leisure

There is not much in the way of organised entertainment in these suburbs. However, because of the Expressway, access to Doha from all of them is relatively simple and quick.

Education

One of the major western expatriate schools, The Gulf English School is located in Gharrafa and The College of the North Atlantic is sited in Duhail. Access to all of the other schools in Doha is relatively simple due to the proximity of The Doha Expressway, although traffic on the this road can be heavy during peak periods.

Rayyan

Located on the western side of Doha, Rayyan until fairly recently was an independent town. However the urban sprawl of Doha means that Rayyan is now a Doha suburb.

Accommodation

Accommodation in Rayyan tends to consist of traditional large Qatari family houses, although there are a limited number of small villa and flat developments.

Shopping & Amenities

Day-to-day requirements are readily available locally and the main shopping areas of Doha are easily accessible.

Entertainment & Leisure

There is little in the way of organised entertainment in Rayyan. However, Doha is close and Rayyan is the home to the main horse racing track in Qatar.

Setting Up Home

Education

Most of the major western expatriate schools are within relatively easy reach of Rayyan.

Sheehaniyah

Located on the Doha to Dukhan road about 30 minutes from central Doha, Sheehaniyah until recently was of little interest as a place to live and was only noted as the main centre of Qatari camel racing. Recently, a small number of compounds have been built and the town is growing slowly. There are a limited number of amenities and shopping would have to be done in Doha. Because Sheehaniyah is located outside Doha schools aren't easily accessible.

SETTING UP HOME

Moving Services

There are numerous moving companies available in Doha. The prices vary, but this is one area where the old saying is true: you get what you pay for. Get a couple of quotes from a few companies before making a decision. Many international employers will pay for your relocation and may have a particular moving company that they prefer to deal with. Relocation allowances are generally based on family size and an average estimate of goods that need moving. If you are a book lover, for instance, and have 50 or more books that need moving, these can quickly add to your allowance.

Smooth Moves

- Have any sentimental or important DVDs, books and, CDs with you rather than packed as these can often be stopped by customs and are easier to explain at the airport than by the agent at the port.
- Make sure to get additional quotes if you feel the first one is too high.
- Ask about what items are covered by insurance and to what amounts.
- Be sure someone from the family or a friend is present when the crew is packing to ensure all items arrive intact.
- Photograph anything that you would want replaced (rugs, furniture, etc) if damaged.
- Keep copies of the itemised inventory for delivery reference.

While airfreight is tempting, because it can take half the time of shipping by boat, it is more expensive. In either case remember that your goods have to clear customs once they reach Qatar; in most instances your employer will help provide the necessary paperwork with the authorities. This means any sensitive material such as movies, music, or books that are deemed inappropriate can be rejected from your shipment. If you are unsure about the suitability of any of your items, it's best to check with your employer's HR department or the shipping company, as they are often experienced in the local expectations.

For local moves you can use the professionals, or you could pack your belongings yourself and hire a truck – these can be found in the Najma souk area close to Souk Haraj. Bear in mind that any items broken en route won't be insured; alternatively you could pack yourself and then hire a few labourers and their vehicle to do the heavy lifting for you. This can be a good alternative if you are short on time, but again, if anything is broken, you are using them at your own risk. Rates can be anywhere from QR 50 to QR 100 per hour depending on distance and quantity of goods. It's best to agree upon the pricing beforehand.

When you are leaving Qatar, use a professional relocation firm; they know what they are doing, and will usually cover the liability on goods en route to your next destination. Companies like GAC have plenty of experience in dealing with the Gulf region. You may find that you have many more belongings than when you arrived; if the whole load turns out to be heavier in total weight than your cargo allowance, you can choose to cover the difference out of your own pocket. Alternatively, you may need to decide what to leave behind, depending on the quality and sentimental value of the goods in question.

When shipping goods to another country, it's advisable to take care to fully understand any import duties you may be liable to pay. Depending on the country in question, it may mean that it is cheaper to sell some items locally and buy new when you arrive at your next destination. Shipping companies will be happy to advise you on the best possible options that are most suitable for you and your family.

Allied Pickfords Old Airport, 4455 3455, *alliedpickfords.com*
Clearview Relocation Al Aziziya, 5587 9181, *clearviewqatar.com*
Crown Relocations > *p.41* Umm Ghuwailina, 4462 1115, *crownrelo.com*
Eastern Freight Forwarders 4442 8067, *eff.ae*
Gulf Agency Company Qatar (GAC) > *p.89* Al Souq, 4420 5600, *gac.com/qatar*
Gulf Warehousing Company QSC > *p.83* 4450 8508, *gulfwarehousing.com*
Inchcape Shipping Services Slata, 4432 9810, *iss-shipping.com*
Overseas Cargo Suhaim Bin Hamad St, 4499 5755, *overseas-cargo.com*
Qatar Logistics Al Mansoura, 4455 0991, *qatarlogistics.com*

GAC International Moving

Abu Dhabi	▶
Bahrain	▶
Dubai	▶
Kuwait	▶
Oman	▶
Qatar	▶

Click GAC International Moving
for peace of mind in every move

Relocation in itself is a challenge. And we believe that you already have enough to do without worrying about your forthcoming move. That's why when it comes to moving your home or office, GAC treats each item with care and every move with pride.

With more than 30 years of experience in moving household goods in and out of the Middle East, GAC provides comprehensive high quality door-to-door services for any relocation need. Moves are professionally planned, starting with a free initial survey and recommendations on the most efficient shipment mode. It's another world-class solution from GAC – available in over a thousands locations on earth.

GaC wherever you go

www.gac.com

GAC Abu Dhabi
P O Box 377
Abu Dhabi, United Arab Emirates
Tel: +971 2 673 0500
moving.abudhabi@gac.com

GAC Dubai
P O Box 17041
Dubai, United Arab Emirates
Tel: +971 4 881 8090
moving.dubai@gac.com

GAC Bahrain
P O Box 412
Manama, Kingdom of Bahrain
Tel +973 17 339 777
moving.bahrain@gac.com

GAC Oman
P O Box 740
Ruwi 112, Sultanate of Oman
Tel: +968 2447 7800
moving.oman@gac.com

GAC Kuwait
P O Box 20637 Safat
13067 Kuwait, State of Kuwait
Tel: +965 222 64 164
moving.kuwait@gac.com

GAC Qatar
P O Box 6534
Doha, State of Qatar
Tel +974 4420 5600
moving.qatar@gac.com

MEMBER OF
FIDI GLOBAL ALLIANCE

FAIM

Furnishing Accommodation

Many rented houses in Doha come furnished with all main items. Some come semi-furnished, which usually means with kitchen appliances (such as cooker, fridge and washing machine). It could also mean with air conditioners, although some houses are rented without any air-con so it is wise to check this before you sign any contracts. Doha has lots of furniture shops if you need to fill your house yourself (see p.304 for the best places to shop for furniture). Unfortunately, Doha doesn't have an IKEA (yet), but there are a number of other budget options including Home Center (p.305). Alternatively, for simple, modern furnishings with unidentifiably Nordic design credentials, look no further than ID Design (p.306).

Many international companies will give employees an allowance to buy their own furniture, which then becomes theirs after two years' service. Other firms will provide its employees with a relocation allowance to spend on whatever they wish, while some will offer a choice from a selection of furniture that they already have in storage. Many employers also provide white goods and soft goods – items such as a few linens, towels, and kitchen necessities – so the employee does not have to spend the first few days in an entirely empty facility. It's best to ask prior to relocating so that you know what will be provided for you and decide what you may want to bring with you or purchase once you've arrived.

Second-Hand Furniture

As people arrive and leave Qatar all the time, there are many second-hand furniture sales via company newsletters or word of mouth. Some people put up lists on notice boards in supermarkets and schools, and others have garage sales. It's also worth visiting some of the popular expat hang outs such as sports clubs, and family friendly cafes and restaurants. Qatarliving.com is also a popular place for sale items to be listed, as are the classifieds in the newspapers. Both are an excellent way of picking up good quality furniture at bargain prices.

Household Insurance

Although cases of theft from private properties are still rare in Qatar, isolated incidents do occur and it is best to be prepared for all outcomes. It is advisable to buy insurance cover if you have costly household goods and valuables, as well as for damage or loss of property from accidental incidences of fire and flooding. If you would like to insure your home and contents, there are currently only a handful of companies to choose from, but they will be able to guide you through the relevant types of cover and required procedures.

For a list of companies providing household insurance, see Insurance Companies, p.114.

UTILITIES & SERVICES

Electricity & Water

The Qatar Electricity & Water Corporation (Kahramaa) is the sole distributor of water and electricity. When you rent accommodation make sure both supplies are connected before you move in. This is easily done if your company or the real estate agency hasn't already arranged it.

To set up a new account you'll need a Kahramaa application form, a copy of the lease for your accommodation, a copy of your Qatari ID, your contact number, mailing address, and the electricity and water reference number for your unit. You'll also need to leave a security deposit of QR 2,000. The reference number can generally be found outside your unit on the utility box, and the landline number assigned to your house will be on the exterior doorframe.

Bills can be paid online at kahramaa.com.qa or at km.com.qa, via automatic bank bill payment, over the phone, or at the post office.

In the summer, you should expect higher utility bills because of the rise in heat and corresponding increase in air-conditioning usage. If you do want to try and lower the costs of utilities, try to cool only those spaces that you are directly occupying. Most houses and even apartments have room-specific air-conditioning units – so turn off the unit in the kitchen if you are in the living room, bedroom or dining room.

Electricity and water bills are sent out every month. For the first five months the bills are consumption estimates and from the sixth month an actual meter reading will be taken. This is known as a reconciliation bill and is generally higher than the estimates. Apartment bills tend to be between QR 200 and QR 400 per month, and villas between QR 800 and QR 1,000 per month, though they can fluctuate in the summer when you will need more air conditioning. You can pay your bill online at km.com.qa or at kahramaa.com, at any of the banks in Doha, or at a Customer Service Centre. Customer Service Centre contact numbers include the general helpline on 991.

Electricity

The voltage in Qatar is 240 volts and the frequency is 50Hz. Sockets are of the three-pin British ring main type, although strangely almost all appliances you buy will have European style two-pin plugs, so stock up on adaptors.

Water Suppliers

Tap water in Qatar is perfectly safe to drink but many people like the idea of chilled water on tap and water dispensers are very popular. Refill bottles can be bought cheaply and cost about QR 25 for your initial purchase and around QR 8 for refills. The main suppliers are shown opposite:

Hot Water In Summer

Many accommodation units lack insulated water tanks; money can be saved in the extreme summer heat by turning off the hot water heating system (immersion heaters) and using the water from the cold tank, which is by now very hot anyway from its exposure to the sun. The water from the formerly heated hot tank can then be used as your cold water. Whilst this is sensible and will certainly save you money, washing lettuce becomes a major problem.

Aqua Gulf Pure Mineral Water 4450 1400
Nestle Pure Life (Al Manhal Water) 4460 3332, *nestle-family.com*
Rayyan Mineral Water Co 4487 7662, *rayyanwater.com*
Safa International 4460 6699, *safawaterqa.com*

Gas

There is no mainline gas in Qatar, so if you have a gas cooker, you will have to use cylinders that will be delivered to your residence. The gas cylinders cost QR 375 initially and then QR 15 for a refilled cylinder; as the deliveries are often done during the day when no one is home, getting resupplied can be tricky. If you live in a compound, your security or maintenance staff can let you know when the delivery trucks will be in your area and you can leave the fee with them to pass on. If you want to arrange an order with the gas suppliers directly, try Mashahdi Gas (4442 3016) or Al Shamal Gas Centre (4432 4995).

Sewerage

Most houses in Doha are now connected to the main sewerage system. Some new complexes have been built in areas which are not yet connected to the sewerage system, as are all houses outside of Doha, but these properties will have septic tanks, which will be emptied on a regular basis. If you are living in a private or standalone villa, it's best to check what the maintenance is for your septic tank.

Al Afaf Group 4431 1409, *alafafgroup.net*
Almuftah Group 4444 6868, *almuftah.com*

Rubbish Disposal

Usually, villas have a green bin outside the front door, applied for by the landlord and collected on a daily basis by maintenance staff. Refuse trucks come round and collect the rubbish a number of times a week, depending on which area you live in. If you live in an apartment there will be chutes that are emptied by the municipality rubbish trucks. All rubbish is taken to a landfill, which is located about half an hour's drive outside the city. The concept of recycling is of growing interest in Qatar, though the municipality has not yet taken steps to implement a programme across the city; most of the recycling efforts stem from the post secondary institutions such as the universities at Qatar Foundation and Qatar University. Some compounds do arrange for recyclable materials to be taken to plants in the Industrial Zone. Recycling bins can be found in some parks and schools, and are slated to expand into other parts of the city. For more information, see Going Green, p.14.

Telephone

There are two phone providers in Qatar, Qtel and Vodafone. While Vodafone is still a new player in the Qatar market, focusing mostly on prepaid mobile phone customers, its aim is to expand its services as its customer base grows. At the early part of 2011, Virgin Mobile also entered the market but there was a lot of controversy about the partnership with Qtel and at the time of writing Virgin Mobile's position in Qatar seemed uncertain.

Qtel is the original telephone and internet provider. Landline, mobile and internet connections can be arranged through them, but you need your residence permit first. Once you have residency, you can apply for a telephone line by visiting any of Qtel's shops to fill in an application. Make sure you apply for an ADSL internet connection at the same time, if you require one. Local calls between landlines are free, while calls made to mobiles are charged at reasonable rates. For more information on landline services call 111.

Qtel also offers two calling cards: the Qcard, which can be used from any telephone, payphone (Qatar has over 800 public phones) or mobile; and the Dawli International Card, which has low international rates and can be used from any Qtel mobile or landline.

Mobile Phones

In 2009, the Vodafone Group launched Vodafone Qatar, greatly expanding Qatar's mobile phone services, which had up to that point been solely operated by Qtel. Vodafone offers prepaid and post-paid services. To get started with either service you need to buy a welcome pack (costing QR 25), from a Vodafone store or partner shop. The pack comes with a SIM card and Vodafone phone number, and you will need to present ID when purchasing it.

Vodafone's prepaid service is called Red. Once you've bought your welcome pack you can buy credit (called a Flexi plan) in Vodafone stores and partner shops, to make calls and access other services. With the post-paid service, Freedom, you set up a monthly Flexi plan, which is automatically debited from your credit card or bank account. On both Red and Freedom packages, you receive bonus value and Vodafone minutes, which allow you to call other

Utilities & Services

Qtel tower

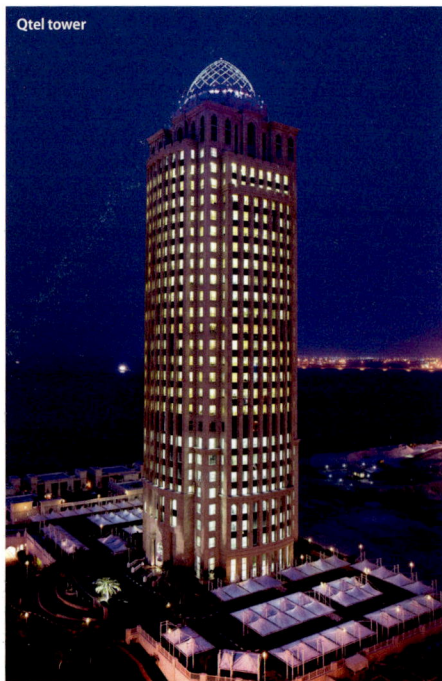

Vodafone users free of charge, each time you buy a Flexi plan over QR 20 – the higher the value of the plan, the more Vodafone minutes you receive. You can also access a range of services including local and international calling, text messaging, roaming and mobile internet. For social networking fans, Vodafone is a good option as you can access Facebook, Maktoob, Orkut and Friendster at anytime for free. There are additional mobile internet packages available if you use a lot of data. Look out for frequent special offers on various services. For more information, including store locations check out vodafone.com.qa or call 800 7111.

Qtel offers a range of mobile phone services, including post-paid, prepaid, residential packages (combining GSM post-paid line, landline and ADSL in one), mobile internet and 3G services.

For a GSM post-paid line you can visit any Qtel shop to fill in an application. Customers get access to a number of services including 3G video calls and mobile email, and the Mozaic Mobile package that includes news, entertainment and ringtones. The company offers a number of packages for post-paid customers, including the 'Friends and Family Service' which provides a 25% discount on calls made to up to three international numbers of your choice (for a fee of QR 25). For further information on GSM post-paid services, call 111.

Qtel's pay-as-you-talk option is called Hala. Hala SIM cards are available at Qtel offices, and the scratch-off recharge cards (with values of QR 30, QR 50 and QR 100) are widely available in shops, supermarkets and Qtel offices. The Hala SIM card is available for QR 200, comes with QR 100 of credit and is valid for 120 days (the validity of this card can be extended). Hala also now allows international roaming. For more information visit qtel.com.qa.

The latest company to turn its attention to Qatar was Virgin Mobile, who made its network available in May 2011. However, despite offering competitive value, excellent coverage and good customer service, the service was, unfortunately, quickly phased out following a regulatory issue. At the time of writing, the partnership's future in Qatar appears uncertain.

People who own smart phones or iPads can avail themselves of the downloading services provided by both telecoms suppliers but beware, if you underestimate the cost of the plan you need, additional time can be very expensive. Also if you go out of Qatar don't forget to disable your roaming facility. Downloading overseas, even in other Gulf states will be charged as international calls.

Television

The inclusion of Al Jazeera English news channel alongside the already well established Al Jazeera Arabic division has made the Qatar network a major regional broadcaster. In addition to the local media, including Qatar Television's Channel One (Arabic) and Channel Two (English), there are a variety of options available from satellite providers. If you just want to access the limited range of free-to-view channels you can buy a one-off decoder from any of the satellite providers. The Orbit Showtime Network offers a wide range of channels, including BBC Prime, BBC Entertainment, America Plus, ShowSeries, OSN Comedy, movie channels, news channels, ESPN, children's channels and many more. It often has promotions which include a free dish, decoder and installation, so check the local press for the latest offers or visit the OSN website (osnetwork.com). Packages cost between QR 87 and QR 398 per month and are available through a number local providers (Starlink, Al Muftah Cable Vision, Al Mashriq Systems, Qatar Multi-Tech and Gulf Security Equipment). OSN also offers the Showbox, a recordable decoder, which costs QR 595 as opposed to the standard HD decoder which is QR 297.

Internet

You can get connected to the internet by applying to Qtel once you have your residence visa. You will need a letter from your sponsor, and it is a good idea to apply for the internet connection at the same time as you apply for your landline telephone. Qtel will provide you with a password and a user name, and will also install the necessary software on your computer, so make sure you have your computer available when the company sends someone to install the internet connection.

Qtel offers a range of packages and services for internet access, the cheapest of which is the Eshtirak dial-up connection for residential use that costs QR 2 per hour, in addition to a QR 20 monthly fee and QR 50 one-off fee. High-speed broadband internet is also available, with 1MB charged at QR 200 a month and 8MB costing QR 600 per month (a Wi-Fi router and installation are free if you sign a year's contract).

It is also possible to access the internet without subscribing to any of the above packages as prepaid dial-up cards (known as Ebhar) can be bought from any of the Qtel customer service centres plus a number of shops and supermarkets. Ebhar prepaid dial-up internet cards are available in denominations of QR 30, QR 50 and QR 100. These allow users to access the net by plugging a computer into any telephone line – time online is deducted from the pre-paid card and not charged to the phone line.

A further dial-up option is 161 Instant Internet. Without the need for a subscription, usernames, passwords or special equipment, users simply plug into any phone line and dial 161 from their computer. Surfing is charged at QR 6 per hour and will appear on the phone bill at the end of the month. You can find more details of all of Qtel's internet packages at qtel.com.qa.

There are Qtel Wi-Fi HotSpots all over Doha, which you can connect to using prepaid HotSpot cards in denominations of QR 30, QR 50 and QR 70. You can also get a mobile broadband service through Qtel. ICTQatar, the telecommunications regulator, also recently launched an initiative to give users free access to a wireless network along the Corniche and in Al Bidda Park, although the patchy signal means the service is temperamental.

There are several internet cafes scattered around Doha too (they charge around QR 6 per hour) mostly within cafes such as Grand Cafe on Salwa Road or the Coffee House at Midmac Roundabout. You can also get 10 minutes' free internet access at the main Post Office in West Bay (4446 4446).

Postal Services

You can find the main Post Office without too much effort. On Doha's Corniche, it is a large building with lots of small arches around the outside. It has a four-level car park that you have to drive through to get to the main entrance. The entrance into the building is on the left-hand side. here are no postmen to deliver mail to your door in Qatar, but instead you can obtain a PO box from any Post Office branch. You need to complete an application form, attach a copy of your ID card and pay the subscription fee. Once

this is processed, a box number will be allocated to you. If you apply to the head office you will be given an electronic card to access your box; other branches use keys. It's first come, first served with regards to the size you get, and there's a flat-rate fee. The annual fee for PO boxes (including electronic key) at the head office is QR 360 for a personal box and QR 300 for renewal; a company box costs QR 560 and QR 500 for renewal. Annual renewal and new subscription fees run from 1 January until 31 December. Fees are calculated pro-rata at QR 25 per month, depending on when you apply (see qpost.com.qa for details). Other branches are opening by the day but only offer one box size. The fees for personal boxes are slightly cheaper (QR 200, including two keys or an electronic key card). There's also a new delivery service called Q-Post Premium, which has been launched for the delivery and collection of important documents from office or home premises, for a fee of QR 15 per item. The documents are tracked through all stages of handling and confirmation of delivery is provided online. Again, see the Q-Post website for full details. Alternatively you can have things sent to your company's box, depending on its policy. Post seems to arrive fairly speedily, although during Ramadan it may take a little longer and during Eid the Post Office will be closed completely.

Courier Services

All of the international courier services operate in Qatar and their rates and delivery times vary. It is best to plan ahead, when possible, as even the fastest services can take a minimum of three business days to get documents or other items to an international location. The most popular courier firms include Aramex, FedEx (through local contractor Falcon Express), and DHL. You should look at their websites to get the most up-to-date information, as prices often change several times during the year depending on the cost of fuel. One of the best, and often overlooked courier services, is operated from post offices by Q-Post and called Mumtaz Post. Simply go into any post office with your package or parcel, preferably unsealed so that the contents can be verified, before sealing it. Mumtaz Post is quick, economical and efficient and they have arrangements for delivery in all destination countries. You will be given a number that will allow you to track your package on the internet, from your original submission point to its final destination. In general, deliveries are not automatically brought to your door in Qatar; if a parcel arrives for you, you will first get a phone call.

Aramex Bu Hamour, 4420 0100, *aramex.com*
DHL Express Ain Khaled, 4458 7888, *dhl.com.qa*
FedEx 4466 1722, *FedEx.com*
TNT 4462 2262, *tnt.com*

Carpet Cleaners & Laundry Services

Most of the homes in Qatar have tiled floors rather than wall to wall carpeting, but rugs are popular furnishings and most need a good clean from time to time. If you have a speciality item that you would like to have cleaned, taking it to a rug shop is a good way to make sure that they send it to an appropriate service. Many carpet shops are happy to come and collect your rugs, take them away for cleaning and bring them back again, and most will request to see the rug (for size, quality and so on) before quoting a price. See Carpets, p.300 for a selection of carpet retailers, or call Oriental Carpet Company on 4447 9794.

If you simply want to give that dirty old rug a wash down, look no further than the local car wash. Some have an A frame outside their premises for jet washing and drying your dirty old carpet; they are easy to spot.

When it comes to getting your washing done, if you don't have your own machine, most neighbourhoods have dry cleaners that also offer a laundry option, usually including home delivery. It's important to hang on to your receipt as most places are very busy and items can get lost. Many places will return stained garments unless you have specifically told them about the stain beforehand, as they don't want to be accused of having caused the damage while cleaning. Expect to pay around QR 10 for having a shirt cleaned, whereas a suit will be closer to QR 25. For quilts and other speciality items such as sheets, chair covers and linens, prices are at least QR 50-80. Another popular service is ironing (pressing), which can be done at the same facility you take your garments to; alternatively, there are many shops in Grand Hamad Street, which just offer pressing services.

Al Ahmadi Laundry & Dry Cleaners Al Sadd, 4444 1840
Al Rayes Laundry & Dry Cleaning 4465 1555, *groupalrayes.com*
Al Thuraiya Laundry & Dry Cleaning Muaither, 4414 1669, *thuraiyagroup.com*
Assiyana Al Asmakh, 4432 2088, *assiyana.com*
Family Laundry Old Airport, 4450 5903
Magic Laundry Industial Area, 4450 3084
Prestige Laundry Fereej Al Nasr, 4432 3040
Special Dry Cleaning & Laundry 4472 0812

Domestic Help

Many local and expat families in Doha have some form of domestic help, either live-in or several times a week. There are a few agencies that can help you to find a live-in housemaid. The advantage of using an agency is that if for some reason the person is not suitable, the company can arrange for them to return home and provide a replacement at no extra cost, as long as it is within six weeks of arrival. Agencies also sort out all of the visa procedures, which can be daunting if you try to do it on your own.

Alternatively, you might find a maid via word of mouth, as families leaving Qatar can provide good references for people who have worked for them. For more information on sponsoring a maid, see p.42.

If you don't need live-in help then weekly cleaning services are generally easy to arrange. Most people find out about a cleaner either through colleagues at work or neighbours. QR 30-60 an hour is the average rate for an independent cleaner, or you can arrange for a similar weekly service through an agency but this will likely increase the price. In either case, you'll be expected to provide the all of the essential cleaning products and supplies.

Modern residential housing

Whether you are at home or not while the person is cleaning is entirely up to you – many people give keys to their regular cleaners, once they have established a relationship of trust with them, but do take care with your selection. Although theft is unlikely, be sensible and store valuable products away. It's also worth being aware that should you be unfortunate enough to suffer a house break-in or theft, the standard procedure is for the police to arrest anyone who has a key.

Note that if you go with an individual outside an agency they are not covered by any theft or breakables insurance policy and you will have to sort out any problems that arise.

Al Baidha Cleaning Company 4469 2696
Al Doha Maintenance & Services 4486 1034, *admsc.com*
Al Mannai Cleaning Company 4435 6424
Al Sayed Cleaning, Maintenance & Rent A Car 4444 1123, *alsayedcleaning.com*
Assiyana 4432 2088, *assiyana.com*
Gulf Energy Technology & Projects 4412 7514, *gulfenergy.com.qa*
Qatar Cleaning Company 4466 2695, *qatarcleaningco.com*
Rose Services & General Cleaning Company 4469 7711

HOME IMPROVEMENTS

Beyond regular maintenance, such as repairs for leaks and to appliances, residents often have a whole range of things they'd like to implement in order to make a space feel more like home. This can range from painting walls to hanging pictures, or pulling up bricks in the backyard to plant trees. The important thing is to communicate with your compound or villa management as policies on such changes can vary. Likewise, apartment blocks are likely to have strict rules on what you can and can't do. In most instances, the labour costs will be at the expense of the tenant as will the cost of restoring any changes to their original condition.

Maintenance

Housing in Qatar requires constant maintenance – thanks, in no small part, to the climate. Air conditioning units can be temperamental and need regular servicing, plumbing problems aren't uncommon and electrics can go haywire. If you are in a compound or apartment, then your first call for maintenance issues should be to the property or compound manager, who is usually available 24 hours. Most compounds have agreements with service providers to respond to plumbing and electrical problems. Beware that delays

Many houses benefit from swimming pools

are likely if problems happen at the weekend. The most common incidences are air conditioner leaks, which can usually be cleaned up in a few hours but may require repeat visits.

If you are renting from a private landlord, you will usually have to go through him first before you hire anyone to carry out work for you; it's therefore preferable to agree on a maintenance contractor at the leasing stage, who you can go to directly without seeking any further landlord approval. If you own the property yourself, there are a few options that you can try when looking for plumbers, electricians or carpenters. The streets around the Najma area have a number of carpenters, and there are quite a few small businesses on Al Arabiya Street where you can locate electricians and plumbers. Recently, due to the Heart of Doha redevelopment scheme, many of the building supplies, electrical and plumbing supplies shops have relocated to Barwa village, between Airport Roundabout and Wakrah.

If you live on a compound it will either provide someone to do the maintenance work for you or give you a number to contact. Be sure to ask around for recommendations for the best maintenance firms.

Builders

Other than painting and gardens, if you'd like to alter your rented property considerably, this should be done in consultation with the landlord, property manager or developer to first make sure they approve of any changes. Additionally, they may be able to suggest specific contractors. Most residences, even apartments, come with a maid's facility, but if you feel yours needs adaptation, this is something to discuss early on in the leasing or buying process with your landlord or developer.

Painters

Painting supplies can be found in many of the general hardware stores on Salwa Road or near the Al Luqta areas. Jotun, Hempel and National paints are popular brands manufactured locally and are readily available. Many of the hardware shops have signboards for a particular brand rather than a shop name, making them easy to spot. Some hardware shops can mix colours on their premises. It's also worth asking the staff in the paint shop if they can send a painting crew to do the work for you; this is a popular service so expect a slight delay.

Alternatively, if you live in an apartment or compound, the maintenance crew are often willing to do some extra work, such as painting; fees are upwards of around QR 50 an hour, depending on the scale of the job. You'll need to provide all the supplies including brushes, tarps, masking tape for doors and so on. If neither of these options are available there are a few companies such as Jassim Decoration Services (4443 0031) who can send painters directly to your home.

If you employ painters on a casual basis take care to ensure that they are skilled craftsmen, and specify exactly what it is that you want done. Many casual labourers are desperate for work and will insist that they can paint, when in reality the truth is often quite the opposite.

Gardens

The dramatic heat of the Qatari summer is the main impediment to creating and maintaining a successful garden; with very little annual rainfall and rapidly diminishing groundwater, plenty of hydration is required. However, the cooler months do provide a relatively adequate climate for many species. September to April is the best time to plant and grow most outdoor vegetation. Many compounds will provide landscaping and a gardener to take care of the public spaces on the property, but a lot of expats take to cultivating their back gardens as personal hobbies. If you have an extensive garden you'll want to make sure someone waters it on a daily basis during the hottest months, particularly if you are away.

If you are starting from scratch with a dried out patch of sand, compost can be obtained from the animal market, off Salwa Road. Another often used option is to collect seaweed from the beaches, mix it with household compost and peat (available from all hypermarkets and garden centres) and dig it into the sand. Almost anything will grow in Qatar, so as long as you secure reasonable soil and sufficient water – the sunshine is nearly guaranteed to be there.

Because grass is a water-intensive plant, most of the homes only have small lawn plots; other alternatives include hardier ground cover plants such as ivy to fill large areas. Bougainvillea, cacti, and small trees are often popular choices because they can take up more space and also provide aesthetic value with less routine care. If you are adamant about having a grassy garden you can always cheat and opt for astroturf. Fake lawns are increasingly popular; they stay green throughout the year and are more environmentally friendly as there is little watering involved (although you do need to hose the astroturf down every few weeks to stop it becoming extremely dry and rough). You can buy astroturf (in varying degrees of quality) at Arabian Trees and Plants (arabiantrees.com).

To find gardeners, many people ask for referrals from those who have lived here for a while, or use the compound's employees, paying them for their time. If you do get a good one, make sure you treat him well and keep him; in an arid country like Qatar a garden is a wonderful asset.

If you are considering a sizeable number of plants or covering a large area, it is often possible to arrange for the staff of a nursery or from the stalls in the Omani Market (p.328) to pay you a visit at an additional fee.

FairGreen International Landscaping New Doha, 4456 8370, *fairgreen-intl.com*
Floranza International Nursery Bu Hamour, 4469 9982, *floranza.net*
Larissa Gardens Bu Hamour, 4460 2529, *larissagardens.com*
Qatar Canadian Company For Nurseries & Ornamental Plants Fereej Bin Omran, 4487 2352, *qatarcanadian.com*

Swimming Pools

Installing home swimming pools is not that common in Qatar as many compounds have pools in their clubhouse. If you don't have one on your premises, you can always pay to have one installed – but it doesn't come cheap. Try making contact with the following companies for maintenance and cleaning supplies.

Al Jabor Trading Company 4432 8500
Arrayyan Pools 4466 3331, *arrayyanpools.com*
Bluewater Swimming Pools & Water Features 4412 2022, *bluewater-qatar.com*
Gemco Swimming Pools 4465 2452
Regency Pools 4466 0012, *regency-pools.com*
Tadmur Roofs & Pools 4466 4850, *tadmur-roofsandpools.com*

Accommodation options

Are you in the wrong job?

At Kershaw Leonard Recruitment we know that no matter what field you specialize in, the environment must be the right one. By getting to know our clients' and candidates' needs, we provide the ideal solutions for both, ensuring that everyone's best interests are met and that no one is pulled in the wrong direction. For more information visit www.kershawleonard.net or contact Tel +974 4455 4379.

The right people people
Kershaw Leonard
DOHA kL *DUBAI* kL *ABU DHABI*

Work, Finance & The Law

WORKING IN QATAR

The lure of a tax-free income is hard to resist, and even though the glory days of supremely fat wages and endless benefits are over, there are still many reasons why working in Qatar is appealing. The country has enjoyed a booming period of growth over the last decade which is expected to continue (see Economic Growth, p.30), largely thanks to its rich reserves of liquefied natural gas (LNG) and in spite of the recent economic downturn.

Since the global recession – when Qatar suffered a 9% redundancy rate during 2009 – the unemployment levels have improved with only around 1% of the population unemployed. In terms of banking, finance and mining, the global crisis appeared to be a mere blip on the radar, with many sectors reporting growth overall starting already in 2010. With the economy holding strong, opportunities for those with specialist skills are abundant, particularly in the gas, oil, finance and construction sectors, and frequently in management or executive roles.

Most job placements won't require you to speak Arabic; however it does pay to learn a few greetings and pleasantries before you arrive (see Basic Arabic, p.18). All workers are entitled to one month's paid leave per year, a flight home at least once every two years and a bonus equal to one month's wage for every year of service worked. In addition to this, some international companies offer paid furnished housing and utilities, medical insurance, tuition fees for dependents, as well as share option schemes. Your employer will normally look after some or all of your relocation costs (including flights for you and your family) and will pay for all necessary residence visas and work permits when you arrive.

Traditionally, the working day in Qatar is broken up into two portions with an afternoon break in between (many local businesses still adopt this model); however most corporations expect hours to be worked in one block, usually with an early start time of around 07:00.

Labour law in Qatar states the maximum working hours per week as 48, though this is rarely the case. The working week is normally Sunday to Thursday, but some businesses now expect employees to work every day except Friday. The average working hours per day are eight, but some positions – such as those in gas and construction – will have you clocking in for much longer.

Spouses wishing to work should have no trouble finding employment, especially if they are formally qualified and experienced in fields such as teaching, accounting, finance, administration or hospitality. Local hire placements do not normally offer the inflated salaries and added benefits of jobs recruited from overseas, but you might enjoy other perks, such as decreased working hours, a less-competitive environment and greater opportunities for advancement.

Historically, immigrant workers from poor economic backgrounds haven't received the best treatment in Qatar, despite the fact that they provide the backbone of labour for the construction and development industries. Thankfully, attitudes toward worker rights and freedoms are changing for the better and Qatar's human rights profile is slowly improving as a result.

Sponsorship

The only real catch for employees in Qatar is that you must be sponsored in order to work here – no person is allowed to reside in Qatar without sponsorship. Although the sponsorship system itself is fairly straightforward, it does effectively tie you to your sponsor, which has its restrictions. If you are being hired from abroad, your company will proceed with all the formalities such as flights and visas in order to bring you here, (see Entry Visa, p.40), then will help you obtain your residence permit after you have arrived (see Residence Permit, p.40).

Approval for residency is a long-winded, bureaucratic necessity, requiring you to submit a stack of paperwork and meet specific medical and character requirements (see Medical Test, p.43 and Fingerprinting, p.43). The whole process takes about four to six weeks and all costs are covered by your employer.

You must remain under employer sponsorship for a period of at least one year before considering switching jobs, and only then if your current employer permits it (see Changing Jobs, p.105). You cannot leave the country without first obtaining approval from your sponsor.

It is important to note that a sponsor is legally responsible for the actions, behaviour and welfare of anyone under their sponsorship. So whilst your company must assist with housing and travel provisions, treat you with respect and courtesy and comply with workplace satisfaction standards, they also assume liability in terms of local law and customs. If, for example, an employed couple is found to be

---

┌ Visa On Arrival? ──────

In early 2010 there were reports that visas on arrival would be scrapped for certain nationalities which had previously qualified for them. After a few weeks of confusion, it was announced that the new regulations had been put on hold indefinitely. As laws are subject to change with little notice, you should always check the latest with your local Qatari embassy prior to travelling.

living together unmarried (see Villa Sharing, p.69) or if a misdemeanour is committed, then the sponsoring company may suffer the consequences.

The same applies for anyone residing under family sponsorship (a married man would sponsor his non-working wife and children) or if you sponsor anyone to work for you, such as a maid, nanny or driver.

Working Hours

Qatari labour law states that employees work a maximum 48 hours per week, except during Ramadan when a maximum of 36 hours per week applies. In spite of the law, many international firms (such as those associated with gas and construction) demand much longer working hours than specified, with reduced Ramadan hours usually only applicable to Muslims. All workers are entitled to public holidays, irrespective of their religion.

On the whole, people tend to work about eight hours a day with office timings varying from company to company. Most employees enjoy a two-day weekend, usually Friday and Saturday, but some companies only allow one day off on Friday. A number of offices work split shifts, but most work straight through the day. Government offices tend to work from 07:00 to 14:00. Commercial offices sometimes work from 08:00 to 12:00 and then from 16:00 to 20:00; or a straight shift through to 17:00.

Shopping centres are generally open from 10:00 to 22:00, but individual shops tend to follow the split shift, usually 08:00 to 12:30 and 16:30 to 21:00.

There are two Eid holidays – Eid Al Fitr and Eid Al Adha. Eid Al Fitr marks the end of the Holy Month of Ramadan and is determined by the sighting of the new moon. Ramadan dates are not always guaranteed, although a rule of thumb is that it begins about 11 days earlier than the previous year. Eid Al Adha falls around 70 days after Eid Al Fitr. Due to the uncertainty in pinpointing actual dates, public holidays are often announced in the daily newspapers at the last minute. Fixed public holidays are listed on p.9.

Business Culture

Business in Qatar is notoriously done at a more leisurely pace than you might be used to – which may be frustrating at first – with Arabs preferring to do business in person, not over the telephone or via email. You should confirm appointment dates and times and tardiness is considered extremely rude. Even so, be prepared for meetings to be cancelled at the last moment, or to sustain an array of interruptions.

Eye contact is very important in the Arab world and maintaining it is a sign of respect and trust. When meeting with people of the opposite sex, wait for them to initiate a handshake; many people do not shake the hands with members of the opposite

Downtown Doha

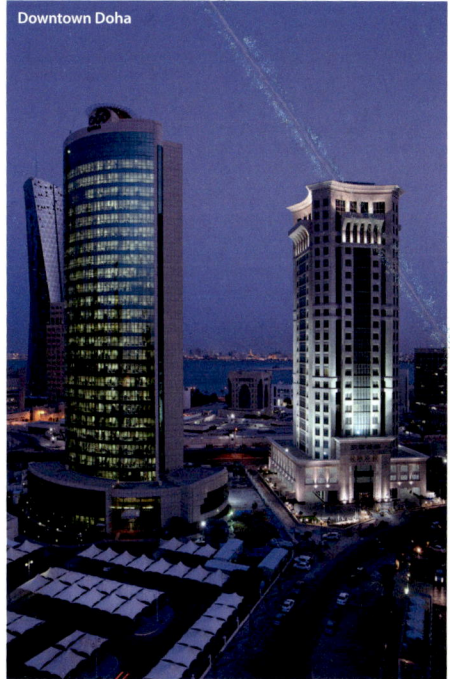

sex who they are not related to (based on religious principles). Don't be surprised if your hand is held for an uncomfortably long period (don't try and let go) and don't be offended if someone does not want to shake your hand at all. You may place your right hand over your heart, which is a signal for showing appreciation, instead. Learning a few words in Arabic is an excellent icebreaker and helps to build rapport.

Business cards are a popular way of introducing yourself, and you may find yourself handing them out continuously so be sure to have plenty at hand. If, in turn, you are given a business card, make sure to look at it and take time to read it as the person may take offence if you simply place it into your pocket.

When making small talk, avoid enquiring about family matters and concentrate on more generic conversation such as sports or general compliments about the country if you are newly arrived. You should accept an offer of something to drink, even if it is a glass of water, as a sign of respect. If offered Arabic coffee or gahwa, accept with your right hand and be sure to leave a small amount in the bottom to signal that you have finished; an empty cup implies that you would like a refill.

When conducting business, it is important to note that the spoken word is very significant in this cultural context. Try not to promise anything that you might not be able to deliver. Follow up on meetings with a phone call of appreciation and work to maintain ongoing contact, therefore keeping your relationships genial and courteous and inviting open communication. Word travels fast in such a small community, so a good reputation for honesty, respectfulness and reliability is crucial.

Finding Work

There is a shortage of qualified professionals in Qatar, especially in high-growth industries such as gas, construction and finance. If you are interested in working here, start by investigating any transfer or secondment opportunities that might be available in your current company. Failing that, start reviewing the job advertisement pages in your local newspapers and on the web.

Some good job search websites in the region include Bayt (bayt.com), Gulf Talent (gulftalent. com), Monster Gulf (monstergulf.com) and Naukri (naukrigulf.com). Sign up to their mailing lists to get job alerts sent directly to your inbox. Most companies advertise vacant positions on their websites, so keep an eye on the online job sections of potential employers, or send an email directly to their human resources department.

Alternatively, you could contact an international recruitment agency, some of whom have offices in Doha (see opposite) or might be located in nearby Dubai (for example, Morgan McKinley morganmckinley.ae). Specialist companies like Genesis Associates (genesisassociates.co.uk), MPH Consulting Services (mphglobal.net) and NES Group (nesgroup.com) are based outside Qatar and source jobs for workers interested in oil, gas and construction sectors.

Registering with a recruitment agency is free of charge, and generally just a matter of contacting the company and providing them with your CV. Web-based companies usually allow you to simply email your current CV or upload it directly through their website, or ask you to complete an online form detailing your employment history and skill level.

Depending on the agency, you may be assigned a consultant with whom you can discuss the kind of job you are looking for. You may also have access to job search tips, hints on how to improve your CV and advice on preparing for interviews.

Your agency will contact you if you have been selected as a potential candidate for a job and put you in touch with the employer to arrange an interview. If you find a job or wish to discontinue your job search, you should issue a formal request in writing for your details to be removed from their database.

If you are already in Qatar and looking for work you can register with a local recruitment agency (see the list below), search the *Gulf Times* or *The Peninsula* newspapers or rely on word-of-mouth. Some expat

websites advertise jobs (see p.23) or you can approach companies in person. It is easy for applications to get lost amid piles of paperwork here, so be sure to check back regularly in case any suitable positions have since come available.

Part-time or freelance opportunities are on the increase, especially for people skilled in teaching, tutoring, writing, photography and administration. It is possible to set up your own small business here (mobile hairdressing, home-made jewellery), but you must have a Qatari sponsor for it to be legitimate (see Setting up a Small Business, p.110).

For further study options, check out the course listings at Virginia Commonwealth University (qatar. vcu.edu) or College of North Atlantic (cna-qatar.com). Smaller companies such as New Horizons Qatar (4446 5000, newhorizons.com) specialise in computer skills training, while Empower Management Consulting (4411 7561, empowermc.com) teaches business strategy, management and leadership development.

Recruitment Agencies

Al Noof Recruitment Services Fereej Al Nasr, 4442 2076, *alnoof.com*
Brunel Oil & Gas Services Al Waab, 4466 6275, *brunelenergy.net*
Cappo Qatar 4495 4625, *cappogroup.com*
Charterhouse Partnership > *p.103* Dubai, +971 4 372 3500, *charterhouseme.ae*
Clarendon Parker Qatar Musheireb, 4437 8855, *cpq.com.qa*
Kershaw Leonard Qatar > *p.98* Old Airport, 4455 4380, *kershawleonard.net*

Networking & Events

Networking is the keystone of doing business in Qatar and valuable agreements – including contracts worth billions of riyals – are commonly awarded based on reputation rather than merit. Therefore it is worth muscling into that corporate 'in-crowd' to ensure that the best opportunities and right information come your way. News is freely exchanged on the local grapevine so as an outsider you could easily miss out on useful insider knowledge, especially with regard to potential pitfalls, which are rarely advertised. Arabs prefer to conduct business in person, so it is important to 'be seen' in Qatar. Visit trade shows, conferences, exhibitions and events and introduce yourself to as many relevant people as possible – representatives from government departments are worth knowing for their extensive and sometimes handy knowledge of official formalities and the law. You should also maintain contact with your associates by telephone, rather than email.

Get started with social networking sites like linkedin.com. A variety of social networking sites based in Qatar are listed on qatarliving.com. Women

Explore further with Charterhouse Partnership

STRATEGIC CAREER DEVELOPMENT

Banking	Sales and Marketing	Healthcare
Finance	Legal and Compliance	Facilities Management
Human Resources	Information Technology	Professional Support
Construction	Insurance	Supply Chain and Logistics

CHARTERHOUSE
PARTNERSHIP
MIDDLE EAST · AUSTRALIA · EUROPE · ASIA

www.charterhouseme.ae
info@charterhouse.ae

Dubai Office:
Tel: +971 4 372 3500
Fax: +971 4 332 8062

Abu Dhabi Office:
Tel: +971 2 406 9819
Fax: +971 2 406 9810

can also join Doha Divas, a group of professional women, mostly under 40, who are into networking and socialising. You can make a request to join the group by visiting its Facebook page. The Qatar Professional Women's Network (QPWN) aims to support the development of professional expats in the community with networking, discussions and visiting guest speakers. To become a member, email info@qpwn.org or join its Facebook page.

Business Councils

Advantage Austria Al Dafna, 4429 2326, *advantageaustria.org*
Australia & New Zealand Business In Qatar 5569 8493, *anzbiq.org*
Dutch Business Council Qatar *dbcqatar.com*
German Industry & Commerce Umm Ghuwailina, 4431 1152, *ahk.de*
Italian Business Council Of Qatar New Al Mirqab, 5547 2952
Qatar British Business Forum Onaiza, 4496 2080, *qbbf.com*
Qatari Businessmen Association Al Dafna, 4435 3120, *qataribusinessmen.org*
Spanish Business Council *sbcqatar.org*
US Qatar Business Council *usqbc.org*

Employment Contracts

An employment contract should be in writing and must be attested by the Ministry of Labour (gov.qa). There should be three copies of the contract: one for the ministry and one each for the employer and employee. Your contract should state your name, address, nationality, job title and identification (usually your passport number), the name and address of your employer, and a breakdown of your job duties and salary, detailing all responsibilities, benefits and exclusions incurred by the role. Allowances such as housing, schooling, flights, shipping, medical insurance and any other inclusions should be clearly stated and defined. The date for commencement of the contract, the contract duration and method of payment should be specified, plus whether it will be in Qatari riyals or another currency, as some employers pay wages in US dollars at a fixed rate of exchange.

By law, you are entitled to paid annual leave and sick leave, a return flight home to your country of origin at the completion of your contract, plus one month's gratuity for each year of service.

Expat women are allowed 50 days' maternity leave and a 60 minute nursing interval per day for the first year after the birth of their child. The quality and range of added benefits (such as school tuition fees) can vary greatly between jobs and employers and are free for you to negotiate before you sign your contract. Your success, however, will depend on the employer. Employers are allowed to impose a probationary

period during which your suitability for the job may be assessed. It must not exceed six months and you must be notified three days before the period ends whether your engagement will continue. If your probation has not been successful, the company must repatriate you as normal, arranging your exit visa (see Exit Visa, p.43), paying for your flight home and honouring benefits (such as shipping) as specified by the contract. Legal entitlements, such as annual leave, are only applicable upon completion of the probation period.

Should you choose to leave before your contract ends or before your notice period has been fulfilled, the company is not required to honour any outstanding annual leave or end-of-term gratuity payment. They may also refuse to pay benefits associated with your repatriation, such as flights and shipping, though most companies will agree to send you home as a gesture of goodwill. Breaking the law could also result in you losing your job, and consequently your employee benefits.

Free Zones

Companies who operate in free zone areas enjoy an array of attractive benefits, including the opportunity to incorporate local business into their venture, whilst still retaining complete 100% foreign ownership, unlike those outside of free trade zones that must be Qatari-sponsored and only 49% owned. Requiring no Qatari sponsor means that free zone companies are allowed to hire and sponsor their own expatriate employees (the process is the same, see Employer Sponsorship p.42). Free zone traders are not taxed, are allowed unlimited repatriation of capital and profits, and are entitled to duty-free import of goods and services – an appealing prospect for start ups and small businesses.

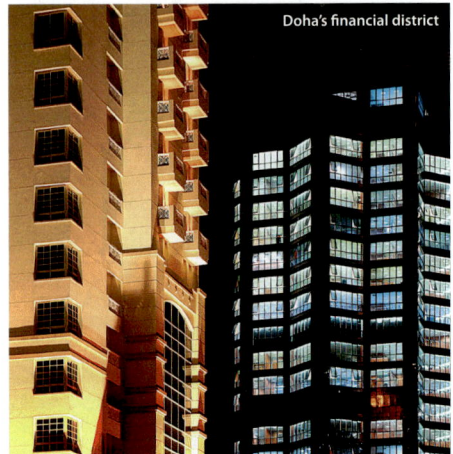
Doha's financial district

In 2006, the government designated 10km in the vicinity of the New Doha International Airport as the country's first free trade zone. Due for final completion in 2015, the zone will allow small and medium sized companies to operate across a diverse range of activities and industries. Examples may include financial advisors, accountants, auditors, law firms, offices for tourism, media, entertainment and business management, as well as desalination plants, cargo storage and cleaning firms.

Qatar Science and Technology Park (4454 7070, qstp.org.qa) in Education City is the country's first dedicated technology free zone. It aims specifically to attract companies interested in applied research and scientific development, in line with Qatar's ambition to become a leader in global technology. Tenants, including Exxon Mobil, Shell, Total and Microsoft, enjoy shared access to local institutes and universities specialising in computer science and business, mechanical, electrical, chemical and petroleum engineering, medical education and research, and advanced vocational training in technical disciplines.

Foreign investment law prohibits 100% foreign ownership of firms associated with banking, insurance, commerce and real estate, unless licensed by Qatar Financial Centre Authority (qfc.com.qa). This government initiative was set up in 2005 to attract and sustain multinational investment by allowing the same benefits as those enjoyed in free zones. The major difference is that companies may operate anywhere in Qatar, therefore taking advantage of local rents.

Labour Law

Labour law is governed by the Ministry of Labour and Social Affairs (4484 1111, gov.qa), where you can obtain valuable information about working in Qatar, including advice on how to resolve a dispute. Because of the complexity of the laws, if you are involved in a labour dispute it is worth seeking the advice of a lawyer.

A printed copy of the labour law is available from the ministry, or you can view it online on the Qatar Embassy website in Washington DC (qatarembassy.net).

In Qatar, employers may dismiss an employee without warning in certain circumstances. If the offence is not a serious one, the employer has to give the employee one written warning before they can be dismissed. The employee has the right to appeal to his or her employer within seven days and if the appeal is rejected, the Ministry of Labour will decide upon the appeal within a further seven days. The ruling is final. Investigative committees may be formed within companies, but only for Qatari nationals.

Laws were introduced in 2005 which allow for free trade unions but only for Qatari nationals. The law did make entitlements for the right to strike, but the conditions are so complicated that it is very difficult to legally do so. Employees of some sectors such as civil servants and domestic workers are not permitted to strike, and workers in public, health and security services must not strike if doing so puts people or property at risk.

An employee has the right to the following public holidays: three days for Eid Al Fitr, three days for Eid Al Adha, and one day on Qatari National Day (18 December). Additional Eid holidays may be announced at the discretion of the government, sometimes as late as the day before. A Muslim employee is entitled to 20 extra days, without pay, to go on Hajj (a religious pilgrimage to Mecca in Saudi Arabia, and one of the five pillars of Islam).

Barwa Al Baraha

In response to international pressure to improve the treatment of migrant workers in the construction and manufacturing industries, the Qatari government has pledged to take assertive action to improve workers' economic, social and civil rights. One positive step toward this goal is Barwa Al Baraha, a QR 2 billion government housing project, the second phase of which was launched in early 2012. With capacity for 53,000 residents, the camp will provide simple recreational facilities such as a cricket ground, tennis and basketball courts, a gymnasium, cinema, supermarket plus on-site medical facilities, and is expected to greatly improve the living conditions and quality of life of Doha's labouring population.

Employees are entitled to three weeks of annual leave if they have been with the company for less than five years, and four weeks for more than five year's service. Most international companies allow four weeks of annual leave after one year of service.

Sick leave is granted after three months of employment and consists of the first two weeks on full pay and a further four weeks on half pay.

Female employees are entitled to 50 days maternity leave and an hour of nursing time each day for the year following the birth. Male employees are entitled to two days paternity leave for the birth of each child.

Changing Jobs

If you decide to change jobs while in Qatar, be aware that your current employer could impose a work ban upon you (see Banning, p.108), especially if your new job is in a similar profession. Before you can switch jobs, you must first obtain a no objection letter (NOC) from your present employer. If your current employer refuses to provide an NOC, your future employer may enter into negotiations with them on your behalf. If successful, you may proceed to transfer your sponsorship to your new employer. It will cost you

Exhibitionist Tendencies

Qatar is capitalising on its exotic location and hospitality prowess with heavy investment in its meetings, incentives, conferences and events sector.

Being an ancient pearling and fishing village, and ideally centred along the European and Asian trade routes, Qatar has welcomed travellers and merchants to its shores for centuries. Now one of the fastest-growing economies in the world, Qatar is capitalising on its unique, exotic location and hospitality prowess with heavy investment in its MICE (Meetings, Incentives, Conferences & Events) sector.

The Qatar National Convention Centre (qatarconvention.com) is a new development, built at an estimated cost of around $1.2 billion. The iconic building offers 40,000 square metres of exhibition space over nine halls and 57 meeting rooms, with an auditorium capable of seating 4,000 people and banquet seating for 10,000. The project has already attracted global attention for its cutting-edge design and dedication to sustainability and the environment. As the world's first green-technology venue, it is on course to achieve a Gold Standard under the US Green Buildings Council's Leadership in Energy and Design (LEED) rating system (usgbc. org). The centre is being actively promoted with an intense marketing scheme. Its first event was the 20th World Petroleum Congress from 4 to 8 December, 2011. Meanwhile, the Doha Exhibition Centre & Tower (qataridiar.com) is due for completion in 2012 and promises to be a major venue for international and local exhibitions. The futuristic and innovative design boasts a 105 storey tower complete with five-star hotel, serviced apartments and residences. Attached to a luxury retail centre and 100,000 square metres of convention space, the entire undertaking is also estimated to cost around $1.2 billion, and like QNCC, is expected to elevate the profile of Doha as the Middle East's leading destination for business tourism. For more information visit qmdi.com.qa.

West Bay business quarter

Major Exhibitions In Qatar

2012

September
5-8	Made in USA, Doha Exhibition Center	madeinusaqatar.com
15-19	'HYA' Abaya Exhibition, Doha Exhibition Center	qatartourism.gov.qa
17-19	GCC-Europe Forum, Doha Exhibition Center	gcceuropeforum.com
25-28	Doha Furniture and Decoration Exhibition-INFDEX, Doha Exhibition Center	qatar-expo.com
26-28	International Exhibition for Pool & Spa, Doha Exhibition Center	htsxpo.com

October
7-10	TowerTech, Doha Exhibition Center	towertech-qatar.net
8-10	Milipol Qatar, Doha Exhibition Center	milipol.com
16-18	7th International Hotel, Restaurant and Food (Diyafa) Exhibition for Qatar, Doha Exhibition Center	qatartourism.gov.qa
16-18	Doha Exhibition Transport and Rail, Doha Exhibition Center	albaidagroup.com

November
6-8	Energy Qatar, Doha Exhibition Center	energy-qatar.com
11-14	Q Money, Doha Exhibition Center	qmoney.info
13-15	Eco-Q, Doha Exhibition Center	eco-q.org

December
5-15	Doha 23rd International Book Fair, Doha Exhibition Center	qatartourism.gov.qa
21-25	'HYA' Abaya Exhibition, Doha Exhibition Center	qatartourism.gov.qa

2013

January
Offshore Middle, East Qatar National Convention Centre	offshoremiddleeast.com
Qatar Motor Show, Doha Exhibition Center	qatarmotorshow.gov.qa

February
Doha Jewellery & Watch Exhibition, Doha Exhibition Center	dohajewels.com
Doha Food Festival, Doha Exhibition Center	qatartourism.gov.qa

March
Multaqa Qatar, Ritz-Carlton Doha	globalreinsurance.com

April
International Wedding Exhibition & Fashion Show (IWED), Doha Exhibition Center	qatar-expo.com
Carpet Exhibition, Doha Exhibition Center	
Environmental Festival, Doha Exhibition Center	qp.com.qa
Qatar Career Fair, Doha Exhibition Center	qatarcareerfair.com.qa

May
Project Qatar, Doha Exhibition Center	projectqatar.com
Cityscape, Doha Exhibition Center	cityscapeqatar.com
Made In Italy, Doha Exhibition Center	madeinitalyqatar.com

QR 1,000 the first time, QR 1,500 the second time and QR 2,000 if you transfer a third time. Most employers will handle the paperwork and cover the costs for you. If you are unable to remain in your current job, and can't transfer your sponsorship to a family member or another sponsor, then you will need to leave the country at the end of your notice period. You will then not be allowed to return to work in Qatar for a period of two years.

Banning

Once you leave your job, you will be banned from working in Qatar for a period of two years. This ban period can be avoided if you obtain a letter of no objection (NOC) from your original employer, but they are not obliged to give it to you. Without an NOC, your employer can prevent you from working for any other company or transferring your sponsorship to work in Qatar until the ban period is over. There isn't really much you can do to obtain an NOC if your employer refuses, which makes for a compelling reason to stay on good terms. Even so, some companies will still impose the two year ban after you have left their service to prevent you from taking up work with a rival company. If your employment is terminated due to a serious offence, then you may be banned from working in Qatar for four years.

Absconding

Anyone who permanently departs Qatar without cancelling their residence visa with their sponsor, or any person who leaves their employer rightfully but fails to depart the country within the 7 day grace period, may be reported as having absconded. Similarly, anyone who consistently fails to report for work or who is found illegally working for a different employer may be guilty of absconding.

If you are still under company sponsorship and they suspect that you have absconded, your employer will file a complaint with the Search and Follow Up department of the Ministry of Interior. If found guilty, your residency will be immediately cancelled and your employment contract terminated. Your company will not be liable for payment of the end-of-service gratuity or other bonuses such as your repatriation costs, that you would normally be entitled to. Depending on the severity of your case, you may be detained, fined and deported.

Any company found guilty of employing or sheltering absconding workers will be fined heavily and may have their licence revoked.

Redundancy

In spite of Qatar's solid economic indicators, redundancy is still a possibility. During the recent economic downturn, stories of job cuts and wage decreases circulated around the globe, with the finance and real estate sectors receiving heavy blows. With so much foreign investment located in Qatar and with a large portion of the economy reliant on construction, Qatar was not immune. While the situation has improved greatly following a recovery that started as early as 2010, it's still good to be aware of your rights. Few laws govern redundancy in Qatar so it is worth checking your contract for any clauses or provisions specific to you and your company. If made redundant, your company must give you the same notice period of termination as specified in your contract for an ordinary end of service. The employer must pay all outstanding wages by close of business following the last day of your employment and they must honour all benefit and bonus gratuities. They must also arrange your exit visa (p.43) and repatriation formalities for you as normal. If you have been made redundant, don't panic. Talk to your employer about continuing your sponsorship for as long as possible. This might give you more time in which to find another job and complete the necessary arrangements for switching your sponsorship to your new employer (see Changing Jobs, p.105). You should determine how long you can stay in any company-provided housing; if the rent has been pre-paid, you might be allowed to live there temporarily beyond the end of your employment. Most of all, don't forget to obtain a letter of no objection (NOC) from your employer before you leave.

Company Closure

The laws regarding company closure remain vague in terms of employee rights, but generally speaking, recourse is very limited. By law, your company is required to pay you any salary owed and you should be repatriated as per the conditions stated in your employee contract, but you will have little chance to resolve any disputes that arise. Once your employment is terminated, your company will cancel your visa and residence permit, which means you will only have seven days to either leave the country or find a new sponsor, so sticking around to argue your point isn't a likelihood.

It is a good idea to investigate the economic stability of any company before you accept a job or promotion, especially if your role requires any financial responsibility or authority. There have been reports of people who have arrived in Qatar to work for a troubled company, or who have accepted management or partnership offers, only to be left in charge of that company – and its accumulated debt – while upper management flee (see Debt, p.117).

If you suspect that your company may be in trouble and there is a risk of foreclosure, you should contact a lawyer for advice or begin searching for another job. If you are suddenly offered an unlikely invitation to become an executive partner or manager or a company signatory, then it may pay to be wary and proceed with caution, especially if the company is small or relatively new. Consult a lawyer immediately if you have been left burdened with company debts or loans.

Voluntary & Charity Work

There are plenty of opportunities to volunteer or perform charity work in Qatar. If you are looking for a great way to fill your time, enhance your resume, expand your friendship circle or entertain the kids with a meaningful experience, the following organisations will be grateful to hear from you. For something less official, voluntary groups such as Doha Mums (dohamums.com) invite members to host and coordinate events, while schools are usually happy to have help with their library and reading programmes or in their Parent Teacher Association.

Cats In Qatar
3393 7645
catsinqatar.com
This group is dedicated to helping people foster and re-home cats and kittens who have been abandoned or whose owners can no longer look after them. For further details email info@catsinqatar.com.

HOPE Qatar
Capital One Villa 4 Bu Samra **5534 8611**
hope-qatar.org
Map **2 J13**
An organisation that provides care and assistance to children with special needs. The centre is always keen to receive new volunteers and has put together Friends of HOPE which organises the various skills and time offered by volunteers. Email info@hope-qatar.org to offer assistance.

Qatar Animal Welfare Society (QAWS)
Nr Qatar Racing & Equestrian Club Muaither
5539 6074
qaws.org
Map **1 B9**
Staffed and funded entirely by volunteers, QAWS is always grateful for helpers willing to walk dogs, clean kennels, provide foster homes or help with fundraising, advertising and administrative tasks. Donations of pet food, animal bedding and other second-hand items are gladly accepted.

Qatar Centre For Voluntary Activities (QCFVA)
Various Locations **4467 5999**
qatarvoluntary.org
This centre specialises in volunteer training and helps connect interested people with a variety of community initiatives and programmes.

Qatar Charity
Ahmad Bin Hanbal St Old Airport **4466 7711**
qcharity.com
Map **2 R13**
A non-government organisation established to support communities in need within Qatar and abroad. With an emphasis on humanitarian relief, volunteers assist with fundraising and project development. See its website for how to pledge your time or to find out how to donate.

Qatar Orphan Foundation (Dhriema)
Off Salwa Rd Bu Hamra **4458 9444**
q-orphans.org
Map **2 K12**
An organisation that seeks to provide care and services to orphans. It assists with finding homes and provides compassionate support.

Feed The World

IIMSAM (Intergovernmental Institution for the use of Micro-algae Spirulina against Malnutrition) works towards the eradication of world hunger through cultivating, distributing and spreading knowledge of Spirulina, a blue-green microalga which is rich in vitamins and proteins. This valuable food source is already helping to feed 90,000 people in Kenya, and the Middle East Regional office of IIMSAM has supported such overseas efforts by raising funds for and awareness of the cause. If you would like to help, either by making a donation or by volunteering, call 4465 3332 or visit iimsam.org.

Qatar Red Crescent
Nr Movenpick Hotel, Museum Rd Slata **4443 5111**
qrcs.org.qa
Map **2 S7**
Qatar branch of the non-profit International Red Cross and Red Crescent Society, providing humanitarian relief to the suffering and promoting human rights through equality. Offers training in first aid and social services and relies heavily on the efforts and donations of volunteers.

Reach Out To Asia (ROTA)
Rota Villa, Al Nasriya St Gharrafat Al Rayyan
4454 1603
reachouttoasia.org
Map **1 A6**
This charity aims to improve the standard of living by fostering educational development. Its goal is to promote access to education through various community projects; volunteers share their expertise through hands-on work and donations.

Social Development Center
Nr Ramada R/A, Suhaim Bin Hamad St
Fereej Bin Mahmoud 4454 2400
sdc.org.qa
Map 2 M10

This non-profit organisation is dedicated to improving family welfare. Its team of volunteers assists with social and humanitarian services and is also invited to participate in awareness and fundraising campaigns.

Working As A Freelancer/Contractor

It is against the law to do any kind of paid work in Qatar without a permit from the Ministry of Labour (see Sponsorship p.100). Workers can be brought in from overseas to take up employer-sponsored postings in the form of a short-term contract, but independent freelancing is illegal. The practise, however, is widespread, especially in traditional occupations that rely heavily upon outsourced work. Jobs are regularly advertised in newspapers and on websites by employers seeking freelancers in media, journalism, research, photography and teaching. Freelance work is a popular activity for spouses here on family sponsorship, especially those who hold specialist qualifications and skills, but you shouldn't move to Qatar with the intention of working freelance as a primary source of income. With regard to the law, providing there is no proof that you are being paid for any work that you do, then you should stay out of trouble.

Working Part-time

Part-time and casual jobs are available in Qatar, but it is illegal to work without a permit (see Sponsorship, p.40). A law was issued in March 2009 prohibiting sponsors from permitting anyone under their sponsorship to work for any other individual or company. However the laws concerning part-time work have recently been changed. It is now legal to undertake part-time work in addition to your primary job provided you've the permission of your employer.

Still, whatever your trade, it is not a good idea to invest too heavily in marketing and self-promotion – if you are suspected of running a small business you may come under fire for illegal trading (see Setting Up a Small Business p.110). Part-time and casual jobs aren't readily advertised in Qatar, so your best option is word-of-mouth or browsing local websites (p.23).

Setting Up A Small Business

The decision to launch a new business anywhere in the world is fraught with risk, especially in the wake of the global economic crisis, and regardless of how meticulously you have studied your market. This may be even more so in Qatar where, as a foreigner, you are legally obligated to go into partnership with a Qatari sponsor to whom you must assign at least 51% of ownership. Your Qatari co-owner does not have to make any contribution to the start-up, financing, management or operation of your company at all, but a good partner may agree to at least assist you with legal and financial formalities. Be aware that your sponsor has complete authority to close your business down at will, so give careful thought to who you choose to go into partnership with.

The exception to this rule is if you open your business in a free trade zone (see Free Zones, p.104), whereby you can retain full ownership and will be entitled to benefits such as import duty exemption, but may have to pay less-than-competitive rental rates. You will also be exempt from paying business tax at the normal rate of 10%.

It is wise to arrange any necessary start-up finance with your bank in your home country before you leave, especially if you are a newcomer to Qatar as a local bank might be reluctant to lend you their money. Furthermore, if you struggle to make repayments, you should still be allowed to leave Qatar, unlike foreigners who have accrued excessive local debt and are consequently prohibited from leaving the country (see Exit Visa, p.43).

Before setting up trade, you must find a location for your business then seek approval from the Qatar Ministry of Economy and Finance (4494 5555), and any other ministry relevant to your type of business, for example, a legal firm must have approval from the Ministry of Justice (4484 2222, moj.gov.qa). To do this, visit the commercial licensing section with a copy of your passport or Qatari ID, a copy of your lease contract and a copy of the memorandum of association. Your licence will be issued three days later, at which point your application is submitted for review by six ministerial departments: the Commercial Stores Inspection Department, Advertisements Permission Department, Industrial Area Division, Health Affairs Department, Housing Construction Department and the Civil Defense Department. After approval has been obtained, you return to the Ministry to collect a temporary commercial register, which you take along to the Qatar Chamber of Commerce & Industry (4455 9111, qatarchamber.com). Your application is checked, approved and once all fees have been paid, you can finally return to the Ministry of Economy and Commerce for your commercial register to be authorised.

Consult professional legal and financial advice at every step and engage the services of the commercial section of your local embassy wherever possible. Qatar's Investment Promotion Department (IPD) provides extensive information and support for businesses (4494 5522, investinqatar.com.qa) or you can enlist the services of a private specialist such as Future Gate Business Services (4467 7801, futuregate.info).

Office tower

FINANCIAL AFFAIRS

Bank Accounts

Opening a bank account in Qatar should be fairly simple. For the sake of convenience, most employees have their wages paid into the preferred bank of their company, but as banks do not charge to have your wage transferred into a different bank from your employer, the choice is up to you. A good selection of local and international banking institutions, including the highly reputable International Bank of Qatar (IBQ), have premises in Qatar all offering a variety of accounts, reward schemes and conveniences such as internet banking. Some banks will send you an SMS to notify you whenever there is activity on your account (such as ATM cash withdrawals and wage deposits).

To open a new account, you will need to provide a letter of no objection (NOC) from your sponsor which should state your monthly wage. You will also need to supply a copy of your passport, a copy of your residence permit (you can't open an account until you have one) and two passport photos. Most banks require that you earn over a specified amount each month to be eligible for a current account, and they may request other supporting documents such as evidence of your address. Some banks may charge a fee if your monthly balance falls below a certain amount; otherwise there aren't usually any fees for keeping an account.

Check Your Balance

Although payment by cheque is rare, if you are found guilty of issuing a cheque without sufficient funds you will be reported to the police and potentially deported on fraud charges (see Cheques, p.117).

Once your account has been opened you will be issued with a debit card and a credit card (if one was requested). Cash is the preferred method of payment in Qatar for small business transactions, at the souks and in some petrol stations, otherwise cards are widely accepted. Bank branches generally open during the morning only, from 07:00 to 13:00, Sunday to Thursday. Branches located inside the shopping malls usually adopt the same hours as the centre which are roughly 10:00 to 23:00.

ATMs (cash machines) are commonplace so you should have no trouble accessing your money. Most banks do not impose a fee for using a rival's machine.

It is a good idea to keep a bank account open in your home country while you are in Qatar in case you need to transfer money back and forth. Speak to your bank before you leave the country in case you need to sign any forms, and ask about any fees, charges or deductions that may apply.

Main Banks

Ahli Bank QSC 4423 2503, *ahlibank.com.qa*
Al Khaliji Commercial Bank QSC 4494 0000, *alkhaliji.com*
Arab Bank 4438 7777, *arabbank.com.qa*
Bank Saderat Iran – Qatar 4441 4646, *bsi.com.qa*
Barwa Bank > p.115 800 8555, *barwabank.com*
BNP Paribas Doha 4453 7537, *bnpparibas.com.qa*
Commercial Bank Of Qatar 4449 0000, *cbq.com.qa*
Doha Bank Al Najada, 4445 6000, *dohabank.com.qa*
HSBC Bank Middle East 4442 4722, *hsbc.com.qa*
International Bank Of Qatar > p.113 4447 8000, *ibq.com.qa*
Mashreq 4408 3111, *mashreqbank.com.qa*
Masraf Al Rayan 4423 5646, *alrayan.com*
Qatar Development Bank 4430 0000, *qdb.com.qa*
Qatar International Islamic Bank 4438 5555, *qiib.com.qa*
Qatar Islamic Bank 4440 9409, *qib.com.qa*
Qatar National Bank 4440 7777, *qnb.com.qa*
Standard Chartered 4424 8601, *standardchartered.com*

Financial Planning

Living in Qatar offers a good opportunity to save, as most people don't pay for their accommodation and there is no personal income tax (see Taxation, p.116). A potential trap is that higher earnings often equals greater spending, especially in the first few months when that big-screen TV is suddenly more affordable.

It is easy to obtain a credit card or bank loan which means it is can be just as easy to rack up serious debt, but be warned that little help is available to you if you do. To avoid getting into any trouble, it might be worth visiting a financial planner, who will advise you on the best way to make the most of your tax-free lifestyle and how to increase your saving potential.

Qatar Financial Centre (4496 7777, qfc.com.qa) has a range of facilities and services on offer to help you with your finances or you can consult a bank, savings company or independent advisor. An independent financial advisor should have knowledge on a broader range of savings plans and products available on the market. Most international banks, and some of the local banks (see Main Banks, p.112), have financial planners who will be happy to meet with you and discuss your options, but they will be inclined to sell packages associated with their institutions.

Banks with an international presence, such as HSBC or Standard Chartered, may be able to extend their assistance to your financial affairs back home, or you can contact Lloyds TSB (+971 4 342 2000, lloydstsb.ae) in Dubai to enquire about financial schemes in the Isle of Man, Jersey and Guernsey (see Offshore Accounts p.116).

Winner of "Best Customer Service in the Middle East" award 2008, 2009, 2010 and 2011, "Best Retail Bank" award 2011, "Best Private Banking Services" award and "Best Credit Card" award 2012.

4447 8000
www.ibq.com.qa

Financial Affairs

While some employers and local banks do offer pension plans, it is worth investigating the offshore schemes available from overseas banks, as they may provide better long-term dividends.

It is extremely important that you know the tax laws in your home country and how they will apply to your foreign income before you leave. Enquire about tax exemptions and how to pay tax on your domestic investments, such as rent and shareholder dividends, while you are away.

If you're buying a property in one of Qatar's new developments such as The Pearl (p.322), the Commercial Bank of Qatar, Qatar National Bank and International Bank of Qatar offer mortgages, as does HSBC Middle East.

Cost of Living

Pint of beer (pub)	QR 35
Taxi (10km journey)	QR 30
Car rental (per day)	QR 100-130
Cigarettes (per pack of 20)	QR 7-10
Cinema ticket	QR 30
Cleaner (per hour)	QR 30
Dozen eggs	QR 9
Chocolate bar	QR 5
Cappuccino	QR 14
Loaf of bread	QR 6
Burger (takeaway)	QR 14
Water 1.5 litres (supermarket)	QR 2
Milk (1 litre)	QR 6
Bottle of house wine (QDC)	QR 30-200
Glass of house wine (restaurant)	QR 40
Text message (local)	QR 0.4
New release DVD	QR 85
Newspaper (international)	QR 20
Mobile to mobile call (local, per minute)	QR 0.30-0.45
Large takeaway pizza	QR 80
24-pack of beer (off licence at QDC)	QR 160
Petrol (gallon)	QR 4.55
Can of soft drink	QR 1.5-2

Financial Advisors

First Finance Company 4455 9988, *ffcqatar.com*
Guardian Wealth Management 4491 5355, *guardianwealthmanagement.com*
International Financial Services 4496 7215, *interfs.com*
KPMG 4457 6444, *kpmg.com*
Qatar Financial Centre Authority 4496 7777, *qfc.com.qa*

Insurance Companies

Aetna Global *aetnaglobal.com*
Al Khaleej Takaful Insurance & Reinsurance Company 4441 4151, *alkhaleej.com*
Allianz Takaful 4403 9777, *allianz.com*

Building Your Wealth

Jonathan Johnson, a senior financial consultant at International Financial Services, provides some advice on how to benefit from tax-free living.

A foreign assignment usually entails improved employment conditions and pay, so most expatriates can take advantage of this opportunity to save money. That said, sometimes this objective is overlooked and many expatriate workers return home with a wealth of memories, but with some regrets that they did not save some of that hard-earned cash.

If you are determined to save, whether the money is to be used for a future property purchase, to clear debts, buy a car, or to top-up a pension, it is most important to employ some discipline from the outset. You will be surprised how quickly your savings will start to grow.

Build An Emergency Fund
Try to gather some savings to be used in emergencies, such as loss of job or unexpected travel. Set up a separate savings account that isn't connected to your current account and try to deposit around 5% to 10% of your earnings into it each month. The minimum amount in your emergency fund should be 3 to 6 months worth of basic living expenses.

Life & Critical Illness Insurance
People often insure their cars and houses without hesitation, but don't consider what may happen if they happen to fall ill. Proper protection planning can alleviate the financial pressures involved in the loss of a loved one and will give you and your family peace of mind knowing that they will be left in a comfortable, position if you are not able to care for them.

Save For Your Retirement
This can be very low on many people's list of priorities since retirement can seem so far away, but it should be a major part of your financial planning. Determining when you can afford to retire and whether you can maintain your lifestyle requires a disciplined attitude to saving regularly and for the long-term. Failing to do so could mean you have to work much later in life than you intended.

For more information contact International Financial Services on 4496 7215 or online at interfs.com.

ARRIVALS

TIME	FROM	FLIGHT NO.	REMARKS

JUST ARRIVED IN QATAR?

WE'LL HELP YOU TAKE CARE OF YOUR URGENT FINANCIAL NEEDS.

As a new arrival, you've got lots to do, so let us handle all your banking needs, with our complete range of products and services.

- Free Current Account - no fees, and no minimum balance required
- Get Personal, Auto or Home finance at one of the most competitive profit rates
- Get a VISA Platinum credit card with worldwide acceptance, and 5,000 complimentary Barwa Bank loyalty points convertible to 5,000 Qatar Airways Privilege Club Qmiles
- Benefit from one of the highest profit paying (historically) Faseel & Jeelkum Savings Accounts
- Our online banking lets you check balances, remit funds, pay your credit card bills and much more locally and worldwide
- Access your funds 24/7 from VISA - enabled ATMs worldwide
- Prestige Banking - enjoy personalized banking services with qualified dedicated Relationship Managers
- 24/7 call center and free SMS banking service

CALL **800 8555**
100% Shari'ah compliant

BARWABANK.COM

بنك بروة
BARWA BANK
the *future* has a bank

Financial Affairs

AXA Insurance (Gulf) 4496 7383, *axa-gulf.com*
Bupa *bupa-intl.com*
Doha Insurance Company 4433 5000, *dicqatar.com*
Healthcare International *healthcareinternational.com*
Libano-Suisse Insurance Company 4466 4406,
libano-suisse.com
MetLife Alico 800 971 011, *metlifealico.ae*
Nasco Karaoglan 4491 4254, *nascoqatar.com*
Oman Insurance Company 4442 2110, *tameen.ae*
Qatar General Insurance & Reinsurance Co
4428 2222, *qgirco.com*
Qatar Insurance Company 4496 2222, *qic.com.qa*
Qatar Islamic Insurance Company 4465 8888,
qiic.com.qa

Credit Cards

When you open a bank account, you will also be offered a credit card, which is convenient as you will already have the necessary documentation with you (passport, ID, proof of earnings). The bank will also automatically link your accounts, making it easier for you to pay off your balance.

You need to earn over a certain amount to be eligible for a credit card (this can be between QR 1,500 and QR 10,000 per month, depending on nationality) and you may authorise an additional card for your partner. Some banks also offer reward incentives (such as air miles) so it is worth shopping around for the best deal. All major credit cards are widely accepted in Qatar, although taxis, some small businesses, petrol stations and market vendors will only accept cash. You shouldn't have to pay any extra fees or charges for paying by credit card.

Incidences of credit card fraud and identity theft are on the increase in Qatar and you should exercise caution. If you lose your credit card, you must report it immediately to your provider. The bank will suspend all activities on your card and will verify your most recent transactions. If you fail to inform your bank that your credit card is missing or has been stolen, you may be forced to pay for any unauthorised purchases that have been charged to your card.

Most banks will call you immediately if an international transaction appears on your account so keep this in mind when shopping on the internet. You should inform your bank before you travel outside of Qatar so they can make a note of it on your account. Without prior notification, your bank may suspend your account once international purchases start appearing, which will put a considerable downer on your holiday.

Offshore Accounts

While offshore accounts used to be associated with the very wealthy or the highly shady, most expats now take advantage of tax-efficient offshore schemes. An offshore account works in much the same way as a conventional account, but it can be adjusted specifically for you. Money can be moved where it will produce the best rewards, and cash accessed wherever and whenever you need it, in your desired currency. Offshore accounts allow for management through the internet, and over the phone, in a range of currencies (most commonly in US dollars, euros or pounds sterling). If you are travelling outside Qatar, try to make sure your account comes with 24 hour banking, internationally recognised debit cards and the ability to write cheques in your preferred currency. To open an account, there is usually a minimum balance of around $10,000. Do some thorough research before opening an account, and check the potential tax implications in your home country. It is important to seek independent financial advice, and not just the opinion of the bank offering you an account. Banks such as HSBC offer good offshore services but will, of course, only advise on their own products. To open your account you may have to produce certain reports or documents from your chosen country. However, for those willing to do the research and undertake the admin, offshore banking can prove to be a lucrative investment.

Taxation

In 2009, the Forbes Tax Misery & Reform Index (forbes.com) found Qatar to be the world's friendliest tax climate. Residents in Qatar do not pay tax on income, including wages and personal bank interest, and there are no plans to alter tax laws for individuals any time soon.

In January 2010, in an effort to boost foreign investment, Qatar introduced a new corporate law, lowering the rate of tax levied on foreign companies to a flat 10%, from a previous rate of up to 35%. Qatari businesses and those that operate in designated free zones such as Qatar Science & Technology park (4454 7070), attract no tax whatsoever.

However, Qatar isn't completely barren of tax. An import duty of 4% applies to most goods, including vehicles, with the exception of essentials such as tea, coffee, sugar, rice and infant formula, which are exempt. Manufacturing items such as cement and steel may attract up to 20% tax while 100% duty applies to alcohol and tobacco imports. There is no tax on exports.

Certain goods and services inside major hotels, including spa treatments and dining may be levied at 5%, with alcoholic drinks taxed at 17%. It's generally best to ask before booking a service what the luxury tax rate is, as it can vary greatly between establishments.

Tax rules differ from country to country so check whether you have to inform the tax office in your home country of any earnings you accrue whilst in Qatar, or capital gains tax on sums of money that you send home.

Cheques

The practice of post-dating cheques was banned in April 2010 when a new commercial law took effect. However, after six months of general confusion, the rule was discarded and individuals are allowed to go back to post-dating cheques. While payment by cheque is far less common than cash or credit, banks and landlords often rely on collecting post-dated cheques as security against loan and rent payments. It is important to note that serious penalties will apply to anyone who issues a cheque without having the necessary funds in their account, with fines ranging between QR 3,000 and QR 10,000 and the possibility of 3-36 months imprisonment existing.

Debt

It is easy to whittle away your salary, and use up the funds you don't necessarily have in Qatar with credit cards widely accepted and banks offering rewards and incentives when you charge your purchases to plastic. As tempting as it is to indulge in greater spending, the penalties in Qatar concerning debt are severe, so it is crucial to keep your finances in check. Credit cards (p.116) and loans are very easy to obtain and usually just require you to show proof of minimum earnings per month. It is up to you to make your repayments on time, and banks and financial institutions offer little support to those who default on payment. Usually, your name and details are simply handed over to the authorities to be dealt with by the police. Anyone who has accrued significant debt will be barred from leaving the country and may face criminal charges resulting in hefty fines or imprisonment. If you find yourself in trouble with the law, you should seek the advice of a lawyer and your local embassy representative immediately. Banks and institutions such as telecommunications provider QTel (p.91) will give you a warning if payment is overdue, usually by SMS notification. To avoid missing your payment deadlines, consider setting up a standing order with your bank so that automatic payment of your bills is made directly from your account. Refer to Money Matters (p.118) for ideas on how to stay out of the red, or consult a financial advisor (see p.114).

LEGAL ISSUES

Civil Law

The legal system in Qatar is based on civil law. A constitution came into effect on 8 June, 2005, which promised freedom and equality, and provides for a 45 member Majlis Al Shura. This functions as the Emir's advisory council, two thirds of which are elected by the public with the remaining members appointed by the Emir. The first elections were held on 1 April 2007. Qatar's legal system used to be based on Shariah

law which has its roots firmly in Islam. Today, the restructured legal system has brought the Shariah and civil courts together to form the Court of Cassation (or Supreme Court), which is the highest court in the country. There are two other levels of court, the Court of the First Instance and the Court of Appeal. All court proceedings are conducted in Arabic (see If You Are Detained, p.120). Few crimes are reported in the media, which can lead people to mistakenly believe that little crime exists in Qatar. Laws in the region are strictly administered and there are certain crimes for which there is zero tolerance, such as possession of drugs and drink driving. The penalties for these and other major offences are severe and could include deportation, hefty fines, or imprisonment. For more information, see Crime p.119.

Law Firms

Al Kaabi Law Firm 4443 6222, *alkaabilawfirm.com*
Al Shahwani & Al Mohannadi Lawyers & Consultants 4435 2014
Arab Law Bureau 4483 0202, *albureau.com*
Behzad Law Office 4466 0333, *behzadlawoffice.com*
Clyde & Co 4496 7434, *clydeco.com*
Dewey & LeBoeuf 4410 1717, *deweyleboeuf.com*
Eversheds 4496 7396, *eversheds.com*
LaLive In Qatar 4496 7247, *laliveinqatar.com*
Latham & Watkins 4406 7700, *lw.com*
Law Offices Of Dr Najeeb Al Nauimi 4431 1124
Patton Boggs 4453 2500, *pattonboggs.com*
Rouhani & Partners 4442 5815, *rouhanilaw.com*
Simmons & Simmons 4409 6700, *simmons-simmons.com*
SNR Denton 4459 8960, *snrdenton.com*
Sultan Al-Abdullah & Partners 4442 0660, *qatarlaw.com*
WongPartnership 4491 2332, *wongpartnership.com*

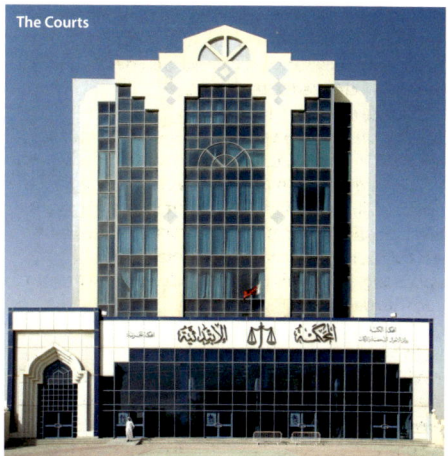

The Courts

Money Matters

If the recent economic downturn taught us all anything, it should be that you are equally as susceptible to money problems as anybody else. Regardless of how secure your job seems, in spite of how well you manage your finances, and even if you are the type of person who accounts for every penny, you are not immune to hardship, so invest some time and pay attention to these insider tips on doing your best to keep on top of your finances.

Respect The Plastic: It is much easier to hand over plastic than cash, so be mindful of how much you are spending every time you pay by credit card. If you're prone to over indulging on credit, leave your card in a secure place at home, reserving it for emergencies only. Be sure to pay off your balance in full each month to avoid trouble with your bank or the law.

Live By Half: Really examine your expenses and be brutal when it comes to deciding what you can live without – fancy restaurants, double lattes, manicures and spa memberships are all luxuries, and cutting them out of your budget could mean surprising savings at the end of the month.

Home Entertainment: Enjoying the multicultural delights on offer is one of Qatar's simple pleasures, but it doesn't always come cheap. Instead, stay in and invite your friends round for dinner and a movie, or you can keep your dinner party costs down by asking everyone to bring a dish.

Shop Savvy: Certain supermarkets may be convenient and stock familiar brands from back home but you'll be paying for it. You'll save a packet if you buy your everyday items from a cheaper grocery store and try to find inexpensive local alternatives to those unmissable favourites.

Dig The Discount: Qatar has some incredible sale periods, so stock up during promotions and take advantage of buy-one-get-one-free offers. Don't be afraid to bargain with staff for their best prices, especially in souks, and always shop around.

Get Packing: There's no such thing as a free lunch but packing your own sandwiches is the next best thing. It's healthier, you'll save money and you don't have to queue to get it.

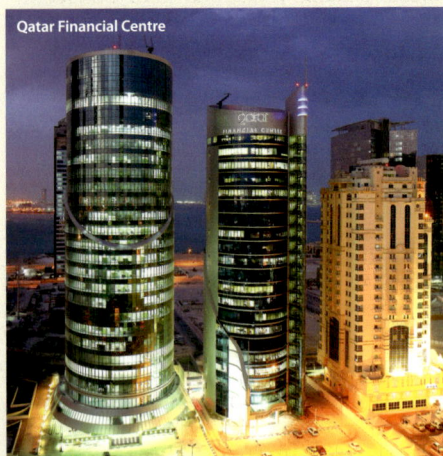

Qatar Financial Centre

Lose The Excuse: Extravagant purchases might cheer you up when you're feeling homesick, but a free video call to loved ones over the internet or a lovingly-typed email, are two cheaper alternatives. Plus, you get to make someone else feel good.

Shop The World: Having the world at your fingertips has its advantages. You can save a lot of money by ordering goods over the internet, even after shipping is added (see Online Shopping, p.287) Better yet, if you know someone is coming to Qatar, get them to buy the item and bring it with them.

Pre-Owned Is Preferred: With the transient nature of the expat population, second-hand goods are regularly advertised for sale on shop notice boards and online forums, some hardly used. Before you splurge at the shops, check out what has been cast aside and you could find a bargain (see Second-Hand Items, p.316).

Book A Summer Break: Telephone and satellite television companies will allow you to suspend your account with them if you plan to be away for long periods, or to freely downgrade the plan you are currently on. Don't be afraid to limit your subscription to only the periods you require it for (such as football season) or cancel your television plan altogether if you find you rarely watch it.

Wills & Estate Law

Drawing up a will is simply one of those essential things that everybody should do, preferably with the help of a lawyer. In Qatar, law is a mix of civil and Shariah law, but in terms of inheritance, Shariah law prevails. In the case of death, your sons and your brother would be first in line to inherit your estate, potentially leaving your wife and daughters with nothing. If both parents died, any children under legal age would go to a guardian, who would then be entitled to their inheritance.

Shariah law is only applicable to your estate in Qatar, so if you own property here or have large amounts of cash in the bank, it is wise to get a Qatar-based lawyer to assist you with a locally viable will, and have it attested by the Ministry of Foreign Affairs and your embassy.

You should at least have a will lodged in your home country to carry out your wishes regarding assets and property outside Qatar. You can either lodge one with a lawyer before you leave, or find a downloadable 'will kit' online. A home-made will should still be formally signed, witnessed and attested. There is also no tax on inheritance in Qatar (see Taxation, p.116).

Family Law

Family law is a mix of civil and Shariah law, and while matrimonial matters are accounted for in the constitution, the application of the law is unclear, and usually just comes down to the discretion of the judge.

The preservation of the family unit in Qatar was highlighted with an Emiri Decree in 2006, requiring that all couples intending to marry undergo medical pre-screening for genetic suitability. This is an effort to reduce the high rate of chronic disease and infection present in Qatari children; a result of genetic mutation caused by inter-marrying.

Qatar has the 12th highest divorce rate in the world. As an expat, if divorce becomes a likelihood, consult the advice of a family lawyer immediately, especially if you are sponsored by your spouse who has the right to cancel your residency (see Sponsorship, p.40 and Getting Divorced, p.129). For this reason, it might be advantageous to begin proceedings back in your home country.

Maintenance payments vary depending on the age of the child and will be decided upon in court, along with visitation rights. Custody is usually awarded to the mother, except where the mother is a non-Qatari woman married to a Qatari man, whereby the courts generally award full custodianship to the father. A divorced mother must obtain permission from her ex-husband to leave the country with his children.

Crime

The official crime rate in Qatar is one of the lowest in the world, making it a desirable place to live in terms of safety. Strict laws and severe infringement penalties are an effective deterrent – the country imposes some of the highest fines for traffic violations in the world (see Driving p.57).

Still, it pays to be vigilant and take sensible precautions with valuables and cash. Petty crime has experienced a significant increase with the recent population boom and incidences of fraud involving identity theft, email scams and card skimming have been reported. Avoid unfamiliar areas at night and be wary of strangers. Media reports of rape, domestic abuse and murder rarely appear, but that doesn't mean that they don't happen.

The most common reason for expats finding themselves on the wrong side of the law is being under the influence. There is zero tolerance for drinking and driving in Qatar and the blood alcohol level is zero, so even one small drink puts you immediately over the limit. Drink-driving, consuming alcohol in public and being intoxicated in public are all considered very serious offences and penalties are severe – you may be arrested, fined, imprisoned and deported. Fault for any traffic accident you have after drinking alcohol will automatically be yours, which is worth remembering after a heavy night when alcohol could still be present in your system. Furthermore, your insurance provider will not be liable to cover you following an accident.

Penalties for illegal drug use, possession or trafficking are severe and unforgiving, with convicted offenders experiencing heavy fines and lengthy jail terms. This applies to those drugs and medications that can be purchased over the counter in other countries but are classified as illegal here in Qatar. See Prohibited Items on p.122 for more information.

Physical or verbal abuse, especially in public, is not tolerated. Fines, imprisonment and deportation may be imposed, depending on the severity of the incident.

To keep on the right side of the law, residents should familiarise themselves with local customs (p.17) as failure to observe them can have serious repercussions. The wearing of inappropriate clothing (short skirts, uncovered shoulders), displays of affection in public, or cohabiting can all result in fines, imprisonment or deportation, as can pregnancy outside of marriage and homosexuality.

Alert your embassy immediately if you are in trouble with the law, and consult a legal professional for advice and representation. Government and community support for victims of crime is rudimentary (see Victim Support, p.122).

If your belongings are lost or stolen you should contact the local police. In the event of theft you must obtain a police statement, which may be required when making an insurance claim, and which is usually only issued once the police investigation is complete.

If bank and credit cards go missing you should contact the bank (see Main Banks, p.112) to have the cards cancelled, and if you lose your passport your embassy or consulate (p.390) will be able to help. As always, it is a good idea to keep copies of your essential documents (passport and residence permit) in a safe place, in case of an emergency.

Metrash

Metrash is a government notification service that sends important alerts to your mobile phone. For individuals, this includes information on expiry dates of your visa, driving licence, and your vehicle registration. It also notifies you if a traffic violation has been recorded. You can subscribe online at the government Hukoomi website (gov.qa) but you must have a post-paid mobile phone contract – pre-paid Hala card numbers are not permitted.

Police

Qatari police are known for being friendly and helpful, and for lacking the ego and pretension of some western authorities. They generally have a good command of English and are usually approachable – assuming you stay on the right side of the law. There is a healthy presence of police around the city who wear a light blue shirt with dark blue trousers and a beret.

There are three types of police patrol units, identifiable by the different coloured Land Cruisers they drive. The standard police are part of the Public Guards Department, and patrol the roads in white vehicles with a blue stripe down the side. They maintain public security and are often spotted directing traffic at roundabouts and intersections.

The Al Fazaa rescue police launched its operation in March 2009, driving distinctive black and white Land Cruisers that are fast, flashy and high-powered. Meanwhile, the Lakhwiya police, meaning 'brotherhood' in the local Arabic dialect, drive red vehicles and represent the Internal Security Force. A white Lamborghini Gallardo, with blue and yellow stripes, joined the fleet of patrol cars in early March.

In the souk area, you will find dedicated traffic wardens, whose sole job is to direct traffic in and around the market. They wear a beige uniform with a white rope sash.

It is not common to be stopped by police, even if you have committed a minor offence. If you have been spotted talking on your mobile phone while driving, for example, an officer will take note of your licence plate and submit details of the offence to the traffic infringement department. You may not even be aware of your offence until you next try to leave the country or go to renew your driver's licence (see Traffic Fines & Offenses, p.59).

If You Are Arrested

If you are arrested you will be taken to a police station and questioned. If it's decided that you must go to court the case will go to the public prosecutor who will set a date for a hearing. For a minor offence you may get bail, and the police will keep your passport and often the passport of another male resident who is willing to vouch for you. Police stations have holding cells, so if you don't get bail you'll be held until the hearing. All court proceedings are conducted in Arabic, so you should secure the services of a translator. If sentenced, you'll go straight from court to jail. Upon being arrested you are advised to contact your embassy or consulate. They can liaise with family, advise on local legal procedures and provide a list of lawyers, but they will not pay your legal fees. The consulate will try to ensure that you are not denied your basic human rights, but they cannot act as lawyers, investigators, secure bail, or get you released.

If You Are Detained

You can be held by the police for up to 48 hours before being charged. You will appear before a judge within four days of your arrest, who then decides whether you will be released, remanded in custody to await trial, held in pre-trial detention pending investigation, or released on bail.

The judge can extend your detainment, normally at the Capital Police Detention Centre, for an extra week at a time to allow authorities time to investigate your case, or indefinitely if you are suspected of being a threat to national security. Criminal cases are usually tried within two to three months with both Muslims and non-Muslims tried under the same court system – a mixture of civil and Shariah law. You will be entitled to legal counsel throughout the process at your own expense – there is no state-funded representation available – or you may represent yourself.

Tips For Women

Stick to the dress code; tight, revealing clothing usually equals unwanted attention. Take extra care out at night and in unfamiliar areas, especially after a few drinks. Never get into an unlicensed taxi or accept a lift from a stranger. Qatar is a safe place but caution and vigilance should be exercised regardless.

Providing your crime didn't involve violence, you may apply for bail. If bail is approved, you will be released to a citizen sponsor and will be prohibited from leaving Qatar until your case has been resolved.

If you are sentenced to prison, you will be transported directly from court to Qatar's Central Jail. Officially, conditions meet international standards but reports from ex-detainees suggest otherwise. Men

explorer

there's more to life...

The ultimate career guide

EXPLORER

The Essential Career Guide

Working in the Gulf

BAHRAIN · KUWAIT · OMAN · QATAR
SAUDI ARABIA · UNITED ARAB EMIRATES

Includes information on choosing the right GCC
country, finding a job and closing the deal, financial
and legal issues, advancing your career, and moving on.

askexplorer.com/shop

askexplorer

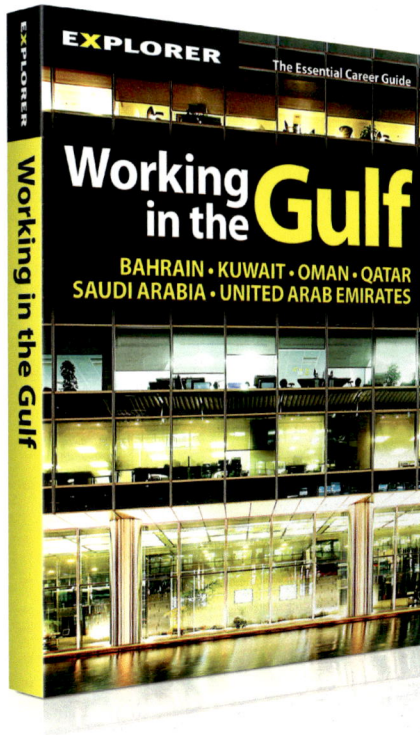

Legal Issues

and women are detained separately. Interestingly, Qatar is one of only six countries where females make up over 10% of total detainees.

Victim Support

If you are the victim of crime such as theft, you should report to the police immediately. Beyond that, there are shockingly few groups or organisations actively helping and supporting victims. Domestic violence in families and abuse against workers frequently goes unreported as there are few support networks available to sufferers. In 2007, the Qatar Foundation for Child and Women Protection (4462 8444) was launched to provide support services to women and minors who are at economic, social, political and psychological disadvantage. The foundation seeks to end all abuse and offences against women and children, offers protection against discrimination, and has established the first dedicated women's shelter.

The National Human Rights Committee (nhrc-qa. org) provides information and advice; otherwise you can seek assistance from your nearest embassy or consulate.

Prohibited Items

In January 2010, The Supreme Council of Health (4407 0000, sch.gov.qa) banned the use and sale of Reductil Sibutramine (the anti-obesity pill).

Medications including codeine, tranquilisers, some antidepressants and some sleeping pills are also banned so it is recommended that you leave these all behind if you can. However, if you do require medicines containing these substances, be sure to carry your prescription with you and a letter from your doctor to verify their use. Although these measures still may not allow you to bring the medication into Qatar, it will at least help keep you out of trouble if you are questioned.

Remember to pick up repeat prescriptions whenever you return to your home country, as Qatar may not have an alternative option available to you. If your doctor can prescribe an alternative, give yourself time to adjust to the new medication, allowing for the possibility of side-effects or unsuitability.

Similar to other countries around the Middle East, the possession, use and trafficking of illegal narcotics in Qatar is dealt with very harshly and should be taken very seriously. Even the smallest amounts of marijuana or hashish could earn you a lengthy prison sentence followed by an immediate expulsion from the country. It is advisable and sensible to steer clear of any involvement in illegal substances; dealing and smuggling illegal items into, out of, or around Qatar, will attract very little sympathy from authorities, including your embassy, so the simple advice is: don't do it.

The financial district lights up in the evening

Observe & Obey

Save yourself from a brush with the law by remembering the following.

Dress Conservatively

Strict dress codes must be observed in Qatar, and even more so during the holy month of Ramadan. Skimpy items like strappy tops, mini-skirts and hot pants are high on the indecency list, even during the blistering summer months. The code is more relaxed at the beach, by the pool and in nightclubs, but make sure you are well covered until you get there. Always dress appropriately and think of all the sunburn you'll avoid.

Crimes Of Cohabitation

You would have to be pretty unlucky to be caught, but Qatari law specifies that unmarried couples must not live together. The sensible choice is to get married or live apart.

Illegitimate Bumps

It is against the law for an unmarried woman to be pregnant. If this happens, the best advice is to get married or get out of the country. You need to show your marriage certificate here in order to obtain prenatal checks and treatment so the authorities will find out one way or another. Severe penalties should be a convincing deterrent.

Remain Orderly

Drinking in public view (unless at a licensed venue or event) and being drunk in public are strictly illegal. The law does not take kindly to people behaving in a disorderly manner in public, especially if alcohol is in any way involved.

Keep The PDAs In Check

Public displays of affection can land you in seriously hot water. Kissing, hugging and even holding hands are all considered indecent and may result in arrest and possibly deportation. You may be able to get away with a quick peck at the airport but, better still, stick to a handshake and a wave.

Bounce Into Jail

Payment by cheque is uncommon, but if you do, always make sure you have enough funds in your account to cover the amount. If not, your bank will report you to the authorities and the police may charge you with a criminal offence.

Don't Have One For the Road

It goes without saying that drinking and driving is illegal. But what many people fail to understand is that there is no safe, legal limit when it comes to drinking and driving here. Even a sip of wine or a strong brandy pudding can put you over the limit, because the limit is zero. If you are driving, stick to soft drinks and water all night. If you are drinking, leave the keys at home and get a cab. You can still be convicted of driving under the influence if there is alcohol in your system the morning after a big night.

Penalty For Possession

There are severe penalties for drug use, possession and trafficking in Qatar. Don't be tempted to participate in any drug-related activities while living in Qatar as it may result in a much-longer stay than you anticipated. It is also important to remember that some items that can be bought over the counter in other countries are illegal in Qatar. If you have been prescribed medication back home and you are unsure whether it contains illegal substances, seek the advice of a medical practitioner in your home country before bringing these items into Qatar.

Respect Ramadan

It is illegal to eat, drink or smoke in public view during fasting hours the holy month of Ramadan (p.20). 'In public view' includes your car, the beach, your workplace and even the gym. You should not chew gum either. Some restaurants inside major hotels have closed-off sections where you can dine out of sight but options like these are becoming less common, so don't count on it. Eating, drinking and smoking in public is only permitted after iftar (the breaking of the fast).

Look Mum, No Hands

It's one of the most widely flouted laws in the history of the legal system, but it is absolutely illegal to drive while talking on your mobile phone. Apart from being dangerous, not just for you but for your fellow road users, it is punishable with hefty fines and point deductions. Invest in a hands-free kit or better yet, switch your phone off while driving – it may be one of the few opportunities to enjoy some peace and quiet in the midst of a busy day.

SHERBORNE

QATAR

Sherborne Qatar School · SQ. 2011/2012. · Photo courtesy Pret-a-Porter

"Confident, Happy and Smiling Children"

- QNSA Accreditation Team

Preparatory School

The Preparatory School is modelled on schools like Sherborne Prep School in the UK which aim to develop the whole child.

The innovative Independent Curriculum provides a challenging and purposeful education, stretching the most able and nurturing pupils in areas they find more difficult.

Participation in Art, Drama, Music, PE and Games and a wide range of co-curricular activities completes the whole child approach.

We develop articulate, confident, courteous and caring pupils ready for, and eager to face, the challenges of the Senior School.

Senior School

The British curriculum prepares pupils for examinations in International GCSEs and International AS/A Levels. Our teachers are qualified and experienced, and have trained and worked in the UK.

Academic success is important and we have a Scholarship Programme to support and stretch the most able. We also encourage creativity through Art, Drama, Music and co-curricular pursuits.

Pastoral care matters, which is why every pupil has a personal tutor who supports and guides both pastorally and academically.

Telephone +974 44596400, Fax +974 44596412

www.sherborneqatar.org

Family &
Education

FAMILY

Ask any expat what the best thing about living in Doha is and they almost always reply with 'the lifestyle' – and for many families the main reason for moving here is for the opportunity to provide a better life for their children. Qatar is a desirable place to raise a family and many people outstay their original employment contracts primarily for this reason.

Qatar is extremely family friendly, with children welcome almost everywhere, and finding little ones dining in a fancy five-star restaurant or reclining in a late-night cinema screening is the norm. The downside to this is that while most establishments are happy to accommodate children, not all of your fellow patrons will be as understanding, so if your kids are being noisy or unruly you may find some unwelcome comments directed your way. Interestingly, this intolerance seems to be largely a western prejudice, whereas most locals tend to believe that the highlights of Qatar should be enjoyed by everybody.

Most families live in compound housing where you'll usually find an instant network of friends for you and your kids. The comfort and reassurance of being able to play in a secure environment with a known group of friends provides much peace of mind to normally anxious parents. Outside of the compound you should have no problem finding activities to entertain kids of all ages too, but you might need to use a bit of imagination. There are plenty of clubs and associations for you to join (see Activities, p.263), and new and interesting things to do are regularly advertised on event calendars.

The level of schooling is high too, with nursery through to secondary and further education available from reputable international institutions offering a range of curricula (see Education, p.137).

Getting Married

A skip down the aisle is entirely possible in Qatar; indeed unmarried couples are not legally allowed to live together (see p.123). But while it's possible, it is not particularly common for expats to marry here, largely because the process is more procedural than celebratory and there is only a limited choice of venues available. Couples are not allowed to marry on property that hasn't been legally approved for a wedding ceremony, so a seaside or garden wedding is out of the question, and not all designated venues can accommodate all religions. Christian churches, for example, may not marry Muslims.

While the marriage ceremony itself may be simplistic, the reception is where you can really indulge. A number of five-star hotels provide stunning facilities and services for weddings, including personal wedding planners and luxurious honeymoon packages. None of them come cheap, but your event will certainly be one to remember.

Some of the upmarket hotels that offer wedding packages include The Ritz-Carlton, The Four Seasons Hotel, and Al Sharq Village & Spa. All provide dedicated wedding planners, but be prepared to put down a hefty deposit and book well in advance. The InterContinental and Marriott hotels offer more affordable packages without compromising on quality. See p.196 for a full list of hotels in Doha, most of which will be delighted to provide you with a quote regarding their wedding services and packages. For those on a tighter budget, there is nothing stopping you from throwing a post-wedding bash in your favourite restaurant or your backyard. See Caterers (p.341) for ideas on staging your own party. If you're wondering where to buy your wedding finery and all that goes with it, see Wedding Items on p.319.

In The Picture

There are plenty of freelance photographers who would be delighted to capture your wedding (see local forums for recommendations) but check with the venue first. Some have strict rules regarding photography on their premises and may even restrict you to using their in-house photographer only.

The Paperwork

If you decide to get married in Qatar, the first thing you need to do is contact your nearest embassy to find out whether your marriage will be recognised in your home country, or any other country where you intend to live together (See Embassies & Consulates, p.390). You will also need to verify that you are allowed to marry your partner if you practise different religions. A Qatari man is allowed to marry a non-Muslim woman, but not the reverse, and the Catholic church will only marry a Catholic person to a non-Catholic person if they are Christian.

Your embassy will require certain documentation to be presented before a marriage may be consented to. This may include passport, birth certificate, passport photos, residence permit, an application form and divorce papers, if applicable. Some embassies will ask you to sign a legal affidavit declaring your eligibility to marry; others require you to swear an oath. Some, such as the British embassy, require you to formally post a notice or intention to marry, allowing anyone opposing the marriage time to object. Church weddings will also require you to produce the above paperwork and extras such as a baptismal certificate.

Certain embassies, including those of Britain, India, and the Philippines, offer civil ceremonies on site, providing certain terms and conditions have been met. Check with the embassy (p.390) to learn more.

Muslims must attend the Shariah Court to be married, or can arrange for an official to solemnise the union at a private residence. Two witnesses must be present, and the bride must have written consent from an immediate male authority (usually the father). A Muslim man is allowed to marry a non-Muslim woman, but permission must first be granted from the government. A Muslim woman is not allowed to marry a non-Muslim man. Non-Qatari Muslims also require a letter from their sponsor.

The fee for a Muslim marriage is QR 300 if the ceremony takes place on private property, or QR 200 if held on official grounds. The government website (gov.qa) has more information.

An Extravagant Affair

Qatari weddings are an opulent display – costing between QR 100,000 and QR 250,000 on average. The celebration is conducted separately, with men-only festivities taking place in an outdoor tent while women gather indoors, often in a luxury hotel ballroom. If you ever get the chance to attend a Qatari wedding, you should accept, simply to experience the spectacle.

Catholics can be married at the Church of Our Lady of the Rosary (p.49) by giving at least three months' prior notice, and only after attending a marriage preparation course. One person must be Catholic and the other also Christian. The priest will meet with you before the wedding to discuss arrangements and decide whether or not he is willing to bless the marriage.

Anglicans can marry at the Church of the Epiphany (p.49), providing at least one partner is a baptised Christian. Couples need to sit three interviews with the church rector to seek approval for the marriage. Two witnesses must be present at the ceremony (they can be supplied by the church for QR 100 each) which takes place in the 30 seat rectory chapel. The fee for marriage is QR 2,500.

Once married, you must register your marriage at the Ministry of Justice (moj.gov.qa), across from City Center Doha, near the Kahramaa building. You need your marriage certificate and an Arabic translation; you do not need to visit in person. Your registration then needs to be attested at the Ministry of Foreign Affairs (mofa.gov.qa). Authentication costs QR 20. It is advisable to also have your marriage attested and registered with your embassy.

There is no legal requirement for you to change your name once you are married, so it might be worth waiting until you leave Qatar to do so. If you do feel the need, take your marriage certificate, current passport and photos to your embassy and follow their necessary guidelines. You will have to get a new passport showing your new name, which in turn means you'll need a new, updated residence permit.

Genetic Screening

Nuptials have become even less glamorous with the introduction of compulsory medical screening. As of December 2009, all couples intending to marry must undergo medical testing to determine genetic suitability. This is in an effort to reduce the alarming rate of transferable defects in Qatari children that occur as a result of inter-marrying between cousins. The free test is performed at a number of authorised health centres (see below). In addition to screening for regenerative genetic defects, the process also tests for infectious and transition diseases and analyses couples' medical histories. The results of the tests take about three weeks and you won't be able to register your marriage without them. However, you cannot fail the test as such; if a problem is identified the doctor will warn of the risks posed, but the decision to marry rests with the couple.

Airport Health Center 4467 5633, *phcc.qa*
Al Gharafa Health Center 4481 4843, *phcc.qa*
Al Khor Health Center 4472 0224, *phcc.qa*
Al Rayyan Health Center 4481 2668, *phcc.qa*
West Bay Health Center 4483 7790, *phcc.qa*

My Qatar Wedding Amanda Williams, Canadian expat

I got married in the local courts here in 2004. I didn't know what to expect but was pleasantly surprised at how easy the whole process is if you have a little knowledge. My husband speaks Arabic so this made it a great deal easier; I would say it would be difficult without someone who speaks Arabic, although not impossible. All women must cover their hair to go into the Islamic court, but that wasn't an issue for me as I am covered anyway. I had already converted to Islam so getting married in the Shariah court wasn't an issue for me, but I know a lot of girls who have had to convert. It used to be that the courts did not conduct mixed religion marriages, although I am told that is no longer the case. The only thing that really surprised me is that you are required to have your father with you, if it is your first marriage, to act as your guardian. We didn't bother with a reception – we just went in, signed the contract and went home. We honeymooned for a month in Syria after that. I am not one for the whole wedding party thing, I would rather skip it and travel.

Family

Having A Baby

Excellent services and facilities are available for birthing in Qatar, so, unless you specifically want to return to your home country to be nearer to family, the only reason why you shouldn't have your baby delivered here is if you are unmarried, which is illegal (see p.128).

Better salary packages in Qatar mean that families can in many cases make a comfortable living on one wage only. As such, one of the parents, usually the woman, stays at home to take care of the kids. Employed expat women are entitled to 50 days' total maternity leave; fathers are entitled to two days' paternity leave. Domestic labour is cheap too, so most families employ a maid or nanny to assist with babies and children to make up for the absence of having family close at hand.

If being away from family is a concern, or if you just need that extra reassurance to get through labour, you can hire a trained doula, or birth partner. Contact Sarah at iceaqatar@yahoo.com for more information or to register for a childbirth training class. There are also excellent community friendship and support groups to assist you, such as Doha Mums (dohamums.com), and pre and post-natal classes, including those run by Aspire Active (aspire.qa), are a great way to meet fellow expectant or new mums. Having access to an instant network of women who have all been there before you is a great reassurance for the inevitable upheaval that comes with having a baby.

Most expats opt to receive care under the private hospital system so that husbands can attend the birth, and because it is often covered by employer health insurance. The public system is perfectly acceptable and, although a little disorganised, is almost entirely free of charge – but men are not allowed to be present during scans or during the delivery (see Maternity, p.167).

Pregnant Out Of Wedlock

Being pregnant and unmarried is a very serious offence in Qatar and penalties are harsh. If caught, you will be arrested, jailed and detained to await deportation. Under Shariah law you may also be sentenced to lashings, especially if you are Muslim.

If you are single and find that you are pregnant, the simple advice is to leave the country as soon as you can and, assuming you intend to return to Qatar, get married. There may have been a time where you could hide your pregnancy until you at least had a chance to marry here, but with the recent introduction of compulsory pre-screening for all married couples, you would almost certainly be caught. Secondly, there isn't really such a thing as a 'quickie' wedding here – most marriages take at least several weeks of necessary arrangements before they can take place (see Getting Married, p.126).

In order to obtain prenatal care here and to actually give birth, you need to show your marriage certificate. If you are unable to produce one, you will be reported to the police immediately, so the authorities are certain to find out, one way or another.

If you leave the country to have the baby, marry your partner before you both return, as it is illegal to live together as an unmarried couple in Qatar (see p.123). If it is determined that you were single and pregnant in Qatar, you may still be arrested and sentenced, even after the baby is born, but this kind of thing is unlikely to occur unless you are already in some kind of trouble with the authorities. Still, your safest bet is to observe local laws and only consider pregnancy if you are married.

Birth Certificate & Registration

You have two months after delivery to register the birth, apply for a passport and obtain a residence permit for your baby, otherwise a daily fine of QR 10 will apply.

The hospital will issue paperwork affirming the baby's birth, which is the first step to obtaining a birth certificate. If you had your baby at Hamad General Hospital (p.164), you will automatically be issued a registration number for your baby; if not, you will need to collect a registration number from the National Health Authority. To do this, simply take all of the paperwork given to you at the hospital where you delivered your baby to the Women's Hospital at Hamad Medical City (see p.166). The registration number will be issued on the spot.

Once you have your Hamad baby registration number, take all your hospital paperwork to the Supreme Council of Health headquarters in the old Asian Games Building on Al Khaleej Street, near Civil Defence Roundabout (sch.gov.qa). Make sure you have the passports, IDs and copies of residence permits for both parents with you. You can request as many copies of the child's birth certificate as you like (QR 20 each), translated into English. You only need one original copy that you can make your own copies from, but extra copies of the Arabic original are a nice idea for family members, or as a memento for your child.

You will be issued with a receipt which you will need in order to collect the birth certificate and a green vaccination record card (see Vaccinations, p.170) approximately one week later. Every baby needs to have a green vaccination card, regardless of whether or not they were born here in Qatar. The card summarises the recommended vaccinations for your baby and is marked with a stamp and date once they have been administered. Government clinics will refuse to immunise your baby without one.

Take the birth certificate to your embassy to apply for the baby's passport. By law in Qatar, the child may be assigned the nationality of either or both parents, assuming neither are Qatari, where different rules apply depending on which parent is the national. If the baby is born in Qatar to non-Qatari parents, the baby has no right to Qatari citizenship.

Wetting The Baby's Head

The Church of Our Lady of The Rosary (p.49) performs baptism ceremonies for those wishing to welcome their little one into the Catholic faith, but most people just wait until they are back home among the company of family and friends. The arrival of a new baby in Qatar is usually met with plenty of visits, gifts and good wishes to the new family. A novel idea for a newborn gift is to visit a scribe at the souks and have the baby's name painted in Arabic. For more gift ideas see Baby Items, p.296.

Depending on the embassy, you will need a certified copy of the baby's birth certificate, both parents' passports, a copy of your marriage certificate, an application form and relevant fee, and you will need to provide two passport photos of the baby. Each embassy has different requirements regarding the photo, and you need to check which colour background is acceptable and how the baby must appear in the picture. Getting a newborn to keep their head straight and look into the lens of the camera may prove to be your biggest challenge of the entire registration process. Once the passport has been issued (usually within two weeks), you may begin the residency process for your baby (see Residence Permit, p.40). This is normally taken care of by your company PRO at no cost to you. You will need to submit the baby's passport, two passport photographs, birth certificate, the green vaccination record card, and the passports of both parents for the residence permit application to be correctly processed.

Babies Born Back Home

For births outside Qatar, you will need to obtain the baby's birth certificate and passport before you and the baby can return. Also bear in mind that most airlines don't allow babies to travel if they are younger than 10 days old. Your baby can enter on a visit visa (see Visas, p.40), after which you have 60 days to obtain their residence permit (see Residence Permit, p.40).

Adoption

It is not possible for a foreigner to adopt a Qatari child. Adoption of other nationalities is possible, but you need to check the regulations of the country where you hold your citizenship and determine which rules apply to you and the child you wish to adopt. You will also need to enlist the cooperation, and ultimately the approval, of the embassy representing the child. Once adoption is successful, you may undertake the residence process for your child as normal (see Residence Permit, p.40).

Getting Divorced

Divorce laws are governed by the country where your marriage licence was issued – which may not necessarily be the place where you got married, or where you now live. The situation becomes more convoluted the more complex your circumstances (for example, you may be from separate countries, or you may not be a citizen of the governing country), but whatever the case, you should first consult a lawyer for advice (see p.117).

If you are residing in Qatar under family sponsorship, bear in mind that your spouse has the right to cancel the residence permits of you and your children at any time. If there is any likelihood of this occurring, or if chances are that your divorce will not be amicable, then your best option might be to return to your home country and start proceedings from there. If you do get divorced in Qatar, then you should

H a v i n g   A   B a b y   I n   Q a t a r Jennie Bonnalie, primary school teacher and mum to India and Poppy

I have had two babies in Doha, both at Al Ahli Hospital. The treatment I received for both births was fantastic. I was in hospital for a week after having both babies, and I really feel that the staff got to know me each time. The nurses are lovely, and although they may not be assertive, they are very forthcoming in terms of care and getting you anything you need. The hospital is spotless, the food is excellent and you get to choose your meals, which is a bonus! Their philosophy is that you are a guest, not a patient, and you do certainly feel that way. The births themselves were fine, and the staff went out of their way to follow my wishes. They are just very cautious and don't want to make any mistakes. My husband was treated really well whenever he visited and there was a guest room for him to stay overnight. A meal was always supplied for him too. The only down side to having a baby here is that there is little or no after care, but I did feel that I could return to the hospital if I had to. Otherwise you have incredible support from other mums in the community. My advice is if you are going to Al Ahli, take a book with you for your appointments because waiting times are getting excessive. And at the end of one appointment, book your next one before you leave, otherwise you might not be able to get one at all. My experience was very positive and I'd happily recommend having a baby in Doha. Just as long as you realise that it is different to how it is in the UK or elsewhere, then you will be fine.

Family

at least register your divorce in your home country as well, to ensure that all foreign property and assets can be divided up accordingly.

Proceedings in the Qatari court vary depending on the nationality of each party, the reasons for divorce and whether there are children involved. Each case is tried by a judge and treated uniquely, so rulings for each divorce may differ considerably.

Maintenance payments will depend on the age of the child and are decided upon in court, along with visitation rights. Custody is usually awarded to the mother, except where the mother is a non-Qatari woman married to a Qatari man, whereby the courts generally award full custodianship to the father. The father won't necessarily be ordered to pay child support for his children, but he will be responsible for their upbringing and entitled to significant access. Boys over the age of 12 have the right to choose to live with their father.

A divorced mother must obtain permission from her ex-husband to leave the country with his children, but an estranged father does not need permission from his ex-wife.

If there is a chance that your marriage may be reconciled, there are excellent counselling services available to you and your partner. Contact the government Family Consulting Centre (p.177) or see Counselling & Therapy on p.177 for a list of independent practitioners.

Single Parents

As a single parent in Qatar, you may actually be better off here than in your home country. Wages for expats who are hired from abroad are usually superior to those offered back home and employment packages include extra benefits such as housing and paid schooling. The nursery and daycare system here is very good and some institutions accept children from as young as 3 months, so engaging in full-time work is entirely acceptable. Better yet, you can follow the lead of most other families and hire a full-time maid or nanny to live in your home and take care of your child while you are at work. Hiring a maid is inexpensive and comes with the added opportunity for you to get out of the house on your own to enjoy a social life.

As the single parent, you will have to sponsor your child so that they can legally live with you (see Family Sponsorship, p.42). Currently, you must earn a minimum of QR 7,000 per month to sponsor a family member. You will also need to show evidence supporting your single parent status, such as your spouse's death certificate or divorce papers.

With family being paramount here in Qatar, single life may sometimes have you feeling like the odd one out, but it won't take long to meet new people and establish a good network of friends for you and your kids. Being a parent, people will automatically assume

that you are married, but other than that there is no social stigma against single parenting.

Babysitting & Childcare

Placing your child in someone else's care is never an easy decision and, for the sake of peace of mind, you'll probably find that word of mouth is the best way to find a babysitter. Ask around among friends and even at your child's nursery or school as a trusted staff member might like the opportunity to supplement their income. Teenagers and housemaids are usually keen to earn some extra pocket money if you feel comfortable enough with the idea. Or you could join forces with another expat parent who is willing to exchange babysitting services with you. Doha Mums (dohamums.com) is planning to launch a babysitting co-op, where a small group of members can get together and mind each other's children. The service will be free and for members only.

Most of the major hotels offer child minding services, but you may need to be a staying guest. The Four Seasons Hotel (p.198) has the Kids For All Seasons service where you can leave your kids (for a fee) while you visit hotel facilities such as the spa or restaurants. The Mövenpick Tower and Suites hotel (p.202) has a separate play room where children are entertained while you relax and enjoy your weekend brunch. Keep in mind, however, that these services may not guarantee one-on-one supervision of your child and that minders might not be suitably qualified in child care or first aid. If this is concern for you, then ask in advance.

It is important to note that maids, nannies and even some school staff may not be formally qualified at all, let alone in childcare, so be wary about who you decide to bring into your home. You should also write down your villa number, your address and draw a map with directions so your babysitter/maid can explain how to find your house. Finding a live-in maid or nanny can be a headache. By law, your full-time maid is supposed to live in your house with you and you must offer them sponsorship. Not all people are eligible to sponsor domestic help and the government decides from which nationality you may recruit your maid. You can hire a maid who is already living in Qatar, or you can recruit someone directly from their home country. There are pros and cons to each method – see Sponsoring a Maid, p.42, for more information.

Activities For Kids

During the winter months, kids can spend plenty of time outdoors enjoying the cooler temperature and mild weather. Parks dotted in and around the city have playground facilities that are clean and well-maintained and are limited to use by families only (see Parks, p.212). The new public beach at Katara Cultural

Village offers an excellent array of water inflatables to play on. Alternatively, beaches such as Al Wakra are only a short drive away and most compounds have good recreational facilities, including swimming pools.

The hotter months can still be enjoyed outdoors in the evenings when temperatures drop, but most activities during the day take place in the comfort of air conditioning. Major shopping centres have play areas for kids, and there are the usual cinemas and bowling alleys. For information on the various options located around town, see Amusement Centres, p.216.

In addition to these, there is a plethora of clubs and associations supporting a variety of sports and hobbies (see Activities, p.264) that your kids can sign up to, and a variety of after-school options on offer to keep kids active.

Aspire Active
Aspire Academy For Sports Excellence Baaya
4413 6219
aspire.qa
Map **2 A10**
Aspire Active runs a daily fitness programme for 12 to 17 year old boys. Classes include boxing, spinning and karate. The training focuses on building core strength and improving hand-eye coordination, endurance and flexibility. Each programme costs QR 350 per year and classes are held weekly at no additional fee.

Circusland
Landmark Mall Umm Lekhba **4487 6111**
landmarkdoha.com
Map **2 E1**
This large play area features carousels, dodgems, arcade games, a soft play area, rides and a children's hair salon. A fee of QR 15 enables children to enjoy all non-token activities. Open from 10:00 to 24:00 daily.

Club Scouts
Various locations
4411 3567
Affiliated to the Direct Service Council of the Boy Scouts of America, this group is open to boys of all nationalities. 11 to 18 year olds can join the Scout Pack which meets three Tuesdays a month. The Cub Pack, for 7 to 10 year olds, meets at various volunteer's houses. Both groups are active and in operation from September to May.

Doha Brownies & Guides
Sherborne Qatar 4459 6400
sherborneqatar.org
The Brownies group is for girls aged 7 to10; for more info and to join the waiting list email kirsty.merriman@gmail.com. The Guides group, for girls aged 10 to14, is based at Compass International School. Email judyandgarymond@yahoo.co.uk for details.

Doha Golf Club
Al Jamiaa St Al Egla **4496 0777**
dohagolfclub.com
Map **1 H1**
The junior academy offers coaching for kids aged 5 to15 years. Tuition includes the fundamentals of golf, swing shape and action, putting and driving. Lessons are available at weekends only, before 15:00.

French Institute Of Qatar
135 Al Inshirah St Onaiza **4493 0863**
institutfrancais-qatar.com
Map **2 M2**
This cultural centre runs activities for children, including music and art classes. The sessions are held in French; however, if your child is not a native speaker, beginners are welcome to join too.

Get active in Qatar

Family

Fun City

Centrepoint Al Sadd **4428 9251**
landmarkgroup.com
Map **2 K8**
Small, nicely maintained, Fun City has a soft play area
and a separate section with dressing-up clothes, slides
and a drawing table. Costs are QR 16 per hour from
Sunday to Wednesday and QR 20 per hour Thursday
to Saturday. The small rides cost extra. There is a kids'
hairdresser upstairs. Children up to 140cm in height
are admitted. Parents suffer from a lack of seating.

Fun City

City Center Doha Al Dafna **4483 9501**
Map **2 Q2**
This Fun City is not to be confused with the Fun City
located at Centrepoint (see above). Formerly known
as X-Treme World, it now has a more accurate name; a
good afternoon's fun can be had with the small roller
coasters and rides on offer. Pay by the ride from QR 5
to QR 20.

Girl Scouts

Various Locations
Affiliated to USA Girl Scouts Overseas, this group
offers a supportive, fun group environment and
activities that aim to prepare girls up to the age of 12
by building skills needed for success later in life. To
sign up your daughter (or to volunteer yourself), email
Margaret Grote at QatarUSAGSO@gmail.com.

Playball

Various Locations **5506 2169**
kidinmecoaching.com
A fun, sport-based fitness and movement
development programme for 2 to 7 year olds,
focussing on developing kids' coordination, balance,
spatial awareness and the acquisition of basic team
sports skills. Contact Nadia Rahim for more info.

Qmotion

Nr Nissan Petrol Station Fereej Kulaib **4411 7911**
qmotion.com.qa
Map **2 K4**
Qmotion's Kids in Motion programme offers different
levels of physical activities for children from 4 to 12
years of age. Classes focus on developing fitness,
strength, motor skills and confidence through fun,
physical games. Course fees for a nine-week course
with two 45 minute classes per week are QR 1,440.

Mother & Toddler Activities

Most parenting groups are intended for mothers and
their little ones, so dads might have a tougher time
finding ways to entertain toddlers. Strictly speaking,
women in Qatar aren't meant to interact with men
that they aren't related to; in practice it's simply not
the norm here for men to take such a hands-on role in
raising children. That said, the number of stay-at-home
fathers is increasing and it isn't too difficult to spot
them when you are out and about with your child.

Qatar is extremely friendly towards families and
you can easily meet other mums or dads without
much difficulty. Playgrounds are the obvious starting
place for families, and there are plenty to choose from
if you are in Doha. Get some exercise pushing the
pram along the Corniche (p.190) or around the Aspire
Zone circuit (p.190) during the cooler months and
summer evenings. For mums with toddlers, joining a
mums' group gives you access to an instant network
of friends, ideas and activities. It's never too early to
teach your kids, so joining a class is a great way to
introduce them to new concepts and socialise at the
same time. Lessons in swimming, yoga, gymnastics
and music are all available for babies, toddlers and
pre-schoolers.

Aspire Active

Aspire Academy For Sports Excellence Baaya
4413 6219
aspire.qa
Map **2 A10**
Aspire Active has a junior years programme for
children aged 6 months to 5 years. The focus is on
stimulating and nurturing development of a healthy
attitude toward fitness, exercise and nutrition. There
is a joining fee of QR 350 per year and classes are held
weekly at no additional fee.

Doha Dolphins Swimming Club

Doha College Fereej Al Soudan **4411 7911**
qmotion.com.qa
Map **2 H12**
Learning to swim helps children to gain confidence
and independence in the water, and these swimming
classes are for children aged 4 months to 4 years.
Small class groups allow for specialised lessons with
experienced and qualified teachers. Arm bands
are used for babies and toddler classes, and parent
participation is an essential part of the programme.
The cost per session is QR45-55 or you can opt for the
very reasonable annual membership of QR 325.

Doha Mums

Various locations
dohamums.com
Formerly Doha Expat Mums & Kids, this is a well-
established mums' group with lots of activities, events
and playgroups for mums and their children. There are
some listings for dads as well, but the wife has to be a
member. Doha Mums organises a plethora of activities
including day trips to nearby stores, picnic days and
even an annual Summer Market. Membership is free
and provides access to exclusive member benefits

and a private forum packed with useful information. Just attend an event and request to join. There are even coffee mornings organised in some of the well known cafes around town to welcome new members. Expectant mums are also welcome to join.

Ghanem Gardens Playgroup
Ghanem Gardens Club House Rawdat Al Khail
Map **2 N10**
This is a friendly mother and baby/toddler playgroup that features toys to play with, singing and art activities, among other things. The group meets on Mondays from 09:30 to 11:30, and sessions cost QR 15 to attend. Contact Lena Kaminskas at lena. ontheroad@rambler.ru for more details.

Mums In Doha
Various Locations
mumsindoha.com
This is a mums' group that started up in Doha in the summer of 2010. It's a bilingual group, offering monthly mums' and kids' activities in Arabic and English including music classes, 'monkeynastix' movement classes for toddlers, arts and crafts sessions and more. Keep an eye on the website for updates.

Music For Me – Parent & Child Music Classes
Various Locations
Music classes for babies, toddlers and pre-school children and parents. Each lesson features singing, dancing, finger-play, marching and movement, bells, shakers, sticks, maracas and balls. Dads are welcome. The price is QR 250 for 10 weeks, with a 20% discount for siblings. Contact Sheryl McKnight at musicformedoha@yahoo.com for full details.

My Gym Children's Fitness Center
Salwa Rd Fereej Abdel Aziz **4464 1429**
mygym-qatar.com
Map **2 P9**
This gym for youngsters is open to toddlers and children from the age of 3 upwards, and aims to improve each child's general health, well-being and self-esteem. All the sessions are designed to be constructive and non-competitive. Classes can take a variety of forms, from gymnastics through to musical games and dance. Experienced and well-trained staff organise and run all the classes, and birthday parties are available upon request. Call for more details.

Ray's Reef
Royal Plaza Al Sadd **4413 0000**
royalplazadoha.com
Map **2 L8**
This is a small yet fun play area at Royal Plaza mall, suitable for younger children and babies. Kids can enjoy soft play and climbing areas, a ball pen and an

art corner. Open from Sunday to Thursday, 12:00 to 22:00, Friday 15:30 to 23:00 and Saturday 10:00 to 22:00. Entry is QR 20.

Summer Camps
Many expat families leave Qatar in the summer months to escape the heat and the lack of summer entertainment. Schools close down for an extended break during this period and families have previously struggled to find ways to entertain the kids indoors. This is beginning to change, as demand slowly increases alongside the rate of the population. Some nurseries (p.137) stay open during the break which is a relief for parents of small children. Centres such as the International Academy for Intercultural Development (p.268) run summer classes in art, dance, performing arts and fitness for kids. There are also several fitness companies and sports teams that run summer programmes, so it's worth contacting the groups listed in Activities and Hobbies, p.263. Evolution Soccer (p.272) offers lively and fun football camps during the summer and other school holidays. Be sure to sign up early.

Keep an eye on local websites for any hotel programmes available for kids – in 2010 the Mövenpick Hotel Tower and Suites (p.202) ran a junior hotelier course that took place once a week over seven weeks. It was open to children aged 6 to 12 years and covered a variety of training throughout the different departments within the hotel.

For those with older children, it's worth checking out the Mövenpick's programme, as events usually run in the evenings when most younger kids are already tucked up in bed. Indoor play centres (see Activities For Kids, p.130) and amusement centres (p.216) are open throughout the summer.

Play time

Family

After-School Activities

There are dozens of clubs and groups that you and your kids can join in Qatar, or courses that you can enrol in (see Activities & Hobbies, p.264), and many schools offer extracurricular programmes for students interested in a variety of disciplines, including art, music, language and sport.

If you wanted to, you could easily consume every afternoon and most of your weekend sending your child to swimming club, English tutoring, guitar lessons and tennis coaching, but registration fees aren't always cheap and the costs of lessons do add up. As long as school work doesn't suffer, then after-school activities can be a fun and educational way of entertaining your child, and can also be helpful to working parents.

Aspire Active (p.131) has launched a timetable of fitness and wellness classes for teenagers that is inexpensive, but there is usually a waiting list. Organisations such as Qatar Scientific Club (p.270) offer activities for children interested in science and technology. These include model aircraft, scuba diving, astronomy and bird watching. The Qatar Toastmasters (p.269) helps alleviate nervousness by teaching public speaking, and Doha Debates (p.207) is a great way to introduce young adults to current affairs and politics.

Volunteering (p.109) is a great way to teach kids the value of helping others, and local organisations are always grateful for help. Walking the dogs at Qatar Animal Welfare Society (p.270) is a nice alternative for kids who are not able to have pets at home.

Support Groups

Moving to a new country is quite an endeavour, but help is at hand to get you through the adjustment period, and any other life problems you might be experiencing. The strong sense of community between expats means it's usually just a matter of speaking up to find specialist care or a friendly ear.

Various nationalities have their own expat websites and social groups set up; these can be an excellent way to help you establish cultural contacts and new friends among likeminded expats (see Meeting New People, p.48).

You can also find support for professionals (see Networking & Events, p.102). If you feel like you would benefit from an outside perspective or need professional support, refer to Counselling and Therapy on p.177.

Al Anon
Various Locations **5507 1842**
aaqatar.org
This support group offers help to people who have family or friends that are affected by alcohol. Free help is available 24 hours a day by calling the number above.

Alcoholics Anonymous
Various locations **5560 5901**
aaqatar.org
Alcoholism can be a problem for some expats. Free support is available to those struggling with alcohol-related problems. All contact is treated with respect and confidence. If you need help, you can call the 24 hour hotline.

Autism Support Group
Villaggio Mall Baaya
Map **2 B11**
Meetings for people whose lives are affected by autism are held at 15:30 on the first Wednesday of each month, and at 09:30 on the last Wednesday of the month at Columbus Cafe in Villaggio Mall. Email pattidoha@yahoo.com for further details.

Overeaters Anonymous
Various locations **5547 3506**
http://sites.google.com/site/oadoha
An association that supports people suffering from compulsive overeating disorder, Overeaters Anonymous encourages members to develop a food plan with the help of a health care professional and a sponsor. Meetings are held every Wednesday evening at 19:30, call Jacki (5547 3506) or Mike (6668 6234) for directions. There is no cost to join.

Qatar Diabetes Association
Rawdat Al Khail **4454 7334**
qda.org.qa
Map **2 N10**
This association is committed to promoting normal, healthy lives for diabetic patients, and to prevent its development to those at risk. The association is supported by volunteers and donations, and aims to raise up the awareness of diabetes in the expat and local community.

Qatar National Cancer Society
Al Rayyan St Fereej Bin Mahmoud **4447 8128**
qncs.org
Map **2 K7**
A society that aims to ease the impact of cancer on patients and their families through education and support programmes. It promotes prevention and supports efforts to cure cancer.

Social Development Center
Nr Ramada R/A, Suhaim Bin Hamad St
Fereej Bin Mahmoud **4454 2400**
sdc.org.qa
Map **2 L10**
This non-profit group assists with individuals and families in harsh economic circumstances through self-empowerment programmes, training and

awareness schemes. It also provides financial, educational and humanitarian aid to eligible beneficiaries.

Think Pink Qatar
Various locations **5516 1167**
A group that promotes awareness to aid in the prevention, early detection and treatment of breast cancer in the community. Breast Cancer Support Group helps women to find the right resources for proper medical treatment and understanding. Membership is open to sufferers of breast cancer and their families.

Death
The death of a family member or a friend is difficult at any time, but even more so in a foreign country with unfamiliar procedures. Contact your embassy to assist you wherever possible.

Certificates & Registration
The police must be notified in the event of a death so that they can issue a report stating that there was no foul play involved. Once this report has been issued, you can collect a Notification of Death certificate from the mortuary at Hamad General Hospital (4439 4444). Take the police report, the death certificate and the documents listed below to the Preventative Health department in the Supreme Council for Health headquarters on Al Khaleej Street near Civil Defence roundabout. The Preventative Health department won't need all of the photocopies listed, but some will be taken by each department you visit (for example, embassies usually require three), so be prepared and take the whole lot with you to hand over as you go. You will need:

- 10 copies of the deceased person's passport
- 10 copies of the deceased person's spouse's passport
- 10 copies of the passport of the person handling the arrangements
- Copies of each person's ID card may also be required
- Approximately QR 100 for fees

The department will issue more paperwork that is needed for the CID office on Sports City Street (the same place that you go to have your fingerprints taken, p.43) to issue a Transfer of Dead Body certificate. After you obtain this, return to the Preventative Health department with all the paperwork. You will be issued with six sets of death certificates.

You should also register the death with the deceased person's embassy (see Embassies & Consulates, p.390). The embassy will require a death certificate and a completed Registration of Death form (available at the embassy). As an indication of cost, at the British Embassy registration of a death costs QR 630 and a consular death certificate costs QR 390. The embassy will cancel the deceased person's passport, which is necessary if the body is to be repatriated. The residence visa must also be cancelled.

Returning The Deceased To Their Country Of Origin
Contact your airline to arrange shipment of the body (Qatar Airways Cargo, 4455 6111), and an undertaker in the country to which the body is being flown. Advise the mortuary of the flight details as soon as they have been booked so they can arrange to transport the body to the airport.

Contact Qatar Aviation Services (4462 1745, qataraviation.com) and provide copies of the deceased's passport and that of the accompanying person. Contact details of the undertaker in the home country will also need to be provided. An airway bill for the body will be issued (cash payment is expected in advance).

The body will need to be embalmed for transit. There are no undertakers in Qatar, but a team of volunteers, run by a man named Nery Alphonso, will help with the preparation of the body. The team do not charge for their services, but will happily accept donations, which they pass on to local charities. A member of the team will come and prepare the body 24 hours before it is due to leave the country. Nery Alphonso can be contacted on 5581 0596. Catholics may seek assistance from Catholic Church of Our Lady of the Rosary (4416 5550).

You will also need a coffin from Gulf Box Sales (4435 5460). It costs around QR 3,000 (again, payment is required in advance) and will be ready in two days once the measurements of the deceased have been taken. The coffin will be delivered to the mortuary on the day the body is being flown home.

On the day of departure, you will have to take the paperwork, together with the deceased's original cancelled passport and the airway bill, to the airport. At Arrivals, go to the customs counter, where you will get one set of papers stamped. Then go to immigration and get the deceased's passport stamped. You will then have to return to Qatar Aviation Services with all the stamped documents.

Local Burial
Expats may be buried in Dukhan Cemetery, approximately 90 kilometres from Doha. Transport to the grave site and burial is provided free of charge courtesy of the Qatar government, but you must purchase a coffin. Local burial usually takes place within 24 hours of death, in accordance with Islamic custom. Cremation is not permitted in Qatar.

Family

Pets

The attitude toward keeping pets in Qatar is fairly liberal, although some compounds have introduced new regulations in response to complaints from residents. Pets that bark, howl and dig up garden beds can be a nuisance, as can unleashed, uncollared dogs, and it is these issues that are likely to irk your neighbours. Pets are not allowed in public parks (including the Corniche) and beaches.

If you are planning to import a pet or are looking to adopt one, verify with your landlord or sponsor whether you are allowed to keep animals in your home. Be certain to do this before you begin the process of importing your pet.

Cats and dogs should be microchipped for identification purposes, wear a collar and be protected against fleas, ticks and worms, which are omnipresent here. If you already have your animal micro-chipped before import, remember to change your address on the chip once your pet has arrived. For new microchips, visit one of the vets listed on the next page. Do not let your pet roam freely around the neighbourhood and avoid them coming into contact with strays that might carry diseases and infections.

The Qatar Cat Coalition arranges for strays to be humanely caught, neutered and returned to their point of capture, and Qatar Animal Welfare Society (qaws.org) does its best to home abandoned pets. If you are interested in adopting a rescue pet, QAWS would be glad to hear from you. There are listings on its website of cats and dogs that are family friendly and are looking for homes.

There are pet shops dotted around Doha where you can buy aquarium fish and accessories (see Pets, p.136), and you can buy rabbits and birds from the pet section of Souk Waqif. Larger animals such as goats, sheep and camels are available for sale at the animal market on Wholesale Market Street off Salwa Road. When shopping for a pet, beware that hygiene standards in pet stores and at the souks may be substandard, and there are few guarantees concerning the age, health and history of the animals on sale.

Bringing Your Pet To Qatar

Most cats and dogs may be imported into Qatar, providing that all vaccinations, including rabies, are present and up to date. The following dog breeds, however, are banned from import: Afghan, American Staffordshire terrier, boxer, bulldog, bull mastiff, bull terrier, doberman, great Dane, Japanese akita, pug, rottweiller, shar pei and Staffordshire bull terrier.

To import your pet you need a permit from the Ministry of Municipal Affairs & Agriculture. This requires presentation of a valid health certificate for your pet (dated within a fortnight of anticipated entry in Qatar), and the animal's vaccination record. Application forms are available in person from the

ministry office, from your sponsor employer, or an agent such as Qatar Pet Travel or Qatar Pet Relocators. An agent may also require photos (if the animal is a dog), passport copies of the owner and flight details or airway bill. Most airlines allow animals to travel as cargo or on the same flight as their owners, but you will need to check beforehand. There are no quarantine rules in Qatar, so your pet will be released immediately after customs.

Taking Your Pet Home

Pets travelling out of Qatar need to be vaccinated against rabies and have all their vaccinations up to date. EU countries require a blood test to show that the vaccinations have been effective. Some countries will require the animals to be de-wormed and have tick and tapeworm treatments before they arrive. Check the regulations of the country to which you are taking your pet for more detailed information.

A health certificate will need to be issued seven days before the animal is due to travel, which can be done at the Government Veterinary Clinic free of charge. Remember to take your pet's updated vaccination record with you. The certificate is valid for one week only and needs to be taken to Qatar Aviation Services at the airport cargo section (4462 1745). Here you will have to book a flight for your pet and pay the amount in full, including handling fees, before you are issued the airway bill (this needs to be done five days before you want the animal to travel). Finally, you will need to make sure you have a suitable travel kennel that is approved by the airline. These are available for purchase from any of the vets and boarding kennels below but you may wish to call first and check that they stock the size you need, especially if you are planning to export a large dog. Extra large crates may need to be ordered from outside the country (you can find one online yourself or ask your vet to help you) so research local availability in advance.

Remember that the necessary procedures need to be completed within five to seven days prior to the animal's departure from the country.

Vets, Kennels & Grooming

Vet services are limited but the standard and quality of service is extremely high. Qatar Veterinary Center and The Veterinary Surgery are both utilised by expats and perform vaccinations, worming, sterilisation, microchipping and general surgery. They also stock specialist pet foods, travel cages, toys and accessories for your pet. Prices are on the moderate to high side, but an alternative is available. Services, including worming, vaccinations, health examinations and surgery are performed at the Government Veterinary Clinic free of charge. There are no official pet sitters or dog walkers in Qatar. Instead, pet owners tend to

---

get neighbours to look after animals for short periods, or house them in a boarding facility during longer periods. Be aware that demand for pet boarding is extremely high, so book as far in advance as possible, especially if you are planning to travel during peak summer seasons and school holidays. Apart from the government clinic, all of the organisations listed below offer kennels, boarding and grooming and will assist you with both importing and exporting your pet. If your pooch needs sprucing up, Pampered Pets offers grooming services and will come to collect your pet from your home.

Government Veterinary Clinic Old Airport, 4456 0444
Pampered Pets Kennels & Cattery Off Al Shamal Rd, 5588 4132, *ppkdoha.net*
Paws & Claws Nr Villaggio, 5528 6335
Qatar Pet Relocator 5528 6335, *qatarpetrelocators.com*
Qatar Pet Travel Ain Khaled, 5542 4030, *qatarpettravel.com*
Qatar Veterinary Center Al Aziziya, 4421 6405, *qatarvet.name.qa*
The Veterinary Surgery 4 Omar St, Fereej Bin Mahmoud, 4436 7187, *dohavets.com*

EDUCATION

The standard of schooling in Qatar is very high; the facilities are excellent, teachers are well-qualified and there is a variety of curricula to suit many nationalities. Added to that, children have the benefit of being exposed to cultures and experiences beyond the scope of schooling opportunities in their home country.

The main difficulty is finding a place for your child. Many expats have turned down the invitation to come to Qatar purely because they have not been able to get their kids into school, even when applying months in advance. There are just simply not enough schools to accommodate the growing number of expat families who live here, and most have lengthy waiting lists. Some schools have to assign a portion of their quota to Qatari nationals or to ESL (English as a second language) students, which places a further limit on space availability. When new schools, or new branches of current schools, do open up, these too fill up very quickly.

School fees are expensive, so if you don't have this included as part of your employment package you will need to factor it into your budget. You may find that it is more financially viable to leave your child to continue their schooling where they are, as a boarder or in the care of family (see Overseas Schooling, p.142). Alternatively, you may consider home schooling as an option (see Home Schooling, p.140).

The school year runs from September to June, split equally between three terms: autumn (September to December), spring (January to March/April) and summer (April to June/July). Schools run from Sunday to Thursday, from around 07:30 to 14:00, and accept children from age 4.

To apply, you will need to submit an application form, a copy of your child's passport, two passport photos, a copy of their up-to-date immunisation record and a copy of their most recent school report. You will need to pay an application fee, then a deposit to secure a place, if offered. Students can join in at any time during the school year, providing there is a suitable place available.

If you can, choose a school in close proximity to where you will be living to capitalise on transit times.

Supreme Education Council > *p.ii-iii*

The body overseeing educational development in Qatar is the Supreme Education Council. Find out more about Qatar's educational developments at english.education.gov.qa.

Nurseries & Pre-Schools

Nursery is a great option for families in which both parents are working full-time. Some establishments accept babies from as young as 3 months and are either open all day, or have late afternoon pick-ups (usually for a fee). Most nurseries are far from being just day-care institutions and follow formal international curricula designed for the educational and social development of your child. The popular ones offer a good balance of learning through structured periods of educational play, promote positive nutrition and encourage open parent participation and feedback.

Even if one parent is not working, nursery is a good opportunity for your child to socialise with other children and to gain independence and self-confidence. All nurseries are open five days a week, but some will allow you to send your child for less than that. Starting with only a couple of hours per day, maybe one or two days per week, then slowly building up their attendance is a good way to ease your child into the idea of going to nursery, especially if they are not used to being away from you.

Rates depend on the age of your child and how often you wish to send them. As a rough idea, expect to pay around QR 2,000 per month (plus registration fee) for a two-year old to attend five days per week. Paying by term works out cheaper. Not all teachers and assistants are formally qualified in education, so if this is something that concerns you, be sure to enquire. You should also check whether the nursery is registered (a government requirement) by contacting the Supreme Education Council on

Education

the corner of Jaber Bin Hayyan Street and E Ring Road (4455 9555, english.education.gov.qa). Several primary schools (such as at Park House and Doha College) have nurseries attached. Students who have attended the nursery are given preference for places in kindergarten and primary, which is a bonus given that waiting lists for school places are long.

Apple Tree Nursery
Al Waab St Al Waab **4481 2147**
appletreedoha.com
Map **2 H2**
Apple Tree follows the British curriculum and uses internationally sourced learning materials. Qualified team leaders promote literacy, movement, music, and arts and crafts in an active, fun environment. Facilities include an outdoor garden, library area, designated sleeping room, sand and water play and an on-site nurse. Hours: 07:00 to 14:00; Age: 1 to 4 years

Central English Speaking Kindergarten (CESK)
Nr Doha College Fereej Al Soudan **4413 5675**
ceskonline.com
Map **2 H12**
This kindergarten offers a strong child-centred approach in a stimulating learning environment that encourages creativity, individuality and self-confidence. It features spacious outdoor play areas, complete with modern indoor and outdoor equipment and age-appropriate toys, and follows the British curriculum. Hours: 07:05-13:15; Age: 18 months to 5 years

Cocorico Nursery
Nr TV R/A, Al Jamiaa St Al Markhiya **4488 1583**
cocoriconursery.com.qa
Map **2 K2**
Offers hands-on learning, critical thinking and social skills as per the progressive learning philosophy of John Dewey. Activities include gym time, circle time, reading, and fun outdoor play to promote the development of language, literacy, gross motor and reasoning skills. Classes are in English and French based on a mixture of American and French curricula. Hours: 06:30 to 15:30, afternoon service until 18:30; Age: 2 months to 3.5 years

Creative Child Nursery School
Riviera Gardens Compound, Al Khafji St Duhail **4479 5916**
creativechilddoha.com
Map **1 E3**
A safe, fun and nurturing environment for children supported by dedicated staff. Children are encouraged to use creativity to explore their world by learning essential social skills and building self-esteem. Hours: 06:30 to 13:30; Age: 1 to 4 years

Elder Tree
Nr Ahli Club, Bilal Bin Rabah St Nuaija **4455 1020**
elder-tree.com
Map **2 R13**
A fun and friendly environment, with excellent indoor and outdoor facilities for children. Staff are committed to the educational and social fulfilment of each child in a nurturing and stimulating setting. French, Arabic & Islamic lessons are included, if desired, and late afternoon pick-up is available. Al Nu'aijah branch (also known as the Al Hilal branch) takes children from 2 months for up to six days per week with monthly or term payment (hours: 06:00 to15:30). There are other branches at Ain Khalid (4498 4984) and Al Markhiya (4488 8493), which are for kindergarten (ages 2 to 5). Attendance for these two branches is for five full days, payment is by term, and the hours are 06:30 to14:30.

The English Kindergarten
Mansour Bin Talha St, Off Al Maadeed St, Bu Samra **4468 0641**
tek.com.qa
Map **1 H12**
This kindergarten is committed to offering children a stimulating and productive experience in preparation for later schooling. The English Kindergarten features arts and crafts, puzzles, soft play, obstacle courses, dress up, circle time, music, movement, cooking and PE. An outdoor area includes a cycling track to keep the youngsters active. The facility follows the British curriculum. Hours: 06:45 to 13:00; Age: 18 months to 5 years

Fun First Nursery
Zone 66, Saha 47 Legtaifiya **4411 0953**
funfirstnursery.com
Map **1 J3**
Fun First provides a safe, nurturing environment in clean, safe surrounds. Children enjoy structured play that encourages creativity and freedom to learn through music, arts and crafts and physical activity. The curriculum follows the Early Years Foundation programme. Hours: 07:00 to 14:00 (early drop off and late pick up are available for working parents); Age: 1 to 4 years

Lifetime Nursery
Nr Al Hilal Petrol Station Al Hilal **4455 1010**
lifetimeqatar.com
Map **2 Q12**
Lifetime provides a dynamic approach to teaching and learning in a safe and happy environment. Each day is broken into a strict schedule of learning units and lessons to stimulate, educate and inspire the child. The nursery follows the American curriculum designed by Time Life International. Hours: 06:30 to 14:00; Age: 2 months to 3 years

Education City

Home Schooling

The shortage of school places available for expat children in Qatar, extensive waiting lists and the high cost of tuition fees have seen some families turning to home schooling as an option for their child's education. Home schooling can also help bridge any learning gaps that have resulted from the transition to Qatar's academic year, as might be the case for students coming from a January to December academic year, rather than the September to June year used in Qatar. The home schooling community is well established here thanks to Doha Home Educators, and student groups meet regularly to participate in classroom lessons and activities. Members organise field trips and extra-curricular activities such as tennis coaching to keep children involved and socialised.

To pursue home education, you must register as a home schooler in your own country. The institution you register with should follow the national curriculum and have government accreditation – check your home country's government website for a list of approved home educators. This will ensure that your child can successfully graduate each class year like children in regular schools, and that any awards they receive will be officially recognised.

The home education company that you have registered your child with will provide a course of downloadable tutorials and lesson plans. Your child must work through and complete these lessons and submit assignments and exams in order to pass the course. You will be able to access online study groups and classes to support your child's progress, and you can meet with other home schoolers in Doha to undertake group activities.

The difficulties you might encounter when educating at home are in designating strict times to supervise and assist your child's lessons, and in creating a quiet, distraction-free study environment. You should commit around four hours per day, preferably in the morning when you and your child are most alert. Although not a formal requirement, home schooling should take place under the supervision of a parent who is not working full-time.

For more information, contact Doha Home Educators (dohahomeeducators@gmail.com) or visit dohahomeeducators.wordpress.com for downloadable resources, links to international home schooling sites, lesson plans, access to classroom support groups and a members-only forum.

Little Angels Nursery
14 Wadi Al Qura Al Maamoura **44602 713**
littleangelsqatar.com
Map **1 H12**
This nursery aims to provide a balance between happiness and an education with an excellent early learning programme. Outside and indoor play areas keep your child busy with physical activities, singing, painting and exploration. The curriculum is loosely based on Montessori methods. Hours: 06:30 to 15:30; Age: 2 months to 4 years

Mary Poppins Nursery
Nr University R/A Onaiza **4493 1793**
Map **2 M2**
Mary Poppins Nursery is a pleasantly small nursery with a bright, friendly atmosphere. Children are split into groups according to age, with babies cared for separately. Reading, colouring, singing and music classes encourage children to develop social, educational and motor skills, and all classes are organised with an emphasis on happiness, good health and well-being. Equipment is clean and well-maintained and the staff are well-trained and dedicated to inspiring young minds. The American curriculum is followed. Hours: 06:00 to 18:00; Age: 2 months to 4 years

Mulberry Bush Nursery
Nr Greenland Plant Nursery Al Maamoura **4450 2545**
Map **1 J12**
The philosophy at this nursery is based on developmentally appropriate learning activities to build a foundation for learning, self-esteem and emotional well-being. It aims to provide creative development in a safe, happy, positive environment. The British curriculum is followed. Hours: 06:30 to 14:30; Age: 2 months to 4 years

Petits Pas
Nr University R/A, Oweina St Al Jebailat **4483 4250**
petitspasqatar.com
Map **2 L2**
Following a combination of French and American curricula, Petit Pas is the only nursery in Qatar that is a member of the World Forum Foundation (worldforumfoundation.org). Lessons are communicated in either French or English to promote learning skills in both languages, and foster a bilingual upbringing. The children enjoy a range of activities that are scheduled in the outside shaded, grassy play area or the bright indoor play room. Lunches are provided on site. Hours: 06:30 to 18:00; Age: 3 months to 4 years

Rising Stars Kindergarten
Al Wazan St Nuaija **4467 3069**
Map **1 L12**
A purpose-built kindergarten with the aim of helping children develop the skills they need for the future, and preparing them for the world of primary school. The atmosphere is fun and bright and focused on creative, emotional and intellectual development by qualified class leaders. It follows the British curriculum. Hours: 06:45 to 12:30; Age: 18 months to 5 years

Starfish Lane Kids
Nr Dahal Al Hamam R/A Al Markhiya **4487 5939**
starfishlanekids.com
Map **2 H2**
The focus here is on learning through fun in bright, colourful and happy surroundings. There is an emphasis on creativity, nutrition and positive reinforcement to promote self-esteem and good values in children. Starfish follows the Australian curriculum, and there is another branch in Al Jelaiah (4411 0355). Hours: 07:00 to 14:00, late pick-up available; Age: 1 to 4 years

Sunbeam School
Nr Al Sadd Sports Stadium, Al Bayyan Gardens Compound Fereej Al Soudan **4444 0108**
Map **2 H10**
The aim of this kindergarten is to encourage children to reach their full potential, not just academically, but developmentally. It features outdoor facilities with a shaded area and sandpit, and offers a variety of classes and activities. The British curriculum is followed, and the school also caters for pupils with special needs (p.152). Hours: 07:30 to12.45. Age: 2 to 5 years

Stop Gap Schooling
If you're moving to Qatar from a country with a different academic year, such as Australia, New Zealand and South Africa, where the school years run from January to December, a bridging programme like that at Cedars Tutoring Centre (p.144) can ensure that your child doesn't miss out on any crucial parts of the curriculum as a result of their transition.

Tiny Town Birtish Nursery
Nr Landmark Mall, Off Arab League St
Hazm Al Markhiya **4483 4553**
tinytown.com.qa
Map **1 G4**
Children are encouraged to learn through exercise, rest and play in a stimulating environment. Tiny Town has indoor and outdoor play areas, and the teaching programme covers arts and crafts, music, early maths, science, language and physical development.

The curriculum is a combination of the Early Years Foundation Stage, is complimented by the Birth to Five Matters programme and encourages learning through play. Contact Mrs Nadene Shameem on 6602 8092. Opening hours: 06:00 to15:00; Age 6 months to 4 years

Tots Corner Nursery
Al Madeed St Bu Samra **4468 8008**
Map **1 H12**
This popular nursery focuses on fun, educational play. A bright environment and plenty of activities keep children happy and content in the company of dedicated, caring staff. The mix of British, American and Australian curricula offers a range of experiences to suit every expat child. Hours: 07:00 to 14:00; Age: 1 to 4 years

Primary & Secondary Schools
The school year runs from September to June, with applications for enrolment not usually accepted before January. You will be able to get your child on the waiting list before enrolment opens if they already have a sibling at the school. Schools will accept enrolments mid-year if there is a place available. Each school has its own enrolment requirements, but generally you need to submit an application form along with the required fee. You will be invited for a formal interview and your child will need to pass an entrance exam. Shortly after, the school may offer you an actual place or a spot on their waiting list. To secure your child's place, you will need to complete a registration form, pay a fee and provide documentation including your child's passport photos, a copy of their passport and parents' passports, a copy of your child's latest school report, and a copy of their residence permit.

You may apply to more than one school, but you will need to pay a non-refundable application fee (ranging from QR 100 to QR 550) for each of your children at each school. You will then need to pay a non-refundable deposit of around QR 3,000 to QR 4,000 (per child, per school) to secure their place, or their position on the waiting list, if one is offered.

The school week runs from Sunday to Thursday from roughly 07:30 to 14:00, with reduced hours during Ramadan (usually only one hour less). The standard of teaching in the international schools is high and generally follows curricula set by Britain, America, Canada or the International Baccalaureate programmes. Most schools have reasonable facilities and offer extracurricular activities for students, but they cater for the status quo, not the budding athlete or the promising musician.

Most expats opt for schools that follow the curriculum of their home country, especially if they only plan to be in the country for a year or two.

Education

Some parents prefer the Montessori method for its relaxed approach to learning, or the International Baccalaureate programme because it is so widely compatible with national curricula throughout the world. Others simply choose a school because it is conveniently located or has a good bus service.

It is essential that you check whether your school is internationally accredited and that the graduate diploma is certifiable outside of Qatar. Furthermore, only the government schools undergo mandatory inspections; private schools (embassy schools in particular) are exempt. Private schools don't always publish their exam results so the only way of determining the academic record is to ask.

School Fees

School fees in Qatar are expensive, so it is helpful if your company includes schooling allowances in your employment package. Primary school fees range from QR 20,000 to QR 58,000 per year. Secondary school fees range from QR 30,000 to QR 58,000 per year. There are three terms per year: autumn (September to December), spring (January to March/April) and summer (April to June/July), featuring approximately 68 teaching days per term. The end of year summer break lasts from late June through to early September. Home schooling (p.140) is also available if you have trouble finding a place for your child, or if fees are beyond your budget.

When enquiring about fees, be sure to request a full breakdown of all fees and charges (including extras) and check for sibling discounts, if applicable. Many schools charge an application fee, plus a registration fee, plus an entrance assessment fee, plus an annual capital fee on top of tuition fees. If your company employer offers schooling as part of your employment package, you should check whether this applies to all years of schooling (some do not pay for pre-schooling) and if it relates to your entire school fees. Some companies may pay a portion of tuition only, or will not pay for extras such as school bus transport.

Overseas Schooling

If your child demonstrates exceptional skills in sport, music or academic disciplines, it may be beneficial to switch their schooling to your home country, where specialist training and a wider range of facilities are more likely to be available. Schools in Qatar don't offer the range of subjects, extra-curricular activities or level of competition that is available elsewhere, simply because there is not enough demand. Nor do they offer incentive programmes such as work experience or community fund-raising. The downside of overseas schooling is that your child may struggle against the social and emotional adjustment of being apart from the rest of the family. Similarly, parents may find it difficult being away from the child.

School Transport

If the school offers a bus service, ask about fees per term and the on-board behavioural policy. Some schools such as American School of Doha have very strict rules regarding riding the bus, and you will need to make sure your child is aware of the penalties for disobeying them. Ask about the bus timetable and determine where along the bus route you live, to get an idea of how long your child will be on the bus for each day. If your house is at the end of the route, you may need to get them out of bed and ready for school much earlier than you expect, and bear in mind that a long journey to and from school can be tiring, especially for children in early primary.

School Uniforms

Most private schools require students to wear a school uniform, and the cost of one entire uniform ensemble can add up quickly. Some schools require that students have school-issued PE bags or swimming caps, or expect you to purchase uniform items from a

Starting School Kirsten Holland, Assistant Head of Primary, Qatar Academy

Readying your child for school is all about talking to them. Start three months beforehand, telling them where and when they will be going to school, what kind of fun things they are going to do there, and reassure them with information such as mummy or daddy is going to take you in the morning and then mummy or daddy is going to come back in the afternoon and pick you up. Use the name of the school so that the child can build an identity and establish a rapport with it. Get them involved in the process as much as possible, drive past the school and point it out to them or show them pictures on the web if you are still overseas. About two weeks before school starts, take them to buy their uniform, new shoes and schoolbag. Don't do this any sooner than a fortnight before school starts, because firstly the items might lose their novelty if they have been looked at for too long, and secondly, children grow very quickly and you don't want tears on the first day when their uniform or shoes don't fit! If you can, take your child to visit the school and meet the teachers a week or so before they start. This will establish a familiarity that will be fresh when they finally begin their attendance. Just explain the whole process as you go, and talk, talk, talk to your child.

Research and development at Qatar Science & Technology Park

Education City

Qatar University

Education

pricey in-house shop. It is worth checking which items are compulsory and which ones can be substituted with cheaper alternatives. You may be able to save on items that don't need the school logo on them.

School Dinners

School lunches aren't normally provided, but if they do happen to be available, check the costs before signing up. Ask about the school's healthy eating policy and whether food allergens such as nuts are banned. The school should also advise you on any items banned from lunch boxes, such as fizzy drinks.

Aspire Academy

Aspire Academy is a high-profile government initiative dedicated to identifying and training the sporting elite of Qatar. Launched in 2004, the institution recruits students from local government schools and from under-developed countries throughout Asia, Africa and Latin America, to study under the leadership of coaching professionals in cutting-edge, world class facilities. The academy follows the Qatari curriculum with an emphasis on cultivating sporting prowess in students. Currently there are approximately 200 student athletes in grades 7 through to 12 receiving specialist training in football, athletics, squash, table tennis, sailing, judo, gymnastics, swimming, tennis, fencing, rowing, shooting and golf. aspire.qa

Al Jazeera Academy

Nr Palm Tree R/A Al Maamoura **4469 3777**
aja.edu.qa
Map **1 H13**
Al Jazeera offers classes from pre-school through to secondary, with boys and girls separated from year 7. The curricula followed are International for primary, and IGCSE for secondary levels, with the option to follow the IB diploma or Cambridge International Diplomas. The school has impressive sporting facilities including a 25 metre heated swimming pool, basketball, volleyball, netball and tennis courts, a football field and an athletics track.

Al Khor International School

Al Khor **4473 4666**
The school is based in the Al Khor Community, owned by Qatar Gas and RasGas. It is managed by Dubai-based Global Education Management System (GEMS) and follows the British national curriculum. It offers primary and secondary education, and has an affiliated nursery school. New premises are being built to expand the primary school's facilities and capacity to 1,700 students.

American School Of Doha

Al Bustan St Fereej Al Soudan **4459 1500**
asd.edu.qa
Map **2 H11**
The American curriculum is followed here, using the American Education Reaches Out (AERO) stimulus. ASD, originally opened in 1988, provides education from pre-kindergarten to grade 12, and is accredited by the New England Association of Schools & Colleges. There is an elementary school, middle school and high school, with teachers from the US, Canada, Europe, the Gulf region and Latin America, and although the main bulk of students are from America, the student population is drawn from over 40 countries.

The Cambridge School

Al Maadeed St Bu Samra **4469 6590**
tcsqatar.com
Map **2 H12**
Situated in Al Maamoura, The Cambridge School follows the English national curriculum from kindergarten to year 9. Its teachers are drawn from across the world, and pupils come from nearly 70 different nations. The school is run by the Taleb Group.

Cedars Tutoring Centre

Abdulla Bin Nawfat St Nuaija **4456 7499**
Map **2 R13**
This school provides British curriculum education from reception through to grade 12 in a small school environment. Its adaptable learning programme focuses on the needs of the individual, with particular attention given to those with language deficiency – both in terms of special needs and English as a second language. There is a bridging programme for recent arrivals who are out of sync with Qatar's academic year. Cedars also offers schooling to children of families who are in Doha but are still waiting for a place at their preferred school. The secondary school is located near the E Ring Road (4451 3012).

Compass International School > p.145

Al Waab Al Abareeq St Al Gharrafa **4487 7445**
cisdoha.com
Map **2 C2**
Opened in 2006, the school currently educates children from 4 to 12 years of age, but aims to offer education through to age 18. With mostly British teachers and around 400 pupils from around the world, it is a multinational school offering the international primary curriculum. Its unique selling point is a specialist Dutch language programme. It currently runs the British curriculum with plans to introduce the International Baccalaureate programme. There is another campus at Rayyan (4411 4288) and a new campus at Madinat Khalifa (4493 2036).

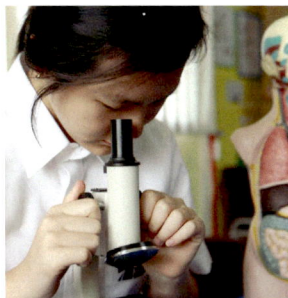

Education

Doha College > p.147
Nr Qatar Decoration R/A Fereej Al Soudan
4468 4495
dohacollege.com
Map **2 H12**
The college has been operating for over 25 years, and continues to excel with high standards of learning and achievement. Students are aged from 3 to 18 and are drawn from over 60 different nationalities; 45% of students are British. Children who attend pre-school at Doha College are normally eligible for entry into primary at the school. It follows the British curriculum.

Doha English Speaking School (DESS)
Al Wabra St Fereej Kulaib **4459 2750**
dess.org
Map **2 J4**
The range of facilities offered at this primary school includes a grassed playing area, a swimming pool and a multi-purpose hall where students can perform theatre productions on a good sized stage. The curriculum is British and priority is given to British passport-holders.

Doha Montessori British School
Nr Al Azizya R/A Ain Khaled **4450 2257**
dohabritishschool.com
Map **1 E12**
This establishment teaches the British curriculum from pre-school and has provided education for children up to year 12 since the autumn of 2010. The school has recently moved into a brand new, state-of-the-art facility that caters for a range of academic and sporting subjects. The student body comprises 65 different nationalities.

Minding The Gap
Qatar Foundation's Academic Bridge Program accepts secondary school graduates who did not meet the criteria for university entry, but wish to do so. Courses are specifically aimed at students looking to study in business, engineering, medicine, arts, foreign services and communication, but other disciplines are also catered for. 4492 7300, abp.edu.qa

German School Doha (Deutsche Schule Doha)
Osama bin Munqith St Bu Samra **4450 5209**
ds-doha.de
Map **2 J12**
The school teaches the German curriculum from a villa in Al Maamoura, and currently caters for kindergarten to year 4, with plans already in the pipeline to extend the educational range in the near future.

Qatar Foundation
Founded in 1995 by decree of the emir of Qatar, Qatar Foundation's initial aim was to simply provide educational opportunities and to improve quality of life for the people of Qatar. The foundation has since proven itself to be far more than that, with an impressive list of world-class educational and research institutes now under its wing. Projects such as Education City have attracted leaders in primary, secondary and tertiary education to Qatar's doorstep. Qatar Science & Technology Park fosters global economic and research development in a collaborative free zone environment, and Qatar National Convention Centre aims to corner the MICE market for Qatar. Ongoing diversification programmes continue to drive Qatar Foundation to the forefront of world technology and innovation (4454 0000, qf.edu.qa).

The Gulf English School
Al Gharaffa St Al Gharafa **4457 8777**
gulfenglishschool.com
Map **1 D4**
Taking pupils from pre-school to year 13, this school follows the British curriculum with Arabic and Islamic studies authorised by the Qatar Ministry for Education. Facilities include four science labs, art and media suites, a 25 metre indoor swimming pool and learner pools, sporting pitches and a gymnasium.

The International School Of Choueifat
825 Al Onaizah St Legtaifiya **4493 3110**
iscdoha-sabis.net
Map **1 J3**
International school following the SABIS Education Programme, from kindergarten to Grade 12. The school demands impeccable performance from its students through its rigorous teachings in discipline, manners and excellence. Campus includes state-of-the-art computer and science laboratories and a range of sporting facilities including an Olympic-sized swimming pool, grass football pitch, ballet studio, multipurpose courts and a gymnasium.

International School Of London Qatar > p.149
Leabaib **4499 5196**
islschools.org
Map **1 D1**
This school takes children from early childhood through to year 10, and is currently working toward full accreditation to both the International Baccalaureate organisation and Council of International Schools. Facilities include modern classrooms, a computerised library, an indoor

DOHA COLLEGE

Excellence for All, Excellence from All

Excellence recognised...

Doha College is pleased to announce its success in being accredited by:

- **Council of International Schools (CIS)**
- **British Schools in the Middle East (BSME)**
- **British Schools Overseas (BSO)**

"An excellent school ... with a credible vision"

CIS, BSME, BSO – January 2012

All three bodies paid tribute to the exceptional high quality of education we offer our students.

We would like to acknowledge the Doha College community for their support in helping us achieve this milestone.

Vision

To be recognised as one of the leading international schools in the world.

COBIS   HMC   BSME

www.dohacollege.com

Education

sports hall and lecture theatre, a full set of science laboratories and ICT rooms, as well as outdoor floodlit football and basketball courts. Plans for a swimming pool are under way.

The Japan School Of Doha
Nr Education City, West Nassiriya
qa.emb-japan.go.jp
Following a curriculum guided by the Japanese MEXT for primary and secondary schools (grades 1-9), this school is also open to non-Japanese speakers and has a wide range of extracurricular activities available. The academic year here starts on 1 April and ends on 31 March the following year.

Adult Education

There are surprisingly few short courses available in Qatar, and most of them are not advertised so do your research and ask around. The College of the North Atlantic (p.150) offers a wide variety of evening certificate courses, in subjects covering banking and finance, business, engineering, English, health sciences (including first aid), information technology, leadership and security services. You can learn a new language at one of the centres listed on p.154. Expats like Lydia Shaw (p.276) run photography workshops as part of their home business. For inspiration on other activities of interest available in Qatar, see Activities & Hobbies, p.263.

Newton International School
Lusail St Legtaifiya **4411 0014**
newtoninternationalschool.edu.qa
Map **1 J2**
Newton offers teaching for pre-school children, right through to year 9, and follows the British curriculum. Pre-school and reception are taught in a separate building from the rest of the school. Classes in these years have a maximum number of 22 children, supervised by a teacher and co-teacher, allowing for plenty of open discussion, and one-to-one tutoring, in a relatively small and focused group. Its staff are drawn from Australia, Britain, Europe and the Middle East. The secondary campus is situated at D Ring Road.

Park House English School
Nr Al Jazeera Academy Al Maamoura **4468 3800**
parkhouseschool.com
Map **1 H13**
Offering the values associated with a 'traditional British education', this excellent private school has around 1,000 pupils of some 50 nationalities, from nursery through to year 13. Founded in 1994, as one of the only international schools in Qatar, it is now based

in a new campus with a sports centre encompassing an all-weather football pitch and 25 metre swimming pool. The school has a primary department for years 1 to 6 and a separate secondary department for years 7 to 12.

Qatar Academy
Education City Al Shagub **4454 2000**
qataracademy.edu.qa
Map **2 A3**
A part of Qatar Foundation, the academy is fully accredited by the European Council of International Schools and follows the International Baccalaureate programme. It has perhaps the most impressive, classroom, academic, extra-curricular, recreational and sporting facilities in the country and offers education from early childhood through to senior years. The Al Khor branch (4454 6750) is a popular bilingual national school with an American curriculum that caters for students from kindergarten through to year 5. There are also plans to expand to senior years in the near future.

Qatar Canadian School
Nr Landmark Shopping Mall Umm Lekhba
4421 7553
qcs.edu.qa
Map **1 F4**
Taking pupils from early childhood through to year 9, Qatar Canadian School follows the Alberta education programme. Facilities are limited at the school, but access is enabled to the outstanding set-up at the nearby College of the North Atlantic (p.150).

Sherborne Qatar > *p.124*
Nr Selah Al Den School, West Nassiriya 4459 6400
sherborneqatar.org
This school is helped and enhanced by its mother school in Dorset, England, which has been in existence since 1550. The British curriculum is taught from early childhood through to year 10, with plans to educate to year 13 from September 2013 onwards. Academic and sporting facilities are excellent and there are plenty of extracurricular activities on offer for students.

University & Higher Education
Education City, the flagship project of the Qatar Foundation, has campuses from some of the best universities from North America, including Virginia Commonwealth University, Weill Cornell Medical College, Texas A&M University, Carnegie Mellon University, Northwestern University and Georgetown University. These offer a wide range of diploma and degree courses over one to four years. There are numerous courses available for students to choose from, including design art, business and computer

A Commitment to **Outstanding** International Education

- International Primary and Secondary School for ages 3-18.
- International Baccalaureate Primary, Middle and Diploma Programmes.
- One of the Supreme Education Council's outstanding schools.

PO Box 18511
North Duhail, Doha
State of Qatar
+974 4433 8600
www.islqatar.org

International School of London
Qatar

Education

Family & Education

science, medical degrees, engineering, and journalism with Northwestern University.

Tuition fees for the American institutions are exactly the same as their stateside affiliates and the qualifications achieved in Qatar equal those attained at their sister schools. The maximum cost for an undergraduate degree in Great Britain is capped at £9,000 (approximately $14,700, or QR 53,800) per year, whereas courses in the American universities often cost as much as $30,000 (£18,600, or QR 110,000) or more per year.

The national university, Qatar University, is a gender segregated, English-Arabic institution. It has a population of 8,000 students, male and female, including Qataris and children of other nationals who are living in the country, as well as scholarship students from the Middle East region.

Boys will need to get a visa through the relevant university, but girls can stay on their father's or husband's sponsorship.

Carnegie Mellon University > p.IFC
Education City Al Shagub **4454 8400**
qatar.cmu.edu
Map **2 A3**
Originally founded in Pittsburgh by the industrial magnate Andrew Carnegie, and later amalgamated with the Mellon Institute, the university is renowned for its strengths in computer science and business studies. Its information systems degree is a bachelor of science programme designed to provide a 'bridge' between human processes and computer technology.

College Of The North Atlantic Qatar
68 Al Tarafa, Duhail North Al Tarfa **4495 2222**
cna-qatar.com
Map **1 F3**
This college opened in 2002 to offer specialised courses in areas such as health sciences, information technology, engineering technology, business and banking studies. The curriculum is Canadian and qualifications are internationally accredited. Full-time and part-time studies are available.

Georgetown University School Of Foreign Service In Qatar
Education City Al Shagub **4457 8100**
qatar.sfs.georgetown.edu
Map **2 A3**
The Edmund A Walsh School of Foreign Service is the oldest and largest school of international affairs in the US. The School of Foreign Service Qatar offers a four-year liberal arts curriculum, with majors in international politics and culture & politics, leading to a BSc in foreign service. The curriculum is identical to that followed by the Washington DC campus.

Northwestern University In Qatar
Education City Al Shagub **4454 5000**
qatar.northwestern.edu
Map **2 A3**
Northwestern University offers two undergraduate degrees from the School of Communication and the Medill School of Journalism, both based in Illinois, USA. Graduates receive the equivalent qualifications to those achievable by their US counterparts. Students are offered the chance to fuse classroom lessons with real world practical work experience while also learning how to create computer animation and short films, allowing them to develop into well-rounded media students.

Qatar University
Nr Doha Golf Club Al Tarfa **4403 3333**
qu.edu.qa
Map **1 G2**
The most significant higher education institution in the country, Qatar University has several colleges including Law, Business & Economics, Arts & Sciences, and Pharmacy. With its roots stemming back to 1973 when the tiny College of Education was established by the emir, the exponential growth (it now has 28,000 graduates) mirrors the economic change experienced in Qatar. Almost all classes are single sex, with a few recent exceptions, and are taught in either Arabic or English. Priority for admission is given to Qatari students but international students may apply.

Stenden University Qatar
Nr Hamad General Hospital, Al Jelaiat St Rumaila **4488 8116**
stenden.edu.qa
Map **2 L6**
Formerly CHN University, Stenden offers bachelor degrees in international business, international hospitality and international tourism management, with full accreditation from the Dutch-Flemish Accreditation Organisation. The curriculum is based on the unique Problem Based Learning concept.

Texas A&M University At Qatar
Education City Al Shagub **4423 0010**
qatar.tamu.edu
Map **2 A3**
Since 2003, Texas A&M (formerly the Agricultural and Mechanical College of Texas) has offered courses in chemical, electrical, petroleum and mechanical engineering, mathematics, the liberal arts, and science. Tuition is in English and the programmes are identical to those taken by students in Galveston, Texas. The university encourages its students to work in groups, as they will do in their working lives, creating a strong college experience which it calls Aggie Life.

Shared Glass collaboration with Fabrica 2011

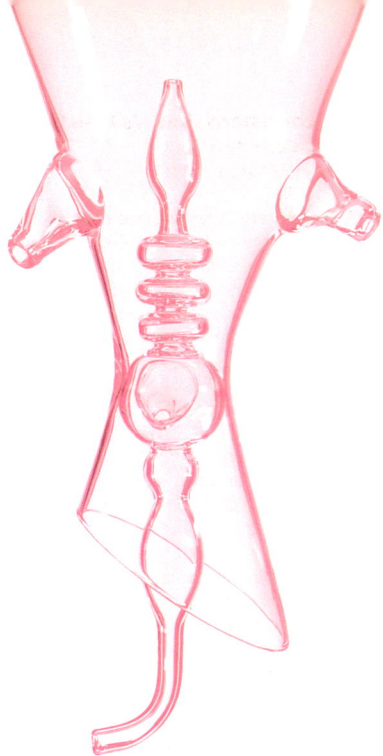

MFA.DESIGN.

The only graduate design
program in the Gulf region

www.qatar.vcu.edu/mfa

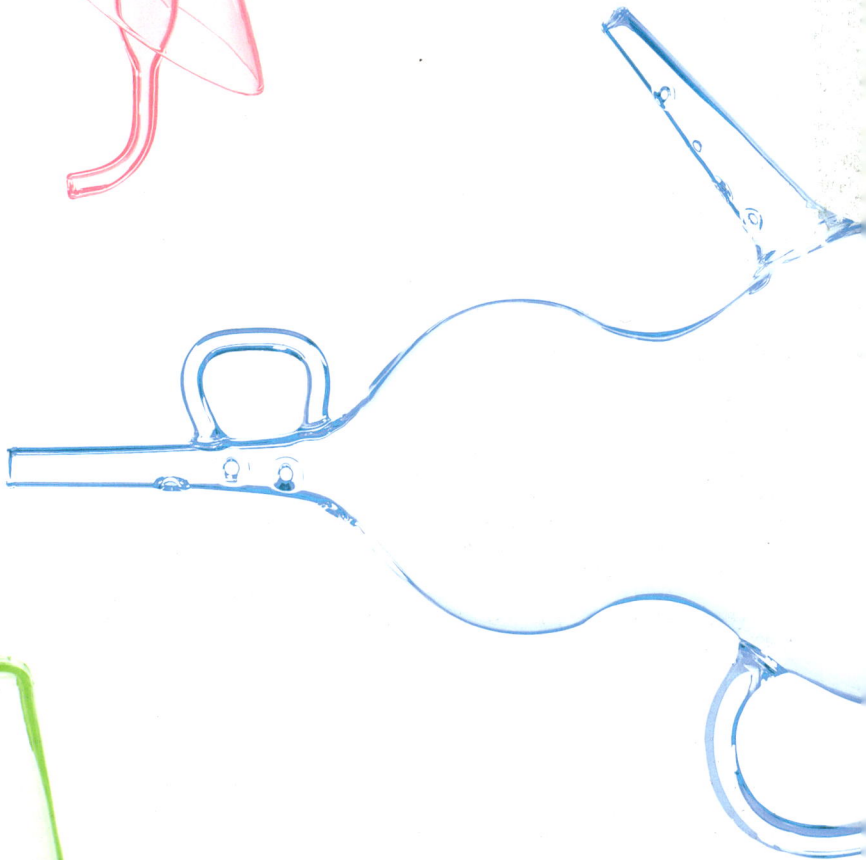

vcuqatar

virginia commonwealth university in qatar
جامعة فرجينيا كومنولث في قطر

مؤسسة قطر
Qatar Foundation

Education

School ahead

UCL Qatar > p.153

Education City Al Shagub **4457 8680**
ucl.ac.uk/qatar
Map **2 A3**

Due to welcome its first students in September 2012, this new facility offers postgraduate degrees specialising in Arab and Islamic studies, cultural heritage and archaeology. In addition, short training programmes will be offered for experienced professionals. The facility is ran in partnership with Qatar Foundation and Qatar Museum Authority.

University Of Calgary Qatar

Nr Doha Racing & Equestrian Club, Al Forousiya St
New Al Rayan **4406 5200**
qatar.ucalgary.ca
Map **1 B9**

The philosophy of this university's flexible, innovative bachelor of nursing degree is focused on evidence-based health care that encompasses the entire family, not just the patient. Graduates are educated to the same standard as students at the Calgary campus, and qualifications are fully accredited by the Canadian government. The university hopes to offer masters and doctorate degrees in the future.

Virginia Commonwealth University In Qatar (VCUQ) > p.151

Education City Al Shagub **4402 0555**
qatar.vcu.edu
Map **2 A3**

Virginia Commonwealth University (VCUQ) was established in Qatar in 1998. This branch of the Richmond-based US university offers four-year bachelor of fine arts degrees in fashion, interior and graphic design, providing a unique Arabic and Islamic context for the study of these creative subjects.

Weill Cornell Medical College In Qatar

Education City Al Shagub **4492 8800**
qatar-weill.cornell.edu
Map **2 A3**

Partnered with the Ithaca and New York City branches in the USA, this is the first American university to offer its MD courses overseas, and upon its launch in 2001, became the first medical university in Qatar. The college has progressive, world-class facilities and is heavily committed to medical research and development.

Special Needs Education

Few schools in Doha are equipped to accommodate children with learning difficulties. As part of the application process, most schools require children to attend an interview and pass an entrance exam. If any learning anomalies are identified during the testing phase, it is unlikely that your child will be offered a place in the school.

Depending on the severity of the learning deficiency, there are several options available that all offer good facilities for children with learning difficulties. However, like regular schools in Doha, places are limited, fees are expensive and there may be long waiting lists, with priority given to locals. Home schooling may be an option for you (see p.140), otherwise contact schools in advance and establish the likelihood of obtaining support for your child before you arrive.

The Learning Centre (TLC), a Qatar Foundation initiative, offers education for children with average or above-average learning potential, but who have a history of problems interfering with their academic progress. TLC cannot accommodate students with severe behavioural problems. Admission is determined after a series of educational and psychological tests.

Sunbeam Centre of Excellence is for children aged 12 and under who have learning difficulties – the curriculum is based on the British Special Educational Needs programme and the centre has qualified staff, teachers, therapists and psychologists. Children are assessed and, if accepted, are carefully matched with other children that will best suit their social skills.

Cedars Tutoring Centre (p.144) offers a limited special needs programme, where possible integrating children with learning difficulties such as ADHA, dyslexia and Down syndrome into their mainstream classes. Children with Down syndrome, cerebral palsy, autism spectrum disorders and genetic disorders can undertake intense educational therapy at Shafallah Center Services including rehabilitation, educational and vocational training, counselling for families and social awareness programmes. Places are very limited and priority is given to Qataris.

The Qatar Society for Rehabilitation of People with Special Needs (4466 3232) runs programmes

UCL

LONDON'S
GLOBAL
UNIVERSITY
HAS ARRIVED

UCL is one of the world's leading multi-disciplinary universities, and the first British university to open a campus in Qatar. At UCL Qatar we offer unique and innovative postgraduate degree programmes in the areas of archaeology, conservation, cultural heritage and museum studies:

• Archaeology of the Arab and Islamic World MA
• Conservation Studies MSc
• Museum and Gallery Practice MA

In addition, we offer short training courses for mid-career professionals working in the cultural heritage sector.

To discover more and apply online visit: www.ucl.ac.uk/qatar

UCL Qatar, PO Box 23689, Georgetown Building, Hamad bin Khalifa University, Doha, Qatar
Tel: +974 4457 8688
Email: admissions.qatar@ucl.ac.uk

Qatar Foundation
Unlocking human potential.

QATAR MUSEUMS AUTHORITY

Education

of rehabilitation and education for people affected by disability, and provides support for families. The society helps adapt houses to provide more suitable accommodation for those with special needs, and produces and imports learning aids and artificial limbs for beneficiaries.

Al Noor Institute for the Blind and the Qatar Social and Cultural Centre for the Blind cater for the visually impaired through a series of initiatives.

There is a speech and language therapy department (4439 3333/4439 7643/7645) in Rumailah Hospital. The service is open to anyone with a health card. High demand for the service means that there may be a waiting list.

Al Noor Institute For The Blind
Nr Qatar Foundation & ROTA Al Shagub **4481 3498**
Map **1 B6**
The institute caters for visually impaired people over the age of 3 years. Younger children receive care visits in their home, helping them to prepare to enter the institute once they are old enough. Job training workshops and activity programmes are available in cooperation with Al Sharq Village & Spa.

Awsaj Institute Of Education (AIE)
Education City Al Shagub **4454 2111**
tlc.edu.qa
Map **2 A3**
AIE offers a comprehensive learning programme for grades 1 to 12, based on the Alternative Education Plan (AEP). Subjects include mathematics, social studies, science, physical education, IT, English, Arabic and Islamic studies. Lessons are in English.

Qatar Social & Cultural Centre For The Blind
Nr Dahl Al Hamman Park Dahl Al Hamam **4487 7544**
blind.gov.qa
Map **2 H1**
Services available to members include courses in computers, Braille, English, crafts and sport. Field trips are also regularly enjoyed in Qatar and abroad. Free transportation is provided to and from the centre for members. Full membership is free for Qataris while affiliate membership (QR 100) is available to expats who hold a residence permit and are under 18.

Shafallah Center For Children With Special Needs
69 Lusail St Al Egla **4495 6666** shafallah.org.qa
Map **1 J1**
The centre accepts children aged between 3 and 21 years who suffer disabilities such as Down syndrome, cerebral palsy and autism. Most students suffer multiple impairments. Specially trained staff work with each student to teach independence and socialisation.

Sunbeam School
Nr Al Sadd Sports Stadium, Al Bayyan Gardens Compound Fereej Al Soudan **4444 0108**
Map **2 H10**
This centre has excellent resources and encourages self-paced working and rest times. Trained specialists offer speech and language therapy.

Special Needs Considerations Tina Santilli, principal, The Learning Centre

Several international schools in Qatar have support programmes for students with special needs, but it really depends on the severity of the learning deficiency and the willingness of the school. Some types of therapy aren't really available in the country, so Qatar is not the place for children who need intensive rehabilitation for even a mild problem such as speech correction. It is not worth sacrificing your child's health, well-being and social development, especially if your child is better off staying where a full range of support and services are available to them. Before you come to Qatar, be brutally honest about your child's needs and thoroughly research school websites to learn about their policies and type of learning support offered. Better still, pick up the phone and make your enquiries directly. Don't even think about coming to Qatar if you have a severely disabled child as there is no support at all for you and your family, unless you speak Arabic, wherein you might be able to seek help from Shafallah Centre. Special needs education is all about meeting the child's needs in a mainstream classroom environment. Everything depends on the level of support that your child requires in class, and it is this issue that scares some schools away. Don't worry about getting your child into a particular curriculum; good schooling is about the right fit, and for me, the programmes are the people.

At The Learning Centre we provide a dedicated level of specialist care to each and every child. Our class sizes have a maximum of 10 students and we actively aim to meet the educational requirements of individuals. This allows students the opportunity to receive a more personalised standard of education, tailored to their needs. We also offer an intense testing and analytical assessment of your child, should you require one, to help both parents and teachers gain an understanding of the learning abilities of the child. We do everything we can to promote the best mental, physical and social development of our students in an innovative classroom environment.

Language Courses

While English is widely spoken in Qatar, it is worth learning some basic Arabic. A few words can go a long way in terms of courtesy, and will certainly help you when dealing with government officials. Understanding Arabic is an advantage when doing business in Qatar – Arabs like to exchange pleasantries at meetings, and deals can be made or broken depending on how well you demonstrate respectfulness. Berlitz Language Center offers morning and evening classes and has a wealth of teaching experience. Arabic courses are also held at the Qatar Centre for the Presentation of Islam and are free of charge. Courses in a variety of other languages are also available.

All primary and secondary schools offer language instruction, usually in Arabic, plus either French, Spanish or Dutch. If English is a second language for your child, Cedars Tutoring Centre (p.144) can offer additional support in a mainstream environment.

Alexander Language Centre Arabic, English, French, Spanish. Al Aghsan Square, Fereej Al Soudan, 4436 4425, *als-alexander.org*

Bell Doha English Language Centre English Nr Souq Al Ali, Al Luqta, 4488 0823, *belldoha.com*
Berlitz Arabic, English, Dutch, Farsi, French, German, Italian, Japanese, Mandarin, Portuguese, Russian, Spanish and Urdu. E Ring Rd, Al Thumama, 4455 0506, *berlitz.ae*
British Council English courses for adults and young learners. 203 Al Sadd St, Al Sadd, 4425 1888, *britishcouncil.org/me-qatar*
English Language Services English Nr Abu Hamour Clinic, 990 Mesaimeer St, Bu Hamour, 4469 9223, *elsmea.com*
French Institute Of Qatar French 135 Al Inshirah St, Onaiza, 4493 0863, *institutfrancais-qatar.com*
German School Doha (Deutsche Schule Doha) German Osama bin Munqith St, Bu Samra, 4450 5209, *ds-doha.de*
Qatar Centre For The Presentation Of Islam Free classes in Arabic and Islamic Studies. Nr Doha English Speaking School, Fereej Kulaib, 4441 1122, *islamweb.net.qa*
Qatar Guest Center Arabic and Islamic Studies Kab Bin Malek St, Airport Rd, 4486 2390, *qgc.com.qa*
Score Plus Qatar English Al Kuwari Bldg, Al Sadd, 4436 8580, *score-plus.com*

Qatar University

Dr. Maroun Khoury
Consultant
Hematology/Oncology

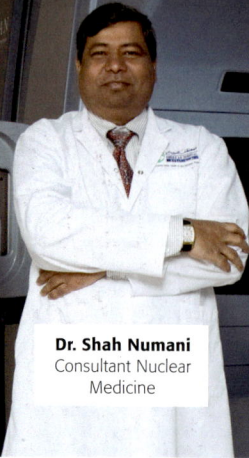

Dr. Shah Numani
Consultant Nuclear
Medicine

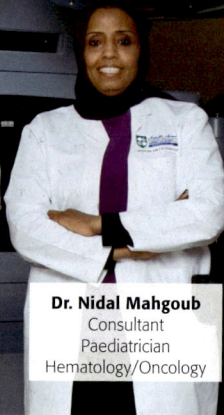

Dr. Nidal Mahgoub
Consultant
Paediatrician
Hematology/Oncology

Dr. Salim Chaib-Rassou
Consultant Radiation
Oncology

In your battle **against cancer**
Think of us as **your army**

The Regional Center for Cancer Care at American Hospital Dubai

Cancer not only affects your health, but also your family and lifestyle. Understanding this, the American Hospital Cancer Care Facility offers a range of current Medical Oncology and Hematology services for adults and children. Our specialists are American Board Certified (or equivalent) and are supported by a team of expert staff trained in advanced cancer treatment techniques in the region.

Clinical Offerings
• Medical Hematology Oncology • Pediatric Hematology Oncology • Radiation Oncology
• Surgery • Palliative Care • Multidisciplinary Approach

For more information, please contact +971-4-377-6369

المستشفى الأمريكي
AMERICAN HOSPITAL
D U B A I   دبي

Delivering better health in the Middle East

Organization Accredited
by Joint Commission International

www.ahdubai.com

The first hospital in the Middle East to be awarded Joint Commission International Accreditation (JCIA)

The first private laboratory to be certified by the College of American Pathologists (CAP)

Health, Fitness & Well-Being

HEALTH

Qatar offers its residents a particularly high standard of healthcare. Both public and private facilities are available, and English is spoken in all establishments.

The country's public health service provides free and low-cost health care for nationals, and these services are also available to expats in possession of a government health card. Medical insurance is normally required to use private health facilities, which is something that many (but not all) employers will provide as a benefit, or else can be taken out by the individual.

The country's relatively small population, combined with the high number of medical institutions, means long waiting lists are not generally a problem in either public or private hospitals (except in the case of some obstetrics and gynaecology services, see p.166). Expats are increasingly using government facilities. However, for many expats the first stop for medical issues is usually a private hospital or polyclinic. These handle everything from general medical complaints that you may see a GP about in some countries, to more serious conditions. The Supreme Council of Health's website (sch.gov.qa) provides a regularly updated list of licensed healthcare practitioners as well as information on the location of health centres and pharmacies.

Healthcare in Qatar is expected to continue to improve under Qatar's six-year National Health Strategy (2011-16) with emphasis placed on educating local health professionals, national health insurance, pharmaceutical production and prevention.

Government Healthcare

At the centre of Qatar's public health system is the Hamad Medical Corporation (HMC), the government's public health care provider. HMC is a network of 40 health centres, 80 dental centres, and a handful of public hospitals in Doha. Of these, Hamad General Hospital, the Women's Hospital, Rumailah Hospital and Al Amal Hospital are located in the Freej Bin Mahmoud area. Al Khor Hospital is situated to the north of the capital. The standards of HMC facilities are excellent, with first rate equipment and many expat specialists on staff. Hamad is recognised as a regional centre of excellence for severe liver disease and infant inherited metabolic disorders, and is increasing focus on organ donation and transplant services.

Hamad is expanding rapidly. In May 2011 the Heart Hospitals Outpatient Clinic opened within Hamad Medical City. A Skilled Nursing Facility is to open in 2014 and plans for Skilled Nursing and Physical Medicine and Rehabilitation, a Children's Hospital and a new Women's Hospital are underway.

Hamad General Hospital houses Doha's main accident and emergency facility, which is probably the most common part of the government health system accessed by expats. There is also an A&E at Al Khor.

For non-emergency treatment, your nearest HMC clinic or healthcare centre will be able to tend to your needs and will refer you to a hospital for further treatment if necessary.

Hamad Medical City

Medical Corporation, Hamad Medical City already contains several hospitals – Hamad General and the Women's Hospital were the first ones to open, followed up by the Fahad Bin Jassim Kidney Centre and the Heart Hospital in 2011. There's also a dedicated cancer research facility and due to open over the coming years are a children's hospital established in partnership with Toronto's Hospital for Sick Children, a rehabilitative care centre for the elderly, plus a medical training facility. Find out more at hmc.org.qa.

The healthcare centres, known as primary health care centres or polyclinics, are available in most main suburbs of Doha and various regional towns around Qatar, and can be identified by a green hexagonal sign outside. Additional facilities at some centres include Healthy Woman, maternity and paediatric clinics, accident and emergency units, dental services, ophthalmology and cardiology specialists.

Waiting times for some specialised services, such as MRI scans, have been reduced with the extension of operating hours. A new primary health care centre for single workers in Abu Nakhla will relieve some of the workload away from Hamad.

For more information on the locations and facilities of the various clinics, see p.160 or visit hmc.org.qa.

Health Card

All residents are entitled to a health card, which is necessary to be seen by a doctor at a government clinic or hospital, and entitles the bearer to subsidised treatment. Your company will usually assist you in obtaining a card, or you can go through the process yourself (see Becoming A Resident, p.29, for details). The Qatar National Health Card, a combined Qatar Identification Card and a health card, is expected to be introduced shortly by the new E-Health Department.

Private Healthcare

Doha has a number of private clinics (also known as polyclinics) and hospitals. Medical facilities are generally of a high standard, waiting times are short, and doctors and nursing staff are well trained and responsive. Unlike in some countries where you may have a family doctor, it can be 'pot luck' who you see when attending clinics.

Many expats have private healthcare for themselves, and sometimes their families, included in their employment packages. Most international companies enrol employees on private health insurance schemes, while some (such as oil and gas firms) have their own medical clinics. Often, Qatari companies do not provide private health insurance, but will pay the QR 100 fee for your government health card (see p.43).

It is not mandatory to have health insurance in Qatar, although the government is considering the introduction of a national insurance scheme for all residents. However, if your preference is for a private medical facility over a public one then it is worth taking out some form of cover as it will offset the relatively high cost of private medical care, as well as giving you more choice over where you get treatment.

There are a large number of international companies specialising in private health insurance in Qatar and elsewhere. Comprehensive health insurance costs from around QR 200 per month for single-person policies, and QR 400 plus for families for regional coverage.

Some international insurance companies offer cover specifically for expats, which includes the cost of hospitalisation, dentistry, some alternative therapies, and medications. You can also pay extra for other options such as medical evacuation to another country in the case of serious accidents or illnesses.

It is important to make sure you are fully aware of exactly what your policy covers before you take it out, and where you stand in terms of issues such as maternity costs and pre-existing conditions.

When you arrive for private healthcare the hospital may require approval or verification from your employer before authorising some forms of treatment – particularly the more expensive ones – and may not just take your insurance card as proof you are insured.

At other times you may be required to show proof that you have the funds already in place to be able to pay, usually by pre-authorising a certain amount on your credit card. Also note that the waiting timeframe for some insurance companies can be very slow, so it's best to be prepared.

For a list of companies providing healthcare insurance, see Insurance Companies, p.114.

Accidents & Emergencies

If you are ever in the situation where you, or someone you know, needs emergency medical treatment, Hamad General Hospital is the place to head (see p.164). Its A&E centre is considered world class and is open to all, regardless of insurance status. The Women's Hospital (p.166) deals with medical emergencies relating to childbirth.

HMC also operates emergency medical service departments at its medical centres in Abu Baker

Siddiq, Airport, Al Sheehaniyah, Mesaimer, Umm Gwailina, Umm Salal, Al Khor, Al Wakra, Al Rayyan, Al Murrah and Al Shamal (see Government Health Care Centres, p.160).

Emergency Numbers

Ambulance, Police & Fire 999
American Hospital (private) > *p.156* 4442 1999
Al Ahli Hospital (private) 4489 8888
Doha Clinic Hospital Emergency (private) 4438 4211
Hamad General Hospital 4439 4444

For urgent treatment for minors, the Pediatric Emergency Center (4439 2948) is located on the corner of Al Sadd Road and Bin Hamad Street.

Al Ahli Hospital (p.163) operates its own smaller A&E section which is open to all, but as a private clinic you will be charged for any services.

If your condition requires an ambulance, call 999. You'll need to give a nearby landmark, and if possible arrange for someone to show the ambulance crew to a villa or apartment if it is a difficult location to find.

The ambulance service, also run by HMC, is remarkably good, given the state of the traffic in Doha. It is staffed by highly trained EMS teams who are fluent in English. Response times are generally good in Doha, but expect delays in remote areas such as Al Shamal or desert locations.

General Medical Care

Government clinics are found throughout Qatar and are clearly marked with a large green hexagon on the front of the building. When you apply for a health card, you will be assigned a clinic based on your address (bring a copy of your lease or electricity bill when applying). The implementation of an electronic number system has reduced waiting times, but you may still be in for a lengthy wait at the health centre depending on the time of day. See the list below for details of the specialties covered at your local clinic; be aware that specialties are normally covered by a visiting physician and so are usually only available on one or two days a week. You can find out timings of the different specialty clinics by calling the polyclinic or visiting sch.gov.qa. If you require treatment from a specialist not listed, your local health centre should be able to refer you to a clinic or hospital that can help. As the reputation of local health services rises, more expats are choosing to use the government system.

Many expats still opt for a private hospital or polyclinic for day-to-day health issues. These handle all medical issues from general complaints through to more serious conditions, surgery and treatment. While most of these clinics operate on a walk-in basis, private hospitals tend to require that you check-in at

Health, Fitness & Well-Being

a service desk, where they will take copies of your ID and your insurance cards or proof that you can pay (usually a credit card).

If you are seeking private specialist services, you can usually call ahead to make an appointment. In some specialist fields, such as women's health and obstetrics, you can choose your doctor and make appointments for future visits.

If the situation is urgent, go directly to the A&E unit of the hospital (see p.163) and you will be seen almost immediately, first by a triage nurse who will assess you, then by a doctor.

Most clinics are not proactive, so the onus is on the individual to be vigilant about ensuring you are up to date on your annual checkups. Many expats wait until their yearly visit to their home countries for these more routine checks, but some clinics, such as the Apollo Clinic (p.161) in Fareej Bin Dirhem, offer well woman and man packages that cover a variety of checks including blood pressure, cholesterol and women specific checks including pap smears, usually for a fee of around QR 500 upwards.

Government Health Centres

Abu Bakr Al Sidiq Health Center Specialist services offered: cardiology, diabetic care, gynaecology, dental, x-rays, New Fereej Al Ghanim 4468 1795, *phcc.qa*

Airport Health Center Specialist services offered: cardiology, ophthalmology, ENT, gynaecology, dental, x-rays. Nr Family Food Center, Al Matar St, Old Airport, 4467 5633, *phcc.qa*

Al Jumailiya Health Center Specialist services offered: gynaecology, dental na, 4478 6338, *phcc.qa*

Al Khor Health Center Specialist services offered: cardiology, diabetic care, ENT, gynaecology, ophthalmology, dental, x-rays. 4472 0224, *phcc.qa*

Al Muntazah Health Center Specialist services offered: cardiology, diabetic care, ophthalmology, gynaecology, ENT, dental, x-rays Rawdat Al Khail, 4443 5784, *phcc.qa*

Al Rayyan Health Center Specialist services offered: general medicine Off Al Rayyan Al Jadeed St, Old Al Rayyan, 4481 2668, *phcc.qa*

Al Shahania Health Center Specialist services offered: diabetic care, gynaecology, dental, 4471 8995, *phcc.qa*

Al Shamal Health Center Specialist services offered: diabetic care, ophthalmology, ENT, gynaecology, paediatrics, dental, x-rays 4473 1232, *phcc.qa*

Al Wakrah Health Center Specialist services offered: cardiology, diabetic care, ophthalmology, gynaecology, dental, x-rays. 4464 4450, *phcc.qa*

Madinat Khalifa Health Center Specialist services offered: cardiology, diabetic care, ophthalmology, gynaecology, ENT, nutrition, dental, x-rays Khalifa St, Madinat Khalifa South, 4486 2655, *phcc.qa*

Mosquitoes

Mosquitoes can be a problem in Qatar; you'll notice them mainly in the months when there is rain (usually December to February) and in the months when the humidity is high (usually July to September). Mozzies seem to be more prevalent in areas that once were marshlands, such as Al Azizya, Al Waab and Al Muraikh.

Mosquito-repellent sprays and plug-ins are available at most supermarkets as well as the larger hypermarkets such as Carrefour (p.325) and Lulu (p.325). If you prefer natural remedies, some pharmacies stock herbal oils, including citronella oil which is said to be a natural repellent. Carrefour usually stocks citronella candles in the camping section and, occasionally, Home Centre will have citronella sticks. Wearing long-sleeved shirts and long trousers are also a good way to avoid being bitten. Malaria is not endemic in Qatar and there are no anopheline mosquitoes here to act as carriers. However, malaria cases are being seen more frequently among the large immigrant labour force who originate from malarial regions such as Pakistan, India, Thailand, Indonesia, Sri Lanka, Sudan and Yemen.

Mesaieed Medical Center Specialist services offered: general medicine Nr MIC Management Bldg, Mesaieed, 4422 3168, *mic.com.qa*

Omar Bin Khattab Health Center Specialist services offered: diabetic care, gynaecology Al Qafila St, New Slata, 4466 7374, *phcc.qa*

Umm Ghuwalina Health Center Specialist services offered: cardiology, diabetic care, gynaecology, dental Umm Ghuwailina, 4443 3892, *phcc.qa*

Umm Salal Health Center Specialist services offered: gynaecology, diabetic care, dental, x-rays na, 4478 9236, *phcc.qa*

West Bay Health Center Specialist services offered: cardiology, diabetic care, gynaecology, dental, x-rays Nr Al Meera Supermarket, Hazm Al Markhiya, 4483 7790, *phcc.qa*

Private Health Centres & Clinics

Al Shefa Polyclinic
Muntazah St Nuaija **4466 0330**
alshefapolyclinic.com
Map **2 Q12**
A full service polyclinic with specialities including internal medicine, dermatology, venereology, orthodontic, ophthalmology, paediatrics, x-ray, MRI, ENT, orthopaedic, speech therapy, obstetrics, gynaecology, ultrasounds, acupuncture and an in-house laboratory.

The Apollo Clinic Qatar
Nr Hafsa Signal, Al Muntazah St Fereej Bin Dirhem
4441 8441
apolloqatar.com
Map **2 Q9**
The largest private polyclinic in Qatar; it's often busy, but delivers good medical care. It handles general and serious complaints. Physicians specialise in internal medicine, obstetrics, gynaecology, paediatrics, endocrinology, diabetology, dermatology, ENT, general surgery, ophthalmology, orthopaedics, pulmonology, dentistry and provide many diagnostic procedures including x-ray, 4-D ultrasound, ECG, PFT and TMT.

Aster Medical Centre
Nr Jaidah Flyover, Wadi Musherib St Musheireb
4444 0499
aster.com.qa
Map **2 P8**
This clinic has general practitioners plus specialists in paediatrics, ENT, obstetrics, gynaecology, dentistry, ophthalmology, orthopaedics, internal medicine, x-ray and dermatology.

Dr Amina's Clinic
Nr Pearl R/A, Al Wakrah **4463 2474**
Map **Qatar Country Map D4**
A private practice specialising in ear, nose and throat. Clinic hours are Saturday to Thursday, 08:00-12:00 and 16:00-20:00; closed on Fridays.

Dr Hassan Al Abdulla Medical Center
250 D Ring Rd Old Airport **4432 3900**
drhassanmedical.com
Map **2 U12**
Dr Hassan specialises in dermatology and venereology. Services at this clinic include laser treatment, plastic surgery and anti-ageing therapies. There is also a dental clinic onsite with dentists specialising in root canals, orthodontics (braces), paediatric dentistry, and oral surgery.

Dr Jagan Chacko
Nr National Showroom, Al Musherib St Musheireb
4444 7879
Map **2 Q8**
A small, private practice run by Dr Chacko that specialises in internal medicine.

Dr Mohammed Ameen Zabib Clinic
Jablah Bin Malik St Bu Hamour **4468 5444**
Map **2 H13**
This private clinic specialises in gastroenterology. The opening times are between 09:00-12:00 and 17:00-19:30.

Dr Mohan Thomas
Nr Centrepoint, Al Sadd St Al Sadd **4444 8899**
Map **2 K8**
A solo practice specialising in ear, nose, and throat. Clinic hours are Saturday to Thursday, 08:00-12:00 and 16:00-20:00; closed on Fridays.

Dr Mohanan's Clinic
Nr Pizza Hut, Dhakira Rd Al Khor **4472 1202**
Map **Qatar Country Map C2**
Dr Mohanan is a physician and GP with more than 30 years experience, based in Al Khor.

Elaj Medical Centre
Commercial Centre, Salwa Rd Rawdat Al Khail
4443 1254
elajqatar.com
Map **2 N9**
Multi-speciality practice offering a number of services including internal medicine, urology, dermatology and rheumatology.

Future Medical Center
Nr Villaggio Mall, Al Waab St Al Aziziya **4451 0051**
fmcdoha.com
Map **2 C12**
Large, multi-specialty clinic with physicians specialising in a number of areas including aviation medicine, cardiology, dermatology, cosmetology, endocrinology, ENT, gastroenterology, general surgery, internal medicine, nephrology, neurology, obstetrics, gynaecology, ophthalmology, orthopaedics, paediatrics and urology. Future Medical Center is open Saturday to Thursday, 08:00-22:00. The Center is closed on Fridays.

KIMS Qatar Medical Centre
Abdulrahman Bin Jassim Al Thani St, Al Wakra
4463 1864
kqmc.com.qa
Map **Qatar Country Map D4**
Dr KMR Mathew is a general surgeon and is the medical director of this clinic. The clinic also employs specialists in orthopaedics, gynaecology, paediatrics and ENT, and there are two dentists.

Naseem Al Rabeeh Medical Centre
Nr Tadamon Petrol Station, D-Ring Rd Nuaija
4465 2121
naseemalrabeeh.com
Map **2 P12**
A multi-specialty clinic with physicians specialising in general medicine, dermatology, paediatrics, ENT, ophthalmology, orthopaedics, gynaecology, radiology and dentistry. Clinic hours are Saturday to Thursday, 07:00 to midnight and Friday from 16:00 to 22:00.

Pharmacies & Medication

Pharmacies are ubiquitous in Qatar. You can find one on almost every street corner and in every strip mall, or shopping mall. Many are open 24 hours and in some instances you can arrange to have your medications delivered to you. Go into your local pharmacy and ask, as this is usually an unadvertised service, so be sure to tip the delivery driver. This service is especially useful for those who take medications on a regular basis such as blood pressure medications and diabetic supplies, or if you wake up too awful to get out of bed.

Medical History

It's worth requesting a copy of your medical history from your GP practice at home and giving it to your new clinic to ensure your medical background is taken into consideration when you seek medical advice. Most insurance policies don't cover holiday vaccinations, so if you plan to travel beyond Qatar, you can save yourself a lot of money and needles if you have a record of which jabs you've already had and the date they were administered.

Each pharmacy is staffed with a qualified pharmacist who is licensed under the Ministry of Health regulations. The pharmacists are knowledgeable and can be consulted for medical advice, but if you have any pre-existing conditions, or are uncertain what's wrong with you, it is always prudent to check with your physician first.

A number of drugs available in Qatar are sold under different brand names to the ones you might be familiar with back home; ask the pharmacist if you are having trouble finding the brand you are accustomed to using as it may be right under your nose on the shelf, hiding behind a different name. Instructions for prescriptions are printed in English, but you should always notify the pharmacist of any other medications you are taking, and whether or not there are any contraindications. Most pharmacies also stock other products such as vitamins, baby care items (such as nappies, wipes, dummies, bottles and so on), skin care products, perfumes, dental care items, blood pressure monitors, blood sugar monitors, bathroom scales, and other toiletries.

Medication is readily available in Qatar. If you are seen by your doctor for a medical condition, even if it's minor, chances are you will leave with one or more prescriptions. A lot of this has to do with culture, as many believe that if you leave the office without a prescription, then the doctor is not a very good clinician. Certain drugs do need a prescription, such as controlled narcotics and antibiotics, just as they would in most countries. On the other hand, drugs such as birth control pills and contraceptives, high dosage

ibuprofen, and even Tamiflu are available over the counter. These drugs would require a prescription in most countries. However, there are certain drugs that you can get over the counter in most countries that do require a prescription in Qatar. If you are bringing a prescription with you from your doctor in your home country, be aware that you may have to renew your prescription with a local doctor as most pharmacies are not authorised to accept prescriptions from foreign countries.

Some pharmacies do import brands from western countries (e.g. Tylenol, Advil, Motrin). If you see a medication you are accustomed to using back home, it might be a good idea to stock up as you never know when you may see it again. If you do stock up, just be aware of the expiration dates and be prepared to pay about double the price you would pay back home.

Prescription medications are generally more expensive in private pharmacies. If you take a medication on a regular basis, it may be wise to obtain a government health card and use one of the government hospitals or clinic pharmacies. There you will find the same medication for virtually next to nothing, or free of charge. Government pharmacies do not honour prescriptions from private clinics.

Prohibited Medications

There are common medications that are banned in Qatar that may be available over the counter or on prescription in other countries. The most common banned drug is codeine which is usually prescribed in tablet form or added to some cough syrups. All GCC countries are discussing a likely ban on e-cigarettes. A ban is in place on the anti-obesity drug, Reductil Sibutramine and, more recently, Avandia, a controversial drug used to fight diabetes. There is also a ban on the use of some tranquilisers, anti-depressants and certain sleeping pills. They are used only in psychiatric patients in extreme cases. Ironically, antidepressants of the SSRI class (such as Paxil or Prozac) are available over the counter. If you use any of the banned medications and carry them with you or travel with them, make sure you have a doctor's prescription or letter confirming your dependence on them. Make sure you bring enough with you as you are unlikely to find these drugs in Qatar. On the other hand, don't overdo it or you may be suspected of possession of illegal drugs for sale. Qatar has a zero tolerance policy for drug trafficking and possession. Offenders risk jail time and hefty fines.

A definitive list of substances that are banned in Qatar can be obtained by visiting the Supreme Council of Health (sch.gov.qa, 4407 0000).

Al Afifa Pharmacy Al Waab St, Al Waab, 4444 0567
Al Bateel Pharmacy Fereej Al Nasr, 4436 6610
Al Fateh Pharmacy Al Aziziya, 4447 6190

Al Noor Pharmacy Fereej Al Soudan, 4450 5625
Al Ousra Pharmacy Electricity St, 4432 0567
Al Salam Pharmacy Fereej Al Soudan, 4466 5551
Diplomat Pharmacy Al Dafna, 4483 9566
Future Pharmacy Al Sadd, 4432 5374
Hyatt Pharmacy Najma, 4435 1165
Khulood Pharmacy Al Markhiya, 4487 7784
Makka Pharmacy Fereej Bin Mahmoud, 4413 1533
Queen Pharmacy Old Airport, 4465 4520

Main Hospitals

The standard of hospitals in Qatar is generally high, both in the public and private sectors, although some patients may find a lack of the sympathetic bedside manner that they may be used to in their home countries. The government has identified healthcare as one of its major priorities in Qatar National Vision 2030 (p.16) and has upgraded all of the country's public hospitals in recent times. The best private hospitals usually boast top-of-the range facilities and specialists, and, for expats who have insurance (p.114), tend to be the preferred choice due to their added comfort, familiarity and ease of access. Some of the polyclinics (see p.160) also offer facilities that you might associate with hospitals in other parts of the world.

Some of the departments in Doha's private hospitals operate in a similar way to private clinics, dealing with general medical care and accepting walk-in patients. If you live close to a hospital, it's worth checking what services they offer, as you might save yourself a drive to a clinic located further away.

Al Ahli Hospital
Ahmed Bin Ali St, Wadi Al Sail **4489 8888**
ahlihospital.com
Map **2 K5**

More like a luxury hotel, Al Ahli is considered to be one of the best private hospitals in Doha. Its lobby and private rooms are constructed around a five-star hotel concept, offering maternity suites and other amenities. There is a 24 hour emergency unit, paediatric care, obstetrics and gynaecological units, chiropractic medicine clinic, as well as a general medical service. The hospital also houses a fertility and IVF clinic.

Al Emadi Hospital
Al Hilal West (D-Ring Rd) Nuaija **4466 6009**
alemadihospital.com.qa
Map **2 R12**

This private hospital has facilities for eating disorders, general, plastic, reconstructive and orthopaedic surgery, dermatology, ENT, rheumatology and maternity, plus there is a dental clinic and an ophthalmology department. It also has an excellent family medicine practice with resident paediatricians and a gynaecology unit, and is also popular within the expat community.

GIVING BLOOD

Giving blood is not as common a practice in Qatar as it is in some other parts of the world. However, many companies and expat organisations organise blood donation drives as part of their charity work in the community. Many Muslims also donate during Ramadan.

While rare, you may occasionally see donation drives at educational institutions such as Qatar Foundation's campus in Education City (qf.org.qa). More frequently, embassies and local volunteer organisations are starting to sponsor drives in shopping malls and at other sites. Keep an eye on the newspapers such as *Gulf Times*, *Qatar Tribune* or *The Peninsula*, which often list community events such as blood drives. Online forums are also a good source of local information (see p.23) and their own social groups often hold donation days.

Doha's main blood donation centre is located inside the grounds of HMC, near the main entrance.

You need to register initially and be checked that you are in good health. You must also be between 18 and 60 years old and weigh at least 50kg. Once registered and cleared, you are taken to the donation room. The donation process itself takes under 20 minutes and less than 500ml of blood is taken.

Another way to give blood is to look for the HMC Mobile Blood Donation Van which travels to work places, as well as to big events including Qatar Heath Expo at the Qatar Convention Center each December. For more information see hmc.org.qa.

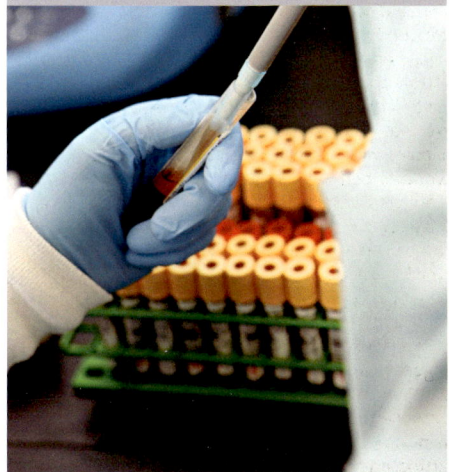

Al Khor Hospital

Al Khor Main Rd Al Khor **4474 5446**
hmc.org.qa
Map **Qatar Country Map C2**
A modern government hospital servicing the thriving
coastal community, this is a full service general
hospital and has recently been expanded. With 116
beds, this government hospital also provides full
outpatient services and is equipped with an ICU, a
pulmonary function test lab and an endoscopy unit. It
also houses Qatar's first breastfeeding centre.

Al Wakra Hospital

Wkeir St Al Wakrah
hmc.org.qa
Map **Qatar Country Map D4**
Open since May 2011, this hospital has 305 beds
and offers health services from maternity care to
surgical operations and emergency care, including a
specialised pediatric emergency clinic.

American Hospital > *p.156*

Nr Radisson Blu Hotel Rawdat Al Khail **4442 1999**
Map **2 N11**
This private hospital has an emergency department
as well as paediatric, obstetrics and gynaecology
units, and it deals with general surgery, orthopaedics,
internal medicine, urology and cardiology. The facility
also houses a diabetic counselling service, a physical
therapy unit and a pharmacy.

Doha Clinic Hospital

Al Mirqab Al Jadeed St Al Sadd **4438 4333**
doha-hospital.com
Map **2 L9**
One of the older private medical facilities in Qatar,
this hospital originally opened as a clinic and, after

numerous renovations, has become one of the most
popular hospitals among expats. While husbands are
not allowed to be present during a C-section at all
hospitals, some expat mums have been able to obtain
approval at this hospital. There are outpatient and
inpatient facilities, which include an x-ray department,
maternity ward and emergency room.

Fahad Bin Jassim Kidney Centre

Nr HMC Fereej Bin Omran **4439 4888**
hmc.org.qa
Map **2 K6**
Part of Hamad Medical Corporation, this state-of-
the-art centre provides care to those suffering from
chronic and acute kidney diseases. It is equipped with
80 dialysis units and 20 private rooms.

Hamad General Hospital

Nr Women's Hospital, Al Rayyan Rd
Hamad Medical City **4439 4444**
hmc.org.qa
Map **2 L7**
Qatar's main government hospital, Hamad has
facilities for surgery, paediatrics, internal diseases,
diabetes, cardiac, anaesthetics and laboratory work.
It also has Doha's primary A&E department, and this
is the place that you are likely to end up should you
experience any sort of emergency, as it is the country's
most advanced and best-equipped facility.

Heart Hospital

Nr Rumailah Hospital & NCCCR Rumaila
hmc.org.qa
Map **2 M7**
Formerly known as the Cardiology Hospital. It is
located next to Rumailah and Al Amal Hospitals in
the Hamad Medical City complex. The Outpatient

Rumailah Hospital

Common Health Complaints

While you are likely to enjoy a generous slice of the good life in Qatar, the sedentary lifestyle, brunches and dusty, dry conditions can take their toll. Here are a few health complaints that you should be aware of.

Bugs

Air conditioning in homes, malls, hotels and offices can feel positively subzero at times, and moving from 40°C outside heat to an icy 18°C indoor climate several times a day can cause a few problems, as can the recycled air that is pumped through air-conditioning units. Furthermore, as Qatar is a transitory place, the many people that come and go from across the globe bring different kinds of germs and bugs with them, meaning your immune system can take a beating. Maintaining an active lifestyle and a good diet will help to fight off those unwanted lurgies. If you do find yourself coming down with a dose of the Doha sniffles, make sure to keep yourself hydrated by drinking plenty of water, and take an extra layer with you to guard against the low air-conditioning temperatures. As a home to international bugs, it's worth keeping a closer eye on your children too; if any strange symptoms occur, a trip to the doctor may be in order.

Putting On The Pounds

When summer arrives the heat and humidity drive many people indoors for a summer of stagnating. Adding to the already unhealthy car culture and all-you-can-eat brunches, it's not uncommon to find a few extra inches appearing around your waistline. Fortunately, there is a good range of gyms and health clubs in Qatar where you can work off the excess, as well as year-round indoor swimming, tennis and squash facilities – so there's no excuse, even in the summer. See Fitness, p.177, for more details.

Diabetes

More people in Qatar die from diabetes-related illnesses than any other condition, and an estimated 20% of the population are sufferers, with the majority of cases being diet-related Type 2. Being overweight is a major contributing factor and local estimates put obesity among children at 40%. The government has launched awareness campaigns to educate the community about cause and prevention. The Qatar Diabetes Association (p.134) is a good source of information and if you suspect that you or your child may have diabetes, all hospitals and polyclinics have diabetes units.

Sun Safety

It goes without saying that extra sun care needs to be taken when out and about in Qatar. The hot sun and high temperatures are recipes for sunburn and heat stroke if you are not prepared. Sun block is widely available in supermarkets and pharmacies. Sun hats, sun glasses, light, loose clothing that covers your limbs, and seeking shade are recommended during the hotter parts of the day and during the summer months. With high temperatures throughout the year, make sure that you drink enough water to remain hydrated; this is particularly important when you exercise and in the summer. Keep a couple of bottles of water in the car in case of emergencies – if you breakdown during the summer, you may be faced with an uncomfortable wait while the police or recovery truck comes to the rescue. You should also be aware of any changes to your skin, such as new moles or ones that change shape or colour, or bleed. Contact a dermatologist immediately if you have any concerns. Early detection of melanoma can save your life.

Dusty Doha

Asthma sufferers may find that the dusty outdoors, and the dry air-conditioned indoors aggravate symptoms and you may need to rely on your inhaler more often than you would at home. A number of health centres offer asthma clinics including Al Ahli, Al Emadi, Aster Medical Centre, American Hospital, Elaj, Hamad General, Qatar Medical Centre and the Women's Hospital.

Health

Annex (OPD) opened in May 2011 and currently the Orthopaedic Evening Clinic has their daytime clinic here. In the second phase admission, catheter, surgery and emergency services will be added.

National Center For Cancer Care & Research
Nr Rumailah Hospital Rumaila **4439 7800**
hmc.org.qa
Map **2 M7**
A state-of-the-art hospital with world-class doctors, NCCCR is mainly used for tumour diagnosis and cancer treatments. They are the first in the world to use a 1.5T Optima MR450W MRI system, which better targets tumours. This government-run hospital has all the latest equipment needed for early detection of cancer.

Patient System

HMC has introduced an appointment system in the Women's Hospital outpatient department, which is designed to reduce the waiting time to see a doctor. Previously given on a walk-in basis, appointments must now be made by calling 4439 8000. A scheduled time and duration for the visit will be determined on a needs-based priority system. Patients who arrive without an appointment will have to return at an arranged time, with the exception of those with symptoms that require emergency attention.

Rumailah Hospital
Nr NCCCR & Heart Hospital Rumaila **4439 7000**
hmc.org.qa
Map **2 M7**
Qatar's first full service public hospital, Rumailah was renovated and repurposed in the 1990s and now has facilities for plastic surgery, ear, nose, and throat surgery, and ophthalmology. With more than 300 beds, it also has a stroke unit and a rehabilitation centre for disabled adults and children, as well as day surgery facilities, a speech and language therapy department and a psychiatric unit. The hospital also houses the HMC Cardiac Care Unit, which offers round-the-clock care for cardiac patients.

Women's Hospital
Nr Hamad General Hospital, Al Rayyan Rd
Hamad Medical City **4439 6666**
hmc.org.qa
Map **2 K7**
This government-run hospital focuses on obstetrics and gynaecology, including IVF. Its maternity facilities are particularly strong for premature babies as there is a neonatal intensive care unit.

Obstetrics & Gynaecology
The best way to find a quality obstetrician or gynaecologist is to ask for referrals from the hospital of your choice or among employees of your (or your spouse's) company. There are a few private clinics in Qatar that offer general medical services, but these are not necessarily vetted through any quality control system, so it is better to go through the relevant department at either a government or private hospital. Most of the private hospitals have equipment for the annual well woman check.

The current medical advice in many countries is that women should have a yearly cervical smear, and women over 35 an annual mammogram as well. Of course, if there is a family history of breast or cervical cancer these exams should be done more frequently and, in the case of mammogram screening, this should probably begin earlier than 35. Consult your doctor if you are unsure. Most clinics do not send out reminders when you are due for a checkup, so be sure to keep track of the times yourself.

Oral contraception and condoms are available without a prescription and some gynaecologists do place IUDs which are available by prescription. The morning after pill is not available in Qatar, so if you are in need of emergency contraception, see your doctor as soon as possible as they may be able to offer other options. Abortion is illegal in Qatar and unmarried pregnant women can be prosecuted.

Maternity Care
Some expats return to their home countries to give birth, but most now opt to stay in Doha to deliver: the local maternity facilities are good (and improving all

Hospital Experience Ann Gavin, 38, Australian expat

After more than two years living in Qatar, I encountered my first serious health condition in early 2010. I had company-arranged health insurance, so I drove myself to Al Ahli Hospital. After registering, verifying my insurance and paying a co-payment of QR 50, within minutes I was in a room and being seen by a doctor. After a barrage of tests, I was told by the general surgeon that I was to be admitted. I was given a private room with satellite TV, free wireless internet and round-the-clock care. The doctors spoke excellent English, listened and were informative. The surgical staff in particular were excellent, and the nurses were caring and considerate. I spent three days in the hospital and was discharged with medications and several follow-up appointments scheduled. In all, the experience cost me just QR 50 and I received excellent care.

the time), so it is no longer necessary for women to travel back home. If you choose to have your baby in Doha, you must first decide which hospital you want to deliver in. Many women are seeking the services of a doula to be present at the birth and to help with post-natal care. Only a few certified doulas practice in Qatar but the International Childbirth Education Association (ICEA) is striving to train more childbirth educators and doulas to fill the rising need.

All of the main hospitals in Qatar have maternity wards, so it's best to have an idea of whether you'd like to use a government hospital or a private one, to narrow your choices. As many people have their babies in Doha, it's best to get on a waiting list for prenatal care as doctors are often fully booked or travelling. All hospitals have private rooms, but operate on a first come first served principle.

The public system is perfectly acceptable and, although a little disorganised, is almost entirely free of charge. Antenatal appointments cost about QR 30. Call Hamad before 14:00 to make an appointment. Make sure you arrive a bit early with health card in hand. The major disadvantage of the public system is that men are not allowed to be present during scans or during the delivery, whereas they are at private hospitals. According to health regulations, no hospital allows men to be present at C-sections.

Breastfeeding Support

Al Khor Hospital (p.164) has a centre for breastfeeding. Plans exist to open a 24 hour breastfeeding hotline and a walk-in clinic at Hamad General. Keep an eye on the press for further announcements.

Most hospitals employ midwives in the maternity unit. Midwives are licensed to deliver babies via natural birth, but in most cases, a doctor will deliver your baby. All independent obstetricians must be affiliated to a hospital, and this is where they carry out their deliveries. If you opt for a private, independent obstetrician and have a preferred delivery hospital in mind, it's worth checking first that your doctor is permitted to deliver there. In the unlikely event that your chosen hospital is full, you will be sent to the Women's Hospital. Ask your doctor for their caesarean rate, as some doctor's rates are substantially higher than others.

Most private hospitals will allow you to have a birth plan including soothing music playing, dimming of lights, having a doula present, and so on. The government hospitals are not usually very keen on birth plans. No matter where you decide to have your baby, note that a water birth will not be possible as they are illegal in Qatar. Epidurals are common for pain relief and for elective caesareans (spinal blocks are also

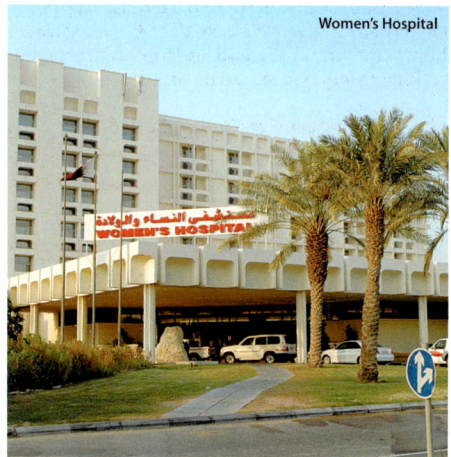
Women's Hospital

available); however, you may need to be persistent if you want to be with your baby immediately following the delivery.

Qatar law requires that women are married before bearing children; if a woman delivers and is unmarried, she could face serious charges.

The Women's Hospital has a fairly large maternity unit, but because it is a government hospital, men are not allowed access into the delivery room – a fact that puts many expats off going there. Bear in mind that its neonatal intensive care unit is the best option for delivery if your baby is born prematurely. Costs vary quite considerably depending on whether you take a private or shared room, but neither option costs more than QR 1,000. A private room costs QR 100 per night per baby.

Most health insurers only cover pregnancy costs if you have subscribed at least nine months prior to falling pregnant. If you don't have insurance you can still deliver privately; you just have to pay for it independently. It costs around QR 8,000 to QR 12,000 for a natural delivery and around QR 10,000 to QR 25,000 for a caesarean, depending on the hospital. The private hospitals offer excellent care, with Al Ahli Hospital proving to be the most popular. Doha Clinic is one of the favourites and Al Emadi's relatively new maternity unit is also attracting interest. Antenatal care is charged additionally; for example, antenatal checkups and three ultrasounds will cost around QR 1,500. Be sure to check on costs at the first meeting with your doctor and ask all your questions before you make a decision on where you would like to deliver. It is best to do the research at this stage so you won't feel as concerned nearer to the birth.

Virgin Health Bank opened in 2011. They are forerunners in cord blood banking and liaise with all hospitals in Doha.

Health

While breastfeeding is certainly promoted in Qatar, it can be difficult to find trained staff to assist you should you experience difficulties or simply just want reassurance. At Hamad you can request for breastfeeding assistance and they will be available to offer help as needed. Al Khor Hospital (p.164) houses Qatar's first multidisciplinary breastfeeding advocacy programme for physicians, nurses, mothers, family and community; a number of resources are available here to help you with any issues or questions you may have. Qatar's only International Board Certified Lactation Consultant (IBCLC) is also among the staff at this Al Khor facility; he happens to be a man.

Elsewhere, assistance is available from Sarah Hannibal (see below) and the breastfeeding support group of Doha Mums (p.132).

Obstetricians & Gynaecologists

Al Khor Hospital Breastfeeding Resource Center

Al Khor Hospital Al Khor **4474 5555**
hmc.org.qa
Map **Qatar Country Map C2**
Located at Al Khor Hospital and headed by Dr. Mohammed Ilyas Khan, who has many certifications including IBCLC. The clinic offers individual consultations, workplace lactation support and training, and houses a growing library. A Lactation Management Clinic meets every Wednesday.

Dr Khudsia Begum

Nr Al Tamim Dental Center, Al Waab St Al Waab **4447 5969**
Map **2 G11**
A female doctor specialising in obstetrics and gynaecology. No appointments necessary; the clinic operates on a first come, first served basis. Dr Khudsia speaks English, Hindi and Malayalam.

Dr Leelamma Abraham's Clinic

Villa 48, Abu Hamour St Bu Hamour **4460 0777**
Map **2 J13**
Dr Leelamma is a female general practitioner with extensive experience in gynaecology, but does not treat obstetric patients. Walk-ins are welcome but as this is a popular clinic, appointments are recommended.

Dr Sonia Abu Saba

Al Emadi Hospital Nuaija **4466 6009**
alemadihospital.com.qa
Map **2 R12**
This female doctor specialises in obstetrics and gynaecology at Al Emadi Hospital. A full range of pre- and antenatal care and expert consultation is available; however, note that Dr Sonia does not deliver babies. Clinic hours are 09:00-13:00 and 17:00-21:30, everyday except Thursdays (09:00-13:00), and Fridays, when it is closed.

Dr Zeenat Rizvi

Al Ahli Hospital Wadi Al Sail **4489 8000**
ahlihospital.com
Map **2 K5**
Dr Rizvi is the head of the obstetrics and gynaecology department at Al Ahli Hospital. She is quite popular, so you may have to wait a few weeks to be able to get an appointment, especially if your own schedule is busy as well and you can only make it on certain days. or at certain times.

Sarah Hannibal

Various Locations **5537 5472**
icea.org
As an International Childbirth Educators Association (ICEA) certified doula, Sarah Hannibal can accompany you to the hospital for birth. Ms. Hannibal is also a breastfeeding counsellor, childbirth educator and doula trainer. Consult ICEA for additional details on the services and available support.

Virgin Health Bank

Qatar Science & Technology Park Al Shagub **4405 1414**
virginhealthbank.com.qa
Map **2 A4**
Virgin Health Bank collects and stores babies cord blood stem cells which can, if necessary, be used later in life by the child or a family member as treatment for over 80 diseases. Virgin Health Bank is licensed by the Supreme Council of Health in Qatar and The Human Tissue Authority in the U.K. They are Sharia compliant. The focus is on providing the highest quality collection, processing and cryopreservation systems possible and educating families on the possible benefits of storing cord blood.

Having A Baby In Qatar Emily Phillips, 30, expat mum

What gets frustrating is when cultural, language or procedural issues come up. We (expats) tend to be defensive because we often assume things would be better back home, wherever that may be. We may be out of our comfort zone, and that is a scary thing if pregnant and feeling vulnerable. Just keep asking questions, get all the info you can so you know what to expect, and relax. Take a hospital tour, meet some of the nursing staff, talk to others. Stress and anxiety are not what you need while you are pregnant.

Serious Medical Conditions

Medical facilities for chronic medical conditions are continually improving in Qatar. Here's the lowdown on the most prevalent serious illnesses in Qatar and where to go to receive treatment for them.

The most prevalent serious medical conditions in Qatar are diabetes, heart disease, kidney disease, kidney stones and obesity. It is estimated that 20% of the population in Qatar is diabetic. There are no distinct statistics on the prevalence of heart disease, kidney stones, and obesity; however, heart disease and obesity can be attributed to the unhealthy lifestyle and poor eating habits adopted by so many in Qatar. Fast food is available on nearly every corner in Qatar and most of the restaurants will even deliver right to your front door. Add to that the fact that a car is almost a necessity as most places are difficult to access on foot and the constant heat makes trying to walk anywhere unpleasant. Kidney stones can be a problem for people who drink a lot of desalinated water (such as tap water and some of the cheaper bottled water brands). While this water is safe to drink, it does contain an abundance of minerals.

The Qatari government is aware of these issues and runs awareness campaigns and classes through Hamad Medical Corporation and the National Health Authority (both contactable on 4439 4444). Campaigns are usually advertised in the local papers or you call for more details. Qatar Foundation also runs the Qatar Diabetes Association (p.134), whose aim is to increase knowledge and understanding of diabetes. The Fahad bin Jassim Kidney Centre (p.164) offers management of kidney disease and dialysis.

There are several specialist facilities available for expats diagnosed with these illnesses. Most government clinics offer diabetic and cardiac care and there are also private clinics specialising in cardiology and internal medicine (see Private Health Centres & Polyclinics, p.160). HMC Cardiac Care Unit at Rumailah Hospital (p.166) is a 24 hour medical unit which deals with heart attacks, unstable angina (chest pain) and cardiac monitoring. A dedicated Heart Hospital opened at the beginning of 2011. The hospitals (government and private) also have nutritionists on board for weight loss and management. The BeautyFull programme at Aspire Active (p.131) offers special nutrition and exercise classes for overweight women.

For cancer sufferers, National Center for Cancer Care (p.166), established by HMC, is a state-of-the-art facility for cancer treatment. It has radiotherapy facilities and a new bone marrow transplant unit is under development. Think Pink (p.135) is a support group for women living in Qatar who are battling with or have survived breast cancer.

With any chronic disease or serious illness it is imperative to seek medical attention as early as possible to improve the chances of survival and minimise any lasting effects. Some insurance policies do not cover pre-existing or chronic medical conditions, so check your paperwork carefully and consider taking out additional cover if you have a family history of disease or are particularly at risk through contributing factors.

Health

Paediatrics

All hospitals in Qatar have a paediatrics department. The department at Hamad General Hospital has a very good reputation, and the Pediatric Emergency Center is excellent and each branch has an outpatient section. The nurses are friendly and are very good with children. However, they do not handle trauma cases such as broken bones or deep cuts, so go directly to Hamad General Hospital or Doha Clinic for these treatments.

There are also private paediatric clinics in addition to the hospitals and government clinics. Many of the private clinics listed under General Medical Care (p.160) have resident paediatricians too; Al Wakra Hospital has a specialised paediatric emergency unit. Whether you choose to go to a private clinic or to a government hospital is your choice, as the care at both will be excellent. Be sure to ask for recommendations from friends and colleagues as word of mouth is usually the best way to find a good paediatrician. Visits to the paediatrician are usually covered by insurance but always check with your insurance company to make sure the doctor falls under your insurance scheme. If you have a government health card and you use one of the government hospitals, the fee will be nominal.

Vaccinations

Under the National Vaccination Program, vaccinations against all childhood diseases are available in Qatar free or for a nominal charge through government clinics, and at a higher fee in private clinics.

The HMC has an excellent service on its website (hmc.org.qa) where you can enter the child's name and date of birth to determine their vaccination schedule through to starting school. This site will also give you the necessary information about other diseases for which you can get a vaccine including hepatitis B and polio. This information is available in English and Arabic by clicking on any of the diseases or vaccines on your baby's personalised time table sheet.

To have your child immunised at a government clinic, you will require a compulsory green vaccination card issued by the National Health Authority. It states the types of vaccinations that are recommended for children and the age when they should be administered. If your baby was born in Qatar, you will be issued with their vaccination card following the baby's birth when you collect the birth certificate. For babies born outside Qatar, you can apply for a card from the National Health Authority inside the Asian Games Building near Civil Defence Roundabout. You will need to produce your baby's birth certificate and evidence of all immunisations that have been administered overseas. Once you have your green card, check the list on p.160 for a nearby government health clinic which offers paediatric services.

TB Or Not TB?

Immunisation against tuberculosis is administered at birth in Qatar. If your baby was born outside Qatar, you will be expected to visit the Vaccination Unit of the Preventative Health Department in Ain Khaled (4406 4222) to have your child immunised.

Paediatricians

Dr Atiya Khalid Bashir
Al Ahli Hospital Wadi Al Sail **4489 8000**
ahlihospital.com
Map **2 K5**
A female paediatrician at Al Ahli Hospital, Dr Atiya is a favourite among expats. Appointments are required.

Dr Mohammed Basha
Aster Medical Centre Musheireb **4444 0499**
aster.com.qa
Map **2 P8**
Dr Basha is a paediatrician based at Aster Medical Centre. Appointments are required, and should be made at least one day in advance.

Dr Samer Rida
Al Emadi Hospital Nuaija **4466 6009**
alemadihospital.co.qa
Map **2 R12**
Specialising in paediatrics, Dr Samer is also the medical director of Al Emadi hospital. Clinic hours are 09:00-13:00 and 17:00-21:30 everyday except Thursdays, when it is only open for the morning session, and Fridays, when it is closed.

Dr Thomas Samuel
The Apollo Clinic Qatar Fereej Bin Dirhem **4441 8441**
apolloqatar.com
Map **2 Q9**
Dr Samuel treats all children's ailments, and gives vaccinations and well baby/child care. Clinic is open Saturday to Thursday, from 06:00-23:00 and on Fridays from 08:00-23:00.

Pediatric Emergency Center
Al Sadd St Al Sadd **4439 6001**
hmc.org.qa
Map **2 L9**
This centre offers emergency services for children up to the age of 12. The centre has an excellent reputation. Make sure to have the child's health card with you. A health hotline is available by calling 4439 6055. It is open 24 hours a day, 7 days a week, 365 days a year. Satellite centres are Al Rayyan (4481 9989), Al Daayen (4412 9488), Al Aiport (4467 7672).

Dentists & Orthodontists

There is an ever-growing number of private dental clinics in Doha offering various treatments. Dental facilities are generally of a high standard, with state-of-the-art equipment; however prices may be higher than some expats are used to, with a simple scale and clean running to QR 500 in some cases and an examination costing upwards of QR 300.

Most employers' healthcare insurance also covers dental work, however, you should certainly verify this with your insurer. If your insurance only covers medical, you may still be covered for oral surgery as some insurance plans place oral surgery under medical rather than dental treatment.

The government dental clinics (see Government Health Centres & Polyclinics, p.160) are excellent and have a high standard of care. You must have a government health card to use their services, but once you do, all treatment is free. The drawback is you may have to wait 2-6 weeks to get an appointment for routine care as they are very busy.

It is recommended that children see a dentist as soon as they have their first tooth. Be sure to find a paedodontist (children's dentist) for your children as they are specially trained to deal with child patients. Furthermore, they will have equipment that is more comfortable for children (such as smaller dental chairs, x-ray film and dental instruments).

Corrective dentistry (orthodontics) and cosmetic dentistry are widely available in Qatar. The combination of higher salaries and time spent away from their home countries makes expats very likely candidates to opt for cosmetic work. In many ways, Qatar is an ideal place to undergo orthodontic treatment: most clinics offer white fillings, cosmetic bonding and professional teeth whitening, and the prices tend to compare favourably against most expats' home countries.

This said, it makes sense to do some research and price comparison between the various clinics: the costs, methods and facilities can vary surprisingly greatly from one dentist to another.

Al Raed Dental Center

Villa 34, Al Waab St Al Aziziya **4450 9673**
rdc-qatar.com
Map **2 A12**
This clinic offers orthodontics (braces), root canal treatment (endodontics), cosmetic dentistry and children's dentistry. Open 08:30-13:00 and 16:00-21:00.

Beauty Dental Clinic

Nr Wholesale Market, Haloul St Bu Hamour
4451 3783
Map **2 G13**
General dentistry, orthodontics and a one-visit teeth whitening using the latest laser system.

Consultant Dental Center > *p.173*

Villa 30, Nr Lulu Hypermarket, Ahmed Bin Hambal St Old Airport **4467 7166**
consultantdentalcenter.com
Map **2 S13**
This well-established practice offers a wide range of services, including: orthodontics, implants, cosmetic dentistry, oral surgery, periodontics, TMJ therapy, crowns and bridges, and root canal treatment.

Dr Ghassan Kahlout Dental Clinic

Nr Gulf Times, C Ring Rd Najma **4441 7224**
Map **2 S11**
This practice offers routine dentistry, tooth whitening, orthodontics, braces and tooth implants.

Dr Hassan Al Abdulla Medical Center

250 D Ring Rd Old Airport **4432 3900**
drhassanmedical.com
Map **2 U12**
Services offered include orthodontics, prosthodontics (crowns, bridges and dentures), laser therapy, oral surgery, implants and children's dentistry.

Dr Johnny's Clinic

Nr Gulf Cinema, C Ring Rd Najma **4427 0760**
Map **2 S11**
Dr Johnny specialises in orthodontics and has over 20 years of experience. He also carries out fillings, crowns and bridges, hygiene and root canal treatments.

Dr Tamim Dental Polyclinic

Nr Qtel Tower, Al Waab St Al Waab **4450 2929**
drtamimclinic.com
Map **2 G11**
This state-of-the-art polyclinic features specialists in orthodontics, paedodontics, oral surgery and prosthodontics (crowns, bridges, and dentures). It is the first clinic in Qatar to offer CEREC (high-tech computer system for ceramic restorations).

First Dental Centre

Al Jamiaa St Al Markhiya **4487 4771**
Map **2 L2**
This small practice has a team of four dentists providing routine dental care including fillings, prosthodontics (crowns, bridges, dentures), orthodontics and endodontics (root canal treatment).

Future Dental Center

Future Medical Center Al Aziziya **4458 0800**
fdcdoha.com
Map **2 C12**
This clinic boasts the largest group of dental consultants and specialists in Qatar. It provides comprehensive dental care services and is fitted with the latest state-of-the-art equipment.

Health

Health, Fitness & Well-Being

German Dental Clinics
Al Mirqab St New Al Mirqab **4441 1711**
implant-qatar.com
Map **2 L9**
This family practice has three German-trained dental specialists. It offers aesthetic dentistry including invisible orthodontics, tooth whitening and veneers, alongside routine treatments and paedodontics.

International Specialized Dental Center
Al Waab St Al Waab **4450 7897**
isdc-doha.com
Map **2 G10**
This multi-specialty clinic offers crowns, bridges, dentures, root canal surgery, gum disease treatment, oral surgery, orthodontics and paedodontics.

The Queen Dental Center
City Center Doha Al Dafna **4493 2888**
Map **2 Q2**
This large dental practice provides treatment in all areas of dentistry, including cosmetic dentistry, orthodontics, paedodontics, oral surgery, and TMJ treatment. Fifteen different languages are spoken in this practice.

Queen Medical
Villaggio Mall Baaya **4419 0888**
queenmedical.com
Map **2 B11**
A multi-specialty clinic offering general and cosmetic dentistry, dermatology, phototherapy, botox, laser removal, physical rehabilitation, opthamology, hypertension, internal medicine and cosmetology. Some underrepresented fields are also found here including routine well child exams, adolescent gynaecological care, learning difficulties, ADD management and diabetes management and endocrinology.

Opticians & Ophthalmologists
The dry, dusty environment in Qatar can cause problems for eyes, even if you've had no trouble in the past. Spending lengthy periods in air-conditioned environments can cause problems for contact lens wearers too. If you're experiencing discomfort caused by the dust, natural tear or refresher eye drops can increase your comfort and are available in most opticians and pharmacies. Sunglasses are an essential accessory in Qatar and prescription lenses are widely available. Everyone has to have an eye test when applying for a driving licence, either at a Traffic Police Department (p.59) or in selected opticians' stores.

Opticians can be found in shopping centres as well as around town. Qatar Optics and Yateem Optician have a few branches in Doha. Many opticians also do eye examinations and can refer you to an ophthalmologist if required. There are ophthalmology departments in several of the clinics and hospitals, including Doha Clinic (p.164), Al Ahli Hospital (p.163), Al Emadi Hospital (p.163), The Apollo Clinic (p.161), Future Medical Center (p.161) and Hamad General Hospital (p.164).

As well as standard treatment and prescriptions, most ophthalmologists in Qatar also do Lasik (laser surgery) to correct vision problems. Lasik surgery is completed in about 20 minutes (for both eyes), but the recovery time can take anything up to six months. It's not cheap though: the cost of Lasik can be up to QR 5,000 per eye.

It is highly recommended to take your children for eye examinations from the age of 6 months. This should be repeated when the child is 3 and again when they begin school. As many as 25% of school age children have vision problems and unfortunately, many go undiagnosed.

Al Jabor Vision Technology
Nr Gulf Cinema Signal, C Ring Rd Najma **4442 7152**
Map **2 R11**
Provides eye tests and contact lenses. These are ordered from Germany, which translates into longer waiting times but results in accurate fittings. The German optometrist is frequently recommended and can help you choose frames.

Al Magrabi Eye, ENT & Dental Center
Nr Doha Airport, D-Ring Al Hilal **4423 8888**
magrabihospitals.com
Map **2 T12**
Magrabi has an excellent reputation in Doha for Lasik surgery but also has centres throughout the Middle East and Africa. Other specialities are ENT and dentistry.

Bahrain Optician City Center Doha, Al Dafna, 4483 8848, *optica.net*
Optic Gallery The Mall, Old Airport, 4467 8100
Qatar Optics Landmark Mall, Umm Lekhba, 4486 6649, *qataroptics.com*
Yateem Optician Al Zaben Complex, Salem Al Mubarak St, Fereej Al Nasr, 4432 3204, *yateemgroup.com*

Alternative Therapies
A growing list of alternative therapies is available in Doha, although many therapies are not certifiable practices in the country and as such are banned by the Ministry of Health. All homeopathic remedies and treatments are banned in Qatar; 'backyard treatments' are officially frowned on, although through word of mouth you will be able to locate therapists who have recognised qualifications from other countries, offering treatments to friends and family. The Supreme Council of Health is working on legislation that will regulate alternative therapies and should open this sector in the future.

WE CREATE SMILES EVERYDAY

المركز الاستشاري لطب الاسنان
CONSULTANT DENTAL CENTER

WE PROVIDE
all of your dental care from simple cleanings to most complex surgery.

OUR MISSION
is to provide a more relaxed and pain free dental visits. Consultant Dental Center where Beautiful Smiles Begin.

OUR GOAL
as a dental team is to provide you and your family with Quality Dental Care in an environment that is both comfortable and caring.

+974 4467 7166 / 4467 7199

www.consultantdentalcenter.com • info@consultantdentalcenter.com

Health

Acupuncture is one of the few alternative treatments which has been recognised officially by the ministry. It is available at Hamad General Hospital (p.164) and Al Emadi (p.163), for pain relief and other health conditions.

A few places in Doha now offer reiki, reflexology and massage therapy, and a number of salons and spas are beginning to include alternative treatments on their therapy menus.

Spa Chakra offers hydrotherapy, as well as naturopathy, a holistic concept which is becoming increasingly popular with high-end spas. Colour therapy is offered by Six Senses Spa (p.184) and the Spa & Wellness Centre (p.184) at the Four Seasons; Six Senses also offers reiki. A number of spas, including The Spa at Doha Marriott (p.196), offer shiatsu massage. Ayurvedic treatments are available at Angsana (p.181).

The International Chinese Bodycare House
Sheraton Doha Resort & Convention Hotel Al Dafna
4483 2543
cbodycare.com
Map **2 R3**
Expanded into three locations, this Chinese medicine clinic performs authentic reflexology, lymphatic drainage, acupressure and traditional acupuncture, meridian therapy, cupping and scraping, performed by trained Chinese therapists and supervised by a medical doctor. They also sell Chinese oils, herbs and teas.

Kottakall Ayurvedic Centre
Nr Lulu Centre, Al Rayyan Rd Al Sadd **4436 0061**
Map **2 L7**
This centre offers Ayurvedic massage using herbal oils. It is a male-only centre, but home visits can be arranged for female customers.

Tao Yuan Foot Centre
Souk Waqif Al Jasra **5528 5711**
Map **2 Q7**
Located near to the restaurant end of Souk Waqif. In addition to manicures and pedicures, this centre offers foot reflexology, cupping, back and full body massages for men and women.

Sports Injuries
Sports are a big part of life in Qatar, and sports injuries are common. Some medical insurance companies cover this, but others don't; it depends not only on your personal policy, but also on the type of sport you engage in. Some policies cover non-contact sports, but won't cover injuries sustained in more extreme pursuits. Policies may exclude all contact sports, so it's worth checking whether your insurance includes your weekly kick-about.

Most sports injuries can be treated at one of the government or private hospitals where there are well-trained therapists and the equipment to deal with most problems (see Main Hospitals, p.163).

There is also a new, state-of-the-art orthopaedic and sports medicine hospital, Aspetar (see below), at the Aspire complex.

Elsewhere, many private clinics offer physiotherapy (including exercise therapy and massage) and orthopaedic therapy, both surgical and non-surgical (see Health Centres & Polyclinics, p.160). For more minor aches and complaints, if all you need is a good rub down, many hotel and day spas offer massages that range from deep tissue and shiatsu to specialised sports massage (p.174).

Chiropractic treatment is becoming more common in Qatar, with a couple of private clinics specialising in it. Chiropractic involves spinal manipulation, and can be effective both alone and in conjunction with other treatments such as physical therapy, psychological counselling, and dietary measures.

Aspetar Qatar Orthopaedic & Sports Medicine Hospital
Aspire Zone, Sports City St Baaya **4413 2000**
aspetar.com
Map **2 B11**
This hospital is part of the Aspire Zone, Qatar's centre for sporting excellence. The hospital primarily exists for the rehabilitation and treatment of the young sporting students of the Aspire Academy, but it is also open to the general public. It has a host of top physicians including orthopaedic surgeons, sports medicine doctors, physiotherapists and podiatrists, and is in high demand. It isn't cheap or covered by the health card, but it is very good and very efficient. Some private insurance holders may be covered for treatment; contact the hospital or your insurer to check.

Doha Chiropractic Center
D Ring Rd New Slata **4465 0012**
Map **2 M12**
Doha Chiropractic Center has qualified chiropractors and massage therapists who can assist you with all types of back ailments such as sciatica, slipped discs and general back pain. Dr. Sharon Hormozi has a good reputation in Doha.

Dr Yasser El Bardini
Al Kindi Medical Complex Al Sadd **4432 3985**
Map **2 J10**
This is a small, solo chiropractic clinic. Clinic hours are from 09:00-12:00 and 17:00-20:00 from Saturday to Wed. Thursday closes at 15:00. Dr El Bardini speaks English and Arabic.

Nutritionists & Slimming

In the past, Qatar's population relied on healthy staples such as whole grains, fish and dates for sustenance, but the ready availability of convenience food and an increasingly sedentary lifestyle have added plenty of inches to the nation's waistline: recent statistics from the Supreme Council for Health estimate that up to 40% of the population is clinically obese and 32% is overweight.

Fortunately help is at hand. From personal trainers to weight loss surgery, there are a range of options available if you are looking to shed some serious weight, and if you are just looking for a helping hand with a healthier diet, there are nutritionists and healthy eating food companies to turn to.

Dietary advice for diabetes is taking the forefront in government campaigns, due to the country's high incidence of Type 2 diabetes. See Serious Medical Conditions, p.169 for details of treatment and support for diabetics. Similarly, eating advice for digestive disorders such as reflux, IBS and coeliacs, plus for allergies and the menopause, is becoming even more prominent.

While there are no official weight loss groups in Qatar, you will find plenty of people in the online community offering support and advice to fellow dieters (see Useful Websites, p.23). In the forums, you will find informal groups that meet regularly to try to keep each other on the straight and narrow. Some people choose to follow Weight Watchers online at weightwatchers.com, and others enlist the help of weight loss professionals in Qatar. Overeaters Anonymous (p.134) is a support group in Qatar.

Most hospitals have dieticians and nutritionists who can give nutritional guidance for medical conditions as well as for weight loss. Some high-end fitness centres, for example Spa Chakra (p.184), have dieticians available to help their members stay trim.

For more extreme measures, weight loss surgery is available. Hamad Medical Corporation (HMC) offers anti-obesity bariatric surgery and most recently gastric plication; gastric band surgery can also be performed in major private hospitals like Al Ahli (p.163) and Al Emadi (p.163). Plastic Surgericenter (p.176) performs liposuction, fat injection, tummy tucks, and arms, thighs and butt lifts.

Most fitness centres and gyms offer personal training services and some of the higher end ones, like that at Spa Chakra (p.184), have an in-house nutritionist to help balance your exercise programme with a good diet. There are also plenty of opportunities to take part in sports (see Activity Finder, p.264) to keep you active and help shift your unwanted weight. Aspire Active (p.131) runs the BeautyFull programme aimed at aiding weight-loss the old fashioned way – through reduced calorie

Keeping fit and healthy on the Corniche

Health, Fitness & Well-Being

intake and an increased amount of physical activity. International women's fitness franchise, Curves (p.178), has three centres in Doha where women can take advantage of its innovative exercise programmes and healthy eating advice. For men, Energie Fitness Club (p.178) offers a six week healthy living programme to help you stay on track.

Hypoxi therapy, the latest weight loss craze to reach Doha, is now available at the Grand Regency's Fat Burning Studio. Art of Abundant Living takes a holistic approach to help you maintain lifestyle changes. Private cooking classes can encourage you to prepare healthy meals.

Art Of Abundant Living
Various Locations 7773 0750
artofabundantliving.com
Nicole van Hattem is a board certified Holistic Health Coach. Individual consultations usually last 6 months but shorter consultations are available. She helps clients define personal goals, define steps to achieve those goals and provides long-term support. She helps with issues ranging from weight loss to lifestyle. Corporate and wellness programmes, employee engagement initiatives, leadership development, workshops and retreats round out her repertoire.

The Nutrition & Diet Center
Al Mirqab Al Jadeed Al Sadd **4436 8820**
dietcenterme.com
Map **2 M9**
At this centre, dieticians and nutritionists analyse your eating and health habits, then devise a lifestyle plan tailored to your dietary needs and goals. Educational assistance is available to encourage and promote a positive approach to healthy eating and exercise. Calorie-conscious meals are on the menu at their flagship cafe. The Diet Shop on Salwa Road (4466 4995) is open for breakfast, lunch and dinner, or the kitchen can prepare a weekly eating plan of nutritious meals that you can ask to have delivered straight to your home or workplace.

Perfect Figure
Wyndham Grand Regency Doha Al Sadd **4434 3446**
perfectfigure.ae
Map **2 K7**
This interesting fat burning studio offers an innovative and exciting approach to weight loss through Hypoxitherapy. Hypoxi machines involve traditional exercise, such as cycling on an exercise bike, with the application of low pressure to problem areas which become activated as you start to exercise. This increases blood supply to these problem areas, which is said to aid faster fat burn.

Cosmetic Treatment & Surgery
Cosmetic surgery is quickly gaining popularity in Qatar, and many services and procedures are now offered by most of the major hospitals in Doha. Hamad General Hospital (p.164) deals with bariatric (weight loss) surgery, while Rumailah Hospital (p.166) houses the government's main plastic surgery department and burns care unit. In the private sector, Al Emadi Hospital (p.163) now has a number of resident and visiting plastic surgeons.

Outside of the main hospitals however, there are still only a small number of reputable clinics. Before engaging the services of a plastic surgeon, it is highly recommended and most sensible to do your research into both the procedure and the clinic's credentials. Plastic Surgicentre has been operating in Doha for a number of years now and has an established reputation. The Ministry of Health is clamping down on non-qualified practices. You can call the Medical Commission on 4467 9111 to check whether a clinic is officially registered.

Non-surgical cosmetic procedures, such as botox, dermabrasion, mesotherapy (tiny injections to disperse fat), and laser hair removal are also becoming more popular. A number of private medical clinics, such as Dr Hassan Al Abdullah Clinic (p.161), offer the more technical procedures, whereas laser hair removal is available at a number of salons (see Beauty Salons, p.180). Dermabrasion facials are offered at various spas and salons, including The Spa at Doha Marriott (p.184) and Villaggio's Medical Spa (4451 7590), and again it pays to do your research.

Dr Saed Kaldari Plastic Surgery Clinic
Nr Al Jazeera Academy, Abu Hamour St
Al Maamoura **4451 5177**
drkaldari.com
Map **1 H12**
Dr Kaldari is a former consultant for the UMAS. in Sweden. His clinic specialises in SmartLipo which is lipsculpting or tightening while under local anesthesia. Also available are Ultrasonic lipolsysis, laser hair removal, rhinoplasty, otoplasty, face lifts, breast augmentations, microdermabrasion, transdermal fillers and mesotherapy.

Plastic Surgicentre
Nr Le Mirage, 147 Najma St Al Hilal **4466 2260**
drmakki.com
Map **2 R12**
The first and most popular dedicated plastic surgery clinic in Doha, it offers a vast number of procedures including, but not limited to, face lifts, rhinoplasty, breast augmentations and reductions, male breast reduction, weight-loss procedures, laser treatments, and minor procedures including mole removal. A full range of non-invasive procedures is also available.

Counselling & Therapy

Starting a new life in a different country can be a stressful process, and whether you are new to the city or not, sometimes it can help just to talk through whatever issues and anxieties you are facing. Mental health services in Qatar are not as developed as in some countries and, for the services that are available, immediate appointments may not be in place because of over-demand.

Rumailah Hospital (p.166) houses Qatar's main psychiatry unit; it has long waiting lists but also deals with emergency cases. Some private hospitals (p.163) have psychiatrists on staff, as do some of the private clinics (p.160), which may also have counsellors and therapists. These professionals can perform a medical assessment, and, if necessary, assist in recommending medical evacuations for mental health reasons. Doha increasingly has counsellors and psychiatrists who work independently from home, who you can find out about with a little digging. There are a number of support groups which operate in Qatar (see p.134) too. The Doha Mums Out of Sync Group provides support to mums with children who have special needs including dyslexia, autism, Down Syndrome, and Cerebral Palsy.

Dr Aju's Clinic

Villa 3, Al Mashaf St Fereej Al Soudan **4436 5051**
drajusclinic.com
Map **2 J11**

Dr Aju Abraham is a UK-trained psychiatrist who runs a private mental health clinic. The clinic offers psychiatric, psychological and therapeutic methods of treatment including psychopharmacology, cognitive behaviour, family therapy, supportive psychotherapy and biofeedback for a range of mental illnesses, including depression, panic disorders, stress related disorders, sleep disorders, adult ADHD, bipolar affective disorder, post traumatic stress disorder, childhood and adolescent behaviour disorders, schizophrenia and eating disorders. Counselling is offered on an individual or family basis.

Family Consulting Center

Mohammed Bin Thani St New Fereej Al Hitmi
4489 2888
Map **2 K6**

This centre offers free counselling services to residents and nationals in matters that range from marital and family to caregiver counselling, as well as awareness and prevention counselling.

Victoria Hensen

TV Roundabout Al Jebailat **5539 5692**
Map **2 K3**

Dr Victoria Hensen is a privately practising clinical psychologist who trained in the US and New Zealand.

She deals with all DSM IV conditions such as post-traumatic stress disorder (PTSD) and anxiety in both children and adults. She offers play therapy and family therapy. She also offers psychiatric diagnosis and can give referrals to other mental health services.

FITNESS
Gyms & Fitness Clubs

With rising rates of obesity, the government is keen to get people active, and has put in place a number of initiatives and events from Schools Olympic Day (qatarolympics.org) to the Aspire Active public health programmes held at the Aspire Academy (p.144). Some companies offer full or part payment of a membership of a hotel health club or gym to encourage employees to stay healthy.

Most compounds and apartment blocks come with some form of fitness facilities, but you can expect anything from a fully kitted-out fitness centre with the latest high-tech machines, to a broken exercise bike and a few odd weights. Many people have access to swimming pools in their accommodation and some of the nicer compounds have tennis courts and other sports facilities.

There are a growing number of independent gyms and fitness centres outside private compounds. Most charge a monthly or yearly membership fee for access to facilities – look out in the local press for joining discounts and special offers. Many gyms offer a daily rate or visitor pass, although this will become a very expensive option if done on a regular basis. Most gyms also run a number of fitness classes including aerobics, spinning and body combat which may be included in the membership fees or paid for on a class-by-class basis.

In addition most hotels offer memberships to their fitness facilities, offering extensive facilities. Although usually more expensive, these gyms are often quieter and sometimes include access to spa facilities, so it's worth ringing around to compare quotes before you sign up. Some independent spas, such as Dados (p.182) and Spa Chakra (p.184) also have great facilities.

If your motivation is your biggest exercise hurdle, there are options ranging from personal trainers to group fitness classes, and if you're serious about getting fit, military-style bootcamps are intensive training sessions aimed at increasing fitness levels in a short time frame. Goal-orientated personal training is also good if your aim is losing weight, whereas dance classes (p.267) offer a more fun approach.

For sociable types, all kinds of sports are on offer in Qatar and are a good way to meet like-minded people. See Activities p.263 for more details. Girls on the Go motivates young girls to live healthy lives through exercise and healthy eating.

Al Massa Active

Radisson Blu Hotel, Doha Rawdat Al Khail **4436 4850**
radissonblu.com
Map **2 N10**
Al Massa is a no-frills fitness centre with separate gyms for men and women. The women's section offers fitness classes including aerobics, dance, pilates and cardio circuits. Monthly membership costs QR 1,100 for men but ask if they have a promotion. Monthly membership for women is QR 750.

Aspire Academy For Sports Excellence

Nr Villaggio Mall Baaya **4413 6000**
aspire.qa
Map **2 A10**
The first-class facilities at this sports academy include the world's largest purpose-built indoor sports dome, seven outdoor football pitches, an Olympic size swimming pool and specially designed fitness rooms. This is in addition to a dedicated medical centre and lecture halls for over 1,000 students. Aspire is also actively involved in the local community, and many schools have fitness classes with Aspire staff. The centre's facilities are open to the public via the Aspire Active classes (4413 6430). There are separate classes for men, women and different ages of children, in a variety of sports and fitness disciplines. Adult classes include spinning, cardio workouts and yoga, with kickboxing, boxing and circuits for the men and Pilates, pre and post-natal classes, BeautyFull weight loss, dance cardio and aquatics for the girls. There is also a range of classes for mothers and babies, toddlers and young children. Aspire organises programmes for those with diabetes, with a specialist weight camp to help children avoid obesity.

Bay Club

InterContinental Doha Al Gassar **4484 4852**
ichotelsgroup.com
Map **1 K3**
Classes include Body Groove, circuit training, Kick Fit, Step A02, spinning and yoga as well as personal trainers. Facilities available are a gym, pool, sauna and steam room. Open to non-members. 1 month membership is QR 1,850.

Bodylines Leisure & Fitness Club

Oryx Rotana Al Hilal **4402 3485**
rotana.com
Map **2 T11**
Bodylines has a fitness centre with personal trainers, a spa with a jacuzzi, sauna and steam room, yoga and aerobic classes. 1 month membership costs QR 1500. Walk-ins are welcome. Weekend use of the swimming pool, sauna, steam room and jacuzzi costs QR 125 for an adult and Q R85 for a child (pool only). Weekday is QR 100 for adults and QR 65 for children.

Curves

Nr Mercedes Showroom, Salwa Rd Al Waab **4469 9955**
curvesme.com
Map **2 G12**
This is the place for women of all ages to head to when supreme fitness is the goal. The 30-minute workout incorporates aerobic and strength training with warm-up, cool down and stretching, and is designed with busy women in mind. The international website curves.com demonstrates the machines used. Three locations in Doha, one off Salwa Road, Nuaija near in Al Ahli Sports Club, 4455 2477, and another in Duhail near Landmark, 4421 7755.

Dana Club

Majlis Al Taawon St Lekhwair **4483 4700**
danaclub.com.qa
Map **2 N4**
Dana Club has a great family set-up, offering a range of exciting activities for kids and adults alike. Facilities include indoor air-conditioned tennis courts, swimming pools (indoor and outdoor), two fitness centres, outdoor sports courts, a billiards room and a children's playground. Fun events, including football tournaments and volleyball matches, are held regularly. An internet cafe and two restaurants are ideal retreats to recover from your exertions. Membership is offered in a variety of packages.

The Diplomatic Club

Al Gassar **4484 7444**
thediplomaticclub.com
Map **1 K2**
Open to select members, the Diplomatic Club has great facilities. There is a gym, a 200m beach, volleyball court, squash and tennis courts, watersports, outdoor pool, kids' club and spa. Lessons and fitness classes are also available. Sports and fitness aside, the club also has a library, beauty salon and four dining venues. Application forms for membership are available at reception.

Energie Fitness Club

Nr Ramez Shopping Centre, Airport Rd Al Thumama **4467 2390**
energie-qa.com
Map **1 P12**
This all-round fitness haven is a men's gym with thoroughly modern facilities and professional support and training services. It offers a large number of cardio machines, plus a weights room, fitness classes, personal training and access to sports medicine therapists. A money-back guarantee is available on its six-week 'empower' healthy living programme. Membership costs QR 850 per month and QR 5,000 per year.

Fitness First
City Center Doha Al Dafna **4411 5999**
fitnessfirstme.com
Map **2 Q2**
Fitness First's first foray in Qatar offers the formula which has made this brand such a success across the world: a large fitness room with multiple cardio machines, free weights and weight machines, plus an extensive range of group exercise classes, steam and sauna. Separate areas for women and men. Membership rates start at QR 400 per month, plus joining fees.

Fitness Qatar
Various locations 3000 8974
fitnessqatar.me
Formerly Fit for Life Qatar. This fitness training company has its own studio or can provide personal trainers to come to your preferred gym. It also runs Boot Camp Qatar, a high-energy, group training class which usually takes place early in the morning in outdoor locations. Mixed classes or women-only classes available. The price for boot camp is QR 750 for 12 consecutive sessions or QR 1,850 for 36 consecutive sessions. An annual unlimited boot camp pass costs QR 5,500.

Pure Leisure & Wellness Centre > *p.81*
Kempinski Residences & Suites Al Dafna **4405 3307**
kempinski.com
Map **2 Q1**
Dermalife Spa-Oceana hydrotherapy allows clients to relax in a bed of colour. Personal trainers are available in addition to a gym, two steam rooms and sauna, cardio and weight machines. Pilates, yoga, reflexology, shiatsu and an indoor pool. Sundays and Tuesdays 09:00-13:00 are for ladies only. A monthly corporate membership for four people costs QR 1,050 per person including the joining fees.

Yama Yoga Studios
Garvey's European Club, Off Salwa Rd
New Fereej Al Ghanim **6617 5802**
yamayogastudios.com
Map **1 D12**
One of the best equipped yoga studios in town with top-rate instructors offering classes from absolute beginners to head-standing experts. Classes are a combination of astanga, vinyasa, jivamukti and vini. Pre-natal classes, children's classes and salsa classes are also offered. Workshops are held regularly by instructors from all over the world. The Absolute Beginners Course is highly recommended for those who have never had any formal yoga instruction. The Garvey's location is a bit of a construction site at the moment. Classes are also held at The Ritz (p.202), the Dana Club and Asas Towers in West Bay.

WELL-BEING
Whether it's shifting excess weight, hitting the park bootcamp-style, being pampered at a health spa, receiving meditation advice from a guru, or limbering up with a body massage: whatever your definition of well-being there's a good chance that someone, somewhere in Qatar will have the necessary facilities and skills to have you feeling better in no time.

Personal Grooming
Looking good is a way of life in Qatar for both nationals and expats, men and women of all social and financial levels. You'll find salons in all shopping malls, hotels and in lots of independent villas around town.

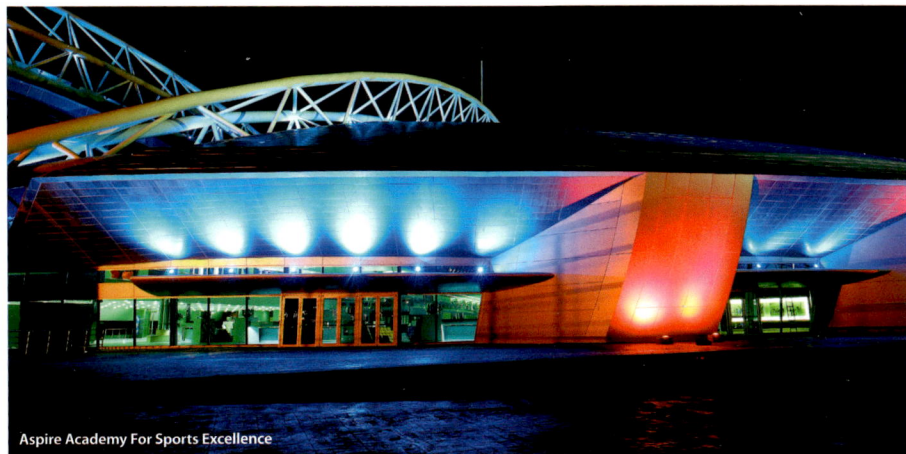
Aspire Academy For Sports Excellence

With certain services such as manicures, pedicures and waxing costing less than in many other international cities, you may find that a trip to the beautician's becomes a more regular diary fixture than at home. Fridays are usually the busiest day so make sure you book ahead; on other days many places accept walk-ins or bookings at short notice.

In the majority of places, you'll only see stylists and therapists of the same sex as the clients, and you'll never see a mixed sex establishment.

There are numerous salons which offer henna painting. The traditional practise which involves henna dye being painted on a woman's hands and feet is still very popular with Qatari and Indian ladies, particularly for weddings or special occasions, like Eid. For tourists, a design on the hand, ankle or shoulder can make a great memento and the intricate brown patterns fade after two to three weeks.

There are growing opportunities for male grooming as well, with barbershops and salons to suit all budgets, and a select number of spas that accept male customers. Whether you're after a short back and sides, a traditional shave, a chest wax or a facial, there's something for all.

Many hair salons and nail bars offer a combination of therapies and services, but as the quality, prices and service vary greatly, trial and error and word of mouth are the best ways to find a dependable salon. Indeed, word of mouth is such a potent method of advertisement, and Doha is so small, that one talkative customer can make very impressionable ripples both positive and negative.

Beauty Salons & Nail Bars

Beauty salons and nail bars are dotted all over Doha, so whether you need plucking, waxing, polishing, threading or buffing, there is plenty of choice from the top of the range venues to the smaller, price sensitive beauty salons.

The more salons there are, the more vigilant the Ministry of Health is becoming with regard to health and hygiene standards. The ministry performs regular checkups on facilities to ensure that they are abiding by official standards – violations mean that the facility is shut down immediately and risks its licence being revoked. This ensures firstly that standards of care remain high in the area, and secondly, prices within the city remain competitive.

As a rough guide, facials start at around QR 150 in smaller salons and can go as high as QR 1,000 in high-end spas. Manicures range from QR 40 for a simple polish through to QR 200 for a more elaborate process. Pedicures start at around QR 50 for a basic treatment and go upwards from there.

With year-round sunshine holding endless possibilities for strappy shoes, flip-flops, sandals and summery wedges, there's no excuse for having less than perfect pinkies. It's worth trying out a few different nail bars to find one that really suits your needs, because the chances are you'll be making regular appearances there. The listings below are a good starting place if you're new to the city. Many spas (p.181) and hairdressers (p.180) offer a side-line in beauty treatments. Day spas such as Dados (p.182) and Bio-Bil (4493 4433) offer pampering services to get you polished and pruned from head to toe.

If you're a shy, retiring type, (or just plan on having a lazy afternoon at home), it's worth asking whether salons can send a therapist to your villa as, while this is not usually an advertised service, many salons are happy to do so for advance bookings and an additional fee.

Al Kazem Beauty Centre Najma, 4443 2417, *alkazem.com*
Al Majedah Beauty Saloon Fereej Al Nasr, 4444 8508
Diva Lounge Beauty Spa Al Sadd, 4431 8488, *divaspaqatar.com*
Doha Beauty Centre & Spa Fereej Bin Mahmoud, 4431 3773, *dohabeautycenter.com*
Dona Beauty Salon Al Sadd, 4444 1301
Donia Beauty Salon Al Sadd, 4436 2254
Franka Beauty Saloon Rawdat Al Khail, 4444 3255
Manila Beauty Salon Fereej Bin Omran, 4443 6164
Marie Claire Bu Samra, 4468 9211
Markaz Funoon Al Henna Fereej Al Nasr, 4444 4033
Meche d'or Beauty Parlour Al Sadd, 4444 1995
Nails Al Sadd, 4413 0222, *andtrading.net*
Paris Nails Umm Lekhba, 4487 8643, *medicalspa-qatar.net*
Pinkies Rawdat Al Khail, 4431 7959
Skin & Soul Hannan Najjar Beauty Center Al Hilal, 4455 2456, *skinandsoul.com*
Stylo Salon Al Sadd, 4436 3626

Hairdressers

Hairdressing salons are never for just 'doing hair'. Most offer a vast menu of other services like manicures, pedicures, facials, waxing, threading, laser hair removal and so on. Even 'doing hair' is not as simple as a cut, colour and blow dry – in Doha you can find salons offering treatments from Brazilian keratin treatments to the Japanese yoko treatment. In addition, many salons offer customised services for little girls, pregnant women and new mamas.

You'll find hairdressers all over Doha – in malls, hotels, beauty salons, and a few independents. As with all services in Qatar, ask for recommendations as standards vary greatly; it's likely that once you've found a salon you like, you'll stick with them. At the top end of the spectrum you can opt for somewhere like Hair Studio, in the Riviera Gardens compound, which is popular with expat women. It offers pricey but well-executed cuts and colours with no fuss.

Prices start at QR 500 for a cut, colour and blow dry. At the other end of the scale, you can get a cheap and cheerful cut at one of the barber shops in the Najma area for around QR 20. Most hotels have a barber's salon where men can get a cut for between QR 60 and QR 100.

There are also hair salons designed especially for kids – most are located in malls close to children's play areas. Head to Fun City in Doha City Center or Circusland in Landmark Mall; there's a salon near to Jungle Zone in Hyatt Plaza too. There is no need to make an appointment for any of these salons – they operate on a first come, first served basis.

There are a number of stylists who will come to your home, which is a great idea if you have small children or if you want the whole family done at the same time. Ask around as numbers are usually passed from one satisfied customer to another.

Cut By Alexandre Zouari W Doha Hotel & Residences, Al Dafna, 4453 5353, *whoteldoha.com*
The Diplomatic Club Beauty Center The Diplomatic Club, Al Gassar, 4484 7407, *thediplomaticclub.com*
Ellie & Gean Sheraton Doha Resort & Convention Hotel, Al Dafna, 4485 4444, *ejhair.com*
Franck Provost Paris Hair Salon Spa & Wellness Centre, Al Dafna, 4494 8844, *andtrading.net*
Glow American Salon & Spa Off Salwa Rd, Al Waab, 4468 9945, *glowamericansalon.com*
The Hair Studio Riviera Gardens Compound, Duhail, 4479 5945
Jean Louis David Renaissance Doha City Center Hotel, Al Dafna, 4417 5771, *andtrading.net*
Lucie Saint-Clair Royal Plaza, Al Sadd, 4447 7725, *lucie-saint-clair.com*
Marie Claire Salwa Rd, Bu Samra, 4468 9211
Rosy InterContinental Doha, Al Gassar, 4484 4830

Health Spas & Massage
Soothing for the body, mind and soul, a massage could be a weekly treat, a gift to someone special, or a relaxing way to get you through a trying time at work. Numerous massage and relaxation techniques are available, but prices and standards vary, so it's worth pursuing the reviews here and asking friends for recommendations. Spas range from those at opulent hotels where every detail is customised for a journey of relaxation, to comfortable independent places which offer fewer facilities but better value for money if you just want someone to loosen your knots. It's worth checking out the treatment menus at beauty salons (p.180) as some offer good value head, neck, shoulder and back massages. Also, some of the fitness clubs (p.177) have spas or massage rooms on site, both for sports and relaxation purposes.

Angsana Spa
Wyndham Grand Regency Doha Al Sadd **4434 3152**
angsanaspa.com
Map **2 K7**
Situated in the Grand Regency Hotel, the Angsana Spa is a calming escape from daily Doha life. Unwind in the privacy of one of eight spacious spa suites, fully equipped with en-suite bathroom facilities. Couples can enjoy simultaneous pampering, followed by a steam and Jacuzzi bath, in the couple's suite. Choose from a lengthy list of Asian-influenced treatments, such as anti-ageing facials, therapeutic body massages and invigorating body polishes derived from green tea and other natural sources. Not to be missed are the hydrotherapy showers and baths, such as the Thunderstorm Shower or Spring Shower, which guarantee head-to-toe cleansing. Book the private hydrotherapy spa suite for the ultimate squeaky-clean spa experience.

The Spa, Doha Marriott

Bliss Spa

W Doha Hotel & Residences Al Dafna **4453 5555**
blissworld.com
Map **2 Q1**

From the cheerful welcome at the door to the luxuriously soft robes, Bliss is an oasis of calm and offers a unique concept in Qatar. With its peaceful and calming interior and its stylish, white leather opulence, it's like stepping into a parallel universe. This is the first Middle East outpost of the cult New York-based 'working woman's spa'. Housed in the so-hip-it-hurts W Hotel, it has a luxe nail lounge with manicure and pedicure stations equipped with personal TVs, nine treatment rooms and cosy lounges. The changing rooms are amongst the best in Doha, offering a full range of grooming products from Paul Mitchell, as well as Bliss' own range, to sample apres treatment. Also on offer is the legendary brownie buffet along with tea, coffee and crackers, and a range of magazines which makes it hard to drag yourself away and back into the real world. Stand out treatments include the Blissage 75 massage and the Triple Oxygen Treatment Facial. Bliss might not be cheap, but for a true escape from Doha's dusty streets, it's well worth the extravagance once in a while.

Bodylines Leisure & Fitness Club

Oryx Rotana Al Hilal **4402 3485**
rotana.com
Map **2 T11**

Located on the first floor of the Oryx Rotana next to Choices restaurant, Bodylines exudes calm, elegance with subdued lighting, luminous swatches of golden velvet softening rich marbled walls and the light scent of ginger. After swimming laps in the pool or working out in the 24-hour gym, guests can relax in the Jacuzzi or steam room. A wide range of massages are available. The Microfoliant Scrub smoothes desert-stressed skin, while the Sea Mud Wrap cleanses and nourishes with plant extracts. Schedule-bound business travellers can also benefit with express back, shoulder and neck massages.

Dados Spa > p.183

Al Seal Residence, Conference Centre St Al Dafna **4498 0033**
dadosbeauty.com
Map **2 Q2**

Vibrant and hip, Dados is an unashamedly girlie, glam spa that offers a refreshingly fun beauty experience. In addition to treatments, you can find some funky clothing items on sale here. After sampling the must-have fashion pieces adorning reception, book yourself a well-deserved spot of pampering – the novel range of delectable treatments includes indulgent massages, great scrubs and traditional Hammam treatments; alternatively, pop into the nail bar or hair salon. Little girls and pregnant mamas are catered for by bubbly,

expert staff who leave you feeling as bright and glossy as the decor. The best part? Prices are reasonable and your pampering comes guilt-free knowing that a portion of your treatment fee goes directly to charity.

Jaula Spa

Grand Hyatt Doha Al Gassar **4448 1056**
doha.grand.hyatt.com
Map **1 K1**

Luxurious and resplendent, Jaula offers a truly outstanding spa experience. Guests utilise private, purpose-built suites in which everything from changing and showering to therapy is performed, letting you escape into your own haven of welcome solitude. Exceptional treatments promote wellness and harmony and are delivered by skilled staff who use all-natural products from marine and botanical sources that focus on rejuvenation, hydration and deep relaxation. Massages, facials, scrubs, wraps and waxing are all on offer, using enriching oils, minerals, clays, salts, seaweeds and algae. The spacious, earth-inspired decor mixes warmth, symmetry and serenity, as the ideal backdrop for the superior quality of products, therapies and personalised service available. Prices are, unsurprisingly, on the high side but Jaula is an extravagance worth treating yourself for.

Lady Siam Massage

Nr Toys 'R' Us, Al Kinana St Al Sadd **4435 4115**
Map **2 L9**

This is a ladies-only salon mainly offering Thai massage treatments, and aromatherapy massage using essential oils. Tailored more towards a quick respite from a hard day's work, rather than a full blown splurge, prices start at QR 120 for a full body massage, but look out for monthly promotions when the price comes down to QR 100.

Ozone Gym & Spa At La Cigale Hotel > p.199, 338

La Cigale Hotel Fereej Bin Mahmoud **4428 8888**
lacigalehotel.com
Map **2 M9**

This gem of a spa feels like an oasis of calm in the midst of busy streets and the madness of the Ramada junction. The treatment rooms are decorated with fresh orchids and divinely fragrant smells fill the air to create a soothing atmosphere. The treatment menu is varied with a particular focus on skin therapy (including anti-cellulite LPG) and a full range of massage and Hamman treatments. Various packages, including combinations designed to aid slimming and relaxation, are also on offer. After your treatment, you'll get to relax some more at the spa's excellent sauna, steam room and swimming pool area; then park yourself in the actual relaxation room where a yummy platter of fresh fruit and drinks awaits.

dados | بادوش

all about beauty, fun & fashion

**Flaunt your Gorgeousness with Dados Beauty
and Spark up your Fashion Style with Dados Boutique!**

hair & nails

traditional hammam

pamper your face & body

DADOS BEAUTY
Al Seal Residence, West Bay, Doha, Qatar
Telephone No. (+974) 4498-0033
www.dadosbeauty.com

trendy brands

Irresistable Accessories

DADOS BOUTIQUE
The Pearl Qatar Porto Arabia 47 2 La Croisette
Telephone No. (+974) 4495-3876 ext. 1471
boutique@dadosbeauty.com

Well-Being

PURE > *p.81*

Kempinski Residences & Suites Al Dafna **4405 3307**
kempinski-residences.com
Map **2 Q1**
Centrally located in West Bay, PURE is well equipped
for those serious about fitness. The brightly lit and
spacious workout areas are divided into separate
spots for cardio and other fitness pursuits. Afterwards,
you can take a dip in one of the two indoor pools, or
head for the steam room to soothe the muscles. The
spa treatments on offer cover all the essentials, should
you wish to book a spot of pampering. Whether you
worked a sweat at the gym or enjoyed a relaxing spa
treat, don't forget to indulge in some fresh juices
before heading out – made with fresh ingredients, the
selection is truly refreshing.

Six Senses Spa At Sharq Village & Spa

Sharq Village & Spa Al Khulaifat **4425 6999**
sixsenses.com/six-senses-spas
Map **2 U8**
Six Senses provides the ultimate destination for
luxurious pampering and this beautifully designed
spa is a true retreat. Evocative Arabic windtowers and
souk-like passageways give an exotic but reassuringly
natural feel, while the excellent service ensures five-
star treatment throughout. A spa butler will escort you
to the spacious changing room and walk you through
indoor and outdoor passageways to one of the
treatment rooms. This tranquil journey lasts to the final
stroke of your massage and infuses through your time
in the peaceful relaxation room. Some of the treatment
highlights include the Hammam and the hot stone and
four hands massages. Classes such as tai chi, Moksha
(heated) yoga and meditation are also on offer and
personal training is available in the fitness centre. Be
sure to arrive early to make the most of the sauna, spa
and hot and cold plunge pools. There are even private
outdoor pools that can be used at your leisure.

Spa & Wellness Centre

Four Seasons Hotel Al Dafna **4494 8801**
fourseasons.com/doha
Map **2 R2**
This is not just any regular spa – among state-of-
the-art facilities, there are some features within the
wellness centre which are unique to Doha: loosen up
in the hydrotherapy lounge and pool, plunge into
cool and warm pools, soak your feet in the reflexology
bath, relax on a heated Roman-style laconium bed, or
try meditating in the colour therapy room. Spa guests
will also have access to the hotel's beautiful private
beach, swimming pool and fitness centre, where
personal trainers are available. The various treatments
on offer include wraps, scrubs and signature Thai
massages. The spa itself has separate areas for men
and women, while the hydrotherapy lounge is mixed.

Spa Chakra

Alfardan Towers, 61 Al Funduq St Al Dafna
4499 9250
Map **2 Q3**
This sleek and futuristic award-winning spa offers a
high-tech relaxation experience in elevated surrounds.
Situated on the 39th floor, the spa's facilities include
a Vichy shower and a colour therapy-enhanced
swimming pool with spectacular city views. A full
range of treatments for men and women is available
including facials, massages, anti-ageing and beauty
treatments, and naturopathy consultancies. While
you wait, opt for some pre-massage hydrotherapy to
maximise the benefits of your chosen treatment. The
therapy rooms are on the clinical side and lack the
aesthetic touches of some luxury spas, but each one is
kitted out with top notch facilities including a private
bathroom. A gym, weights room, personal trainer
and nutritionist services complete the spa's fitness
offerings. Memberships are available.

The Spa, Marriott Doha

Doha Marriott Hotel Al Khulaifat **4429 8520**
marriott-doha.com
Map **2 V8**
This spa offers treatments to pamper every inch
of your body, from therapeutic back massages
and Turkish baths, to full body scrubs and facial
treatments. Other treatments include body wraps,
foot baths, manicures, pedicures, therapy baths and
beauty treatments including waxing. There is a lap
pool available for those in search of a more cardio
workout, and a steam room, and the compact fitness
centre offers fitness counselling and personal training.
Fitness classes are also available. Just call the spa for
a timetable.

The Spa, Ritz-Carlton Doha

The Ritz-Carlton, Doha Al Gassar **4484 8173**
ritzcarlton.com
Map **1 K1**
With delightfully tranquil views of the sea, the Ritz-
Carlton Spa is an oasis of relaxation, well-being and
serenity. Beyond the typical treatments, this spa offers
state-of-the art health and fitness facilities for all
guests to use. Spa members, hotel guests and pay-per-
use visitors may work-out in the fitness room with or
without the help of a personal trainer, attend a group
fitness class or book a time slot in the indoor squash
or tennis courts. After a good work-out, members
and guests can enjoy the outdoor pool, indoor
Roman bath, steam-room, sauna and spa treatments.
Spa facilities are separate for men and women. Try
a Perfect Date massage, an Arabic body treatment
derived from honey and dates, or the wonderfully
relaxing signature massage, aptly named The Ritz
Carlton Massage.

Hammam at Ozone Spa

Dados Spa

Six Senses Spa

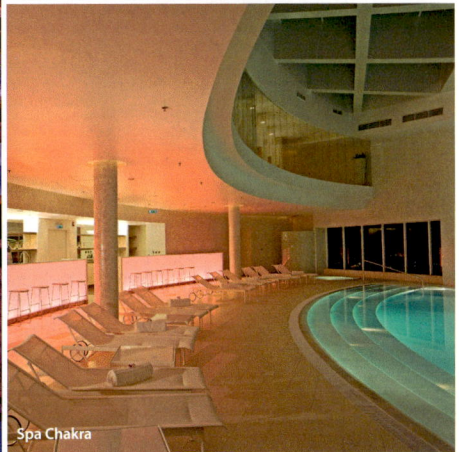
Spa Chakra

SUKAR PASHA
OTTOMAN LOUNGE

EXPERIENCE THE OTTOMAN LIFESTYLE

Whether you are coming alone or as a group, you will find Sukar Pasha Shisha Lounge a casual, yet highly luxurious location; a haven where ancient flavors and aromas will seduce your senses.

Sukar Pasha Ottoman Lounge
Katara Cultural Village
Doha, Qatar

Tel: +974 44082000
Fax: +974 44082002
Email: info@sukarpasha.qa
Url: www.sukarpasha.qa

OPEN DAILY
12pm – 6:30pm (Drinks & Shisha)
6:30pm – 12:30am (Dinner)

Discover Doha

DISCOVER DOHA

As a fast growing country with significant plans for the future, Qatar is keen to keep strengthening its position as a tourist destination as well. However, it is very selective about how this is achieved and the attractions it offers: while the shopping and fine dining sectors continue to improve, culture, education, sport and business tourism are the key focus of Qatar's national and international marketing efforts.

The stunning Museum of Islamic Art (p.207) stands as a proud symbol of Qatar's past and future. Other major projects that have already now been completed include Katara Cultural Village (p.207), formerly known as the Cultural Village, the Arab Museum of Modern Art and the ultra-modern Qatar National Convention Centre (p.33).

Elsewhere, entire cities have been built, one of which, The Pearl (p.33), rests on reclaimed land. To the north of West bay, the massive Lusail Project includes Entertainment City and Energy City, along with office space, residences, hotels, resorts, shopping and dining.

Recently, Doha proudly flew the esteemed flag of Arab Capital of Culture in 2010. The city is still enjoying reverberations from this event with increased art gallery space and cultural offerings. In addition to the Museum of Islamic Art and the Arab Museum of Modern Art, there are a few interesting private collections which are open to the public by prior appointment. These include Sheikh Faisal bin Qassim Al Thani Museum and the Orientalist Museum (p.208), both of which are well worth visiting; if you don't want to handle the administration yourself, there are tour companies who will arrange access for you (see Main Tour Operators, p.228). There are also a number of forts and sites of archaeological interest to visit but, because Qatar was a Bedouin country with a mobile population, there are few historical sites of note.

Cultural attractions aside, Qatar boasts a host of outdoors attractions. Being a peninsula, the country has long stretches of beaches and coastline, much of which is unspoiled and easy to get to. One of the greatest pleasures is camping in the desert or on the beach. Camping in Qatar is easy – requiring far less paraphernalia than camping in cooler climes, so even if you're not an outdoorsy person, you should give camping a try at least once while you're living in the country (see Camping, p.218). A particularly popular camping site with residents and visitors is in the dunes around the natural wonder of the Inland Sea (see Khor Al Udaid, p.243).

Those of a sporty disposition are well-catered for as well. The 2006 Asian Games, when athletes, officials and spectators from over 40 countries converged on the Qatari capital, were a turning point in the country's appeal as a sports destination. Building on the success of the Asian Games, Doha has built an infrastructure to attract annual sporting events, such as the Qatar ExxonMobil Open (p.24) and QTA Qatar Total Open (qatartennis.org) where the world's top tennis players compete at Khalifa International Tennis and Squash Complex. In 2011 this venue hosted the Asian Football Cup, which attracted thousands of fans to the region.

Also a legacy of the 2006 games, the Aspire Zone is a world-class sports facility which hosts major sporting events such as the IAAF World Indoor Championships. In addition to numerous public facilities, the centre runs fitness classes and houses a sports academy.

In 2010, Qatar ecstatically won the bid for the 2022 Fifa World Cup (p.27). One can expect even more building projects as a result of this winning bid; even more so if Qatar's ambitions to host the Olympic Games in 2024 are actualised.

Other sporting events which can be enjoyed by Qatar's residents include horse racing at Qatar Racing and Equestrian Club (p.225), motorsports at the Lusail International Circuit (p.26), the Commercial Bank Qatar Masters (p.25) and the Qatar Table Tennis Open. A range of powerboat competitions, including the Oryx Cup UIM World Championship, are hosted by Qatar Marine Sports Federation (qmsf.org).

The capital, Doha, is framed by the Corniche – a pedestrian walkway around the bay, where walkers, joggers and cyclists can enjoy views of the turquoise Arabian Gulf. Along the Corniche and throughout the city, there are public parks which offer shade, cafes, toilets and plenty of space for children to run off steam (see Parks, p.212). Soaring temperatures from May through to October mean that much of the population retreats indoors, but there are plenty of indoor entertainment centres to keep kids busy (see Activities For Kids, p.130). Doha residents have welcomed the opening of Doha's first water park (see Aqua Park, p.216).

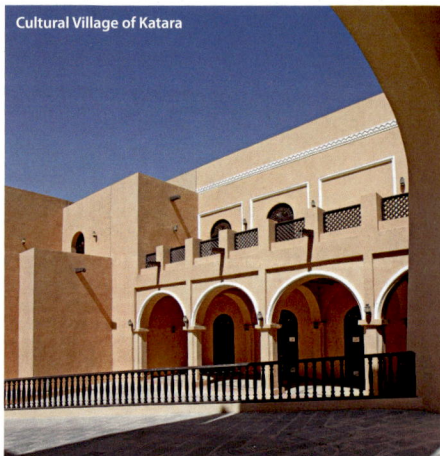

Cultural Village of Katara

One of Doha's highlights is its sprawling souks – particularly the beautifully revamped Souk Waqif (p.330), which has been renovated and expanded using traditional building methods and is home to stores selling traditional wares, as well as cafes and restaurants with street-seating that are perfect for an enjoyable and relaxing evening with friends, or simply to sit alone and people watch. Having exhausted the souks, shoppers can take their pick of Doha's many shopping malls from the Venetian-inspired Villaggio (p.335) to deluxe boutiques on The Pearl (p.33). For those who still can't find what they're looking for, an eight kilometre-long business and shopping area, Barwa Commercial Avenue, is being constructed on the south edge of the city.

PLACES OF INTEREST

Doha's main areas to explore are described over the next few pages. If you're new to the city, these are good places to start if you want to get a feel for your new home. Following Places Of Interest, different attractions are described, so if you're looking for something specific, that's the place to start.

When exploring the city, note that while Doha is quite compact, increasing traffic and major road improvements mean that it can be slow-going getting across town. The city's plethora of roundabouts (a hangover from its days as a British protectorate) are now being replaced by traffic lights. The city is, at present, a mass of building work, and will be for some time yet. Residents tend to use the names of nearby buildings or landmarks to describe a location, so pay attention to your surroundings as well as to street names. Street maps usually show the Corniche and bay at the top, which is logical; the bay is actually in the east, not the north, as often implied (see Pull-Out Map).

Al Sadd & Al Rayyan Road

Al Rayyan Road heads west from Doha Fort (p.206) and the souk area, all the way out of town and towards the district of Al Rayyan on the outskirts of Doha. The main hospital, Hamad General Hospital (p.164), is on this road, near Sports Roundabout, and the Women's Hospital (p.166) is next door. These are now part of the QR Hamad Medical City development (p.32), along with a growing number of other institutions of different specialisms. The apartment blocks on Mohammed Bin Thani Street, near the civil defence (fire station) building, were built for the athletes at the 2006 Asian Games and are now home to medical staff. The turrets of the Castle Gardens compound on the corner of Mohammed Bin Thani Street and Ahmed Bin Ali Street are good landmarks to help orient new residents. Al Sadd Street, which runs

parallel to Al Rayyan Road, is a busy commercial area with restaurants and shops, including the Royal Plaza shopping mall (p.336). From the Al Sadd signal, where Al Sadd Street meets the C Ring Road, turning south (right from Al Sadd Street) will take you to La Cigale – one of Doha's most exclusive hotels, with restaurants including Le Central (p.364), a deluxe foodhall and, contender for best bar in the city, Sky View Bar (p.373). Running between Al Rayyan and Al Sadd is Jawaan Street, which has the Grand Regency (p.206) and Millennium (p.200) hotels and Al Asmakh Mall, more commonly known as Centrepoint (p.4428 9141).

Al Dafna & Al Gassar (Diplomatic Area & West Bay)

The area which encompasses the north end of the Corniche from Qatar National Theatre to the Sheraton, the Diplomatic Area and much of West Bay, is officially known as Al Dafna, but many people still refer to it by its former names. Just after the Sheraton Hotel is the Diplomatic Area, home to various embassies and consulates. This district is still undergoing a lot of development, with towering hotel, apartment and office blocks springing up all the way from City Center Doha to the opulent West Bay Lagoon on the mainland entrance to The Pearl. In 2009 the trendy W Hotel (p.204) opened and now houses some of Doha's most exclusive night spots, Crystal lounge (p.371) and Wahm (p.373), as well as designer restaurants Spice Market (p.368) and Market By Jean-Georges (p.365). The Kempinski Residences (p.200), Merwebhotel Central (p.200) and the Oryx Rotana (p.202) are among the other hospitality destinations already open here and in the pipeline are others, including the Hilton Doha, a Renaissance hotel, a Shangri-La, and a Marriot.

At the heart of Al Dafna is City Center Doha (p.331). This enormous mall has 350 shops, an ice rink, bowling alley and children's amusements; parking here can be a nightmare. Opposite City Center Doha is Qatar Financial Centre, the capital's financial hub.

If you head out of Al Dafna from City Center Doha along Al Wahda Street, you will reach another useful landmark – Arch Roundabout (also known as Rainbow Roundabout). If you take a right here and head up Lusail Street (Al Istiqlal Street), you will pass Qatar International Exhibition Centre, with its red roof, on the right; this is the temporary home of the Qatar Tourism Exhibitions Authority (4499 7499, qatartourism.gov.qa) and is where many of Doha's international congresses and trade fairs are held. Behind this is the InterContinental hotel (p.198) and the St Regis hotel.

Staying on Lusail Street, you'll see Katara (p.207). Although a few buildings are still to be completed, Katara has been open to the public since April 2010 and has quickly become a hub of weekend activity. It houses an opera house, a public beach, museums and galleries. The Qatar Photographic Society (p.276), Qatar Fine Arts Society (p.265), and the Qatar Museums Authority Gallery all hold periodic exhibitions. It was also the venue for Qatar Marine Festival (4499 4300), Doha Tribeca Film Festival (p.26) and Katara International Kite Family Day, all of which are expected to become annual events well worth attending. On the left hand side of Lusail Street are a number of massive villas, some of which are international embassies.

Al Waab & Around Villaggio

Al Waab Street runs north of and parallel to Salwa Road. To the left of Al Waab Street, heading away from town, are a number of popular villa compounds, behind which is the site of the vast Al Waab City development (p.85).

Authoritative Friends

Qatar Museums Authority is responsible for all of Qatar's museums and heritage sites. Get the latest openings info online at qma.com.qa, or join the QMA in the 21st century by keeping up with developments through its Facebook page.

Rising above Al Waab Street, you'll see the Aspire Tower, which is a very useful landmark for navigating the Doha area. Below the tower is Aspire Zone which was the focal point for the successful 2006 Asian Games. Also on this site is Aspire Academy, which offers top class coaching and training facilities for various sports, and aims to nurture the Qatari sporting champions of tomorrow. There is also an impressive range of fitness classes held at the site which are open to the general public (see Aspire Active, p.131). Neighbouring the Aspire Zone is the Khalifa Stadium with its graceful arch, and Aspetar Orthopaedic and

Sports Medicine Hospital (p.174) is also within the complex. The Grand Heritage Doha Hotel and Spa (p.198) just opened within the Aspire Zone.

For those that prefer flexing their plastic rather than their muscles, Villaggio shopping mall (p.335) is next to the Aspire Zone, and the slightly ageing, but still popular, Hyatt Plaza (p.336) is further along Al Waab Street.

Behind Hyatt Plaza is Aspire Park (p.212), a large but rather empty expanse of a public park, which features a sprung jogging path and a manmade lake. Next to this is Aspire Play Park (p.212) which is popular with younger children.

After Hyatt Plaza, a left onto Al Furousiya Street takes you to Doha Zoo (p.216), while a right takes you to the Racing and Equestrian Club (4480 8122) where you can watch horse racing for free or pay for riding lessons; heading straight on takes you past the new drag racing circuit in Doha Industrial Area (see Motorsports, p.225).

Doha Corniche

The Corniche is arguably the most picturesque area of Doha and a great place to explore whether you've got half an hour or a whole day. Just east of the 'proper' start to the Corniche, on Ras Abu Abboud Street, sit the Marriott hotel (p.196), Doha Sailing Club (p.278) and the very smart Sharq Village and Spa (p.204). Coming from the airport, signs still point the way to Ras Al Nasaa, an Iranian restaurant which has been demolished.

On the seaside, directly across from the large construction site which is to be the National Museum of Qatar (p.208), an unofficial fish market has sprung up. Each morning, throngs of people can be seen waiting for the fishermen to bring in the daily catch. Continuing along the Corniche, just before the port

The Clock Tower

is Halul Cafe, a pleasantly shabby place to smoke a shisha, drink Turkish coffee, and play chess or cards.

Impossible to miss is the striking series of balanced cubes which is the renowned Museum of Islamic Art (p.207), designed by IM Pei, who was responsible for the Louvre extension in Paris. The museum, which opened in December 2008, houses one of the world's largest collections of Islamic art and stands alone as a phenomenal work of architecture.

Hot Spot

You'll notice signs in the parks along the Corniche advertising Wi-Fi hotspots, but the signal is often weak. Souk Waqif is another Wi-Fi hotspot and a good place to get online. Here you'll notice people enjoying a post-work juice while making the most of the free connection. At some cafes and restaurants you may be lucky enough to locate an electrical socket to power your computer.

Further on is the start of the attractive pedestrian stretch of the Corniche (which is perfect for early risers to jog along) that loops in a semi-circle all the way around the bay, ending at the unmistakable Aztec pyramid-shaped Sheraton hotel (p.204). Soon after the Museum of Islamic Art, a jetty leads to a small harbour for fishing boats and dhows. The dhows can be rented for the day through local tour companies (p.228) to take you around the bay, or to one of the near-lying islands (p.243). At the entrance to this jetty, on the Corniche, is the much-photographed pearl sculpture. Grand Hamad Street runs away from the Corniche close to the pearl sculpture and leads to the souk area (p.323).

Continuing along, on the left, you'll see the Emiri Diwan (presidential palace) (diwan.gov.qa), with its expansive lawns and cascading water feature. Behind the Diwan are the Clock Tower and Grand Mosque (this is not open to the general public). The large building next to the Diwan is the Ministry of Interior, and past this lies Rumeilah Park (also called Al Bidda Park, p.214), which is very popular with families, especially in the evenings and at weekends. The park has a takeaway cafe, toilets, children's play areas, and a Heritage Village, which has been built to resemble a traditional Qatari hamlet but which is only open during Ramadan and Eid and for cultural events. At the far end of Rumeilah Park is an amphitheatre and a collection of small shops (most of which seem to be permanently closed) running along a small canal. At the opposite end of the canal to the amphitheatre is a small heritage house which contains rudimentary displays of women's traditional handicrafts. More interesting than the displays is the building itself, which resembles a traditional Qatari home. It has sporadic opening times. The Qatar National Theatre

(p.343) is next to Rumeilah Park, and following this is the National Library, which is closed awaiting the construction of new premises.

Snap Happy

You should be careful with your camera when in the vicinity of the Diwan, as the authorities tend to get a little sensitive if you take pictures of official buildings or royal palaces.

On the Corniche itself it's impossible to miss the giant Oryx figure, Orry, the mascot for the 2006 Asian Games. Next to him is the only watering hole on the Corniche, the popular Al Mourjan restaurant (p.351) which, previously called Balhambra, serves a Lebanese spread along with tea, juices and shisha, in high-end surroundings with stunning views of the Gulf from its terrace. From here Palm Tree Island (p.243), formerly a popular, shaded beach area, is visible and notably void of greenery. The view of the skyline from this area changes each and every year as more striking towers of glass pepper the shoreline of the modern commercial and financial area (see Doha's Striking Skyline, p.34).

Changing Names

New residents should note the change in roundabout names: there had been a roundabout near the Qatar National Museum (called Museum roundabout); that road is currently under construction and the roundabout no longer exists. Today the roundabout nearest to the Museum of Islamic Art has become known as the Museum Roundabout, rather than Customs Roundabout, as it used to be called.

There is a also a very pleasant patch of green beside the water just before you reach the Sheraton, with a shop and cafe, children's playground, toilets, and plenty of space to sit and relax and enjoy a picnic (see Sheraton Gardens, p.214). You will almost always see families taking full advantage of this space during the cooler months. Near to this is the Msheireb Enrichment Centre (p.206); although this is mainly to showcase the masterplan for the Dohaland development (p.33), it also has a display of interesting historical photos of Doha. The Corniche is a very popular destination and the parks and roads around here get very busy and congested especially on weekend evenings.

Khalifa Street & Al Luqta Street

Khalifa Street runs from the Oryx Roundabout near the Corniche to the three-level interchange by the Immigration Department, where it becomes Al Luqta

Street and continues west. This road heads cross-country, eventually reaching Dukhan (p.80) on the west coast. At the top end, near the Oryx Roundabout, is Khalifa International Tennis and Squash Complex (p.280), which is the venue for the annual ExxonMobil tennis tournament for men (p.24), which attracts some of the best players in the world. Just beyond that is the magnificent State Mosque (p.33) which will be open to worshippers soon.

Further along Khalifa Street on the left is the Al Jazeera and Qatar TV headquarters, just before the appropriately nicknamed TV Roundabout. There are a few independent restaurants around here which are popular with expats and locals. To the south of Khalifa Street is Doha English Speaking School (p.146). Continuing on Khalifa Street you will reach the Traffic Department where you go to arrange driving licences and to register vehicles (see Getting Around, p.51). Just after the Traffic Department lies the newly completed, triple-decker flyover, where Khalifa Street meets the D Ring Road.

The Immigration Department is just by the interchange, and on the left hand side of the road is the Weaponry Museum (p.240), which is currently closed. From here Al Luqta Street continues over the 'sloping roundabout' (just about the only hill in Doha), west towards Education City, which is run by the Qatar Foundation.

Education City is an impressive regional centre for teaching and research excellence, and is home to a number of international university campuses including Carnegie Mellon, Georgetown, Texas A&M, Virginia Commonwealth, and Cornell (see Universities and Higher Education, p.148). A series of dramatic new buildings adorn the landscape including the wavy-roofed Qatar Science and Technology Park (4454 7070, qstp.org.qa) and the nearly completed Qatar Convention Centre (p.33), which looks as if a giant, steel sidra tree is growing through it. Mathaf: Arab Museum of Modern Art (p.207) is located at the far end of Education City.

Behind Education City is a huge dome which is being built to house Al Shaqab Riding Academy (p.273), where visitors will be able to view thoroughbred horses and take lessons at the riding school. Some of the buildings have been completed while others are still under construction.

A few kilometres out at Sheehaniyah is Sheikh Faisal bin Qassim Al Thani's fascinating museum (p.238). This is a large, private collection, which can only be viewed by making an appointment, but it is worth the trip. It is an eclectic selection of ancient weaponry, textiles, woodwork and metalwork, currency, vintage cars, and much more. Further along are the oryx farm (p.238) and the camel racetrack (p.237) – it is advised that people contact a tour company (p.228) for trips to these places.

Salwa Road & Bu Hamour (Markets Area)

This is not so much an area, but more a main artery that heads in a straight line from the Ramada Interchange out of the city, eventually reaching the Saudi Arabian border and the highway which leads to the UAE (see UAE Roadtrip, p.252). Much of the south end of Salwa Road is under construction; drivers anticipate the addition of flyovers will relieve some of the common traffic jams in this area.

The Ramada Interchange is another Doha landmark. Where Salwa Road and Suhaim Bin Hamad Street (C Ring Road) cross, each of the four corners has several restaurants and shops. The abundance of fast food places has earned it the name 'cholesterol corner'. You can find a Chili's (p.356), Pizza Hut and Dairy Queen here, alongside plenty of other international and regional chains. Near the Ramada Interchange you'll also find Jarir Bookstore (p.298). Mega Mart (p.325), a popular grocery store among expats longing for a taste of home, is located at The Centre shopping mall near Radisson Blu (p.202), which houses a vast range of eateries and bars including Pier 12 and Bubbles champagne bar.

Away from the city centre, Salwa Road heads south-west towards the triple-decker interchange (known locally as Midmac Interchange) with the newly constructed D Ring Road (Al Amir Street). Further along on the right hand side, just before the D Ring interchange, you'll find Café Bateel (p.356), which does some of the best bread and pastries in Doha and makes a lovely place to stop for lunch. After the interchange, Salwa Road turns into a seemingly endless parade of shops and garages set back from the road. There isn't that much variety, but if you want car spares, tyres, or furniture, you'll be spoilt for choice. Skater boys (and girls) will like the Skate Shack (p.297), selling bikes, skateboard gear, and watersports equipment (it's on the left as you drive away from Doha, just after the roundabout for the wholesale markets). 16km past the Industrial Roundabout is the new Aqua Park (p.216).

The markets are worth exploring for the experience alone, even if you have no intention of buying anything. Nearest Salwa Road are the fruit, vegetable and fish markets. Soon after, the huge bales of straw on trucks beside the road announce your arrival at the livestock market where traders buy and sell sheep and goats. The camel market is nearby too.

Souk Area & Souk Waqif

Souks are bazaars or markets that sell virtually everything. The area that extends inland from the port is the traditional shopping district, with a mixture of slightly shabby low rise concrete buildings and more attractive older designs. Qatar's first souk, Souk Waqif (p.330), still exists today and has undergone an extensive renovation project. After the Museum of Islamic Art, Souk Waqif is the second jewel in Qatar's cultural crown. Sympathetically redeveloped, it retains its old-world character and is filled with cafes, restaurants and hundreds of tiny shops; it makes for an interesting place to explore.

The souk used to be the weekend market where the Bedouins would come into town to trade their meat, wool, milk and other goods and while it has been redeveloped and enlarged, it is not a twee tourist attraction – you can still buy anything from a fishing net to a Gulf Fulla doll. There's a fantastic range of items to buy, from Arabic perfumes and oils to beautifully embroidered bukhnoqs (head coverings adorned with gold and silver thread and worn by young Qatari girls) and heavyweight camel hair cloaks worn by men in the winter. Follow your nose and you'll find shops selling vast piles of spices, herbs and nuts. At weekends, traditional activities including music, henna painting and weaving take place in the main square.

Covered alleys run throughout Souk Waqif, with one broad street stretching diagonally from Al Koot Fort (p.206) towards the car park beside Hotel Souq Waqif (p.198). This street is lined mainly with cafes and restaurants with a few one-off shops. If you need a break, try a light lunch at Zaatar W Zeit, a popular Lebanese fastfood chain, and be sure to get a spot in the shade. In the evening, roof-top dining at Tajine (p.369) Moroccan restaurant is popular with tourists. For shisha and juice any time of the day or evening, stop at Al Koot Cafe.

Children may be thrilled to discover dolled-up rabbits on the street south of Hotel Souq Waqif; parents may be less so, as some of the animals here are visibly ill, while others are kept in constraining cages with a multitude of mates. For some, this area of the souk is thus best avoided, but if you find yourself

here, having a small bottle of disinfectant hand solution at the ready will keep bacteria on children's wandering hands in check.

Once off the main thoroughfare, the souk can be overwhelming for first-time visitors. The more cautious might find a late morning or early afternoon visit less intimidating, while the adventurous will enjoy the bustle of Thursday evenings in the souk. The winding lanes are disorientating and you will get lost, but it's all part of the experience and shopkeepers are generally friendly and happy to point you in the right direction. Single women may find themselves on the receiving end of unwanted stares, particularly on Fridays, the only day of the weekend for many workers, but while you might be stared at, you won't be hassled. The souks are safe places, even if you find yourself completely lost, and the best way to minimise the staring is to dress conservatively and cover your shoulders and knees. Single men should note that there may be restricted 'family' access on Fridays; dressing smartly will decrease your chances of being turned away. The souk is generally open from 09:00 or 10:00 to 13:00 and then again from 16:00 to 22:00. On Fridays, shops often open in the afternoon only.

The wider souk area is a jumble of streets and smaller souks (see Markets and Souks, p.326), centred around the high spiral of Fanar, the Islamic Cultural Art Centre (p.207). Parking in the area has been expanded with a big carpark at each end of Souk Waqif on Jasim bin Mohammed Street and Abdulla bin Jasim Street and the new, air-conditioned, underground car park by the Grand Mosque; despite these being paid car parks, it can still be hard to find a parking spot at the weekend. The area around the souk is also being redeveloped: immediately behind the Emiri Diwan, construction has begun on what is to be the new heart of Doha (p.33).

Heading south-west along Wadi Musheireb Street (which is the beginning of Salwa Road), from the junction with Al Diwan Street, there is a big selection of electronics and lighting shops. To the east, this street comes out near Al Koot Fort, at the busy roundabout with a wooden dhow in the middle (Dhow Roundabout). Just off Ali bin Abdullah Street is Souk Najada, full of cheap electronics and clothes, and within its courtyard you can see the Windtower House (p.209), which was once a museum but is now closed. On Jasim bin Mohammed Street, next to the souk parking lots, stands the Doha (or Al Koot) Fort (p.206), which is still closed for renovations. Next to the Fort you can often find camels resting in the sun.

Musheireb and the area that extends inland from the port is not a residential district as such, although there are some old villas and many of the shops have low-rent apartments above them. With such a variety and quantity of shops this is a popular area where expats and locals alike can enjoy rooting around for

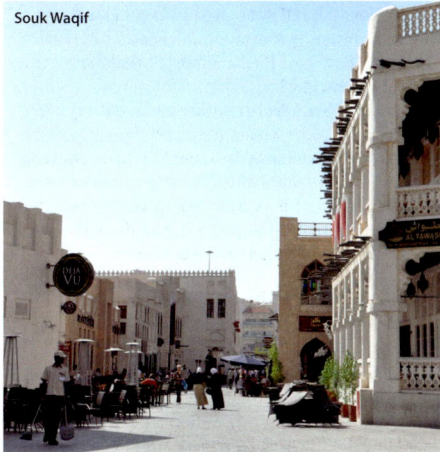
Souk Waqif

bargains. Single women should again be aware that this is a male dominated area, and that they may find themselves on the receiving end of unwanted attention. On Fridays and in the evenings, this area can be heavily congested, with parking usually proving problematic.

The Gold Souk

Around the bus station, off Al Ashat Street, is the Gold Souk, home to lots of tiny jewellery shops (and a few discreet imitation designer watch and handbag sellers). They sell imported and locally made gold and some will make up your own designs at a reasonable price. As befitting to a jewellery market, precious stones adorn many pieces. Some incorporate glass instead of gems but jewellers usually inform buyers of this and gems should come with authentication certificates. Buyers can also find a few pieces of silver. Most of the gold sold is 21 carat so, depending on where you are coming from, it may be more yellow in tone than the gold you are used to, but it is certainly of a high quality. All the gold in Qatar is tested and marked, so you can be sure that you're buying the real thing. It is sold by weight according to the price of gold that day. For more on buying gold and diamonds, see p.306.

Best Price?

The souks are great places to perfect your bargaining skills. You should never accept the first price you are quoted unless there is a sign in the shop that says they have fixed prices. You should take a leisurely stroll through the souk, comparing prices at various stores before you make any conclusive purchases (see Bargaining, p.290).

West Bay Lagoon & The Pearl, Qatar

Heading north past Katara Cultural Village, Lusail Street crosses Legtaifiya (West Bay) Lagoon. Until recently, there was a lot of major construction work going on around here, with the Lagoon shopping plaza and the distinctive Zig Zag Towers (p.35) apartment blocks being finalised in 2011. Both facilities are now complete. The Grand Hyatt (p.198) and The Ritz-Carlton (p.202), two of Doha's plushest hotels, are in this area, with further hotels under development.

Turning right from Lusail Street, passing The Ritz-Carlton and crossing a manmade causeway will take you to the gateway of The Pearl. From the bridge you can drive straight into the underground carpark, which is clearly signposted. Alternatively, continue straight, past the car park and shops, to cross the cobblestone bridge to Marsa Arabia. Here is a large parking lot from which you can enjoy gorgeous views of Doha's skyline framed by the towering construction

of The Pearl and the luxury yachts in the marina. Residents can often be seen walking and jogging on La Croisette, Porto Arabia's boardwalk, during cooler times of day.

Nicknamed the Arabian Riviera, The Pearl is a series of interconnected islands. It is a stunning feat of construction worth a visit just to witness it, if nothing else. Some parts of The Pearl are still under construction. When fully completed you will find posh villas, apartments and private islands here, in addition to designer shops and five-star restaurants. Porto Arabia, now fully open to the public, is setting the standard with high-end dining, shopping and residential facilities to suit well-monied patrons. Timid forays into being a cultural destination are also being made. A regional art exhibition and workshop attracted local and regional artists, residents and tourists.

The island is a wonderful place to stroll at leisure. Walks along the promenade are reminiscent of Italian rivieras. You can enjoy indulgent coffee and cakes at the Chocolate Bar (p.352), an exquisite tea at Dalloyau or a leisurely Lebanese lunch at Burj Al Hammam (4495 3876) before sauntering round the deluxe boutiques of Hermes, Missioni, Ferragamo, Armani, Cavalli, Lancel, Hugo Boss, Ferre, Maserati and the likes. Afterwards, tuck into delicious Italian fare at Bice (p.355), or opt for one of the many other eateries now open here. With sixteen cafes and restaurants The Pearl doesn't lack for fabulous international cuisine. Among the highlights is Megu (p.365), a beautiful restaurant providing modern Japanese food in a chic, international environment, and Pampano (p.366), a classy haunt serving up nouveau Mexican. Tsé Yang (p.370) is hailed as the poshest Chinese restaurant in Doha and has people returning for the atmosphere as well the delicious food. Carluccio's (p.356) is affordable and serves equally affordable wine with your plate of freshly made pasta. French continental cuisine is represented by Le Relais de l'Entrecôte and Les Deux Magots and Liza (p.364) provides an upscale atmosphere where you can enjoy a Lebanese meal.

Should you need assistance with carrying your purchases, or are feeling a little indolent after over-indulging at dinner, onsite transportation is available in the form of golf buggies, which can be found close to the shops and in the Marsa Arabia carpark waiting to ferry guests to their desired destination.

Dog owners have found a much-appreciated haven in the more remote north sections of the Pearl where they can walk with their canines for a few kilometres along the beach.

Back on the mainland, and heading further north on Lusail Street, is the site of the massive Lusail City development which will eventually house 200,000 people. Work is still in the early stages, but there are plans for an Energy City, Entertainment City and Media City, as well as schools, restaurants and shops (p.33).

Alfresco living in Souk Waqif

DOHA HOTELS

Most of Doha's five-star hotels are located in West Bay, which is the area that also has the most beaches. Occupancy rates in Doha's hotels are generally very high, as visitor numbers (both business visitors and tourists) are increasing faster than new hotels can be built. More expensive hotels usually provide direct access to the beach and comprehensive sports facilities, a spa and a collection of restaurants. Nearly all of the popular western chains are either represented in the city, or have an opening planned for the near future.

There are also a number of good four, three and two-star hotels, which provide a more affordable option. Apartment hotels or serviced apartments are another option if you are visiting the city and prefer a bit more independence; they're also perfect for residents who have guests visiting for extended periods (see Serviced Apartments, p.68).

The licensing laws for serving alcohol in Qatar mean that whether you're going out for Friday brunch, after-work drinks or a romantic dinner, you'll probably be heading to a hotel, so you'll soon become familiar with all of the places listed in this section. For a full listing of Doha's restaurants and bars, see Going Out, p.339.

Many hotels offer seasonal discounts to GCC residents, particularly in the hot summer months when the number of international tourists dips. Keep an eye out for special offers and sign up to hotel newsletters, as summer prices offer huge discounts, and a few weekends in luxurious surrounds might be just the thing to get you through the sweltering months.

Al Bustan Hotel
Museum St Slata **4432 8888**
albustanhotel.info
Map **2 T7**
Close to the popular areas of Doha, including the Corniche, and very near the airport, Al Bustan is popular with business travellers and visitors who want to experience the buzz of the city. Home to one of Doha's favourite restaurants, the Albatross (p.352), the hotel also has a recreation centre and the standard rooms are comfortable and affordable.

Ascott Doha > p.186
Diplomatic Area Al Dafna **4497 1111**
somerset.com
Map **2 Q2**
This brand-new serviced residence has stylish two and three bedroom apartments that boast excellent amenities and a convenient location in the heart of Doha's diplomatic district with easy access to a number of shopping malls, restaurants and the Doha Exhibition Centre. The leisure facilities include a fully-equipped gym and two swimming pools; a spa and a restaurant are due to shortly.

Best Western Hotel Doha
Old Salata St Al Mirqab **4422 1133**
dohaseefhotel.com
Map **2 R7**
This hotel is centrally located on the edge of the souk area. It offers 130 suites and 50 rooms, along with a rooftop pool. The staff can help arrange trips including island cruises, and desert safaris.

Century Hotel
820 Malik Bin Anas St Umm Ghuwailina **4445 5111**
centuryhoteldoha.com
Map **2 T8**
Situated near the airport and Corniche, Century Hotel's central location means that you're within a short distance from a wide range of attractions. Nearby, you'll find the varied dining options of Souk Waqif (p.330), while business travellers get to benefit from easy access to the financial district. The in-house facilities include a restaurant, health club and business centre.

Courtyard By Marriott Doha City Center
West Bay City Center, Al Wahda St 4419 5555
marriott.com
Map **2 Q2**
Open since 2011, this new hotel features meeting room facilities, a health club, spa, swimming pool and various restaurants and bars. Extended stay suites are available for stays of over three months. Situated within West Bay, the hotel is ideally located for business guests, while the adjoining mall offers leisure visitors retail therapy right on their doorstep. In-house eateries will include Cucina, New York Steakhouse, Brasserie Centre-Ville, Champions sports bar and Ipanema Brazilian Churrascaria.

Doha Marriott Hotel
Ras Abu Aboud St Al Khulaifat **4429 8888**
marriott-doha.com
Map **2 V8**
Located close to the airport, this modern hotel is favoured by business travellers as it provides a wide range of facilities including rooms with high-speed internet access. Its restaurants Salsa (p.368) and Asia Live (p.354) are popular, as is the Marriott's Friday brunch where patrons can select dishes from a range of restaurants. The 350 room hotel has a fitness centre, spa, whirlpool, outdoor swimming pool, children's pool and playground, and a well-maintained beach.

Ezdan Hotel & Suites
Al Kharais St Onaiza **4496 9111**
ezdanhotels.com
Map **2 P3**
Ezdan Hotel and Suites is situated within a vast, self-contained complex close to West Bay. It's an ideal base for business travellers. The hotel tower comprises 200

Discover Doha

EXPERIENCE A NEW LEVEL OF HOME COMFORT
SOMERSET SERVICED RESIDENCE

Somerset West Bay Doha
Diplomatic Area, PO Box 26026
Doha, Qatar

Somerset Al Fateh Bahrain
Juffair, PO Box 75771
Kingdom of Bahrain

SOMERSET
SERVICED RESIDENCE

Warm and engaging, Somerset Serviced Residences is ideal for executives and their families seeking a work-life balance and an enriching lifestyle. Choose from either Somerset West Bay in Doha or Somerset Al Fateh in Bahrain in the GCC and make yourself at home. Because life is about living.

For further information and reservations, please visit www.somerset.com or email enquiry.doha@the-ascott.com or enquiry.bahrain@the-ascott.com

Managed by

THE
ASCOTT
LIMITED
A Member of CapitaLand

Somerset Serviced Residence is managed by The Ascott Limited, a member of CapitaLand. It is the largest global serviced residence owner-operator in Asia Pacific, Europe and the Gulf region, managing the *Ascott, Citadines* and *Somerset* brands in over 70 cities across more than 20 countries.

rooms and suites and 344 serviced apartments, while the other three towers house 1,500 fully furnished suites ranging from studios to three bedroom apartments. A business and convention centre, salons, a fitness club, supermarket, spa and entertainment centre are just some of the amenities on offer.

Four Seasons Hotel
Corniche St Al Dafna **4494 8888**
fourseasons.com
Map **2 R2**

This world-class hotel has a private beach and an exclusive marina. Facilities at the hotel are excellent with a luxurious spa, tennis courts, and indoor and outdoor swimming pools. Dining options include Nusantao: Sea Kitchens and Il Teatro (p.360), one of Doha's favourite Italian restaurants. The highest standards of service will impress business travellers and cosmopolitan visitors.

Grand Heritage Doha Hotel & Spa
Nr Aspetar Baaya **4445 5555**
grandheritagedoha.com
Map **2 A10**

This hotel's warm elegance makes it an appealing five star choice within the Aspire Zone. The location and setting aside, the draws include 133 beautiful rooms and four duplex suites, all kitted out with custom-made Nespresso coffee and tea machines as well as luxurious wardrobes. The other facilities include a well-equipped gym, an indoor lap pool, spa, and a meeting room for 120 people. Within the hotel are Victoria, an authentic tea lounge, and Figus, which also serves innovative Mediterranean cuisine.

Grand Hyatt Doha
West Bay Lagoon Al Gassar **4448 1234**
doha.grand.hyatt.com
Map **1 K1**

One of Doha's newer hotels in town, the Grand Hyatt has raised the bar for five-star hotels in Doha. To say that it is grand is an understatement – the giant crystal chandelier hanging in the lobby sets the tone for things to come. Most of the hotel's 249 rooms have terraces or balconies with sea views, and dining highlights include the Thai restaurant Isaan (p.360) and Mediterranean-inspired The Grill restaurant (p.360). Guests can also enjoy the divine Jaula spa (p.182), a 400 metre private beach, and children will find plenty to entertain them at the Kids' Club.

Hilton Doha
Diplomatic District St, West Bay Al Dafna **4423 3333**
hilton.com
Map **2 S2**

Open since April 2012, this brand-new hotel boasts a scenic location in the Diplomatic district. The spacious

rooms offer sweeping views of the Arabian Gulf; the Executive Rooms also have private balconies. In addition to a spa and stretch of private beach, the leisure facilities include six restaurants, and bars offer a wide variety of dining and entertainment options. For business travellers, there are seven flexible meeting rooms as well as a business centre and a dedicated Executive Lounge.

Holiday Villa Hotel & Residence City Centre
Al Muntazah St, Al Muntazah Rawdat Al Khail **4408 4888**
holidayvilladoha.com
Map **2 P11**

This new hotel's location makes it a good choice for business travellers and other visitors who appreciate being close to the city centre. The hotel has 734 guest rooms, three meeting rooms and two main ballrooms that can accommodate events of up to 300 guests.

Hotel Souq Waqif
Al Jasra **4443 3030**
hotelsouqwaqif.com.qa
Map **2 Q7**

One of the few boutique hotels in town, this little gem sits on the edge of Souk Waqif. If you want a slice of heritage then this is the place to stay, as the hotel is built in a traditional style and sits amid the hustle and bustle of the souk. If you stay here, the chances are your fellow residents will be dignitaries and diplomats, but prices are surprisingly reasonable for a five-star hotel. Each of the hotel's 11 rooms and two suites are luxuriously decorated. Hotel facilities are a little limited but include a seafood restaurant and in-room massage including shiatsu and reflexology styles.

InterContinental Doha
Al Istiqlal Rd, West Bay Lagoon Al Gassar **4484 4444**
intercontinental.com/doha
Map **1 K3**

Located on the edge of West Bay Lagoon, 25 minutes from the airport, this five star hotel has Doha's longest beach and largest free-form pool. The hotel's architecture blends modern design and traditional Arabic elements. With friendly staff and top-notch venues, including Greek restaurant Mykonos (p.365), tex-mex Paloma (p.366), and the trendy Lava club (p.372), this hotel has great facilities for both business and leisure visitors.

InterContinental Doha The City > *p.201*
Onaiza **4015 8888**
intercontinental.com/dohathecity
Map **2 P2**

Thanks to its great location in West Bay, the area's many attractions are just moments away from this new hotel. In-house, you'll find a health and fitness

An Exceptional Experience for the Senses

The most impressive landmark to grace Doha skyline, La Cigale Hotel lives up to its reputation and introduces a new level of comfort to hotel and leisure facilities in the Qatari city. The hotel offers luxurious rooms and suites, a range of world class restaurants, business and leisure facilities as well as extensive entertainment choices. The multi-purpose luxurious ballrooms and meeting rooms are equipped with state-of-the-art audio and visual equipments, suitable for conventions, banquets, wedding celebrations, exhibitions and fashion shows.

60 Suhaim Bin Hamad Street, Doha, Qatar | Tel: +974 4428 8888 | Fax: +974 4428 8000 | Email: info@lacigalehotel.com | www.lacigalehotel.com

club as well as eight restaurants and lounges. These include Doha's highest restaurant, Strata (p.369), chocolate lounge Criollo (p.358), and Hive (p.371), a popular after-work drinks spot. Two more restaurants are set to open shortly to give the hotel's appeal as a dining and nightlife destination a further boost.

Kempinski Residences & Suites > p.81
Off Diplomatic St, West Bay Al Dafna **4405 3333**
kempinski-residences.com
Map **2 Q1**
From the cafe to the six-bedroom, duplex suite, Kempinski is a well-lit, luxurious space. Centrally located in the business district, it is currently the tallest building in Qatar at 62 storeys. Kempinski comprises 370 fully serviced suites, from roomy one-bedroom suites to palatial six-bedroom penthouses. Especially popular with large and extended families, the suites can be rented for private business meetings, VIP dinners or parties and for short or long term stays. Residents enjoy free access to the Kids Club where children are 'edu-tained'; non-residents can purchase a four hour day pass. The tower also houses spacious fitness facilities, two swimming pools, steam room, and Pure Leisure and Wellness Centre. The Gourmet House's (p.360) German baker has Europeans enthralled with freshly baked goods twice daily.

Get Away

When residents feel the urge to get out of Doha for the weekend, many people opt for a camping trip in the desert or along Qatar's coast, but if you don't like sand in awkward places, there are a few resorts and hotels which will guarantee you peace and quiet, and a few home comforts. Sealine Beach Resort (p.243) is a popular getaway south of Doha en route to Khor Udeid (the Inland Sea). Al Sultan Beach Resort (p.235) in Al Khor has a good range of facilities including a large pool and private beach, but its restaurants are unlicensed, while Al Ghariya Resorts offers self-catering accommodation on Qatar's north-east coast (p.235).

La Cigale Hotel > p.199, 338
60 Suhaim Bin Hamad St Fereej Bin Mahmoud **4428 8888**
lacigalehotel.com
Map **2 M9**
A short ride from the airport, La Cigale boasts 225 guest rooms and suites, with exclusive amenities. In the few years that it's been open, it has established a reputation for first-class hospitality and service. The hotel's deluxe touches include Murano crystal chandeliers and real gold-leaf papering in the lifts. With a range of dining venues, including live cooking

stations at Le Cigalon (p.364), the tasty and authentic Italian restaurant, Di Capri, and three bars, including one of Doha's best night spots, Sky View bar (p.373), it's easy to warrant an entire day spent within the confines of the hotel. If necessary, you can work off any over indulgence at Ozone Gym and Spa (p.182), the hotel's premier health and fitness centre.

Le Park Hotel
Jawaan St Al Sadd **4425 5555**
leparkhotel.com
Map **2 K7**
Located next to the Grand Regency in the congested Al Sadd area, Le Park Hotel is a four-star hotel aimed at business travellers. It has a gym and business centre for guest use, and a restaurant serving international fare.

Mercure Grand Hotel Doha City Centre
Musheirib St Al Jasra **4446 2222**
mercuredoha.com
Map **2 Q8**
While its location in the heart of the business district means that it's convenient for business travellers, holidaymakers are also attracted to this grand hotel. It offers 172 rooms, three suites and three large conference rooms, as well as the swimming pool, a fitness centre with sauna, tennis courts, squash courts, a mini shopping centre and three licensed restaurants, including La Villa (p.361).

Merwebhotel Al Sadd
Al Sadd St Fereej Bin Mahmoud **4447 1111**
merweb.com
Map **2 N8**
Centrally located close to the C Ring Road, this hotel has 126 rooms, a coffee shop and restaurant. The hotel group has two other locations across Qatar (see below).

Merwebhotel Central Doha
Ras Abu Aboud St Old Al Ghanim **4409 4444**
merweb.com
Map **2 S8**
Open since 2010, this hotel features 218 stylish rooms, all of which are kitted out with high-tech touches. There are accessible rooms for guests with disabilities, a bar, restaurant, and a health club which features an outdoor pool, sauna, steam room, whirlpool and massage rooms.

Millennium Hotel Doha
Jawaan St Al Sadd **4424 7777**
millenniumhotels.com
Map **2 K8**
The impressive Millennium Hotel is located adjacent to Al Asmakh Mall in the busy Al Sadd area. There are three unlicensed restaurants, a spa, fitness centre, club

AT THE RIGHT ADDRESS, A WHOLE NEW PERSPECTIVE ON DOHA LIVING.

Soaring high into the city's skyline, the new InterContinental Residence Suites Doha The City has arrived in Doha, bringing a new perspective to living the high life. Take pleasure in knowing that you'll experience the unsurpassed level of service you'd expect from InterContinental, with a choice of residence suites from one to four bedrooms. Enjoy access to eight of Doha's finest restaurants & lounges, the relaxing health club and the rooftop pool. Experience living from an InterContinental perspective, taking you to new heights.

Do you live an InterContinental life?

InterContinental®
DOHA THE CITY

InterContinental®
RESIDENCE SUITES DOHA THE CITY

For reservations or for further information, please call **+974 4015 8888**
email dohareservations@ihg.com or visit intercontinental.com/dohathecity
©2010 InterContinental Hotels Group. All Rights Reserved.

In over 170 locations across the globe including DOHA • HONG KONG • LONDON • NEW YORK

Doha Hotels

lounge and indoor rooftop swimming pool. The hotel is a short drive away from the beach, Doha Golf Club and the Corniche.

Mövenpick Hotel Doha

Corniche Rd Slata **4429 1111**
moevenpick-hotels.com
Map **2 S7**

Breathtaking views of the Corniche are on offer at this hotel. Close to both the airport and the Museum of Islamic Art, the hotel offers good amenities for business travellers, including Wi-Fi and a business centre. The boutique styling also attracts tourists who will enjoy being located near many of the tourist locations. Leisure facilities include a spa, swimming pool and whirlpool and gym, a restaurant, coffee lounge and cocktail bar.

Mövenpick Tower & Suites Doha

Diplomatic St Al Dafna **4496 6600**
moevenpick-hotels.com
Map **2 R2**

Mövenpick's second hotel in Doha is located at the entrance of West Bay. It offers 26 floors of suites and modern rooms for both short and long-term travellers. This contemporary hotels offers all the latest in technology, without losing the charm and warmth of Mövenpick's traditional Swiss roots. All rooms have self-catering facilities and the tower has three eateries including Wok Mee Noodle House (p.370).

Oryx Rotana

Nr Doha International Airport Al Hilal **4402 3333**
rotana.com
Map **2 T11**

Close to Doha International Airport, the Oryx Rotana is an affordable, five-star retreat for business travellers. The hotel is recognisable from the outside by the peak of the triangular, glass atrium and thin, blue shafts of light criss-crossing the towers. Inside, the eight-storey high atrium allows expanses of light into the modern interior. 400 rooms and suites have access to a temperature-controlled outdoor pool, a large state-of-the-art fitness centre and the spa, Bodylines (p.182). Nine versatile meeting rooms can be used for dining events or board meetings, and can be transformed into a theatre. There are five excellent dining options: popular with residents are the Jazz Club; the lobby bistro, Sky Lounge; buffet-styled Choices; tapas at The Cellar; and poolside refreshments at Splash.

Radisson Blu Hotel, Doha

Salwa Rd Rawdat Al Khail **4428 1428**
radissonblu.com
Map **2 N10**

Previously known as Ramada Plaza Doha, this vast hotel was renovated and upgraded during 2012. In addition to the 584 modern rooms and suites, the hotel's draws include a large swimming pool and fitness facilities that range from gyms to squash, tennis and badminton courts. The hotel also has a business centre and meeting rooms. You can eat and drink your way around the world at the Radisson's numerous restaurants and bars, which include a champagne lounge, Bubbles On Two, Shehrazad Lounge Bar and Terrace, Ruby Wu's, and Pier 12 which serves some of the best seafood in Doha. If you're still feeling hungry, step outside to 'Cholesterol Corner' (p.192) and take your pick from a host of fast food eateries.

Renaissance Doha City Center Hotel

Al Wahda St Al Dafna **4419 5000**
marriott.com
Map **2 Q2**

Open since 2011, the Renaissance Doha City Center is part of a new wave of openings in West Bay and is directly connected to the Courtyard By Marriott. It features 234 rooms and 23 suites, meeting room facilities, a health club, spa, swimming pool as well as a number of restaurants and bars.

The Ritz-Carlton, Doha

West Bay Lagoon Al Gassar **4484 8000**
ritzcarlton.com
Map **1 K1**

All of the Ritz Carlton's 374 rooms and suites are exquisitely decorated, with breathtaking views over the sea or marina. The beach club offers watersports, while the luxurious spa has every pampering treatment imaginable. The hotel has a variety of restaurants, including upmarket Italian Porcini (p.367), and La Mer (p.361) serving French haute cuisine. It serves one of Doha's best afternoon teas in The Lobby Lounge (p.365). The hotel also runs a popular wine club (p.267) and holds regular events such as Cinema Under The Stars in the cooler months. Sign up to the hotel's newsletter for regular updates on events and promotions.

Safir Doha Hotel

Cnr of Al Najma & Al Arab St Najma **4445 5333**
safirhotels.com
Map **2 R10**

The new Safir Doha Hotel offers 133 guest rooms and suites with a relaxing rooftop bar. Due to its close proximity to Doha International Airport and the central business district, the hotel predominantly caters to guests travelling to Qatar for work. Dining options include the Flavors restaurant, The Lounge Cafe and the Leisure Deck serving delicious international fusion cuisine. There are also excellent business facilities including state-of-the-art board rooms.

Swiss-Belhotel Doha, only 8 minutes from Doha International Airport, located in the bustling business district of International Banks, offers 78 plush serviced Apartments.

swiss-belhotel doha

فندق سويس بل–الدوحه

P.O.Box 17522, Jabr Bin Mohammed Street
Al Hikma Road, Old Salata, Doha, Qatar

Doha Hotels

Sharq Village & Spa

Ras Abu Abboud St Al Khulaifat **4425 6666**
sharqvillage.com
Map **2 U8**

Taking guests on a nostalgic journey to earlier
times, the Sharq Village and Spa is reminiscent of a
traditional Qatari village, but with all the modern-
day elegance and facilities of a five-star hotel. The
suites and villas are arranged across the property
and connected by interesting and visually stunning
winding pathways. Guests and day visitors can enjoy
the divine Six Senses Spa (p.184) and Doha's only
beachfront restaurant, Al Dana (p.350).

Sheraton Doha Resort & Convention Hotel

Al Corniche St Al Dafna **4485 4444**
sheratondoha.com
Map **2 R3**

Overlooking Doha's attractive Corniche, the Sheraton
is one of Qatar's oldest hotels and is often used as a
landmark when promoting the country. It has a good
range of sports facilities and restaurants, and there is
often a cultural or business event taking place in the
hotel. Standing amid 70 acres of landscaped gardens,
the 363 room hotel has direct access to the beach.
Homely Mediterranean restaurant La Veranda (p.361)
is perennially popular, as is the Irish Harp pub (p.371).

Somerset West Bay > *p.197*

Off Diplomatic St Al Dafna **4420 3333**
somerset.com
Map **2 Q1**

Located in West Bay, close to City Center Doha and the
Corniche, this serviced residence is under the globally
successful The Ascott Limited, and is a convenient
place for those in Doha on business as well as those
in search of more leisurely ways to spend their time
in the city. Its spacious, well kitted-out serviced
apartments offer attractive views of the Arabian Gulf.
Facilities include an indoor swimming pool, sauna,
fitness centre, the American Grill diner (p.351), maid
service, babysitting and meal delivery.

Souq Waqif Boutique Hotels

Souq Waqif Al Jasra **4433 6666**
swbh.com
Map **2 Q7**

Looking for a boutique stay in Doha? The brand-
new collection of tiny but all the more atmospheric
and luxurious five star hotels in and around Souq
Waqif may be just the ticket. Ranging from 14 to 37
room properties, the boutique establishments are
all different in style. Therefore, whether you're in
the mood for traditional Arabic or something more
modern and contemporary, there's an address to
suit. See the group website for further details of the
individual properties.

St. Regis Doha

West Bay Al Gassar **4446 0000**
stregisdoha.com
Map **1 K3**

Located equidistant to The Pearl and Doha's
diplomatic district, the St. Regis is a new luxury option
right on the beach. The 336 rooms and suites offer
stunning views; some come with private terraces to
boot. Nearby, you'll find the myriad cultural attractions
and dining options of Katara Cultural Village. However,
there's plenty to keep guests entertained in-house
as well: choose between restaurants that include
Gordon Ramsay's Opal (p.366) and Hakkasan, or book
a relaxing pampering treat at the Remède Spa.

Swiss-Belhotel Doha > *p.203*

Jabr Bin Mohammed St Al Mirqab **4407 8888**
swiss-belhotel.com
Map **2 S7**

Located only a short distance from the Museum of
Islamic Art and the airport, this hotel offers a range
of hotel rooms and serviced apartments for long and
short stays. Guests are able to choose from four dining
venues and are also able to take advantage of the
hotel's large swimming pool and excellent fitness and
business facilities.

The Torch Doha

Al Waab St, Aspire Zone Baaya **4446 5600**
thetorchdoha.com
Map **2 B11**

At 300m tall, The Torch is a Doha landmark and staying
at the hotel that occupies 17 floors of this iconic
building is a great choice if stunning vistas feature
high on your wish list – with 360° views across the
whole city, hotels rarely come more scenic than this. In
addition to its 167 luxurious guest rooms and suites,
the hotel has a large health club and excellent fitness
facilities as well as a number of good dining options,
including the aptly named Three Sixty, a revolving
restaurant at 240m.

W Doha Hotel & Residences

Off Diplomatic St, West Bay Al Dafna **4453 5000**
whoteldoha.com
Map **2 Q1**

When the W Hotel opened in 2009, it shook up
Doha's conservative luxury hotel scene with its
funky, contemporary style. Black chandeliers and
bold prints dominate the decor and the overall vibe
is decidedly funky and non-conventional. That said,
the service is second to none of the more traditional
luxury establishments. As well as a selection of quirky
boutiques, a fully equipped fitness centre and Bliss
Spa (p.182), the W houses some trendy restaurants
and bars, including Spice Market (p.368) and the
Crystal lounge (p.371).

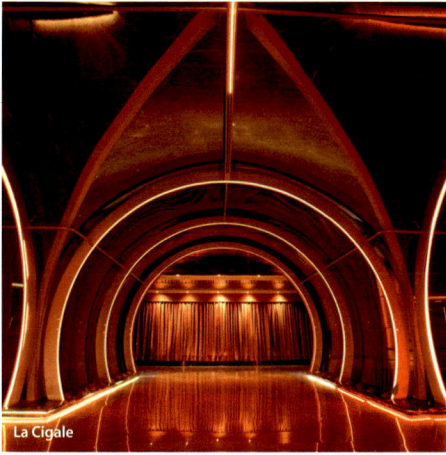

La Cigale

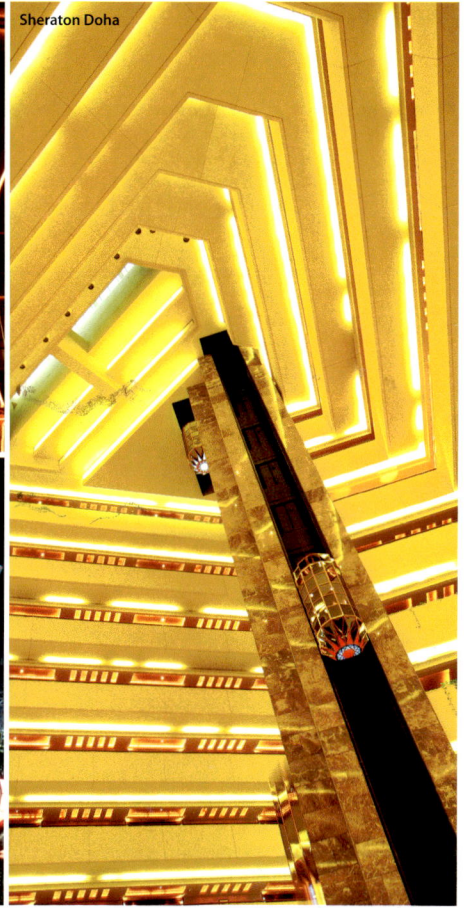

Sheraton Doha

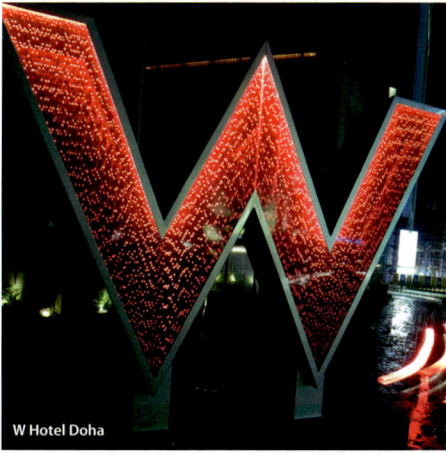

W Hotel Doha

Ezdan Hotel & Suites

Wyndham Grand Regency Doha
Nr Sports R/A, Sheikh Jawaan St Al Sadd **4434 3333**
wyndhamgrandregency.com
Map **2 K7**
Known simply as Grand Regency, this impressive hotel is situated in the Al Sadd area, 15km from the airport. It has 246 rooms including 21 suites, a business centre, meeting room facilities and a ballroom, plus a gymnasium and fat burning studio. There are four unlicensed restaurants, including Chopsticks (p.357), Tangia (p.369) and Grand Gourmet (p.360).

ART & CULTURE

Heritage & Cultural Sites
The pride of Doha is the Museum of Islamic Art (p.207) on the Corniche, which opened to worldwide acclaim in December 2008. It no longer stands alone as one of the few open museums in Doha. Since December 2010 Mathaf: Arab Museum of Modern Art (p.207) has housed part of Qatar's substantial Arab art collection, and is on display in a temporary location near Education City. For a taste of Qatar's heritage, the reconstructed Souk Waqif (p.330) is like a living museum. It is a great place to witness classical Arabian architecture, to experience traditional bartering and to enjoy the local culture of street-side dining and shisha cafes. Katara, the newly opened Cultural Village (p.207) was built to display many examples of Qatari architecture and heritage and is becoming well-loved by residents. High-quality exhibitions are regularly shown at the QMA Gallery (p.209) and this is where you'll find the Arab Postal Stamps Museum (p.206). Katara is also the venue for prestigious events including the Doha Tribeca Film Festival and will host some large outdoor music concerts in the near future. Other museums, such as the Orientalist Museum (p.208) and Sheikh Faisal Bin Qassim Al Thani Museum, just outside Doha (p.232) can be visited by prior appointment, and the quirky Al Khor Museum (p.234) is worth a visit if you are in the area.

Qatar has acquired an impressive collection of textiles, jewellery, coins, photographs, armour, fossils, rocks and minerals; much of this is in storage following the closure of museums such as the Weaponry Museum and Al Wakra Museum, or awaiting exhibition space in one of the many museums planned or under construction in Doha. Other institutions such as The National Heritage Library (p.208) are still at the planning stage.

There are a few forts and heritage sites in Doha, but many are closed for refurbishment. There is a small heritage house in Al Bidda Park (p.214) which is worth a look as an example of a traditional Qatari house; the Heritage Village, which backs on to the park close to the children's play area, is only open during special events. Finding out opening times for the few museums and heritage venues that are open can be tricky, and actually finding the right building or place can be even trickier. It may be best to use a tour operator (p.228) to find out which sites they visit. A good website for directions and coordinates for some of Qatar's heritage sites (although some of the other information is out of date) is heritageofqatar.org. Qatar Museums Authority (qma.com.qa) is responsible for the country's museums and has some useful information on heritage sites around the country.

Msheireb Enrichment Centre
Rebranded to reflect Qatari roots, the former Knowledge Enrichment Centre remains moored off the Corniche near the Sheraton Park. The Centre is primarily an information centre about the Msheireb project, formerly Dohaland, and also known as The Heart of Doha (p.33). Visitors must first cross a bridge to reach the barge. Inside is an architectural model of Msheireb which involves the reconstruction of the Musheireb district using traditional architecture. There are also some historical photos depicting the development of Doha. Conferences, workshops and other events are planned for the future. Admission is free, but note that children under 12 are not permitted entrance. The centre is open Monday to Thursday 09:00-20:30 and Saturday 15:30-18:30, closed Sunday and Friday. 3319 7482 mec.msheireb.com.

Arab Postal Stamps Museum
Katara Cultural Village Al Gassar **4409 1077**
katara.net
Map **1 K3**
The Arab League stamp collection was transferred to Qatar from Cairo in 2010. It is comprised of 280,000 stamps representing 22 Arab countries, and a small library. Admission is free.

Doha Fort (Al Koot Fort Museum)
Jassim Bin Mohammed St Al Jasra qma.com.qa
Map **2 Q8**
This white Moorish-style fort is being restored so it is not open to the public at the moment but you can still get close to it. Unfortunately, the Handicrafts Museum located within is also closed for the foreseeable future. Located on the corner of Jasim bin Mohammed and Al Qalaa streets, on the edge of Souk Waqif (p.330), it was built in 1927 to protect the souk from thieves. It is one of the last remaining military forts in Doha. One of the more fascinating features of the structure is the roofless, wall-less mosque that sits in the courtyard. Visitors can also note the irregular turrets.

Fanar Qatar Islamic Cultural Center

Abdullah Bin Jassim St Al Souq **4425 0250**
fanar.gov.qa
Map **2 R7**

Fanar is a cultural education centre which aims to educate non-Muslims about Islam and to deepen the faith of newly converted non-Arab Muslims. To reach these goals Fanar hosts events including free Arabic classes, art and calligraphy exhibitions, as well as Friday morning services for English-speaking Muslims. It also occasionally houses exhibits such as the Islamic Culture and Civilization Exhibit in 2010. The spiral minaret of the Qatar Islamic Cultural Centre is easy to spot on the Doha skyline towering above Grand Hamad Street.

Katara Cultural Village > p.iv, 186, 353

Off Lusail St Al Gassar **4408 0000**
katara.net
Map **1 K3**

Katara, also known as just Cultural Village, is not a traditional museum but rather a unique development that brings together various artistic elements in Qatar including music, dance, theatre, photography, painting and sculpture. It has quickly become a hub of activity and sparked some of the most interesting cultural commotion in town, hosting events as diverse as the Doha Tribeca Film Festival, the Marine Festival (4499 4300) and, most recently, International Kite Family Day. The site, which is designed to recreate a large Qatari village, allows artists to meet and collaborate on their different projects. It is open to the public, with two concert halls designed for opera, ballet and large theatrical productions, an outdoor amphitheatre which holds 5,000 people, as well as galleries, workshops, cafes, restaurants, souks, and Doha's first public beach (p.214). The Qatar Fine Arts Society, the Qatar Photographic Society, and the QMA Gallery are already operating within the centre; the village was inaugurated in April 2010 with the opening of Qatar Marine Festival. Restaurants at Katara have quickly reached almost cult status and most of them are usually full at peak dining times. Khan Farouk serves up Lebanese; L'wzaar has the best fish and chips in town and is family friendly; Sukar Pasha serves Turkish directly on the boardwalk and Mamig is among the city's favourite restaurants, serving Armenian and Lebanese food. On hot days, La Gelateria Fina at the far end of the boardwalk cools with homemade ice cream.

Mathaf – Arab Museum Of Modern Art

Off Al Luqta St Education City **4402 8855**
mathaf.org.qa
Map **2 B3**

Since December 2010 modern Arab art has had 5,500 square metres of display space to call home. Located in a converted school building in Education City,

the works span from 1840 to the present and every Arab country is represented. Mataf aims to foster communication within the art community and the community at large. Hands-on workshops, curatorial tours, poetry readings, film screenings and night tours aid this end. The popular artist encounter series creates a platform for artists in Doha to share their knowledge with children and adults. The Global Art Forum (Gaf) introduced Mataf to the international art scene as experts from around the world participated in panel discussions. The library, Maktaba, is stocked for both academic and casual users. A small gift shop and cafe are located near the exit. Free admission. Open 11:00-18:00. Friday 15:00-21:00. Mondays closed.

Further exhibition space is temporarily located in the grounds of the Museum of Islamic Arts (p.207) at Al-Riwaq Exhibition Hall, a building which resembles a shipping container. Entry to Al-Riwaq is QR 25 for adults, 16 and under and students with valid ID are free. Entry to Mataf is free.

The Doha Debates

The Doha Debates is part of the Qatar Foundation and publicly promotes dialogue and freedom of speech in Qatar. Renowned international journalist Tim Sebastian (former host of BBC's Hard Talk) invites four speakers a month to address controversial issues facing the Arab and Islamic worlds. The debates are broadcast around the world on BBC World News. Past topics have included controversial issues including women in Islam and Israeli/Palestinian conflicts. They follow the traditional Oxford Union style of debate, where two teams argue over a central motion. The audience is invited to participate, and at the end a vote is taken and the chairman announces the result. If you would like to attend the debates as a member of the audience, apply online at dohadebates.com. The debates run from September to May and are held at Education City. Details of upcoming motions are on the website.

Museum Of Islamic Art

The Corniche Al Souq **4422 4444**
mia.org.qa
Map **2 R6**

This is Qatar's pride and joy. Built on an island of reclaimed land on the Corniche, this geometric design in pale limestone is an impressive addition to the skyline. The building itself is simple yet beautiful, with stunning details drawn from Islamic influences. Outside the building are calming pools of water, while the interior (designed by Jean-Michel Wilmotte) holds a pair of glass-sided staircases that sweep up from the entrance hall. There are two floors of permanent

Art & Culture

exhibition galleries, a temporary gallery, a 200 seat auditorium, a library and a cafe. The Education Wing is now open, and runs classes in art for both school students and laymen, inspired by the collection, and a monthly series of lectures, plus activities for schools.

Entry to the museum is free of charge, as are the informative audio guides, available in various languages. Allow at least two hours to explore the collection. For more details on the exhibits within, see Exploring The Museum Of Islamic Art, p.207.

A wide range of temporary exhibitions rotate in the exhibition space located near the main entry. A fee of QR 20 is often charged with one day allocated as free to the public. These exhibitions are often a fantastic display of objects such as those found in The Pearl Exhibition, or the recent Dutch Masters Exhibition.

National Heritage Library
Cnr Ras Abu Aboud & Jabir Bin Mohd Sts
Al Salata Al Jadeeda qma.com.qa
Map 2 S8

This collection of 100,000 books, manuscripts, maps and scientific instruments all relates to the Arab world. Some date back to the early 15th century, when the first printing began in Europe. Housed in a large villa in a quiet side street, with its polished dark wood and spiral staircases it feels like the library of a large stately home. There are some very valuable items, including one of only four sets of volumes detailing Napoleon's expedition to Egypt in 1798. The foreign language section has books in Latin as well as modern European languages, with many volumes given over to explorers Sir Richard Burton and TE Lawrence (Lawrence of Arabia). Among the works in Arabic are some beautiful hand-drawn copies of the Quran. This museum is really intended for historians and researchers, but enthusiastic amateurs may visit and they are happy to give tours to small groups. Opening hours are 07:30 to 12:45 and 16:00 to 18:45; the library is closed on Fridays and Saturdays. A new home for the library is being designed and will be at Qatar Foundation's Education City and managed by the Cultural Development Center, which is also working to digitise the collection (see Key Developments, p.32). Special exhibitions will be held throughout Doha, including in Katara.

National Museum Of Qatar
Museum Park St Slata **4452 5555**
qma.com.qa
Map 2 T7

The museum has been under renovation for a number of years and is still currently cordoned off by large fencing. The renowned architect Jean Nouvel designed the expansion. Initial estimates suggested the museum could open in 2006 but there are still no signs of walls in sight. If it does ever eventually open

the museum has considerable plans to showcase Qatar's history, with various archaeological artefacts, coins, jewellery, traditional clothing, household items and tools. There were even talks that there would also be an area recreating a Bedouin scene. Other features will include a section on Qatar's geology which will take an interesting look at the oil industry throughout the ages. A large aquarium should also contain marine creatures native to the local shores. The museum development is located only a short distance from the Corniche, and is based around the restored Old Salata Palace of Sheikh Abdullah bin Qassim. For updates on the reopening, it is recommended that you call the National Council for Culture, Heritage & Arts on 4466 8777.

Open Sites

While many of Doha's heritage sites are under development, there are some interesting places outside the capital that are worth visiting. There are forts or archaeological sites of interest in Zubarah (p.236), Zekrit (p.238), Umm Salal Mohamed (p.233) and Al Jassasiyeh (p.236) – as most of these are open sites, there's nothing to stop people going in and looking around, although some, like the rock carvings at Al Jassasiyeh, can be hard to locate. If you have your heart set on seeing a particular site, it's worth contacting a tour company (p.228) to see if they're running trips there to make sure you don't turn up to discover the site closed, being redeveloped or under excavation; but if you're happy to go with the flow and take on an expedition, there are interesting things to do in all of these areas. Be considerate; don't touch or climb on the sites.

Orientalist Museum
Off Al Muthaf St, Nr Qatar National Museum Slata
qma.com.qa
Map 2 T7

Tucked away behind the Qatar National Museum, this small white building is home to an impressive collection of Orientalist paintings and drawings, mainly by European artists, showing life in the Arab world in the 19th century. The inside is suitably sumptuous for a collection which contains works by major names from the Orientalist movement including Eugene Delacroix, Eugene Fromentin and Jose Villegas y Cordero. There's even a small landscape by celebrated English artist JMW Turner. The paintings were collected by art lover Sheikh Hassan bin Mohammed Al Thani over 15 years, and he donated them in 2005. To view the paintings you need to make an appointment twith Fathi Hamzaoui, who talks you through the major artists and their work (his English is reasonable, but he prefers French or Arabic).

Qatar Explorer

Art & Culture

Windtower House
Off Grand Hamad & Ali bin Abdulla St Al Jasra
Map **2 R8**

This is one of the last traditional windtowers in Qatar. You will find it off Grand Hamad Street and Ali bin Abdullah Street; it is actually enclosed within the downmarket Najada Shopping Plaza (Souk Najada). Windtowers, known as barjeel in Arabic, were used in the days before electricity as a primitive form of air conditioning. They function in the opposite way to a chimney, by sucking fresh cool air into a house. This building once housed the Ethnographical Museum, but the museum is closed and the house is no longer open to the public, although it can be viewed from outside.

Art Galleries
The art scene in Doha is slowly beginning to show its colours. The pinnacle is, of course, the Museum of Islamic Art (p.207) and since 2010 art fans in the city have enjoyed the collection at Mathaf Arab Museum of Modern Art (p.207) too.

Aside from such headline-grabbing art museums, there are a few smaller galleries around the city. The Orientalist Museum (p.208) contains an impressive collection of Orientalist paintings and drawings, mainly by European artists, depicting life in the 19th century Arab world; it is open by prior appointment only. The gallery at VCUQ showcases both students' work and that of international artists.

PechaKucha Nights

PechaKucha is a creative networking and showcasing formula which involves concise 20 screen slideshows, with just 20 seconds dedicated to each slide. Doha hosted three successful PechaKucha nights at the Waqif Arts Centre. After this venue closed in 2010, they moved to the VCUQ Atrium where PechaKucha Doha Vol. 4 took place. Look out for updates in Doha and around the world at pecha-kucha.org.

Rotating exhibitions can be seen at Katara (p.207). The Qatar Fine Arts Society (p.265) is based there and holds up to 10 exhibitions a year. The Qatar Photographic Society (p.276) gallery at Katar has an exhibition which changes on a monthly basis. The Qatar Museums Authority Gallery (p.209) presents high-quality exhibitions which rotate approximately on a bi-monthly basis. Fanar Qatar Islamic Cultural Centre (p.270) sometimes hosts displays of Islamic art and calligraphy. Exhibitions are occasionally held in hotels, such as the premier of the Art Wanson Gallery's exhibit at the Grand Hyatt in 2010. To find out about other temporary art exhibitions, check the relevant centre's website, sign up online to hotel newsletters and keep an eye on the local media.

Al Markhiya Gallery
Souk Waqif Al Jasra **4442 8007**
almarkhiyagallery.com
Map **2 Q7**

This small but esteemed gallery is located in the middle of the Souk Waqif. Al Markhiya's mission is to promote regional art, whether that be painting, sculpture or photography, by networking with international galleries. Paintings by new and established artists are featured here.

QMA Gallery
Katara Cultural Village Al Gassar **4452 5555**
qma.com
Map **1 K3**

Opened in 2010 under the umbrella of the Qatar Museums Authority, the QMA Gallery regularly rotates exhibits approximately every two months. Exhibits are usually of high quality. The gallery opened with a photography exhibition from the renowned Magnum photographers. Recent shows include GCC Heritage Without Borders Archeology Exhibition and the Doharama exhibition which juxtaposed old photos with recent images of Doha.

Virginia Commonwealth University Gallery > p.151
Virginia Commonwealth University In Qatar (VCUQ) Al Shagub **4402 0555**
qatar.vcu.edu
Map **2 A4**

Located within the Virginia Commonwealth University campus, this gallery is simply referred to as The Gallery. Exhibitions display student art as well as internationally acclaimed work.

Doha's art scene is thriving

Exploring The Museum Of Islamic Art

Doha-based writer Frances Gillespe takes a tour of Qatar's cultural pride and joy.

MIA's geometric interior

Whether you approach by car or on foot along the wide sweep of the Corniche, the Museum of Islamic Art (MIA) creates a stunning visual image. Standing on a specially constructed island 60 metres off Doha Corniche, it's at its most spectacular in the late afternoon, when the slanting rays of the sun create golden highlights and subtle shadows on the many-angled facades.

When prestigious Chinese-American architect IM Pei, then in his late eighties, was approached by the Emir to design it, he drew inspiration from the 13th century sabil (ablutions fountain) of the 9th century Mosque of Ahmad bin Tulun in Cairo, Egypt. Pei was also influenced by an 8th century fort at Sousse in Tunisia. 'There,' he wrote, 'I felt I was coming closer to the essence of Islamic architecture, where sunlight brings to life powerful volumes and geometry plays a central role.'

The stand-alone island was Pei's suggestion, to ensure future buildings would never encroach on the museum. Behind the building, a park of approximately 64 acres of dunes and oases will, when completed, provide not only some shelter from the onshore winds but also create a picturesque backdrop.

Opened on 22 November 2008 by His Highness Sheikh Hamad bin Khalifa Al Thani, this world-class museum is the pride of the people of Qatar and has drawn thousands of visitors from around the globe. Clad in honey-coloured stone, it consists of a five-storey main building and a two-storey education wing, connected across a central courtyard.

You gain entrance via a pedestrian bridge; as you approach, your eye is drawn to the building's angular surface planes, which step back progressively as they rise around a high domed atrium, concealed from outside view by a central four-sided tower. On each side of the tower an eye-shaped opening captures and reflects subtly-patterned light within the faceted dome.

Entering the museum, you are drawn into the airy, spacious atrium by the light flooding in through the vast sheet glass walls. From the windows you can enjoy spectacular vistas of the West Bay area and the sea. Looking upwards from the atrium, the circular, pierced metal chandelier, measuring an impressive 12 metres in diameter, is unmissable. Beneath it, two graceful curved stone staircases rise from the atrium to the first floor – this is a good place to start exploring the museum's exhibits.

Before you set off, pause for a moment to notice how the shape of the five storey building, topped by a stainless steel dome, changes as the structure descends: the circular perimeter of the dome evolves into an octagon, then a square, which in turn is transformed into four triangular column supports.

Upstairs, the interior, designed by Jean-Michel Wilmotte & Associates, features grey porphyry stone and exotic Brazilian lacewood. To protect the fragile antiquities, the galleries have subdued lighting and no natural light enters the space. Despite this, on entering the first gallery, initial impressions are of the rich colours glowing from the wealth of objects on display. The assemblage of carpets, textiles, calligraphy, metalwork and miniature paintings includes pieces that cover over a thousand years of Islamic art.

The collection, which includes manuscripts, ceramics, metal, glass, ivory, textiles and precious stones, is showcased as a journey through time, countries and cultures. The oldest piece dates from the ninth century and the most recent from the 17th. Originating from Spain, Egypt, Syria, Iraq, Turkey, Iran, India and central Asia, the collection testifies to the wide scope and richness of the Muslim territory, which stretched from Cordoba in the west to Samarqand in the east.

Highlights include a 10th century cast bronze fountain head in the form of a hind from a palace courtyard fountain in Spain, a planispheric astrolabe, also 10th century, from Iran or Iraq, and a silk carpet known as the Timurid Chessboard Garden Carpet made for the Samarqand ruler Timur and dating from the 14th-16th centuries. There are priceless jewels – a cup carved from a solid emerald, a jade amulet worn by the Moghul emperor Shah Jahan in the 17th century, and a dazzling golden falcon from Moghul India inlaid with gems and enamel.

Among the most unassuming but impressive of the treasures on display is a 9th century white earthenware bowl from Iraq with a Kufic inscription in blue, which translates as 'what is done is worthwhile.' Many feel that this could well stand as a fitting motto for the Museum of Islamic Art.

The iconic MIA at night

PARKS, BEACHES & ATTRACTIONS

Parks

Doha is dotted with parks but you need to know where to look to find some of the more hidden ones. The larger parks, especially those along the Corniche, are popular destinations for a picnic or meeting up with friends or kids for an afternoon of play. Some parks are closed for refurbishment; most notably Rawdat al Khail Garden (Al Muntazah), one of the oldest parks in Doha, which has been closed for years; residents still await signs for the refurbishment work to begin. The Aspire Park, a large park at the Aspire Zone featuring a vast expanse of grass and a lake, is the newest of Doha's parks and there are plans for the development of 12 further parks and the construction of a community hall in Al Rayyan. Still more parks and playgrounds are planned throughout the city and suburbs of Doha.

Doha loves its parks and they are well maintained, with most having cafes and toilets. All are free to enter and some can be accessed round the clock; however, several are only for families so single men will not be permitted entry. Grassy areas, such as those at Airport Park, are frequently taken over by impromptu cricket games, especially on Fridays.

Aspire Park

Nr Villaggio Mall Baaya
Map **2 A12**

This is Doha's largest and most famous park. It covers 88 hectares (the size of more than 80 football pitches) and has a large lake, horse riding trails, a sprung jogging track for the fitness minded, shaded seating areas, a restaurant and plenty of parking spaces. Although more than 700 trees have been planted, there is not an overabundance of shade, so the park comes into its own during the evenings and in the cooler months (between November and April). You can walk under the arched fountains for a cooling treat or stroll up the man-made hill for views of the surrounding area. It is located near to the Villaggio Mall (p.335).

Aspire Play Park

Nr Villaggio Mall Baaya
Map **2 A12**

This small play park is very popular in the evenings with local families and has slides and swings. Nearby is lots of paved space for cycling and roller skating or just running around to let off steam. To get there, drive between Hyatt Plaza and Villaggio Mall, turn right at the guard gate and take the first left. A small entry fee of QR 5 is required for entry by car to this area. Alternatively, park in one of the parking areas just outside the gate and walk across to the play area. There is plenty of parking and toilets are also available.

Fun In The Sun

While most parks have shady trees scattered about, most play areas are usually uncovered. Make sure you take basic precautions before letting your kids exhaust themselves playing under the hot sun – apply sun screen, cover them up with a hat and loose clothing, and make sure you have plenty of water.

Busamra Park (Al Khulaifat Park)

Al Khulaifat Park Street South New Fereej Al Khulaifat
Map **2 L12**

What this park lacks in size, it gains in charm. It is encircled by shady alcoves, filled with open grassy areas, and complete with a play area for toddlers and older children. Nearby, off Al Khulaifat Park Street North is another beautifully landscaped park for women and children only, which is closed in the morning for maintenance and only open from 14:00 to 20:00.

Dahal Al Hamam Park

Cnr of Al Markhiya & Arab League Sts Dahl Al Hamam
Map **2 G1**

This sizeable park has lots of grass and an enormous paved area. It's well equipped with good play equipment on sand, which is usually shaded. There is a cafe selling snacks and drinks that opens after 17:00. The park opens from 14:00 until 23:00, so you can picnic and play until well after bedtime. Entry is free,

BREATHE EASY Amanda Williams, long-term resident of Doha and mother of three

I feel extremely safe and don't get panicked if my child wanders out of sight in the playground or shopping mall. I did find it a bit disturbing when we arrived here 11 years ago to have my toddler whisked away at a beach by one of the staff. I was hysterical. I jumped up and started to look for him almost in tears, only to find him coming out of the restaurant with a huge ice cream cone. The member of staff just thought my son was cute and wanted to show the lady in the coffee shop. I still cringe a little every time something like this happens here but I appreciate the different approach to children and the innocence involved. My children have remained children a lot longer here than they would back home, although my family feels my 13 year old son can be very naive. On the other hand they see that he has enjoyed his childhood while he is still a child. I can't imagine raising my children anywhere else now that we have been here.

Qatar parks

but like many other parks in Doha it is open to families only. There are toilets and plenty of places to park. Recycling bins are available.

Rumeilah Park (Al Bidda Park)
The Corniche Al Rumeilah
Map **2 N5**

Located opposite the Corniche, this is a popular family park that tends to be busiest on Fridays. It has an open-air theatre and a collection of small shops running along a small canal. At the opposite end of the canal to the amphitheatre is a small heritage house which contains rudimentary displays of women's traditional handicrafts, but in itself is an interesting example of a traditional Qatari home. It has sporadic opening times. There is also a small kiosk where you can buy refreshments. At the far end of the park, beyond the children's playground is a fenced off area called the Heritage Village that was built to resemble a traditional Qatari village. It is open only for Ramadan, Eid and special cultural festivals.

Community Parks
Most neighbourhoods have small public parks well worth a visit. These are usually lush, quiet oases in hard to find corners. Finding them is often a matter of catching a glimpse of a red play roof peeking out over the top of a wall, and driving in erratic circles until you find the park entrance, such as Naeeja West Park off Rawdat al Khail Street.

Sheraton Gardens
Nr Sheraton Hotel Al Dafna
Map **2 Q3**

At the north end of the Corniche, just before the Sheraton Hotel, this is another popular park providing great views across Doha Bay. There's plenty of parking available in the car park or on the road nearby, and you'll find a little kiosk selling drinks and snacks, but the play area and the immediate area surrounding it are not shaded. There are a few benches further down the Corniche but there are no public toilets. The location right at the water's edge makes this a nice, short stop for an early morning snack. Just off the Corniche, close to the snack kiosk is the floating Msheireb Enrichment Centre (p.206).

Beaches
Qatar is not short on beaches, but, for the most part, it is predominantly the private ones owned by the hotel leisure clubs that have any facilities, so be prepared to take your own food, drinks, deck chairs and shade.

The hotels on the north side of Doha, such as the new Grand Hyatt (p.198), Diplomatic Club (p.280), the InterContinental (p.198), and the Sheraton (p.204), have well-maintained private beaches. Further south,

the luxurious Sharq Village and Spa (p.204) offers public access to the beach; Tuesdays and Wednesdays are ladies only. The Four Seasons (p.198) offers public access to their beach on weekdays. Prices vary from QR 180 for a day pass during the week to QR 20,000 for an annual family membership at somewhere like the Diplomatic Club (p.280) which includes beach access. Hotels will occasionally run specials which allow women to access their beaches for free, so make sure to check with the individual hotels for any specials.

Swim Safely
Although the waters off the coast generally look calm and unchallenging, very strong rip tides can carry the most confident swimmer away from the shore very quickly. Take care when swimming around Qatar's coast as there are no lifeguards.

Doha's first public beach has opened at the Katara Cultural Village (p.207). Entrance to the well-maintained area costs QR 100 per person, but this is money well-spent thanks to the level of facilities on offer; there are water inflatables to keep the kids amused and plenty of sunloungers for parents. And as an added bonus, you'll of course find all other facilities of Katara within easy reach.

Popular spots south of Doha include Al Wakra (p.240), by the dhow harbour, and the stretch of coastline extending from Messaieed down past the Sealine Beach Resort (p.243) to the Inland Sea (p.243). On the west coast, there are beaches at Zekrit (p.238) and along the coast by the Dukhan (p.239) oil fields, including the palm tree beach near Umm Bab (p.240).

North of Doha offers the most options for beach lovers. Simaisma (p.234) on the road to Al Khor is worth a visit, as are Al Khor itself (p.234) and the area to the immediate south-east. The northern tip of the country has many fine beaches with shallow waters, including those around Al Huwailah, Fuwairat (p.235), and Al Ghariya (p.235).

The Qatar National Green and Clean Campaign organises volunteers to clean up the beaches but the beaches in Qatar can still be littered, and broken glass is a real problem; it is a good idea to wear beach shoes. During the summer, jellyfish lurk in the waters around Qatar so you should carry a bottle of white vinegar, which will help ease the pain of a sting.

Wildlife
Despite the hot climate and arid conditions, there are a surprisingly large number of opportunities to get up close to some interesting wildlife in Qatar. The clear waters around the coast are teeming with exotic wildlife, including turtles and dolphins, making Qatar an interesting place for snorkelling and diving. For more on these activities see Out and About (p.217).

Doha Zoo

The coastal areas are also home to flamingos and a variety of interesting birds, and it's worth getting involved with the Qatar Natural History Group (p.266) if you are a keen ornithologist. To find out about the wildlife highlights beyond Doha's city limits, see Out of Doha, p.232. For native wildlife closer to Doha, the camel racetrack at Sheehaniyah (p.237) and the nearby Oryx Farm, are popular destinations to which tour operators regularly run trips.

Al Shaqab

Nr Educational City Al Shagub **4454 6320**
alshaqab.com
Map **2 A4**

Owned by the Emir, Sheikh Hamad bin Khalifa Al Thani, this farm provides the opportunity to view some of the highest quality thoroughbred Arabian horses, many of which are world champions. Located in old Rayyan, behind Al Rayyan Football Club and next to Education City, the stud has world-class facilities to care for the horses, including a therapeutic pool. There's also a riding school providing classes for all ages and abilities; for lessons call 4454 6320. Visits by appointment only for individuals or groups can be made directly with the farm. Al Shaqab is expanding and for safety reasons groups are currently limited to five people at a time. A visitor's centre and museum will be integrated within the new facilities which are scheduled to open in 2011.

Doha Zoo

Al Furousiya St Fereej Al Murra **4468 2610**
Map **1 B12**

Doha Zoo sees thousands of visitors each year. It is home to about 1,500 animals from around the world including lions and giraffe. The larger animals do not seem to have much space and can be seen pacing up and down looking less than happy. Environmentally conscious children and adults might find this upsetting. Perhaps the greatest attraction is the generous, shaded play area and lovely gardens to the right of the entrance. A cafe is available for light refreshments. Dream Park (p.216), a new attraction, provides pay-by-the-ride, whirling entertainment for children of all ages. Tuesday afternoons are for women and children only, and Wednesday afternoons are reserved for families. A nominal fee of QR 2 is charged for children aged 18 and under. Adults pay QR 5.

Amusement Centres

Qatar is working hard to expand its appeal on the entertainment front, as well as the cultural front. The entertainment sector got a boost when the new waterpark opened in 2010 (see Aqua Park p.216). Marah Land (p.217), another outdoor amusement park, has also recently opened just south of Doha in Al Wakra. In longer term plans, two theme parks

are at the drawing board stage within Lusail City (p.33). Among these is Entertainment City; originally scheduled to open in 2009, the opening date is yet to be confirmed but the facilities are meant to include a water park, a theme park, housing for 200,000 residents, restaurants, theatres and shopping. However, as construction has not yet begun it seems likely that it will be a few years more before visitors can get their thrills on any roller coasters here.

Until these large-scale theme parks come to fruition, residents and tourists from toddlers to teens can enjoy the tame rides and video games at the amusement centres listed below. For indoor play centres for toddlers and young children, also see Activities For Kids, p.130 and Mother and Toddler Activities, p.132.

Aqua Park

Salwa Rd, 16km from Industrial R/A
4490 5872
Map **Qatar Country Map C4**

Located 16 km out of town along Salwa Road, the first phase of the Aqua Park had its soft opening at the end of 2010 to mixed reviews. While it is not the Wild Wadi of Dubai, residents can get a cooling thrill in the chilled water rides: a 200m lazy river; wave pool with waves reaching up to 1.5m; water slides, the highest reaching 20m; an activity pool with five slides and waterfalls; lagoon with juice bar; Jacuzzis and more. It also features a dry land area, with paintballing, soap football pitches and a BMX park. A resort is being built next to the park. When fully complete the park will cover 100,000 square metres and the resort 200,000 square metres. A strict, although slightly vague, dress code is in place. No zippers, buttons or other metal pieces on clothing; women should cover shoulders and legs to the knee; one piece swimsuits are not permitted. Most expat women wear long biking shorts. Men must wear long shorts. Women are likely to feel less on display on Tuesdays as it is Ladies Day; boys up to age 8 allowed. Entry is QR 100, under 2s are free. Open daily 10:00-22:00.

Dream Park

Nr Doha Zoo, Al Furousiya St Ain Khaled
Map **1 B12**

At 8,000 square metres, Dream Park is hailed as the largest outdoor amusement park in Qatar. Until Marah Land opens in Al Wakra, it is also the only dry outdoor entertainment park. Pay-by-the-ride has a few rides for children of all ages such as a Ferris Wheel, a haunted house and the thrilling Ranger. Small retail shops make it feel a bit like a miniature Disneyland. Be warned that the park is especially popular during the cooler months and Eid holidays. Plans are to expand to 16,000 square metres with restaurants, shops, more rides and entertainment.

Gondolania Theme Park
Villaggio Mall Baaya **4403 9888**
gondolania.com
Map **2 B11**

This exotically named entertainment centre is located near Villaggio Mall. There is a bowling centre, a go kart track, video games and a range of exciting rides including a rollercoaster, boat ride, Ferris wheel, carousel, bumper cars, and more. Large trampolines and a soft play area for under 10s have opened and are perfect for getting a bit of exercise in for children. The rides are charged via tokens which can be purchased at the entrance. Benches and cafes offer comfortable spots for parents to sit back and enjoy themselves. Fast food restaurants are nestled within the centre for even greater convenience. Enquire about special packages for schools or for special events such as kids' birthday parties.

Jungle Zone
Hyatt Plaza Baaya **4469 4848**
Map **2 A12**

Jungle Zone is packed with activities, all jungle-themed, to keep kids entertained. In addition to its usual attractions, it can also organise your child's birthday party or school outing. Entrance costs QR 55 at weekends (Thursday to Saturday) and QR 40 from Sunday to Wednesday. It is located next to the food court in Hyatt Plaza.

Marah Land
Al Wakrah
Map **Qatar Country Map C5**

The second branch of Dream Land follows the same concept as the original located at the zoo, but at

25,000 square metres, it's much bigger. Open since 2011, the attractions on offer include the usual entertainment rides and games, along with a bicycle and recreation area.

Winter Wonderland
City Center Doha Al Dafna **4483 9163**
Map **2 Q2**

Winter Wonderland is City Center Doha's ice-skating rink; located in the middle of the mall, it can be seen from each floor. When the temperature outside gets unbearable, it's a great way to cool down. The rink is open every day. Skaters are charged QR 35 for one hour and 45 minutes of skating, and spectators can pay QR 10 to watch from the stands. You can buy snacks and drinks at the food area next to the rink.

OUT & ABOUT

Qatar has much to offer beyond Doha's city limits. The landscape that stretches away from the city has great potential for exploring and leisure-time activities. Getting out into the deserts and remote coasts by 4WD is a must-do while you're a Doha resident, and once you're out there, you'll find some super camping spots to take advantage of too. The sea that surrounds the country is also a great adventure playground, and the warm Gulf waters provide a wonderful opportunity to try snorkelling, diving and boating.

Boating

Unsurprisingly, there is a considerably sized informal boating culture in Qatar, particularly around Doha, and especially at weekends. A number of

Get out on the water

Owning A Boat

If you are thinking about buying a boat, be aware that the marinas are expensive. Currently, charges are in the region of QR 500 per foot per year (around QR 15,000 per year for a 31 foot boat) and on average, fees increase around QR 2,000 each year. Most marinas are full and there are waiting lists for berths.

The first marina within the Lusail City development is scheduled to receive boats mid-2011, which should help to ease the growing waiting lists. Once complete, Lusail Marina (mourjan-lusailmarina.com, 5584 3282) hopes to become the premiere marina facility, able to accommodate 10 – 40 metre boats.

The alternative is a trailable boat under about 20 feet, which can easily be launched from either of the public slipways in Doha and, assuming you have space, kept at home. The slipways are both off Doha Corniche, one at the old Navigation Marina in the Dhow harbour, and the other at the southern end of the Corniche in front of the Halul Cafe.

All motor boats in Qatar must be registered annually; this is a simple process that costs QR 50 and is carried out at the Coastguard office in the Doha Port area, next to the old RAFCO Marina. This office is the most user friendly Government office in Qatar. Should you be unwise enough to buy an unregistered boat, you will have serious problems either using it or selling it on.

For safety reasons, if you are taking a boat any further than the confines of Doha Bay, you have to check out and in as you leave and return at the Police Barge next to the main Doha shipping channel. Some of the marinas in outlying areas, such as The Ritz-Carlton, will do this for you by fax as you leave the marina.

companies provide boat charters, offering everything from cruises of a couple of hours to scuba diving excursions in remote locations (see Main Tour Operators, p.228). Large sailing yachts, speedboats and other motorboats can be hired for private charter and corporate events; other companies offer outings on dhows and also cater to weddings and birthday parties. Fishing trips are also available and dhows can be hired informally along the Corniche (see Boat Tours, p.227).

The year-round favourable weather conditions and calm waters off the coast mean that sailing (p.278) is a popular sport in Qatar, but most people who own boats primarily use them for trips to local islands (p.243), for the purpose of swimming, picnicking, barbecuing and camping. Whichever type of boat you have or want to hire, there are plenty of places to explore.

If you're venturing further afield, Explorer's *Dubai Yachting and Boating* has handy maps, suggested cruising areas around the UAE coast, details of marinas, local rules and regulations, and contains a comprehensive contacts directory, as well as offering advice on buying and mooring a boat. With so much invaluable information, this is the ultimate resource for boaters old and new. Buy online at askexplorer.com/shop

Camping

Constant sunshine and some idyllic locations make camping a much-loved activity in Qatar. In general, warm temperatures and next to no rain means you can camp with much less equipment and preparation than in other countries, and many first-timers or families with children find that camping becomes a favourite weekend break. For most, the best time to go is between October and April, as in the summer it can get unbearably hot sleeping outside.

Choose between the peace and tranquillity of the desert, or camp on the beach and wake up to a morning dip in the sea. Many good camping spots are easily accessible from tarmac roads so a 4WD is not

Carry When Camping

Before you set off to pitch up, there is some basic equipment which you should consider taking to make your stay in the great outdoors a little more comfortable, and to get you out of any sticky situations what may arise:

- Tent
- Lightweight sleeping bag (or light blankets and sheets)
- Thin mattress (or air bed)
- Torches and spare batteries
- Cool box for food
- Water (always take too much)
- Camping stove, or BBQ and charcoal if preferred
- Firewood and matches
- Insect repellent and antihistamine cream
- First aid kit (including any personal medication)
- Sun protection (hats, sunglasses, sunscreen)
- Jumper/warm clothing for cooler evenings
- Spade
- Toilet rolls
- Baby wipes
- Rubbish bags (ensure you leave nothing behind)
- Navigation equipment (maps, compass, GPS)
- Mobile phone (fully charged)

THOUGHTFULNESS
BEYOND IMAGINATION

At the heart of the desert lies **Lusail Marina, the first marina of the Lusail development,** a new generation of marina combining leisure and relaxation with style and perfection. Our exclusive setting and prestigious services let you live a unique yachting experience. We not only promise to exceed your expectations, but also guarantee a highly personalised tailor-made service.

Your ultimate yachting lifestyle destination in

LUSAIL
MARINA
Doha, Qatar

A Mourjan Marinas IGY destination

Claim your place and be part of the new wave of marina destinations
T: +974 5584 3282 E: lusailmarina@mourjanmarinas.com www.mourjanmarinas.com

Lusail Marina, Doha, Qatar • Festival Marina, Dubai, UAE • Almouj Marina, Muscat, Oman • Port Tarraco, Tarragona, Spain

A SUBSIDIARY OF   GSSG   مجموعة غانم بن سعد ال سعد وأولاده القابضة
GHANIM BIN SAAD AL SAAD & SONS GROUP HOLDINGS

always required. You can camp just about anywhere, but there are some stand-out spots that are super places to pitch up.

Some of the best beaches for camping are on the northern coasts at Fuwairat and Al Ghariyah. The western beaches off Route Q39 between Dukhan to Umm Bab, such as Palm Tree Beach (p.240), are quiet places to pitch your tent, while closer to Doha, Simaisma beach (p.234) is a popular spot.

For desert camping, the area south of Mesaieed (p.242) has the biggest dunes and around Khor Al Udaid (the Inland Sea) and a number of tour companies have permanent Bedouin-style camps there. All of Doha's tour companies offer trips to Khor Udeid, so if you fancy sleeping under the stars but want someone else to arrange the logistics and supply the gear, then this may be the best option for you (see Main Tour Operators, p.228).

If you're lucky enough to own a boat, or have an obliging friend who does, you can pitch up on Arabian Gulf islands close to Doha, such as Safliyah and Banana Island (p.244), and in more remote areas, such as Sharao'uw Island (p.244).

Diving

If there is one feature that makes diving in Qatar pleasurable it is the water temperature. Early in the year the sea temperature reaches its minimum of 16°C, which although a little cool, is quite manageable if you wear a 6mm wet suit. By July and August, it reaches a slightly uncomfortable 35°C. Although the wet suits have long disappeared by this time, most divers still wear lightweight Lycra suits to protect themselves against jellyfish stings.

In between these cool and hot periods the water is close to or just below body temperature and is extremely pleasant.

Fish & Ships

Marine life in the seas around Qatar, particularly around wrecks, ranges from macro life, such as nudibranches and shrimps, to very occasional whales and whale sharks, and everything else in between, including groupers, and lobsters, dolphins, squid, cuttle fish, lion fish, snakes and a variety of rays.

Despite the hype, coral reefs in Qatar are a disappointment – there are few of them and most are dead, although they do have prolific marine life. Offshore wrecks are another matter altogether; despite being quite a distance offshore, up to a 90 minute ride in a fast boat, they are well worth the trip and numerous. There are dozens of wreck sites around Qatar, including dredgers, dhows, tankers and barges. Most are in around 20 metres of water. The deepest

known wreck, the 50 Metre Tanker, is actually in 49 metres of water at high tide. Some of the offshore wrecks verge on the spectacular. The best is known, for obscure reasons, as the MO wreck; the real name of the boat is the Alexion Hope. The MO was a Greek cargo ship that was abandoned after coming under attack in one of the Gulf wars, and drifted into Qatari waters, where the authorities sank the ship to prevent it causing any damage to the offshore oil platforms. This caused great delight amongst the scuba divers of Qatar, who could not believe their good fortune in acquiring a genuine shipwreck in just 20 metres of clear water.

Within a few kilometres of the MO is the Macdeem, a supply boat that hit an oil platform in the Shargi oilfield. Having been badly damaged the boat sank in the field and is again in about 20 metres of water, sat on the bottom of the sea, completely upside down and interesting to see.

Will It Bite Me?

The answer to that question is a resounding no. Although there are creatures in the waters around Qatar that are capable of biting or stinging you, attacks by marine creatures are unheard of. If you leave the wildlife alone, it will leave you in peace to admire the tranquil under water scenery. You are generally too big to be considered as prey.

Another nearby site, known appropriately as 'Steptoes', is an industrial dumping ground consisting of old barges, cranes and general oilfield debris. This site attracts big fish; whale sharks have been spotted here too. Under the guidance of an experienced lead diver, it is feasible to drift dive from the Macdeem to Steptoes on one tank of air.

Other dive sites in Qatar include the Old Club Reef, an 18 metre deep training site, (p.243) near the Sealine Resort, Dolphin Reef, another 18 metre artificial reef (p.239) near Dukhan and Five Mile Reef, a shallow six metre dive, which lies around 40km south-east of Doha (p.244).

The best way to access any of these dive sites is by enlisting the services of a dive company or by joining a dive club (see Activities and Hobbies, p.263).

Caving

There is no real pot-holing in Qatar, and few decent hiking routes, but there are a number of underground caverns formed by water erosion. Construction of new roads in Doha was delayed after contractors stumbled across previously unknown caves. The best known and most accessible is Dahl Misr (White Caves), located in the desert, off Salwa Road, about a kilometre south of the Satellite Earth Station.

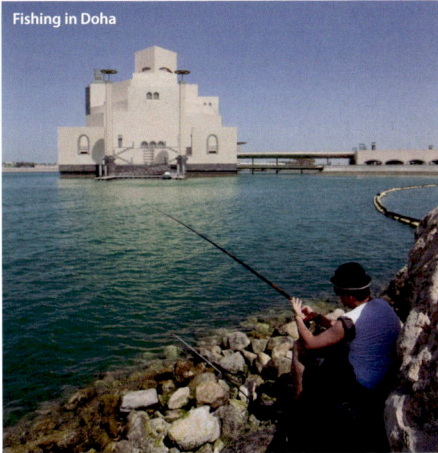

Fishing in Doha

Fishing

Whether you drop a line from a boat or cast a rod from the shore, you will find that the clear waters of the Arabian Gulf are rich fishing grounds; your catch can include anything from sardines to barracuda. The corniches of Doha and Al Khor are particularly popular spots with shore fishermen. For those who do not have access to a boat, it's relatively easy to organise a fishing trip through one of the operating tour companies in the area or by hiring a dhow to take you out on the waters (see Boat Tours, p.227). Note that the setting of fishing nets within 5km of the shore is strictly prohibited.

Off-Roading

With the vast areas of virtually untouched wilderness, dune bashing is a popular pastime. Every other vehicle on the road in Doha seems to be a 4WD, but unlike in many countries, in Qatar there's ample opportunity to truly put them to the test in an off-road environment. Dune bashing, or desert driving, is one of the toughest challenges for both car and driver, but once you have mastered it, it's also the most fun. Apart from sand driving, most of the other off-road driving that you'll encounter in Qatar is on sabka (salt flats), with some rocky driving areas on the west coast. Driving on sabka and rock is much easier than sand but you need to be careful that sharp rocks don't damage your tyres; always make sure to carry a spare. While there are no formal desert driving courses available in Qatar, a number of local 4WD agents organise informal camping parties to Khor Al Udaid from time to time where advice on driving techniques on sand are given. Check with the agents, for example Jeep. For a beginner's guide to desert driving, see p.222.

For the biggest and best dunes in Qatar you will need to head south. The area to the south of the

Sealine Resort towards the Inland Sea (see Khor Udeid, p.243) is a popular weekend driving destination, and more fun driving can be found south of Route Q55 near the Singing Sand Dune (p.242).

If you want a wilderness adventure but don't know where to start, contact any of the major tour companies (see Main Tour Operators, p.228). All offer a range of desert safaris.

For real driving enthusiasts, a journey to the largest sand desert in the world should be on your bucket list while you are living in the region. The Rub Al Khali (Empty Quarter) stretches through southern Saudi Arabia, covering a vast area of the western UAE and reaching into Yemen, but is most accessible around Liwa, located in the emirate of Abu Dhabi. As it is absolutely possible to drive to the United Arab Emirates from Qatar, you are able to take your own trusted vehicle; just be sure that it has been fully serviced before you venture out on long distances. For further information and details about this epic trip of a lifetime, see p.252.

Drive With Care

To protect the environment from damage, you should try to stick to existing tracks rather than creating new tracks across virgin countryside. While it may be hard to deviate from the track when wadi bashing, dunes are ever-changing so obvious paths are less common. Although the sandy dunes may look devoid of life, there is a surprising variety of flora and fauna that exists.

Snorkelling

The warm clear waters of the Gulf make snorkelling in Qatar a pleasant pastime. The equipment required is minimal – just a mask, a snorkel and, if you are so minded, a pair of fins. The seabed around the country is like the land, mostly sand, but there is always something to see. In the shallow sandy areas keep your eyes open for a small fish that can be seen cohabiting with a crayfish. It is difficult to tell what the role of the fish is in the partnership as it appears that the crayfish does all the work. There a few coral reefs in Qatar and on most of the ones that do exist the coral itself is regretfully dead. Two highlights easily reachable from the shore are a live coral reef just off Fuwairat beach on the north east coast (p.235) and a shallow rocky outcrop called Six Metre Reef, which is about 200 metres from the shore of the beach next to Dukhan Beach Club on the west coast (p.239). Depending on the state of the tide the top of this outcrop can be only a metre below the surface and marine life is abundant. If you have access to a boat, Jinan Island (p.244), Five Mile Reef (p.244) and Banana Island (p.244) are all good snorkelling spots.

Beginners' Guide To Desert Driving

Driving on sand is good fun – all that is needed is a 4WD vehicle and a little bit of skill. As long as you use some common sense, that skill is not hard to acquire. There are, however, a number of things to take into account.

Remember that you are off to play in a real life wilderness and there are inherent dangers that you must be prepared for. A well-maintained vehicle is an essential, as are food and water – you should always take more water than you think you'll need. Take a mobile phone in case you need to summon emergency help and, while not essential, a cheap handheld GPS is also a good idea. It will not only give you your exact location, it can also help you retrace your route back to civilisation if you get lost. A towrope and a spade are absolutely crucial for when you become bogged down. Additionally, your essentials should include a basic first aid kit and, of course, don't forget the sunscreen.

You will also need a tyre gauge, because unless you deflate your tyres to about 12 PSI (just less than 1 Bar) before you start, you are not going to get very far at all. Deflating increases the surface area of the tyre in contact with the sand, providing added traction for the soft conditions and saving your engine from being overworked, but remember not to take corners too fast or too hard, as this can cause tyres to come off their rims.

On sand, driving with high ratio 4WD engaged is normal; this can be lowered to the low range if you are experiencing traction problems or are stuck. You will use first and second gears a lot, but on more open and flatter tracks, you will get into third and even fourth, and at times it will feel very similar to driving on the road.

The key to driving on sand is maintaining controlled momentum and always looking ahead so you can plan for obstacles before you reach them. You'll need lots of engine revs and a determination to keep moving. Following the tyre marks of others is sensible, based on the principal that if someone else has already been there and not become stuck, it's unlikely to happen to you either. When the track starts to undulate or you head into the dunes, slow down, keep a steady pace and stay alert for obstacles. You should try to use the accelerator more than anything else, barely touching the brakes or clutch. If you do brake, do so lightly and smoothly to avoid sinking into the sand.

At first, even small dunes can seem quite extreme, so take things cautiously. Approach the dune head on, plan your ascents to take the smoothest route and try to reduce your speed so that you coast over the top of a dune at close to walking pace so you will be in control for the descent. Remember that you never know what's over the other side of the dune until you are over the crest, and some beautifully crescent-shaped dunes hide a potentially lethal danger for the unwary – while the forward edge may be sloping gently, the back edge can be almost sheer. Approach the crest with caution and go easy on the gas – it is far better to fail to make a climb because you were going too slowly than to end up jumping over the top of a dune.

As you go over the crest the last thing you are likely to see over the end of your car bonnet is sky, lots of sky! But don't panic, because as soon as you are over the top and going downwards, you will see the sand again. Once on the downward slope there is no going back; you are committed and your car will be incapable of reversing back to the crest. Drive slowly and point straight down the dune, letting the engine control the speed rather than using the brakes.

Don't stop in areas of soft sand or facing uphill if you can help it. Attempting to set off from stationary pointing uphill will almost certainly result in your car staying exactly where it is or, worse, coming to rest with its floorpan sitting on the desert floor. If you are in this situation it is better to carefully reverse yourself downhill.

But be aware, there are hazards to blindly following others' tracks, particularly if you are leading the convoy. The tracks you are following may be being followed by another car heading in the opposite direction and the last place you want to meet is on the crest of a dune. For the same reason, don't stop on the blind side of a crest or anywhere else that others cannot clearly see you.

Don't worry too much about getting stuck; it happens to everyone. If you do get stuck, don't keep revving the engine – chances are it will just dig you in further. Get out of your car to assess the situation, and try to work out how it happened so you can learn for next time. Usually, clearing a little sand from around the wheels and a few people pushing will get most cars out of minor problems. If you can, lift the car up and get something under the wheels to give some grip – the loose mats from inside the car can be very useful for this. If you are in deeper, you may need to dig the car free, lower the tyre pressures more or get someone to tow you out.

Quicksand can be another trap for the uncautious, especially in beach areas where seawater ebbs and flows inshore. This can also be a problem in some more innocuous inland areas if there has been a lot of rain. If you sink in quicksand you will need a winch or crane, or possibly even a new car if the tide comes back in before you are extricated.

Always ensure that you drive in convoy with at least one other vehicle to provide assistance when stuck, and never drive beyond the limits of your experience, regardless of anything others may do. Under no circumstances should you abandon or fail to help anyone in distress.

Enjoy playing in the sand; with a little practice you will soon become adept at handling it, but be wary of overconfidence; the desert does not make allowances. For reasons of mutual assistance it is sensible to travel in groups of vehicles.

Discover Doha

SPECTATOR SPORTS

The Qatari government has big plans to develop the nation into the regional hub for sports-related tourism. This was demonstrated by the staging of the Asian Games in 2006 and by various bids for global sporting events, including the successful bid to stage the 2022 FIFA World Cup. The result of this policy is that the country boasts some of the finest sports stadia in the world with more to come.

As part of the master strategy to develop tourism and spread the name of Qatar through sporting prowess, a centre of excellence, Aspire Academy, has been established (p.178). Here, any Qatari showing ability in a particular sport will be developed according to programmes set up by top-class trainers and coaches. Aspire's facilities, from its competition areas to its spectator facilities, are magnificent in every respect. Athletes gain experience in their specific discipline through international events organised by Aspire and as a spectator you can watch some of the world's top contenders in action, free of charge.

The most popular sport in Qatar is football, with motorsports coming second in popularity, but trailing a long way behind. The facilities for watching football are up there with the best, but other sports have not been neglected; billions of riyals have been spent on excellent spectator facilities, particularly for tennis and motorsports.

Annual sporting events are not guaranteed to take place at the same time each year, although some events, such as major tennis internationals, can usually be pinned down to within a month, and the cooler months between October and April are when most sporting events are held.

If you're more interested in playing sport than watching it, check out Activities and Hobbies, p.263

Camel Racing

Arabs may have a long-standing association with horses, but in many people's minds, the enduring image of a traditional Bedouin will be a man in long robes, surrounded by camels. This association is not too far from reality in Qatar's epicentre for camel racing sport in Sheehaniyah (p.237), about 20 kilometres west of Doha, on the road to Dukhan. There are a collection of camel breeding farms and studs, complete with a 10 kilometre camel-racing track and grandstand. There are no charges for spectators and plenty of seating in the grandstand, although for a better view, you can follow the race in your 4WD along a track which runs around the main race course. When the race gets underway, the owners and trainers follow the camels in pickup trucks, often with drummers in the back, for the encouragement of the animals. It is well worth following them for the exciting atmosphere, but don't get too close. Contact

Qatar Camel Racing Committee at Al Shahaniya Race Track on 5546 4783 for more information.

Until very recently the camel jockeys were very small boys. Qatar took a lead in abolishing this system and commissioned Qatar Scientific Club to design radio controlled robot jockeys. These replacement robot jockeys have been widely adopted throughout the Gulf. It was an imaginative and innovative step forward for human rights, but the wobbling robots do look surreal.

Top Competitions

Aspire Academy for Sports Excellence (aspire.qa) was set up by the Qatari government with the purpose of developing Qatari sporting talent into the best in the world. Apart from aiding their athletes to take part in overseas international competition, Aspire often organises international events of their own to test and develop the skills of local sportsmen and women against the best in the world.

These events range from high diving through to athletics and gymnastic disciplines, such as the annual FIG Artistic World Cup (dohagym.com), but unfortunately are usually not advertised particularly well. If you are keen to watch the top sportsmen of the region and, in many cases, the world, keep a close eye on the local press.

Football

There is no spectator sport in Qatar bigger than football, and Qataris can be fanatical about it. The successful bid for World Cup 2022 will see many changes to the country's landscape as new stadiums are built to Fifa regulations.

Organised football has grown since it began in the late 1940s and a blurred line exists between the country's two main football bodies – the national authority is the Qatar Football Federation, and the Qatar Football Association (4494 4411, qfa.com.qa) runs the national leagues.

The domestic competition consists of 18 teams, which are formed into two leagues. The top 10 compete in what is known as the Q-League. Each year the bottom two teams in the top league are relegated and two teams are promoted from the lower league. Many of the teams, particularly the very wealthy Q-League sides such as Al Arabi, Al Sadd and Al Rayyan, operate from state-of-the-art, purpose-built stadiums and command a loyal following.

Teams are made up of the most talented locals, with the addition of international, and often world-renowned, players who are usually reaching the tail end of their playing careers. This applies particularly to European and South American players; high calibre international coaches are also brought in to manage

Al Sadd Sports Club

offers major prize money and attracts some of the world's best players. It is not unknown for local golf aficionados to spend part of their annual leave watching the Masters – it is an opportunity to watch the best golf at close quarters without the usual hindrance of crowds. The governing body is the Qatar Golf Association (4483 7815, qga.com.qa).

Horse Racing

Horse racing is a popular sport in the Gulf and in Qatar it takes place throughout the winter months at the impressive Qatar Racing and Equestrian Club (4480 8122, qrec.gov.qa), located on the western edge of Doha at Al Rayyan. Races are scheduled every Thursday from 16:00 until about 21:00 and are extremely popular. The appeal probably has a great deal to do with the fact that spectating is completely free of charge and onlookers stand a chance of leaving the track a much wealthier person than they arrived. Although gambling is prohibited, race-goers can enter free raffles to guess the winning horses; prizes are substantial, and often include cars. The course is floodlit, and good coverage is broadcast on huge TV screens. The events are well attended, and consequently if you are travelling by car, a certain amount of patience is required in order to get out of the car park at the end of the evening's racing.

Other forms of equestrian sport are also catered for, including an Arabian horse show in March, also held at the Qatar Racing and Equestrian Club (the local press will provide the exact timings of the event) and the Desert Marathon, which takes place during the relatively cooler winter months, in the desert south of Messaied. A course is laid in the valleys between the sand dunes, and riders from around the world compete in the event. Rules regarding the treatment of the animals are extremely strict and veterinary doctors at various stages of the course have the power to withdraw any horse that is showing signs of excessive stress. To watch this sport all you need is a four-wheel drive vehicle and a picnic. Just sit in the desert and wait for the riders to pass by. Keep an eye on the local press for timings.

the local teams. The season runs through the cooler months from October to April. At end-of-season league deciders and some international matches there are usually draws held for the spectators with very substantial prizes; the chance to win one of 20 Toyota Land Cruisers is not beyond the realms of possibility.

International matches and friendly tours by top European and South American teams are frequent and can see stadiums filled to capacity. These games are usually played at the stadiums belonging to the larger Q-League teams or at Khalifa Stadium next to the Aspire Academy.

Football fans can watch local games for free, but prices for international exhibition matches have recently started to rise and entry can now cost as much as QR 100. Football violence is unheard of.

An amateur event that is thoroughly enjoyed by partisan spectators, but also attracts others, is the traditional grudge match between English and Scottish expats, an annual event that has taken place for over 50 years. Check out the Qatar Football Association's website, or watch the local press for more information as the venue varies from year to year.

Golf

In January each year the Doha Golf Club (p.273) in West Bay hosts the Qatar Masters PGA Championship (p.25) on its pleasant course, designed by Peter Harradine. The event, like many in the region,

Motorsports

Qatar Motor and Motorcycle Federation (4437 9884, qmmf.com) is the governing body for motorsports in Qatar and is responsible for the purpose-built Losail racetrack (circuitlosail.com), situated on the north side of Doha, about 10km from Doha on the new Al Khor Road. Designed primarily as a motorcycle track, Losail is the setting for the Qatar round of the MotoGP championship (p.26), usually held in March, and, until 2010, was also a venue for the Superbike World Championship. The circuit is renowned for its laidback atmosphere, with crowds in the low thousands, and is a popular track with all the top stars.

Spectator Sports

The track does have its limitations for spectators, who are restricted to the large stand on the fast starting and finishing straight as visibility can be obscured by the pit buildings opposite. However, the stand does provide ample shade from the hot Arabian sun, offers a good view of the action in the pits, and the outfield action can be followed on huge television screens located opposite the stands.

The track is also occasionally used for car racing. As is normal for most events in Qatar, entrance fees are lower than the international standards, but this depends on the status of the event taking place.

A Grand Day Out

If you're a Formula 1 fan you've moved to the right region with Abu Dhabi and Bahrain hosting Grand Prix races. In recent years, the Bahrain race has been among the first ones of the season in March/April, while the Formula 1 Etihad Airways Abu Dhabi Grand Prix has been either the season finale or the penultimate racing event in October/November. Due to some unrest, the Bahrain Grand Prix was cancelled at the start of 2011, but in 2012, the race was back on. For more info on travelling to Bahrain and Abu Dhabi see Out Of Qatar, p.244 and for F1 race information, visit formula1.com.

Several other motor racing events are staged in the country each year, including the Qatar International Rally (p.24), an event which takes place over a period of three days in January, again organised by Qatar Motor and Motorcycle Federation.

The location of the rally sites, which take full advantage of the country's desert terrain, vary from year to year and are usually announced in the local media in the run up to the event. All that is required is a four-wheel drive vehicle to get you to the more remote spectator points. If you fancy getting even closer to the action, Qatar Motor and Motorcycle Federation always advertises for marshals and stewards to carry out trackside duties – call 4437 9884 for information on how to get involved.

A new addition to Qatar's catalogue of motor sports entertainment is drag racing for cars and bikes. A course with full facilities including a quarter mile track and a drift demonstration pad has been constructed at Street 52 of Doha Industrial Area. Arabian Drag Racing League, Freestyle drifting, Sand Drag competitions, as well as the recent addition of the Formula Drift event are popular with residents and locals alike. At the moment racing takes place on an ad hoc basis, but events are prominently displayed in the local press and on the Qatar Racing Club website (qrczone.com, 4450 9357). Entry is free to the public, with a charge of QR 50 for the VIP area.

Rugby

Doha Rugby Football Centre (p.278) organises and participates in both national and Inter-Gulf events from their club and ground off Salwa Road. Spectators are welcome; non-members must pay a small guest entry fee. Aussie Rules and Gaelic football matches are also held here. Check the website for details of upcoming competitions.

Tennis & Squash

Although primarily the home of tennis in Qatar, the purpose built Khalifa International Tennis and Squash Complex (p.280) also hosts important international squash competitions. Facilities for watching are first class and you can enjoy displays by the biggest stars of both sports for negligible prices.

Men's tennis players compete in the annual Qatar ExxonMobil Open (p.24), which usually takes place in early January. With $1 million prize money up for grabs, most of the world's leading players turn up to compete. For more information on the tournaments, contact the Qatar Tennis Federation (qatartennis.org). Ticket prices range from QR 10 to QR 50 per match and up to QR 450 for a season ticket for the whole competition. Both of these competitions have become extremely popular of late and tennis fans are advised to book tickets in advance to avoid disappointment. Bookings can be made at the tennis complex itself, at booths set up in shopping malls and online through the Tennis Federation website, although the online option can become difficult to use as soon as tickets are in short supply.

The Qatar Classic Squash Championship also usually attracts the cream of the world's players to the Khalifa complex, but the timing of the event is variable. Spectator facilities are good and attending a game will not break the bank. Unusually for Qatar, the competitions for men and women occur at the same time. Contact the Qatar Squash Federation for the latest information (4470 2777, qatarsquash.com).

Watersports

Given the clear blue water of the Gulf, the shelter afforded by Doha Bay and the ideal viewing location of Doha Corniche, it is hardly surprising that powerboat racing has become a popular spectator sport. In the case of the large and immensely powerful Class 1 boats, the vessels are clearly visible throughout the entire course, including a fast stretch directly in front of the spectators. The excitement of watching smaller Formula 200 boats can be experienced even closer up.

Jet ski and pleasure boat racing competitions are also organised and most events take place between October to May to avoid the summer heat. Details of races, which have in the past been prone to last minute additional contests being added to the schedule, can be found on the Qatar Marine Sports Federation website (qmsf.org). It is also advisable to check the local press.

TOURS & SIGHTSEEING

Most of the tour companies offer similar packages for trips in and around Doha. The absolute must-do is an excursion to the desert and Khor Al Udaid (the Inland Sea), camping overnight if you can. Most of the big tour companies have permanent Arabic tents pitched there in the cooler months and after some exhilarating dune bashing, they will cook a barbecue dinner and bring out the shisha.

Because the tour companies are fairly small local operations they can be flexible in arranging whatever you want to do. Most trips have a minimum number, and the bigger your party the cheaper it will be.

The range of trips offered includes: desert safaris, dhow cruises, wildlife tours taking in the oryx farm and camel racetrack, heritage tours taking in outlying towns Al Ruwais and Al Khor and archaeological sites such as the ruins in Zubarah, fishing and diving trips, watersports, sand boarding and quad biking excursions and Doha shopping and city tours.

Sand Boarding & Skiing

For thrills and spills, desert style, try sand boarding on the dunes. You won't reach the breakneck speeds of snowboarding, and if you do fall off you'll land in lovely soft sand. This must-try activity is offered by most of the tour operators (p.228).

Activity Tours

If you are interested in more active pursuits, you can experience many sporting adventures on the sand or sea. There are a number of tour companies that will arrange trips with fun activities like sand skiing or boarding (which is not quite as easy as you may think), or watersports tours which include activities such as jet skiing, parasailing, water skiing, and banana boat rides. Diving and fishing tours are also available (see p.220).

Boat Tours

Day or evening dhow cruises that either sail around Doha Bay or venture further afield to one of the small islands are very relaxing and give you the chance to see Doha from a whole new perspective. A traditional meal is provided and there may be music and entertainment too. The trips usually last around three or four hours. Boats leave from Navigation Dhow Harbour off the Corniche. There are various

View of The Pearl Qatar by night

Tours & Sightseeing

options, depending on how long you want to go for, and how many people are in your group. As well as the large dhows operated by tour companies, there are also plenty of dhows that can be rented out on a less official basis. The dhow harbour is the area to look around, and sometimes you can barter a better deal with these more impromptu outfits. Phone numbers are usually displayed on the boats. Make sure you look at the smaller, less expensive dhows where the road turns into a T junction.

Some establishments, including hotels such as Best Western Hotel (p.196) and clubs such as the Diplomatic Club (p.280) have a boat or yacht for hire for fishing, watersports and sightseeing tours. Similarly, Ronautica (4496 5801, ronauticame.com) at The Pearl Qatar has yacht charters available including day trips and fishing excursions (4495 3894).

Palm Tree Island Boat Company
Nr Sheraton Doha Resort & Convention Hotel
Al Dafna **4486 9151**
Map **2 R3**

This company owns a dhow which will take you for a pleasant trip in the bay around the island at the very reasonable cost of QR 20 for adults and QR 15 for children; this includes a soft drink and snack. No booking is required.

Museum of Islamic Art atrium

Regatta Sailing Academy
InterContinental Doha Al Gassar **4442 4577**
regattasailingacademy.com
Map **1 K3**

The Regatta Sailing Academy has a range of sailing vessels to suit all requirements, including funboats, dinghies, and even two 30 foot yachts that can be used for pleasure or racing. The academy is staffed by fully qualified British Royal Yacht Academy instructors, who provide full instructions about the safety of the lagoon area and any coaching tips that may be needed before you are permitted to venture out into the waters of Doha Bay.

Main Tour Operators

As Qatar steps up its tourism efforts and opens the country up to more visitors, there are more and more tour operators being established.

Tour companies usually provide pick-up and drop-off from your hotel or house. Prices are fixed and there may be a stipulated minimum number of passengers on certain tours. If you do not have the minimum number of people you will still be able to do the tour, but the price per person will most likely sky rocket.

Al Jasra Travel
25 Ibn Dirham St Al Mansoura **4443 0737**
aljasratravel.com
Map **2 R11**

Al Jasra Travel offers a full programme of land and water tours in and around Doha and across the city. These include half-day city tours, archaeological site tours, water sports tours, including dhow cruises, fishing trips, jet skiing and diving. Half day, full day and overnight sand dune tours and a desert roses safari tour are also readily available.

Arabian Adventures
Al Asmakh St Fereej Al Asmakh **4436 1461**
arabianadventureqatar.net
Map **2 Q8**

Tours to sites around Doha, include city tours, fishing trips and a heritage tour to the oryx and camel racetrack, while a desert safari offers the chance to explore the sand dunes in 4WD vehicles.

Black Pearl Tourism Co
Al Sadd St, Bin Jeham Al Kuwari Complex Al Sadd
4435 7333
blackpearl.co
Map **2 L8**

Black Pearl offers country tours and desert tours, including a half day camel trek. One of its most popular tours is the five-hour dhow cruise, which includes a swimming stop just off Safliyah Island. The sea camp is one of the largest in Qatar.

Gulf Adventures Tourism
29 Aspire Zone St Baaya **4422 1888**
gulf-adventures.com
Map **2 B10**
A range of tours are offered to all the major tourist destinations around Doha including the Inland Sea and the capital's cultural sites. The day-long Grand Sightseeing Tour takes visitors to many major spots in Qatar from Al Shahaniya to Souq Waqif.

Qatar International Adventures
Al Matar Al Qadeem St Old Airport **4455 3954**
qia-qatar.com
Map **2 V13**
An extensive range of tours is on offer including shopping, watersports and desert excursions. The company's Bedouin-style campsite near the inland sea is fitted with showers, so it's perfect if you fancy sleeping under the stars but like your home comforts.

Qatar International Tours
Al Hail Bldg, Matar St Old Airport **4455 1141**
qittour.com
Map **2 V12**
Choose between watersports and fishing trips, or stay on dry land and explore the country's cultural sites, Doha Zoo or Doha's shopping highlights. Alternatively, head inland and dig for fossilised desert roses, or camp out under the stars. Online booking available.

Regency Travel & Tours
Sheikh Suhaim Bin Hamad St Al Sadd **4434 4444**
regencyholidays.com
Map **2 L8**
Regency offers a broad range of half, full and overnight tours to all of Qatar's major tourist and heritage attractions.

Safari Tours
A safari is a must-do in Qatar. Unlike in Africa where it involves spotting wildlife, a safari in this part of the world means a trip into the desert. You will be picked up in a powerful 4WD to head into the dunes for some thrilling off-road driving and spectacular scenery. Drivers need to be experienced, as travelling up and down near-vertical dunes is potentially lethal, so it's best to use a reputable tour company.

Desert tours usually head south out of Doha, stopping at Sealine Beach Resort (p.243) to meet up with other cars in the convoy and deflate tyres, before heading across the sand to the Inland Sea. Seatbelts are compulsory and as you defy gravity, skimming round the edge of enormous sand dunes, you will understand why. It will feel like the car is about to somersault off the edge, but put your faith in your driver and just enjoy this exhilarating ride. When you stop at the Inland Sea, you can try sand boarding or

Traditional handicrafts

swim in the calm, shallow water. Watching the sun set over the desert dunes is a memorable experience and a great photo opportunity.

If you want to experience an authentic desert safari experience, you can choose to stay in the desert overnight – most tour companies have their own permanent campsites set up among the dunes, where you can enjoy an Arabic barbecue accompanied by music, belly dancing, a puff or two on a traditional shisha pipe and an evening under the stars all tucked up in a sleeping bag.

Shopping Tours
To immerse yourself in one of the nation's favourite pastimes, a shopping tour gives you a good taste of the old, with a healthy dose of the new. The trip begins with a tour of the souks where you can barter for goods ranging from spices, fabric and perfumes to traditional handicrafts and even falcons. The tour then moves on to show you the best of Doha's modern shopping malls.

Country Tours
Several companies offer trips out of Doha. Khor Udeid (the Inland Sea) is the most popular destination for a day trip or a night's camping in an Arabian tent. Several companies, like Qatar International Tours (p.229), also do a trip north of Doha which takes in Al Khor with its corniche and dhow harbour, before moving on to the fort and ruins in Zubarah, and finally visiting the fishing harbour in Ruwais. Also popular is the tour to the oryx farm, camel racetrack and equestrian club in Shahaniya. Heading west, you can arrange to camp on the beach at Zekrit, with the chance to spot dolphins and turtles.

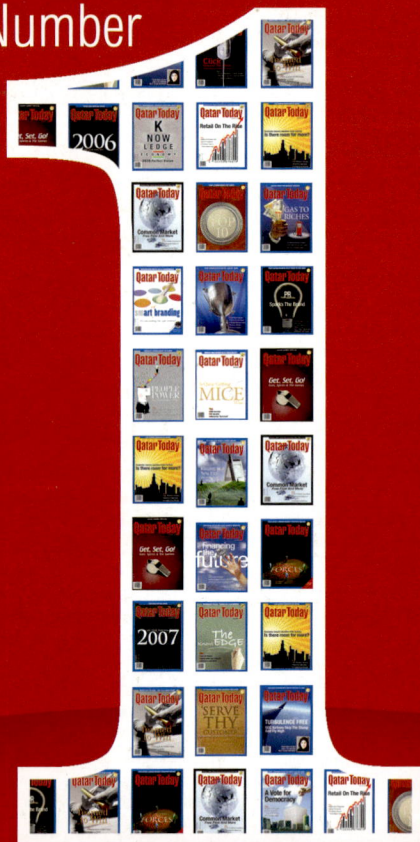

Out Of The City

OUT OF DOHA

While tourism beyond Doha is still in its infancy, there are a number of interesting places outside the capital which are worth exploring. For a weekend break within the country, many residents head south for a night or two at the Sealine Beach Resort (p.243). This small resort, run by Qatar National Hotels, is a peaceful patch right on the beach that offers watersports and a variety of sporting activities. For others, camping in the desert, or on a remote beach, is the perfect antidote to city life. Most Qatar residents make the trip at least once to the Inland Sea (Khor Udeid, p.243) in the south-east, which provides an opportunity to drive through the mountainous dunes and witness the impressive waterway as it meanders like a river through the desert with Qatar on one bank and Saudi Arabia on the other.

While there are plenty of ways to spend your weekends within Qatar's borders, if you feel like a change of scenery, a true getaway will involve a flight and Doha is within easy reach of some interesting places. The five other GCC countries warrant some exploration while you're living in the region too, so whether you're after the big city lights, diverse nightlife and limitless shopping of Dubai (p.255), high octane excitement at the Abu Dhabi (p.251) Formula 1 Grand Prix race, the untamed beauty of Oman (p.245) or simply a relaxing getaway in one of the region's many five-star resorts, there is plenty of choice accessible in under 90 minutes by air.

Because Qatar is essentially a one-city state with almost all the commercial, ceremonial and sporting activities taking place in the capital, the names Doha and Qatar have become almost interchangeable. Despite Doha's dominant position in the country, there is much more to the rest of Qatar than meets the eye. Indeed, for some things such as beaches, unless you want to pay to sit on one belonging to a five-star hotel, you have to go outside of Doha to find them.

The interior of the country varies between barren desert plains and impressive sand dunes; along the coast you'll find rocky outcrops, mangrove swamps and remote beaches. For many residents, weekends during the cooler months are spent pursuing outdoor activities such as camping, dune driving and watersports. If history and heritage are of more interest to you, Qatar has a number of archaeological sites at various stages of excavation, and a collection of forts scattered around the country. Beyond Doha's city limits the isolated farms, desert terrain, salt flats (sabka) and small villages provide a complete contrast to city life and afford a glimpse of how life in the country used to be.

For those interested in exploring beyond the capital, the country can be split into three distinct land areas, which radiate out from Doha to the north, the south and the west. Each of these areas can feasibly

be covered in a daytrip or a two-day camping trip, but there are also a number of towns and villages that, due to newly constructed roads, are within easy reach of Doha, both as interesting places to visit and as satellite commuting towns. Located within a 40km radius of Doha, these locations are attractive to commuters, as they offer lower rents and more space, and to weekend visitors looking to sample a different pace of life to the city. For more information on living in these areas, see Residential Areas, p.78.

Beyond Doha, the country's attractions and places of interest are easiest to visit if you have your own vehicle and some areas, particularly Khor Udeid, the Ras Abruk Peninsula and desert regions, require the use of a 4WD vehicle. Alternatively, tour companies based in Doha operate visits to a number of the locations – Khor Udeid (the Inland Sea) (p.243) being one of the most popular destinations. Other tours include desert safaris, dhow cruises, heritage tours taking in the oryx farm and camel racing, a northern tour going up to Zubarah fort and the nearby excavated ruins, Al Ruwais and Al Khor, fishing and diving trips, watersports, sand boarding and quad biking, and Doha shopping and city tours. Because the tour companies are fairly small local operations they can be flexible in arranging whatever you want to do. Most trips have a minimum number, and the bigger your party the cheaper it will be per person (see Main Tour Operators, p.228).

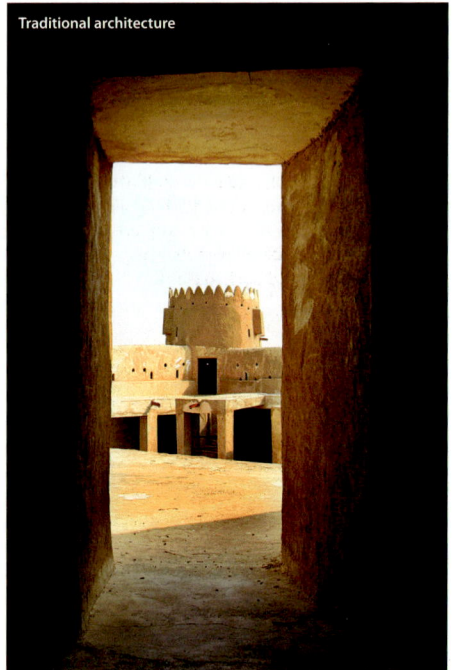
Traditional architecture

It's worth finding out about the activities of social organisations and clubs as some of these organise regular picnics and camping trips around the country for their members (Social Groups, p.48; Activities & Hobbies, p.263). The Qatar Natural History Group (p.270), for example, organises excursions to remote areas for those interested in local flora and fauna, archaeology and geology.

North Of Doha

If you have a spare day or fancy a weekend camping, the coastal drive from Doha all the way round to Dukhan and back to Doha is worth exploring. The easiest way to travel to the north from Doha is take the new Al Khor Road (Route Q1A), although if you want to visit sites such as the Barzan Towers (p.234) and Umm Salal Mohammed fort (p.234) you will have to make a diversion to the parallel Shamal Road (Route Q1). The Al Khor Road starts at Doha Golf Club (p.273) and travels north until it reaches Al Khor town. A new road (Route Q141), on the north side of Al Khor, joins the Shamal Road which eventually takes you to the northern-most tip of Qatar. En route it passes close to the Al Jassasiyeh carvings and numerous sandy beaches such as those at Fuwairat and Al Ghariyah, which are perfect for camping if you're making a weekend of it.

At the top end of the peninsula you'll pass plenty of traditional old fishing villages, which, while not dedicated 'heritage sites' as such, can still give you an idea of how life may have been before the advent of the modern world. Madinat Al Shamal is a relatively new town that primarily acts as an administrative centre for the smaller towns and villages in this northern part of the country. The north-west coast has a number of fortifications and ancient buildings, including those at Al Jemail (also spelt Al Gamel) where you'll find an abandoned fishing village with the ruins of houses and a small mosque. Further down the coast is Zubarah with its striking fort. From Zubarah you can head back to Doha.

Umm Salal Mohamed
Map **Qatar Country Map C3**

The most straightforward way to Umm Salal Mohamed is to head north on Shamal Road (Route Q1), but you can also access it from the Al Khor Road, and it makes a worthwhile detour en route if you are heading further north. From the second Golf Club Roundabout on Al Khor Road, turn inland and follow the road for about 6km, then join the Shamal Road heading north for a further 6km, looking out for the signposted road to Umm Salal Mohamed on the left.

Umm Salal is a traditional village that has only recently started to witness change. The Barzan Towers can be seen to the right as you enter the village, and in the centre of the village is Umm Salal Fort.

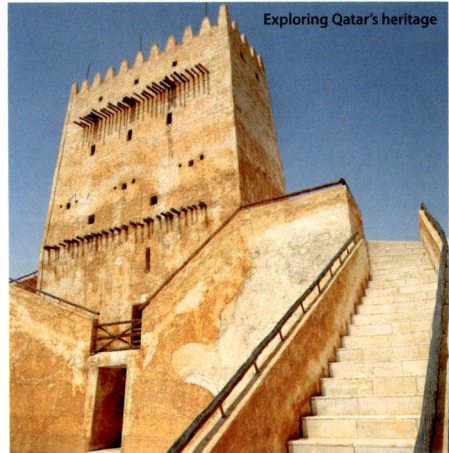
Exploring Qatar's heritage

Both Umm Salal and its neighbour Kharatiyat are within easy commuting distance of central Doha, and modern compounds and small shops have started to spring up in the area. Access is much improved now that good progress has been made on the Doha Expressway, which is being constructed to replace the Shamal Road.

Slightly north of Umm Salal is the village of Umm Salal Ali. There are burial mounds on the northern edge of the village, which are said to be associated with the Dilmun civilisation and date back 5,000 years.

Lusail City

Shortly after the Doha Golf Club roundabout on Al Khor Road leaving Doha, you'll see a triple fence which stretches for almost 20km to the turn off to the village of Simaisma (p.234), securing the land between the road and the sea. Although this is largely desert at the moment, it encloses the area that is to become the new town of Lusail. There are to be marinas, entertainment areas, an Energy City, residential areas, shopping malls and many more dedicated zones. Completion is a long way off, but when finished it will be as big as Doha and will join on to the northern edge of Doha's West Bay area (see Key Developments, p.32).

On the opposite side of Al Khor Road, 13km from the Golf Club Roundabout is Losail International Circuit (losailcircuit.com), a purpose-built motorcycle track that hosts the Moto GP Grand Prix, and numerous other motorcycle and car racing events (see Motorsports, p.225).

If you're stuck for inspiration for a gift for the petrol head in your life, book a car or motorbike track day at Losail, or for the ultimate thrill, opt for a night time track session.

Out Of Doha

Barzan Tower

Umm Salal Mohamed qma.com.qa
Map Qatar Country Map C3

The towers, built at the end of the 19th century, served as watch towers and as such offer views over the surrounding countryside. The 'T' shaped tower is considered a unique architectural style in the Gulf region. They were recently restored and are open to the public at no charge, 24 hours a day.

Umm Salal Mohammed Fort

Umm Salal Mohamed qma.com.qa
Map Qatar Country Map C3

This rundown fortification was constructed as a residence for Sheikh Jasim Bin Mohammed during the late 19th and early 20th centuries. It is notable for its thick high walls and impressive facade. The fort is not open to the public as it is still inhabited.

Simaisma

Map Qatar Country Map D3

Six kilometres north of Losail Circuit on the Al Khor Road is the Simaisma flyover. Turn off here to visit Simaisma, a sleepy little fishing village on the shore that is just awakening to the first rumblings of development. Simaisma has a good beach, with a large area of hard sand (sabka) behind it, making it a popular spot for camping and dog walking. There is also an 800 metre long public jetty, which shelters a small fleet of fishing boats, and a private jetty a little further along the beach.

The sea here is very shallow and at low tide the water disappears almost to the end of the jetty leaving a large expanse of white sand, meaning that children can paddle in complete safety. Simaisma and its surrounds are popular with birdwatchers for the fairly prolific resident birdlife ranging from owls to flamingos.

Nuisance Neighbours

Because of its proximity to Bahrain, over the centuries Zubarah has been the venue for many battles and skirmishes between rival tribes from both sides. Indeed, until about 2000 it was actually claimed by Bahrain on the grounds that it had been settled 200 years previously by exiles from Bahrain. There is a sheltered bay to the west of the fort that is an archaeologically interesting, shallow scuba diving site. Unfortunately it is also a military area and permission to enter is not easy to obtain.

Development is just starting to hit Simaisma and a number of new compounds have been built. Rents are reasonable for Qatar and it is within 25 minutes commuting time of both Doha and Ras Laffan Industrial City (see Residential Areas, p.78). Along with the new housing developments, new shops are gradually starting to open. There are a few mosques in Simaisma, including one near the beach, but none are open to non-Muslims and they hold little interest to the general public.

Al Khor

Map Qatar Country Map C2

Al Khor is a small coastal town with an attractive waterfront. If you're after a change of scenery from Doha, the Corniche is a great location for a picnic lunch or dinner and is a popular spot at weekends, especially during the cooler months. Sadly the Corniche has fallen into disrepair, but plans are afoot to carry out refurbishment. The fish market in the dhow harbour is a great place to buy fresh seafood from the day's haul. There is also a quaint little museum on the waterfront that is free of charge. Next to the museum is a shaded area with a children's playground and pleasant views of the harbour and out to sea – another good spot for a picnic. After visiting the museum you could drive further along the Corniche and visit the old watchtowers that still stand guard over the town.

Located inside a naturally protected harbour with a south facing entrance providing shelter from prevailing winds, the town has existed here in one form or another since prehistoric times. Until its economy was hard hit by the Wall Street Crash in the late 1920s, followed hard on its heels by the advent of Japanese cultured pearls in the 1930s, it was the centre of the Qatari pearling industry and consequently the most important city in the country. Remains of abandoned traditional villages dating from this period and before can be found by taking a short detour either north or south along the coastline.

Today the harbour supports an active fishing fleet, consisting mainly of traditional dhows, although the sails are long gone and they are now powered by diesel engines. The fish market is located in the dhow harbour which is generally open daily from early morning to late evening, with the exception of a short period when it closes for Friday prayers. The market is worth visiting, if for no other reason than to inspect the variety of marine life that is dragged from the Gulf. The activity around the dhows behind it can provide some nice opportunities to capture a bit of local colour.

Despite being the 'second city' of Qatar, Al Khor was for many years considered a bit of a backwater. The development of the nearby Industrial City of Ras Laffan and the construction of the Doha to Al Khor road have changed that dramatically and Al Khor has entered a phase of rapid growth, with new compounds seemingly appearing daily. For Al Khor residents, there are adequate shops, many of which are branches of Doha-based businesses, and a new mall is due to open in 2011. For more on living in Al Khor, see Residential Areas, p.78.

Al Sultan Beach Resort

Al Khor Corniche Al Khor **4472 2666**
alsultanbeachresort.com
Map **Qatar Country Map D2**

Located near to the harbour entrance in Al Khor is Al Sultan Beach Resort. A medium-sized, five-star hotel, it has an ornate Arabic style with plenty of gold and marble decor, but the facilities are good. It has a private beach, a large swimming pool, Jacuzzi and fitness centre. There are two main restaurants but neither are licensed. Day visitors are welcome for a fee.

Dhakira

Map **Qatar Country Map D2**

Follow the road north from Al Khor and in the next sheltered bay you will find the village of Dhakira (also known as Thakira). This fishing village has become a dormitory area for Al Khor, but has a pleasant small harbour and extensive mangrove swamps. There are a couple of shops in the village and if you're feeling peckish, the juice bar (a small wood and aluminium shack situated on the sharp bend in the road as you leave the houses to approach the harbour) serves up delicious takeaway egg, cheese and chilli sandwiches in Indian paratha bread for a mere QR 3.

Huwailah, Fuwairat & The North East Coast

Map **Qatar Country Map C1**

Three kilometres north of Al Khor, on the corner of Al Khor Industrial Area, is a right-hand turn leading to Ras Laffan Industrial City. Ras Laffan is a huge petrochemical area and a major source of the nation's prosperity. This is where the gas from the prolific offshore fields is brought ashore, processed and exported around the world as LNG. It has a tightly controlled security area.

The newly constructed road (Route Q141), which leads past the Ras Laffan turning, joins up with Shamal Road (Route Q1), after about 20km, at the Highland Service Area (a petrol station with a minimarket). Shamal Road will be renamed Doha Expressway when it is completed; currently both names are used for the same road. From here, head north along Shamal Road towards Ruwais. To your right, between the road and the sea, are many old villages dating from Qatar's pearling past. Some are abandoned, but a few are still partially inhabited, so make sure that you don't enter anyone's property uninvited if you go exploring. That said, visitors are usually welcomed and people here are likely to be as curious about you as you are about them. There are empty beaches that are perfect for camping and picnicking, and mangrove swamps and creeks where you can enjoy canoeing, windsurfing, kite surfing and snorkelling. Flamingos are commonplace in the shallow waters and you may be lucky enough to spot dolphins swimming off the coast. Be sure to take your own watersports equipment and picnic, as there are no facilities whatsoever. This remote area is off standard tour operator itineraries, but some companies will arrange bespoke trips (p.288). While this means that you're unlikely to be disturbed by other visitors in this area, you should make sure that you know what you're doing before you take to the water, as there is no one to help if you get into trouble.

In the 1700s, Huwailah village, south of Fuwairat, was a major pearling centre. Between Huwailah and Fuwairat are the most significant rock carvings in Qatar, which some people believe may date from prehistoric times. It is possible to explore all the way up the coast in a 4WD vehicle and well worth the effort. There are deserted beaches, abandoned settlements and mangrove swamps almost all the way to Ruwais.

Mosque Etiquette

Throughout the country there are plenty of small mosques, some of which are very old, that are still used for daily prayer by local Muslims. Unlike more relaxed Islamic countries where tourists are allowed to enter and explore certain mosques, Qatar is more conservative. Non-Muslims are not necessarily forbidden from entering some of the mosques (although some mosques, such as the Grand Mosque on the corner of Jasim bin Mohammed Street and Al Rayyan Road, are totally off limits), but it is unusual and there are no organised tours. To respect the Islamic faith, it may be better to appreciate the beauty of Qatar's mosques from the outside – even if you see them advertised on various websites as heritage sites. If you do happen to gain access to the inside of a mosque remember to dress appropriately. That means shorts, sleeveless tops and low-cut shirts are out, and women should cover their hair.

Al Ghariya Resorts

75km North of Doha, Ghariya 4472 8811
alghariyaresorts.com
Map **Qatar Country Map C1**

Located slightly further north of Fuwairat, Al Ghariya Resorts offers self-catering apartments and villas, many of which have beautiful sea views. There is an indoor swimming pool, three restaurants serving traditional Arabic food, and various indoor and outdoor play facilities to keep the children amused. There is also a fishing marina and equipment is available to buy onsite. Alternatively, if you choose to stay the night, you can fish directly from your villa or chalet. The resort welcomes day visitors who are charged a very reasonable QR 30 for use of the pool, play areas and fishing marina.

Out Of Doha

Al Jassassiya Carvings

60km North of Doha, Nr Huwailah & Fuwairat
Map **Qatar Country Map C1**

These rocky hills that overlook the north-eastern coast of Qatar, between the two villages of Al Huwailah and Fuwairit, contain various stone carvings and engravings. There are about a thousand depictions, cut into the horizontal surfaces of the rock, to explore. Among other things, you'll notice crude carvings of boats and cup-shaped rings, which are thought to have been used for the traditional Arabian games of al aliya and al haloosa, which were played using stone counters. Others believe that the depressions were designed simply to catch rain water. The carvings were first photographed in 1962 by a Danish archaeological team and were later catalogued in 1974. Al Jassassiya is considered the most significant of several similar sites in the country.

It is an open site and anyone can simply go and look around. There are no entrance fees.

Al Jassassiya is around 75km north of Doha, on the road to Al Huwailah. As the area may be difficult to find, and the carvings could prove difficult to spot, you may want to take along someone who's been before, or arrange a trip through a tour company (p.228). In the past the Qatar Natural History Group (p.270) has organised visits here.

Ruwais

Map **Qatar Country Map C1**

Continuing north either on the Shamal Road (Route Q1) or up the coastal tracks, you will eventually reach the northern tip of the country at the pleasant fishing port of Ruwais. This town (sometimes referred to by locals as Shamal), is centre of the administrative area of Madinat Al Shamal. This town is a marine entry point into Qatar and dhows trade between here and neighbouring Bahrain. For the adventurous spirit, it is possible to travel to Bahrain from here, but you will need to have your exit visa ready and to make private arrangements with a dhow owner. Even in a slow moving dhow Manama is only a three to four hour ride away, and your dhow captain may even throw in a fishing stop along the way.

The sea around Ruwais is very shallow and access to the harbour is via narrow channels. The shallow water mixes with the white sand forming an emulsion which, when viewed in the morning sunlight, gives the sea a translucent tropical island blue hue; the effect lessens in the afternoon.

Ruwais is too far from Doha for feasible commuting, but is the nearest town to the projected Qatar to Bahrain Causeway and consequently it is expected to become a boom area in the near future (see Key Developments, p.32). Apart from the harbour, there is little of interest for daytrippers in Ruwais, but it makes a pleasant stop en route to Zubarah.

Al Rakiyat Fort

Northwest of Doha qma.com.qa
Map **Qatar Country Map B1**

This fort was built between the 17th and 19th centuries, and restored in 1988. It is made of stone and mud and, similar to other forts in the country, is rectangular with a tower at each corner; three square and one round. The fort is located near a camel farm, just off the coastal road between Zubarah and Ruwais. You'll have to drive off-road for a few hundred metres but it is possible in a normal car. The site is open to the public, but apart from the building itself there's little else to see.

Zubarah

Map **Qatar Country Map B1**

From Ruwais, travelling 30km south westwards towards Zubarah, you will pass a number of derelict villages along the seaward side, including that at Al Jemail (also spelt Al Gamel). There you can explore an abandoned fishing village with the ruins of houses and a small mosque. The settlement was built at the beginning of the 19th century and abandoned in the 1930s, before being inhabited again from 1945 until the 1970s. The ruined mosque lies at the heart of the village, showing how faith is central to the traditional Qatari way of life. Eventually you will reach Zubarah Fort, which is worth a stop. If you follow the track down the side of the fort to the beach you will come across the remains of a partially excavated village originally established in Neolithic times. It was at its most prosperous from the mid 18th century, and indeed in more tribal times became a haven for exiles from the island of Bahrain. There have been a couple of archaeological digs and there may be more in the future. Two areas have been reconstructed (the north house and the south house) and two further areas have been excavated – a souk area and a section, beside the sea, which was once metal workers' workshops.

Heritage Hotline

Some of the forts and museums listed in this chapter do not have individual phone numbers, but you may be able to get additional information by calling the Qatar Museums Authority on 4452 5555.

From Zubarah Fort take the road heading south-east for 35km and after travelling past many of the northern farms you will find yourself back at the Highland Services Area. To get back to Doha from here, either turn right onto the Shamal Road (Route Q1) in the direction of Doha or go straight ahead and retrace your track down the road to Al Khor (Route Q141) and then follow the Doha Road (Route Q1A).

Whichever way you choose all you really have to do is follow the signs for Doha.

Al Zubarah Fort
Zubarah Madinat Al Shamal qma.com.qa
Map **Qatar Country Map B1**
Located 110km from Doha, on Qatar's north-west coast, Zubarah fort was built in 1938 (although it looks much older), during the reign of Sheikh Abdullah bin Jassim Al Thani. It was erected beside the ruins of a neighbouring fort. The impressive Foreign Legion-style fort has a square structure, with high, thick walls, and has circular towers in three of its corners and a rectangular tower in the fourth. The fort once served as a coastguard station and, until the mid 1980s, it was still being used by the military. There are a couple of cannons outside and a few museum exhibits inside. Entry is free, but you should tip the guide.

West Of Doha
To go west from Doha you have to head for Wajbah along Rayyan Road. Wajbah is a place that is easily recognisable because the palace of Qatar's Emir, Sheikh Hamad, is situated there. Set back from the road, the palace was constructed about 15 years ago and is a private residence for the Emir and his family. Understandably, security is fairly heavy and casual visitors are not encouraged and neither is photography. Wajbah Fort, one of the oldest forts in the country, is near to the Emir's palace, but it too is closed to the public.

From Wajbah follow the Dukhan Road (Route Q3) through Sheehaniyah and then on to Dukhan via a brand new eight-lane highway (Route Q3). From Dukhan you can turn south to Umm Bab, again following a new road (Route Q39). Heading a further 40km south, you will reach the Salwa Road (Route Q5)

from where you can head back to Doha or you can drive to the Saudi Arabian border, 18km away at Abu Samra. However, if all you want to do is go to the Saudi border, take the Salwa Road directly from Doha. The distance is 90km.

Al Wajbah Fort
15km Northwest of Doha Wajbah qma.com.qa
Map **Qatar Country Map C4**
With its high towers and thick walls, this fort is considered one of the oldest in the country. It was the site of a famous battle in 1893, when the people of Qatar (under the leadership of Sheikh Qassim bin Mohammed Al Thani) defeated the Ottoman forces. As a result, the name of Al Wajbah evokes a strong feeling of pride among local people. The fort's two large towers have in the past been open to the public and free of charge to visit; it's unclear if or when the fort will reopen. To reach the fort, if driving from Doha, take the first left turn after Wajbah Roundabout before you reach the Emir's palace, go over the speed bumps and turn right at the end of the gravel track.

Sheehaniyah
Map **Qatar Country Map B3**
About 16km from Wajbah, the first place of interest is Sheikh Faisal Bin Qasim Al Thani's private museum, on your left just before you reach Sheehaniyah. This eclectic museum can be visited by prior arrangement and is well worth the effort. Sheehaniyah itself (previously known as Shahaniyah) is the centre for camel racing activities in Qatar. Camel studs and stables are spread over a distance of 6km, to the right of the main Dukhan Road, with the 10km camel racing track complete with grandstand behind. As long as you are polite and don't bother the animals, no one seems to mind you looking at and taking photographs

Inside Zubarah Fort

of the camels. Races are held regularly in winter; for race information telephone 4487 2028 (mornings only). See Camel Racing p.224 for more information. Near to the stables, along the Lujmiliya Road (formerly Jemeliyah Road) is an oryx farm; in the opposite direction, towards Rawdat Rashid, is Al Wabra Wildlife Preservation. Both are only accessible to the public through tour company visits.

Sheehaniyah is within easy commuting distance of Doha and recently accommodation compounds have started to appear.

Observe The Oryx

The Arabian oryx is the national animal of Qatar. It has been suggested that this timid animal is the source of the legend of the mythical unicorn; although a healthy oryx normally has two horns. The largest oryx farm in the world is located in Sheehaniyah, west of Doha. It is closed to the public, but a few tour companies can arrange visits there.

Sheikh Faisal Bin Qassim Al Thani Museum
1km before Al Samariyah R/A 4486 1444
sheikhfaisalmuseum.com
Map **Qatar Country Map C3**

Sheikh Faisal's personal collection, housed at his farm near Sheehaniyah, is considered by many to be one of the best museums in the country; it is certainly the most eclectic. Located inside a huge rectangular fort complex, it is home to thousands of fascinating and rare exhibits. The first hall contains a large collection of Islamic art, including glass and ceramics, jewellery, and metalwork. There's an impressive range of ancient weaponry too, with guns, daggers, swords and armour, some dating back to the 15th century. The second hall has more Islamic artefacts such as doors, furniture, and a selection of antique carts. This hall is also where you'll find the sheikh's impressive collection of vintage cars, including Model T Fords and classic 50s motors complete with fins and lots of chrome. Hall three displays old currency, while hall four contains rare books and manuscripts with examples of Arabic calligraphy. The fifth hall is home to various fossils and archaeological finds from around the region and elsewhere; six has textiles, clothing and embroidery from the Ottoman era. One corner of the museum is recreated as a traditional Qatari house, and there is also a library with over 12,000 books covering history, religion and poetry. To visit the museum you have to ring in advance to make arrangements. It's easy to get there by car and is signposted, but you can also ask one of Doha's tour companies to arrange a visit. Take drinks and snacks as there is no cafe.

Al Wabra Wildlife Preservation
Nr Sheehaniyah Al Wabrah awwp.alwabra.com
Map **Qatar Country Map C3**

If you go into Sheehaniyah village and follow the road out towards Rawdat Rashid for about 5km, you will come to a right hand turn, 2km down this road you will reach Al Wabra Wildlife Preservation. Within the premises are a number of facilities that incorporate laboratories, animal nurseries and artificial rain, as well as natural imported food. The farm is associated with international animal breeding programmes. This project is the brainchild of Sheikh Saoud bin Mohammed bin Ali Al Thani, who with his passion for nature, has joined forces with international teams of experts in a quest to conserve rare and endangered species. You can find out more about the breeding programme and the farm at http://awwp.alwabra.com. The farm is not open to the public, although occasional educational visits can be arranged by emailing office@alwabra.com or gm.office@alwabra.com.

Zekrit
Map **Qatar Country Map A3**

About 25km from Sheehaniyah you will begin to notice odd geological formations on the right hand side of the road which, while on a smaller scale, are reminiscent of the rugged scenery of American Wild West movies. One of them, known locally as 'the hole in the wall', even has a hole through its middle that you can walk through. After passing Dukhan Industrial Area on your left, turn right at the next intersection following the signs for Zekrit village. Once past the schools and the new hospital, you have a choice of going off road and exploring the strange desert formations, following the myriad of tracks, or going straight ahead to Zekrit village.

This area is best explored with a 4WD, because of very rough tracks and extremely rocky off-road terrain. It's accessible in a normal 2WD car, but a 4WD will give you better ground clearance. If you use a normal car, stick to the main tracks.

As you approach Zekrit village, Zekrit Bay will appear on your left. This is a very shallow inlet that is popular with kite surfers. Zekrit is an ancient village and had strong associations and trading ties with Bahrain in the past. It is here that supplies were brought in from Bahrain in the early days of oil development in Qatar, until a tarmac road connected Doha to the west coast. A little further north of the village some of the old channel markers marking the slightly deeper water for the incoming dhows can still be seen.

A climb up the small hill in front of the village reveals old, possibly prehistoric, graves hewn from the solid rock. Many visitors do not realise their original purpose and visitors have been known to unwittingly barbecue in them. If you stand on top of this higher ground and look at the tops of the surrounding hills (known as jebels), the remains of other burial mounds dating from the Dilmun culture can be seen, though none are complete, most having lost their actual mounds many years ago.

In standing with its ancient role as a trading post, Zekrit once had a small fort, the foundations of which have recently been excavated on the northern edge of the village.

Ras Abruk Peninsula
Map **Qatar Country Map A2**

The surfaced road ends in Zekrit village and from here to Ras Abruk, the track is very rough. Head north, along the coast if stopping at one of the many rocky coves or beaches takes your fancy, or inland if you want to have a better look at the jebels, many of which are full of fossilised sea shells and seaweed.

About 10km north of Zekrit, on high ground in the centre of the peninsula, you will find the 'Film Set'. This is a castle-like building situated next to an existing oasis and was originally purpose built for the making of a major television serial for Qatar TV (in Arabic). Various buildings within the set, filmed from different angles, gave the illusion of a traditional village with streets of blacksmiths workshops, houses and stables. A fishing village, complete with small dhows with sails, was also built on the shore close by, but this has now been dismantled. If you wish to inspect the film set, there is no charge, but you're advised to tip the caretaker.

About a kilometre further up the main track, look out for a gap in the rocks to your left leading to a valley. The traditional houses in this valley were also purpose built for the film and most of them were set on fire during the filming of a major battle scene.

The whole of the peninsula has now been classified as Ras Abruk Nature Reserve and attempts have been made to introduce endangered animal species and in some cases find replacements for animals that used to live there. These animals tend to congregate around the Film Set oasis, but don't be too surprised if anywhere on the peninsula you come across foxes, gazelle or ostriches. Take particular care with the ostriches; they are generally timid and tend to flee if approached, but if you accidentally corner one you may find yourself on the receiving end of a sharp claw.

Travelling north for another 8km will take you across two causeways to the end of the peninsula. This is an eerie and atmospheric, but attractive, area of coves and cliffs that finally leads to a headland near a coastguard station.

The islands that you can see offshore are part of the Hawar Chain, a disputed area between Qatar and Bahrain until recently, when they were finally ceded to Bahrain under an international agreement. Some of them are surprisingly close to the Qatari shoreline.

Fossil Hunting In Qatar

In ancient times, what is now Qatar was seabed or, at best, a series of small islands sticking out from a shallow sea. Consequently, the desert areas are prolific with marine fossils. In areas of hard sabka (salt flats), you are likely to come across fossilised shells exposed by desert erosion. A commonly found fossil is the spiral-shaped shell of a gastropod (resembling a cone-shaped spring); these can be found up to 5cm long and occasionally larger. Fossilised oysters, arranged on top of each other just like in the sea, are common around rocky outcrops, particularly in the desert south-west of Sheehaniyah, towards Umm Bab.

The quarries around Umm Bab are worth a look as gastropods and even large fossilised bones are sometimes unearthed through quarrying work.

Also in Umm Bab, very close and east of the flyover, is a shale embankment that is full of fossilised sharks' teeth, but don't expect any large trophies – most are smaller than a match head.

Further north, on the Ras Abruk Peninsula, some of the rocky outcrops appear to be full of cavities; if you look carefully you can see that the cavities are actually fossilised seaweed. On top of the outcrops, small fossilised shells can be found.

Dukhan
Map **Qatar Country Map A3**

Situated at the end of Route Q3, about 75km from Wajbah, is Dukhan. A company town owned by Qatar Petroleum, Dukhan is where Qatar's first oil discoveries were made in the 1930s. It's also as far west as you can go: from here the road turns south following the west coast (Route Q39). Just outside the town's main security gate is a small shopping centre with a reasonable supermarket and a few fast food joints, handy if the kids are getting restless. On the coast is the Qatar Petroleum Beach Club but, like the rest of Dukhan, it is only open to QP employees and their guests.

Both north and south of the beach club there are, however, some nice beaches that are open to all. Both areas have some attractive shaded seating areas. For competent swimmers, there is a nice six metre deep rocky reef about 200 metres offshore of the southerly beach, which is a good spot for snorkelling. For dive enthusiasts, Dolphin Reef, an 18 metre deep, man-made scuba diving area, attracts dolphins and, occasionally, large fish. Although tour operators do not visit the site, Doha SubAqua Club (p.268) organises occasional dives here. If you have your own boat and are prepared to tow it from Doha, the reef is located 4km directly offshore from the QP Beach Club (although you will have to launch it from the beach).

Out Of Doha

Desert Roses

If you use one of the gates in the camel fence along the road between Sheehaniyah and Dukhan and turn left into the desert from one of the small villages along this road you will find the hard packed desert (sabka) is sprinkled with marine fossils of varying sizes. If you dig in some of the sandy areas heading towards Umm Bab, you may also find buried slabs of desert roses. These are formed by crystallised sand and in Qatar they are usually dark grey coloured. A 4WD is essential but be careful not to damage your tyres on sharp rocks. If you don't have your own vehicle, you can join a Desert Rose tour with a tour operator (p.228) who will take you to the area and provide digging equipment.

Umm Bab
Map Qatar Country Map A4

There are good beaches, camping and picnic spots in the 25km from Dukhan to Umm Bab (along Route Q39) and the road is excellent. If you have a 4WD, it is also possible to drive down the coast and coastal desert, but beware of sharp rocks.

Umm Bab, as you would expect of Qatar's cement manufacturing centre, is a dusty place. However, if you turn off the main road at Umm Bab flyover and head for the shore, you will reach Palm Tree Beach, named for obvious reasons. It is a pleasant place to camp and picnic although there are no amenities whatsoever; there is a very small shop on the road down to the beach, but don't plan on buying much more than milk or bottled water there.

The road then continues along the west coast for 40km until it meets the Salwa Road (Route Q5) from Doha, which will take you to the Saudi Arabian border. On the shore side there are numerous areas for coastal exploration and on the inland side, the desert is a good area for fossil hunting.

South Of Doha

To reach the south of Qatar from Doha, head past Doha Airport and on to Al Wakra on Route Q7. From Al Wakra, you can choose whether to divert along an alternative road to Mesaieed to take in, en route, the unusual phenomenon of the Singing Sand Dune (p.242). Alternatively, follow Route Q7 and go directly to the industrial town of Mesaieed (formerly Umm Said) from where you should follow the signs for Sealine Resort. Around the Sealine, the desert starts with a vengeance and becomes inaccessible without a 4WD. Off-roaders can travel through the dunes until reaching Khor Udeid, also known as Khor Al Dhaid, but best known as the Inland Sea (p.243). Camping in this area is an essential experience for all Qatar residents.

Al Wakra
Map Qatar Country Map D4

Situated 8km from Doha Airport's most southerly point, the fishing town of Al Wakra has almost become a suburb of Doha. Much development has taken place there recently and it is within commuting distance of Doha, with a number of good schools in fairly easy reach (see Residential Areas, p.78).

Al Wakra is a small town with pleasant beaches and a recently developed harbour that houses many of Qatar's fishing dhows, in addition to private boats. There's a park near the car park by the dhow harbour, which is green and pleasant enough, but with facilities that could use a little work. The long jetty is an interesting place for a stroll. Along the shore are the remains of some traditional houses. Al Wakra beach is a popular place for dog walkers from Doha and with families at the weekend, although there is little in the way of facilities on the beach itself. Al Wakra museum is closed indefinitely for refurbishment.

History On Hold

Qatar has an interesting culture and history and there are a few museums, forts, and heritage sites around, but many of them, including the Weaponry Museum, Handicrafts Museum National Museum and Al Wakra Museum, are currently closed for refurbishment. Officials seem uncertain if these museums will be reopened or the collections incorporated into new museums such as the Museum of Islamic Art (p.317) and Arab Museum of Modern Art (p.206). Finding out when you can visit the few that are open can be tricky, and actually finding the right building can be even trickier. Until everything settles down, it may be best to use a tour operator (p.228) to find out which museums are accepting visitors.

Abu Manaratain Mosque
13km Southwest of Doha
Map Qatar Country Map D4

Abu Manaratain Mosque, located on the seafront to the left of the jetty, is a unique building in Qatar and one that creates an attractive photographic opportunity. The mosque is not particularly old itself, dating back to the 1940s, but it is built on the site of earlier mosques and the traditional methods of construction, using coral and rock surrounded by a baked mud roof to keep the heat of the sun out, can be seen. As always, non-Muslims should limit their appreciation to the outside of the mosque. While you're in the neighbourhood, seek out the wonderful fish market nearby where the freshest catch of the day will be available and cooked for you on the spot.

Traditional architectural details

Sheikh Ghanim Bin Abdulrahman Al Thani House

Beach Rd, 13km South of Doha qma.com.qa
Map **Qatar Country Map D4**

Another building of traditional architectural interest is the house of Sheikh Ghanim bin Abdulrahman Al Thani, located along the beach road about 500 metres north of Manaratain Mosque. It was originally built by one of the prominent pearl traders in Al Wakra, as a warehouse and small factory to produce debis, a time-honoured date-based food used to flavour fish dishes. The house features traditional wind towers, which were the only form of cooling available before the advent of air conditioning. It also has attractive wooden channels to drain away water during the very infrequent, but heavy Gulf storms. It is interesting to note that modern Qatari housing is usually built with no guttering or water drainage at all. The building is open to visitors 24 hours a day; just speak nicely to the security guard.

Convoy Companions

When driving off-road in sand, it's vital that you are always accompanied by at least one other 4WD vehicle who can help tow you out if your get really stuck. That extra pair of hands could literally be a life-saver. You should also ensure that you have at least one experienced off-road driver who can lead the pack. For a beginners' guide to desert driving, see p.222.

The Singing Sand Dune

Map **Qatar Country Map C5**

From the roundabout in the centre of Al Wakra, head west for about 20km. On the way, you'll pass through the bleak village of Wakair, and will eventually reach Route Q55, which links Salwa Road with Mesaieed. At this junction, you have three options: turn right to pass by Al Udeid Army Camp (the main coalition air base for the Middle East and jocularly known throughout Qatar as 'the secret air base'); driving straight ahead will take you off road to limitless expanses of almost uninhabited rocky desert to explore (it's easy to get lost, so take a compass or GPS to find your way back to the road); and finally, a left turn will take you southwards to the Singing Dunes. 2.8km from the junction on Route Q55, turn right on a small surfaced road. Follow this road for just less than 6km, where it turns into hard desert. In front of you will be large crescent-shaped sand dunes. Park your car and, armed with a plastic bag or something to use as a sledge, climb the dune. If the sand is absolutely bone dry – ideally in the afternoon of the dry season– it will resonate and sing to you.

The sheltered area at the crescent side of the dune is a popular place for gatherings. From more official

events, such as Dunestock (p.343), an annual rock concert organised annually by Doha Players, to carol singing around bonfires during the festive season and desert outings organised by various activity groups, you'll often find other people enjoying the desert here. It's also a popular destination for tour groups (p.227).

Digging For History

Most of the archaeological and historical sites are located in unpopulated areas, are tricky to find and lack signposts. Some of Qatar's historic forts have been restored and some have ongoing excavations underway. Be aware that you may drive for hours to find a fort, only to discover there is no information available on its history. Most have no proper gates so can be visited anytime. A good website for directions and coordinates (although some of the other information is out of date) is heritageofqatar.org. If you are feeling less adventurous you could ask a tour company to arrange a visit.

Mesaieed

Map **Qatar Country Map D5**

Mesaieed is an industrial area with a large secure area containing a port, steelworks, oil refineries and manufacturing facilities. The town is rapidly expanding, but mostly with property built to house company employees. Unless you want to use the shops there is nothing of interest there.

Sealine resort is signposted from Mesaieed, so follow the signs but take care, as this road is often very busy with 4WD vehicles and large trucks. Follow the road around the industrial area perimeter fence and on to Sealine where the road ends and the soft sand starts.

All along the Sealine Road there are tents, from which quad bikes of all sizes can be rented. There are low dunes all around that you can practise on, but take care, especially if you have children with you – the desert is unforgiving and, in inexperienced hands, these powerful machines can be incredibly dangerous.

Without owning a 4WD, you will not be able to progress much further, although you can drive on the compacted desert as far as the first dune and to the beach on the south side of Sealine Resort. The beach is very popular here, especially at weekends when unfortunately it tends to get very litter strewn. If you are picnicking or camping here, or anywhere else in the desert, make sure that you take your rubbish away and leave the vicinity in the same natural state as you arrived. The big sand dune behind the beach is usually busy, particularly on Friday afternoons, with adventurous 4WD drivers showing off their skills while trying their best to reach the top. It is a popular spectator sport.

Old Club Reef

10km past Mesaieed (or 4.5km from the end of the surfaced road at Sealine, if you're coming from the other direction), just past the chemical plant fence, there is a turning to your left, leading to Old Club Reef. This is a very popular 18 metre deep artificial reef, used as a training dive site by diving agencies based in Doha and sometimes by recreational scuba divers. It consists mainly of old buses, cars, vans and large industrial debris, which have been sunk and then roped together to assist underwater navigation.

Sealine Beach Resort
Mesaieed **4476 5299**
merweb.com
Map **Qatar Country Map D5**
The Sealine Beach Resort is a popular weekend break destination for Doha residents. It offers long-term and day visit facilities with villas, chalets, rooms and suites, plus three pools, including a children's play pool with slide, extensive watersports facilities offering activities such as waterskiing, jetskiing and windsurfing, and a range of eateries including beach and pool bars. There are also tennis courts, a beach volleyball court and a gym, or you can opt for camel riding or horse riding.

South Of Sealine
Map **Qatar Country Map C6**
The dunes from Sealine to Khor Udeid are impressive, if sometimes a little overcrowded at weekends. The next 35km south of Sealine Resort can be driven partly along the shore if you feel like it or via any of the multitude of tracks running through the wilderness area. It can be as hard or as easy as you like. You can have a heart-stopping ride through the high dunes or an easier trip on the mostly hard flat sabka. If it is your first time, take all precautions and travel with others, as there are multiple pitfalls and getting lost is easy. See p.222 for essential advice on desert driving.

Khor Udeid
Map **Qatar Country Map C6**
Khor Udeid, better known as the 'Inland Sea', is a wide inlet with narrows in the centre, which widens out to a large shallower seawater lake. The border between Saudi Arabia and Qatar runs down the centre. The Qatari side is edged with impressive dunes and the Saudi side is rocky. Due to its location as an international border, boats are not allowed to operate in the Khor Udeid Area. The water is tidal and the strong currents make the narrows a dangerous spot for swimmers. Never swim across the narrows – apart from the dangers of currents, turning up unannounced on Saudi shore in swimming gear and with no passport is not recommended.

Having said that, swimming around the shore is very popular and away from the narrows area the currents are perfectly normal. Some of the big steep dunes slope straight into the water, so you can start high up and run down them straight into the sea.

The Inland Sea is a popular daytrip destination for tour companies, so if you don't have your own 4WD, enlisting the services of a professional allows you to enjoy this area of outstanding natural beauty. The trips vary from half day to overnight camps and some of the tour companies have opened permanent camp sites where you can try sand skiing, ride camels and experience a taste of traditional Bedouin life (see Main Tour Operators, p.228).

Khor Udeid is also an important area for resident and migratory bird species, such as flamingos, cormorants, waders, gulls and terns. On two of the small islands in the middle of the narrows are enormous osprey nests, which have been built up by the birds over years. While trying to access the islands is not recommended, from the shore the birds can often be seen peering over the edge of the nests. Plans to make the Inland Sea a protected conservation area are under discussion.

Due to its easy accessibility from Doha, Khor Udeid can get very crowded, particularly at the weekend. Litter is a serious problem and many visitors come away disgusted by the quantity of rubbish and litter left by visitors, especially along the shore areas.

The Islands

There are a number of islands around Qatar's coast which are interesting boating destinations for camping, picnics, diving, snorkelling and general exploring. Some of them lie within short reach of Doha, and can be accessed by boat charters (p.227) or private dhow hire along the Corniche (p.228), but some lie further afield and involve a boat charter either through a tour company (p.228) or a boat charter company (p.228). When out on the water, you can observe an unusual feature of most Qatari seagulls – unlike their noisier cousins elsewhere, they appear to be almost mute.

If you are lucky enough to own a boat, or have access to one through friends, there is a thriving boating community and culture in Qatar (see Boating, p.217). If you are willing to sail around the peninsula or trail your boat across the country, there are a number of places of interest which are only accessible by boat, such as Dolphin Reef (p.239).

Palm Tree Island
Map **2 Q5**
This is the small island in Doha Bay and it can be sailed around on the dhows moored along the Corniche. Palm Island has one tree and little else on it; oddly it is an acacia tree and there is not a palm tree in sight.

The island was previously developed as a daytrip resort. In those days, there was a group of palm trees at the north end of the island (where the island got its name) and an acacia tree, which flourished. The resort fell into disrepair, the buildings were levelled and the palm trees with them. The acacia tree and the misleading Palm Tree name remained.

Al Safliyah Island
Map 1 P4
This is Doha's party island and is located on the north side of Doha Bay, opposite the Sheraton Hotel and the Pearl Qatar. Rocky and deep on the south side, it is shallow and sandy on the northern side with a long sand spit that runs to within 750 metres of the Sheraton Hotel at low tide. In all but the most extreme conditions it is sheltered on both sides. It's a popular destination at weekends, but swimmers and boaters should be aware of unskilled people driving rented jet skis from the mainland. At sunset, desert hares and desert rats, which hop around like tiny ghostly kangaroos, can sometimes be seen.

Aliyah Island
Map Qatar Country Map D3
Located slightly further north of Safliyah and accessed either via the Pearl channel from Safliyah or from The Ritz Carlton channel, this island is treacherous with shallow rocks on its northern side and waters too shallow for easy boat access on its southern side, but it has small bays on its western side; these are sheltered but should be entered slowly as there are shallow mud banks surrounding them.

Once ashore, Aliyah is an interesting place to explore from a natural history point of view. Expect flamingos, cormorants and desert hares. Perhaps most interesting are the gulls that build completely unprotected nests on the ground, leaving the eggs to incubate in the sunshine during the day and only returning at night to keep them warm. The birds have no predators on the island and visitors should observe the nests from a distance.

Banana Island
Map Qatar Country Map D4
This large, banana-shaped island lies close to the Doha shipping channel, 8km west of Doha port. Its shape gives it extremely good protection from the prevailing northerly wind. The shallow rocky side is good for snorkelling and the sheltered south side is deep with a stony shore apart from one good beach. It is a popular destination at weekends, but less busy than Safliyah.

Five Mile Reef
Five Mile Reef is also known as Rubble Tower, by virtue of a feature that was once in the centre of it but was long ago replaced by two narrow steel towers. It

should be navigated with care as it is five miles long, two miles wide and very shallow. The centre of it dries out at low tide. It is an excellent snorkelling spot, about 40km south-east of Doha which takes about an hour to get there in a fast boat.

Sharao'uw Island
A low lying island with both a rocky shore and a sandy shore, situated about 70km south-east of Doha, Sharao'uw has a nice sheltered bay and is usually deserted. It is good for overnight camping and has a sizeable population of long-eared rabbits.

Jinan Island
Map Qatar Country Map A3
Located off Qatar's west coast, 2km from the Ras Dukhan headland, this small flat rocky islet is the most southerly of the Hawar chain and the only one of the islands belonging to Qatar (be careful as the Bahrain Hawars start less than 1km north). Sometimes known as Bird Island, this is another place where visitors can observe the strange ground nesting habits of the gulls. Access to the island's only bay should be carried out very slowly to avoid rocks and you will need to wear shoes to get ashore. It is not recommended for picnicking as the birds smell. The south of the island develops into a very shallow and extensive rocky reef, which is good for snorkelling. For more on exploring the west coast, see p.237.

OUT OF QATAR

Out of Qatar, the other five GCC countries (Bahrain, UAE, Oman, Kuwait and Saudi Arabia) are all accessible in under 90 minutes by air. You can opt to drive to the UAE and Bahrain, but this requires visas for the brief passage through Saudi Arabia, and the journey to Dubai, for example, takes around seven hours. Most residents choose not to travel beyond the borders of Qatar by car because of the restrictions placed on women travellers when they reach Saudi. However, it is possible and if you feel like taking on an adventure, it could turn out to be the roadtrip of a lifetime (see p.252 for more details).

Most people prefer to fly, and Doha is within easy reach of some interesting places. The rest of the GCC provides ample diversions for weekend breaks and regional vacations, and some are serviced by low-cost airlines, making a weekend away all the more affordable (p.260). Flight connections to regional destinations such as Amman, Damascus and Beirut are also excellent. Should you feel like stretching your wings further, the enormous new airport development will eventually transform Doha into a regional travel hub (p.33), but until then Dubai and Abu Dhabi are only an hour away and connect to destinations across the globe, meaning that the rest of the world is just a short hop away.

Depending on your nationality you may be eligible for a visa on arrival in certain GCC countries. Just remember, if you are in Qatar on a visit visa and you leave, you will need another one to get back in. However, access is a little easier now as the Qatari government allows 33 nationalities to obtain visas on arrival (see p.40).

Oman

Oman is a peaceful and breathtaking place, offering visitors a depth of history, culture and spectacular scenery. The capital, Muscat (p.246), has enough attractions to keep you busy for a good long weekend, including beautiful beaches, some great restaurants and cafes, the mesmerising old souk at Mutrah, and the Sultan Qaboos Mosque. Out of the capital you will find many historic old towns and forts, and some of the most stunning mountain and wadi scenery in the region. Salalah, in the south, has the added bonus of being cool and wet in the summer.

Flying to Muscat from Doha takes around 90 minutes and Oman Air flies direct (omanair.aero). To fly to Salalah, you will need to connect in Muscat.

For further information on Oman check out the *Oman Residents and Visitors' Guide, Oman Off-Road Explorer* and *the Oman Trekking Explorer* – see askexplorer.com/shop.

Mussandam

The UAE's northern neighbour, Musandam, is an isolated enclave belonging to Oman. The region is dominated by the same Hajar Mountains that run through the eastern UAE. As the peninsula juts into the Strait of Hormuz, it breaks up into a myriad of jagged, picturesque fjords. Spending a day exploring the fjords on a wooden dhow is a must for any visitor to the region. Most of the trips originate from the region's capital, Khasab, and daytrips from Khasab Travel & Tours (+9714 266 9950) cost around Dhs.550 per person and include lunch, soft drinks and an informative guide.

Alternately, you can access the famous Wadi Bih off-road route from Dibba and spend a weekend camping atop some of the region's most magnificent mountains. Check out the *UAE Off-Road Explorer* for route details.

Visas

Visas for Oman are required whether entering by air or road, and different regulations apply depending on your nationality and how long you want to stay. Nationalities are split into two groups – check out the Royal Oman Police website, rop. gov.om, for full lists (click on 'Directorates', 'DG of Passports', then 'Types of Visas'). People in group one can get a visit visa at the border – it's usually free for visitors but Dubai residents are likely to incur a Dhs.30 charge for single entry or Dhs.100 for multiple entry. Residents from group two, however, will need to get a visa from the Oman consulate or embassy in advance, which may take a few days to process. The charges are the same for both groups.

Nizwa

After driving deep into the Hajar Mountains, you'll find Nizwa, the largest city in Oman's interior. This oasis city offers fascinating sights and heritage, including the 17th century Nizwa Fort and the Jabrin Fort, notable for its apparently haunted passageways and male and female prison cells. Make your way up to the top of Jabrin Fort for a fantastic 360 degree view of the surrounding area.

Salalah

Home to several museums and souks, Salalah is best known for its lush landscape. The scenery is especially attractive during the summer months, when the area catches the Indian monsoon. Salalah is also a major frankincense producer and you can visit the farms along the Yemen border to witness how it is extracted.

Oman's rocky coast

MUSCAT

Sandwiched between spectacular rocky mountains and beautiful beaches, Muscat is one of the Middle East's most striking cities.

Muscat is one of the most attractive and charismatic cities in the Middle East, and once you've visited you'll understand why many count it as their favourite regional city. It is visually striking, perhaps because it looks so little like a normal city; rather than a bustling CBD characterised by countless skyscrapers, gridlocked traffic and dirty smog, Muscat has many separate areas nestling between the low craggy mountains and the Indian Ocean. There is no one area that defines Muscat on its own – each part has its own distinctive character and charm.

Great care has been taken to ensure that, while it is definitely a modern city, there is a cohesive and traditional Arabic element which has been retained. Visit the old town of Muscat or the Mutrah Souk for an idea of what life has been like for decades for the people that still live in the area.

Muscat is clean and features a lot more greenery than you may be used to in Doha. With beautiful beaches, bustling souks, a collection of great restaurants and cafes, and some fascinating museums, you'll need at least a few days to fully discover this friendly city. The main areas worth exploring are around the old town and the fishing port of Mutrah, although taking long walks along the beach in Qurm or exploring the natural lagoons in Qantab are also worthwhile activities.

The Old Town Of Muscat

The old town of Muscat is situated on the coast at the eastern end of the greater Muscat area between Mutrah and Sidab. It is quiet and atmospheric, based around a sheltered port that was historically important for trade. The area is home to some very interesting museums. Muscat Gate Museum is located in one of the fortified gates of the old city walls, and illustrates the history of Muscat and Oman from ancient times right up to the present day. The view from the roof over the old town is worth the visit alone. Bait Al Zubair is in a beautifully restored house and features major displays of men's traditional jewellery, including the khanjar, women's jewellery and attire, household items, and swords and firearms. The Omani French Museum celebrates the close ties between these two countries, and is on the site of the first French Embassy. Other highlights include the striking Alam Palace, home of Sultan Qaboos, and Jalali Fort and Mirani Fort overlooking the harbour.

Other Areas

Although primarily a residential area, Qurm has some great shopping, good quality restaurants and cafes and the city's largest park, Qurm National Park & Nature Reserve, which features a large boating lake, a fountain, the Sultan's rose garden and many meandering pathways. Qurm is home to arguably the best beach in Muscat and also to some of the top hotels, all of which have superb leisure facilities.

Mutrah

Mutrah rests between the sea and a protective circle of hills, and has grown around its port, which today is far more vibrant than the port of Muscat's old town. Mutrah Corniche is lined with pristine gardens, parks, waterfalls and statues. Further east you'll find Riyam Park, where a huge incense burner sits on a rocky outcrop, while nearby is an ancient watchtower overlooking Mutrah – the view from the top is lovely and well worth the steep climb. One of Muscat's most famous shopping experiences lies in this area: the Mutrah Souk. It is always buzzing with activity and is renowned as one of the best souks in the region.

Sultan Qaboos Mosque

Mutrah Fort

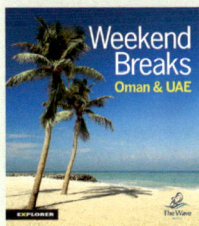

Weekend Breaks
Oman & UAE

Get the lowdown on the best weekend breaks in Oman and the UAE.

The villages of Al Bustan and Sidab provide an interesting diversion from the main Muscat areas. Head south along Al Bustan Street out of Ruwi on the spectacular mountain road to get to the village of Al Bustan and the Al Bustan Palace Hotel, one of the most famous hotels in the region.

Further down the coast, the mountains increase in height and the landscape gets more rugged. However, this undulating rocky coastline hides a number of beautiful secluded coves. These bays, mostly reachable by roads winding over the mountains, are home to the beaches of Qantab and Jassah, the Oman Dive Center (omandivecenter.com) – one of the top dive centres in the world – and the new Shangri-La Barr Al Jissah Resort. Many of the bays in this area have stretches of sandy beach sheltered by the rocky cliffs, and crystal clear waters that are perfect for snorkelling, diving and fishing.

Outside Muscat

Not much further out of Muscat than the Shangri-La Barr Al Jissah Resort, Yiti Beach, while once a popular daytrip from Muscat, is now sadly becoming off limits due to the construction of a huge development called Salam Yiti. As Sifah beach, a little further down the coast, is very popular. The well-travelled path past the last of the houses in As Sifah leads to a beach which slopes gently towards the ocean at low tide. If you're keen to snorkel, head towards the northern edge of the beach. If you enjoy hiking, you can explore the headlands on foot (and maybe even find a secluded beach or two further along).

There are some excellent off-road routes you can do from Muscat within a day, or on an overnight camping trip. For more information on off-roading in Oman, get a copy of the *Oman Off-Road Explorer*.

Oman Hotels

The Chedi Muscat
18th November St, Way No 3215, North Ghubra 32
Muscat **+968 24 524 400**
chedimuscat.com
This beautiful boutique hotel on the shore is famed for its clean lines, luxury and an impressive sense of calm. The stunning spa and outstanding restaurant don't hurt either. With an infinity pool, private beach and library, this is a destination for a break from bustle and perhaps isn't an ideal choice for families.

Crowne Plaza Muscat
Off Qurum St Muscat **+968 24 660 660**
ichotelsgroup.com
This established hotel boasts cliff top views over Al Qurum and the beach below. Many of the 200 guest rooms benefit from the striking vistas and several of the restaurants also boast outdoor terraces. There's a large swimming pool, gym, spa and dolphin watching trips available, making this hotel a great choice for those looking for relaxation and for visitors who want an action-packed break.

InterContinental Muscat
Al Kharjiya St Muscat +968 24 680 000
intercontinental.com
An older hotel that has recently undergone a major facelift, the InterContinental continues to be popular for its outdoor facilities, international restaurants and regular entertainment in the form of dinner theatres and visiting bands. Alfresco restaurant, Tomato, is a must-try. Trader Vic's, with its legendary cocktails, is perennially popular. All of the rooms have views of Qurum Beach, landscaped gardens or the mountains.

Oman Dive Center
Nr Qantab & Barr Al Jissah, Bandar Jussa Muscat
+968 24 824 240
extradivers-worldwide.com
Just south of Muscat, a stay here is an amazing and sociable experience; and one that is highly enjoyable whether you're a diver or not. You can book a barasti hut (they are actually made of stone, with barasti covering) for an average of RO.66 for two people (depending on season). The room price includes breakfast and dinner in the centre's licensed restaurant. For keen divers, the centre offers dive training and excursions, as well as boat tours in the surrounding area.

Shangri-La's Barr Al Jissah Resort & Spa
Off Al Jissah St Muscat **+968 24 776 666**
shangri-la.com
With three hotels catering for families, business travellers and luxury-seekers, the Shangri-La is one of the most gorgeous resorts in the region. The hotel has several swimming pools and enough play areas to keep children occupied for days. The exclusive, six-star Al Husn is incredibly luxurious and perfect for a weekend of out-of-town pampering.

Six Senses Zighy Bay
Zighy Bay, Musandam Daba +968 26 735 555
sixsenses.com
Located in a secluded cove in Musandam, the resort has been designed in true rustic style and is made up of individual pool villas. Like all Six Senses resorts, the focus here is on relaxation. The spa treatments available are of the highest quality and expertly prepared dinners can be enjoyed from the comfort of your own villa, or from the mountainside restaurant with breathtaking views of the bay.

Bahrain
Just a 45 minute flight away, near neighbour Bahrain is small enough to be explored in a weekend. With traditional architecture, miles of souks, excellent shopping and some truly outstanding bars and restaurants, you can choose from a cultural escape or fun-packed break. Formula 1 fans won't want to miss the Grand Prix that usually takes place in April – see the *Bahrain Mini Visitors' Guide* for more on what to do on this lively island.

Visas On Arrival
Citizens of 35 countries (which include the USA, Canada, Japan, New Zealand, most EU countries, Norway and Switzerland), can obtain a two-week tourist visa at the airport for BD 7 (BD 5 for US and UK passport holders; British visitors also qualify for a three month visa for the same price); it is advisable to have dinars on hand but other currencies are accepted. Citizens of GCC countries do not require visas to enter Bahrain. Citizens from all other countries require visas from the appropriate embassy prior to arrival. For full details visit evisa.gov.bh.

Bahrain Attractions

Bahrain Fort
Nr Karbabad Village, Karbabad Manama
This impressive 16th century Portuguese fort is built on the remains of several previous settlements, going back to the Dilmun era around 2800BC. There are several large, informative notices dotted around the area, and some information booklets are available in English. Entry is free and the fort is open from 08:00 to 20:00 every day including Friday. The village at the entrance to the fort is worth a visit on its own. Nearly every square inch of the place, from walls to satellite dishes, is covered in brightly coloured murals.

there's more to life...

Your indispensable guide to living in Oman

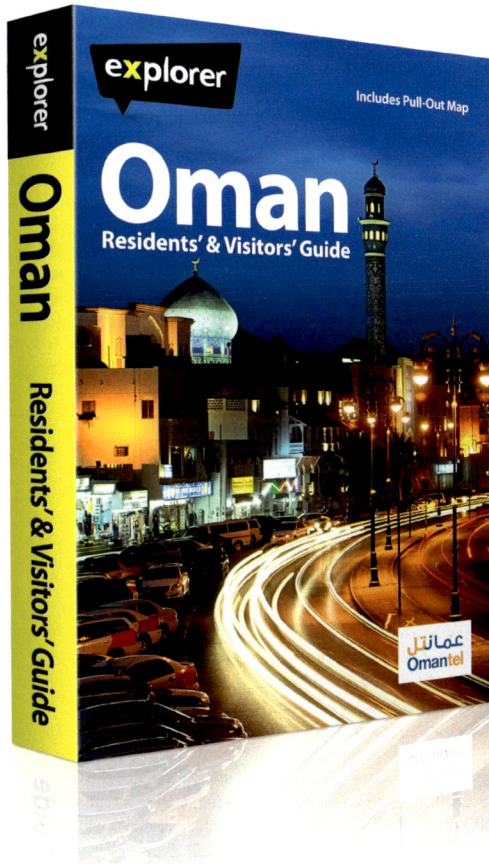

ask explorer.com/shop

Sponsored by
Omantel

Bahrain National Museum
Nr Al Fatih Highway, East Corniche Manama
Situated on the corniche, this museum documents
Bahraini life before the introduction of oil. Children
will love the Hall of Graves and the museum often
hosts impressive international exhibits.

Beit Al Qur'an
Nr Diplomat Radisson Blu Hotel Manama
+973 1729 0101
The building may not look like much from afar, but a
closer inspection reveals stunning details such as walls
covered in beautiful Arabic calligraphy. The museum
displays examples of historical calligraphy and Islamic
manuscripts. Entrance is free, but donations are
welcome.

The Burial Mounds
South of Saar Village & West of A'ali Village
Manama
One of the most remarkable sights in Bahrain is the
vast area of burial mounds at Saar, near A'ali Village,
at Hamad Town and at Sakhir. The mounds were built
during the Dilmun, Tylos and Helenistic periods and
are anything from 2,000 to 4,000 years old. The largest
burial mounds, which are known as the Royal Tombs,
are found in and around A'ali Village.

La Fontaine Centre Of Contemporary Art
92 Hoora Ave Manama **+973 1723 0123**
lafontaineartcentre.net
This place is a true architectural gem. There are wind
towers, cool corridors, a Pilates studio that has to
be seen to be believed, a world-class restaurant,
an extensive spa, regular film screenings and art
exhibitions. These make La Fontaine a unique jewel
in Bahrain's crown. The enormous fountain in the
courtyard is worth a visit.

Bahrain Hotels

Al Areen Palace & Spa
Nr Bahrain International Circuit, Umm Jidr Manama
+973 1784 5000
alareenpalace.com
Located close to the F1 International Circuit, this
all-villa resort offers an extensive spa, outstanding
restaurants and good conference facilities.

Al Bander Hotel & Resort
Nr Bahrain Yacht Club Sitra **+973 1770 1201**
albander.com
Located at the southern end of Sitra, this resort has a
wide range of facilities including swimming pools and
watersports at their private beach. Rooms are either
cabana style or in chalets, and there are activities for
kids and a variety of food and dining options.

Political Unrest

At the start of 2011 the situation in Bahrain
became unstable; by 2012, the situation appears
to have calmed but it's still best to check the
latest travel advice with your embassy. The status
of affairs in the other GCC countries remained
calm throughout (with the exception of minor
problems in limited areas in Oman and in the east
of Saudi Arabia). As always when travelling to a
foreign country, it is advisable to seek and observe
the recommendations issued by your national
embassy before travel.

Novotel Al Dana Resort Bahrain
121 Sheikh Hamad Causeway, Al Muharraq
Manama **+973 1729 8008**
novotel.com
Conveniently located on the causeway just minutes
from the airport and close to the city, yet with its own
beach, this hotel is a great choice for families. There's
also a large pool, an indoor and outdoor play area, and
good watersports facilities.

The Ritz-Carlton, Bahrain Hotel & Spa
Off King Abdulla The Second Ave Manama
+973 1758 0000
ritzcarlton.com
The hotel has one of the best beaches in Bahrain, in a
man-made lagoon surrounded by lush gardens. The
600 metre private beach sweeps round the lagoon
with its own island and private marina. Along with
the nine quality dining venues and comprehensive
business facilities, hotel residents have access to all of
the club facilities, including the racquet sport courts,
the luxurious spa and watersport activities.

Kuwait
Kuwait may be one of the world's smallest countries
but its 500 kilometre coastline has endless golden
beaches that remain refreshingly tranquil. In Kuwait
City, meanwhile, you'll find attractions of a more
urban kind: from the Grand Mosque to the Kuwait
Towers, there are many architectural splendours to
explore, while Al Qurain House (which still shows the
scars of war with its immortal bullet holes) gives you
a fascinating, if tragic, insight into the troubled times
of the Iraqi invasion. There is also Green Island: home
to restaurants and a children's play area, this artificial
island also grants a great alternative view of Kuwait's
beautiful shoreline. For accommodation options,
try the Four Points by Sheraton (+965 2242 2055,
fourpointskuwait.com), Courtyard Kuwait City (+965
2299 7000, marriott.com) or the Radisson Blu Hotel
(+965 2567 3000, radissonblu.com). For stylish, design-
conscious stays, look no further than Hotel Missoni
Kuwait (+965 2577 000, hotelmissoni.com).

Saudi Arabia

The Kingdom of Saudi Arabia has some incredible scenery, fascinating heritage sites, and diving locations that are among the best in the world. Sadly, due to the difficulty in obtaining tourist visas, few expats are likely to experience this diverse and intriguing country. Limited transit visas, available through agents, allow visitors a three-day stay in the kingdom en route to another country, such as the UAE or Bahrain. Recent press reports suggest that the Kingdom will issue more tourist visas in order to boost tourism, and give better access to business travellers now that it is part of the WTO. Until then, take a look at sauditourism.com.sa/en to see what you're missing.

UAE

The UAE has plenty to offer weekend breakers and you may find yourself going back multiple times to multiple destinations and experiencing different types of trips each time. The cities of Dubai and Abu Dhabi are around a 90 minute drive from each other but are destinations in themselves that both warrant a weekend's exploration. Outside of the cities, there are further places to explore within the emirates of Dubai and Abu Dhabi, including luxurious desert resorts and in the western region of Abu Dhabi emirate, the Liwa Oasis in the Rub Al Khali (the largest sand desert in the world). Outside of these two emirates, there are further possibilities – choose between the beautiful beaches and clear seas of the east coast, the cultural heritage and fascinating museums of Sharjah, the dramatic mountain ranges of the northern emirates and the sleepy towns in between.

With frequent flights to Dubai, Abu Dhabi and Sharjah direct from Doha, and a rise in low-cost operators driving down prices, you may just find yourself visiting the UAE time and time again.

Abu Dhabi

Dubai may be the UAE's bold and brash member, but Abu Dhabi remains both the nation's capital and the richest of all the emirates, with a blossoming, burgeoning city to prove it. In recent years there has been a greater commitment to tourism, and projects such as Yas Island with its Grand Prix racetrack (p.226) and the development of the Desert Islands, are proof of that. The city lies on an island shaped liked a scorpion and is connected to the mainland by causeways. It is home to numerous internationally renowned hotels, a selection of shiny shopping malls and a sprinkling of culture in the form of heritage sites and souks.

Abu Dhabi is marketed as the cultural capital of the UAE and is home to an annual jazz festival, a film festival and a music and arts festival, and hosts numerous art exhibitions throughout the year. Find out more from the Abu Dhabi Tourism and Culture Authority (adach.ae).

Abu Dhabi Attractions

Al Bateen
Abu Dhabi

This is one of Abu Dhabi's oldest districts and home to a dhow building yard, the Al Bateen Marina, a few historically accurate buildings and the future Al Bateen Wharf. It's a nice area to walk around, with plenty of open green spaces.

The Corniche
Off Corniche Rd Abu Dhabi

Corniche Road boasts six kilometres of parks that include children's play areas, separate cycle and pedestrian paths, cafes and restaurants, and a lifeguarded beach park. There is plenty of parking on the city side of Corniche Road, and underpasses at all the major intersections connect to the waterfront side. Bikes can also be rented from outside the Hiltonia Beach Club for Dhs.20 per day.

Ferrari World Abu Dhabi
Yas Island Abu Dhabi **+971 2 496 8001**
ferrariworldabudhabi.com

This indoor family amusement park houses the world's fastest rollercoaster which, travelling faster than 200 km/h, simulates the experience of driving in an F1 car.

Heritage Village
Nr Marina Mall Abu Dhabi **+971 2 681 4455**

Located near Marina Mall, this educational village offers a glimpse into the country's past. Traditional aspects of Bedouin life are explained and craftsmen demonstrate traditional skills.

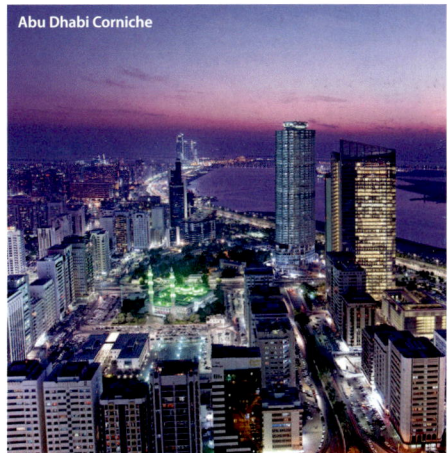
Abu Dhabi Corniche

UAE Roadtrip

Qatar is a small country, just 150km long and 80km wide. Sometimes it's necessary to get out and see what the surrounding countries have to offer.

The obvious choices for a regional getaway are the United Arab Emirates and the Kingdom of Bahrain. It's possible to drive to both of these countries, but whether you're heading for the UAE or Bahrain, your roadtrip will involve driving through Saudi Arabia. Gaining permission to enter Saudi can be tricky – a transit visa will need to be arranged in advance, women have to be accompanied by either a brother or husband to cross over into Saudi, and once they do they are not allowed to drive or show their hair. For these reasons, many people choose to fly to Qatar's near neighbours, but if careful preparations are made, driving is not as difficult as it first appears. If you fancy turning a journey into something a bit more adventurous, then a roadtrip is worth considering.

Planning Your Trip

Obviously the first prerequisite is that you have a roadworthy car. If you are going all the way to Dubai, one capable of making a seven-hour 700km journey, mostly across a baking desert, is an essential. Make sure you check your tyre condition and pressure, oil levels and brakes before setting off, or have a mechanic do it for you, and don't even think about it if your car is prone to overheating.

The second essential is paperwork, and your transit visas have to be obtained in advance. The process takes about a week and you will need an agent to do the work for you. The cost is about QR 80 per passport and you will need to provide the agent with the following documents:

- Original passports of all of the travellers
- A copy of your vehicle's registration certificate (Istamara)
- If you are not the registered owner of the vehicle you will have to provide an NOC letter, addressed to the Saudi Arabian Embassy (the agent will provide the template), from either your bank if the vehicle is registered in their name or your company if they are the registered owners
- A No Objection Letter from your employer to give you permission to obtain a Saudi visa. This is not required for dependants if they are travelling with a parent, as long as they are the sponsor

Once issued, your transit visa is valid for a 30 day round trip, on condition that you take no longer than three days from entering to leaving Saudi Arabia, on both the outward and return journeys.

In addition to the above, other essential documents are a passport with six months' validity remaining, a Qatar driving licence, Qatar ID for every passenger and a Qatar exit visa (the same as is required for departure from the airport).

Exploring Liwa

Any women travelling with the party must wear an abaya, a loose-fitting, full length dress and headscarf (usually in black) during the Saudi portion of your trip. There are plenty of stores in Doha which sell abayas (see tip box on p.326). Also remember that women are not permitted to drive in Saudi.

On The Road

From Doha, Salwa Road (Route Q5) takes you just over 100km to the Abu Samrah border post. Here you go through normal departure checks and your vehicle's papers will be inspected. 8km down the road, you will reach the Saudi Arabian border post. Inside the immigration building is a series of desks: at the first show your Qatari paperwork; at the second show it to the Saudi immigration officials, and at the third purchase your Saudi car insurance (QR 100; valid for two weeks).

Once over the border and about 5km down the road, you'll see a see a large sign that says 'UAE/Emirates'. Check your fuel gauge here before you rush off across the desert; there is a fuel station very close to here on the left, and then there are no more until you cross into the UAE, 135km down the road.

Leaving Saudi is simple, with similar procedures to your entry; however, the entry into the UAE is more time consuming. Firstly you have to park your car and get a visa from a building on your left. Nothing is signposted in English and there seems to be little logic to the queuing system, so ask for the counter that issues On Arrival forms and fill one out for every passenger. Then find the queue for retina verification and get your forms stamped. Take the completed forms back to the original counter and pay QR 100 per person and you will be issued with your visas. Then collect your car and proceed towards the Customs checkpoint. Just before you reach it you will be sold UAE vehicle insurance, valid for 2 weeks, which costs Dhs.100.

Abu Dhabi Emirate

On the UAE side of the border, you will be in the emirate of Abu Dhabi, but it's another 360km to Abu Dhabi city and a further 150km to Dubai. The road to Abu Dhabi (E11) follows the coastline of the Arabian Peninsula, with a few hotels dotted along the coast, including the luxurious Desert Island Resort and the five-star Danat Jebel Dhanna (p.254). Heading south through the wilderness of Abu Dhabi's western region, Al Gharbia, you'll come to the Liwa Oasis, a green fertile area which stretches over 150km, and the Rub Al Khali (the Empty Quarter), the world's largest sand desert which stretches into Southern Saudi Arabia and Yemen. In the Empty Quarter, the sand dunes rise to over 300m, making for some intense off-road driving and camping in untouched surroundings. Exploring the Liwa area is an experience not to be missed while you're living in the region: it's an epic trip of a lifetime.

Dubai

If you are heading to Dubai, you should obtain a road toll tag, known as a Salik tag, from any petrol station. It costs Dhs.100 (which includes Dhs.50 credit) and each time you pass through a toll gate, Dhs.4 will be deducted from your account. You may be fined if you travel through a toll gate without one or if you've run out of credit. Top up cards can also be purchased from petrol stations. For more info, visit salik.ae.

The return journey is similar to the outbound with the addition that there is a Dhs.25 exit tax to pay as you leave the UAE.

Top Travel Tips

- Both Saudi and UAE border posts will accept any GCC currency in payment.
- Fuel is cheapest in Saudi and most expensive in the UAE.
- With the exception of ADNOC stations in Abu Dhabi, no petrol stations in the UAE accept credit cards for fuel, but many have an ATM so that you can withdraw cash to pay with.
- There are strict customs laws against importing alcohol, pork, drugs, pornography and firearms – if you are caught with any of these you will be arrested. If you try to bring plants back in to Saudi you will be sent to the quarantine area; this means that you have plenty of time to socialise with queuing truck drivers at the border post instead of going home.

Saudi Arabia Transit Visas Agents
Al Ahli Club of Kuwait, Near MidMac Roundabout (Near the Mercedes Garage)
4431 3077

Al Ishan Services
Souk Asiri, Off Grand Hammad Street
4443 4050

Sheikh Zayed Grand Mosque
Shk Rashid Bin Saeed Al Maktoum St Abu Dhabi
+971 2 441 6444
szgmc.ae
One of the largest mosques in the world, this architectural masterpiece can accommodate 40,000 worshippers. It features 82 domes and the world's largest hand-woven Persian carpet. It is open to non-Muslims every day except Friday, and complimentary tours run at 10:00 from Sunday to Thursday.

Sir Bani Yas Island
Abu Dhabi **+971 2 406 1400**
desertislands.com
Half nature reserve, half luxury resort and spa, Sir Bani Yas Island is the centrepiece of Abu Dhabi's Desert Islands development plan. Home to the Arabian Wildlife Park, and Desert Islands Resort and Spa by Anantara, the island has thousands of free-roaming animals. Hiking, mountain biking and 4WD safaris, as well as snorkelling and kayaking trips, are available and you can reach the island by a private seaplane.

Yas Island
Abu Dhabi
yasisland.ae
Yas Island has emerged as Abu Dhabi's latest tourism hotspot; in addition to hosting the annual Formula 1 Grand Prix at the Yas Marina Circuit, the island boasts several resorts with luxurious spas and restaurants, a world-class golf course, and Ferrari World, which houses the world's the fastest rollercoaster. du Arena and Flash Forum stadiums also stage regular concerts by internationally acclaimed musicians. Most recently, the largest IKEA in the UAE opened its doors to eager shoppers in 2011 and, looking ahead, more hotels and a waterpark are set to open by 2013

Abu Dhabi Hotels

Al Raha Beach Hotel
Nr Al Raha Mall Abu Dhabi **+971 2 508 0555**
danathotels.com
Excellent service, a gorgeous spa and unsurpassed comfort in an idyllic boutique beach setting just outside Abu Dhabi city.

Visas On Arrival

Citizens of the following countries receive an automatic visit visa on arrival in the UAE: Andorra, Australia, Austria, Belgium, Brunei, Cyprus, Denmark, Finland, France, Germany, Greece, Hong Kong, Iceland, Ireland, Italy, Japan, Liechtenstein, Luxembourg, Malaysia, Malta, Monaco, Netherlands, New Zealand, Norway, Portugal, San Marino, Singapore, South Korea, Spain, Sweden, Switzerland, United Kingdom, United States of America and Vatican City.

Danat Jebel Dhanna Resort
Jebel Dhanna **+971 2 801 2222**
danathotels.com
Located 240 kilometres west of Abu Dhabi city, close to Sir Bani Yas Island, this resort features plenty of watersports, a private beach and sand golf.

Emirates Palace
Corniche Road West Abu Dhabi **+971 2 690 9000**
kempinski.com
Emirates Palace is the ultimate in ostentatious luxury, with 14 bars & restaurants, 394 rooms and suites with butler service, an amazing collection of pools and a private beach. Be warned, without a reservation you won't be getting anywhere near this exclusive

Yas Viceroy Abu Dhabi

property. Large, open-air concerts are held in the 200 acre palace gardens in the cooler months. Check the website for details of what's on.

Fairmont Bab Al Bahr
Nr Al Maqta & Mussafa Bridges Abu Dhabi
+971 2 654 3333
fairmont.com
One of the UAE capital's newest luxury hotels, the Fairmont Bab Al Bahr is located on the creek near to Souk Qaryat Al Beri, Abu Dhabi's modern Arabian souk. In easy reach of the airport and ADNEC, with some great dining options including a Marco Pierre White steakhouse, it's a good choice for business or pleasure.

Hilton Abu Dhabi
Corniche Rd West Abu Dhabi **+971 2 681 1900**
hilton.com
This 10 storey luxury hotel on Corniche Road has three swimming pools and a private beach, plus a wide range of watersports. Each room boasts enviable views, and the hotel houses some of the best restaurants in the city, including Bocca.

InterContinental Abu Dhabi
Bainouna St Abu Dhabi **+971 2 666 6888**
ichotelsgroup.com
Adjacent to the marina, the hotel is surrounded by lush parks and gardens. With five restaurants, four bars and 330 deluxe rooms offering views of the city and the Arabian Gulf, the hotel is popular with business travellers. Following the hotel's recent renovation, many of the restaurants and bars are worth a visit.

Jumeirah At Etihad Towers
Nr Emirates Palace, West Corniche Abu Dhabi
+971 2 811 5555
jumeirah.com
Part of the impressive Etihad Towers development, this recently opened hotel offers a prime Corniche location, 382 fabulous rooms and suites and excellent leisure facilities.

Le Meridien Abu Dhabi
Nr Old Abu Dhabi Co-Op Society Abu Dhabi
+971 2 644 6666
lemeridienabudhabi.com
Famous for its health club and spa, private beach and Culinary Village, there is a children's swimming pool and activities including tennis, squash and volleyball.

Rocco Forte Hotel Abu Dhabi
Shk Rashid Bin Saeed Al Maktoum Rd Abu Dhabi
+971 2 617 0000
roccofortehotelabudhabi.com
This luxurious hotel is a great option if you're in town for one of the many conferences and events that take

place at the nearby ADNEC. The 281 rooms are of top calibre and while there is no beach, the hotel's pristine 25m pool and an excellent spa more than make up for this.

Shangri-La Hotel, Qaryat Al Beri
Qaryat Al Beri Complex Abu Dhabi **+971 2 509 8888**
shangri-la.com
Overlooking the creek that separates Abu Dhabi island from the mainland, the 214 rooms and suites all have private terraces. The adjoining Souk Qaryat Al Beri houses a variety of shops and restaurants connected by waterways.

The St Regis Saadiyat Island Resort
Saadiyat Beach Abu Dhabi **+971 2 498 8888**
stregissaadiyatisland.com
One of the first resorts to open on the pristine island development of Saadiyat, this is a great choice for a luxurious escape away from the crowds.

Yas Viceroy Abu Dhabi
Nr Yas Marina Abu Dhabi **+971 2 656 0000**
viceroyhotelsandresorts.com
Striking and futuristic, the Yas Hotel is a modern work of art. Straddling the grand prix track of Yas Marina Circuit, it's the ultimate place to stay during race weekends, while top-notch restaurants, an impressive sky bar and the Ferrari World (p.251) theme park next door ensure plenty of distractions for visitors throughout the rest of the year.

Dubai
Cliches tend to trip off the tongue when describing Dubai – the city of gold, sleepy fishing village transformed into modern metropolis, the Vegas of the Middle East, and so on. The truth is that while the emirate boasts an incredible number of attractions claiming to be the tallest, biggest or longest, it's not all bright lights – the atmospheric old town around the Creek, and the restored Bastakiya area are musts for any visitor wanting to scratch Dubai's cultural surface. Dubai is also a great place for families and from amusement parks and aquariums to child-friendly hotels and restaurants, you'll find plenty of ways to keep the kids busy. Beyond the city, the desert opens up further possibilities and many visitors choose to combine a city break with a relaxing luxury desert retreat such as Bab Al Shams (p.258).

That said, if it's bright lights you're after, Dubai outshines the rest of the region. The emirate has been successful in its quest for economic diversification, and its focus on tourism revenues has resulted in a fantastic array of superlative-laden attractions for tourists and residents alike. From skiing on real snow at Ski Dubai (p.257) and plunging through shark-infested waters at Aquaventure (p.256), to shopping 'til you drop' at Dubai Mall (p.256), a weekend trip to Dubai promises an action-packed break. Its selection of five-star hotels, restaurants, bars and clubs will ensure a well fed and watered stay, and luxury spas and clean beaches provide ample opportunities to relax.

For more help on planning a trip to Dubai, log on to askexplorer.com where you can find listings of up-coming events and further information about Dubai hotels and attractions, and where you can order a copy of *Dubai Mini Visitors' Guide* – the essential guide for your weekend break.

Dubai Attractions

Aquaventure
Atlantis The Palm Dubai **+971 4 426 0000**
atlantisthepalm.com
Metro **Nakheel**
The ultimate destination for thrill seekers. The Leap of Faith gets the adrenaline pumping with a 27 metre near-vertical drop that shoots you through a tunnel surrounded by shark-infested waters, while the Rapids take you on a tumultuous journey down a 2.3km river, complete with waterfalls and wave surges. For the little ones, there is Splashers, a fun water playground. Open daily from 10:00 until sunset. Entrance for those over 1.2m is Dhs.210, and Dhs.165 for those under that height. Children younger than 2 years old and Atlantis hotel guests get in for free.

At The Top
Burj Khalifa Dubai
burjkhalifa.ae
Metro **Burj Khalifa/Dubai Mall**
In less than 60 seconds, a high-speed lift whisks visitors up to the 124th floor of the world's tallest tower. From the Burj Khalifa observation deck, you can survey a 360 degree view of the city. Advance bookings are Dhs.100 for adults and Dhs.75 for children; tickets bought on the day cost Dhs.400.

Dubai Aquarium & Underwater Zoo
The Dubai Mall Dubai **+971 4 448 5200**
thedubaiaquarium.com
Metro **Burj Khalifa/Dubai Mall**
Located, somewhat bizarrely, in the middle of The Dubai Mall, this aquarium displays over 33,000 tropical fish to passing shoppers free of charge. For a closer view of the main tank's inhabitants, however (which include fearsome looking but generally friendly sand tiger sharks) you can pay to walk through the 270° viewing tunnel. Also well worth a look is the Underwater Zoo, which includes residents such as penguins, piranhas and an octopus. If you're feeling really adventurous, you can even go for a scuba dive in the tank (call ahead to book), ride a glass-bottomed boat or feed the sharks.

The Dubai Mall
Nr Interchange 1, Financial Centre Rd Dubai
thedubaimall.com
Metro **Burj Khalifa/Dubai Mall**
One of the world's largest shopping malls, The Dubai Mall is a shopper's paradise housing some 1,200 stores, including the famous New York department store, Bloomingdales and countless designer boutiques. Even if you're not in town to shop, you should make a trip to the mall anyway to view the many attractions within. There is an Olympic sized ice rink, an indoor waterfall, a 22 screen cinema, Sega World indoor theme park, KidZania edutainment centre, the Dubai Aquarium and Underwater Zoo and some great alfresco dining venues with views of the spectacular musical displays of the Dubai Fountain.

Dubai Museum
Al Fahidi Fort Dubai **+971 4 353 1862**
definitelydubai.com
Metro **Al Fahidi**
Located in Al Fahidi Fort, this museum is creative, well thought-out and interesting for all the family. The fort was originally built in 1787 as the residence of the ruler of Dubai and for sea defence, and then renovated in 1970 to house the museum. All aspects of Dubai's past are represented. You can walk through a souk from the 1950s, stroll through an oasis, see into a traditional house, get up close to local wildlife, learn about the archaeological finds or go 'underwater' to discover the pearl diving and fishing industries. There are some entertaining mannequins to pose with too. Entry costs Dhs.3 for adults and Dhs.1 for children under 6 years old. Open daily 08:30 to 20:30 (14:30 to 20:30 on Fridays).

Heritage & Diving Village
Nr Shk Saeed Al Maktoum House Dubai
+971 4 393 7139
definitelydubai.com
Metro **Al Ghubaiba**
Located near the mouth of Dubai Creek, the Heritage & Diving Village focuses on Dubai's maritime past, pearl diving traditions and architecture. Visitors can observe traditional potters and weavers practising their craft the way it has been done for centuries. Local women serve traditionally cooked snacks – one of the rare opportunities you'll have to sample genuine Emirati cuisine. It is particularly lively during the Dubai Shopping Festival and Eid celebrations, with performances including traditional sword dancing. Open daily 08:30 to 22:00 (Fridays 15:30-22:00). The village is very close to Sheikh Saeed Al Maktoum's House, the home of the much-loved former ruler of Dubai, which is a good example of a traditional home and houses a number of interesting photographic exhibits.

Take A Tour

View the city from the upper floor of a double-decker bus, learning some fascinating facts about Dubai along the way. Big Bus Tours (bigbustours.com) allows you to hop on and off at various attractions, while the amphibious Wonder Bus takes to water (wonderbustours.net).

Jumeirah Mosque

Jumeira Rd Dubai **+971 4 353 6666**
cultures.ae
Metro **World Trade Centre**

This is the most beautiful mosque in the city and perhaps the best known, as its image features on the Dhs.500 banknote. The Sheikh Mohammed Centre for Cultural Understanding (cultures.ae) organises mosque tours for non-Muslims on Saturday, Sunday, Tuesday and Thursday mornings at 10:00. Visitors are guided around the mosque and told all about the building, and then the hosts give a talk on Islam and prayer rituals. The tour offers a fascinating insight into the culture and beliefs of the local population, and is thoroughly recommended. You must dress more conservatively than elsewhere in town – no shorts and no sleeveless tops. Women must also cover their hair with a head scarf or shawl, and all visitors will be asked to remove their shoes. Cameras are allowed, pre-booking is essential and there is a registration fee of Dhs.10 per person.

KidZania

The Dubai Mall Dubai **+971 4 448 5222**
kidzania.ae
Metro **Burj Khalifa/Dubai Mall**

This new addition to Dubai Mall offers kids the chance to become adults for the day. Billed as a 'real-life city' for children, youngsters can dress up and act out more than 75 different roles, from policeman to pilot and doctor to designer. The KidZania city even has its own currency, which children can earn and spend. It's intended to be both fun and educational.

SEGA Republic

The Dubai Mall Dubai **+971 4 448 8484**
segarepublic.com
Metro **Burj Khalifa/Dubai Mall**

This indoor theme park located in Dubai Mall offers a range of thrills and spills, courtesy of the nine main attractions and the 150 arcade games. A Power Pass (Dhs.150) gets you all-day access to the big attractions, which include stomach-flipping rides like the Sonic Hopper, the SpinGear and the Halfpipe Canyon. Unlike many other shopping mall amusement centres, SEGA Republic is for all ages, and features some truly unique thrills.

Ski Dubai

Mall Of The Emirates Dubai
skidxb.com
Metro **Mall of the Emirates**

Ski Dubai is the Middle East's first indoor ski resort, with more than 22,500 square metres of real snow. The temperature hovers around – 3 celcius, even when it's closer to +50 outside, to make for a cooling excursion from city life. Competent skiers and boarders can choose between five runs and a freestyle area, skiing and snowboarding lessons are available for beginners, and there is a huge snowpark for the little ones. Slope pass and lesson prices include the hire charge for jackets, trousers, boots, socks, helmets and either skis and poles or a snowboard. Freestyle nights are held every other week on Mondays from 20:00 to 23:00.

Souk Al Bahar

Nr The Dubai Mall Dubai **+971 4 362 7011**
soukalbahar.ae
Metro **Burj Khalifa/Dubai Mall**

With atmospheric passageways, Souk Al Bahar is designed to resemble a traditional souk. It houses a host of designer boutiues and shops selling Arabian wares such as carpets, paintings, jewellery, clothes and perfumes, but its main attractions are the restaurants and bars, many of which have terraces with views of the Dubai Fountain and Burj Khalifa.

Souk Madinat Jumeirah

Al Sufouh Rd Dubai **+971 4 366 8888**
jumeirah.com
Metro **Mall of the Emirates**

This modern shopping mall is a recreation of a traditional souk with confusingly winding passageways, authentic architecture and interconnecting waterways traversed by motorised abras (traditional boats). It houses a collection of boutique shops, galleries, cafes and bars and the al fresco dining venues are always buzzing during the evenings of the cooler months.

Wild Wadi Water Park

Jumeirah Rd Dubai **+971 4 348 4444**
jumeirah.com
Metro **Mall of the Emirates**

Spread over 12 acres beside Jumeirah Beach Hotel (p.258), this waterpark has a host of aquatic rides and attractions to suit all ages and bravery levels. Depending on how busy it is you may have to queue for some of the rides, but the wait is worth it. The highlights include Wipeout (a permanently rolling wave that's perfect for showing off your body-boarding skills) and the four-seater Burj Surge. The park opens at 10:00; closing time varies throughout the year. Admission is Dhs.205 for adults and Dhs.165 for kids; family and season passes are available too.

Dubai Hotels

The Address Downtown Dubai

Emaar Blvd Dubai **+971 4 436 8888**
theaddress.com
Metro **Burj Khalifa/Dubai Mall**

Even at over 300 metres in height, The Address is dwarfed by its neighbour, the Burj Khalifa – but breathtaking views, beautiful interiors and eight dining outlets (including Neos, the panoramic bar on the 63rd floor) make this one of the most popular spots in town. There are also two more The Address hotels, located at Dubai Mall and Dubai Marina, while The Address brand runs the small boutique hotel at The Montgomerie golf course and The Palace – The Old Town in Downtown Dubai.

Al Maha, A Luxury Collection Desert Resort & Spa

Dubai Desert Conservation Reserve, Dubai – Al Ain Rd Dubai **+971 4 832 9900**
al-maha.com

Set within the 225 square kilometre Dubai Desert Conservation Reserve, with breathtaking views of picturesque dunes and rare wildlife, this luxury getaway was named as one of the best ecotourism models by National Geographic in 2008. Al Maha is designed to resemble a typical Bedouin camp, but conditions are anything but basic. Each suite is beautifully crafted and has its own private pool and butler service. Activities include horse riding, camel trekking and falconry. There is also a superb spa.

Armani Hotel Dubai

Burj Khalifa Dubai **+971 4 888 3888**
dubai.armanihotels.com
Metro **Burj Khalifa/Dubai Mall**

The new Armani Hotel was one of the most talked about new openings in 2010. The chic hotel is fittingly located in the extravagant Burj Khalifa which towers over Dubai. The hotel's eight restaurants, lounge bar, and spa can all be enjoyed, if you can fork out from Dhs.4,000 for a night stay.

Atlantis The Palm

Crescent Rd Dubai **+971 4 426 0000**
atlantisthepalm.com
Metro **Nakheel**

With a staggering 1,539 rooms and suites, all with views of the sea or the Palm Jumeirah, Atlantis is certainly one of Dubai's grandest hotels. It has no less than four fancy restaurants featuring the cuisine of Michelin-starred chefs, including a branch of the world-famous chain Nobu. It is also home to Aquaventure, the biggest water park in the Middle East, and the Lost Chambers aquarium.

Bab Al Shams Desert Resort & Spa

Nr Endurance Village Dubai **+971 4 809 6100**
meydanhotels.com

Bab Al Shams ('The Gateway to the Sun') is a beautiful desert resort built in the style of a traditional Arabic Fort. Each of its 115 rooms is decorated with subtle yet stunning Arabian touches, and pristine desert dunes form the backdrop. The authentic, open-air, Arabic desert restaurant is highly recommended. There is a kids' club, a large swimming pool (complete with swim-up bar), lawn games and the luxurious Satori Spa.

Burj Al Arab

Nr Wild Wadi, Jumeira Rd Dubai **+971 4 301 7777**
jumeirah.com
Metro **Mall of the Emirates**

Standing on its own man-made island, this dramatic Dubai icon's unique architecture is recognised around the world. Suites have two floors and are serviced by a team of butlers. To get into the hotel as a non-guest, you will need a restaurant reservation.

Crowne Plaza Dubai Festival City

Al Rebat St Dubai **+971 4 701 2222**
ichotelsgroup.com
Metro **Emirates**

On the banks of the Creek, this Crowne Plaza is excellently positioned within the Festival City complex. One of its highlights is the Belgian Beer Café, an atmospheric bar that serves a great selection of European beers and is extremely popular with Dubai residents and visitors alike.

Hilton Dubai Creek

Baniyas Rd Dubai **+971 4 227 1111**
hilton.com
Metro **Al Rigga**

With very flash yet understated elegance, this ultra-minimalist hotel features interiors of wood, glass and chrome. Centrally located and overlooking the Dubai Creek, with splendid views of the Arabian dhow trading posts, the hotel has two renowned restaurants in Glasshouse Brasserie and new Dubai gastronomic darling Table9 by Nick and Scott.

Jumeirah Beach Hotel

Nr Wild Wadi, Jumeira Rd Dubai **+971 4 348 0000**
jumeirah.com
Metro **Mall of the Emirates**

Shaped like an ocean wave, with a fun and colourful interior, the hotel has 598 rooms and suites and 19 private villas, all with a sea view. It is also home to some excellent food and beverage outlets, including Uptown for happy hour cocktails and a great view of the Burj Al Arab. Kids and families will love Wild Wadi Water Park, which is located here.

Le Meridien Dubai
Airport Rd Dubai **+971 4 217 0000**
lemeridien-dubai.com
Metro **Airport Terminal 1**
383 rooms in an ultra convenient location, a stone's throw from Dubai airport and the Aviation Club, guests and visitors can enjoy many excellent restaurants inside the hotel, many of which share a large alfresco terrace in the cooler months. The hotel is also home to trendy nightspot The Warehouse and Antipodean restaurant Yalumba, which offers a famous Friday brunch.

Madinat Jumeirah
Nr Burj Al Arab, Jumeira Rd Dubai **+971 4 366 8888**
jumeirah.com
Metro **Mall of the Emirates**
This extravagant resort has two hotels, Al Qasr and Mina A'Salam, with no fewer than 940 luxurious rooms and suites, and the exclusive Dar Al Masyaf summer houses, all linked by man-made waterways navigated by wooden abra boats which whisk guests around the resort. Nestled between the two hotels is the Souk Madinat, with over 95 shops and 44 bars and restaurants to choose from.

One&Only Royal Mirage
Al Sufouh Rd Dubai **+971 4 399 9999**
royalmirage.oneandonlyresorts.com
Metro **Nakheel**
This stunningly beautiful resort is home to three different properties: The Palace, Arabian Court and Residence & Spa. The service and dining (opt for the Beach, Bar & Grill for a romantic evening out; try delectable Moroccan cuisine in the opulent Tagine; or enjoy cocktails with a view in The Rooftop and Sports Lounge) are renowned, and a luxury spa treatment here is the ultimate indulgence. This hotel's sister resort, One&Only The Palm, is located directly across the water on The Palm Jumeirah. A ferry service connects the two properties.

Park Hyatt Dubai
Nr Dubai Creek Golf & Yacht Club Dubai
+971 4 602 1234
dubai.park.hyatt.com
Metro **Deira City Centre**
Enjoying a prime waterfront location within the grounds of Dubai Creek Golf & Yacht Club, the Park Hyatt is Mediterranean in style with low-rise buildings, natural colours and stylish decor. The hotel has 225 rooms and suites, all with beautiful views, as well as some great dining outlets and a luxurious spa, which features a luxury couple's massage option. Excellent restaurants inside the hotel include The Thai Kitchen and Traiteur.

The Ritz-Carlton, Dubai
The Walk, Jumeirah Beach Residence Dubai
+971 4 399 4000
ritzcarlton.com
Metro **Dubai Marina**
Even though it is the only low-rise building amid the sea of Marina towers behind it, all 138 rooms have beautiful views of the Gulf – the Ritz-Carlton was, after all, here years before the rest of the marina was built. Afternoon tea in the Lobby Lounge is a must, and there are several other excellent restaurants and a very good spa onsite. The Ritz-Carlton has also added another property to its offerings, with a new 341 room hotel in the DIFC area.

Shangri-La Hotel Dubai
Sheikh Zayed Rd Dubai **+971 4 343 8888**
shangri-la.com
Metro **Financial Centre**
Featuring great views of the coast and the city from Sheikh Zayed Road, this hotel has 301 guest rooms and suites, 126 serviced apartments, a health club and spa, two swimming pools and a variety of restaurants and bars including majestic Moroccan Marrakech and seafood specialist Amwaj.

The Westin Dubai Mina Seyahi Beach Resort & Marina
Al Sufouh Rd Dubai **+971 4 399 4141**
westinminaseyahi.com
Metro **Nakheel**
Set on 1,200 metres of private beach, The Westin has 294 spacious rooms and suites with all the luxury amenities you would expect of a five-star hotel. The other facilities include the aptly named Heavenly Spa and a slew of popular dining spots such as Italian Bussola, tapas haunt Senyar and wine bar Oeno.

Atlantis The Palm

LONG-WEEKEND TRIPS

Make the most of a long weekend by heading off to one of many great travel destinations within easy reach of Qatar.

Qatar's central location in the Middle East and the increasing number of routes available via Qatar Airways, and other carriers, makes it an ideal base for exploring the region and beyond. Destinations across the Middle East and Asia are popular with expats during long weekends and short holidays and you'll find that heading abroad is a common way to spend the Eid holidays for Arabs and non-Arab alike. Egypt, Syria, and Lebanon are only three hours away, while Sri Lanka, the Maldives, India and South Asia are also a short flight away, making them excellent choices for a long weekend away.

In general, it pays to book your travel a few months in advance, if possible, so as to get the best rates. As travel is a popular hobby for many Qatar residents, it's important to consider the time of year and day of the week when heading to the airport, as seasonal queues can delay check-in, so leave yourself plenty of time to make your flight. To save yourself time, use online check-in, where available, and get an e-gate card to fast-track through customs.

Egypt

Egypt is an ideal trip for history fans. It's one of the oldest civilisations in the world and home to famous historical sites such as the Pyramids and Sphinx. It also has some amazing scenery: there is the moon-like White Desert and the isolated Siwa Oasis in the west, the Red Sea and the vast Sinai Peninsula in the east, and, of course, the Nile. Cairo's chaotic streets are a constant adventure and the city has an active nightlife. Following the period of unrest in 2011, it's advisable to check the latest travel advice from your embassy. Fly direct to Cairo with Qatar Airways or Egypt Air.

India

India is a land of many guises, from the beautiful beaches of Goa to the vibrant city of Mumbai and the imposing mountains of Kashmir to the peaceful backwaters of Kerala. India's variety means that you might have trouble deciding on just one destination – but it's close enough to Qatar for you to go back time and time again. It's best to avoid the summer monsoon, but if you do get caught in the rain, you can take advantage of good off-season deals. Some areas such as Ladakh in northern India and the desert state of Rajasthan receive very little, if any, rain all year. Fly direct to Delhi, Mumbai or Kochin with Jet Airways or Qatar Airways.

Jordan

Jordan is packed with religious and historical sites, incredible architecture, and friendly, welcoming people. The capital, Amman, offers enough dining and cultural attractions to fill up a few days, but to truly experience the country, you'll need to get out of the city. Head south to feast your eyes on Petra, the ancient city built into solid rock canyons. On your way, don't miss the opportunity to float atop the waters of the Dead Sea. History and religious experts will be fascinated by the many holy sites that dot the country, and movie buffs shouldn't miss a trip to Wadi Rum, where Lawrence of Arabia was filmed. For flights to Amman, your best bets include flights via Abu Dhabi, Dubai or Sharjah in the UAE; check with Etihad Airways, Emirates, Air Arabia or flydubai.

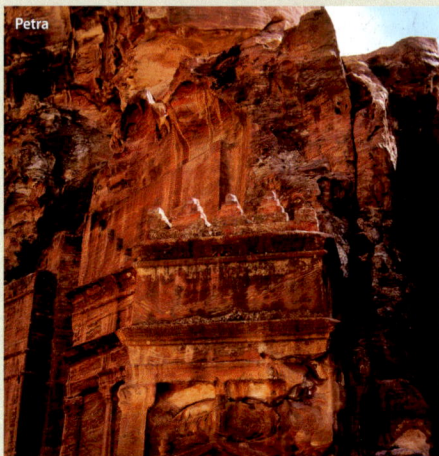

Petra

Lebanon

Lebanon's blossoming development as a vibrant tourist destination has suffered some knockbacks recently with conflicts both internally and externally. But, never a nation to take things lying down, it is doing everything possible to rebuild itself. Beirut's nightlife is considered by many to be the best in the Middle East, and its culinary excellence is well known. Outside of Beirut is just as interesting; the massive Roman temples in Baalbek are not to be missed, and the many villages scattered throughout the country hold the key to Lebanon's incredible hospitality. Fly direct to Beirut with MEA Air Liban or Qatar Airways.

Sri Lanka

The beauty of Sri Lanka, apart from the short flight time and negligible time difference, is that you can either have a fantastic holiday on a small budget, or a luxurious holiday of a lifetime. Colombo has enough attractions to occupy travellers for at least a day, although most holidaymakers choose to spend their time in the lush mountains or on untouched beaches that are found across the island. Fly direct to Columbo with Qatar Airways or SriLankan Airlines.

Syria

With Damascus, the oldest continuously inhabited city in the world, Aleppo, one of the great food capitals of the world, and untouched countryside, Syria has a lot to offer. However, an unstable political situation since 2011 means that travel is not advised at the time of writing; check for the latest advice with your embassy. Once it is safe to go, the old part of Damascus is a joy to explore on foot thanks to the many souks and unique architecture. The ancient city of Palmyra (known as Tadmor in Syria) is a must for anyone

interested in the country's incredible past. Syria is also a great choice for budget-minded travellers, as flights to and from Qatar are cheap and you could spend an entire week eating only the delicious street food. Fly to Damascus via the UAE with Etihad Airways, Emirates, Air Arabia or flydubai.

DIRECTORY:

Air Arabia – airarabia.com
Egypt Air – egyptair.com
Emirates Airline – emirates.com
Etihad Airways – etihadairways.com
flydubai – flydubai.com
Jet Airways – jetairways.com
MEA AirLiban – mea.com.lb
Qatar Airways – qatarairways.com
Turkish Airlines – turkishairlines.com
SriLankan Airlines – srilankan.aero

Turkey

Perfectly placed between contrasting cultures of east and west, Turkey is a popular holiday destination with beautiful landscapes, great weather, sun, sea and mountains. To top it up, Istanbul is an amazing city – full of history, great food and a amazingly vibrant nightlife. Alternatively, take a road trip to the capital, Ankara, for a taste of Turkish student life and a glimpse of the country's most modern city. If you need a break from big-city life, head south to the equally impressive Bursa, where you'll find the iconic Ulu Cami mosque and huge, communal thermal baths; in the winter season, it is even possible to ski around the mountains here. Fly direct to Istanbul from Doha with Turkish Airlines, or via the UAE with Etihad Airways, Emirates, Air Arabia or flydubai.

Turkey

Qatar's No.1 News &
Business Magazine

Qatar's Only Monthly Arabic
News & Business Magazine

30 Years of Media Excellence

Qatar's No.1 Fashion Title

An Annual Publication
That Focuses On
The Country's Development

Qatar's First Student
Community Magazine

BEST OF NEWS, BUSINESS & LIFESTYLE

As the only media house in Qatar bringing out three leading monthly magazines,
Oryx Advertising Company is known for its quality publishing.

All our publications are leaders in their categories and are the choice of
premium international, regional and local brands.

Offering an unmatched circulation and readership, our publications
deliver reach and quality unrivalled by any other medium in Qatar.

ORYX
ADVERTISING CO. W.L.L.

P.O. Box: 3272 Doha - Qatar. Tel: (+974) 44672139, 44550983,
44671173, 44667584 Fax: (+974) 44550982
Email:qtoday@omsqatar.com Website: www.omsqatar.com

To find out how our publications can serve as
powerful advertising mediums
please call us at +974 44550983

Follow us on
- www.facebook.com/qatartoday
- www.twitter.com/qatartoday
- www.facebook.com/glam
- www.twitter.com/glam

Qatar Today   قطر اليوم

GLAM   CAMPUS   Progress قطر

Activities & Hobbies

ACTIVITIES & HOBBIES

Making friends is a key part of settling into your new life. Joining a social club or taking part in group activities is a good way to meet people who share the same hobbies as you – and there are plenty of chances to do so in Qatar.

With the exception of a short period in July and August when it becomes very humid, Qatar's location is an ideal one for participating in outdoor activities. Even then, if it is water sports that take your fancy, there are plenty to choose from; if you have always wanted to try a water-based activity, Qatar is the place to give it a go. The great weather and warm sea should help tempt you into jumping on to a wakeboard, parasail or jet ski. There are also several good companies that offer diving trips for varying fees; costs will often include equipment hire and any training needed to participate.

If you prefer to be on dry land, a few tour operators offer desert safaris and dune-bashing tours, which can include overnight camping; this is a great way to get your adrenaline flowing while taking advantage of the region's natural landscape.

As befits a country that is intent on building sports based tourism, Qatar has developed first-class facilities, and not only for spectators. As a result, football, tennis and motorsports enthusiasts can participate in many events.

There are also a variety of social groups, classes and clubs that are organised by residents. The listings in

Beauty School

Whether you want to learn cutting or crimping, make-up or massage, highlighting or holistic therapy, you can study it at Tajmeel, Qatar International Beauty Academy. Short courses, workshops and full and part-time diplomas are offered at the modern campus near to Ramada Interchange. Part of Qatar Foundation, Tajmeel is managed by an experienced team from the Yorkshire College of Beauty in the UK. For more info and to download the course prospectus, visit qatarinternationalbeautyacademy.com.

this chapter pick out some of the highlights, and it's worth keeping an eye on local newspapers, websites such as Qatar Living (qatarliving.com) and magazines such as *Marhaba* and *Qatar Happenings* for details of upcoming events. And, as always, word of mouth is an excellent way of discovering what's going on in Qatar.

Art Classes

Brush & Canvas
Al Dana Club, Nr Khalifa Tennis & Squash Complex
Lekhwair **4455 3764**
aparnashere.com
Map **2 N4**
Doha-based artist Aparna Shere conducts weekly art classes for adults at Al Dana Club on Tuesdays and Thursdays from 18:30 to19:30. Techniques taught

Activity Finder

include canvas painting, portraits, watercolours, acryllics, sketching and oil pastels.

Fanar Qatar Islamic Cultural Center
Abdullah Bin Jassim St Al Souq **4425 0250**
fanar.gov.qa
Map **2 R7**
The Qatar Islamic Cultural Centre hosts regular workshops in painting, drawing and pottery. It also showcases works of Islamic art and calligraphy and offers free Arabic lessons.

French Institute Of Qatar
135 Al Inshirah St Onaiza **4493 0863**
institutfrancais-qatar.com
Map **2 M2**
Art classes are offered at the French Cultural Centre; although teaching is in French, translators are usually available for English speakers. The courses are in 9 week blocks (two classes per week) and cost around QR 1,050 for adult drawing and about QR 400 for children's painting classes. In addition, the centre runs courses in French language, music for children and babies and theatre classes. Contact the centre directly for details of its latest class schedule.

Qatar Fine Arts Society
Katara Cultural Village Al Gassar **4408 1471**
katara.net
Map **1 K3**
The Qatar Fine Arts Society has been around for 29 years. The society holds three-day workshops where international participants can eat, drink, have fun, and, of course, paint. It has a small library open to the public with books and pamphlets in Arabic, English, French and Chinese. Open Sunday to Thursday 07:30 to 13:00 and 16:00 to 20:00.

Virginia Commonwealth University In Qatar (VCUQ) > p.151
Education City Al Shagub **4402 0555**
qatar.vcu.edu
Map **2 A3**
The School of Art at VCU (p.152) offers various community evening classes, including portrait drawing, history of art, jewellery making, watercolours and Islamic art. Costs range from QR 1,000 to QR 1,400. High demand for places means that some courses fill as soon as advertised, so keep an eye on the local papers for new course announcements. The school also arranges various exhibitions with a gallery open from Sunday to Thursday, from 10:00 to 18:00 (see Art Galleries p.209).

Aussie Rules
The Doha Kangaroos compete in the AFL Middle East. The team trains from August to March at the American School of Doha and plays its home games at the Doha Rugby Club. The friendly club welcomes new players of all skill levels. It runs Auskick kids' clinics and holds social events throughout the year. See website (dohakangaroos.com) for more information.

Baseball

Qatar Little League
American School Of Doha Fereej Al Soudan **6650 2928**
qatarlittleleague.org
Map **2 H11**
This baseball league is open to boys and girls aged 4 to 16; for girls aged 10 to 18, there's also a fast-pitch softball league. In total, there are 30 teams across six leagues. If you have children who are interested in playing or wish to volunteer to help organise, call (6650 2928) for more information on registration, location and timings.

Basketball
Many of the basketball courts in Doha are in health clubs and therefore are reserved for use by members only. However, there are places where you don't have to join to play; some of the health clubs allow non-members to use their courts, as long as they are accompanied by members.

Cabana Club
Radisson Blu Hotel, Doha Rawdat Al Khail **4428 1621**
ramadaplazadoha.com
Map **2 N10**
Although there is no fee to play basketball on this court, it is for the use of Cabana Club members and Radisson Blu hotel guests only. It is advisable to book one day in advance.

Evolution Basketball
Doha College Fereej Al Soudan **7730 3435**
evosoccer.com
Map **2 H12**
Boys and girls aged 6 to 16 are welcome to attend the fun training sessions. See the website for timings and locations.

Qatar Quilt Guild
This active group is made up of quilters from around the world. Monthly meetings are held at 16:00 on the last Wednesday of each month, when quilters can share their latest works and learn new techniques. Regular competitions and talks are held and there is a lending library of quilt books. Annual membership costs QR 120. Find out more at qatarquiltguild.blogspot.com or email qatarquiltguild@gmail.com.

Activities & Hobbies

Birdwatching

Not only does Qatar have a range of local bird species resident throughout the year, it is also a stop-off point for migrating birds moving to new climates during the spring and autumn. The mangrove area just north of Al Khor is particularly rich with bird life. In winter, both the east and west coasts play host to flocks of migrating flamingos and, in recent years, smaller flocks seem to have given up migrating and become permanent residents.

Qatar Natural History Group
Doha English Speaking School (DESS)
Fereej Kulaib qnhg.org
Map **2 J4**

Bird watching is one of the many interests of the Qatar Natural History Group, which holds regular meetings at DESS on the first Wednesday of each month, from October through to June.

Meetings start at 19:00 and speakers from both the local community and overseas make regular presentations on the subjects of natural history, archaeology, astronomy and wildlife, in addition to bird watching. Bird watching trips are organised to many locations in Qatar.

Single membership costs QR 50 per year and family membership QR 100 per year. The group currently has over 350 members. Contact April Conkey (chairman@qnhg.org), or Fran Gillespie (pr-representative@qnhg.org), or simply turn up at one of the meetings for more information. New members must join using the online application form and pay fees in person at one of the monthly meetings.

Bowling

Qatar Bowling Center
Nr Mannai R/A Al Bidda **4432 9178**
qatarbowlingcenter.net
Map **2 N7**

The Qatar Bowling Center has 32 lanes. The entrance fee is QR 15 and then each game costs QR 12 (including shoe rental). Entrance is free for members. Membership costs QR 200 per year for individuals and QR 400 for a family membership. There are some league teams that play regularly (usually on Friday, Sunday and Tuesday evenings) and hold tournaments. Tuesday mornings are reserved for ladies only. The centre has a small food court where you can get snacks and soft drinks, as well as a pro shop, pool and billiards tables.

Winter Wonderland
City Center Doha Al Dafna **4483 9163**
Map **2 Q2**

The Winter Wonderland bowling centre has an eight-lane bowling alley. Although it's therefore slightly smaller in size than its neighbour at the Qatar Bowling Center, it's a fun spot to head for with a group of friends or family. One game costs QR 12 at all times of the day. Alternatively, you can pay QR 500 for the 'Strike Gold' membership card, which lets you play 100 games at your leisure. Packages are available for schools and colleges.

Boxing

Qatar Boxing Federation
Aspire Academy For Sports Excellence Baaya **4494 4266**
Map **2 A10**

The primary function of this federation is to promote boxing in Qatar. However, if you are a keen boxer and would like to practise regularly, you can contact the organisation and fill in the information form, and you will be able to use the facilities. You will have to undergo a medical test before you start.

Canoeing & Kayaking

The calm waters of the Gulf are ideal for sea kayaking, and you can rent kayaks from some of the hotels that offer watersports. If you enjoy kayaking, it's worth investing in your own boat as there are some great spots around Qatar's coast that can only be fully accessed by kayak, such as the shallow waters around Dhakira (p.235) and the mangroves north of Fuwairat (p.235). If you paddle a few hundred metres offshore around Fuwairat, there is a good chance you could be paddling among dolphins and turtles. As these places are remote, there is nowhere to hire equipment, so you need to bring your own and be a competent paddler and swimmer.

Bay Club
InterContinental Doha Al Gassar **4484 4852**
ichotelsgroup.com
Map **1 K3**

The Bay Club has kayaks available to hire for QR 20 per half hour. Non-members also have to pay a day visitor fee of QR 350 for access to the club at weekends.

Sealine Beach Resort
Mesaieed **4476 5299**
merweb.com
Map **1 D5**

This resort is a haven for aquatic fanatics, as it offers many water sports from its beautiful stretch of private beach, including pedal boating, jet skiing and aqua cycles. Kayaks are available for hire for QR 50 per hour. Don't expect to paddle across the Arabian Gulf though, as you will be restricted to the confines of the resort for safety reasons. Life jackets are provided. Entry fees to the resort are QR 50 per person Saturday to Thursday and QR 195 on Friday.

Chess

Qatar Chess Association
Nr Green Steps R/A, Off Muntaza St Nuaija
4494 4292
qatarchess.com
Map **2 P12**
The Qatar Chess Association is the umbrella body for competitive chess in Qatar and can give you information on where to look for competition and tournaments at all levels of the game. The Chess Association also hosts the annual Qatar Open Chess Championship (p.25), which is open to male and female entrants of all nationalities. Find out more and register for the competition online.

Cookery Classes
Cookery classes are offered by various hotels, including the Grand Hyatt (p.198) and Sharq Village & Spa (p.204). The best way to find out about upcoming events at hotels is to sign up to the e-newsletter on their websites. If there are no classes scheduled, the hotels are usually quite flexible and, as long as you can get together a minimum number of people, they are quite happy to arrange something for you. At both Sharq Village and the Grand Hyatt, customised lessons are available and you can work together with the chef to design a lesson that specifically appeals to your group.

Some of Doha's social groups, such as American Women's Association (p.48) and Doha Mums (p.48), also organise cooking classes for their members which are normally hosted at one of the hotels.

The Ritz-Carlton, Doha
West Bay Lagoon Al Gassar **4484 8000**
ritzcarlton.com
Map **1 K1**
The Ritz-Carlton Doha offers a monthly cooking class under the supervision of one of the hotel's many expert chefs. The theme varies, but classes in French and Italian cuisines are always in demand. Each class includes a three-course meal. A children's cooking class is on offer too, for kids to try their hand at cake decorating and preparing easy meals. The Ritz-Carlton also runs a popular wine club. Meetings are held for nine months of the year (not in summer and not during Ramadan).

Cricket

Evolution Cricket
Various locations **6631 9641**
evosoccer.com
Evolution Cricket offers cricket coaching for girls and boys aged 6 to 16 years. Courses cover basic skills development in a fun atmosphere. Prices are QR 700 for a 10 week course. One to one coaching, cricket camps during school holidays and birthday parties are also offered.

Qatar Cricket Association
Off Wadi Musheireb St Fereej Abdel Aziz **4431 4154**
qatarcricketassociation.org
Map **2 P9**
As a nation with a major part of its workforce originating from the Indian subcontinent, it is hardly surprising that cricket features high on the list of activities available in Qatar. Games are played anywhere, from dusty sand strips to organised cricket clubs. It is probably the most popular participation sport in the country. The Qatar Cricket Association (which organises the national league) regulates the game in Qatar. The Qatar Veterans' Cricket League is affiliated to the Qatar Cricket Association and organises softball matches of 20 overs each. These games are even more popular than standard cricket matches.

Cycling
Except for a few hot summer months, the conditions for cycling remain perfect for most of the year: you can expect to be pedalling under clear, blue skies from September to May.

Qatar Chain Reaction
Various locations qatarchainreaction.org
Qatar Chain Reaction is a group of avid cyclists who organise road rides every week. In addition, they have time trials, group social events and also cater for mountain bikers. For more information, look up the website or email info@qatarchainreaction.org. There is no membership fee.

Qatar Cycling Federation
Nr Khalifa Stadium Al Aziziya **4447 5522**
Map **2 C12**
This group is open to members of the public who are keen cyclists. It organises regular rides, as well as individual and team races in the categories of road racing, time trials, mountain biking and triathlons. The federation's official team has also participated in many international races.

Dance Classes

Cabana Club
Radisson Blu Hotel, Doha Rawdat Al Khail **4428 1621**
ramadaplazadoha.com
Map **2 N10**
Salsa dancing lessons are available at the Cabana Club. The dance techniques are taught with enjoyment in mind and classes are suitable for all levels. Call for timings and further information.

Doha Scottish Country Dancing Club
Doha English Speaking School (DESS)
Fereej Kulaib **5523 9861**
scotsinqatar.com
Map **2 J4**
This dance class is all about having fun and keeping fit – anyone with a sense of humour is welcome. Informal sessions take place on Mondays at 19:00 and last for about two hours. All you need to wear are comfortable clothes and soft shoes; just bring a soft drink and the class fee of QR 10. Beginners are most welcome.

International Academy For Intercultural Development
Al Mansoura St, Nr Muntazah Park Al Mansoura **4432 0974** iaidonline.com
Map **2 Q11**
Specialising in Indian classical dance, the classes at the International Academy for Intercultural Development are affiliated to the Nalanda Dance Research Centre in Mumbai. The academy offers seven years' worth of certificate courses for children. Examinations are conducted on a regular basis by a visiting professor from Nalanda. For an individual, a month's package of Indian classical dance lessons (two per week) costs QR 450. The academy also offers classes in other forms of dance, including jazz, Latin American, ballet and ballroom.

International Centre For Music
Villa 81, Ahmed bin Hanbal St Old Airport **4467 1354**
Map **2 S13**
The International Centre for Music offers Royal Academy ballet classes, but also has a wide range of other dance styles such as modern, salsa, tap and hip-hop. The centre even includes some traditional styles like ballroom and Irish dancing. Costs can vary, depending on the class, so call for more information.

Isabelle Mojansky
Various locations 5521 6579
Teaching children aged 4 to 16, Isabelle Mojansky offers dance classes in classical ballet, jazz and modern. All disciplines are taught twice a week and they are held at either Doha College or the Sheraton Hotel. Classes cost QR 50 for a one hour lesson. Call for timings and more information.

Line Dancing
Doha Rugby Football Centre, Nr American School of Doha Fereej Al Soudan **4442 9149**
Map **2 H11**
The Doha Rugby Club is not only home to male and female rugby but every Monday from 10:00 to 11:30 it also plays host to a line dancing class. Sessions are open to all and booking in advance is not necessary. For more details, contact Theresa Pearson (4442 9149).

Skills Development Centre
Omar Bin Khatab Health Centre R/A, Nr Al Muntazah Park Al Mansoura **4465 5433**
sdcqatar.org
Map **2 Q11**
This centre specialises in Indian dance concentrating on folk dance, classical dance and cinematic dance. To learn an Indian dance style, it is recommended that you attend three classes a week. Beginners are welcome, although you should arrive with the understanding that it could take a bit of time before you can compete with the Bollywood stars.

Yama Yoga Studios
Garvey's European Club, Off Salwa Rd New Fereej Al Ghanim **6617 5802**
yamayogastudios.com
Map **1 D12**
As well as a full yoga timetable, including astanga, vinyasa, jivamukti, prenatal and kids' yoga, this studio offers salsa dance lessons. One-off sessions cost QR 60, with 10 session passes which are valid for three months available for QR 550. For details of the schedule (which changes from month-to-month) and details of other branch locations visit the website.

Darts

Doha Darts League
Doha Rugby Football Centre Fereej Al Soudan
dohadartsleague.com
Map **2 H11**
The Doha Darts League begins its season in the autumn with teams consisting of six players (three men and three women) competing. Matches are played every Thursday at 19:00 at the Doha Rugby Club and the sign up fee is QR 50 per player. For more information about how to sign up your team, contact secretary@dohadartsleague.com.

Diving

Doha Sub Aqua Club
Nr Sharq Village & Spa Al Khulaifat **5589 0819**
dohasubaquaclub.com
Map **2 V8**
DSAC was founded in Qatar in 1977 and offers a range of diving courses based on internationally accepted British Sub Aqua Club (BSAC) qualifications. The course lasts for six weeks and includes pool practise, lectures and sea dives. Further qualifications, such as Sports Diver, Diver Leader, Advanced Diver and Instructor, are available. Divers qualified with other agencies are welcome to join. Both shore dives and offshore wreck dives are organised on a weekly basis. The club has its own clubhouse and hosts get-togethers from about 19:30 each Tuesday.

Pearl Divers

Farig Al Nasser St Al Sadd **4444 9553**
Map **2 L4**

Pearl Divers is a five-star PADI facility where internationally qualified instructors can help you become fully proficient and confident underwater. Training to become a PADi-certified open water diver can be completed in about one week.

Q-Dive Marine Center

Souk Al Najada Al Najada **4437 5065**
qdive.net
Map **2 Q8**

This centre offers a full range of diving services and equipment rental. It arranges diving, snorkelling and fishing trips, either with a speedboat or on a classic dhow. It also offers a range of diving courses accredited under PADI. The shop is the Qatar distributor for renowned brands like Zeagle, Sherwood and Genesis. The proprietor, Khaled Zaki, is also an enthusiastic underwater film-maker.

Qatar Divers

Doha Marriott Hotel Al Khulaifat **4431 3331**
qatardivers.com
Map **2 V8**

Whether you're a beginner or an advanced diver, Qatar Divers is a great place to learn. A full range of PADI courses is on offer and you can buy scuba equipment at the centre.

Scubalatif.com

Various locations **5589 5575**
scubalatif.com

Diver training and PADI-certified courses are on offer by a Doha-based instructor and marine biologist who is truly passionate about life underwater and happy to share his vast knowledge.

Spike Hughes

Various locations **5564 2188**

Professional diver Spike Hughes runs PADI courses from beginner to advanced levels, including underwater navigation, deep diving, nitrox and rebreather courses. He also operates trips to offshore wrecks and is an expert on decompression procedures.

Drama Groups

Doha Players

Education City Al Shagub **5575 5102**
Map **2 B4**

For over 50 years, Doha Players were an extremely active amateur dramatics group, staging well supported and regular productions at the purpose-built Doha Players Theatre. Tragically, in March 2005,

Taking a stroll on the Corniche

the theatre was the target of a suicide bomb attack and it has now been demolished. The Players are currently in the process of moving into their new temporary home, a villa close to the Education City, which will allow them to again host small scale productions and social events at its own location. Larger productions are staged at outside premises. As always, the Players welcomes new members. Full membership costs QR 100 per year. Student membership is QR 50, and family membership is QR 150. Log on to the website for more information on how you can join this community-driven organisation.

Public Speaking

For those looking to perfect their public speaking skills, Qatar Toastmasters Club has been helping people deliver killer speeches since its inception in 1997. It is open to all and meets every first and third Sunday of the month at Merwebhotel Al Sadd (see qatartoastmasters.net for more details). Alternatively, Talking Matters Toastmasters Club (talkingmattersdoha.com) meets on the second and fourth Monday of the month at the Oryx Rotana. Contact Ian Rodwell on 3326 4770 for more info. Both groups welcome new members.

Environmental Groups

Sustainable development and environmentally sound policies are a key concern of Qatar. At the grass-roots level, there's plenty you can do to get involved and help advance development towards a green, eco-aware tomorrow.

Qatar Animal Welfare Society (QAWS)

Nr Qatar Racing & Equestrian Club Muaither **5539 6074**
qaws.org
Map **1 B9**

Qatar Animal Welfare Society (QAWS) was formed to improve the lives of the many abandoned or ill-treated cats and dogs in Qatar. With the support of the local community, a haven was built on the outskirts of Doha that gradually expanded to provide shelter for rescued animals ranging from donkeys to possums.

Disaster struck in 2009 when the facilities were burned to the ground. Many animals were saved and temporarily re-housed with volunteers, but help is still needed from people who care about animal welfare to build new facilities, raise funds and donate materials or time. The society is always looking for people who can sponsor an animal or foster a pet temporarily.

Qatar Green Center

Prototype University Building, Arab League St Duhail **4483 8138**
Map **1 F3**

Qatar Green Center is part of the Ministry of Municipal Affairs & Agriculture and is responsible for maintaining the general cleanliness and tidiness of public spaces as well as the 'greening' of towns and cities, which involves landscaping and planting. The centre regularly recruits volunteers to participate in tree planting, beach cleaning and other public services.

Qatar Natural History Group

Doha English Speaking School (DESS) Fereej Kulaib qnhg.org
Map **2 J4**

This society is open to anyone who has an interest in the environment and environmental affairs. Regular meetings are held at DESS on the first Wednesday of each month, from October through to June. Meetings start at 19:00 and speakers from both the local community and overseas make regular presentations on the subjects of natural history, archaeology, astronomy, wildlife and bird watching. Field trips and rambles are organised on most weekends to locations in Qatar and, occasionally, further afield.

Single membership costs QR 50 per year and family membership QR 100 per year. The group currently has over 350 members. Contact April Conkey (chairman@qnhg.org) or Fran Gillespie (pr-representative@qnhg.org).

Qatar Scientific Club

Ain Khaled **4469 6200**
Map **1 G13**

The Scientific Club has over 4,000 members split into various groups. Interests include model aircraft, scuba diving and astronomy, but there are many other topics covered. The club is not only for adults and there are many activities aimed at introducing children to science, scientific activities and modern technology. Call for more information on joining and the current list of activities and events.

Sustainable Qatar

Friends of the Environment Centre, Nr Family Counseling Center New Fereej Al Hitmi **5516 2764**
sustainableqatar.pbworks.com
Map **2 K6**

This is an independent, voluntary organisation that seeks to raise awareness of sustainability and offer opportunities for the community and individuals to engage in environmental projects. Membership is QR 50 for individuals and QR 150 for organisations on an annual basis. Meetings are held regularly and feature guest speakers who give advice on environmental issues that affect the local area. The group's online wiki has a number of useful resources including details of upcoming environmental events in Qatar.

Fencing

Qatar Fencing Federation

Nr Independence R/A Onaiza **4470 8555**
Map **2 M3**

This association caters for those who are serious about fencing. The federation regularly sends a Qatar team to the Fencing World Championships and the Asian Games. However, the association is not only for professional contenders but is also open to members of the public who are interested in fencing basics. Beginners can play on Saturday, Monday and Tuesday evenings from 16:00 to 19:00.

Flower Arranging

The Ritz-Carlton, Doha

West Bay Lagoon Al Gassar **4484 8000**
ritzcarlton.com
Map **1 K1**

Flower arranging is a surprisingly popular activity in Doha. If you're looking to get started too, lessons in this delicate are available at The Ritz-Carlton Doha (also open to non-hotel guests). During the course of a workshop, participants learn at least three arrangements in classes. As an added bonus, morning tea is included in the price and, afterwards, participants get to take the flowers home to show off their new skills.

Aspire Tower & Khalifa Stadium

Activities & Hobbies

Flying

Qatar Aeronautical College

Ras Abu Aboud Rd Doha International Airport
4440 8888
qac.edu.qa
Map **1 P9**

Although primarily geared up to train airline personnel, Qatar Aeronautical College also provides instruction for people wishing to acquire a Private Pilots Licence, with the initial course involving 45 hours of flying, as well as land-based training and a post-graduate PTD course. Visit the website for a full course curriculum and application details.

Football

Football is the national sport in Qatar, both at a professional and amateur level. At grass roots level, teams are usually formed by employees of companies and named after the firms. Keen footballers are advised to watch the local press and enquire among fellow workers and friends to see where the current teams are being formed. The one big event of the year at amateur level is the traditional grudge match between England and Scotland, an annual event that has taken place for over 50 years. Regardless of national pride, it is an event that is enjoyed every year by expatriates of all nationalities. Check out the Qatar Football Association's website, qatarfootball.com, for more information. If you prefer watching football of a higher calibre, Qatar's national leagues have garnered a loyal following. International teams occasionally visit Qatar for friendlies and their training sessions are often open for the public to spectate. See Spectator Sports on p.224 for more information.

Evolution Soccer

Qatar Foundation Al Shagub evosoccer.com
Evolution Soccer has a range of offerings for football fans of different ages and skills levels. There are various football-based activity programmes for girls and boys aged 3 and above, both at a fun and a friendly-competitive level. Individual coaching, football camps during school holidays and birthday parties are also offered. There is also a ladies' soccer session (for over 14 years olds) held weekly at Doha College. The Evolution Soccer Academy is a professional soccer training school; trials are open by invitation only.

Gaelic Games

Qatar GAA has two men's and two women's Gaelic football teams. Training is held on Tuesday evenings from 20:15 until 21:30 at the Doha Rugby Club. For more information, email pro.qatar.asia@gaa.ie or call the Doha Rugby Football Centre on 4468 3771. For more information visit qatargaa.com.

Gardening

Doha Garden Club

Various locations dohagardenclub.com
It may at times seem like an impossible task, but this group of keen gardeners explores the possibilities of growing beautiful gardens in the region's challenging weather conditions. The club meets on the first Sunday of every month (September to May) between 09:30 and 12:00. There is an annual Charity Garden Tour, in which various private gardens around Doha are opened up for viewing. The membership fee is QR 120 per year, plus QR 45 per meeting and QR 60 for non-members.

Qatar Horticultural Society

Various locations **5573 9965**
Guest speakers give regular talks on horticultural topics such as landscaping, propagating houseplants, plants that can survive Qatar's climate, and flower arranging. The group has built up a fairly large library of books on various gardening subjects, which members can borrow. Every year, the society hosts the annual Flower and Vegetable Show, where people from all over Qatar exhibit their vegetables, pot plants and roses.

Golf

There are four golf clubs in Qatar: Mesaieed Golf Club, Dukhan Golf Club, Ras Abu Abboud Boat & Beach Club and Doha Golf Club. The first two are brown courses in remote locations and are for the use of Qatar Petroleum employees only, although occasional open tournaments are organised at both clubs. The one at Ras Abu Abboud Boat and Beach Club is a very small green course and is also restricted to Qatar Petroleum Company employees. The only club open to the general public is the excellent green course at

Doha Golf Club

Doha Golf Club. There are plans for the construction of a further green course as part of the Lusail development, located just north of Doha.

Doha Golf Club
Al Jamiaa St Al Egla **4496 0777**
dohagolfclub.com
Map **1 H1**
Doha Golf Club is open daily to members and non-members. It has a 7,312 yard, 18 hole Championship Course and a floodlit nine-hole Academy Course. It is also home to several restaurants, lounges and conference rooms. Individual membership costs QR 24,500 per year (plus a QR 5,000 one-time registration fee) with other weekday and family packages available. Non-members can expect to pay QR 590 for 18 holes on the Championship course during the week and QR 795 at the weekend. The shorter Academy Course is just QR 200 for nine holes during the week.

The club's Golf Academy is a state-of-the-art teaching and practice facility with custom-built chipping, putting and bunker areas and a driving range (QR 40 per bucket of balls). Lessons are available from around QR 70 for 30 minutes, with packages, workshops and clinics also on offer. Club, shoe and buggy rental are all available.

Gymnastics

The Gymnastics Academy
Doha English Speaking School (DESS) Fereej Kulaib
gymnasticsacademydoha.net
Map **2 J4**
Classes and training are on offer at various locations by this well-established academy; see the website for timings and additional information.

Qatar Gymnastics Club
Khalifa School, Al Wabra St Fereej Kulaib **5529 6360**
Map **2 J3**
This club provides gymnastic facilities and training for children from the age of 4.

Hockey

Doha Hockey Club
Al Rayyan Sports Club New Al Rayan
dohahockeyclub.com
Map **2 B4**
The hockey scene in Qatar is an informal affair, but there are enough enthusiasts to make sure newcomers will be able to find a game. The teams usually play on astroturf pitches owned by the Qatar Hockey Federation and the Qatar Olympic Committee at Al Rayyan Sports Complex; training takes place twice a week at the Al Rayyan sports club. All interested players, men or women, are encouraged to join in and costs are fairly low, covering only the hiring

of the ground. Players should bring a stick and shin pads, although beginners can borrow equipment.

Horse Riding

Al Khor Riding Centre
Nr Simaisma Flyover Al Khor **4432 3245**
Map **2 C2**
This riding centre, situated north of Doha on the road to Al Khor, specialises in one-on-one tuition at all levels of showjumping. From Doha, follow the Al Khor Road (Route Q1A) until you reach the Simaisma flyover (it says Al Dayyan Municipality on it). Keep going and about 3km further north there is a slip road leading to a radio mast. Take this turn, go under the road and you will see the farm.

Al Samariyah Equestrian Centre
Baytur Compound, Al Samariyah Al Khor
wix.com/10searle/asec
Map **2 C2**
Open seven days a week for lessons and catering for both adults and children above the age of 4, horses here range from Shetland ponies to Arabian stallions. All abilities are welcome, from complete beginners to experienced riders. The school is open to members (membership fees of QR 350 a year for adults, QR 250 for children and QR 700 for a three-member family) and non-members with fees based on membership status and whether group or private lessons are requested. Hacks, for example, cost QR 100 for members and QR 120 for non-members while private lessons are QR 200 for members and QR 280 for non-members.

Al Shaqab Riding Academy
Nr Educational City Al Shagub **4454 6233**
alshaqab.com
Map **2 A4**
This new specialist centre and riding academy offers lessons and equestrian training for all. Instruction is available for all levels and kids aged 6 or more are welcome too; contact the centre for additional information.

Sealine Beach Resort
Mesaieed **4476 5299**
merweb.com
Map **2 D5**
At this beach resort, you can enjoy a ride along the sand and surf. Camel rides are also available; however, these tend to be of the 'led round on a lead' variety. If you can ride, you can hire a horse unaccompanied for one hour for QR 150 but bear in mind that you will not be allowed to take it outside of the resort boundaries. Sealine is a popular weekend getaway for Doha residents. Entry fees to the resort are QR 50 per person Saturday to Thursday and QR 195 on Friday.

Activities & Hobbies

Activities & Hobbies

Ice Hockey

Qatar International Ice Hockey League
Villaggio Mall Baaya qiihl.com
Map **2 B11**

The fact that an ice hockey league even exists in Qatar is shocking; that it bears a heavy Canadian slant is less suprising. QIIHL organises ice hockey teams in a very active league, playing mainly in and around Doha but also competing in inter-Gulf matches. For more information and to contact the organisers, fill in the form on the QIIHL web page.

Qatar Minor Ice Hockey Association
Villaggio Mall Baaya qataricehockey.com
Map **2 B11**

The Qatar Minor Ice Hockey Association (QMIHA) is a non-profit organisation operated solely by volunteers to provide a quality hockey programme for children aged 5 to 17 in five age groups. The programme runs from September to March with each group playing approximately 12 league games during the season. There are additional practise sessions throughout the year.

Ice Skating

Gondolania Ice Arena
Villaggio Mall Baaya **4451 9993**
gondolania.com
Map **2 B11**

The Olympic-sized Ice Arena is part of the Gondolania family entertainment centre, located in the middle of the foodcourt at Villaggio Mall. The rink is occasionally used for ice hockey tournaments and private events but for the majority of the day, you can walk almost straight on to the ice without booking. It costs QR 30 to QR 35 for a 105 minute skating session; full-day passes cost QR 100. Coaches are usually around to give you a hand and, no matter what your level, you can also book private lessons.

Winter Wonderland
City Center Doha Al Dafna **4483 9163**
Map **2 Q2**

Winter Wonderland in City Center Doha has a full-size ice skating rink that can be used for recreational skating or for training – while there are also several ice hockey leagues that use the facility. A single skating session costs QR 35 per person while the entrance fee for non-skaters is QR 10. Alternatively, a full day pass costs QR 100. Various membership packages are available: Silver Monthly Membership costs QR 400 and allows unlimited access from Sunday to Wednesday, while Gold Monthly Membership costs QR 750, and allows unlimited access at any time. Extra services include skate hire and skate sharpening

Winter Wonderland at Doha City Center

(QR 75), and professional lessons are available upon request (packages start from QR 500).

Karting

The Karting Track
Villaggio Mall Baaya gondolania.com
Map **2 B11**

Although situated at the rear of the children's play area in Villaggio Mall, make no mistake that this go-kart track is intended for adults. Up to 10 karts race in each session with times being recorded for the fastest laps. Costs for 10 minute sessions are QR 60 from Sunday to Wednesday and QR 70 from Thursday to Saturday. Safety helmet use is compulsory, but if you do not own one, reasonably priced helmets can be purchased from the track operators.

Kitesurfing

Qatar Kitesurfing Club
Various locations **5535 0336**

One of the fastest growing and most exciting sports on the water is kitesurfing. The main venues are the shallow waters of Zekrit Bay on the west coast and the similarly sheltered and shallow waters off West Bay in Doha. Qatar Kitesurfing Club organises activities for those interested in learning from a registered IKO instructor or perfecting their skills in this growing pastime. To get started in this exciting sport, try Jonathan (5535 0336) for lessons (Fridays and Saturdays) or Acrum who is available during the week (5589 9217).

Martial Arts

Cabana Club
Radisson Blu Hotel, Doha Rawdat Al Khail 4428 1621
ramadaplazadoha.com
Map 2 N10
Apart from being able to defend yourself, the benefits of karate include improved physical fitness and energy levels. The Cabana Club has lessons for beginners and advanced students, in age groups of 6 to 10 year olds, 10 to 14 year olds and adults.

Doha Aikido
Sheraton Doha Resort & Convention Hotel Al Dafna
5562 4178
dohaaikido.com
Map 2 R3
This martial arts class offers the Yoshinkan form of Aikido, which is primarily defensive and non-competitive. Sensei Joe Scarlato has over 10 years' experience. Classes are held on Saturday, Monday and Wednesday from 19:30 to 21:00, and from 15:00 to 17:00 on Fridays.

International Academy For Intercultural Development
Al Mansoura St, Nr Muntazah Park Al Mansoura
4432 0974
iaidonline.com
Map 2 Q11
The International Academy for Intercultural Development offers Shotokan karate classes for beginners, intermediate and advanced students. Those who take karate seriously should be able to get to black-belt status in two or three years. Every three months there is an examination to assess your readiness to proceed to the next level. The monthly cost is QR 450 for children and QR 550 for adults.

Korea Taekwondo Center
Salwa Rd, Nr Jarir Bookstore Rawdat Al Khail
4465 9066
Map 2 N10
Taekwondo classes are available for men, women and children and are split into three levels: beginners (white and yellow belts), intermediate (green to red belts) and advanced (senior red and black belts). The coach, JK Shin, is a seventh-dan black belt, a member of the Qatar national taekwondo team and the coach for Korea's national taekwondo team.

Motorcycling

Qatar Motor & Motorcycle Federation
Bld 59, Salwa Rd 24 Rawdat Al Khail 4437 9884
circuitlosail.com
Map 2 N10
Qatar Motor & Motorcycle Federation is the governing body for motorsports in Qatar, and holds several motorcycle rallies throughout the year. The federation is always on the lookout for keen volunteers. Visit the website to download a volunteer application form.

Track Days
Wanna-be Sebastian Vettels and Valentino Rossis can test their skills behind the wheel on track days at Losail International Circuit. The facilities will please any petrolhead. Rates are from QR 400 to QR 1,200. Find out more by logging onto circuitlosail.com.

Motorsports

Qatar Motor & Motorcycle Federation
Bld 59, Salwa Rd 24 Rawdat Al Khail 4437 9884
circuitlosail.com
Map 2 N10
Several motor racing events are staged in the country each year, including the Qatar National Rally and the Qatar Road Racing Championship. They are organised by Qatar Motor & Motorcycle Federation, which also provides advice on driving skills. Find out more information about upcoming events, and how you can get involved, through the federation's website.

Radio-Controlled Cars
An informal group of enthusiasts have built themselves a race track, complete with obstacles and grandstand, next to the roundabout on the eastern edge of the Golf Club (near the entrance to the Lusail construction site). There are no contact numbers, but if you want to participate or even just watch they are there most weekends.

Mountain Biking

Qatar Chain Reaction
Various locations qatarchainreaction.org
The lack of mountains in Qatar has not deterred Qatar Chain Reaction, a group of avid cyclists who organise mountain bike rides every week. It also arranges road races and group social events. For more information look on the website. There are no membership fees.

Activities & Hobbies

Quad Biking

Tents are located all along the side of the road to Sealine Resort near Mesaieed, from which quad bikes of all sizes can be rented. Behind the tents are low dunes that you can practice on, but beware, especially if you have children with you, these are powerful machines not toys and they can kill in inexperienced hands. Costs are variable depending on the size of the machine, but expect to pay between QR 400 to QR 600 per hour.

Music Lessons

International Academy For Intercultural Development

Al Mansoura St, Nr Muntazah Park Al Mansoura
4432 0974
iaidonline.com
Map **2 Q11**

The International Academy for Intercultural Development offers music classes in instruments such as keyboards, piano and guitar. For something a little different, you can also take voice training in disciplines like Carnatic and Hindustani vocals; the quality of instruction is good and when it comes to developing a more unusual talent during your stay in Qatar, there's hardly a better way. Call the academy for more information on timings and prices.

International Centre For Music

Villa 81, Ahmed bin Hanbal St Old Airport **4467 1354**
Map **2 S13**

This centre offers classes in piano, violin, guitar and flute. Singing lessons are also on offer for those looking to stretch their vocal cords. More advanced students can take examinations and get certificates under the Associated Board of the Royal Schools of Music. Contact the centre directly for more information about class timings and costs, as well as the qualifications you can complete here.

Orchestras & Bands

Historically, musicians looking for like-minded people to play music with tended to gravitate towards Doha Players (p.269) – new members are still welcome to join and this remains one of the best addresses in town to get involved in the musical circles. Alternatively, if you are a concert musician, talk to the Qatar Philharmonic Orchestra (qatarphilharmonicorchestra.org), which is run by Qatar Foundation (p.146) on a professional basis. If you are a keen vocalist, get in touch with Doha Singers (p.279). For beginner-level training or to brush up on your musical talent, contact one of the music schools listed above.

Paintballing & Laser Games

Qatar Paintball Centre

Villaggio Mall Baaya **6678 2121**
qatarpaintballcentre.com
Map **2 B11**

It may not look like much from the outside, but there are plenty of thrills to be had inside Qatar Paintball Centre. Up to 40 people can play at a time on the two outdoor fields. Equipment and overalls are provided but closed running shoes are required. There are different packages available including: QR 100 for one hour's play with 100 paintballs, or QR 200 for 300 balls. The minimum age is 12 with monthly tournaments open to everyone over the age of 15. The centre is open each evening from 18:00 to midnight.

Photography & Film

In October 2009, in conjunction with the New York based Tribeca Film Festival, Qatar Museums Authority (QMA) launched a world-class international film festival, the Tribeca Film Festival Doha. This has become an annual event and one of the most important events on the social calendar, incorporating both international and national movie premieres. There is also an interesting training workshop dedicated for budding film makers, conducted by internationally renowned masters of the art (see Qatar Calendar, p.24).

Lydia Shaw Photography

Various Locations **5514 6828**
lydiashawphotography.com

Lydia Shaw is a professional photographer who also runs digital photography workshops and Photoshop classes. The photography course aims to give a basic understanding of digital photography and SLR use; lessons run for six weeks with two hours of tuition per week. The Photoshop course is for those with no prior knowledge of the software and includes eight hours of tuition over four weeks.

Qatar Photographic Society

Katara Cultural Village Al Gassar **4467 7793**
http://en.qpsphoto.com
Map **1 K3**

The amateur photography scene is alive and well in Qatar with the Qatar Photographic Society. Founded in 1985, it holds the distinction of being the first photographic society in the Arab world. It has over 200 members and aims to promote photography in Qatar, encourage new talent and provide a forum where photographers can share knowledge and showcase their work. The Qatar Photographic Society cooperates with Sheikh Saoud Al Thani to present the prestigious Al Thani Award for Photography to the best photographers in the Gulf. From time

Sheehaniyah Camel Racetrack

Motorbike enthusiasts

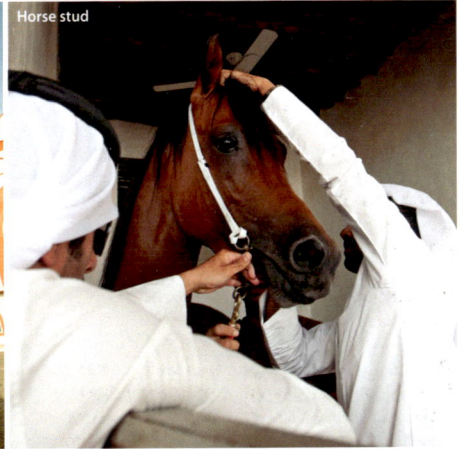
Horse stud

Powerboat racing

to time, courses are held for members on various aspects of photography including still life, portrait and digital shooting. The society organises exhibitions of members' work throughout the year. Annual membership costs QR 200.

Rugby

Doha Rugby Football Centre
Nr American School of Doha Fereej Al Soudan
4468 3771
doharfc.com
Map **2 H11**

Doha RFC was formed in 1974 and today it has mini's and youth's teams, an under 16 side, senior first and second XVs, a vets' team, a Gulf-recognised colts' side, two ladies' teams that have won virtually every tournament in the last two years (including two successive wins at the renowned Dubai Rugby 7s) and even a touch rugby side. Perhaps one of the reasons for the centre's success is its dedicated army of supporters, known to number as many as 700 at some local matches. Like all rugby clubs, the social aspect is, in many cases, every bit as important as the sport.

Contact Doha RFC to enquire about training as timetables obviously vary according to the team you hope to join. Full membership costs QR 1,800 for the full season, with many other levels and discounts available. Complete membership fees and a downloadable application form is available on the doharfc.com site.

Running

The only two hazards that might hamper your running in Qatar are high temperatures and crazy drivers. On the whole though, the climate is bearable for most of the year (and absolutely perfect in the winter),

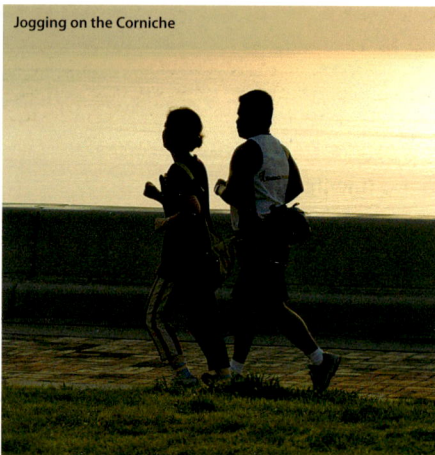

Jogging on the Corniche

and there are plenty of routes around the less busy roads allowing you to avoid the cars. Running along the Corniche (p.251) is a particularly enjoyable and favoured spot, and proves to be a very popular location for Doha's joggers. There is also a sprung running track at Aspire Park, p.212 for those looking for a more comfortable surface to run on.

Bay Club
InterContinental Doha Al Gassar **4484 4852**
ichotelsgroup.com
Map **1 K3**

The InterContinental Doha's Bay Club gathers together running enthusiasts of all fitness levels for a weekly run. Runners meet on Wednesday evenings at the Corniche and there is no need to book and no charge. Contact the club for more information.

Doha Bay Running Club
Nr Sheraton Doha, Doha Corniche Al Dafna
dohabayrunningclub.webs.com
Map **2 R3**

This club meets weekly on Fridays at 05:30, starting at the Sheraton end of the Corniche and usually running 10 kilometres. There are no fees and anyone can join.

Qatar Hash House Harriers
Various locations **5551 9603**

The Qatar Hash is a mixed hash (running race) held on Monday afternoons. There is a family barbecue on the first Monday of every month, at which kids are welcome.

Sailing

The year-round favourable weather conditions and the calm waters off the coast mean that sailing is a popular sport in Qatar. Events and regattas are regularly held.

Doha Sailing Club
Al Sharq Al Khulaifat **4443 9840**
qmsf.com
Map **2 V8**

This members-only club is affiliated with a number of international sailing associations, including ISAF, RYA and Asian Sailing Federation. Coaching is available for members, and various events and get-togethers take place regularly.

Qatar Motor & Motorcycle Federation
Bld 59, Salwa Rd 24 Rawdat Al Khail **4437 9884**
circuitlosail.com
Map **2 N10**

Strangely, dhow racing both internally in Qatar and competition against teams from the UAE falls under the auspices of the Qatar Motor & Motorcycle Federation (as does international powerboat racing). It holds regular practice sessions and owns a large fleet of traditional racing dhows.

Qatar Sailing & Rowing Federation
Ras Abu Abboud Rd Al Khulaifat **4442 0305**
qatarsailing.org
Map **2 V8**
The Qatar Sailing & Rowing Federation promotes sailing in the country with the support of the Doha Sailing Club. The club has a variety of boats suitable for all ages, including Optimist, Laser 4.7, Laser Radial, Laser Standard and catamaran. Racing takes place every Friday and regattas are organised on a regular basis. Tuition is offered for beginners and a try-sail will cost you no more than a phone call to the club.

Regatta Sailing Academy
InterContinental Doha Al Gassar **4442 4577**
regattasailingacademy.com
Map **1 K3**
The academy has a range of equipment suitable for sailors of all ages, including Lasers, catamarans and sports boats. You can seek the advice of several fully qualified British Royal Yacht Association instructors, and get some pointers in the safety of the lagoon before progressing to the waters of Doha Bay. A detailed price list for tuition and boat hire is available on the website.

Scrabble

Qatar Scrabble League
International Academy For Intercultural Development Al Mansoura
Map **2 Q11**
Qatar Scrabble League is a competitive group that welcomes youth players looking to get into tournament scrabble. Current youth players' ages range from 7-15 years. It also welcomes adult players who are willing to play with and mentor the youth team. The group is part of the World English Scrabble Players Association (WESPA) and members have previously taken part in the World Youth Scrabble Championship, the annual Gulf Scrabble Tournament and various other international competitions. New members are selected from the Tournament Scrabble for Beginners course run by IAID and QSL, or via referrals, subject to assessment. Membership is QR 75 for under 17 year olds and QR 100 for adults.

Shooting

Qatar Shooting & Archery Association
Nr Police Training Centre Duhail **4495 3114**
qatarshooting.asia/home-en
Map **1 E2**
Although this organisation used to be solely for members of the national shooting team, it is now open to the public. People can practise clay target shooting, skeet shooting and trap shooting, and there are regular precision shooting events. Facilities are the same as used for training by the national team. The range is located on the northern outskirts of Doha, opposite the College of the North Atlantic building.

Singing

Doha Singers
American School Of Doha Fereej Al Soudan
dohasingers.com
Map **2 H11**
Membership of this choir varies but currently stands at around 60 or 70 adults, who meet weekly to rehearse a wide variety of songs. The choir gives several concerts per year, and often performs alongside the Doha Community Orchestra. All enthusiastic amateur voices are welcome, but as singing is from printed scores, some experience and the ability to read music is useful. Rehearsals take place weekly on Monday evenings, at the American School in Doha from 19:00 to 20:30. It's recommended to make initial contact by email.

Skating, Rollerskating & Rollerblading
Qatar is generally a flat country and there are plenty of areas to be found with disused roads that are ideal for both rollerblading and rollerskating. Two of the most popular areas in Doha are the Corniche (p.251) and around the Aspire Zone complex (p.212). Museum Park (p.210) and Aspire Play Park (p.212) also have large paved areas which are good for skating and practising new skills. Be sure you check for signs giving details of permitted activities in parks and public areas as skating may be banned in certain areas of the city.

Snooker
Many major clubs, hotels and resorts in Doha have at least one snooker table, which is often available for use by members of the public. Prices usually vary between QR 5 to QR 25 per hour of play, although this does not include any entrance fee you may have to pay.

Qatar Bowling Center
Nr Mannai R/A Al Bidda **4432 9178**
qatarbowlingcenter.net
Map **2 N7**
The Bowling Center has nine snooker tables. Entrance is QR 15, and each game (one hour) costs QR 25. It is not necessary to book in advance, unless you plan to play during peak times or at the weekend. You can become a member – annual membership costs QR 200 and members will only have to pay the game fee. Family membership is also available, offering good value at QR 400.

Squash

Many hotels and fitness clubs have squash courts, although these are often reserved for members and hotel guests. Members-only courts are available at the Cabana Club (4428 1621), the Sheraton (4485 4444), The Ritz-Carlton (4484 8000) and the Bay Club (4484 4444). Members can usually take guests. Qatar Squash Federation is the governing body for the sport and it organises the annual Qatar Classic Squash Championship (qatarsquash.com).

The Diplomatic Club
Al Gassar 4484 7444
thediplomaticclub.com
Map **1 K2**

Squash courts are available to non-members; the cost is QR 100 per person per hour and you must play with a coach.

John Lord Duffers League
Various Locations squashleagues.com

This fun squash league is for young and old, men and women, serious players and 'duffers' alike. Depending on your ability, you will be assigned to play at one of five levels, and you will get to compete against four different opponents each month. Although it is a fun league, there is a healthy sense of competition and, as an added bonus, i's of course a great way to get in or stay in shape. Games are played at various locations in Doha – you will decide with your monthly opponents where to play.

Khalifa International Tennis & Squash Complex
Majlis Al Taawon Rd Lekhwair 4440 9666
qatartennis.org
Map **2 N4**

Although primarily the home of the Qatar Tennis Federation, there are a number of squash courts at this club. The courts have recently undergone renovation. Timings and prices can be subject to change, but as a general rule of thumb, courts are usually open from 08:00 to 23:00, and to hire a court for one hour costs QR 30. Call the club for more detailed information.

Swimming

Bay Club
InterContinental Doha Al Gassar 4484 4852
ichotelsgroup.com
Map **1 K3**

Swimming lessons are available here for members and non-members. A private lesson costs QR 120 for an hour and QR 100 for half an hour. It is recommended that people who are serious about learning book a package of 10 one-hour sessions at a cost of QR 1,000. Members get a 10% discount off all lessons.

Cabana Club
Radisson Blu Hotel, Doha Rawdat Al Khail 4428 1621
ramadaplazadoha.com
Map **2 N10**

You can learn to swim here under the watchful eye of qualified instructors in a temperature-controlled swimming pool. Both group and individual lessons are available, with kids' lessons for under 14s. Each session is eight lessons.

Doha Dolphins Swimming Club
Doha College Fereej Al Soudan 4411 7911
qmotion.com.qa
Map **2 H12**

The staff of this club includes 13 qualified and experienced instructors, as well as 22 trained instructor's assistants. Membership costs QR 325 a year, although you will pay extra for certain programmes including children's swimming classes, adult classes and training squads.

The Ritz-Carlton, Doha
West Bay Lagoon Al Gassar 4484 8000
ritzcarlton.com
Map **1 K1**

The Ritz-Carlton Doha is equipped with a 25 metre swimming pool. Lessons are offered for members and non-members. Swimmers are advised to call the club for details of timings, costs and lessons.

Table Tennis

Cabana Club
Radisson Blu Hotel, Doha Rawdat Al Khail 4428 1621
ramadaplazadoha.com
Map **2 N10**

Table tennis is available at the Cabana Club from 19:00 to 21:00. Call the club for more information.

Qatar Bowling Center
Nr Mannai R/A Al Bidda 4432 9178
qatarbowlingcenter.net
Map **2 N7**

There are three table tennis tables at the Qatar Bowling Centre. Entrance costs QR 15, and then an hour of table tennis costs a further QR 20 (including bat hire). Booking is not required, but it is recommended, especially during busy times. You can become a member of the Bowling Centre – annual membership costs QR 200 and a family membership (two adults and two children) costs QR400. Members receive various benefits, including not having to pay the entrance fee.

Tennis

The Khalifa International Tennis and Squash Complex, home of the $1 million Qatar ExxonMobil Open, has hosted some of the game's greats over the last few years (see p.24). In addition to the facilities listed below, quite a few upmarket housing compounds have their own tennis courts.

Bay Club
InterContinental Doha Al Gassar **4484 4852**
ichotelsgroup.com
Map **1 K3**
There are two courts available for hire at QR 30 per hour (advance booking is recommended) for members only. On Fridays and Sundays between 18:00 and 20:00 there is social tennis, where you can meet other players. Social tennis is free for members and costs QR 25 for non-members. Private lessons are available at a cost of QR 120 for non-members and QR 110 for members.

Cabana Club
Radisson Blu Hotel, Doha Rawdat Al Khail **4428 1621**
ramadaplazadoha.com
Map **2 N10**
Private tennis lessons are available here. Prices depend on the number of lessons you are looking for; discounts apply if you go for one of he packages. Also, members qualify for cheaper rates. Contact the club directly to enquire about the available packages and memberships.

The Diplomatic Club
Al Gassar **4484 7444**
thediplomaticclub.com
Map **1 K2**
There are two outdoor, floodlit tennis courts which are open between 07:00 and 22:00. However, be advised

that non-members must play and pay for a coach which will cost QR 100 per lesson.

Elite Tennis Academy
Aspire Academy For Sports Excellence Baaya **5566 4747**
elite-tennisacademy.com
Map **2 A10**
Elite offers private and group tennis coaching for adults and children of all ages and levels of skill. Youngsters between 4 and 17 years of age can join the Mini Tennis sessions on a short court, where the emphasis is on participation and fun. Children will learn the basic skills of tennis whilst getting fit and enjoying the sunshine. Elite also offers a new workout programme called Cardio Tennis, which is a high-energy and predominantly drill-based fitness class. The tennis instructors are following the American IFT, USTA teaching standards.

Khalifa International Tennis & Squash Complex
Majlis Al Taawon Rd Lekhwair **4440 9666**
qatartennis.org
Map **2 N4**
These are the courts that have been played on by some of the game's international superstars during the $1 million Qatar Open. They can be hired for a rate of QR 25 – QR 40 per hour (depending on whether you want to play on the new or old courts). The courts are open from 08:00 to 23:00 on weekdays and 06:00 to 23:00 at weekends, and booking is required. Lessons cost QR 600 per month for adults and QR 400 for children, for three lessons a week.

Game, set and match

Activities & Hobbies

Activities & Hobbies

The Ritz-Carlton, Doha
West Bay Lagoon Al Gassar **4484 8000**
ritzcarlton.com
Map **1 K1**
There are two indoor tennis courts available for hire at The Ritz-Carlton Doha. The club is currently open to both members and non-members; however, it is advisable to book these busy courts at least a week in advance to avoid disappointment.

Sealine Beach Resort
Mesaieed 4476 5299
merweb.com
Map **Qatar Country Map D5**
As well as their wide range of watersports, Sealine Beach Resort also has tennis courts available for hourly hire. The cost of hiring the tennis court for one hour is QR 100 (which includes the use of rackets and three tennis balls). It is wise to book a court in advance, as it can get quite busy, particularly at weekends. Entry fees to the resort are QR 50 per person Saturday to Thursday and QR 195 on Friday.

Sheraton Doha Resort & Convention Hotel
Al Corniche St Al Dafna **4485 4444**
sheratondoha.com
Map **2 R3**
The facilities at this hotel are for the use of members only. However, members may take guests so it's best to get networking quickly as the grounds and courts are state-of-the-art. There is an indoor and an outdoor court, but making a reservation is highly recommended to ensure availability. Private coaching is also available. for those who are looking to improve their game.

Triathlon
There are no triathlon or iron man clubs in Qatar, although there are a number of keen competitors in the country who regularly compete in Gulf events, mainly in the UAE. Local hotels occasionally arrange events that are open to all, as do oil company owned housing communities. For details of these you have to keep an eye on the local press.

Volleyball

Filipino Volleyball Association
Philippine International School of Qatar Al Messila **4462 9248**
filipinovolleyball.bravehost.com
Map **2 G5**
You don't have to be from the Philippines to play with the Filipino Volleyball Association of Qatar. All keen volleyball players and those looking for a new, fun hobby are welcome – the only prerequisites are that you are not a professional club player, and you pay the

annual membership fee of QR 20. Matches are played on Fridays from 17:00 on the volleyball court at the Philippine International School of Qatar (near the New Rayyan branch of Qtel).

Watersports
Watersports are offered by some hotels and clubs in Doha; usually, a day visitor fee is charged for beach access, in addition to charges for the activities. The Sheraton Doha (p.204) offers parasailing, among other watersports. The Diplomatic Club allows non-members to do wakeboarding for QR 200; a wakeboarding lesson costs an extra QR 100. The Sealine Beach Resort (p.243) has a wide range of watersports on offer, including jet skiing, which costs QR 400 per hour. Entry fees to the resort are QR 50 per person Saturday to Thursday and QR 195 on Friday. An alternative option is to join a watersports trip organised by a tour operator (p.228) or to hire a boat (see Boat Tours, p.227). Check out the Activity Finder on p.264 for a list of groups to find out if there's a one dedicated to your favourite aquatic sport.

Yoga
Yoga and Pilates are offered by a number of gyms and fitness centres in Doha, including Aspire Active (p.131) as part of its programme of public fitness classes, and at the Six Senses Fitness Center at Sharq Village Resort and Spa (p.204).

International Academy For Intercultural Development
Al Mansoura St, Nr Muntazah Park Al Mansoura **4432 0974**
iaidonline.com
Map **2 Q11**
Hatha yoga classes are held on three days of the week. All abilities are welcome and there are mixed gender classes, as well as sessions for women only. Prices are QR 450 per month and registration costs QR 100.

Yama Yoga Studios
Garvey's European Club, Off Salwa Rd New Fereej Al Ghanim **6617 5802**
yamayogastudios.com
Map **1 D12**
Yama Yoga Studios offers a peaceful, stress-free environment and knowledgeable yoga instructors who help people become happier and healthier through the regular practise of yoga. 20 classes a week are offered, aimed at people of all ages and stages of life. Classes draw from a number of traditional lineages of yoga with particular focus on astanga to build strength, stamina and mindfulness. Prenatal yoga, Jivamukti yoga and tai chi are also available. Costs are QR 60 for single classes or QR 550 for a 10 session pass, valid for three months.

there's more to life...

Push the boat out

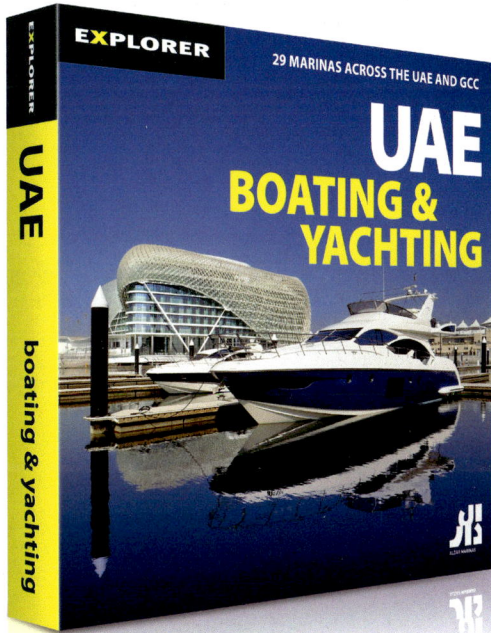

Includes how and where to buy a boat, boating skills, rules, regulations and where to sail, along with information on 29 marinas across the UAE and GCC.

askexplorer.com/shop

askexplorer

Sponsored by

ALDAR MARINAS

Shopping

SHOPPING

It is fair to say that shopping in Qatar is a national pastime for all nationalities. Each evening, especially at weekends, the malls are packed with window shoppers and those looking to drop some serious cash. The shopping scene in Qatar has developed in leaps and bounds over the past couple of years – as the population has expanded, so has the retail potential. Many international brands and retailers have taken the opportunity to move into a new and growing market. From high-end boutiques (p.326), right down to funky little one-man stores in the souks (p.326), traditional and modern blend together to bring surprises and bargains.

Qatar should keep most shopaholics happily swiping their credit cards, and the odd bargain can be found amongst the eye-wateringly expensive range of designer brands. There may be a few items that you can't find, but you'll get over your disappointment by discovering a whole new world of things to buy.

Big shopping centres all house major international brands, and because there is no sales tax or VAT you might find some things cheaper than in your home country, but this is not always the case. Some people may find electronics cheaper than back home, but it really depends on what you compare it to and when you buy the item. Imported clothing brands are often more expensive than they are back home, but if you wait for the sales, you can benefit from sweeping markdowns on stock.

Until the end of 2010, an annual shopping festival was run each summer. Prices were often reduced by up to 50% in many shops. Stores, including supermarkets and hypermarkets, also ran raffles where you stood the chance of winning a new car, holiday or even solid gold. Although the official Government sponsored festival no longer seems to exist, many of the traders in Doha have carried on with the spirit of the festival.

Ramadan is also a good period to snare a bargain, as many shops drop their prices or have special offers. This is also a great time to buy a new car.

The traditional markets, known as souks (p.326), are a must for residents and tourists alike. Many are clustered together near the Souk Waqif area so you can wander from one to the other quite easily. Souk Waqif (p.330) is a landmark in Doha and one of the most beautiful in the Middle East. It's not just a shopping destination – dozens of great eateries are opening in the area as well. Souks are particularly enjoyable for shoppers who like a good rummage, and there are great bargains to be had.

In 2009, the opening of The Pearl Qatar (p.84) changed the luxury shopping scene in Doha forever. The impressive development is not just a manmade island for residential purposes: it also happens to host one of the Middle East's most impressive designer store collections outside Dubai. Where else in the world can you buy saucy lingerie from Agent Provocateur (p.304), have a coffee, then test drive a Rolls Royce?

Nearby, the Doha shopping scene has received another major boost with the recent opening of the Lagoona Mall (p.332). Located less than 1km from The Pearl, it makes shopping in West Bay and the surrounding areas even more exciting thanks to a selection of stores selling everything from highstreet fashions to designer gear, homewares and jewellery.

Outside Doha, the shopping scene remains more limited, although new and growing communities in Al Khor and Al Wakra signal a future change. Al Wakra (p.86) boasts dozens of small supermarkets, but the main shopping destination is the new Barwa Village, Qatar's first attempt at out of town shopping. The former fishing village of Al Khor, which is now morphing into a major town, has a bustling little open-air fish market on the harbour front and has the soon to be opened Al-Khor Mall, housing a branch of the major hypermarket, Lulu. Generally speaking, if you can't find what you're looking for in Doha, chances

Quick Reference

are you won't find it in the surrounding area either, so a shopping trip to nearby Dubai or Abu Dhabi might be the answer.

Online Shopping

While most things can be bought and sold in Qatar, the market is still relatively small and there are occasions when the whole country runs out of a particular product, if you can't find something in particular you may want to look at what's on offer further afield. The variety and convenience of online shopping makes it an appealing venture for many and, if you are craving particular items from back home, searching on the web is often your best bet. There are very few stores with an online presence in the country, but you may find some international stores offer delivery to Qatar. For books and DVDs, amazon.com is a great resource. It delivers to Qatar and, depending on the delivery option you choose, the items can arrive surprisingly quickly. The same company's UK branch amazon.co.uk is another option.

Discount Cards

There are a few stores in Qatar that offer discount cards; these include Jarir Bookstore (p.298), which offers a scheme that gives you a 10% to 15% discount, and Home Centre (p.305), which sends privilege card holders credit vouchers to use any time expect during sales. Qtel (p.91) has also launched its own loyalty scheme called Nojoom, allowing subscribers to accumulate points against money they spend each month. Points can be redeemed for extra airtime, frequent flyer points for Qatar Airways and movie tickets (register at qtel.com.qa). The Air Miles scheme is also available in Qatar, Bahrain and the UAE. It allows those registered with the scheme to generate air miles each time you shop at connected outlets. The points can be redeemed for a variety of products and services including flights and electrical goods. For more information and to register visit airmilesme.com.

UK fashion retailer ASOS (asos.com) also delivers to the region, and its affordable translations of the latest designer styles make it a great option for adding some funky pieces to your wardrobe. You can also purchase more high-end fashion from designers like Stella McCartney and Oscar De La Renta at Net-A-Porter.com.

Local online store dohasouq.com offers a limited range of items for home delivery, including flowers, sweets, electrical appliances, car hire, games and cakes. Orders can be placed online domestically, or from abroad, for delivery in Qatar. For second-hand items, check postings on qatarliving.com where many residents advertise their unwanted items.

You'll also find that online facilities for Qatar-based banks may be less advanced than what you're used to. However, of course you'll still be able to access your offshore accounts as usual.

The Green Box (4411 7911, the-box.me) is a great new site that has started operating in Qatar. The site offers a weekly delivery of fruit and vegetables to your home, with a range of products sourced from Europe. You can buy a 5kg or 10kg mixed box of organic or non-organic stock (prices start from QR 155) and the company has recently started to sell poultry.

Many people who are hankering for items from their home countries often choose to use shipping companies Aramex and Borderlinx (see Shipping p.283), which offer services where you can establish personal mailing addresses in the US and UK so that internet purchases can be forwarded on to you.

Refunds, Exchanges & Consumer Rights

Larger shopping outlets have fairly generous returns policies that are probably similar to reputable shops in your home country. Major chains like Carrefour (p.325) or Home Centre (p.305) will return your money if the merchandise is still in its original condition, as long as you present your receipt and return the item within the deadline (seven days in most cases). Sometimes you will have to insist on speaking to the manager if you want a cash refund rather than a credit note. The manager will always have the final say and will have to sign the paperwork if a cash refund is given.

You will get a better result if you stay calm and don't let yourself get frustrated in your dealings with the shop assistants. Be firm, but reasonable and aim for an amicable resolution. If you are making a purchase, always take note of the returns policy before you hand over your money; it should be displayed somewhere in the shop, but if it isn't then ask to see it.

If you are purchasing from a large store in a shopping centre, your rights are at the discretion of the manager. If you feel you are not being heard or you have been treated unfairly, you can try approaching the mall management offices and lodging a complaint. Put it in writing and request an appointment with the manager. Even at this stage, it is always better to aim for an amicable resolution. Until such time as there is an official consumer watchdog organisation in Qatar, your best bet is to be careful where you make your purchases, be aware of returns policies, and always keep your receipts – without them you won't have a leg to stand on.

Exchange policies at the souks are non-existent – shop owners may exchange an item for you or simply refuse to do so. Getting an item exchanged depends on each shop owner and your rate of success can fluctuate from one day to another. Souk vendors are usually friendly and helpful, but the fact that any returns are going to affect the money that goes into their own pockets may make them inflexible. For this reason, and also because some items may be of lower quality than at larger, more reputable shops, it is probably not wise to make any expensive purchases at the souks.

In May 2008, Sheikh Hamad bin Khalifa Al Thani signed the country's first consumer protection laws. The law enshrines the consumer's right to get fair compensation for any damage resulting from buying or using a commodity or service. It has also made it mandatory for the providers to replace the goods – in case of damage – or refund money, or repair the damage without any extra charges. The new law also allows the establishment of a consumer association, although this is currently still in the pipeline. The Consumer Protection Department in the Ministry of Economy and Commerce (english.mofa.gov.qa or through gov.qa) has also taken a more active stance and fined companies for violations including not adequately displaying the price on consumer goods. In 2009, many stores were prosecuted for violating the new law but some smaller outlets are slow to change. Your best advice is to keep all proof of purchase and be politely firm. However, for advice and complaints, call the hotline: 4494 5500.

Window shopping

Shipping

Should you have gathered some token pieces from your time in Qatar and wish to ship them home, there are several reputable companies able to assist you. However, this is not a very common practice and although some goods in Qatar might be cheaper than in your home country, by the time you add the cost of shipping, insurance and possible import duty, you probably will not be saving anything.

Deliveries Outside Doha

Shop staff may look at you in complete disbelief if you tell them you live outside of Doha city, and delivery of goods outside of the city boundaries can be problematic, sometimes taking days extra to arrive.

Assuming that you still want to ship, air freight is much quicker than sea freight, but it is also vastly more expensive. A cheaper solution is to find someone who is shipping something back to the same country; you may be able to share their container.

Goods Delivery Promises

Shops often run what looks like a very efficient delivery service, whilst you are in their shop. But then they subcontract the work to casual carriers who will stop work at a certain time of day, whether their deliveries are complete or not. This can be most frustrating if you have taken time from work to receive the deliveries. Often ringing the supplier will result in the phone not being answered; the major hypermarkets in Doha are the biggest offenders in this respect. Another regular inconvenience is the delivery driver who has got ahead of his schedule and telephones you to demand that you immediately leave work and return to your home, four hours before the prearranged time, because he is sat outside your house and waiting.

For importing goods, shipping company Aramex offers Qatar's residents the 'shop and ship' service where, for QR 160, you can establish personal mailing addresses in the US and UK, so that internet purchases can be shipped to you. With many companies including amazon.com offering free shipping for local orders, your purchases are sent to the addresses in the UK or US and then redirected through Aramex to you in Qatar. As a rule of thumb, the shipping rate for Qatar is QR 70 per kilogram. Borderlinx (borderlinx. com) also offers a similar service. The shipping companies listed below are reputable and they offer a worldwide service.

Beauty
Defined

Customer Care +974 4436 1111   www.51east.com.qa   FIFTY ONE EAST 51°

Shopping

Aramex Jaber Bin Ghaith St, Bu Hamour, 4420 0100, *aramex.com*
DHL Express Al Thuraya Complex, Salwa Rd, Ain Khaled, 4458 7888, *dhl.com.qa*
Federal Express Falcon Express, Nr Lulu Hypermarket, Old Airport, 4455 4191, *fedex.com*
First Flight Couriers (Middle East) WLL Nr Alma Tower, C-Ring Rd, Najma, 4443 1678, *firstflight.net*
Mumtaz Post (EMS) Al Tyseer, Nr Doha International Airport, Airport Street 42, Al Hilal, 4462 7779
UPS Gulf Agency Co Qatar, Airport Rd, Old Airport, 4432 2444, *ups.com*

How To Pay

There should be no difficulty parting with your cash; shops inside the malls accept cash, debit cards and credit cards. Cheques are not accepted, even if they are from a local bank, and smaller retailers, including the stalls in the souks, will only accept cash. Virtually all types of credit cards are accepted, including Visa, MasterCard, American Express and Diners Club and several banks encourage you to use your credit card whenever possible by offering discounts and loyalty programmes. Debit cards are becoming a very popular way to pay, as they save you the trouble of having to draw cash and you don't incur credit card interest charges. The most common debit card system is Visa Electron, which is offered by most major banks and accepted almost everywhere, except petrol stations. ATMs (or cash machines) are also widely available in malls, banks and even in some government buildings – you'll also find exchange bureaux in all the main malls, souks and banks.

Bargaining

Bargaining may seem strange to you at first, but it is an accepted way of doing business in this region. Most shop owners in the souks expect you to bargain with them, so the first price they quote is usually a vastly inflated one. Offer half of what they ask and work upwards from there. The key to bargaining is to remain pleasant at all times, but remain firm. Don't get flustered or irritable – the friendlier you are the more likely you are to get a good discount. A great technique is to say you are going to have a look around for a better price and walk out of the shop. Owners have been known to follow customers out into the street offering lower prices.

It is not normal practice to ask for discounts in shopping centres or department stores, as prices are fixed, but if you feel comfortable doing so, there is no harm in trying. Some of the smaller shops will offer you a discount to get the sale; while in jewellery shops you will almost always get a discount on the first price quoted.

The calculator is often used as a bargaining tool. Shop owners will tap away at the keys with great

flourish and will then present their offer. At this stage, you can simply clear the screen and type in your price and hand the calculator back to the vendor who will engage in more furious tapping. Eventually you will agree on a price; once this happens it would be considered bad form to leave without making the purchase. It's supposed to be fun so enjoy it – a skilled bargainer gets the best prices. After some difficult economic times, many retailers will offer a discount if you pay with cash, or throw in something extra like a DVD player with the purchase of a TV for example.

Sending Gifts Home

Sending gifts to your friends and family back home shouldn't be too taxing – there are many online stores ready to send your presents to international destinations. For cards and flowers, moonpig.com is a great online store where you can customise your own cards by uploading photos – it also offers a reminder service so you never forget important dates. Interflora (interflora.co.uk) also delivers a selection of gifts internationally and can often accommodate next-day delivery.

Shoes & Clothing Sizes

When shopping for clothes, deciphering sizes can become a bit of a pain, but the good news is that most clothes have international sizes printed on the label. Take note that a UK size 10 is a US 6; therefore the UK sizing is two sizes higher than the US sizing. To convert European sizes into US sizes subtract 32, so that makes a European 38 into a US 6. Also, a European 38 makes a UK size 10. When trying to figure out your shoe size; the general rule is that a women's UK 6 is a European 39 or US 8.5 and for men a UK 10 is a European 44 or US 10.5. If all this is way too difficult to remember, you should check around the store to see if a conversion chart is available or ask one of the shop assistants to help.

Plus & Petite Sizes

Until recently, women looking for clothing in size 14 and up were forced to go farther afield for fashionable offerings. All this has changed since Evans opened its branches in Landmark Shopping Mall (4488 0567) and Villaggio Mall (4413 5272), offering figure flattering clothing including trendy jeans, dresses, and great casual tops. Designer brand MaxMara has a plus-size label called Persona, which plies its high-end European catwalk fashion from a canal-side store in Villaggio Mall. Trendy store Splash (which has plus-size label Scarlett) and Marina Rinaldi's LaGrande Dame (4413 5560) are in Villaggio Mall. Department stores Debenhams (p.323) and Marks & Spencer (p.324) also have a good range. For affordable pieces and current fashion head to H&M, while Punto Roma (4413 5064, Villaggio Mall) offers modern designs in European sizes 40 to 54 (UK sizes 12 to 22).

The Pearl Qatar

Top 10 Things That Are Cheaper In Qatar

Soft Drinks

A can of Coke or Pepsi costs just QR 1.5 when bought from a corner stop, a petrol station or a supermarket. The price per can is even cheaper when you buy your favourite drink by the case. Unfortunately, this bargain price does not always survive the transition to restaurant menus, where a can of pop can set you back a shocking QR 15 or more – that is quite a mark up.

Petrol

Filling up your car here is cheaper than in many other countries and often significantly so. For a gallon of petrol you will pay QR 5.50 at a Doha pump, but the same would cost you the equivalent of around QR 10 in South Africa, QR 17 in the UK, QR 8 in America, QR 11.50 in Australia, QR 10.50 in Canada, QR 14 in India and a whopping QR 19 in parts of Europe.

Cinema Tickets

You will pay between QR 35 and QR 55 for a cinema ticket in Doha (QR 55 is usually for a 3D movie). The downside is that here in Doha, there are no concessions if you are a child, a student or a pensioner, and the ticket price is the same, no matter what time of day it is (whereas in other cities, morning and matinee shows are cheaper).

Street dining in Souk Waqif

Tailoring

Whipping up a new suit or having a dress custom made for you is a costly affair in most countries. In Doha, where cheap tailoring and fabric are the highlights of the souks, you can have a suit made up for as little as QR 500, a long dress for around QR 100 or a blouse for QR 50.

Home Help

Having a cleaner come in a few times a week to hoover and dust your home for you is seen as a luxury in most countries, but in Qatar it is an affordable convenience. For as little as QR 30 per hour, you can hire a cleaner (p.94) to help you around the house with cleaning and even ironing. You can also get a live-in maid; salaries vary anywhere from QR 1,500 a month to QR 2,500 a month.

Personal Grooming

Having pretty feet and hands comes cheap in Qatar; you can get a manicure and pedicure at any of the nail salons for around QR 100. Men can also neaten for a snip at several salons in the Musheireb area where a shampoo, hair cut and a head massage costs around QR 40.

Al Zubara Fort

Trips To Dubai

With flydubai (flydubai.com) now operating between Doha and Dubai, the price of enjoying a weekend getaway in the emirate has dropped significantly. A round trip ticket will cost you QR 500 and sometimes even less, depending on how far in advance you purchase your ticket and the time you choose to fly. Hotels can be on the expensive side, but as a GCC resident you can often get good rates. See Long-Weekend Trips (p.260) for suggestions of other short haul destinations.

Eating Out

Enjoying a three-course meal for two and a few drinks in a fine-dining restaurant will probably cost more or less the same as in other cities, but cheap, street-side dining is one of Doha's great bargains. Whether you snack on a QR 5 chicken or beef shawarma at one of the many places in the Al Sadd area, or feast on a QR 25 Indian or Pakistani style chicken tikka meal complete with salad, chips and rice (which feeds four) from Sara (4442 7024) in Musheireb, it will be hard to find such delicious, authentic food at a cheaper price.

Cigarettes

That QR 7 pack of Marlboro Lights would set you back the equivalent of over QR 30 in the UK, QR 15 in the US and QR 25 in Australia. It's good news for visiting relatives, who always want to take a few sneaky cartons back home, but bad news for smokers who have little financial incentive to quit here.

Cultural Hotspots

Entrance to most museums in Doha is free, including the esteemed Museum of Islamic Art (p.207). A visit to the Doha Zoo (p.216) will set you back QR 5 per adult and kids under 6 years old get in free. A visit to the Camel Racetrack (p.237) is also free, (call 4487 2028, to inquire about the dates before heading there).

Tailoring & Bespoke Services

There is no shortage of tailors in Doha and once you find a good one you should be able to have anything you want made – whether that's a wedding dress, a suit or more casual items. Tailors can usually follow your own drawings and instructions, work from a picture from a magazine or duplicate an existing garment. This often makes tailoring a cheaper option than buying from designer stores.

Word of mouth is usually the best way to find a tailor who is competent and reliable. The area around Souk Waqif is full of little tailoring shops for both men and women. Just walk into a few of the outlets and ask about the materials and what they specialise in. You don't even have to buy the materials from the tailors, as there are plenty of textile shops in the same area that should have something suitable. There are several tailors in Al Mansoura just past the Jaidah Flyover, the souk area (especially Souk Faleh, p.328) and around Al Rawndaq, on Al Taribya Street.

You can also head to the souks for your fabric; Souk Al Asiery (p.328) holds an extensive array of inexpensive fabric, from cotton to lace, while Souk Al Dira (p.328) nearby has high-end fabrics – some costing up to QR 1,000 a metre for silk. These fabrics are often used to make abayas and Indian saris. One of the most famous fabric stores is Bombay Silk (4441 2715), with a staggering range of material in all colours. The store has recently relocated to a brand new location on Salwa Road (near the LG Showroom) with a further branch at Barwa Village near to the Al Wakrah area.

It is worth noting that the complete redevelopment of the centre of Doha in the Heart of Doha project is causing many of these businesses to relocate to other areas or sometimes simply to close down; at the time of writing the situation is very fluid.

After you've picked your material and have been measured, you will probably have to haggle for the best price. A shirt should cost you around QR 80 and a suit around QR 300 to QR 400. Prices are extremely reasonable and standards of workmanship are generally very high. Shirts can be tailored in a day, but for suits you will have to allow a week or so. Many places will also do small alterations including hemming trousers (QR 10 to QR 20).

Al Awadi Textile & Tailoring Souq Najada, 4443 0059
Al Misk Textiles & Tailoring Abdulla Bin Thani St, Musheireb, 4432 1141, *almisktailor.com*
Glorex Trading Company Nr Q-tel, Al Musheirib St, Fereej Mohd Bin Jasim, 4441 3967
The Raymond Shop Al Watan Center, 4441 3967
Samraa Center Textiles & Tailoring City Plaza, Al Sadd
Sara's Secrets Al Sadd, 4432 1030
Tash Haute Couture Textiles Al Awadi Group, Nr Royal Plaza, Al Sadd, 4432 9449, *tashtextiles.com*

WHAT & WHERE TO BUY

With so much choice, there should be little problem finding what you need. From kids' toys to souvenirs and home entertainment, this section lets you know what is out there and the best places to hunt down whatever it is that you're after.

Alcohol

The sale of alcohol is closely monitored and restricted to licensed establishments in Qatar. Qatar Distribution Company (QDC) is the sole importer of alcohol and supplies licensed hotels, clubs and restaurants. It also runs the only liquor store in Qatar. In order to purchase alcohol to take home and consumer, you will need to apply for a QDC liquor licence, which will have a stipulated monthly allowance for purchases (this will be calculated against your salary). You will also have to pay a substantial deposit, the amount of which is dependent on your allowance. This deposit is however refundable when you leave Qatar. With only one shop serving all liquor licence holders in Qatar, be prepared for very long queues ahead of public holidays when people stock up and buy in bulk just before the store closes. Bars and restaurants will serve alcohol only to those over the age of 21 and most of the four or five-star hotels have a licence to sell alcohol for consumption on the premises. Most independent restaurants (those not in hotels) do not have liquor licences. This includes the popular restaurants and cafes found in Souk Waqif, Katara Cultural Village and the various shopping malls.

Neither visitors nor residents are permitted to import alcohol into the country, although you may purchase duty-free alcohol when exiting the country. Upon arrival at Doha International Airport, all of your bags will be screened for alcoholic beverages and any shipments from abroad will also be screened. Customs authorities will confiscate any alcohol they find, but you may collect it upon your departure from the country.

Qatar Distribution Company

Nr Qatar Technical College, Street 668 Al Maamoura
4469 9412
Map **1 H13**
QDC offers a wide range of alcohol and a selection of over 700 wines from all over the world – it also sells cigars and liqueur-filled chocolates. Its prices are expensive compared to similar shops in non-Muslim countries, although not unreasonable. After a few shopping trips you should discover the 'best buys' including affordable Old World and New World wines. QDC is closed on Fridays and for all major public holidays (look out for signs in the shop).

Art

While it may not have the variety of some other cities, Qatar's art scene has enough to offer the most avid art lovers, with galleries holding monthly exhibitions by both local and international artists. Qatari Hosh Art Gallery, in Souk Waqif, (6619 1440) sells work by Qatari artists. Works of art are more expensive here but the gallery is worth visiting for its great selection. The collection also includes framed and unframed pieces, glass paintings, acrylic oil canvases, pencil drawings and watercolour paintings.

Shopping malls are often used by local artists to display and sell their work and occasionally exhibitions are held in the display centres at the Katara Cultural Village (p.362) where they sell their pieces.

In the Souk Waqif area is Al Markhiya Gallery (4442 8007, almarkhiyagallery.com) which holds regular exhibitions for both local and established talent from the region. Here you'll find paintings, calligraphy, sculptures and photographs for sale.

Auction house Sotheby's (4452 8333, sothebys. com) has recently opened an office in Doha and it held its first auctions in March in 2009. As well as dealing in a collection of fine art, jewellery and other interesting pieces, its experts can assist with valuing your own items.

For more modest pieces, Home Centre (p.305) and Homes R Us (p.305) sell canvases that are great for decorating your villa or flat. You can also make your own work of art at Café Ceramique (4476 1100) where you will be able to pick and paint a piece of pottery which is then fired and glazed, to be collected a few days later.

Alternatively, if you're looking for something unique and individual to your home, office or property, visit mackenzieart.com to enquire about customised paintings or wall art in any colour, texture or style suiting to your tastes.

Art & Craft Supplies

Whether arts and crafts are a serious hobby, a part-time passion or you simply want to get creative with the kids, you should be able to get your hands on anything you need in Doha. For junior artists, basic supplies can be picked up cheaply at any supermarket or toy department, but for sparkles, glitter and other fun kids' art materials, try Jarir Bookstore (p.298), which is an especially good place to start if you are a beginner. The store stocks specialist hobby materials for silk screening, dyeing fabric, painting, drawing and needlepoint, plus good quality paints in a range of colours and a reasonable selection of brushes and craft items such as lollipop sticks; if you aren't sure what you are doing, you can wander upstairs and find a book to teach you how. Some of the other bookstores in Doha, such as Ibn Al Qayyim Bookstore (4486 3533), stock an adequate selection of drawing materials, paper and

supplies. Daiso (4469 8999) and Banzai (4431 3115) are Japanese stores that are great for oriental paper and craft products such as synthetic flowers, stamps, stick-ons, cut-outs and decorations. If scrapbooking is your thing, I Spy Bookshop (p.298) and Ibn Al Qayyim Bookstore (4486 3533) have a range of materials to get you started. For the more serious artist, Colour Note Company (p.295) has the best range of professional supplies and will order anything you need (if it doesn't already stock it). Likewise, Alwan (4411 5268) has a very good range of supplies, and the stationery branches of Al Rawnaq are also worth a browse. If you prefer someone to do the work for you, there is a cluster of artist shops on B Ring Road, such as Al Ahram Arts (4443 1989) and Al Bayan Neon (albayan-neon.com) that do commercial screen printing, decorative wall painting, stamps, engraving, banners and signboards, but are also happy to quote for individual projects.

Al Rawnaq Stationery
Al Markhiya St Al Markhiya **4488 1878**
Map **2 K3**

This is a cheap and cheerful shop housing an amazing stock of stationery, blank canvases, coloured paper, cheap paints, brushes, drawing material and various odds and ends. It's a great option for cheering up your kids' bedrooms on a shoestring, with cheap wall stickers, rugs and posters. There is another branch on Airport Road called Al Rawnaq Trading Complex (4466 9555) that also sells toys, kitchenware and household goods, or visit the branch in the Fabric Souk (4441 4505) for buttons, feathers, felt and ribbon.

Alwan
City Center Doha Al Dafna **4411 5268**
citycenterdoha.com
Map **2 Q2**

A variety of arts, crafts and hobby supplies are on offer here, including equipment for painting, drawing, sketching, batik, marbling, stencilling, spray painting, 3D craft painting and origami. Its stores also stock a good range of paints from Daler Rowney, Colour & Co, Giotto, Javana, Hobby Colours, Das Colour, Solo Goya, Liquitex, Louvre and Tulip, with Dynasty brushes and Phoenix canvas products. Another branch is located in The Centre (4443 4782).

Colour Note Company
Nr Doha Clinic, Al Mirqab Al Jadeed St Al Sadd **4432 2868**
colournote.net
Map **2 L10**

A fantastic selection of quality art supplies, mostly sourced from Europe, is sold here. Items available include plaster of Paris, wax, moulds, wires and quality products made by Pebeo. If you can't find what you want here then they will order it in for you.

Shopping

Baby Items

Basic baby items are all readily available in Qatar, but there isn't as much variety as you would find in some bigger cities around the world. For basic supplies, all supermarkets and pharmacies sell nappies, baby wipes, baby food, formula, dummies and bottles. Stores such as Babyshop and others listed below have a good selection of budget clothing, nursery essentials, prams, car seats, feeding items and toys.

For clothing, there are several popular brands such as Adams Kids (4487 0903); Carters (4469 8999); Osh Kosh B'Gosh which is at the Hyatt Plaza (4469 7339) and Landmark Shopping Mall (4486 2012); Pumpkin Patch at City Center Doha (4493 0774), The Mall (4466 4597) and Villaggio Mall (4450 7620); and Tape L'oeil at Landmark Shopping Mall (4487 5222) and Villaggio Mall (4450 7659). Babycare (4437 5796) in Emporium (p.323) stocks a high-end range of baby clothing and nursery furniture from Escada, Kenzo and Paquito.

There are toy departments in all major supermarkets and you'll find toys for sale in speciality shops and corner stores all over the country, but be mindful of safety standards when purchasing cheaper items. Early Learning Centre (4486 6579), Kiddy Zone (p.311) and Toys R Us (p.311) are popular for toys and gifts. If you see something you like, buy it straight away as it may not be there on your next visit.

Popular clothing stores such as Gap, H&M and Next can be found in the main malls, and they all stock good quality baby clothing.

Dirt-cheap clothing can be found at Al Safeer Center (4462 6177), Jamil Fashion (4462 1082), Sana (4443 0180) and in the children's clothing departments of all major supermarkets, but you may need to have a good look through to find a good-quality bargain.

Max (4493 4760) and Shoemart (p.304) are both excellent for cheap, good quality shoes for babies, or, at the other end of the scale, try Jacadi Paris (4432 1725) for luxury newborn items.

Al Rawnaq Stationery (p.295) is terrific for decorating your nursery with cheap wall stickers, rugs, canvas prints and posters. Baby slings, disposable nappy sacks and stylish nappy bags won't be found anywhere, so bring them with you if you plan to use them, likewise any other light items (such as cot mattress protectors and night lights) that you might be able to pick up more cheaply back home. If you're shipping items from abroad, you should bear in mind that some brands, such as Bugaboo, aren't available here so you won't be able to find accessories that match.

There are plenty of international websites that offer shipping to Qatar, so if you're struggling to find an item or brand, it's worth seeing if it can be ordered from overseas. Some good UAE-based options are Bubs Boutique (bubsboutique.com) and Just Kidding (justkidding-me.com). For a funky selection of clothing, toys and accessories from Australia, try Baby's Got Style (babysgotstyle.com), The Hip Infant (thehipinfant.com.au) or Ten Little Indians (tenlittleindians.com.au), or visit UK-based Dribble Factory (dribblefactory.com) for fun slogan tees. My Precious Kid (mypreciouskid.com) has a range of goods that promote child safety and Letterbox (letterbox.co.uk) has plenty of newborn gift ideas.

The classifieds and forum sections of local websites (see list p.23) are crammed with pre-loved baby clothes and nursery furniture and you can usually pick up a pretty good bargain. Don't forget to put your used items up for sale once you have finished with them.

Babyshop
City Center Doha Al Dafna **4483 8508**
landmarkgroupme.com
Map **2 Q2**

You'll find everything you need to get you started, from bibs and bottles, to cribs and car seats. Nursery furniture, travel essentials, bedding, feeding items, baby monitors and toys are abundant, but popular items such as breastfeeding pillows and stair gates are rarely on the shelves. Prices vary greatly depending on the brand (there's the more affordable in-house Juniors range or Ferrari and Maclaren products). Clothing is cheap and basics, such as newborn sleepsuits, come in multipacks. Two other branches are located in Centrepoint (4428 9201) and near the Mannai Roundabout (4444 8179).

Chicco/Tuc Tuc
City Center Doha Al Dafna **4483 0880**
chicco.com
Map **2 Q2**

Like most Italian engineering, Chicco products are sleek and cleverly-designed. Items are excellent quality and meet high safety standards. Transport systems usually fit into each other, so you can buy a removable car seat that fits into a pram base. The colours and styles of all baby products have been extensively researched to stimulate your baby. Prices are on the higher side but it is worth paying the extra for the quality. You'll also find an outlet in Villaggio Mall (4450 7068).

Mamas & Papas
Villaggio Mall Baaya **4451 7879**
mamasandpapas.com
Map **2 B11**

Pick up well-designed, stylish products for babies and mums-to-be here. There is a good variety of items including toys, car seats, pushchairs, cribs, nursery items, decorations, maternity clothes and feeding items. Although this is one of the more costly options, it remains popular for gifts and newborn essentials.

Mothercare
City Center Doha Al Dafna **4483 0475**
mothercare.com
Map **2 Q2**
This long-established store remains a firm favourite for baby essentials. It has a particularly good selection of clothing, cots, bedding, pushchairs and car seats as well as dummies, bottles and bibs. There are branches in City Center Doha (4483 0475), inside Debenhams at City Center Doha (4483 2668), Hyatt Plaza (4469 7288), Landmark (4486 8440) and The Mall (4467 8844) and each store has a designated baby changing and feeding room.

Prenatal
Villaggio Mall Baaya **4413 5519**
prenatal.com
Map **2 B11**
The stylish range of products offered here is presented in a spacious store which is easy to browse in. Maternity wear, nursery items, gifts and newborn clothing and essentials are all available. It also has a branch in Landmark Shopping Mall (4486 1712).

Bicycles
At first glance, Qatar may not seem like the most bicycle-friendly place in the world, but there is a very active cycling scene; the country is, after all, mostly flat, if a bit hot in summer. Road and mountain biking are popular and you can find an adequate (albeit expensive) range of quality-built equipment for both. Serious cyclists tend to stock up on gear in their home country then ship it over, or they may order goods online. A very popular website that ships to Qatar is UK-based Chain Reaction (chainreactioncycles. com); its site features almost every cycling-related item or accessory you can think of. Another good site is probikekit.com which also has a good range of gear. US-based companies Performance Bike (performancebike.com) and Jenson (jensonUSA. com) offer shipping to Qatar by arrangement. All have an impressive range of items available, along with fantastic offers and sales.

Skate Shack (p.297) on Salwa Road has the best selection of brands and Sportmart (4443 0311) stocks Specialised frames and gear. Strings & Wheelz (p.297) is expanding its range of bicycles to include Cannondale, Specialized and Schwinn products and GO Sport (p.304) also have bikes, accessories and clothing for all ages.

Children's bikes and tricycles are available at Babyshop (p.296), Smart Kids Toys (p.311), Toys R Us (p.311) and most toy stores and supermarkets.

If you are looking for something cheaper and probably Chinese made, for yourself or the kids, a collection of shops selling bicycles and accessories are located along Al Mansoora Street in Najma and

there are is another group of bicycle shops around TV roundabout, but make sure you are not compromising on safety. Toys R Us and Carrefour also sell mid and lower range cycles.

Local riders group, Qatar Chain Reaction (qatarchainreaction.org) has a classifieds section for people wishing to buy and sell used bikes, equipment and gear.

Skate Shack
Al Ain Complex, Salwa Rd Ain Khaled **4469 2532**
skate-shack.com
Map **1 E12**
You'll find top brand name bicycles such as Trek and Gary Fisher, and a wide range of safety gear, such as lights, helmets, and protective pads at this store. You'll also find a range of clothes, spare parts and padlocks – the shop assistants are helpful and knowledgeable and they are willing to order a specific model if it isn't in stock. Not all bikes are on display so you will need to ask the staff if you can't find what you are after.

Strings & Wheelz
Villaggio Mall Baaya **4450 7871**
Map **2 B11**
This store stocks bicycles, clothing and accessories from Cannondale, Schwinn and Specialized. New equipment arrives all the time and the shop strives to expand its range. Staff are very helpful and will help you locate everything you need. The store also carries Wilson and Dunlop equipment for racket sports such as tennis, squash and badminton.

Books
The availability of English-language books and magazines in Qatar has improved greatly over the last few years. Most mainstream English-language titles can be found locally in one of the many bookstores of Doha; see below for listings. This said, it must be noted that avid readers may still feel limited by the selection on offer. For example, searching for a specific author's collection, finding out-of-print titles or books in other languages is challenging. However, you can of course always resort to ordering from an online retailer such as amazon.com – provided you don't mind the delivery delay.

The largest booksellers are Virgin Megastore and Jarir Bookstore, with a few retailers catering to a specialised audience. For instance, Marks & Spencer (p.324) sells a variety of British cookery and novelty books and I Spy Book Shop specialises in children's books. Grocery stores Carrefour, Lulu Hypermarket and Megamart sell international magazines and newspapers, along with a tidy selection of best-sellers. Keep in mind that international periodicals may be sold a short time after their initial release and they can be two to three times more expensive than you would pay back home. Moreover, you will find that exposed body parts and other illicit content are censored. Despite the expanding options for buying English-language books in Qatar, many residents continue to buy their books abroad, or sign up with Aramex or Borderlinx's shop & ship services (see shipping p.283) to purchase books from amazon.com and other online retailers. Buying abroad or online offers the ease of purchasing books in your preferred language and eliminates the need to scour the local bookshops in search of a specific title or author. While buying books online may be cheaper than buying the same titles locally, delivery costs can add up. Expect to add another week or two onto the retailers' delivery time when ordering online and be aware that customs officials may investigate your shipment.

A fast, easy and inexpensive way to expand your book collection is to visit a used-book fair sponsored by schools and other organisations. Doha Mums' (p.132) have monthly book-swap coffee mornings at the Starbucks in Landmark Mall (p.334).

For the growing number of people who own iPads and the many makes of Android Pads, the obvious solution is to download electronic books and magazines on line from the likes of Amazon and Kobo. The selection is immense, they are yours within a few seconds of deciding what you want and cost is much less than a printed book or magazine.

Family Bookshop
Barwa Village Al Wakra **4413 5331**
Map **Qatar Country Map D4**
Family Bookshop is a small neighbourhood store between Salwa Road and Al Waab Street (near Aspire Park). Since its branch in the Sheraton closed in June 2009, the store has crammed as many books as possible into its limited floor space. The vast majority of its books are written in English, ranging from mainstream fiction novels to self-help guides and cookery books. Shoppers looking for children's books will find a good range of colouring books, storybooks and novels. It also sells a decent selection of maps, travel guides, reference manuals and study guides.

I Spy Book Shop
City Center Doha Al Dafna **4493 4482**
ispybookshop.net
Map **2 Q2**
I Spy Book Shop has an engaging selection of educational toys and books for children – there is also a small selection of children's books in French. There is a good assortment of mainstream fiction and non-fiction, textbooks, cookery books, travel guides and business titles. The store will obtain books in any language, from any part of the world, by special order via its website, over the phone or in store.

Jarir Bookstore
Nr Ramada Intersection, Salwa Rd New Al Mirqab **4444 0212**
jarirbookstore.com
Map **2 M10**
A similar collection of Arabic and English language books to Virgin Megastore, but there is a much wider selection of international magazines and newspapers in many different languages. You can buy a beverage from its Costa coffee bar too. Also on sale are a collection of electronics, home office supplies and stationery. You may order in books, as long as they are stocked in one of its GCC branches. Another outlet is located in Jarir-Al Rayyan Showroom (4411 4322).

Virgin Megastore > p.xiv, 284
Villaggio Mall Baaya **4413 5824**
virginmegastore.me
Map **2 B11**
This well-known store holds books in Arabic, English and French, including new releases, classics, magazines and reference books – you'll also find some guidebooks, coffee table books and maps of Qatar. There are sections for children and teens and the latest DVD and CD releases. If an item isn't in stock, they can also order books from their warehouse in Dubai. The outlet in the Landmark Shopping Mall (4418 2242) sells a similar assortment but the selection is much smaller.

Camera Equipment
There is an adequate range of photography equipment available in Qatar and you'll find many of the newest camera models, although they may take a while to hit the shelves. Most brands are stocked here (with the exception of Leica), but considering the lack of tax, prices aren't as low as they are in some other countries.

Digital models dominate the shelves of electronic shops, supermarkets and photo processing outlets. Shops around the old Sofitel (now the Mercure Hotel) area carry a wide range of brands that might cost you less if you are prepared to haggle. Bear in mind, however, that you may save money but you will have better buyer protection and returns options from the larger outlets.

You might find a better choice online and save money by taking advantage of currency exchange rates. Two popular US websites for cameras and photography equipment are Adorama (adorama.com) and B&H Photo (bhphotovideo.com), or you can try Kremlin Optics (kremlinoptics.com), Precision Photo (bocaphoto.com), or T4 Cameras (t4cameras.co.uk) based in the UK or Camera Farm (camerafarm.com.au) in Australia. Used and collectible photographic equipment can be purchased at Classic Cameras (bpwltd.com), Collectible Cameras (collectiblecameras.com) and Canadian store Harry's

Pro Shop (harrysproshop.com). Used books, manuals and reference guides can be purchased at Camera Books (camerabooks.com) or Spanish-based online store Kowasa (kowasa.com). Berger Brothers (berger-bros.com) is another good camera store that will accept international orders by telephone. Closer to home, digital cameras are available for purchase at cellcamshop.com and ellamart.com.

Salam (p.324) carries top-end equipment from Canon, Manfrotto, Nikon, Noritsu and Pentz. Fifty One East (p.323) stocks Sony cameras, tripods, lenses and accessories while Jumbo Electronics (p.309) carries Olympus. Virgin Megastore (p.312)) at Villaggio Mall has a good range of Canon and Sony cameras and Jarir Bookstore (p.298) stocks various cameras and accessories. For underwater cameras and camera housings, head to Al Mushiri (p.299).

Wherever you buy your camera equipment, be sure to keep your receipt and check that the warranty you get is an international one (especially important if you are buying a camera to take back to your home country). Don't just take the retailer's word for it, actually ask to open the box and read the warranty yourself to make sure.

There is no shortage of places where you can drop off your memory card for photo processing but the service isn't cheap. Gulf Colours (4444 0343), Fuji Film (4487 5077) and Kodak Gallery (4483 9522) have branches around Doha that can print photos from memory card and CD. For a cheaper alternative, you can upload your prints onto specialist printing websites such as Foto.com (foto.com) and have your order sent to you. For servicing and repairs under factory warranty, Canon and Nikon cameras should be taken to Salam (p.324), while Sony models can be taken to the service centre at Fifty One East (p.323). The main branch of Jumbo Electronics (4442 3303) and Kings Camera Tech (p.299) in the old Sofitel area both perform general repairs and maintenance.

Al Mushiri

Nr Paradise Hotel, Gulf St Fereej Bin Mahmoud
4442 3030
Map 2 N8

This specialist electronics store has a good range of Ricoh and Agfa devices, plus Minolta binoculars and CNC underwater cameras and housings. Friendly and informed staff will help you with your selection and assist you with any after sales advice and care.

Kings Camera Tech

Nr Q-Tel, Abdullah Bin Thani St Musheireb
4435 5679
Map 2 P8

You'll find a wide range of digital SLR and compact cameras from brands such as Nikon and Fuji. Also on sale are tripods, camera cases and accessories. The staff are very welcoming and knowledgeable and love to talk cameras – they can also service most types of cameras on site.

Salam

The Mall Old Airport 4467 2200
salams.com
Map 2 R13

Until recently, Salam was the sole dealer for official Nikon merchandise in Qatar. Today, they carry a good range of high-end cameras and accessories from both Nikon and Canon. There is a photography studio, photo processing lab and maintenance and servicing facility for both Nikon and Canon too. There is another branch of the store at 63 Maysaloun Street (4448 5555).

Car Accessories

For most people in Qatar, cars are regarded as sheer necessity and any serious vehicle customisation and modification is limited to a specialist market. With a bit of legwork, you can indeed pimp your ride into something spectacular, but be prepared to invest plenty of time, patience and money into your project. A good starting point is Car Seat Qatar (p.300), on Salwa Road, or wander through the multitude of shops near the Crazy Signal on the B Ring Road. Al Ansari Accessories (4444 5785) is one of the most popular. Head out to Area 23 of the Industrial Area for customised paint shops and car-parts dealers.

Car 2000 (4441 0104) and Al Obeidly (4441 1412), both near the Crazy Signal, have a good range of car stereos, speakers and MP3 players, or continue along B Ring Road toward Sana Roundabout to find Car Music (4431 4647) and Lebanon Rock (4442 9651). There is a handful of stores in the old Sofitel area, such as Bashir Radio (4442 3516), or try along Commercial Street of Al Gharafa, where you'll also find people to install parts. Al Mater, Al Qateem Street in the Old Airport Area has several shops near the car wash centres.

GPS systems are available at Carrefour, PC One (4450 2555), Virgin Megastore (Villaggio Mall branch) and the electronics section of Jarir Bookstore (p.298). Jassim Al Lingawi Trading (4441 3356), in Souk Jabor, specialises in Garmin handsets, maps and software while Consolidated Gulf Company is the sole retailer for Nokia GPS products. Visit the website cgulfc.com for store locations and timings.

Basic stocks of standard accessories are available from Carrefour and Giant Stores including, car stereos, steering wheel covers, floor mats, air fresheners, jump leads and tools. For more sophisticated tools, car maintenance products and garage equipment, the Teyseer Service Centre (teyseer.com.qa) has branches on Salwa Road, in the Industrial Area and opposite the airport.

Window tinting is widely available and is often used to beat the sun and heat. Before you proceed, you must obtain a permit from any branch of the traffic department (see list on p.44). The permit costs QR 24, payable to the cashier. You do not need to show your ID or have any documentation (such as a letter of consent from your employer) to obtain the permit. If you are pulled over by the police and cannot produce evidence of a permit for your window tinting, the police will ask you to peel the tinting from your windows and you may be liable for a fine.

The percentage of all window tinting must be within legal limits; tinting of the front and back windows is illegal but the side passenger windows may be tinted up to 70%. Cheap tints can fade in the searing summer heat, may not come with a warranty and are unlikely to offer much UV protection, however, they cost around QR 80 per window and can be performed at just about any garage or accessory shop.

Several companies along Salwa Road (on the right after Al Aziziyah Roundabout when heading toward the Industrial Area) offer tinting that meets US standards for solar protection against UVA and UVB, with a five year warranty. A few of these stores are: Titanium (4468 7299, titanium-tint.com), Llumar (4487 6655, llumar.com) and Zeibart (4450 2829, ziebart.com). Any branch of Auto Magic (carmaxx-qatar.com) will do a similar job for around QR 500 (or cheaper). It will cost you around QR 1,500 to tint four windows on an SUV and around QR 1,200 for a sedan car – which should keep the inside of your vehicle around 70% cooler.

Car Seat Qatar

Teyseer Service Centre, Decoration R/A Bu Samra
4469 2621
carseatqatar.com
Map **2 J12**

The sole agents in Qatar for KAHN, Lehmann and Remus products, and approved retailers of ART Tuning, Hamann, Arden, Gemballa, JE Design, HRE Wheels and Real Wheels. Exterior car accessories on offer include alloy wheels, chrome accessories, exhaust systems, spoiler kits and tyres, or you can deck out your interior with leather or wood finishings.

Carpets

Traditional carpets are a popular souvenir for residents and visitors to Qatar, but it pays to do your research before you buy. Most retailers are honest and genuinely helpful, but the range of choice is so varied that it is worth knowing the difference between the various piles and weaves, and how to feel a carpet for its quality. Some basic advice on how to inspect a carpet is to turn it over and view its backing. If the pattern is clearly depicted on the reverse, and if the knotting is neat, then the carpet will be of a higher quality.

The type of carpet you buy greatly depends on how you intend to use it. You can pay tens of thousands for a good quality carpet that will be a good long-term investment. Cheaper carpets serve a useful purpose in the large, concrete houses of Doha. Sturdily made from synthetic materials such as polypropylene, they help to reduce noise and keep your house warm in the cooler months, plus they are colourfast and easy to clean.

You can pick up good-sized floor rugs for only a few hundred riyals in home stores such as Homes R Us (p.305), Home Centre (p.305), Ramez Stores (4465 5170), The One (p.306) or the furniture outlet of Al Shaheen (4435 8635) on Airport Road. Still machine-made, but slightly better quality, are carpets made from wool or wool blends (wool and nylon mix). These tend to come in more attractive designs and a wider variety of colours. Nabco Furniture (p.306) has a good selection from Belgium, or try the furniture shops around Decoration Roundabout, Souk Haraj (p.328) or Reshi (p.306) in Landmark Mall (p.334). Department stores such as Doha City (4441 2734) are good for a wide range of bargain pieces, or wander through the various outlets dotted around Souk Waqif, such as Darriche (p.317).

The most expensive carpets are made from smooth and durable high-quality silk; these usually come from Iran. Handmade examples can fetch around QR

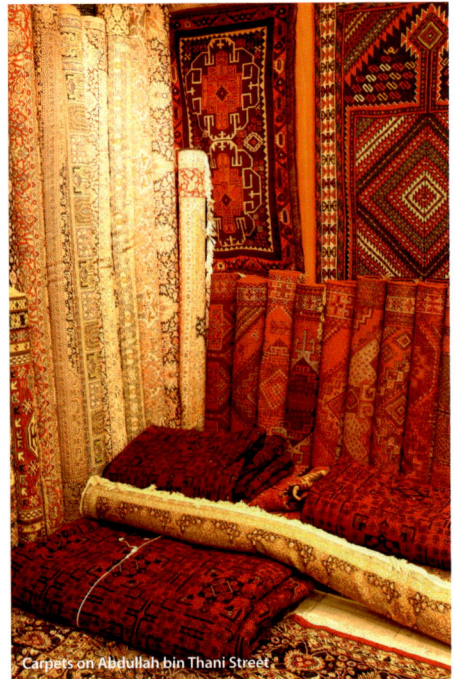

Carpets on Abdullah bin Thani Street

35,000, but you may be able to grab one during sale periods for as little as QR 15,000. Original Art (4413 1325) in Royal Plaza has a small selection of quality floor coverings.

You should haggle for a better price whenever you shop for a carpet, even during sale periods, and don't worry if lots of carpets are rolled out before you. Each store has an impressive array of styles and types of carpets for sale and most vendors will be happy to show you their collection without pressuring you too much to buy. International shipping is also available at many outlets upon request.

Al Mansoora Carpet Centre
Al Mansoora St Al Mansoura 4432 8855
Map 2 Q10

A good stop for when you need to buy a range of synthetic carpeting, rugs and underlay sold finished or per metre – hallway runners start from as little as QR 5 per metre. Staff will gladly come to your home and take measurements for big projects or wall-to-wall carpeting. Delivery and carpet laying services are also available.

Bradran Carpets
City Center Doha Al Dafna 4483 1298
bradran.com
Map 2 Q2

Be wowed by this store's beautiful range of Persian rugs and carpets in all sizes and weaves. Styles include the tougher, coarsely woven rugs sourced from Hamadan and Hariz, the large, distinct magenta-hued rugs from the Mashad region, Kurdish influenced designs of Quchan, and the world-famous intricate and delicate creations from Isfahan and Tabriz. Also visit its branch in The Mall (4467 8886).

The Homesmiths
City Center Doha Al Dafna 4483 0887
homesmithsonline.com
Map 2 Q2

Homesmiths has an exquisite range of home furnishings including Kashmiri, Persian and Turkish carpets, antique and reproduction furniture from China and India, and hand-made and hand-embroidered curtain fabric and bed linen.

Kashmir Handicrafts Emporium
Al Mirqab Al Jadeed St Fereej Al Nasr 4443 2761
the-rugman.com
Map 2 K10

Gathered together in this store are a selection of beautiful pieces from Kashmir and Afghanistan which are hand-made from pure wool. Knowledgeable and friendly staff will assist you in choosing from a vast selection on display. Carpets come in a variety of oriental-style colours and sizes.

Oriental Carpet Company
Al Jazeera St, Off C Ring Rd Fereej Bin Mahmoud 4447 9794
Map 2 M8

A favourite with expats, OCC has a wide selection of carpets on offer. The staff are friendly and helpful without pushing you into a sale. The choice ranges from durable wool rugs to stunning hand-made silk pieces. Items are reasonably priced and you will always walk away with a discount, whether you asked for one or not.

World Of Handmade Carpets
Nr Jaidah Flyover, Al Muntazah St Rawdat Al Khail 4432 2472
Map 2 N10

Features a large selection of quality carpets and home accessories, such as side tables and fancy lighting. Friendly staff are pleased to explain the various types of rugs and carpets that are on display and can advise on the different styles and colour choices.

Computers

The vast majority of computer shops, with the exception of a few stores, are located in the Musheireb area. Fifty One East (p.323) is an authorised Apple retailer and it also sells Sony VAIOs. Here you can find the latest gadgets, accessories and the latest computers. This store is also slated to become the anchor tenant for the new Lagoona Mall (p.332).

For the past few years, Fifty One East has been operating an electronics service centre on Salwa Road (4425 7844). Here it offers after sales support and IT consultation for the brands it sells. Jarir Bookstore (p.298) sells international brands of computers and accessories like HP, Apple, Dell, Sony and Toshiba. It is also an authorised service centre and provides IT support for HP and Dell.

Computers are stocked at a wide variety of shops including Carrefour (p.325), Lulu Hypermarket (p.325). the upperfloor of Giant Stores in Hyatt Plaza is always worth checking, as usually their prices are slightly lower than the rest; all of these stores also offer technical care and repairs at a reasonable rate. Emax (p.308) has a wide selection of electronics (and competitive prices). The computer selection is big and comprises brand names like Sony, LG, HP, Toshiba and Acer. Its staff are friendly, knowledgeable and will give you great information about the electronics you are looking to purchase. Virgin Megastore (p.312) has an excellent selection of PCs, as does PC One (4450 2555) on Salwa Road, which also provides after sales support to its customers. You can buy computers at Computer Arabia (4466 7555) and the Smart Computer Centre (4441 0790).

Most of the retailers in the Musheireb area (p.320) can build a machine to your specifications, which is usually cheaper – the disadvantage is that you will not get an international warranty. When buying an international brand, make sure that you get a warranty card and that it is stamped by the dealer otherwise it will be void if you leave Qatar.

Prices are likely to be similar to those in your home country, but look out for regular promotions; these will usually take the form of bundled software or accessories. Software piracy is a problem in Qatar, so when buying software make sure is from a reputable store like Jarir Bookstore, Fifty One East, or Office1.

Family Computers
Al Rayyan Complex, Al Rayyan Rd Musheireb
4432 4070
fccqatar.com
Map **2 P7**
A good selection of Dell and HP products and accessories, and its skilled and highly trained professionals can service any type of machine. It provides after-sale computer servicing as well as onsite support for all IT related problems. The store also handles warranty claims and is a Microsoft certified partner. It has a service centre (4432 5634) and a branch for software solutions (4443 5361).

National Computer Centre
Al Rayyan Complex, Al Rayyan Rd Musheireb
4435 1200
nccqatar.com
Map **2 P7**
While this store mostly caters to large companies, you will find that its computer repair service is one of the best. Besides repairs and upgrades, you can also buy or rent computers and purchase all related computer accessories and software. Brands on offer include Dell, HP and Acer.

Office1
Anwar Center, Nr Midmac, Salwa Rd New Slata
4465 9244
office1qatar.com
Map **2 L11**
At this authorised Apple reseller you will find all the latest computers and accessories by the brand as well as Sony and HP products – it also provides after sales support and repairs. The staff are very friendly and knowledgeable and are always willing to answer any questions.

Technical Care Center
Al Mirqab Al Jadeed St Fereej Al Nasr **4444 4248**
tcc-qatar.com
Map **2 K10**
This is the main branch of this well-established store which has several outlets in Doha including the Landmark Shopping Mall (4486 5842), Hyatt Plaza (4468 8377) and City Center Doha (4411 5255).

Offering a personalised service to its customers, it provides after sales support and repairs for all types of electronics.

Fashion
You can get your hands on a good variety of international brand names and all the latest fashion in Doha, which makes cruising the malls and shopping areas so appealing. Despite being tax free prices are usually higher than in your home country, especially if you are buying designer clothes, but the sales several times a year mean you can score fantastic deals on designer labels.

Various designers, including Louis Vuitton, Ralph Lauren, Hermes, Valentino and Dolce and Gabbana, now have a presence in Doha's shopping malls. However, if your passion lies in highstreet fashion, you will be right at home with a variety of stores, from Europe and the US, all of which can be found in the main shopping malls (p.330). Stores like Oasis in The Mall (4467 4339) and Villaggio Mall (4413 5278) and Splash in Centrepoint (4413 1927) and City Center Doha (4483 1139) offer very affordable and trendy women's clothing.

The latest addition to the Doha shopping scene, Lagoona Mall, is home to a number of fashion retailers ranging from highstreet fashions to designer gear; see p.332 for more detailed information on the store

Shopping on Salwa Road

selection here. At The Pearl (p.322), boutiques for high-end designers such as Dior, Hermes, Alexander McQueen, Armani, Roberto Cavalli, Hugo Boss, Chloe and Vera Wang nestle together in the elite surroundings. However, this section is not just about shopping; take a stroll along the marina and enjoy the beautiful views it has to offer. The marina is filled with stunning yachts, which can be admired while sitting at one of the many outdoor cafes and restaurants. The sheer size of The Pearl development may tire out even the toughest of shoppers, so try hopping on board one of the water taxis. It costs QR 40 for the day and will leave you more time to look around the shops.

Some five-star hotels have their own upscale boutiques, including the Ritz Carlton (p.202) where you can find Kuwaiti-based fashion paradise Palmera Fashion (p.326). For something a little bit different head to Bombay Silk on Salwa Road or Barwa Village near Wakra, here you can buy beautiful silk fabrics and have them made into whatever you like – this is also a good place to buy a saree (a traditional Indian outfit).

For accessories and fashionable handbags try Zara, Claire's, H&M, Uterque, Coccinelle and Accessorize (which are located in most large malls). You can also find cheaper items in Splash (4483 1139) and Xanaka (4413 5101). At the latter, many of the clothing tags have been cut off, but if you take a closer look you will find that some of them actually originate from Mothercare (p.297), Gap and other well-known brand names. Some stores in Souk Waqif (p.330) stock beautifully crafted tunics and shawls as well as designer knock-off sunglasses, handbags and watches. The counterfeit market is not as big as it is in nearby regions, and it is mostly contained to the Souk Waqif and its surroundings areas. There are several tailors (p.294) in Doha, which is great because you can get garments custom-made really easily – head to Souk Al Asiery (p.328) to buy your fabric.

Those looking for a bargain should head to Sana (4443 0180) in Um Ghuwailina where you will find plenty of clothing for the entire family at great prices. Outlet Exclusive in Al Mana Towers on Al Sadd Street carries designer clothes at prices that won't break the bank. Here, you'll find discounted stock on clothing and accessories for men and women (featuring labels that will make you swoon such as Stella McCartney, Alexander McQueen, Armani, Balenciaga and Roberto Cavalli).

When it comes to men's fashion, you'll find a good variety of shops and the selection is growing. Stores such as Marks & Spencer (p.324), Zara, Massimo Dutti and Next offer great selections – whether you are looking for that weekend T-shirt and jeans combo or for more formal office wear. Other stores with excellent men's fashion are Christian Audigier (4451 9775), Gap, Banana Republic and Pull & Bear. Boggi Milano (4413 5098) sells Italian suits and men's

Designer style

accessories. Places like Topman, River Island and Celio (4450 7651) are quite popular with the younger crowd due to their excellent selection of casual, sports and trendy clothing. Those looking for more designer attire will find a satisfying mix in the luxury extension at Villaggio Mall where you will find Dunhill (4413 3478) and Ermenegildo Zegna (4413 4765).

Most shopping malls have numerous international shoe shops, and a few local stores. Department stores (p.323) also offer a good selection of shoes. Salam (p.324) is the place to head if you are after designer labels, although many upmarket outlets can be found in the malls. Outlets such as Next, Oasis, H&M and Monsoon have limited selections, with Monsoon being particularly good for pretty girlie flip-flops. Sport stores (p.317) are your one-stop for sport shoes for the entire family.

Kids' shoes are widely available in most children's stores such as Pumpkin Patch, Prenatal and H&M (which have various outlets in the main malls). Due to the climate in Doha, kids mostly wear sandals and open toe shoes. If you come from a colder climate and are looking for winter shoes before going away on a seasonal trip, it can be challenging to find a suitable pair. Shoe Mart has a good selection of children shoes such as sandals, sports shoes, formal shoes and flip flops.

What & Where To Buy

Lingerie

The market for racy underwear in Qatar is a crowded one. Popular brands include La Senza (4487 0181, liwastores.com) at Villaggio Mall and Nayomi (4483 1299, nayomi.com.sa) in City Center Doha, which offer frilly smalls at all prices. Jennyfer Secret (4486 2091) at Landmark Shopping Mall and Oysho (4413 5091) in Villaggio Mall are popular with the younger crowd, while Soleil Sucree (4413 5504) and Bendon (4450 7334, bendongroup.com) cater to the top end at Villaggio Mall. Department stores like BHS (p.323), Highland (p.324), Debenhams (p.323) and Marks & Spencer (p.324) all offer an extensive international range. Other stores offering lingerie are Valege Paris (4413 1344) and Change (4413 1177, change.com), both in Royal Plaza. For high-end underwear of the more daring kind, visit the Agent Provocateur store at The Pearl (6690 0225).

Shoes

Adidas City Center Doha, Al Dafna, 4483 9124, *adidas.com*
Aldo City Center Doha, Al Dafna, 4438 3823, *aldoshoes.com*
Birkenstock Royal Plaza, Al Sadd, 4444 8483, *birkenstock.com*
Boudoir Royal Plaza, Al Sadd, 4432 5350, *boudoir.me*
Brantano Shoe Citi Landmark Mall, Umm Lekhba, 4487 3161, *brantano.com*
Dune Landmark Mall, Umm Lekhba, 4486 4183, *dune.co.uk*
Florsheim Landmark Mall, Umm Lekhba, 4487 0181, *liwastores.com*
Foot Locker Villaggio Mall, Baaya, 4413 5315, *footlocker.com*
Geox Villaggio Mall, Baaya, 4450 7194, *geox.com*
Go Sport Villaggio Mall, Baaya, 4451 7574, *go-sport.com*
Grant Shoes City Center Doha, Al Dafna, 4483 9995
H&M Villaggio Mall, Baaya, 4450 7628, *hm.com*
Hush Puppies City Center Doha, Al Dafna, 4483 2760, *hushpuppies.com*
Kurt Geiger Landmark Mall, Umm Lekhba, 4486 0133, *kurtgeiger.com*
Mango City Center Doha, Al Dafna, 4411 5953, *mango.com*
Milano City Center Doha, Al Dafna, 4483 1340, *alshaya.com*
Monsoon Villaggio Mall, Baaya, 4450 7650, *monsoon.co.uk*
Next Villaggio Mall, Baaya, 4413 5633, *next.co.uk*
Nine West Hyatt Plaza, Baaya, 4468 2919, *ninewest.com*
Oasis Villaggio Mall, Baaya, 4413 5278, *oasis-stores.com*
Pull & Bear Landmark Mall, Umm Lekhba, 4487 7801, *pullandbear.com*

Puma Villaggio Mall, Baaya, 4450 7306, *puma.com*
Pumpkin Patch Villaggio Mall, Baaya, 4450 7620, *pumpkinpatch.co.uk*
Reebok Villaggio Mall, Baaya, 4450 7871, *reebok.com*
Salam The Mall, Old Airport, 4467 2200, *salams.com*
Shoe Mart City Center Doha, Al Dafna, 4483 8560, *shoemartgulf.com*

Furniture

The style of furniture in Qatar ranges from functional through cheerful to outrageously over the top. While most tastes are catered for, there is less variety than in other gulf countries and, until the new IKEA opens in Doha Festival City, there is an obvious gap in the market.

Villas are often let furnished, so most furniture buys tends to be an effort to add a personal touch to your home. If you feel like a having a go at making your own furniture or shelving, go to Souk Haraj (p.328), tucked a few streets behind the Airport Road in Najma. You can buy wood, nails and tools or have pieces made to order to your specifications.

The best places for baby furniture are Mothercare (p.297), Mamas & Papas (p.296), Chicco (p.296), Babyshop (p.296) and Prenatal (p.297). For older children, themed bedding sets and room decorations are available at several stores including Homes R Us (p.305), Home Centre (p.305), Nabco Furniture (p.306), KiddyZone (p.311), Doha City (4441 2734) and New World Centre (4443 2712), and the towel and linen departments of Carrefour and Lulu Hypermarket.

There are a string of shops along Salwa Road selling expensive and moderately priced furnishings. Apollo Furniture (4468 9522) is popular for good-quality furnishings, barbecues and outdoor furniture, as is Articles (p.306) at the Royal Plaza (p.336). Qatar Decoration (4468 4808) has been known to outfit various palaces and luxury villas, while Ka International (p.306) has a huge range of furniture, soft furnishings and bed linen sourced from around the world.

King Koil (4468 6814, kingkoildoha.com) is the place to go for good quality mattresses and Love Sac (4468 1233, lovesacqatar.com) specialises in comfy seating. Nabco Furniture (p.306) has a large selection of furniture and decorations over two floors. Further down near Dasman Centre is the furniture branch of Al Shaheen (4435 8635), along with several other worthy outlets.

Cheap bedding, towels and curtains are available from most supermarkets (p.324) and department stores (p.323), but the quality and durability may be less than great. A more stylish range of items are on offer at Dwell at City Center Doha (4493 4775) or Landmark Shopping Mall (4487 0181). The White Company (p.306) also stocks a premium range. If 1,000 thread count Egyptian cotton is what you want, Frette has a gorgeous store in the Royal Plaza (4436 0560) and another in Landmark Mall (4487 4331).

Funky and affordable, The One (p.306), at Landmark Mall and Villaggio Mall, stocks cool couches and colourful accessories. High quality, stylish pieces with sleek lines and finishings are on offer at BoConcept (4411 5054) in City Center Doha, Singways Casa (p.335) at Villaggio, Living In Interiors (4495 3510) near Museum Roundabout and Ligne Roset on Salwa Road (4431 1843).

Shop In The UAE

If you can't find what you are looking for in Qatar take the short trip over to the UAE where many contemporary designer furniture stores, including Roche Bobois (+971 4 399 0393) and Objekts of Design (+971 4 328 4300), have good selections; shipping to Qatar is usually easy to arrange.

Bombay at The Mall (4441 2715) offers high-end 'faux antique' items including four-poster beds and lush leather chairs – with a price tag to match. For an ethnic feel, Reshi (p.306) at Landmark has luxury cabinets, display units, rugs, wall art and ornaments. Teak and wooden antique and reproduction furniture, paintings and artworks can be found at Artefacts of Arabia (p.317), Cottage Crafts (4468 5229), Darriche (p.317) and Oriental Carpet Company (p.301). Ghassan's (p.306) is a literal hole in the wall just off C Ring Road that stocks beautiful real-wood furniture from India and Sri Lanka.

Genuine antiques are hard to come by, but head for Souk Waqif for that rustic touch. Many vendors will try to convince you of the provenance of a particular item, but more often than not, the item probably hails from 21st century India or China.

Curtains and Venetian blinds are usually on the pricey side, especially if you need them made to order. You can browse the range at Al Jawhara Curtains & Furniture (4468 9897), Al Shark Exhibition (4442 2906), Curtain Palace (4432 1999) and Sedar (4469 4442), or simply buy some fabric in the souks and have curtains cheaply made to your specifications by a tailor.

For super cheap furniture that you won't mind leaving behind at the end of your contract term, Souk Haraj in Najma has dozens of small shops selling everything from dining suites to kitchenware and hardware. With the transient nature of the population it is also worth considering second-hand furniture and household goods. Check the classifieds section of expat website qatarliving.com, or the various newspapers (p.22). You should also try looking at advertisements posted on shop noticeboards.

The best times to look for bargains are in summer, during Ramadan and also in April (for pre-summer stock clearances). Delivery is also available upon request at most stores for an extra fee.

Budget Furniture

Home Centre
City Center Doha Al Dafna **4483 9400**
homecentrestores.com
Map **2 Q2**

Spruce up your entire house with the classic or modern furniture sold here for every room. There is also a huge range of towels, wall art, linen, cushions and throws. Branches are located in City Center Doha (4483 9400), near the Jaidah Flyover (4435 5300) and Centrepoint (4413 1930).

Homes R Us
Hyatt Plaza Baaya **4469 8999**
homesrusgroup.com
Map **2 A12**

Showrooms are divided into sections representing every room in the house, with an endless range of hard and soft furnishings, accessories and home essentials. Prices and quality are both excellent.

Contemporary Designer Furniture

Armani/Casa
Porto Arabia The Pearl Qatar **4495 3510**
armanicasa.com
Map **11 L2**

As you would expect from high-end designer Armani, the range of furniture and soft furnishings are elaborate, glitzy and of fantastic quality.

Natuzzi
Al Mana Towers Fereej Bin Mahmoud **4421 4440**
natuzzi.com
Map **2 M9**

Luxurious Italian detailing meets comfortable, cleverly-designed living, Natuzzi specialises in stylish, elegant furnishings which includes sofas, armchairs, flooring, tables and accessories.

Modern Furniture & Home Décor

Apollo Furniture
Nr Decoration R/A, Salwa Rd Bu Hamour **4468 9522**
apollofurnitureonline.com
Map **2 H13**

This store stocks Silentnight bedding, Aimbry lighting and Marinelli seating, plus an excellent range of antique reproduction, Indonesian-style and contemporary furniture. Sofas, curtains and linen can be purchased from the showroom floor or custom made to order. There is also a good selection of outdoor garden furniture, gas heaters and barbecues.

What & Where To Buy

Articles

Royal Plaza Al Sadd **4413 1188**
royalplazadoha.com
Map **2 L8**
You'll find a little bit of everything here, from cute nursery furniture to outdoor wicker furniture and barbecues. Dining suites and sofas vary from slick to novel designs and there is a stack of crockery, candle holders, vases, cushions and extras to match.

ID Design > *p.66*

The Mall Old Airport **4467 8777**
iddesignqatar.com
Map **2 R13**
This ultra-modern European store stocks a great range of stylish furniture and accessories. There is a good selection of kids' furniture, and once you've taken your pick of the sofas, beds and office furniture, you can take advantage of its free home delivery and installation (within the city centre).

Kas

Landmark Mall Umm Lekhba **4486 8585**
kasaustralia.com.au
Map **2 E1**
Bright colours, edgy designs and quality fabrics are the staple at this Aussie retailer. There is a second branch of the store in the Royal Plaza (4413 1351) also selling floor cushions, bean bags, throws, sheets and towels in funky stripes and dots or simple, elegant white.

Dwell City Center Doha, Al Dafna, 4493 4775, *liwastores.com*
Ka International Salwa Rd, 4493 0642, *ka-international.com*
Nabco Furniture Al Matar st, Al Thumama, 4466 6646, *nabcofurniture.com.qa*
THE One Landmark Mall, Umm Lekhba, 4488 8669, *theoneplanet.com*
Qatar Decoration Company Nr Decoration R/A, Salwa Rd, Fereej Al Soudan, 4468 4808
The White Company Landmark Mall, Umm Lekhba, 4486 0789, *thewhiteconpany.com*
Zara Home Landmark Mall, Umm Lekhba, 4486 3062, *zarahome.com*

Wooden furniture

Artefacts Of Arabia

Landmark Mall Umm Lekhba **5561 4573**
artefactsofarabia.com
Map **2 E1**
An eye-pleasing range of imported furniture, art and collectibles from India and South East Asia can be found here, in addition to a good collection of Middle Eastern paintings and artwork. Don't be disheartened if you find the stall has disappeared; the owner occasionally closes up when he ventures away on buying trips.

Ghassan's

Green Door Villa, 50 Aseer St Fereej Bin Mahmoud **4443 7448**
Map **2 L8**
Real wood furniture, imported from India and Sri Lanka, is sold here in addition to a range of handicrafts and carpets – free delivery is also offered. This hidden treasure can be a little difficult to find; from the street, you will only see a dark green door with a small gold name plate on the upper left corner.

Bombay The Mall, Old Airport, 4466 6869
Reshi Landmark Mall, Umm Lekhba, 4486 4795

Gold & Diamonds

There are numerous outlets selling gold jewellery and diamonds, many of which are located inside the shopping malls, clustered in the Al Sadd area and in the Gold Souk (p.328). Gold is available in 18, 22 or 24 carats and is sold according to the daily international weight; meaning that prices don't change much from store to store. Prices vary depending on the workmanship that has gone into the piece, but it's always possible to bargain and ask for a discount, especially if you buy from a store in the souk.

Walking through the Gold Souk, you will be amazed at the wall-to-wall wonderland of glittering gold and diamond shops. Located on Ali Bin Abdullah Street and the surrounding area, the souk is home to stores like Marhaba (4431 8055), Al Faizan (4432 9689) and Princess Jewellery (4435 3515), all of which offer certified diamonds and gems. You'll find that pearls, silver, platinum and titanium are also sold at most of the outlets and several of the stores can make up individual pieces; just bring a photograph or a sample of what you would like to have made and the shop should be able to copy it. Gold pendants with your name written in Arabic make for a great gift, as do cartouche bars (gold bars that have your name written in Latin one side and in Arabic on the other side). Jewellery cons are rare; nevertheless, always ask for a certificate of authenticity before you buy, particularly for diamonds.

Every mall has at least one jewellery store and you'll find branches of Damas (4484 6267, damasjewel.com) and Ali Bin Ali Establishment (p.307) everywhere. Several more major brand names have opened in the shopping malls and you'll find international names like Cartier, Tiffany and Co, Harry Winston, Tod's and Chopard in Villaggio Mall.

Department store Fifty One East (p.323) also has a line of custom-made jewellery and timepieces for sale. If you're on the hunt for a new watch, whether it's a Tag Heuer, Anne Klein, Timex or Tissot, you will find a big selection at Rivoli (4483 3679) in City Center Doha. The Louis Vuitton store in Villaggio Mall has a special watch salon which sells exclusive and bespoke items.

Akshaya Jewellery Nr Najma Signal, Al Mansoura, 4442 9790, *akshayajewellery.com*
Al Majed Jewellery Al Majed Group Bldg, Al Sadd, 4447 8478
Al Majid Home Jewellery Al Sadd St, Al Sadd, 4432 4440, *almajid-jewels.com*
Al Makki Jewellery & Watches Al Sadd St, Al Sadd, 4444 7733, *almakkijewellery-watches.com*
Al Sailan Gem & Jewellery Royal Plaza, Al Sadd, 4436 1195
Al Sulaiman Jewellery & Watches Gold Souk, Old Al Ghanim, 4444 2556, *alsulaimanjewellery.com*
Al Wajba Jewellery City Center Doha, Al Dafna, 4483 3535
Alfardan Jewellery City Center Doha, Al Dafna, 4483 0100, *alfardan.com.qa*
Ali Bin Ali Establishment Royal Plaza, Al Sadd, 4413 1392, *alibinali.com*
Almuftah Jewellery Almuftah Centre, Al Sadd St, Al Sadd, 4444 1320, *almuftah.com*
Blue Salon Suhaim Bin Hamad St, Fereej Bin Mahmoud, 4446 6111, *bluesalon.com*
Cartier Royal Plaza, Al Sadd, 4413 1381, *cartier.com*
Damas Exclusive The Mall, Old Airport, 4467 7200

All that glitters

Diamond & Diamond Royal Plaza, Al Sadd, 4413 1010
Lone Star Jewelry Gold Souk, Old Al Ghanim, 4443 6187, *lonestarjewels.com*
Malabar Gold Lulu Hypermarket, Al Gharrafa, 4407 4000, *malabargoldanddiamonds.com*
Sky Jewellery Souk Waqif, Al Jasra, 4441 1802
TAG Heuer City Center Doha, Al Dafna, 4411 5969, *tagheuer.com*

Home Appliances

Company provided accommodation is usually leased on a semi-furnished basis, so most major kitchen appliances, such as oven and refrigerator, will be fitted already. Some companies do include cookware and kitchen utensils as part of the residential package, but this is not common. You'll also find that some houses use gas cookers and some use electric gas cylinders can be ordered and delivered to your home (see Setting Up Home p.88).

Products are imported from all over the world, so plugs may not be compatible with those fitted in your home. There is also a problem with incompatible voltage, mainly due to people importing 110V North American appliances. If you must do this, make sure you connect your appliance via a 240V/110V transformer.

All of the listed stores sell a good range of electronic appliances including microwaves, fridges, kettles, washing machines, irons, blenders and water coolers. Most stores conveniently offer home delivery and installation upon request. You may have to shop around to buy specific brands and items, or move your search online. Products should come with a warranty of at least one year – if you are doubtful of the international validity then ask to open the box and check the paperwork yourself. Carrefour (p.325) and Lulu Hypermarket (p.325) both have good selections of household names like Black & Decker, Kenwood, Sanyo, Sony, Samsung, Braun, Bosch and LG, and have a good variety of kitchen appliances and general electronics. These hypermarkets tend to be a little bit cheaper than retailers in major shopping malls. Both offer home delivery, sometimes free for purchases over a certain amount.

One of the biggest retailers is Jumbo Electronics, with branches in City Center Doha (p.331) and on Salwa Road. Panasonic and National appliances can be bought from Nasir Bin Abdullah & Sons (p.309). Techno Q (p.309) on Salwa Road offers a selection of high-end goods from brands like Yamaha and Denon. Al Mushiri (p.299) sells Humax and Bernina products as well as a variety of other home appliances. You'll find the Philips brand at Almana & Partners (4431 1072), Pioneer at Ahmad al Uthman (4437 3446), Sanyo at Domasco (4441 6147) and Sharp at Al Muftah Group, or you can visit the large Darwish Trading (p.308) showrooms for Kenwood and Hoover. Al Emadi Electronics

What & Where To Buy

(4442 3312) near Arab Roundabout is the place to buy Blue Star, Thomson and Zanussi products. For high-end and hi-tech home appliances, you can always head to Bang & Olufsen (4487 3240) which has a showroom in Landmark Mall.

Tavola (City Center Doha, 4493 1101 and Royal Plaza, 4413 1222), Table Arts (City Center Doha, 4411 5278 and on Salwa Road, 4469 0236) and the newly opened Lakeland Plastics (City Center Doha, 4411 5243) are favourites for fancy kitchen items and cookware including KitchenAid mixers and products from Cuisinart, Wilton and Le Creuset.

In the old Sofitel area, around National Square, you'll find a street dedicated to electronics shops, with televisions, stereos and other such goods filling the shop fronts. Some of the items are well-known brands, others you may have never heard of and may be cheaper but slightly lower quality. This area is likely to be redeveloped in the very near future as the Heart of Doha project encroaches on it. Emax (p.308) has a good mix of popular and lesser-known brands, or a stroll through Souk Nasser Bin Saif (p.328) should expose an endless selection of well-priced goods.

For second-hand items, people leaving Qatar often post lists of goods for sale on noticeboards in supermarkets and schools. It's also worth checking the online forums (see Useful Websites, p.23).

Almuftah Group

Almuftah Centre, Al Sadd St Al Sadd **4444 6868**
almuftah.com
Map **2 L9**

Head here for household appliances and white goods including televisions, vacuum cleaners, fridges and washing machines. Brands include Black & Decker, GE, NEC, Pyrex and Sharp. Delivery and installation services are available, as well as after sales care and support.

Darwish Trading Company

Airport Rd Old Airport **4455 2266**
darwish-trading.com
Map **2 V12**

The domestic appliances division of Darwish has a huge showroom on Airport Road. Inside you'll find a wide range of white goods and kitchen appliances such as pots, pans, blenders, coffee machines, deep fat fryers, woks and utensils.

Home Audio & Visual

When the temperature goes up, most residents head indoors, which makes having a good home entertainment system an important consideration when it comes to kitting out your home. One big advantage of buying in this region is that there is a good cross section of well-known and lesser-known brands so you can pick up a widescreen television without the overblown price tag. There are dedicated electronics shops specialising in certain brands, but it does pay to shop around at the larger stores to compare prices.

Virgin Megastore (p.312) at Villaggio stocks some Sony goods and merchandise; Techno Blue (4437 0756) sells Samsung. 51 East stocks various electronics and it is also an authorised Bose dealer, while Nasir Bin Abdullah & Sons (p.309) in the old Sofitel area is the place to pick up a good range of Panasonic products. The ever popular Apple brand is also available at iSpot (4411 5204) in City Center Doha, or at PC One (4450 2555) and e-Pro Solutions (e-pro.com.qa). Almana & Partners (4431 1075) and Video Home Electronic Centre (4441 0060) have a good range, or you can browse the listings on Doha Sooq (dohasooq.com).

Supermarkets such as Carrefour and Lulu Hypermarket also stock a range of electronics, from TVs to audio systems and games consoles. They are likely to be a bit cheaper here, and in the souks you will have a better chance of picking up unknown brands from China and Korea. If you are on the hunt for a real bargain, second-hand items are frequently posted on the classifieds section of Qatar Living (qatarliving.com), QatarDeals (qatardeals.com) and various expat websites (p.23).

Games consoles and their accessories are also available at Saqr The Entertainment Store (p.309), or at branches of Virgin Megastore (p.312) and Carrefour. Be sure to enquire about broadcast region codes and compatibility when buying games and DVDs, particularly if you have brought consoles from back home. Qatar uses PAL format and it falls under DVD region 2, but you can buy other regions and formats.

Most stores will offer to deliver and install your purchases in your home, which is handy if you are planning to mount a television to your wall or to set up a complicated surround sound system.

Bang & Olufsen

Landmark Mall Umm Lekhba **4487 3240**
bang-olufsen.com
Map **2 E1**

With price tags to match its slick designs and reputation for innovative technology, Bang & Olufsen is a dream shop for gadget enthusiasts. This store stocks a stylish range of products that look impressive and deliver high-quality sound and pictures. Home integration systems and car audio systems are its speciality.

Emax

Al Asmakh Mall Al Sadd **4413 1920**
emaxme.com
Map **2 K8**

A wide range of electronics products are on offer here including televisions, speaker systems and games consoles. The store also stocks home appliances (fridges, microwaves, washing machines), computers and toys. The main showrooms are in Al Rayyan (4421 3969), plus there are kiosks located in Centrepoint (4428 9302), Landmark (4486 5946) and Villaggio (4451 7893) malls. Extended warranties, insurance and installation are available on purchases.

Jumbo Electronics
City Center Doha Al Dafna **4483 8953**
jumboqatar.com
Map **2 Q2**
With 16 branches in Qatar, Jumbo is one of the largest retailers in home electronics in the country. Products include an assortment of home entertainment systems, kitchen appliances, computers and mobile phones from brands such as Brother, GE, Kenwood, LG, Morphy Richards and Motorola. Visit the website for more information on its showroom locations across the whole country.

Nasir Bin Abdullah & Sons
Panasonic Bldg, Musheirib St
Fereej Mohammed Bin Jasim **4441 7575**
nas-goc.com
Map **2 Q8**
Panasonic audio and video entertainment systems can be bought here. The store also stocks Viera plasma televisions, Lumix digital cameras and camcorders, and general home appliances. As an added bonus, a loyalty card is available for frequent shoppers. This outlet is an authorised JVC retail and servicing centre; other branches are located in Souk Ahmed Bin Ali (4441 3901), Markhiya (4487 4861), Al Wakra (4464 0661), Al Khor (4472 6190) and Al Aziziyah (4468 5492).

Saqr The Entertainment Store
Landmark Mall Umm Lekhba **4487 0500**
Map **2 E1**
These well-stocked stores sell a wide range of CDs and DVDs, in addition to a selection of video games and consoles which include Sony PlayStation and Nintendo Wii. Other branches are located on Al Markhiya Street (4486 9988), Hyatt Plaza (4469 7282), The Mall (under the name Moods, 4467 0096) and Souk Nasser bin Saif (4442 5959).

Technical Care Centre
Landmark Mall Umm Lekhba **4486 5842**
tcc-qatar.com
Map **2 E1**
There are six branches of this shop in Doha which specialises in electronic dictionaries in English and Arabic, including Islamic reference devices from the American Franklin, Najm and Scholar brands. Digital voice recorders, memory cards, and video games and consoles can also be bought here.

Techno Q
Nr Decoration R/A, Salwa Rd Bu Hamour **4468 9494**
technoq.com
Map **2 H12**
For technology enthusiasts, this showroom is a treasure trove of treats with an array of professional audio and video equipment from brands such as Audiotechnica, Creston, DBX, Denon, JBL, Panasonic and Samsung. You'll also find LCD and plasma televisions, DVD players and recorders, projectors, microphones, mixers and amplifiers.

Hardware & DIY
Carrefour has a good selection of tools and hardware, but your best bet when locating tools for DIY jobs is to head either to Barwa Village near Wakra, which has good parking facilities, or to the string of speciality shops along the B Ring Road that sell paints, tools, hardware, flooring, taps and fittings. Shibam Trading Centre (4432 4693) is a licensed dealer in Villeroy & Boch tiles, taps and porcelains and Al Feroz International Trading (4432 1909) stocks power tools and hardware from AEG, Nicholson and Pro-Tech. Further along the road, Qatar Trading Company (4425 2666) has Yale tools and equipment. Back towards Al Matar Street, Al Khoory Building Materials (4415 1049) boasts a good supply of hardware and tools for amateurs and professionals. Nearby, New World Centre (4443 2712) and Doha City (4441 2734) have a basic and affordable range of bathroom taps and accessories. For a more expensive range of items, visit the stretch of flooring and accessories shops along the Airport Road between E Ring and the Porsche dealership.

Souk Haraj (behind Dasman Centre in Najma) has a row of traders selling various types of wood. You can buy what you need for your DIY project, or have one of the workers build something for you to your specifications. If you need something specific made for your home, such as built-in wardrobes, a staff member will happily follow you home, take some measurements, and then provide you with a quote.

The Tool Souk (Souk Waqif, p.330) sells every kind of instrument you might require for simple DIY jobs in the house and garden, with the exception of hand drills (which you'll find at Carrefour). To get there, enter Grand Hamad Street from the Corniche end and, after the first set of lights, take the first slip road on your right and turn right – the Tool Souk will be in front of you. The best place to find parking is in the basement car park on the corner as the road bends to the left. It isn't advisable for women to visit the souk; you won't be in any danger, but the slack-jawed stares may make you feel uncomfortable.

If you need paint to jazz up your flat or villa, there are a number of shops around Doha selling a good variety of colours and all the accessories you'll need.

They can mix thousands of colours, but unfortunately they don't offer tester pots – you just have to take your chances by buying a litre (which isn't too expensive). The most popular paint stores are Hempel Paints (4431 5430, hempel.com), where you'll find almost every colour of emulsion and enamel paint you can imagine (its staff will help with colour matching); Al Shaab Paints (4460 0209, alshaabgroup.com) and Jotun Paints (4441 2728, jotun.com).

Health Food & Special Dietary Requirements

The range and availability of health food in Qatar is increasing with demand and, while the market isn't awash with specialist food shops, almost all major supermarkets now stock a range of items for those with special dietary requirements. You should readily find products that are free of wheat, dairy and gluten including pasta, bread, biscuits, cakes, flours and cereal, along with sugar-free sweets and chocolates (including Green & Blacks), meal replacement drinks and bars (including SlimFast), hard and soft tofu, quinoa, milk made from rice, soy, almond and hazelnut and alternative peanut spreads such as cashew paste. Prices are usually high, with Family Food Centre (p.325) tending to offer the least expensive products and the widest variety. Stock doesn't last long, so buy in bulk when you can. Some health food will be kept in the medicine aisles or the organic section, so ask an assistant if you can't find what you're looking for.

Shoprite (4477 2397) and MegaMart (p.325) sell Weight Watchers products such as frozen meals and soups and Lulu Hypermarket (p.325) has a small selection of Linda McCartney vegetarian meals.

Multivitamins and dietary supplements for adults, pregnant women and children can be found in most pharmacies and supermarkets. City Chemist (4483 9200) and Good Life Chemist (4483 9100) in City Center Mall are both very good. Khulood Pharmacy (4487 7784) on Burger King Roundabout is one of the largest in the country and has especially helpful staff.

GNC Live Well is a popular chain that sells products to promote dietary and sports nutrition, including energy bars, vitamin supplements and protein powders. Branches are in City Center Doha (4483 3675), Bin Mahmoud (4436 4701), The Mall (4467 8888) and Villaggio Mall (4450 7350).

The Nutrition & Diet Center (p.176) has a clinic on Al Kinana Street that can help you with any special dietary needs. Its healthy-eating cafe, The Diet Shop (4466 4995) on Salwa Road, offers low-calorie meals. The store can also prepare a weekly eating plan of nutritious meals that can be delivered to your home.

Kids' Items

There is a high concentration of shops selling toys and items for children and a good range of international stores and smaller outlets. Toys R Us (p.311) is an obvious choice for toys, games, clothing, bicycles and furniture, but Royal Toys (p.311) is a noteworthy rival. Smart Kids Toys (p.311) in Royal Plaza has educational toys from Maisto, Playmobil, Crayola and Lulu Caty. Sanrio (4435 6000) stocks the popular Hello Kitty brand. For video games, a wide range is stocked (for various consoles) at Saqr The Entertainment Store (p.309), Jarir Bookstore (p.298) and Carrefour (p.325).

When it comes to clothing, there is plenty of choice, whether it's high-end designer brands or factory seconds from Sana (4444 0244) in City Center Doha. Many of the department stores (p.323) have children's gear but for real indulgence Blue Salon (p.323) has a section dedicated to premium brands such as Armani Kids, Baby Dior, Calvin Klein Kids, Orchestra and Roberto Cavalli. Salam (p.324) is another place to kit out your kids in designer wear as it stocks kids' clothing ranges by DKNY and Moschino. You can also try Babycare in Emporium (p.323), which is another high-end retailer. Limited Too (in City Center Doha 4483 1015 and Villaggio Mall 4413 5268) has a funky selection of clothing and accessories for older children, and Claire's Accessories is great for hair accessories, beads, bags and jewellery for girls. Branches of the store can be found at Hyatt Plaza (4468 3088), Landmark (4487 1964), The Mall (4467 5344) and Villaggio Mall (4413 5266).

For babies and younger children, Babyshop (p.296) and Mamas & Papas (4451 7879) have a good range and Mothercare (p.297) and Next have outlets in all the main malls. Prenatal (p.297) stocks the essentials and have some great outfits at reasonable prices. Oshkosh B'gosh (4469 7339), Carters (4469 8999) and Pumpkin Patch (4450 7620) sell bright, colourful and practical clothes. Monsoon (p.304) has a great range of party clothes for girls.

Most shops that stock children's clothes also sell shoes, and several, such as Shoe City (4487 3161) and The Athlete's Foot (4450 7477), offer a foot measuring service to ensure you have the correct fit. Shoe Mart (p.304) stocks a range of colourful shoes for babies and children from a variety of brands. The ever popular Crocs brand is available at GO Sport (p.318), Debenhams (p.323), Merch (p.324), Shoe City, and Sun and Sand Sports (p.318).

School uniforms are predominantly purchased from the school itself or from an authorised dealer, such as Zaks (p.311). A cheaper alternative is to have a uniform tailor-made and just sew on the school logo, which is usually available from the school, or you can try Hollywood Fashion (4441 2893) in Al Muntazah. Popular tailors are VIK Uniforms (4487 5760, in Bin Omran), Sterling Tailors (4432 2975, in Musheireb) or upstairs at Modern Educational Stationery Supplies (4435 6515) on the Airport Road. While there, you can pick up cheap stationery, pencils and school books, but the selection and prices are far better at nearby Al Rawnaq (p.295). I Spy Bookshop (p.298) in Doha City Center also has an excellent range of educational books, readers and wall posters for children.

KiddyZone

City Center Doha Al Dafna **4483 4638**
Map **2 Q2**
A one-stop shop for kids' toys featuring branded merchandise. The store sells both board and electronic games, DVD movies, children's bedding, clothing, fancy dress costumes and dining ware from Barney & Friends, Thomas the Tank Engine, Ben 10, Hannah Montana, Bob the Builder, Dora the Explorer and Freej. There are also two other stores located in City Center Doha (the store is known as Space Toys) the Hyatt Plaza (4469 0507) and Landmark Shopping Mall (4421 7215).

Royal Toys

Al Furousia St Al Sadd **4451 6660**
Map **2 M9**
The store's two outlets (you'll find another branch in Al Gharafa, 4421 8486) have everything your child could wish for, from Lightning McQueen beds and mini-Hummers to life-size toy barbecue sets, dolls, action figures, play tents and princess playhouses. The range of toys for both outdoor and indoor play is substantial. Major brands on sale include Peg-Perego, Step 2 and Little Tikes.

Smart Kids Toys

Royal Plaza Al Sadd **4442 7968**
Map **2 L8**
Sells an impressive range of toys, puzzles and board and electronic games, including Vtech educational toys, Wii consoles and Sony Play Stations. Also on sale

are arts and crafts from Crayola, Spy Gear accessories, soft toys, trolley bags and a small selection of Groovy Chick bicycles. Branded games and toys feature Mickey Mouse, Barney, Cars, Hannah Montana and Lulu Caty.

Toys R Us

Suhaim Bin Hamad St Al Sadd **4443 5904**
toysrusme.com
Map **2 L8**
This international superstore is a popular destination to pick up toys and gifts for kids, plus there is a selection of baby essentials and educational toys. Larger items include bicycles, sand pits, swings, slides and sporting equipment – games, costumes, stocking fillers and electronics are on offer. Buy well in advance of Eid Al Fitr and Christmas periods when stocks disappear fast.

Zaks

Nr Decoration R/A, Salwa Rd Bu Hamour **4450 6940**
zaksstore.com
Map **2 H12**
Here you'll find uniforms, including sports kits and school bags, for most of the private schools in Doha. Prices are generally reasonable. Opening hours are Saturday to Thursday 10:00 to 19:30. The store will soon offer online shipping and free delivery.

Maternity Items

The need for fashionable maternity clothing has spurred a growing market with a decent selection of items now on offer, but the range is still quite limited in Qatar and you might baulk at the prices. Babyshop (p.296) has some good basics, Dorothy Perkins (4413 5638) and H&M (4486 4144) stock fun, fashionable items, and Debenhams (p.323), Marks & Spencer

International brands in Doha

(p.324), Mothercare (p.297), Mamas & Papas (p.296) and Prenatal (p.297) all have stylish clothes for yummy mummies. You will have to search around for nursing bras, underwear, swimwear, adjustable separates and evening wear, as stores are somewhat inconsistent with their availability. A good idea is to get on the mailing list of stores such as Change (4413 1177) in Royal Plaza, who will then advise you when new stocks of maternity underwear and swimwear have arrived. Rather than shop around for choice and for correct sizing, you could order online instead. Popular websites are Fig Leaves (figleaves.com) and Stella Maternity (stellamaternity. com), both of which you can have shipped to you using Aramex (p.288), and Just Kidding (justkidding-me.com) which is based in the UAE.

If you find an item you like, you can take it to a tailor (p.294) who can copy it using different fabrics and colours to see you through your pregnancy. You can also ask them to add adjustable elastic tape to your favourite trousers so that they can grow with your bump – Bombay Silk (4441 2715) is a particularly good option. Pepka Wear (5545 5783) has a talented female seamstress if you aren't comfortable being measured by a man.

Pharmacies such as Boots (4450 7325) stock prenatal vitamins, creams for stretch marks and body moisturisers that are safe for use during pregnancy. Breast pads, pumps, sterilisers and bottles are widely available at most pharmacies, in Mothercare (p.297) and in the maternity sections of department stores.

V-shaped breastfeeding pillows are available but they are often in short supply; occasional stockists include Babyshop (p.296), Mothercare (p.297) and Toys R Us (p.311). Alternatively, you could have one made by your local tailor and order one made to fit your body shape. Download a picture from the internet to explain exactly what it is you need, and be sure to request that the filling be very firmly packed.

Babycare shops also have items to help you prepare for the arrival of a newborn, such as bags, changing mats and baby carriers, but stocks are extremely limited and the choice is fairly ordinary. Baby slings, grobags, disposable nappy sacks and cot mattress protectors are very difficult to find, so try the online stockists mentioned on p.287 or ask friends to bring items from abroad when they come to visit.

Music & DVDs

Despite the prevalence of downloaded films and music, the latest Hollywood offerings can be found in many supermarkets, independent shops and at a few outlets in some of the shopping malls around Doha. You should be aware that music and DVDs are censored and any items that are deemed offensive will be either edited or unavailable in the region. BlueRays, DVDs and CDs are widely available but they are usually more expensive than in your home country. Virgin

Megastore offers a great selection of international music and books. Supermarkets like Carrefour also sell a good selection of DVDs and CDs at great prices, although they may not have the latest releases. Giant Stores (p.325) has its own video store which is located on the second floor of the centre; it charges just QR 10 per DVD to rent. If you are looking for something specific, just ask for it and they will do their best to find it for you. The Family Food Centre (p.325) stocks a good range of new and fairly recent releases for sale.

Film Rentals

There are a few places where you can rent movies in Doha. Giant Video (4469 2996) offers the latest releases of mainstream Hollywood or Bollywood titles and it has a reasonable rate and a flexible returns policy. For those looking to watch movies from the comfort of home, Orbit-Showtime Network (osnetwork.com), offers an online pay-per-view service which features old and new films and TV series.

If your conscience permits, it is possible to get the latest releases on pirated DVDs. Just take a wander around the souk area and you will no doubt be approached by someone offering you DVD copies. They are cheap, but you risk getting them home and discovering that the quality is terrible. Piracy is illegal in Qatar, as it is elsewhere in the world, although it is quite unlikely that the police will raid your house to bust you for that copy of Happy Feet.

You could also shop online; there is greater variety and you will be more likely to get hold of the latest releases. Amazon (amazon.com) has a great selection, but it can take long for items to arrive unless you opt for the pricier shipping methods.

Virgin Megastore > p.xiv, 284
Villaggio Mall Baaya **4413 5824**
virginmegastore.me
Map **2 B11**

Virgin Megastore offers the biggest selection of music and DVDs, as well as books and electronics, in town. Its sizeable range is organised by genre to make it easier for you to find what you are looking for. You can also find DVD box sets of your favourite comedy TV show or film.

Falcon Video Nr TV R/A, Al Markhiya, 4486 9988
Moods Music Shop The Mall, Old Airport, 4467 0096
Rotana Music Hyatt Plaza, Baaya, 4469 7282

Musical Instruments

While the selection on offer for musical enthusiasts isn't as widespread as you'll find in other countries, there are a few stores selling a basic range of instruments. Al Najoom Music Store (4443 7215) has an excellent range of musical instruments from leading brands including Fender, Yamaha and Roland. It also has a ready stock of pedals, amplifiers and accessories. The Star of Musical Instruments and Electronics on Al Kahraba Street has a decent selection; it sells a good range of musical instruments and accessories including acoustic and electric guitars, drums, bass and keyboards. Many brands are on offer such as Korg, Roland and Yamaha and its staff can also help you with special requests. Badie Studio and Stores (4442 3554) at Clock Roundabout stocks various instruments including guitars and basses and technical items such as mixing desks, digital recorders and pedals. You can also buy Ibanez, Korg, D'Arrio and Roland branded items here.

Virgin Megastore (see above) at Villaggio Mall and the Salwa Road branch of Fifty One East (p.323) stock Yamaha instruments, and a range of trumpets, saxophones, flutes, keyboards, trombones and miniature drums. Larger supermarkets and hypermarkets sell basic keyboards which are fine for beginners. Traditional Arabic instruments, such as the oud, are available at shops in Souk Waqif and make a great souvenir; a basic 12-string oud, suitable for a beginner, should only cost you around QR 600.

Digital Downloads

Getmo Arabia (getmo.com) and iTunes (apple.com/itunes) are your best bet if you are looking for a place to download your favourite music or movie. Both your iPod and iPhone applications can be downloaded through these websites. In order to use iTunes you must have a credit card registered to a UK or US address.

The International Music Centre (4467 1354) sells a variety of musical instruments and offers courses and lessons. Otherwise, there are plenty of tutors willing to offer part-time tutoring in a variety of disciplines, including traditional Arabic music. Check the classifieds sections of expat websites for advertisements regarding the plethora of private tutors available, as well as for second hand musical instruments and gear. Some music shops may be able to repair instruments (especially strings) and order a specific item for you from overseas if you can't find what you're looking for.

Outdoor Goods

For entertaining at home, Apollo Furniture (4468 9522) stocks high-quality garden furniture and a wide range of Australian barbecues. Other stockists of quality outdoor furniture include Homes R Us (p.305), Home Centre (p.305), Nabco Furniture (p.306) and Carrefour, while Royal Toys (p.311) has a huge choice of kids' play equipment, such as slides, swings, climbing frames and trampolines.

In spite of the sweltering summer temperatures, exploring the great outdoors is a popular year-round pastime in Qatar, but especially during the cooler months. While there are no specialist camping shops, the basic gear is readily available at Carrefour (p.325), GO Sport (p.304) and Giant Stores (p.325) in Hyatt Plaza. You'll find tents, picnic furniture, sleeping bags, mats, GPS units, Coleman cool boxes and barbecues at reasonable prices. Items are suitable for weekend campers but would not withstand extremes, so if you are intending to do anything more strenuous you should consider ordering your kit online. Websites that ship to Qatar are Altrec (altrec.com), Outdoor Gear (outdoorgear.co.uk) and Simply Hike (simplyhike.co.uk), or Backwoods Camping (backwoods-camping.co.uk) will accept international orders with prior arrangement.

Mannai Trading (4455 8484) has a range of outdoor equipment in its Salwa Road automotive showroom including hard to find gems such as car-battery operated fridges. Go Sport (p.304) sells its own line of camping equipment alongside other imported brands, plus you can pick up good quality hiking boots and gear, walking poles and Camelbaks here. Shoemart (p.304) stocks hiking boots from Timberland and Cat, or you can buy directly from their independent stores. Windbreakers, cast-iron cooking pots and gas ovens are available for sale at Souk Waqif (p.330).

GPS units are available at Carrefour, Virgin Megastore (p.312) at Villaggio Mall, Jarir Bookstore (p.298), the Nokia outlets of Gulf Consolidated Company (cgulfc.com) and PC One (4450 2555). Jassim Al Lingawi Trading (Souk Al Jabor, 4441 3356) specialises in Garmin handsets, maps and software and stocks a full range of fishing, diving and marine equipment. Go Sport (p.304) also has a range of fishing equipment or try Dolphin Establishment (4442 5291), just off Al Rayyan Road (you can buy tackle in Souk Waqif).

There is a small handful of specialist dive shops in Qatar: Qatar Divers (4431 3331), located in the marina of the Marriott Hotel, stocks Oceanic and Ocean Reef equipment and is a certified PADI dive centre. Pearl Divers (4444 9553) on Al Merqab Al Jadeed Street and the World Marine Centre (4436 0989) in Al Bustan both stock equipment that can be bought or rented for diving and spear fishing. For more on these shops, see the Activities chapter on p.263.

Speed Marine Establishment (4464 1682, speedmarinegroup.com) sells jetskis and outboard engines and offers a comprehensive servicing centre for engines, boats and trailers. It also specialises in roadsters and quad bikes. New and pre-owned luxury yachts are on sale at ART Marine (+9714 338 8955, artmarine.net).

Party Accessories

Most supermarkets, hypermarkets and newsagents stock a range of invitations, balloons, candles, paper plates, decorations and party bags in various themes. However, if you're planning a bigger party with a large number of guests, you may have trouble finding everything in the same theme, so it makes sense to plan ahead: if you can, start collecting bits and pieces as far in advance as possible, stocking up on matching items; hopefully by the time the big day arrives, you will have plenty of matching party items.

Crazy Party (4450 7777) in Villaggio Mall has a wide variety of seasonal choice. Celebrations Palace (4469 6959) has bouncy castles for hire, and Toys R Us (p.311), Gulf Greetings (4486 2889) and the toy shops in the souks stock a limited range of party gifts, decorations and fancy dress items.

Alternatively, you could extend your search beyond Qatar's borders by going online. UK based Heroes For Kids (heroesforkids.co.uk) has an endless range of party products for children's birthday celebrations and international delivery is available. US store Oriental Trading Company (+1 800 875 8480, orientaltrading.com) will accept international orders by telephone.

If you need a fancy dress costume, it is worth calling on the services of a tailor (see Tailors p.294) to whip up your design rather than scouring the limited selection in stores.

Cakes are available at branches of Cafe Bateel (4444 1414), Fauchon (4432 4888), LeNotre (4455 2111), Opera Cafe (4467 8885), Patisserie Suisse (4432 1213), London Bakery (4432 2555) and the bakery section of all major supermarkets, while Tasmeen (4431 5151) in The Centre is popular for cupcakes. Ice-cream cakes are available at Baskin & Robbins (baskinrobbinsmea.com) and Cold Stone Creamery (Hyatt Plaza 4451 4934, Villaggio 4413 5591). To save you money, Tavola at City Center Doha (4493 1101) or the Royal Plaza (4413 1222) has decorative cake tins and cake toppers for home baking, or you can find a private cake designer by searching online classifieds; Happy Cupcakes (qatar-cupcakes.blogspot.com) and Luli Tuli Cupcakes (see its Facebook page) both come highly recommended.

Events
Royal Plaza Al Sadd **4413 1155**
Map **2 L8**

Stocks a good variety of party supplies including disposable tableware, decorations, pinatas, party bags, balloons and banners. The staff have plenty of ideas for hosting themed parties such as a beach party or baby shower, or to celebrate seasonal holidays. Children's party settings come branded with popular characters such as Hannah Montana and Bratz. You can also head here for fancy dress costumes.

Party Kingdom
Nasrallah Centre, Khaleej St Fereej Bin Mahmoud **4435 3501**
Map **2 N9**

Suppliers of party equipment and accessories including costumes and decorations – it also offers bouncy castle hire. A party planning service is available (call 4421 2095 for information) with plenty of options including themed decorations, popcorn and candy floss machines, henna and face painting.

Party Mania
Al Muntazah St Rawdat Al Khail **4441 8810**
partymaniaqatar.com
Map **2 N10**

Items for sale include costumes, decorations, balloons, banners and disposable tableware. You can also hire a number of items including a bouncy castle, popcorn machine, a slide or lighting system. Cartoon characters, face painters, henna artists, entertainers and DJs are also offered or you can utilise their full party planning service to take care of everything for you.

Perfumes & Cosmetics

There are plenty of shops selling perfumes and cosmetics catering to the glamorous ladies and gents in the region. Paris Gallery in the Royal Plaza (4413 1310) and the Hyatt Plaza (4468 9674) is well known for stocking virtually every brand of makeup and perfume; its prices are reasonable and it often has good promotions. Department stores like Debenhams (p.323), Highland (p.324), Merch (p.324), and Salam (p.324) also stock a good range of cosmetics, with all major houses (such as Estee Lauder, Clinique, Lancome, and Clarins) represented. While in the Middle East you should try some authentic Arabian perfume, such as Amouage, which is known as one of the most valuable types of perfume in the world. You will find several stores in the mall dedicated to selling Arabic scents including oud, which is a luxurious, strong smelling perfume. Frankincense and other scents like amber, sandalwood and musk can also be bought here. Fifty One East (p.323), Ajmal Perfumes (4431 9852) and Arabian Oud (4413 1027) are good for Arabian scents. Also visit dedicated stores Karisma Cosmetics (4469 2327), Khaled Perfumes (4431 1917). Souk Waqif has numerous shops selling ready-made perfumes, or you can have your own scents blended for you. Other souks have perfume shops, although keep an eye on whether the fragrance you are buying is authentic – more than a few fakes are sold to unsuspecting shoppers.

The British beauty stores Body Shop (4465 9624), and Boots (4450 7325) as well as international brands, Mac (4413 5069) and Sephora (4450 7345) are all found in most shopping malls; they have a wide selection of international products and brands. The staff at Mac will gladly help you choose your cosmetics and they may also demonstrate how to use them if you ask nicely and they aren't very busy. Skin products and makeup are widely available at most major supermarkets and pharmacies. If you have special makeup requirements (for sensitive skin or teenage skin, for example) and can't find what you are looking for in the shops, all the top hotels have excellent salons and spas where you may find appropriate brands.

4U

City Center Doha Al Dafna **4483 9240**
salams.com
Map **2 Q2**

4U is owned by Salam (p.324) and there are various outlets in many of the malls in Doha. The store stocks a great range of branded products such as Lancome, DKNY, Clinique and Shisheido. It hosts regular makeup demonstrations which focus on different brands each time, and it also holds a 'ladies' day out', which features skin analysis sessions with its trained skin experts.

Amouage

Fifty One East Al Dafna **4442 2815**
amouage.com
Map **2 Q2**

Made in Oman, Amouage, often regarded as 'the world's most expensive perfume', is a high-end branded scent that can be found in stores such as Fifty One East, Paris Gallery, 4U and Salam. The brand is the epitome of luxury and its range of perfumes include a selection of beautiful scents and unique creations. Fifty One East in City Center Doha and the new flagship store at Lagoona Mall also stock more generic perfume brands.

Faces

Landmark Mall Umm Lekhba **4487 9519**
faces-me.com
Map **2 E1**

Faces stocks every major international brand of makeup and perfume including Clinique, Bobbi Brown, Estee Lauder and Guerlain. The excellent staff are very helpful and knowledgeable and always ready to answer your questions. You can get all your makeup, skin care products and perfume shopping done here in one go. Another branch is located at Villaggio Mall (4450 7189).

L'Occitane

Villaggio Mall Baaya **4450 7585**
loccitane-me.com
Map **2 B11**

Head here for natural skin products and fragrances; all of the products are certified 100% organic and are made using ingredients like almond, orange, rose, lavender, shea butter and green tea.

Pets

Laws regarding exotic and endangered breeds are openly flaunted in Qatar and the buying and trading of pets is a highly contentious subject among expats. Pet shops are of a notoriously poor standard; animals are kept in small, often unclean cages and, may not be to the standards you'd expect back home. Pets can be ludicrously expensive to buy and often don't come with guarantees regarding their age or state of health. If you are particularly sensitive to animal rights issues, it may be best to steer clear of the pet shops and some areas of the souks. You should also bear in mind that even buying collars or bowls from unscrupulous dealers is keeping them in business.

Exotic scents

What & Where To Buy

A safer option is to adopt from animal welfare shelter, Qatar Animal Welfare Society (see p.109), which rescues all kinds of animals and pets (often from local pet stores) and sadly, those that are left behind when their owners leave Qatar. You can view the pets needing homes on its website qaws.org.

You can buy fish and accessories for your aquarium at specialist dealer Aqua Art (4468 2000) on Salwa Road. Its stunning showroom displays feature rare and exotic fish, aqua plants and corals from around the world and the team of experts can build and design customised aquariums, ponds and fountains. Aquatic Solutions (4450 0928, aquaticsolutions.com) can also help you design and build a freshwater or marine aquarium. Many of the pet stores stock fish and aquarium accessories, but a good specialist store is Golden Fish (4431 0304) in the Mansoora/Najma area. When buying fish, try to buy newer stock and avoid those with damaged or bloodied fins and wounds as they may carry disease.

For something just a little bit more exotic, head to the falcon souk in Souk Waqif (p.330). Walk inside and you will be confronted with dozens of these magnificent birds, hooded in the traditional way and sitting on their perches.

The Veterinary Surgery (4436 7187) and Qatar Veterinary Centre (p.137) stock pet essentials including pet food, litter boxes, medicines, travel kennels, toys, grooming equipment and bedding. If your pet has a special dietary requirement, contact either clinic for assistance; they will usually order stock in for you.

All supermarkets and hypermarkets sell a range of food and basic supplies for dogs, cats and for some smaller breeds of pets such as birds and rabbits.

Second-Hand Items

Due to the transient nature of the expat population in Qatar, second-hand goods and items are frequently on offer. Just search the classifieds section of local websites (p.23) or check out the advertisements on supermarket noticeboards.

Second-hand furniture is available from Souk Haraj in Najma (p.328) but the quality is usually fairly average. With a good rummage through you should be able to find some interesting pieces for your home.

Used cars are frequently advertised online on expat websites as well as a few dedicated sites, including Qatar Online (online.qa) and Qatar Sale (qatarsale.com), but be wary of the vehicle's condition and history; you don't want to buy something that has been thrashed in the desert. Oasis Cars (4431 1909) has a wide range of used vehicles on offer and it can assist with transfer of ownership, registration and licensing and also offers a car repair and cleaning service. Most new car dealerships have an added showroom for pre-owned cars that are usually sold with warranty and after sale servicing care. See New Car Dealers, p.62. Several privately advertised cars will claim that this statement should be treated with the utmost suspicion. Adverts for four-wheel drive cars will invariably state that the vehicle has never been off road, which does make you wonder why the seller bought it in the first place.

Souvenirs

When you explore the traditional souks, neighbourhood shops and modern shopping malls, you will come across a variety of Middle Eastern souvenirs to suit all budgets and tastes. Similar souvenirs are sold in most GCC countries, so the only challenge is finding something unique to Qatar. Before you purchase the first stuffed camel that you see, discover the wide range of distinctive mementos and keepsakes available around town.

The most obvious place to hunt for the perfect souvenir is Souk Waqif (p.330). Here you will find endless choice, from craft to kitsch, and can practise your negotiation skills when bartering with shopkeepers for the best deals. If you are in the mood for big-ticket bargaining, consider buying an intricately designed Persian carpet (p.300) or a unique piece of hand-crafted furniture as a lifelong keepsake from one of the many carpet and furniture stalls. You will also find cheaper, more portable souvenirs throughout Souk Waqif (p.330). There are several places to buy colourful textiles, including fabrics, pashminas, table linens and decorative pillow covers, which are substantially less expensive compared to similar goods sold in western countries. Traditional scents like the aromatic Arabian oud, incense, oils and perfumes (p.314) are also popular. You can even purchase a shisha pipe filled with flavoured tobacco. Foodies may appreciate a jar of regionally produced

Antique shops at Souk Waqif

honey, plump dates or a blend of unusual spices. For kids, there are plenty of soft toys and trinkets, including the obligatory camel or oryx paraphernalia to be found at a plethora of toy stalls.

Just a short walk from Souk Waqif is the Gold Souk (p.328) where you can buy a wide variety of jewellery – you can even have a necklace designed with your name written in Arabic.

Beyond the souks, you will find small souvenir shops and stalls in the major shopping centres, along with a few specialty shops scattered around town. These shops and stalls sell postcards, photographs, sports apparel, key chains and other small trinkets themed around Qatar. Some stalls specialise in Muslim prayer beads and other beaded jewellery.

Artefacts Of Arabia
Landmark Mall Umm Lekhba 5561 4573
artefactsofarabia.com
Map 2 E1
This store does not have a shop in the Landmark or Villaggio Malls, but look out for its temporary displays. In addition to a great selection of imported furnishings, Artefacts of Arabia sells antique pearl boxes, Moroccan-influenced gilded mirrors, Arabian framed art and paintings and festive candleholders. It also sells a variety of souvenirs from the region, key chains, postcards and photographs.

Darriche
Souk Waqif Al Jasra 4434 2366
Map 2 Q7
A short walk from Souk Waqif, Darriche sells high-quality imported wooden furniture from India and Southeast Asia, carpets, mirrors and light fixtures. Additionally, Darriche stocks candleholders, wooden figurines and a variety of decorations and knick-knacks.

Museum Of Islamic Art
The Corniche Al Souq 4422 4444
mia.org.qa
Map 2 R6
For the ultimate in high-end souvenirs, head to the Museum of Islamic Art's gift shop for its assortment of art and architecture books, children's colouring books, stationery, jewellery, scarves, ties or tea sets. Its coffee table books make the perfect gift for any art lover.

New House Complex
B Ring Rd Rawdat Al Khail 4441 9908
Map 2 P9
Sensational is the only way to describe the New World Complex (not to be confused with the similarly named New World Centre/Souq Nabina), which is packed with low-cost dinnerware in almost any shape you can think of. A helpful employee will gather together the items you point out and will guide you around the store. The staff will also help to find items to match the Arabic coffee cups, silver serving trays and dining sets on offer.

Qatar Souvenirs
Villaggio Mall Baaya 4492 9444
Map 2 B11
Several Qatari mementos are displayed on this small stand in the Villaggio Mall. It specialises in postcards, and framed miniature art, but you will also find key chains and apparel including caps and T-shirts.

Sports Goods
Several large stores in Qatar offer a good cross section of basic sports equipment, clothing and footwear. You should find it easy to locate the usual sports brands and accessories for core sports such as running, basketball, football, swimming, tennis and squash. Some stores also stock gym equipment like treadmills, exercise bikes and weights. Yoga mats and accessories are on sale at GO Sport (p.318), Reebok in Villaggio (4450 7871) and at Yama Yoga Studios (p.179). Olympic Sports (p.318) and Sportmart (4443 0311) stock darts, boards and flights.

Adidas has a store in City Center Doha (4483 9124) and Villaggio Mall (4450 7645) and Kappa products are available at Centrepoint (p.336) and inside Splash (4413 1927) at City Center Doha. Athlete's Foot (4450 7477) stocks New Balance and Converse shoes, and Body Action Performance (4450 7299) in Villaggio stocks a range of active wear for women.

Clubs that organise specialist sports, such as Qatar Kiteboarding (p.318) and Qatar Paragliding (p.318) also sell new and used equipment. Magic Swell (magicswell.com) is a Dubai-based retailer in kitesurfing gear and sportswear that delivers to Qatar.

Skate Shack (p.297) has a wide range of watersports gear including water kites, wind surfers, wakeboards and water skis. It also sells wetsuits, life jackets and safety helmets. You can buy bicycles, skateboards, ice hockey equipment and roller blades here too. If it is scuba gear you're after, try Qatar Divers (4431 3331), the World Marine Centre (4436 0989) or Pearl Divers (4444 9553). For fishing rods, reels and GPS equipment head to Jassim Al Lingawi Trading (4441 3357).

Golf is extremely popular and clubs, balls and bags are available in most sports shops. The Qatar Golf Academy Pro Shop (p.318) and the Golf Shop (4450 7870) in Villaggio Mall are the best places to purchase decent kit. Next door to the Golf Shop is Saddles & Spurs which sells equestrian equipment and Strings & Wheelz which sells gear for cycling and racket sports. Call 4450 7871 for more information.

Children's items are available at most of the general retailers or check Carrefour for a limited range of swimming goggles, arm bands, UV-resistant swimwear and anti-slip pool shoes. You can find rollerblades, kites, bicycles, scooters and junior tennis, golf and baseball kit at Go Sport (p.318), which also stocks beachwear for all ages. Quiksilver (4483 1360) sells stylish swimwear. There is a limited range for women at Change (4413 1177) in Royal Plaza, or visit the beachwear sections of department stores like Debenhams (p.323) and Marks & Spencer (p.324). If you are unable to find what you are looking for, Wiggle (wiggle.co.uk) will ship items from its voluminous range of cycling, running and swimming gear to Qatar.

Galaxy Sports

City Center Doha Al Dafna **4483 0322**
transindgroup.com
Map **2 Q2**

This is a bulk distributor of sporting goods, shoes equipment and apparel from leading brands including Nike, Adidas, Reebok, Slazenger and Yonex. There is another branch of the store in Souk Al Jabor (4443 0322).

Go Sport

Villaggio Mall Baaya **4451 7574**
go-sport.com
Map **2 B11**

A comprehensive retailer that stocks clothing and equipment for running, swimming, camping, football, cycling, tennis and skating – to name a few. Exercising equipment is available and kids' sports and activities are well catered for. The range of goods includes an in-house line as well as international brands.

Olympic Sports

City Center Doha Al Dafna **4483 0122**
olympicsp.com
Map **2 Q2**

Large showrooms stock everything from clothing to equipment and offer after sales technical servicing on all of their machines. International brands include Umbro, Prince and the perennially popular brands Nike, Reebok and Adidas. You'll also find Victorinox knives and a good range of swimwear from Speedo (for adults and children) and Canadian line, Christina. They are also the main port of call when sports trophies need engraving

Qatar Golf Academy Pro Shop

Doha Golf Club Al Egla **4496 0755**
dohagolfclub.com
Map **1 H1**

Carries an extensive range of golfing equipment and merchandise including products from the shop's very own brand. Golf clubs, balls, bags, trolleys, umbrellas, clothing, tools and accessories are available from some of the world's leading brands, including Callaway, Odyssey, Ping, Titleist and TaylorMade.

Qatar Kiteboarding

Al Wakra **3347 4176**
qatarkiteboarding.com
Map **Qatar Country Map D4**

This is a popular destination where keen kiteboarders can buy all their equipment, with a good selection of brands on sale. These include Ozone, GoPro, Crazyfly, Nobile, Iride, Mr Kitesurf, JD Instruments, Prolimit and Best Kiteboarding. The store also has an online classified section where you can advertise any of your used goods.

Qatar Paragliding

Al Wakra **3347 4176**
wix.com/ovidiustaicu/qatarparagliding
Map **Qatar Country Map D4**

An official distributor of Advance, Gin, Ozone, Independence and Sky products. Used goods are advertised on their online classifieds section-products posted include gliders and harnesses.

Speed Marine

Al Wakra **4464 1682**
speedmarinegroup.com
Map **Qatar Country Map D4**

The store stocks a complete range of water craft including SEADOO jet-skis, Cobra, Johnson and Yamaha ATVs, Evinrude and Bombardier outboards and accessories. A complete on-site service centre specialises in engine, boat and trailer maintenance. Other branches can be found in Al Gharafa (4442 3283), Museum Road (4441 0109) and Salwa Road (4469 4353).

Sportmart

Nr The Centre Mall, Salwa Rd Rawdat Al Khail **4443 0311**
transindgroup.com
Map **2 N9**

The exclusive retailer for Specialized bicycles and gear, Sportmart has a little bit of everything on offer. Along with shoes and apparel, you'll find darts and boards, treadmills, rollerblades, swimming gear and sunglasses.

Sun & Sand Sports

City Center Doha Al Dafna **4483 7007**
sunandsandsports.com
Map **2 Q2**

This large showroom stocks a good range of home gym equipment including treadmills, rowing machines and weights. Plenty of other sports are catered for including football, basketball, running and swimming, plus the adjoining outlets of Columbia and Timberland stock clothing for outdoor sports such as hiking.

Textiles & Haberdashery

The fabric souk is the most comprehensive place
to shop for fabric, buttons, scissors, interfacings
and ribbon, as well as some speciality items such
as dupioni silk. It incorporates an area around Souk
Al Dira (p.328) and Souk Asiery (p.328) with tons of
unnamed shops and stores selling all kinds of fabric
and haberdashery. Across the road from the main souk
is the fabric branch of Al Rawnaq (4441 4505), which
is a great place to get started. It stocks felt, thread,
yarn, buttons, feathers, ribbon and sewing supplies
among other fabric – and its prices are pretty good. Its
range of costume jewellery is also great for decorating
clothing and cushions and for arts and crafts.

Parking can be a bit of an issue around Souk Dira
unless you go very early in the morning – it is often
easier to park in Souk Waqif and walk there. Souk
Faleh (p.328) has ready-made abayas and fabric and Souk
Waqif has a few shops selling dress fabric. Bombay Silk
(4441 2715) on Salwa Road has silk fabrics imported
from India and offers a tailoring service. The arts and
crafts section of Jarir Bookstore (p.298) occasionally
has a few items of interest such as Velcro and quilt
batting. Visit Qatar Quilt Guild online (qatarquiltguild.
blogspot.com) or email qatarquiltguild@gmail.com for
more information on where to buy goods for quilting
and quilt batting, and to share tips and techniques
with Doha's active quilting circle (p.265).

Wedding Items

There are a few shops in town that can help you with
organising your big day. Most hotels have wedding
planners who can assist you with the preparations,
which can be quite expensive, but will cut out some
of the hassle involved in trying to put things together
yourself. The Four Seasons Hotel has wedding
consultants who will work with you to make your
wedding day special. They will organise everything
from flowers to linens, to cakes and transportation.
Lenotre (4455 2111) also offers event planning
services for weddings.

There are several wedding dress shops in Doha.
Allegra Evening Wear Salon (5581 7777) features
traditional and modern designer wedding gowns with
price tags that range from QR 19,500 to QR 26,400.
Most of the gowns are made with hand-crafted
fabrics that are beaded with Swarovski crystals. While
there are options, finding a particular style from
international designers is difficult and having a dress
custom-made is probably the best plan. Places like Al
Fareesha Ladies Tailor, located on Al Sadd Street, can
help you make your dream wedding gown a reality.
Unfortunately, hiring a wedding dress, or the groom's
suit, is not possible in Qatar; however, you may find a
second-hand dress in Pepka Wear (5545 5783).

For all your bridal accessories, including lingerie
and shoes, head to Debenhams (p.323). The store
has a good selection of concession stores which sell
evening wear, accessories and shoes – it is also a great
place to buy bridesmaid dresses, or to purchase outfits
for the mother of the bride and the groom. Monsoon
sells a good range of evening wear for women and
has several stores in Qatar, including City Center Doha
(4483 2769). Arabella (4436 3202), located in the Royal
Plaza, has a good selection too. Monsoon is also a sure
fire hit for bridesmaid's dresses and flowergirl outfits,
accessories and shoes.

L'uomo (4442 0207) on Al Sadd Street and Boggi
(4413 5098) in Villaggio Mall, are good places to
purchase evening wear for men. Both stores feature
classic Italian suits, but L'uomo has slightly cheaper
price tags. You could also opt to have a suit made for
you at one of the many tailors in Qatar. Prices for a
custom made suit range from QR 500 to QR 800.

Most hotels can help with making the wedding
cake; but for a more affordable option, Patisserie
Suisse (4432 1213), Opera (4468 8344) and Cafe Bateel
(4444 1414) can be commissioned to create a wedding
cake. Fauchon (4432 4888) offers catering services as
well as wedding cake creation services. Most of Doha's
florists will work with you to create and design floral
arrangements, hall decorations and the bride and
bridesmaids' bouquets. Gulf Gardenia (4447 7708) can
help with flower arrangements as well as with other
wedding preparations. You can also contact Al Arabia
Flowers (5573 6214), Casa Flora (4432 8111), Royal
Flowers (4444 4469) and Plaza Hollandi (4467 1384,
plazahollandi.chapso.de). Gulf Colours (4443 9399) has
professional photographers and videographers who
can capture the day for you, and it also has a wedding
section in its store with classic and modern wedding
invitations. Lydia Shaw (lydiashawphotography.com) is
a solo photographer who specialises in portrait shots
and also shoots weddings.

Colourful textiles

PLACES TO SHOP
Shopping By Area

Al Mansoora Street
Fereej Bin Dirhem
Map 2 Q10

Beginning with the furniture branch of Al Shaheen, the Najma end of this cluttered street is choked with furniture, fabric and curtain stores that you could spend hours rummaging through. The shops are crammed with goods and the quality is usually very cheap, but then again, so are the prices. Parking is extremely difficult along this part of the main street, as well as in nearby side streets, so either come early in the morning or just before 16:00 when the shops reopen for the evening. The whole area is always busy with people, bicycles and cars which gives it a lively, bustling feel, especially during the evening periods when hundreds of local residents wander out to enjoy the streets at night. Just past the Najma Street junction is a collection of very basic bicycle and accessories shops, but don't expect to ride your next triathlon on any of the available models. You'll find cheap frames, tyres and parts and some shops will help you with maintenance. A short drive further along towards the Al Muntazah end of the street is Al Mansoora Carpet Centre (p.301) where you can buy cheap rugs and floor coverings, as well as a couple of aquarium stores such as Golden Fish (4431 0304).

Al Mirqab Al Jadeed Street
Al Sadd
Map 2 J10

This thin, humble street between C and D Ring Roads, which is usually known by its less formal name of Family Food Road because of the Family Food Store at the end of the street, was jam-packed with shops many of which were regularly frequented by expats. There was a mix of everything here, including fabric shops, tailors, pharmacies and grocery stores, and a few are still there. However, the centre section of this street is gradually being demolished and the shops are being replaced with commercial office blocks. The most popular destinations at the time of writing are Thai Snack (p.370), Colour Note Company (p.295) and Kashmir Handicrafts Emporium (p.301).

The street always seems to be heavy with traffic and you may need to scour the side streets to find a parking spot. A word of warning: even if you do find a parking spot outside one of the shops on Al Mirqab Al Jadeed Street itself, don't be surprised if you return to your car to find that one (or several) cars have parked behind you, blocking your exit. Shops are generally closed for a few hours in the afternoon (with the exception of the grocery stores) and on Friday mornings.

Al Sadd Street
Al Sadd
Map 2 J9

Al Sadd Plaza, on the corner of C Ring Road, was the first shopping mall in Doha but is now utilised as an office block. These days, shoppers tend to gravitate to Royal Plaza (p.336) a little further along the road to indulge in high-end retail spending. Al Sadd isn't exactly the type of street you would spend much time wandering along (it is a major six-lane thoroughfare), but it is worth taking the time to pull into the car parks to take a look around. There are groups of discount clothing and shoe shops gathered along sections of the street, plus jewellery stores and a good number of places to eat, including some quality restaurants serving Arabic and Lebanese food. Several worth sampling are Al Damashqi (formerly Automatic, 4442 5999), Al Khaima (4444 6962) and Al Majlis (4444 7417). Branches of Fauchon (p.358) and Cafe Opera are also present.

B Ring Road
Rawdat Al Khail
Map 2 N9

B Ring Road is a winding arterial road stretching from Ras Abu Abboud all the way around to Al Muntazah. It is almost always heavily congested with traffic and parking can be difficult to find, but this is largely due to the popularity of the shops situated along the road. With the low prices and friendly service, it is a wonder that more westerners aren't aware of the hidden gems along B Ring Road. Between Ras Abu Abboud and Al Matar Street are a huddle of car stores, selling auto spare parts, tyres, upholstery and automotive accessories, plus several auto electricians and car detailers. Oasis Car dealership is on the corner, opposite the Mobil petrol station popular for its car cleaning service. Across from Al Matar Street, and right up toward Jaidah Flyover, are several tool and hardware shops such as Al Feroz and Qatar Trading, lighting showrooms and commercial artist shops that specialise in neon signboards and professional printing. New House Complex (4441 9908) is about halfway along this strip, and stocks a fantastic range of cheap crockery, cookware, coffee pots, trays, pots and serving dishes. On the opposite side of the road and a little further along is Shibam Trading Centre (4432 4693), licensed retailers of Villeroy & Boch tiles, taps and bathroom accessories. Expect most shops to be closed during the afternoon and on Friday mornings.

Musheireb
Map 2 Q8

The Musheireib area (better known as the old Sofitel area) has numerous shops selling everything from cheap clothing to top-of-the-range electronics. There really is a mix of everything here and the alluring

Uncover the shopping secrets of the souks

Places To Shop

fluorescent signage above each shop gives you the urge you to explore and spend. Branches of Jumbo Electronics and Nasir bin Abdullah (p.299) are located here, which are good for perusing home appliances, and Al Mushiri (p.309) at the Bin Mahmoud end is good for for camera equipment. It is very busy at weekends and in the evenings, when the parking situation is a nightmare. You may find you are better off paying for parking in nearby Souk Waqif then setting out on foot. It is not advisable to visit alone on Friday evenings if you are a woman; the streets are overrun with male workers and although you will be safe, the number of stares and looks that you'll attract are likely to make you feel uncomfortable. Much of this area will disappear in the very near future as part of the Heart of Doha redevelopment scheme.

The Pearl Qatar

North of West Bay The Pearl Qatar **4446 3444**
thepearlqatar.com
Map **1 M2**

With an extraordinary collection of high-end designer retailers and boutique shops, The Pearl is worth a visit to simply surround yourself with luxury. Branches of enviable brands such as Hermes, Armani, Kenzo, MaxMara, Jimmy Choo, Vera Wang, Chloe, Missoni, Roberto Cavalli and Alexander McQueen offer fresh-off-the-catwalk haute couture, handbags, jewellery

and fashion accessories. If your Louboutins need a rest, you can stop for a break at world-famous Alison Nelson's Chocolate Bar (p.352), or sip an espresso on the boardwalk while watching extravagant yachts sail by. Evening visitors will not be disappointed by the range of fine dining options including the delectable Japanese restaurant Megu (p.365).

Salwa Rd

Fereej Abdul Aziz
Map **2 N9**

Salwa Road slices through Doha then continues out of the city to the border of Saudi Arabia (over 80 kilometres away). There are plenty of reasons to visit the Doha stretch of Salwa Road but you will need a car to navigate the distances between shops, or simply just to get you safely across to the other side of the road. Being a busy causeway, shoppers tend to head directly to a specific outlet then leave again, as it is near impossible to wander along on foot, especially in the heat. While there are shops, banks, cafes and businesses running the length of the entire thoroughfare, many of them housed in newly constructed rows of buildings, shops that sell similar goods tend to be clustered together. Examples include the fast food outlets around Ramada Junction (known locally as Cholesterol Corner), the furniture shops around Decoration Roundabout, and the

The fashion boulevard at The Pearl

vehicle showrooms dotted along the way toward the wholesale markets located at the western end. A couple of standalone stores popular with expats are Jarir Bookstore (p.298), Studio Qatar (4458 2341) for framing and Zaks (p.311) for school uniforms. Many of the shops are closed during the afternoon and on Friday mornings. Traffic, which is more like a race track than a suburban road, is a nightmare for most periods of the day and night but parking is usually plentiful.

The Souk Areas
Al Souq
Map **2 R7**

The souks are great places to practise your haggling skills and to bag a bargain; they also offer a vibrant glimpse into traditional Qatari trade and culture. The bustling market atmosphere is especially lively at night. A neat trick is to arrive as little as ten or fifteen minutes before the shops are due to open and you will almost always find a parking space – otherwise expect chaos.

Souk Waqif (p.330) is a must-see for visitors to Qatar, being a sanitised, reconstructed for tourist version of the original Souq Waqif, but it is just as worthwhile to venture into the rest of the souk district that begins on the other side of Grand Hamad Street. The Gold Souk (p.328) is worth a visit just to see the dazzling range of heavy Indian designs and ornate bridal jewellery. Parallel to the Corniche run a number of souks, stretching from Souk Faleh near the Fanar Centre, to Souk Jabor. These incorporate much of what is collectively known as the fabric and the abaya souks, and includes Souk Faleh (p.328), Souk Nasser Bin Saif (p.328), Souk Al Asiery (p.328) and Souk Al Dira (p.328). Along this stretch you'll find plenty of hole-in-the-wall shawarma and samosa shops. The new out of town shopping area at Barwa Village near Wakra has all the makings of a modern souq.

Department Stores
Doha has plenty of department stores, most of which are international brand names. Many of the stores anchor the major shopping malls and some provide concession outlets of well-known brands. With names like Marks & Spencer and Debenhams on mall listings, you should find a good variety of products for the whole family.

Bhs
Landmark Mall Umm Lekhba **4487 4271**
bhs.co.uk
Map **2 E1**
Well-known for its abundant range of items for the whole family, this UK department store also has a branch in Al Mana Towers (4431 4347). The popular store carries everything from children's clothing to bedding and a small range of household items. You

will also find it has a well-stocked lingerie section with brands including Triumph, Bellissima and Wonderbra, and good clothing and shoe departments for both men and women.

Blue Salon
Suhaim Bin Hamad St Fereej Bin Mahmoud
4446 6111
bluesalon.com
Map **2 L8**
Blue Salon is one of the premier department stores in Doha. It carries a range of brands including Armani, Valentino, Zegna, Aigner and Diesel. The store sells all the typical products found in a department store, and you can purchase your linens, electronic goods and fashion items for men and women. The ladies' section is laden with high-end brands including Moschino, Luisa Cerano and Maurizio Galante.

Debenhams
City Center Doha Al Dafna **4483 8913**
debenhams.com
Map **2 Q2**
A true department store in every sense, you can get your cosmetics, buy your bathroom towels and pick up clothes for the kids in this one store. Unlike Marks & Spencer, it has a good variety of concession stores covering evening and cocktail dresses, suits for men, shoes, lingerie and swimwear. The accessories department includes handbags by brands like Liz Claiborne, Rocha, Lisi and Faith and its large children's section carries clothing and accessories for newborns up to teens. Household items such as blankets, pillows, vases, photo frames and bedding are also available.

Emporium
Nr Ramada R/A, Al Dhiya St New Al Mirqab
4437 5796
emporiumqatar.com
Map **2 M10**
This store is best described as a mini mall which houses a number of designer shops. You will find a range of high-end stores include Kenzo, Escada, Betty Barclay, MaxMara, Laurel, More & More, Babycare and Ciel. The centre opens from 10:00 to 13:00 and from 17:00 to 22:00, Saturday through to Thursday. On Friday, the store opens from 17:00 to 22:00. There is plenty of parking.

Fifty One East > *p.289*
Lagoona Mall Al Gassar **4425 7777**
51east.com.qa
Map **1 K1**
Fifty One East is Qatar's premier luxury department store catering to the needs of Doha's elite. This new Lagoona Mall branch offers one the widest selections of the most prestigious brands and products – there's

even a Rolex concession store. Calvin Klein and True Religion Jeans are good for casual clothes, while Marchesa, Azzaro and J. Mendel offer deluxe evening gowns in beautiful fabrics and sophisticated designs. Cosmetics are also well represented with brands such as Chanel, Dior and Guerlain. For menswear, you'll get to sample the impeccable cuts of Brioni, the top-notch leather pieces of Moreschi, and the classy Parisian styles of Lanvin. If you are looking for the finest watches, jewellery, fashion, cosmetics and electronics, then this is the place to shop. Other branches are located in Al Maha Centre and City Center Doha.

Highland
The Mall Old Airport **4467 8678**
Map **2 R13**
Highland is a two-level department store which has recently undergone a makeover. It sells a variety of items from high-end cosmetics and perfumes to luggage, bed linen, and household items such as lamps, photo frames, mirrors, and bedding. The bedding range is expensive, but the designs are beautiful and of good quality. The children's section upstairs caters more for younger kids, and even has a small collection of nursery items (cots and bedding); you'll also find the home ware section here. On the first level you'll find cosmetics, clothes for men and women, and the luggage department – which stocks Samsonite luggage and a selection of ladies' handbags. The clothing range on offer is small, but fashionable men can find labels including New Man and ICU. For women there is Roberto Cavalli and Krizia. This eclectic store also has an interesting souvenir section, where you can take home a crystal falcon if your heart so desires.

Marks & Spencer
Landmark Mall Umm Lekhba **4488 0101**
marksandspencerme.com
Map **2 E1**
Those not familiar with Marks & Spencer are in for a treat; it is a great department store that is very popular with both expats and locals and definitely one to add to your list of good shops. Both locations in Doha (there is also a store in Villaggio Mall, 4451 6363) have a great selection of fashion items for the whole family as well as a wide selection of men's suits. A particular bonus is that trousers are available in various lengths. The ladies' section has a lovely range of the latest fashion and clothes are available in a wide range of sizes, from petite to plus-size. Children's clothing ranges from newborns right up to trendy teens and its underwear section is famous. You will find underwear and sleepwear for everyone, but the women's section is a haven of pretty colours and styles ranging from sexy to sensible. There is a range of 100% cotton underwear, which is great for the hot climate. There is

also a small range of household items such as photo frames, cushions, candles and vases. In the UK, M&S is renowned for its food hall, and while in this branch the food section is relatively small, it does sell quality non perishables like biscuits, chocolates, coffee and tea.

Merch
The Mall Old Airport **4467 4314**
merch.com.qa
Map **2 R13**
Merch is another high-end department store, and its defining feature is its enviable cosmetic and perfume section, which houses a variety of international brands. You can also pick up the usual range of handbags, accessories and fashion items for men and women found in other department stores. The store has another branch on Salwa Road (4465 8656).

Salam
The Mall Old Airport **4467 2200**
salams.com
Map **2 R13**
Salam is a well-known name in this part of the world: its department stores Salam Plaza (63 Maysaloun Street) and Salam Studio in The Mall (4467 8467),carry a wide range of designer clothing and accessories. Other items you can find here are cosmetics, perfumes, luggage, household goods and shoes. If it's upmarket, good quality merchandise you want, Salam is the place to go. This is reflected in the prices though, so it's not the place for avid bargain hunters (except during sales).

Supermarkets & Hypermarkets
Most supermarkets and hypermarkets, certainly the larger ones, are located in one of Doha's many shopping malls. Most of the stores stock a good variety of international items, although you may have to traipse through several different shops before you can find all the items on your shopping list. While there are great local products to choose from, it can be frustrating when you happily come across your favourite product from back home, only to discover a few weeks later that it has sold out. So if you see something that you would love to use often, stock up.

Al Meera
Various Locations **4011 9111**
almeera.com
Al-Meera is the local version of the Co-operative Society and was founded with government support to proved basic food staples to Qatar's citizens at prices they could afford. It still does, but now with the addition of most products found in supermarkets; in fact, in most instances, the Al Meera shops are indistinguishable from normal supermarkets. Prices

tend to be cheaper than the glitzy malls, although it has to be admitted that service can be a bit offhand.

Carrefour
City Center Doha Al Dafna **800 7323**
carrefourqatar.com
Map **2 Q2**
You should be able to find most things you need at Carrefour without burning a hole in your pocket. The biggest branch of the store is located in City Center Doha, but there are also outlets in Landmark Mall (4452 0777) and Villaggio Mall (4413 9666). The store is well known for its wide international product range, and its excellent fish and vegetable sections. Besides groceries you can shop for home goods, electronics and beauty products. The store also offers a guarantee on all of its electrical goods and takes all forms of payment including GCC currency, US dollars, Euros and major credit cards. Opening hours are from 08:00 to 24:00 (throughout the year), during Ramadan from 09:00 to midnight; closing from 11:30 to 12:30 for Friday prayers.

Dasman Centre
Nr Toyota Tower, Airport Rd Najma **4431 3115**
dasman.biz
Map **2 T10**
This store opened its doors to the public in 1994 and since then it has grown to three locations, in Markhiya (4493 1096) and Al Gharafa (4487 7868) and the branch on Al Matar Street. The last is the biggest branch and it features 2,000 square feet of retail space. The supermarket stocks a good range of international and local products and provides high-quality goods at very affordable prices. It also offers a good range of household items, electronics, cosmetics and perfumes. Its stores open from 08:00 to midnight every day, with the exception of the Al Gharrafa branch which opens from 08:00 to 03:00 daily.

Family Food Centre
Off Al Rayyan Al Jadeed St Old Al Rayyan **4481 1456**
family.com.qa
Map **2 B6**
The Family Food Centre has three locations in Doha – on Al Matar Street (4462 2722) and in Al Nasr (4442 2456) – but the New Rayyan location is the largest. The store is well known in expat circles for its wide range of international foods, but it also has a good range of food products for customers with special dietary requirements (including vegans). The bakery is a crowd pleaser; featuring freshly made bread every day and other items like muffins, croissants, pies and cakes. The store also offers a catering service – call 4442 5182 for more information. The store opens from 07:30 to midnight Saturday to Thursday and closes from 10:30 to 12:30 for Friday prayers.

Giant Stores
Hyatt Plaza Baaya **4469 2996**
giant-stores.net
Map **2 A12**
Located inside Hyatt Plaza, Giant is a two storey grocery store which has a spacious layout that never feels too crowded. There is a large vegetable section which has a high quality assortment of fresh products imported by air from Lebanon, Syria and Europe. The meat section is well-stocked and is run by helpful staff – you can occasionally find pre-packed Halal beef from the US. Up the escalators are an electronics department and a toys and stationary section. There is also a video store called Giant Video (4450 7040). Giant is also located on Airport Road (4469 4848) and has a further two branches, at the top of Al Matar Street and at VW roundabout. These two branches are known locally as the "Tiny Giant Stores". Stores are open from 08:30 to 23:00 daily, except for Fridays when they close from 11:30 to 12:30 for Friday prayers.

Lulu Hypermarket
D Ring Rd Old Airport **4466 7780**
luluhypermarket.com
Map **2 T12**
Set over two levels, Lulu Hypermarket holds a multitude of items covering groceries, electronics, clothing and household goods. The hypermarket is extremely popular with Asian expats, and there is a great variety of Asian products. Increasingly, more international brands are being added to the stock, making it more popular with western expatriates. Lulu also has its own brand items, which are often a cheaper alternative to some of the imported brands. The store is renowned for its weekly in-store promotions and raffles (where you may be able to bag a car with your weekly shop). On the second floor is a branch of electronics store Emax (p.308). A new major branch is located at Al Gharaffa (4407 4000); this branch is particularly noted for its high quality vegetables. The third branch, opposite the Hamad Hospital does not stock food.

During the late 2012 a further branch is slated to open in the new Al Khor Mall, in Al Khor Town.

Mega Mart
The Centre Rawdat Al Khail **4444 0018**
Map **2 N10**
MegaMart is a small grocery store that stocks mostly western products; therefore it's very popular with the expat community. It's not cheap, but people make this their regular shopping haunt largely due to the fact that you can pick up many products from back home. It has a good selection of fruit and vegetables, including organic fruit, as well as a good fish and meats section. Also on sale is a premium range of products from UK supermarket brand Waitrose,

Places To Shop

hopping

and a range of organic food for children. If you see something you like you should stock up, as you may not see them again for a while. You can also find a great variety of international food products from Mexico, India and the US. There is another branch of the store on Al Rayyan Road, known as Mega Mart Express (4488 3001). The store opens from 08:00 to 23:00 daily. Mega Mart has opened a new branch at Barwa Village near Wakra (4411 1077 / 4411 1099).

Boutiques & Independent Shops

Due to the sponsorship laws in Qatar, there are technically no independent stores operating in the country, by definition. However, Doha does have all kinds of shops and outlets that are effectively separate from the usual range of chain retailers and department store brands. Many of the shops in Royal Plaza and The Pearl are regarded as exclusive boutiques, simply because they have no other branches elsewhere in the country.

Boudoir
City Center Doha Al Dafna **4411 5280**
boudoir.me
Map **2 Q2**
The kind of accessories store you could easily lose yourself in, Boudoir is packed to the rafters with girlie bling, sparkles and ruffles. Hand-crafted jewellery, flowing kaftans and bejewelled footwear are examples of the gorgeous items on offer. For an original gift idea, you can also have names and words crafted into wearable art. Another branch of the store is located at the Royal Plaza (4432 5350).

Cugini
The Pearl Qatar 4495 3876
cugini.com.qa
Map **1 L2**
The staff at Cugini hand-pick clothing, jewellery and accessories from lesser-known designers around the world. The eclectic mix of fashion on display is original, fiercely trendy and in line with the store's philosophy that style is personal, passionate and evolutionary.

Owned by a pair of vivacious cousins, the store made its mark in Qatar when it became the first boutique to open on the illustrious boardwalk at The Pearl Qatar.

Stylish Abayas
Souk Faleh, also known as the 'Abaya souk', has at least 30 stores selling abayas at different prices. You can get one for as cheap as QR 80 or spend over QR 1,000 for a more extravagant style. You can also have one custom-made; this allows you to choose the fabric and design you want. A cheaper range can be found at Souk Waqif (p.330).

Palmera Fashion
The Ritz-Carlton, Doha Al Gassar **4484 8000**
ritzcarlton.com
Map **1 K1**
Boutique fashion at its best, this store specialises in luxury designer clothing, handbags, jewellery and accessories for men and women. The range of high-end brands on its racks includes creations by Gucci, Marni, Yves Saint Laurent, Salvatore Ferragamo, Dolce & Gabbana, Prada and Fendi.

Markets & Souks
Taking your weekly shop to the souks should provide a more organic experience and a great alternative to mall hopping. Doha's souks are filled with a great variety of local and international items and while you can pick up most of the things sold in the shopping centres and supermarkets, you can generally get them cheaper in the souks because you can bargain (see Bargaining on p.290) with the traders.

On the whole, these bustling markets are fascinating not only from a shopper's point of view (you could spend an entire morning rummaging around), but also because of the cultural experience – it is a good chance to get up close and personal to a traditional form of business.

Bargaining is a skill that should be practised and enjoyed. Vendors are friendly and eager to make a sale, and they expect a bit of negotiating from their

FASHION FORWARD Heba Al Okar, co-owner of independent boutique, Cugini

Being a small boutique, we are able to develop and nurture fashion in Qatar in a way that the big brands are unable to. We have found that as much as everybody loves the well-known brands, people are always looking for something different, and this is where we have found our appeal. At Cugini, we are not only working with one brand or label; we select our pieces from many designers, some well-established and others up-and-coming.

Being Qatari, without the governance of foreign sponsorship laws doesn't necessarily give us any edge over our competitors; the truth is, if you have a good concept, a good location and if you truly believe in what you are doing, then you will succeed. Cugini was the first boutique to open on The Pearl, and we believe that our journey is made significant by this benchmark; just like The Pearl itself, we are growing into something amazing.

ooter:
326 Qatar Explorer

customers. Start by shopping around first so that you know what something is worth, and use that as a starting point for your negotiations. Remember that souks are traditional areas often predominately populated by men, so it's wise for ladies to dress conservatively, with shoulders and legs covered. If you wear something tight or revealing be prepared to be gawped at.

Souk Waqif (the Old Souk) is an extraordinary place, where you can buy a traditional Qatari outfit, then walk up the street to eat at a Moroccan restaurant (see Tajine, p.369) before picking up some kitchen appliances on your way home.

Outside Souk Waqif, all of Doha's main souks (the Omani Market, Fruit and Vegetable Market, Fish Market and Animal Market) are situated in the same area south-west of the city, off Salwa Road.

Animal Market

Wholesale Market St Bu Hamour
Map **1 F13**

The Animal Market doesn't get too many expat visitors, and since most westerners are not on the lookout for camels or goats, it is the kind of place you would go to simply out of interest rather than to shop around. The vendors are friendly and eager to talk to you, although their English is often very basic. In case you are interested (and you have a big back garden), a young camel will set you back around QR 5,000, and you can get an adult one for QR 10,000 upwards. Sheep and goats go for about QR 500 each, and if you pay a bit more the sellers will prepare the animal for eating. The animal market is located next to the Fish Market, and along with livestock you can also buy pets. However, a big word of warning: these animals are usually kept in poor conditions and many carry diseases. On the positive side, it is an excellent place for purchasing manure for your garden; delivery can be arranged.

Barwa Village

Off Al Wakrah Rd Al Wakra
Map **Qatar Country Map D4**

This purpose built business area is a creditable attempt to establish out of town shopping with adequate parking facilities, something that is normally lacking in Doha. Most of the small businesses established here have been displaced from the area being redeveloped as the Heart of Doha, in the centre of Doha.

Modern buildings house the businesses, which have been grouped on the familiar souk principle of placing similar traders in specific areas. There are areas for building supplies and DIY, furniture, curtains, electrical white goods, electronics, textiles, opticians and others. The centre of the development houses branches of MegaMart and Centrepoint.

For those who have ever experienced the stress and trauma of trying to park in the old central area of Doha before its redevelopment, to buy something as mundane as a door handle or light fitting, this development cannot be praised highly enough.

Sweet Like Chocolate

Sugar aficionados will delight in Doha's abundance of chocolate shops, which stock premier chocolates from around the world. Do as the locals do and head straight to Patchi, which has several locations including one at Villaggio Mall (4450 7862, patchi.com). It sells delicious chocolate-covered dates and delectable bonbons, wrapped with grandeur. If you want to impress, The W Hotel's Teuscher (4453 5383) has irresistible pralines and truffles, including sugar-free options. Maya La Chocolaterie (Landmark Shopping Mall, 4486 2264) and Alison Nelson's Chocolate Bar at the The Pearl Qatar (p.33) offer a tasty selection to be enjoyed in store or as a takeaway.

Fish Market

Salwa Rd Bu Hamour
Map **2 G13**

You can't miss the Fish Market; just walk along Salwa Road until you see loads of people carrying blue plastic bags, and it won't be long before you recognise the smell. It is not a place for those with weak stomachs; the odour is enough to make you turn around and go to the supermarket instead. But the fish is sold fresh daily and is slightly cheaper than from a supermarket (and can be significantly cheaper if you can drive a hard bargain). The market opens at 04:00, and the earlier you get there the better choice you have (and the less overpowering the smell is). The stalls are all set up in an air-conditioned building, and a cleaning and gutting service is provided for QR 1.

Those looking for a fresh catch can also head for the Corniche in the morning and late afternoons. Next to the Hawar Cafe and the slipway, fishermen set up impromptu tables of fish and other seafood, straight off the boats. They will even gut it there for you. Prices are even cheaper than the Salwa Road market.

Fruit & Vegetable Market

Salwa Rd Bu Hamour
Map **2 G13**

At this market you'll find a good selection of fresh fruit and vegetables, and the prices are usually cheaper than at supermarkets. Buying in bulk is better value for money than buying by the kilogram, but always make sure you check the fruit at the bottom of the box to determine it hasn't been squashed. Vendors are happy to let you sample the fruit before you buy it. As you enter the souk, a man will follow you around with a

Places To Shop

trolley or wheelbarrow. Don't worry; he is only trying to make a living by collecting all your purchases as you go. Once you've finished shopping he will then take it all to your car and help you load it in. It's up to you how much to pay, but anything from QR 5 upwards is appreciated. All the market stalls are covered, providing shade all day, so it doesn't matter what time you go. But earlier in the morning is better, when the produce is fresher.

Gold Souk
Off Ali Bin Abdullah St Old Al Ghanim
Map **2 R8**
With gold reaching record prices around the globe, it remains a bargain commodity in this part of the world. Many expats prefer to take gold rather than cash back to their home country. The government regulates the purity of gold, so you can be sure of great quality. The gold on display here ranges from the spectacular Indian and Arab bridal jewellery through to humble bracelets, all in 18 carat or 22 carat. The Gold Souk can be found just off Ali Bin Abdullah Street.

Omani Market
Nr Wholesale Market Bu Hamour
Map **2 G13**
The Omani Market features plants, pots, garden materials and a selection of woven mats and baskets, which are imported from Oman and, increasingly, Iran and India. There are a few stalls selling nuts and dates and exotic incenses such as frankincense and myrrh. There are also a number of excellent nurseries in the surrounding area selling pots and plants. The choice of pots isn't huge, but it is worth taking the time to browse through all the plants. Don't forget to bargain with the friendly and enthusiastic vendors to ensure you get the best price.

Souk Al Ahmed, Souk Al Asiery & Souk Al Dira
Al Ahmed St Al Souq
Map **2 R7**
These three souks make up the area known as 'the fabric souk', and are great stops for those who wish to recreate the latest catwalk look or design their own creations. Souk Al Ahmed, also known as the 'bridal souk', is an air-conditioned two-storey building off Grand Hamad Street that houses dozens of bridal specialist tailors. Souk Al Dira, which is also known as the 'button and bow souk', is the place to buy fabric by the metre. You'll find a good range of fabric here from simple cotton right through to the finest silk. Stores in this area also sell all manner of accoutrements to ensure you have everything you need to make a one-of-a-kind creation. Much of the current structure was destroyed by fire in October 2009, but fortunately, a good section of the souk survived. Souk Al Asiery

is a cheaper version of souks Al Ahmed and Al Dira, and you should be able to find some good bargains here. This is the place to find all kinds of fabrics at knockdown prices.

Souk Al Jabor
Al Ahmed St Al Souq
Map **2 R8**
You will find everything from perfume to toys, cheap shoes and tacky souvenirs in this jumble of a souk. Located on Al Ahmed Street, you will need to take your patience with you and be prepared to spend some time rummaging to find the things you need.

Souk Faleh
Al Souq
Map **2 R7**
The line of shops that make up Souk Faleh sell a mixed range of low-priced items – some for as little as QR 5 to QR 10. Also known as the 'abaya souk', you'll find gorgeous fabrics for traditional dress which you can have measured and fitted to suit, along with ready-made abayas that range from basic to glitzy.

Souk Haraj
Al Mansoura St Najma
Map **2 S10**
This quiet little gem on Al Mansoura Street is as close as Doha gets to a flea market. Shops here sell locally made furniture at great prices. The carpentry and metalwork stores, located just off the main square, also sell curtains, carpets and assorted items of furniture. The majority of the furniture is imported from India and Pakistan. You can also pick-up second-hand crockery, jewellery and tools. The area has become a little sanitised in the last few years, following a major fire and the construction of purpose-built business premises. It is also the place to look if you want to hire labour. If you walk out of one of the wood-selling establishments you will immediately by surrounded by a mob of labourers all waving saws and claiming to be skilled carpenters, and offering to saw your piece of wood into smaller pieces. The streets around Souq Haraj are also the place to look if you have bought a large item too big to take home in your car. Casual drivers park their small lorries and pick up trucks around the edge of the souq. Be prepared to negotiate with them and then give them a tip.

Souk Nasser Bin Saif
Al Ahmed St Al Souq
Map **2 R7**
This is the electronics souk, where you should be able to find everything a new home requires, and then some. CDs, DVDs and even the old audio cassette tapes are on sale here.

Shopping

Exploring the souks

Places To Shop

Shopping

Souk Waqif

Off Grand Hamad St Al Jasra
Map **2 Q7**

With its cobblestone labyrinth of alleyways, mud walls and wooden beams, it's hard to believe this version of Souk Waqif is just a few years old. The souk's history dates back to a time when Doha was a tiny village divided into two by Wadi Musheireb. The Bedouin brought their woven products, camel milk, camel meat and dates to the market to trade for dried goods. The seawater flowing into the area meant that merchants had to stand up all day. The actual site of Souk Waqif (the 'standing market', or to taxi drivers the 'old souk') sits between Al Souk Street and Grand Hamad Street.

Under supervision of Sheikh Hamad bin Khalifa Al Thani, the government moved in 2004 to restore the souk it to its original glory. The result, engineered by Mohammed Ali Abdullah, is one of the most stunning market areas in the Gulf region. The open-air area has become a place of cultural activities, entertainment and also dining, with the opening of dozens of new restaurants. But this is more than just a tourist attraction – locals and residents alike head here to purchase items ranging from cooking pots to traditional dress.

The souk is known for its spice market, offering pungent delicacies from around the Gulf, Middle East and Asia. Other offerings include honey from Yemen, pashminas from Kashmir and 'antiques' from India. Along the central outdoor area you can find men weaving traditional Bedouin blankets and cushion covers for majlis style furniture. Also within the souk are galleries such as Al Markhiya Gallery (p.209). Most stalls open in the morning but it's livelier after 16:00.

Souk Waqif's bird market

Thursday & Friday Market

Salwa Rd Ain Khaled
Map **2 F13**

Located opposite the Fish Market, this market is only operational during the evening on two days of the week. In its heyday, it was one of the busiest markets in the city. But sadly, after a fire several years back, it is now a shadow of its former self. Vendors sell assorted goods such as perfume, clothes, carpets, fabric and household items. There are a few permanent shops in the area selling similar items, but the selection is poor compared with what you will find in the market.

Shopping Malls

The malls in Qatar remain popular venues with both expats and locals, not only for the wonderful selection of shops, but for catching up with friends over a cup of coffee or enjoying a bite to eat. There are malls scattered across Doha, and one being built outside of Doha at Al Khor. Some of them are huge and bustling with shoppers. What the centres all have in common are attractive interiors, a good range of shops, and plenty of air-conditioning (which comes in handy during summer). Some of the centres have cinema complexes, foodcourts, and children's entertainment areas.

Most of the malls tend to have huge sales twice a year, at the beginning of summer and towards the end of the year. There used to be a shopping festival held over the summer and most shopping centres had shows and family entertainment running throughout the event. Although this was stopped in 2010, many of the malls continued to observe the spirit of the festival and have some excellent promotions running throughout the summer months.

Parking is free at the malls and you'll have no trouble finding a spot during the day. However, trying to find a parking space at one of the popular malls in the evenings and at weekends brings the words 'needle' and 'haystack' to mind. Parking gets even more hectic during public holidays and during Eid. However, even though car parks are full, the centres themselves never seem to feel overcrowded. At some malls, Thursday evenings and sometimes Fridays are reserved for families only, so no single men are allowed to enter. One thing to remember when out shopping is that supermarkets close at 10:45 for Friday prayers and reopen at 12:30.

Doha is growing rapidly and you can already see a number of new shopping centres under construction; give it a few years and there should be plenty more places to spend, spend, spend.

Many malls now employ contract companies, based in their car parks, who will clean the outside of your car, a very useful service in dusty Qatar. The cost is QR 10 or QR 15 and it is normal to give a QR 5 tip to the cleaning staff.

City Center Doha

Al Dafna **4483 9990**
citycenterdoha.com
Map **2 Q2**

This is one of the largest shopping complexes in the Middle East – you could spend an entire day in this mall and still not get to experience everything it has to offer. Situated in the Diplomatic District of West Bay, also known as the 'New Business District', it is one of the best-known landmarks in Doha. With its well-lit and spacious interior, the centre is welcoming for the whole family. There are three levels selling a variety of international and local merchandise. Some of the most popular shops include a large Debenhams and an even larger Carrefour (p.325). Numerous cafes are scattered throughout the mall if you need to take a break, or for something more substantial, head to Noodle House (p.366), or Pizza Express.

There are also plenty of ways to entertain kids within the mall. There is an ice rink on the basement level and a bowling alley. The third level is home to Fun City (a great children's entertainment centre), two food courts, and a Fitness First gym. A 14 screen multiplex cinema shows all the latest movies and there is even a ballroom and function hall, as well as a comprehensive business centre. Banks are available inside the mall and there are a number of cash machines (ATMs) located on each floor. City Center Doha is open from 10:00 to 22:00 Saturday to Thursday, and from 14:00 to 22:00 on Fridays.

City Center Doha Stores

Books & Stationery
Alwan Stationary
Early Learning Centre
Hallmark
I Spy Bookshop
Mustafawi Exhibition
Space Toys & Stationery

Department Stores
4U
Fifty One East
Ansar Gallery
Avenue
Debenhams
Highland
X-PO Center

Electronics & Computers
Axiom Telecom
Cozy Cars
Digital House
Fono Telecom
ISPOT
Jumbo Electronics
Mobile Master
National Computers
  Services
Radio Shack
Starlink
Technical Care Center

Fashion
Boudoir
Camaieu
CHICCO
Gerry Weber
Giordano
Indigo Nation
Kenneth Kole Reaction
Kipling
Limited Too
Mango
Max Fashion
Mothercare
Next
Paris Moda
Promod
Quiksilver
Splash
Springfield
Sunglass Hut
Tosca Blue
Truworths
Vero Moda
Women'secret

Footwear
ALDO
Adams/Hush Puppies
Fantino Shoes
Foot Locker

Grant Shoes
Hush Puppies
Milano
Nine West
Shoe Mart
Tamima Shoes

Furniture & Home Appliances
Al Afghani Bazaar
Al Tawoos Furniture
Bois & Chiffon
Camel Kiosk
City Life Style
Classicx
Dana Gallery
Dwell
Home Centre
KIA International
Konooz
Modern Home
Table Arts
Tavola
The Homesmiths
Villeroy & Boch
World Handicrafts

Kids' Items
Baby shop
Chicco

Limited Too
Pumpkin Patch
Mothercare

Perfume & Cosmetics
Abdul Samad Al Qurashi
Ajmal Perfumes
Al Faisaliya Perfumes
Al Fardan
Al Muftah
Arabian Oud
Asgharali
Bottega Verde
Jarir Perfumes
Khan Al Saboun
M.A.C
MIKYAJY
Rasasi
Syed Junaid Alam
Tashayer & Top Moda
Teeb Al Tiab
The Body Shop

Health & Fitness
Fitness First
Foot Care Center
GNC Live Well
Good Life Chemist

Places To Shop

Lagoona Mall > *p.333*
Nr West Bay Residential Lagoon Al Gassar
4433 5555
lagoonaqatar.com
Map **1 K1**

Doha's latest mall is an exciting addition to the West Bay shopping scene. Located at the base of the iconic Zig Zag Towers, the gigantic mall spans 128,000 square metres and houses some 160+ shops and an atmospheric European-style piazza which is surrounded by some great cafes and restaurants. The mall is anchored by two high-end department stores which specialise in luxury brands: Fifty One East (p.323) and Paris Gallery (p.314). From Rolex to Mouawad, you'll also find a number of top-end jewellery brands represented here. For everyday fashions, the mall is home to familiar highstreet names including Mango, La Senza and Springfield, as well as a few sportswear stores. The other draws include a small handful of homeware stores; try Marina Homes Interior (marinagulf.com) for funky, stylish furniture or pick up some classy tablewares and kitchen appliances at Tablearts (tableartsqatar.com). If all that shopping leaves you in need of a bit of sustenance – or simply a relaxing break – the selection of restaurants and cafes includes a wide range of international cuisines. The mall opening hours are from 08:00 to 13:00 and 20:00 to 01:00; Fridays, 20:00 to 01:00 only. For complete store listings, see the below or log onto lagoonaqatar.com for the latest shop openings and brand launches.

Lagoona Mall Stores

Department Stores
Fifty One East
Paris Gallery

Electronics & Computers
Bang & Olufsen
Bose
Fifty One East
i-Space

Eyewear
Al Jaber Opticians
Fifty One East
Occhiali
R.B.
Sun Fashion
Yateem Optician

Cafes & Restaurants
A Zigo Zago
Bert's Café
Burger Gourmet
Caffe Vergnano 1881
Chili's
Layali
Marrakech Restaurant
Outback Steakhouse
Saladbar Green is Better
Tamarind Indian
Wagamama

Fashion
Adolfo Dominguez
Al Motahajiba
Boggi Red
Cortefiel
DKNY
Fifty One East
Goelia
Gymboree
Hanayen
Jezequel
Kayra
La Senza
Mango
Nara Camicie
Pandora
Pepe Jeans
Point Zero
Porsche Design
Pronovias
Riva
Spiegelburg
Springfield
SuiteBlanco
Super Dry

US Polo
Veleno

Footwear
Clarks
Fifty One East
Mephisto
Moreschi

Gifts & Crafts
Bin Salem
BlueBell
Wrapt

Perfumes & Cosmetics
Abdul Samad Al Qurashi
Fifty One East
Fruits & Passion
Paris Gallery
Silkor
Skin and Soul Beauty Center

Home Furnishing
Fifty One East
Kare
Marina Homes Interior
Tablearts
Zone

Jewellery & Watches
Al Jaber Watches
Al Majid Jewellery
Al Muftah Jewellery
Al Zain
Boucheron
Crōnō
Fifty One East
Mouawad
Paris Gallery
Rolex

Mobiles & Accessories
Axiom Telecom
Fifty One East
i-Space
Qtel
Starlink

Sports & Outdoors
Adidas
Lotto & Reebok
US Polo

Supermarkets
Carrefour

Enrich your Senses

with Spectacular Sensations

LAGOONA

NOW OPEN WITH FIFTY ONE EAST AND INTRODUCING NEW STORES
FOR THE FIRST TIME IN QATAR

UNVEILING NEW STORES SHORTLY

www.lagoonamall.com

Places To Shop

Landmark Mall

Al Shamal Rd Umm Lekhba **4487 5222**
landmarkdoha.com
Map **2 E1**

Since opening, Landmark has undergone three extensions. The mall covers an area of 60,000 square metres, designed in the style of a Qatari castle. It is a popular mall, which features a variety of international and local stores that are suitable for all kinds of shoppers. Inside you'll find renowned brands like Monsoon, Mango, Mexx and Karen Millen, all stocking the latest international fashion. The mall is also popular with expats for its two large UK department stores Marks & Spencer and BHS.

Stop for refreshments at one of the mall's many cafes, including the first Starbucks in Doha. The mall has a food court housing many typical fast food outlets like McDonald's, Hardee's, Pizza Hut and Subway, but there are also a few restaurants including TGI Friday and Pizza Express.

Landmark hosts a number of events, and during special occasions and festivals (like Eid) there is plenty of family entertainment within the mall.

Be aware that at weekends parking can be difficult to find and it is not unusual to end up in a mini traffic jam. Parking is free and can be found around the perimeter of the centre. Carrefour opens at 08:00, and the rest of the shops open at either 09:00 or 10:00. On Fridays, all shops open at 13:00. The centre closes at 22:00 every night.

Landmark Mall Stores

Books & Stationery
Gulf Greetings
News Centre

Department Stores
Bhs
Carrefour
Marks & Spencer

Electronics & Computers
Apple (Office One)
Bang & Olufsen
Digital House
Emax
Nokia
Samsung
Technical Care Center
Virgin Megastore

Eyewear & Opticians
Oculis
Qatar Optics
Sunglass Hut

Fashion
Aftershock
Bershka
Brantano Shoe Citi
Esprit
Evans

Fat Face
Gant
Gap
H&M
Jennyfer
Karen Millen
La Senza
Lacoste
Mango
Massimo Dutti
Mexx
Monsoon
Oysho
Pimkie
Pull & Bear
Reiss
Salsa
Stradivarius
Women'secret
Zara

Footwear
Barratts
Cesare Paciotti
Dune
Florsheim
Geox
Kurt Geiger
Mango Touch
Milano

Nine West
Roberto Botticelli

Furniture & Home Appliances
Bhs
Dwell
Frette
Reshi
KAS
The One
The White Company
Wedgwood
Zara Home

Accessories
Claire's
Colours & Beauty
Damas
Fashion Line
Folli Follie
Furla
Mango Touch
Reserve Naturelle
Segue

Kids' Items
Adams Kids
Deep Impact
Early Learning Centre

Kiddy Zone
Mexx
Mothercare
Oshkosh B'gosh
Reset
Sergent Major
Tape A L'oeil
United Colors of Benetton
Zara

Perfume & Cosmetics
Boots
Faces
The Body Shop

Sports & Outdoor Goods
Adidas
Foot Locker
Reebok
Sports Corner

Souvenirs & Gifts
Plaza Hollandi Flowers
Romeo Gifts
Sweet Heart

Supermarkets
Carrefour

Villaggio Mall

Al Waab St Baaya **4413 5222**
villaggioqatar.com
Map **2 B11**

One of the most unique malls in Doha, Villaggio Mall is located in the shadow of the Aspire Tower (p.35), next to the Khalifa Stadium. As you pass through the doors you are transported to an Italian village on the sea with gondola rides on the canal and the illusion of blue skies between villas and storefronts. Villaggio comes complete with cafes, a French bistro (Paul), family restaurants, a new branch of Dean and Deluca – a gourmet food store with its own cafe, Carrefour, a Virgin Megastore, the largest Quiksilver in the region and every conceivable brand name store in between. The extensive food court encircles a full-size ice hockey rink complete with electronic scoreboards. All the standard fastfood outlets sit alongside Le Pain Quotidien, Sarai (Mediterranean), Thai Chi (Thai-Chinese fusion), Pizza Express, Indian eatery Ashas and TGI Friday. A recent addition to the mall is the Milan-inspired 'luxury extension' which features a six-screen multiplex (see p.342) and a host of designer brands including Louis Vuitton, Christian Dior, Gucci, Dolce & Gabanna and Prada. There is free parking (some of it covered) around the mall. Note that in early 2012, there was a fire that forced the closure of the mall for an unspecified time until all necessary safety checks could be completed. See villagioqatar.com or call 4413 5222 for information on current opening hours.

Villaggio Mall Stores

Department Stores
Marks & Spencer

Eyewear & Opticians
Oculis
Pearl Opticians
Solaris

Fashion
BCBG Maxazria
Banana Republic
Bendon
Bershka
Bottega Veneta
Burberry
Camaieu
Celio
Christian Audigier
Christian Dior
Dolce & Gabbana
Dorothy Perkins
Dunhill
Ed Hardy
Evans
Fendi
Gap
Gucci
H&M
Karen Millen
Lacoste

Lucky Jeans
Mamas & Papas
Mango
Marc Jacobs
Massimo Dutti
Miss Selfridge
Monsoon
Next
Oasis
Oviesse
Oysho
Pimkie
Prada
Promod
Pull & Bear
Ralph Lauren
River Island
Salsa Jeans
Soleil Sucre
Topshop/Topman
Valentino
Villa Moda
Von Dutch
Wallis
Whistles
Xanaka
Zara

Footwear
Geox

Hush Puppies
Milano
Tod's

Furniture & Home Appliances
Singways
Tanagra
The ONE
Zara Home

Jewellery & Accessories
Bulgari
Cartier
Claire's
Louis Vuitton
Mont Blanc
Swatch
Tiffany & Co.
Virtu – Rivoli

Kids' Items
Al Jazeera Children
Bon Point
Carter
Chicco
Cool Cat
Limited Too
Pumpkin Patch
Tape A L'oeil

Perfume & Cosmetics
Al Jazeera Perfumes
Boots
Faces
Hamel El Misk
L'Occitane
MAC
Sephora
The Body Shop

Sports & Outdoor Goods
Adidas
Body Action
Foot Locker
GO Sports
Golf Shop
Nike
Puma
Quiksilver
Reebok
Saddles & Spurs/Strings &
   Wheelz
Thawab Guns
The Athele's Foot
Xtep

Supermarkets
Carrefour

Places To Shop

Shopping

Al Asmakh Mall

Jawaan St Al Sadd **4444 2401**
Map **2 K8**

Al Asmakh Mall, commonly referred to as 'Centrepoint' among local residents, is the little mall with big shops. Babyshop has children's toys for all ages, playhouses, cots, beds and clothing. Close by you'll find Splash, with very reasonably priced clothes, and Shoe Mart with a broad selection for children and adults. There are some fast food places, but nothing like the range in the larger malls. Home Centre has a good range of furniture and takes up a large portion of the top floor. Opposite Home Centre is a small children's play area called Fun City (p.132), which is a great distraction for bored kids and tired parents. The area isn't as big and overwhelming as other children's play areas but it is brighter and very clean. There is also an optician where you can buy sunglasses, and a small electronics shop selling well known brand names. There is street and underground parking, which is well illuminated with easy access to the mall.

Hyatt Plaza

Al Waab St Baaya **4499 9666**
hyattplaza.com
Map **2 A12**

You really can't miss Hyatt Plaza. You'll recognise it from the enormous shopping trolley in the carpark, which you can see from the roundabout by Khalifa Stadium. The trolley is an advert for Giant (p.325), the excellent supermarket located within the centre. This mall is not on the same scale as Landmark or City Center Doha, and has a limited selection of shops and boutiques, but the big furniture shop Homes R Us is popular. There is a smattering of high-street brands including The Body Shop and Mothercare, as well as a larger than average Paris Gallery. A shop not to

The Mall

miss is the quirkiest shop in the mall, possibly even the quirkiest in Qatar: Daiso, the Japanese discount store (4469 8999), where you can get anything from ceramics to chopsticks – and it is as cheap as chips; anything that is not specifically priced is QR 10. There is a large food court situated next to the children's play area, with a fair selection of food outlets. Wi-Fi (cards available from the customer service booth for QR 30 or QR 50) is available throughout the plaza and Starbucks is a great place to sit and watch the world go by. If you have children to amuse, Jungle Zone, a mini version of a theme park, is a decent attempt to keep the little ones happy. While the theme park is not really the best place to leave kids while you wrestle with Giant's trolleys, it does have a soft version of a rollercoaster as well as eight other attractions. Be aware that finding parking, especially at weekends, can be challenging to say the least.

The Mall

D Ring Rd Old Airport **4467 8888**
themalldoha.com
Map **2 R13**

The Mall was the first shopping centre to open in Doha, in the mid 1990s. Since then it has grown into one of the most popular places for shopping and meeting friends. Radio Shack, Paul Frank, Birkenstock, Mont Blanc, Givenchy and Monsoon are among the outlets open. There is a three-screen cinema inside the mall, showing the latest American, European and Arabic films. A food court houses KFC, McDonald's and The Royal Garden Indian Restaurant. Chili's, the popular American restaurant, is also here along with Italian chain restaurant Biella. If you like to be creative with your coffee, Café Ceramique, on the upper level allows you to paint your own ceramic plates, cups and bowls while having a snack. The Mall is host to a number of exhibitions and special events throughout the year. It is very popular with families during festival times, when there is plenty of entertainment.

Royal Plaza

Al Sadd St Al Sadd **4413 0000**
royalplazadoha.com
Map **2 L8**

This luxury retail destination offers a white glove service where you can pre-book a gentleman to assist with your shopping and carry all those bags. Small but perfectly formed, its three retail levels consist of boutiques such as Cartier, Mont Blanc, Levi's, Givenchy, Oilily and Morgan to name a few. There are a variety of features available that including a gift idea service, limousine services, baby changing facilities, complimentary strollers, lost and found, shoe polishing, mobile recharging and wheelchairs. The art deco-style Movie Palace is a plush place to catch the latest English, Arabic and Hindi releases.

![La Cigale Hotel logo]

An Exceptional
Experience for the senses ...

WORLD
TRAVEL
AWARDS
WINNER
2012
Qatar's Leading Hotel

DI CAPRI

Relish in an innovative menu and revel in authentic Italian cuisine from the region of Capri, an island off the Gulf of Naples.

LE CIGALON

Savour delectable buffets of international flavours and Lebanese specialties and watch the chefs at work in the open kitchen.

LE CENTRAL

Enjoy the fresh catch of the day and a selection of Mediterranean dishes complemented by a bountiful appetiser station with 25 starter choices.

YEN SUSHI BAR

Luxuriate in an array of sushi and sashimi creatively crafted and presented through a rotating belt.

ORANGERY
CAFÉ TROTTOIR

Relax amongst orange trees and delight in salads, pizzas, juices, coffees and desserts. Outdoor and indoor seating available.

SHISHA GARDEN

Indulge in an assortment of Oriental mezzeh, BBQ grills and flavoured shisha in an outdoor terrace against the backdrop of a water fountain and greenery.

LA CIGALE
TRAITEUR

Browse through a wide array of food items including 70 types of homemade chocolates, 180 types of artisan cheese, cakes, pastries and ice cream.

MADISON
PIANO BAR

Be entertained by our resident one-man-show who performs classical and pop songs every night, excluding Sundays where a special DJ night takes place.

SKY VIEW

Take in the breathtaking view of the city and unwind to melodious composition from the DJ. Located on the 11th floor, Sky View serves light meals and beverages.

CLUB - 7

A fashionable event & entertainment venue with resident DJ on Thursdays & Fridays and world's top DJs on selected nights.

Going Out

GOING OUT

As the sun goes down, you'll notice a shift in the pace of life in Doha. Around sunset in the cooler months, you'll see families congregating in parks and public spaces like the Corniche for alfresco suppers, after which the roads get busy again (possibly even more so than during the day) with people heading out late to eat, smoke shisha, catch up with friends or hang out in the malls.

Dining out is practically a national pastime in Doha, and from celebrity chef-endorsed fine dining to casual street cafes, the capital's residents are spoilt for choice. If you fancy a glass of wine with your meal, you should head for a hotel restaurant as these venues are usually licensed to serve alcohol. Indeed, with Doha's hotel dining scene excelling in both variety and quality, you'll find no trouble to track down the perfect dinner spot. Competition between hotel restaurants remains high, meaning that quality and service consistently outdo expectation.

The licensing laws also mean that you're unlikely to have a 'local' on your street corner as you might back home. Instead, you may have a roster of four or five favourites across the city to enjoy. The upside of the hotel bar scene is that you're likely to find yourself hanging out in some truly amazing venues that, because of location and cost, you might never have considered trying back home.

Depending on the venue, you may need to present identification and, in some places, buy a membership card, to gain entry to the licensed establishments (see Door Policy, p.342). You're advised to carry ID with you whenever you're out on the town.

Out of the city, the going out options are somewhat limited and, with the exception of the Sealine Beach Resort (p.243), the restaurants situated in out-of-town hotels generally favour function over form, so if you want to eat out or dance the night away you need to be in the capital.

Doha also has an extensive selection of excellent independent, non-licensed restaurants, so don't let the absence of a stiff drink deter you from exploring some of the capital's finest culinary offerings.

Away from the dining scene, there are a number of ways to spend your evenings, from comedy nights (p.343) to classical concerts (see Nightlife, p.342).

EATING OUT

Doha's dining scene is growing all the time, offering everything from basic budget canteen-style places to top notch designer dining. On the whole, prices are reasonable in comparison to some other parts of the world, although if you add a glass of wine or beer, you'll notice the hit to the final bill, as in some places a

bottle of wine can equate to more than your total food bill. Spending an evening dining and hanging out in the cafes of Souk Waqif (p.330) is an absolute must. It has a number of great independent restaurants such as Tajine (p.369), as well as tiny kebab houses, shisha cafes and coffee shops. The busiest nights are Wednesday, Thursday and Friday, when it may be a good idea to book ahead. Katara Cultural Village offers a similar experience; see p.362 for more information on this leisure hotspot. Elsewhere, the boutique-style restaurants on The Pearl offer fine dining – but be warned, it won't come cheap.

Friday brunch is a Doha institution and, while it's a popular choice for celebrating birthdays and special occasions, its also part of the average week for many expats and nationals. Restaurants and hotels of all levels and budget put on extensive spreads for a fixed time period, available for a fixed price, with some like the Gallery Brunch at Doha Marriott (p.196) allowing you to select dishes from a number of restaurants. All-you-can-eat options, including a choice of house beverages or soft options, are usually available in licensed venues.

Nearly all restaurants are family-friendly and it's not uncommon to see children eating alongside their parents in fine-dining venues even late at night. Some restaurants have special family sections, and some offer entertainment for the kids, particularly on Fridays during brunch, so that you can enjoy your meal in peace while the kids are otherwise occupied.

Each new hotel that opens usually brings with it a raft of new restaurants.

Hygiene
The Supreme Council of Health (sch.gov.qa) is the official body responsible for hygiene standards in Qatar's restaurants and cafes. Most outlets are quite hygienic and street food barely exists, so you shouldn't worry about food poisoning even in places which look quite basic.

Food Allergies
A cautionary word, if you have a food allergy – you need to be careful in Doha as menus can be very vague about listing ingredients. Language difficulties, ignorance about food allergies, and a desire to always say 'yes' to customers mean that you may be told a dish is safe to eat when it isn't.

Taxes & Service Charges
Depending on where you eat, you may find that your bill includes a few additions. A 7% government tax is added to many hotel restaurant bills, and a service charge of 10% (and sometimes more) could also appear. Sometimes these charges are hidden in the prices, but this should be clearly explained on the menu. This service charge is not voluntary, and it's

unlikely that your waiter will see any of it, so if you've received good service, leaving a little extra in cash is always appreciated. With smaller restaurants, tipping is always welcome, although it is not mandatory. As well as waiters, you'll find that taxi drivers, doormen, petrol pump attendants, manicurists, and people who pack your shopping or wheel your trolley to your car earn very little, and a tip can make a difference.

Independent Reviews

All of the outlets in this book have been independently reviewed by writers based in Qatar. Their aim is to give clear, realistic and, as far as possible, unbiased views of each venue, without back-handers, hand-me-downs or underhandedness on the part of any restaurant owner, nightclub promoter, crafty PR guru or persuasive barista. If you feel you have been unwittingly led astray, or your much-loved local or hidden gastronomic gem has not been included, let us know by emailing info@askexplorer.com.

Cultural Meals

Souk Waqif is a great place to get a taste of local colour. The cafe hub that stretches through one end of the souk is a hive of activity in the evenings with people eating, drinking coffee, smoking shisha and catching up with friends. It's a place where locals, expats and tourists enjoy people watching as the evening unhurriedly whiles away. On the Corniche, Al Mourjan (p.351), sits in the building that used to house the Balhambar restaurant which was known for its traditional Qatari fare, rustic surrounds and stunning views; the new restaurant benefits from the view, and serves up the highest quality Arabian cuisine, but its elegant design is anything but rustic. If you're looking for something a little more rough around the edges, try Assaha Lebanese Traditional Village (p.354). Other consistently reliable Arabian restaurants with their own dose of cultural charm are Layali (p.364) and The Tent (p.370). If you fancy heading out of the city, all the major tour operators offer trips to the desert where you can enjoy an Arabian barbecue in the sand dunes, and then lie back with a shisha pipe and count stars (see Tour Operators, p.228).

Vegetarian Food

Many international chain restaurants have a vegetarian option or two on the menu. Also, many of the Arabian appetisers, such as hummus, baba ganoosh and the various traditional salads, are vegetarian. There are also plenty of independent Indian restaurants which serve only vegetarian food, often very cheaply.

Takeaways

Fastfood is very popular in Qatar and delivery vans and bikes from KFC and Pizza Hut zip around all day. Shawarma is a popular local snack consisting of rolled pita bread filled with lamb or chicken carved from a rotating spit, vegetables and tahina sauce. You'll see countless roadside stands offering shawarma for as little as QR 3 each, and they make a great alternative to the usual fastfood staples. Those watching their weight should try the Diet Shop (4466 4995) on Salwa Road, who deliver calorie-counted meals to your door. Because food is reasonably priced, getting a restaurant or hotel to cater for a party at home is not necessarily super-expensive (see p.341). They can even supply tables, rugs, shisha pipes and waiters, so you can impress your friends without breaking the bank.

Caterers

For parties, special occasions and business lunches or dinners, there are numerous options for arranging outside catering, allowing you to relax and enjoy yourself and concentrate on anything but the cooking. In addition to specialist companies, many hotels and restaurants have catering departments, so pick your favourite and ask if they can help you out. Depending on what you require, caterers can provide just the food or everything from crockery, napkins, tables, chairs and waiters, to doormen and a clearing up service afterwards. Costs vary according to the number of people, dishes and level of service required. Opera (4468 8344) and Fauchon (4432 4888) are renowned for their off-site catering. Cupcakes (web.mac.com/tasteofheaven) will arrange your party for you at a venue of your choice. They will take care of everything from menu planning and catering, to photography and decorating. Beautiful bespoke cakes and cupcakes are also made to order.

Diet Shop cafe

If you need a party venue, compound halls are a convenient choice, and for kids' birthday parties you can hire shopping mall play areas. Circusland at Landmark is one of the most popular ones, Jungle Zone (p.217) in Hyatt Plaza includes entertainers and photographers in their pricing, while Ray's Reef at Royal Plaza (p.336) is good for younger children. Cafe Ceramique (4476 1100) is fun for older kids and Eli France Cafe (4435 7222/222) has a great upstairs party hall. Fast food restaurants such as McDonald's, Hardee's, Burger King, KFC and Dairy Queen are always popular with children and most will come to your chosen venue to play host. For something a bit different you can host parties at Landmark's Cinemaland, Jumpzone at InterContinental (p.198) or Qatar Bowling Centre (p.266). The major hotels cater for parties ranging from small gatherings to lavish receptions (see Doha Hotels, p.196). For restaurants and cafes, simply browse this section of the book.

to hotel bars and clubs, requiring guests to show their passport or Qatar identification card prior to entry. Hotel guests are usually only required to show their passport, whereas Qatar residents are required to show their Qatari ID and apply for a membership card. Your ID will be scanned on the door and a membership card printed, which you can use for future visits. As each hotel (sometime each bar) has its own card, you may find yourself carting around a lot of plastic on a night out. Some places charge a fee for membership, with the top end charges being QR 100-150.

In Doha, as in other places around the world, certain bars and nightclubs have a 'selective' entry policy. Generally speaking, dressing up, rather than going casual, usually helps, and if you're in a large party (especially all males) it can help to break up the group.

The Yellow Star

This classy yellow star highlights places that merit extra praise. It might be the atmosphere, the food, the cocktails, the music or the crowd, but any review that you see with the star attached is sure to be somewhere that's a bit special.

Driving Under The Influence

Drinking and driving is illegal in Qatar. There is zero tolerance; if you are caught with even a hint of alcohol in your system you will be sent to prison. Be responsible and always take a taxi or order a limousine to get you home at the end of the night (see p.57 for phone numbers).

NIGHTLIFE

Bars, Pubs & Clubs

You can't expect authenticity from Doha's pubs, but then when they're mostly in hotels, in the desert, in the Middle East, that shouldn't come as a surprise. What you can look forward to is some inviting, friendly spots with a decent selection of draught and bottled beers, and reliably good bar grub. Some of the city's members' clubs also have licences, including Doha Golf Club (p.273). Doha also has its fair selection of trendy night spots where you can get dressed up and mingle in chic surrounds to upbeat soundtracks. While there are no superclubs or independent clubs to speak of in Doha, there is no shortage of places to dance the night away. Most of Doha's larger hotels have a night club, and standards are definitely improving; international DJs frequently stop off in the capital to spin some tunes.

The law in Qatar states that drinkers must be 21 or over, but wherever you're heading and regardless of your age, take your ID, as the chances are you'll need to show it on the door in order to gain entry.

Door Policy

The drinking age in Qatar is 21. In late 2009, the government introduced new regulations for visitors

Cinema

Doha has plenty of cinemas for movie-lovers, and catching a flick is a popular way to spend an evening for all residents. Qatar's first IMAX screen opened at Villaggio Mall's Cineco 13, bringing the full 3D, surround-sound, larger than life experience to cinema goers. Almost all the major releases come out here and they're not far behind the western release dates – but movies with what is considered 'unsuitable' content, such as Brokeback Mountain, Black Swan and Love & Other Drugs, never see the light of day and others suffer from gratuitous editing, that may skip out a third of the film. However, gruesome horror pictures are very popular in the Middle East and most will be shown in full here. There is also a big market for Arab and Bollywood films. English language films aren't dubbed, but have Arabic subtitles.

Other than the heavy hand of the editor, there are other little idiosyncrasies to film-going in Qatar, such as people chatting to each other or answering their mobile phone in the middle of a film. It's a good idea to take a pashmina or sweater with you, as the air conditioning can be extreme.

Film listings are given in the local papers, and some cinemas have schedules online. Book in advance for big new releases as these viewings are often sold out.

Away from the big screens, keep an eye out for one-off or seasonal showings. Hotels like The Ritz-Carlton have outdoor screenings of popular movies in the cooler months. Art house and independent cinema is hard to come by, but the now annual Doha Tribeca Film Festival (p.26) is a definite highlight for film buffs and culture vultures alike.

Aspire Ladies Cinema Aspire Ladies Club
aspirezone.qa
Cineco Villaggio Mall, 4493 4934
cinecomovies.com
Cinema Land Landmark Mall, 4488 1674
qatarcinemas.com
Cinema Palace Royal Plaza, 4413 0000
qatarcinemas.com
Grand Cinecentre City Center Doha, 4483 9064
Gulf Cinema C Ring Rd, 4467 1811
qatarcinemas.com
Mall Cineplex The Mall Old Airport 4467 8666
qatarcinemas.com

Comedy Nights
There is only one comedy venue in Qatar, the Radisson Blu, but amateur theatre group Doha Players (p.269) sometimes holds cabaret nights for members.

The Laughter Factory
The Laughter Factory, a company that brings in international comedians to tour the Gulf, comes to Doha once a month for two nights. Three stand-up comics try to avoid the hecklers and get maximum laughs. The standard is usually pretty good, and most of the comics are British (but you get a few other nationalities too). The shows take place in the Shehrazad Bar (4428 1555) and often sell out, so get your tickets in advance from the hotel. Entry is QR 120, and shows start at 20:00. The bar serves pub food before the acts start, a DJ plays afterwards and the shows are non-smoking.
Radisson Blu Hotel, Doha Rawdat Al Khail **4441 7417**
thelaughterfactory.com
Map **2 N10**

Concerts & Live Music
There are now two purpose-built concert venues, both located at the Katara Cultural Village in West Bay, one of which has been designed especially to host opera and ballet productions. The other is a huge outdoor amphitheatre which is slated to hold major events throughout the year. Check the local newspapers for more up to date information.

The Doha Philharmonic Orchestra holds regular concerts, usually in the concert hall at Aspire, but sometimes in open air venues. Tickets are usually sold from Virgin Megastores at Villaggio and Landmark malls and normally cost between QR 50 and QR 250.

In general, Qatar gets plenty of politicians and business people visiting, but very few entertainers

make their way through the country. On occasion, big names do make an appearance – Placido Domingo and Andrea Bocelli played at The Pearl in 2008, and Bryan Adams caused much excitement at Al Sadd stadium a few years ago. Enrique Iglesias was drafted in for an inter-college class of 2009 graduation celebration in Education City and Qatar's biggest music concert 'The Big Day Out' featured Toploader as the headlining act in 2011. The big hotels occasionally stage concerts as does the Qatar National Theatre (p.343), but sometimes marketing can be vague or non existent and you only find out about the event after it has happened. The annual Dunestock festival (dunestock.net.qa) was hugely popular, showcasing local talent in the great outdoors near to the Singing Sand Dunes, but its future looks uncertain. If you can't live without live music, you'll have to scrutinise the local media for tiny press releases or make a habit of checking the forums (see Useful Websites, p.23). Otherwise, sign up for a weekly newsletter or real-time Twitter updates by doha-nights.com to find out what's coming up.

Theatre
The best-known theatrical company in Qatar is Doha Players (p.269). Made up of keen amateurs (some of whom are very talented) and volunteers, the group has been staging English-language productions in the capital for over 50 years. It no longer has its own theatre, but the company has raised funds and is now drawing up plans for a new venue. In the meantime, Doha Players has been using various venues around the capital including Garvey's (p.358), Doha Sailing Club (4443 9840) and, for bigger productions like the annual pantomime and musicals, the College of the North Atlantic (p.150).

The recent opening of the Katara Cultural Village (p.207) is expected to give a boost to performing arts in Doha, with multiple venues on the cards including an opera house, an amphitheatre and a concert hall.

Qatar National Theatre
The National Theatre is located on the Corniche. Its 490 seat auditorium usually plays host to performances in Arabic, but English language shows performed by visiting companies are sometimes held here. As part of the 2010 Doha Capital of Culture celebrations (p.26), the National Theatre hosted operettas, poetry recitals, musical soirees, plays and exhibitions – some of which were in English. As with all types of entertainment in Qatar, to find out when such events are coming up, it pays to keep an ear to the grapevine and an eye on the papers.
Nr National Theatre R/A Al Dafna **4483 1246**
qatartourism.gov.qa
Map **2 N5**

RESTAURANTS BY CUISINE

American
American Grill, Somerset West Bay	p.354
Applebee's, C Ring Rd	p.354
Bennigan's, Khalifa International Tennis & Squash Complex	p.355
Chili's, Souq Rawda, Salwa Rd	p.356
Fuddruckers, Khalifa International Tennis & Squash Complex	p.358
Johnny Rockets, Al Emadi Centre, Salwa Rd	p.360
Ponderosa, Salwa Rd, Nr Ramada Junction	p.367
T.G.I. Friday's, Landmark Mall	p.369

Asian
Asia Live!, Doha Marriott Hotel	p.354
Wok Mee Noodle House, Mövenpick Tower & Suites Doha	p.370

Cafes & Coffee Shops
Alison Nelson's Chocolate Bar, Porto Arabia	p.352
Cafe Bateel, Salwa Rd, Nr Midmac Interchange	p.356
Criollo, InterContinental Doha The City	p.358
Gourmet House, Kempinski Residences & Suites	p.360
Lobby Lounge, InterContinental Doha The City	p.365
Orangery Cafe Trottoir, La Cigale Hotel	p.366
Ras Al Shawah, Nr Sheraton Park	p.367
Red Velvet Cupcakery, Katara Cultural Village	p.367
The Lobby Lounge, The Ritz-Carlton, Doha	p.365

Chinese
Beijing, Off Salwa Rd, Nr The Centre	p.355
The Noodle House, City Center Doha	p.366
Tse Yang, Porto Arabia	p.370

European
Garvey's, Garvey's European Family Club	p.358

Far Eastern
Chopsticks, Wyndham Grand Regency Doha	p.357

Filipino
Al Jazeera Filipino Restaurant, Nr Jaidah R/A	p.350

French
Fauchon, Souq Najad, Salwa Rd	p.358
La Mer, The Ritz-Carlton, Doha	p.361

Greek
Mykonos, InterContinental Doha	p.365

Indian
Star Of India, Khalifa St, Nr TV & Radio R/A	p.369
Taj Rasoi, Doha Marriott Hotel	p.369
The Garden Restaurant, Al Najma Souq	p.358

International
Al Hubara, Sheraton Doha Resort & Convention Hotel	p.350
Al Khaima, Al Sadd Rd, Nr Qtel	p.351
Aroma Cafe, Kempinski Residences & Suites	p.354
Bistro 61, Alfardan Towers, 61 Al Funduq St	p.355
Blue, Grand Heritage Doha Hotel & Spa	p.356
Choices, Oryx Rotana	p.356
Cosmo, Millennium Hotel Doha	p.357
Crepaway, Al Mouthanna Complex, Salwa Rd	p.357
Flavours, Grand Heritage Doha Hotel & Spa	p.358
Grand Gourmet, Wyndham Grand Regency Doha	p.360
Le Cigalon Restaurant, La Cigale Hotel	p.364
Market By Jean-Georges, W Doha Hotel & Residences	p.365
Neo Restaurant, Souq Najd, Salwa Rd	p.366
Opal By Gordon Ramsay, St. Regis Doha	p.366
Richoux, City Center Doha	p.368
Seasons Restaurant, Mövenpick Hotel Doha	p.368
The Cafe Restaurant, InterContinental Doha	p.356
The Lagoon, The Ritz-Carlton, Doha	p.361
The Square, InterContinental Doha The City	p.369
Victoria, Grand Heritage Doha Hotel & Spa	p.370

Italian
All'Aperto, Doha Marriott Hotel	p.354
BiCE Ristorante, Porto Arabia	p.355
Carluccio's, Porto Arabia	p.356
Ciao, Haya Complex, Salwa Rd	p.357
Di Capri, La Cigale Hotel	p.358
Il Teatro, Four Seasons Hotel	p.360
La Veranda, Sheraton Doha Resort & Convention Hotel	p.361
Porcini, The Ritz-Carlton, Doha	p.367

Japanese
Megu, Porto Arabia	p.365
Yen Sushi Bar, La Cigale Hotel	p.370

Lebanese
Al Liwan, Sharq Village & Spa	p.351
Al Mourjan, The Corniche	p.351
Al Tabkha, Porto Arabia	p.352
Assaha Lebanese Traditional Village, Al Hilal Bldg, Hamad Al Kabir St	p.354
Beirut Restaurant, Al Kahraba St	p.355
Burj Al Hamam, Porto Arabia	p.356
Liza, Porto Arabia	p.364

Spice Market

Al Majlis, Middle Eastern — p.351
Automatic, Middle Eastern — p.355

Millennium Hotel Doha
Cosmo, International — p.357
Zaman Restaurant, Lebanese — p.371

Wyndham Grand Regency Doha
Chopsticks, Far Eastern — p.357
Grand Gourmet, International — p.360
Tangia, Moroccan — p.369

Al Souq
Al Mahmal St, Nr Souq Aseiry
Thai Noodles, Thai — p.370

Baaya
Grand Heritage Doha Hotel & Spa
Blue, International — p.356
Flavours, International — p.358
Victoria, International — p.370

Fereej Abdel Aziz
Al Meera Complex, B Ring Rd, Nr Jaidah Flyover
Aryaas, Vegetarian — p.354

Nr Jaidah R/A
Al Jazeera Filipino Restaurant, Filipino — p.350

Off Salwa Rd, Nr The Centre
Beijing, Chinese — p.355

Souq Rawda, Salwa Rd
Chili's, American — p.356

Fereej Al Nasr
Al Mirghab St, Off C Ring Rd
Thai Snack, Thai — p.370

Salwa Rd
Nando's, Portuguese — p.365

Salwa Rd, Nr Midmac Interchange
Cafe Bateel, Cafe — p.356

Fereej Al Soudan
Haya Complex, Salwa Rd
Ciao, Italian — p.357

Fereej Bin Mahmoud
La Cigale Hotel > p.199, 338
Di Capri, Italian — p.358
Le Central Restaurant, Mediterranean — p.364
Le Cigalon Restaurant, International — p.364
Madison Piano Bar, Bar — p.372

Nr TV & Radio R/A
Al Sayad Restaurant, Middle Eastern — p.351

Al Khulaifat
Doha Marriott Hotel
All'Aperto, Italian — p.354
Asia Live!, Asian — p.354
Corniche, Mediterranean — p.357
JW's Steakhouse, Steakhouse — p.360
Pearl Lounge Club, Bar — p.372
Salsa, Mexican — p.368
Taj Rasoi, Indian — p.369

Sharq Village & Spa
Al Dana, Seafood — p.350
Al Liwan, Lebanese — p.351
Cigar Lounge, Cigar Bar — p.371

Al Mirqab
Al Mouthanna Complex, Salwa Rd
Crepaway, International — p.357

Al Sadd
Al Sadd Rd, Nr Qtel
Al Khaima, International — p.351

Megu

there's more to life...

Never get lost again

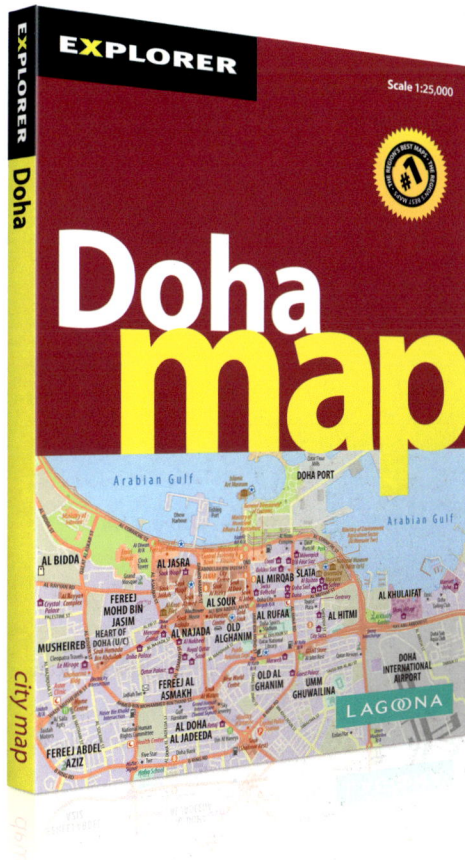

askexplorer.com/shop

askexplorer

Sponsored by

RESTAURANTS & CAFES

Al Dana   Seafood

The airy, open spaces in Al Sharq Village's signature seafood restaurant encircle a beautifully laid-out market-style fish counter in the centre. Most of the fish on display are fresh from the Gulf. The restaurant is covered in flashes of blue and turquoise and a few contemporary chandeliers pull everything together. Diners can either choose a fish and preparation method, order from the ample sushi menu, or pick and choose from the extensive a la carte selection. To really take advantage of the restaurant, stick to the sushi and fresh fish options for your main course. Group and private cookery lessons are available.

Sharq Village & Spa Al Khulaifat **4425 6666**
sharqvillage.com
Map **2 U8**

Al Hamra   Middle Eastern

Al Hamra offers casual dining with a full Arabian menu, and makes a great place to stop by for a quick bite alone, or to catch up with friends. It is close to the souks (behind Al Reem Pharmacy) and is popular with weary shoppers in need of a break. The fresh juices

are a good way to boost your energy levels and the thyme-flavoured breads and traditional mint tea are recommended. It's also a good spot for breakfast.

Al Rayyan Complex, Al Rayyan Rd Musheireb **4443 3297**
Map **2 Q7**

Al Hubara   International

At the far side of the Sheraton's lobby, Al Hubara is open for breakfast, lunch and dinner. Served buffet style, there is a good range of international cuisine to choose from, including Arabian, Japanese and Italian dishes. The helpful staff ensure you can relax and enjoy your meal. The restaurant has a separate room for families, which doubles as a non-smoking area. This is a popular venue for lunchtime meetings, as well as for those seeking a lingering break from work.

Sheraton Doha Resort & Convention Hotel Al Dafna **4485 4073**
sheratondoha.com
Map **2 R3**

Al Jazeera Filipino Restaurant   Filipino

This small eatery appeals to families and singles alike, with heaped plates of food at bargain prices. For less than QR 20, this restaurant offers a variety of fried rice and dishes like the Canton Guisado, fat noodles mixed

Al Mourjan

with stir-fried veggies, chicken and shrimp. Another favourite is the QR 15 tapsilog, white rice topped with an egg and fried beef. Alternatively, you can't go wrong with any of the whiteboard specials. It's basic, but you'll leave full to bursting. To find it, take the first right after passing Sports Corner at Jaidah Roundabout.
Nr Jaidah R/A Fereej Abdel Aziz **4442 3831**
Map **2 N9**

Al Khaima   International

Al Khaima literally translated means 'the tent', and diners here can relax in traditional tented surroundings around the clock as the restaurant is open 24 hours. Known for its quality Arabian cuisine, each dish is accompanied by fresh, warm, oval-shaped bread. The food is quite addictive, and if you can't finish your meal you can always ask the helpful staff to wrap it up for you to take home. There is lots of space in the restaurant, making this a great venue for families with children.
Al Sadd Rd, Nr Qtel Al Sadd **4444 6962**
Map **2 K8**

Al Liwan   Lebanese

Not just your average buffet, Al Liwan offers an extensive array of tasty Lebanese cuisine. Start with hot and cold Lebanese mezze, salads and bread straight from the oven. The fresh seafood and koftas are particularly good and regional main courses change regularly, so there is always something new to try. Those with a sweet tooth will love the well-stocked dessert station which offers everything a pudding lover could ask for, from cheesecake to apple pie, with many a chocolate treat in between.
Sharq Village & Spa Al Khulaifat **4425 6666**
sharqvillage.com
Map **2 U8**

Al Majlis   Middle Eastern

This popular restaurant is known not only for its food but also for the authentic dining experience that goes with it. The upstairs level has intimate cubicles with curtains that can be drawn for extra privacy, but for the real deal you should dine seated on the Arabian cushions and carpets. The food is traditional Arabian too, with assorted mezze and grilled meats. Al Majlis is known for its dish of hammour fish with baby shrimp on a sizzling iron pan smothered in onions and cheese – a must-try for all seafood lovers. To find it, turn right after the 'White Thread' shop at the Qtel end of Al Sadd Street.
Al Sadd Rd, Nr Qtel Al Sadd **4444 7417**
Map **2 K8**

Al Mourjan   Lebanese

Whether you dine indoors in the immaculate white furnished dining area or outside enjoying the gentle

Al Liwan

breezes coming off the Corniche, a visit to Al Mourjan is a wonderful way to pass an evening as you linger over a vast Lebanese spread so big that it may not all fit on your table at once. The terrace seating offers views of the Corniche all the way to the Islamic museum in one direction and the Sheraton in the other. The staff, in crisp uniforms, make sure you are well looked after. After dinner, you can choose one of over 300 shisha pipes for a smoke under the stars.
The Corniche Al Dafna **4483 4423**
almourjan.com
Map **2 N5**

Al Sayad Restaurant   Middle Eastern

By far, one of the best deals in town are the roasted chickens served at Al Sayad Restaurant. For just QR 15, you can get your mitts on one of the delicious pieces of poultry that can be seen neatly lined up, turning gently on a spit. You'll find similar eateries around Doha, and some places offer their chickens spiced, but they're just as delicious eaten plain, with a simple Arabian bread and garlic sauce accompaniment. To enjoy the experience to the full, order a takeaway, hop in the car, drive five minutes down the road and eat it while sitting on the Corniche. Be sure to ask for napkins and be warned – it's not one for a first date.
Nr TV & Radio R/A Al Jebailat **4487 7357**
Map **2 K3**

Restaurants & Cafes

Going Out (side tab)

Al Sayyad — Middle Eastern

For a relaxing night with an out of town feel, this restaurant is a good choice. Set just off the beach at the Diplomatic Club, with outside seating for the cooler months, it offers a great choice of seafood and feels like a million miles away from the city. Sit back and enjoy the authentic Arabian salads while you take your pick from the menu. If you can't decide, the waiters are on hand with helpful advice.
The Diplomatic Club Al Gassar 4484 7444
thediplomaticclub.com
Map **1 K2**

Al Shaheen Restaurant — Middle Eastern

Set on the top floor of the pyramid-shaped Sheraton Hotel, this restaurant enjoys impressive views of the city and coastline from all sides. The service can be disorganised and the traditional live entertainment a little overbearing, but don't let this put you off too much as the menu offers a good chance to try some great Arabian dishes in luxurious surroundings. The food is beautifully presented and portions are ample, and for less adventurous diners there are western dishes too.
Sheraton Doha Resort & Convention Hotel Al Dafna 4485 4821
sheratondoha.com
Map **2 R3**

Al Shami Home Restaurant — Middle Eastern

This Lebanese restaurant is a good place to introduce visitors to Arabian cuisine. It offers an array of juicy grilled meats, seafood, soups and fresh juices. The staff are courteous and knowledgeable, and ready to recommend dishes for those struggling to pick something from the lengthy menu. For those looking to finish the meal off with coffee, conversation and hubbly bubbly, Shami also offers shisha, flavoured tobacco smoked in a pipe that draws the smoke through a bowl of water. Delivery service is available.
C Ring Rd, Nr Ramada Signal New Al Mirqab 4443 3666
Map **2 M10**

Al Tabkha — Lebanese

Since its recent opening in on The Pearl, Al Tabkha has brought a slice of Lebanese home comforts to Qatar. Head here for a casual evening over a great selection of Levantine culinary staples from irresistible mezze to sumptuous shis.
Porto Arabia The Pearl Qatar 4495 3876
Map **1 M2**

Al Tayeb Restaurant — Middle Eastern

This tiny budget restaurant boasts delicious chicken and lamb kebabs and is well worth hunting down in Souk Waqif. Al Tayeb's menu is short and sweet – in addition to kebabs, this eatery offers kidneys, livers and hearts by the skewer. Add-ons include bread, yogurt and roasted vegetables. Unless it's a really stuffy day, opt for a seat at one of the tables outside the restaurant, and enjoy the company of stray cats and those strolling through the souk.
Souk Waqif Al Jasra
Map **2 Q7**

Albatross Restaurant — Middle Eastern

This pleasant, eastern-style restaurant is popular with local families and visitors alike. The food is international with a Lebanese flavour, and the generous portions are beautifully cooked and served in a relaxed atmosphere by friendly and knowledgeable staff. For a different experience, there is a tented section next door (see The Tent, p.370) where you can relax on typical Arabian-style seating and enjoy a shisha pipe.
Al Bustan Hotel Slata 4432 8888
albustanhotel-qa.com
Map **2 T7**

Albisana Kunafa > p.iv, 186, 353 — Middle Eastern

A honeyed taste of Palestine and Jordan is on offer at Albisana Kunafa. The bistro-style venue specialises in two iconic Middle Eastern desserts: kunafaand mohalibya. The former is served hot and created using a traditional Palestinian/Jordanian recipe which features Nabulsi cheese, honey and a sprinkling of pistachio. Mohalibya, a milky jelly with seductive flavours of honey and rose water, meanwhile, is served cold to make it the perfect summer treat. Both options are a delicious way to end your meal and Albisana Kunafa's popularity among the locals is testament to their authenticity.
Katara Cultural Village Al Gassar 4408 1200
katara.net
Map **1 K3**

Alison Nelson's Chocolate Bar — Cafe

Everything from the Chocolate Bar's decor to the menu is innovative and supremely cool. Relax inside the club lounge on pristine white sofas, or outdoors on garden chairs under oversized umbrellas. The menu features classic comfort foods such as grilled cheese, alongside eclectic concoctions (try the chocolate tortellini). Chocolate is woven cleverly throughout the menu, however a refreshing range of healthy salads, light snacks and fresh fruit juices allow for guilt-free pleasures. Fall in love over delectable hot chocolate or indulge in fondue with friends. Moderate prices and warm, speedy table service provide even more reasons why you won't want to leave.
Porto Arabia The Pearl Qatar 4495 3878
chocolatebarnyc.com
Map **1 M2**

Red Velvet
c u p c a k e r y

SIMPLE, ELEGANT
AND TOO
SCRUMPTIOUS
FOR WORDS
THE WASHINGTON POST

"Seduce you from the first bite to the last crumb"

From the *finest* French chocolate and the *best* European butter to the *aromatic* vanillas of the Bourbon Islands in Madagascar

Katara - Valley of Cultures
Building 24, West Bay, Doha
Tel: +974 44080700 | Fax: +974 44081655
Email: redvelvetdoha@redvelvetdoha.com
www.redvelvetdoha.com

Red Velvet Cupcakery - Doha
@RedVelvetDoha

Red Velvet
ARLINGTON, VA   RESTON, VA

Restaurants & Cafes

Alison Nelson's Chocolate Bar

All'Aperto — Italian
Translated from Italian, all'aperto means 'open', which fits the beautiful open-air dining space. An unpretentious but well-presented menu of pasta, pizza and salad awaits diners at this popular restaurant. Outdoor tables, surrounded by clambering vines, make it a great spot for a family dinner or a relaxed get-together with friends. Start with an antipasti platter while you decide on a delicious main course.
Doha Marriott Hotel Al Khulaifat **4429 8888**
marriott-doha.com
Map **2 V8**

American Grill > p.197 — American
Tucked away at the back of the Somerset, American Grill is a bright and pleasant place for a pit stop in West Bay, that won't break the bank. The American-Arabian breakfast buffet is eclectic but there's plenty of fill up on and bottomless coffee to wash it down. Later in the day, you can pop in by for a selection of grilled and fried sandwiches, burgers and mains, or a coffee. Big screen TVs allow you to catch up on the news as you eat, and there are always plenty of newspapers for your perusal.
Somerset West Bay Al Dafna **4420 3333**
somerset.com
Map **2 Q1**

Applebee's — American
Applebee's offers American-style dining geared towards families. The large menu should please all tastes. The restaurant has a young, vibrant feel to it, with happy, energetic staff who are extremely knowledgeable about the food. You can even catch up on the latest television action, as there are screens by the bar for all to enjoy. The shared appetiser dishes are always fun, but the portions are so generous you may not even make it on to the mains. There are several branches in Doha including an outlet in City Center Doha (4493 4880).
C Ring Rd New Al Mirqab **4436 0747**
applebees.com
Map **2 M9**

Aroma Cafe > p.81 — International
The Kempinski's all-day dining haunt serves modern European food in a classy, low-key setting that's equally suited for business lunches or a quiet dinner-a-deux. The brasserie-style starters and mains come in generous portions and the clean decor lets the great quality of the food do the talking. A mouth-watering dessert menu completes the experience. For those short on time, the three-course lunch option is served promptly and, at QR 99, is also of excellent value.
Kempinski Residences & Suites Al Dafna **4405 3333**
kempinski-residences.com
Map **2 Q1**

Aryaas — Vegetarian
This bustling, family-friendly restaurant specialises in delectable South Indian fare at bargain prices. Best known for its dosas – lentil-rice crepes stuffed with a variety of options, including very spicy potatoes – Aryaas is a vegetarian's dream. The dosas are served with three types of chutney and a bowl of spicy broth called sambar. The restaurant's variety of Indian sweets are a perfect finish after a light but satisfying dosa lunch or dinner. The gulab jamun, fried balls of dough dunked in a sugary syrup, are definitely worth a try. Another branch is located in Al Mansoura (4436 0097).
Al Meera Complex, B Ring Rd, Nr Jaidah Flyover Fereej Abdel Aziz **4441 9661**
Map **2 N9**

Asia Live! — Asian
This award-winning restaurant offers an exciting range of Asian fusion cuisine with exotic flavours set to tingle your taste buds. Enjoy your favourite dish from China, Japan, Singapore or Thailand in a pagoda setting reminiscent of the Orient. The live teppanyaki station is a novel attraction, or choose from the extensive a la carte menu or sushi corner. Portion sizes are generous and vegetarians are well catered for. The Peking duck is said to be the best in town – enjoy with a glass of sake, beer, wine or spirits, or treat yourself to a cocktail.
Doha Marriott Hotel Al Khulaifat **4429 8472**
marriott-doha.com
Map **2 V8**

Assaha Lebanese Traditional Village — Lebanese
This Lebanese restaurant is set in a lovely stone building, designed to feel like an old village. It is

Qatar Explorer

actually quite new, but has a special atmosphere. It's very big, but doesn't feel cavernous because there are lots of different rooms with cosy nooks and crannies. The food is very good, with grilled meats and traditional mezze, and the bread is fantastic. To find it, go up Grand Hamad Street from the Corniche, cross the A Ring Road, and it's on the right past Olympic Sports.

Al Hilal Bldg, Hamad Al Kabir St Al Doha Al Jadeeda
4435 5353
assahavillage.com
Map **2 R9**

Automatic   Middle Eastern

The Automatic chain of restaurants has been serving great quality Arabian food in a casual setting across the Middle East for years. The menu sports a good selection of inexpensive mezze and salads as well as grilled meat, fish and kebabs. The portions are a good size and are served hot and fresh to your table by efficient and friendly waiting staff. It's popular for takeaway, and a good option for grabbing your morning pastry and coffee.

Al Sadd Rd, Nr Qtel Al Sadd **4442 5999**
Map **2 K8**

Beijing   Chinese

This independent restaurant is nestled in a private villa off the busy Salwa Road. It has both indoor and outdoor seating which is suitable for large groups, as well as more intimate private dining areas separated by cubicles. Beijing has friendly, knowledgeable staff who can help you choose from the extensive menu, which features a good selection of great tasting traditional Chinese favourites.

Off Salwa Rd, Nr The Centre Fereej Abdel Aziz
4435 8688
Map **2 N9**

Beirut Restaurant   Lebanese

Feel like a local by pulling your car up to the front door of this predominantly takeaway restaurant. Soon enough, a waiter will run out to your car window to take your order. Serving a good selection of Lebanese food, Beirut is known to many residents for its fabulous hummus and foul, a traditional bean dish popular throughout the Arab world.

Al Kahraba St Fereej Mohammed Bin Jasim
4442 1087
Map **2 P8**

Bennigan's   American

This enormous wood-panelled restaurant is very popular with families. The food is the usual American diner-style fare, with a good range of choices – unless you're vegetarian – but the major plus point for parents is the vast carpeted indoor play area. It is a bit

short on things to play on, but is very good for serious running around, and there is an outdoor play area too. Be warned though, this is a very popular place for class outings and is best avoided at the end of term, unless you like the noise of swarms of overexcited children letting off steam.

Khalifa International Tennis & Squash Complex Lekhwair **4483 8700**
bennigans.com
Map **2 N4**

BiCE Ristorante   Italian

This posh Italian restaurant has perfected the art of fine dining, serving up generous portions of flavourful pastas, seafood, steak and pizza. Open for lunch and dinner, BiCE is ideal for both business people and romantics. The bright and open design, impeccable service and view of Doha's skyline well complement the main attraction – creative meals designed by a chef from Milan, Italy. You can't go wrong with his specials of the day, or anything that contains lobster. If you can tear yourself away from temptation, skip the breadbasket and save room for BiCE's delectable desserts.

Porto Arabia The Pearl Qatar **4495 3876**
Map **1 M2**

Bistro 61   International

One of Doha's best kept secrets, Bistro 61 is a quirky cafe-style restaurant that has a little bit of everything to offer. The Elizabethan-style furnishings, including revivalist Tudor chairs, embroidered cushions and ornate chandeliers, kick you into relaxation mode while the ultra-modern glass ceiling and floor to ceiling window breathes sparkling sunlight into the airy space. Ideally situated in West Bay, the location is perfect for business lunch meetings, hence a daily three-course menu has been specially designed. The menu, featuring page after page of scrumptious starters, pizzas, sandwiches and grilled mains and an impressive list of hot drinks, fruit juices, sodas and smoothies, is easily one of the best in town.

Alfardan Towers, 61 Al Funduq St Al Dafna
4498 9393
hdc-global.com
Map **2 Q3**

Food Restrictions

Qatar is a Muslim country, and as such, independent, chain and hotel food outlets do not serve any dishes containing pork. There is zero tolerance towards pork items, and people are not permitted to bring it into the country for personal consumption.

Restaurants & Cafes

Blue

Blue — International

A bit of an underappreciated gem in Doha's fine dining scene, Blue offers an array of international culinary delights: in addition to some of the best sushi in town, the menu ranges from the likes of pumpkin curry soup to superb steaks. The desserts are also worth a try, particularly the signature cheesecake which comes with delightfully a local kick as it's made of dates. Impeccable presentation and friendly service complete the picture.
Grand Heritage Doha Hotel & Spa Baaya **4445 5555**
grandheritage.com
Map **2 A10**

Burj Al Hamam — Lebanese

For a taste of high-end Lebanese cuisine, the Burj Al Haman is a fine choice. Nestled in the corner of Porto Arabia, the restaurant offers incredible views of the marina as you dine inside a stunningly spacious room clad with chandeliers, white pillars, modern furniture and high ceilings – an ideal venue to impress guests. The food is an impressive array of traditional Lebanese treats including cold mezze plates of hummus, moutabal, tabouli and fragrantly flavourful grilled lamb and shish toouk.
Porto Arabia The Pearl Qatar **4495 3876**
burjalhamam.com
Map **1 M2**

Cafe Bateel — Cafe

As you head out of Doha on Salwa Road, Cafe Bateel is easy to miss – but you really should try to seek it out. Menu options include superb salads, soups and sandwiches, plus heartier main courses that lean towards Indian but also include Italian, Arabian and seafood. The interior complements the food, with inlaid wooden alcoves, gypsum walls, Arabian cushions and barasti palm ceilings. Bateel's prize

attractions are its delectable sweets, cakes, pastries and bread; it even sells icecream. Be sure to stock up on baked goods before you leave, but you're bound to be back again soon.
Salwa Rd, Nr Midmac Interchange Fereej Al Nasr **4444 1414**
Map **2 K11**

The Cafe Restaurant — International

Serving breakfast, lunch and dinner, this is the InterContinental's buffet restaurant, where there's an impressive display of international cuisine. Children are welcome, and during a Friday brunch you will even find entertainment to keep them busy them while you eat in peace. The food is excellent, superbly presented and the choices plentiful. The set price means you can try as much as you like and not worry about the bill. The surroundings are fresh and bright and the service is first rate. There are also weekly Asian, seafood and Lebanese nights.
InterContinental Doha Al Gassar **4484 4444**
intercontinental.com/doha
Map **1 K3**

Carluccio's — Italian

Carluccio's is a great outdoor dining venue on cooler evenings. During the hot summers the cool interior provides a casual and relaxing ambience in time-honoured Italian style. The restaurant considers itself to be an ambassador for traditional Italian fare and great emphasis is placed on sourcing the best authentic food from the small producers of each region of Italy. Open from 08:00 to 00:00. Carluccio's operates a delicatessen providing a home delivery service within the Pearl area.
Porto Arabia The Pearl Qatar **6690 1777**
carluccios.com
Map **1 M2**

Chili's — American

This chainknown for its huge signature burgers and sizzling tex-mex disheshas made its mark on Qatar thanks to the very generous portions, seemingly bottomless soft drinks and a relaxed atmosphere. Indeed, with all-American music playing in the background, you could be forgiven for thinking you've been transported to the heart of the Midwest. Other branches are in The Mall (p.336) and City Center Doha (p.331).
Souq Rawda, Salwa Rd Fereej Abdel Aziz **4444 5335**
chilis.com
Map **2 M9**

Choices — International

Choices take their name seriously by offering an astounding array of options in an all-you-can-eat, international buffet with selections that rotate daily.

Going Out

Theme nights are Tuesday Steak Night, Wednesday Indian Night and Thursday Seafood Night. Friday Fest, an expanded, all-you-can-eat-and-drink lunch buffet with a Kid's Corner, is an excellent-value option. Weekdays, breakfast is served from 06:00 to 10:30 and the prices include tea, coffee, fresh juice and water. Lunch is from served 12:00 to 15:30; dinner from19:00 to 23:30. Children 5 and under eat for free; children 6 to 12 get 50% off. Choices offers shisha by the poolside. The Oryx Delight flavour mixes apple, grape and mint in their speciality handmade charcoal.
Oryx Rotana Al Hilal **4402 3333**
rotana.com
Map **2 T11**

Chopsticks   Far Eastern
A delightful jewel of the Orient, Chopsticks is a restaurant of exceptional standards. In rebellion against the tacky decor of a common Far Eastern-themed diner, Chopsticks is refreshingly elegant and formal, with a style that is pleasantly reminiscent of a 1920s art deco cafe. The menu boasts a modest mix of Chinese, Thai and Japanese specialities, including Peking Duck pancakes, sushi and sashimi rolls and crispy beef, that won't break the budget. Even more outstanding than the sumptuous cuisine is the service from immaculately presented staff who simply can't do enough to make your experience memorable.
Wyndham Grand Regency Doha Al Sadd **4434 3333**
wyndhamgrandregency.com
Map **2 K7**

Ciao   Italian
If you want to experience a home-made Italian meal, then Ciao is the place to be. This centrally located independent restaurant goes the extra mile to provide a true taste of Italia, right down to having its cheeses specially flown in. The pizzas and calzones are cooked in an open oven on the main level of the restaurant. When it comes to desserts the tiramisu cannot be missed, although it faces stiff competition from the gelato.
Haya Complex, Salwa Rd Fereej Al Soudan **4468 9100**
Map **2 J12**

Corniche   Mediterranean
Bright and airy, Corniche has few aesthetics to distinguish it from other hotel buffets, but once you've circled the different displays, you'll be pleasantly surprised by the spread on offer. Fresh breads, grilled kebabs, soups, salads, mezze and a selection from the special theme of the day, plus a display of artfully presented desserts, are there to tempt you, and the friendly staff will see that your plate and glass remain full. The Friday brunch (part of the Marriott's gallery brunch, p.196) is popular, with food from

all over the world and entertainment for children. Whatever else, you won't be going home hungry.
Doha Marriott Hotel Al Khulaifat **4429 8404**
marriott-doha.com
Map **2 V8**

Cosmo   International
This large restaurant offers daily lunch and dinner deals. Like the hotel itself, the restaurant is decorated with elaborate touches. Millennium is dry, making it popular with Arab clientele. There is an ample selection of international fare to choose from, but the food isn't outstanding. The sobre ambiance makes it a good choice for a meal with business associates; just make sure that you arrive at the beginning of a sitting as the dishes tend to run out later on.
Millennium Hotel Doha Al Sadd **4424 7777**
millenniumhotels.com
Map **2 K8**

Crepaway   International
The menu at Crepaway, as the name suggests, features a large, lip-smacking selection of sweet and savoury crepes, but that is by no means the limit to the culinary creativity. Open for breakfast, lunch and dinner, it also serves salads, burgers, pizzas and desserts. The good food is definitely matched by the good mood, with the restaurant having the feel of a fun, young and upbeat diner. There's a jukebox, a DJ who can inspire outbreaks of dancing, and occasional karaoke nights too. Crepaway is a lively venue popular with families and Doha's hip and happening crowd. You can even take advantage of the free delivery.
Al Mouthanna Complex, Salwa Rd Al Mirqab **4465 5830**
crepaway.com
Map **2 M10**

Cosmo

Restaurants & Cafes

Criollo > p.201   Cafe

Named after a rare and expensive cocoa bean, Criollo is a chocolate-lover's dream. The finest cocoa from around the world is used to produce exquisite birthday cakes, elegant truffles and hot chocolate to die for. Whether you're looking to treat yourself or pick up some stunning chocolate for gifts, this is the place; it's also a great spot to while away an afternoon with friends. In addition to coffee and hot chocolate, Criollo also boasts a selection of loose leaf teas.

InterContinental Doha The City Onaiza **4015 8888**
intercontinental.com/dohathecity
Map **2 P2**

Di Capri > p.199, 338   Italian

This Italian offers a quirky mixture of modern and traditional, evident in both the decor and the food. The menu is inspired by the famous resort island of Capri and features a selection of exquisitely fresh salads: the Caprese Salad in particular is not to be missed. Homemade pasta dishes, risottos and some hearty meat and seafood options are also available. There's no kids' menu, but the chef who can usually accommodate special requests to create dishes that will keep the young ones happy too.

La Cigale Hotel Fereej Bin Mahmoud **4428 8888**
lacigalehotel.com
Map **2 M9**

Fauchon   French

Although it markets itself as a true 'Salon de Thé', Fauchon actually specialises in various areas. As well as serving gourmet teas, coffees, salads and sandwiches, it dishes up some of the most decadent desserts in the city, and its cakes make impressive gifts. The cafe also does very good outside catering. Simply provide your budget and it will tailor a full scale menu that even includes the china, silverware and a team of uniformed staff to ensure your event impresses the guests.

Souq Najad, Salwa Rd New Al Mirqab **4432 4888**
fauchon.com
Map **2 L10**

The Fish Market   Seafood

The market-style setting for this seafood-lover's paradise fits perfectly with its beachfront location. Friendly, informed staff will guide you through the fish, lobster or shellfish selection which is all on open display, and is prepared to your taste along with a choice of salad, vegetable and beverage accompaniment. The lobster thermidor is to die for – as is the stunning view. Visit on Fridays for the Lebanese seafood brunch or seafood extravaganza buffet in the evening.

InterContinental Doha Al Gassar **4484 4444**
intercontinental.com/doha
Map **1 K3**

Flavours   International

Flavours is Grand Heritage Doha's all day dining restaurant. Its opulent decor and comfy upholstered seats make it a pleasant, relaxed venue for business meetings or family get-togethers. The restaurant's ample buffet offers food from around the world, with an excellent Arabian mezze section, unusual salads and delicious flavoured breads – particularly the olive and tomato kinds – being the highlights. You can also opt for steak dishes or locally-caught seafood, both cooked to order in the open kitchen.

Grand Heritage Doha Hotel & Spa Baaya **4445 5555**
grandheritagedoha.com
Map **2 A10**

Fuddruckers   American

This US chain is a firm family favourite. Children are provided with an elaborate play space outside, allowing the grown-ups some relative peace and quiet in the Americana themed dining area. The menu is big and varied, with Fuddruckers priding itself on its steaks, burgers and potato wedges. You'd better be hungry as portions are certainly on the large side. Wash it all down with bottomless soft drinks.

Khalifa International Tennis & Squash Complex Lekhwair **4483 3983**
Map **2 N4**

The Garden Restaurant   Indian

The Garden is a popular place for a cheap but well-made curry. It's cleverly split into separate dining areas: downstairs is famous for its vegetarian dishes, while upstairs you can eat a la carte or buffet style (all at very reasonable prices). The rich reds and golds of traditional Indian restaurants are abundant, and there is a choice of open tables and separate booths where you can draw the curtains. The waiters are welcoming and full of smiles, the menu is varied, and the food is excellent. Takeaway and delivery are both available.

Al Najma Souq Najma **4436 5686**
Map **2 S10**

Garvey's   European

Re-badged as a family restaurant and minus its alcohol licence, Garvey's retains its relaxed feel and remains a favourite among expat families. Dine in the main area whilst cheering for your favourite football team. The menu is simple but diverse whether you crave fish 'n chips from home or local roast lamb. Be sure to enquire about their specials and note that healthy options are available. Only fresh ingredients are used which is an added bonus considering the prices are a bargain. Open for breakfast, lunch, and dinner, and a party room complete with kids' entertainment can be hired.

Garvey's European Family Club Al Aziziya **4468 7381**
Map **1 E12**

Il Teatro

Asia Live!

La Mer

The Grill

Restaurants & Cafes

Going Out (sidebar)

Gourmet House > p.81 — Cafe
Authentic, European-style bread makes Gourmet House a firm favourite among Doha expats. The in-house baker is German and some of the specialities include deliciously dark rye bread and soft pretzels. A superb assortment of pastries, pies and cakes, as well as a small selection of sandwiches and homemade ice cream, are also available for takeaway or consumption on the spot. You can also pick up other gourmet items from olive oil and balsamic vinegar to jams and tea.
Kempinski Residences & Suites Al Dafna **4405 3333**
kempinski-residences.com
Map **2 Q1**

Grand Gourmet — International
Set amid the splendour of the prestigious Wyndham Grand Regency Hotel, the namesake Grand Gourmet offers a unique upmarket buffet experience. The international selection has a wide variety of entrees, appetisers, salads, mains and desserts, or you can choose from steak, seafood, mezze or low-calorie healthy options from the a la carte menu. Italian cuisine is showcased every Saturday evening, Arabian cuisine is on Fridays, while seafood night is every Wednesday where you can watch your fish being prepared before you in the live kitchen. Or, if you fancy indulging in Far Eastern flavours, head to Grand Gourmet on Mondays. Open daily for breakfast, lunch and dinner.
Wyndham Grand Regency Doha Al Sadd **4434 3333**
wyndhamgrandregency.com
Map **2 K7**

The Grill — Steakhouse
Polished wooden furnishings and warm, ambient lighting set the mood for this contemporary interpretation of the relaxed, casual barbecue. Sit either indoors or on the terrace, and sample the tantalising selection of starters on offer at the salad bar while waiting for your main meal to be grilled to perfection. Choices include Australian wagyu beef, seafood, chicken and duck, washed down with a glass or two from the endless selection of international wines, champagnes and beers. A final visit to the dessert bar rounds off this culinary journey where the presentation is first class, the service is excellent and the quality and taste of the food is outstanding. Open for breakfast, lunch, dinner and Friday brunch.
Grand Hyatt Doha Al Gassar **4448 1234**
doha.grand.hyatt.com
Map **1 K1**

Il Teatro — Italian
The Four Seasons is known as one of Doha's top hotels, and its flagship restaurant, Il Teatro, upholds its reputation. Il Teatro creates a warm atmosphere with its Venetian elegance, picturesque views of the bay and welcoming staff. The menu is quintessential Venetian cuisine, centring on fresh vegetables and seafood. Vegetarians will appreciate the homemade pastas, whereas meat-eaters will enjoy the premium selection of beef. Italian wine-lovers will delight in the variety, including several types of grappa.
Four Seasons Hotel Al Dafna **4494 8888**
fourseasons.com/doha
Map **2 R2**

Isaan — Thai
To eat at Isaan is to experience Thai warmth and hospitality as well as some of the most unique and entrancing food in Qatar. Served tapas style with a range of small plates shared with fellow diners, the Thai chefs use the freshest ingredients sourced locally and regionally, as well as from Asia. Standouts on the menu include red curry grouper and chicken grilled on sugar cane. Be warned, some dishes are not for the faint-hearted but the knowledgeable and understanding waiters will ask the kitchen for mercy.
Grand Hyatt Doha Al Gassar **4448 1234**
doha.grand.hyatt.com
Map **1 K1**

Johnny Rockets — American
Johnny Rockets is a classic American diner, complete with colourful 1950s-style booths and enthusiastic singing staff (put YMCA on the jukebox and see what happens). The menu is loaded with traditional favourites including burgers with all the trimmings, hot dogs and chicken dishes. Milkshake fans are also well catered for. If it's a little early in the day for the full burger experience, between 07:00 and 13:00 the restaurant offers a breakfast menu featuring such delights as French toast and pancakes.
Al Emadi Centre, Salwa Rd New Al Mirqab
4455 2792
johnnyrockets.com
Map **2 M10**

JW's Steakhouse — Steakhouse
The Wild West meets a refined gentleman's club in this lively saloon, where hearty steaks, a well-stocked bar and refined service are prime. Novelties are delivered aplenty, starting with the huge chalkboard menus, the lobster tank, the braces-clad staff and the bullhorn-edged serving boards. The extensive wine list and cigar cabinet add to the appeal, and even vegetarians are catered for with a cursory nod or two. Stop by for a drink with friends or try one of their famous US-certified Angus steaks – if they were any fresher they'd moo. Surf 'n' turf is the house speciality in this highly likeable carnivore haven.
Doha Marriott Hotel Al Khulaifat **4429 8499**
marriott-doha.com
Map **2 V8**

Qatar Explorer

Kebab King — Middle Eastern

This is a typical kebab house with brightly coloured chairs surrounding Formica tables. The staff are friendly and helpful and the menu caters to carnivores and vegetarians alike; even the health conscious will be happy with the wide range of dishes on offer. Grilled fish and meat of various kinds are served up with rice, salad or vegetables. The menu offers some very good curries as well. The restaurant also delivers.
Ras Abu Aboud St, Nr Sana Fashion Slata **4441 0400**
kebabkingrestaurant.com
Map **2 T8**

La Mer — French

Everything about La Mer speaks opulence, from the glittering chandeliers to the exquisite French five-course taster menu with paired wines. The atmosphere is fittingly subdued, with just a hum of conversation beneath the pianist's strains. The service is discreet and faultless. If you want just a sip of the high life, the bar area affords some wonderful views and some delicious cocktails. La Mer is a treat to be kept for a truly special occasion or a truly important client.
The Ritz-Carlton, Doha Al Gassar **4484 8000**
ritzcarlton.com
Map **1 K1**

La Veranda — Italian

Perched on the end of the Corniche, La Veranda has a homely feel inside and intimate tables outside, with further seating on a grass terrace. The classic Italian fare on offer is fresh and well presented, and the staff are friendly. Whether you dine here at lunch with friends over a bottle of wine and the glinting turquoise sea, or on a candlelit evening with a loved one, it would be a crime not to make the most of La Veranda's stunning alfresco location in all but the hottest weather.
Sheraton Doha Resort & Convention Hotel Al Dafna **4485 4444**
laverandadoha.com
Map **2 R3**

La Villa — Mediterranean

This spacious, typically Mediterranean restaurant is on the top floor of the Mercure Grand in the heart of the city. There is a good choice of dishes, some of which are prepared with an unexpected twist. All are creatively presented and delicious. The service is friendly, although the staff's knowledge of the wine list can be a little limited. There are great views of the Doha skyline and the bustling city below, but the traffic can be noisy. The hotel is on Al Muntazah Street, close to the junction with Wadi Musheireb Street.
Mercure Grand Hotel Doha City Centre Al Jasra **4446 2222**
mercuredoha.com
Map **2 Q8**

L'Wzaar Seafood Market > p.iv, 186, 353 — Seafood

Buzzing, colourful and unashamedly flashy, L'Wzaar is a favourite among the in-crowd. Yet the atmosphere is pleasantly casual and the prices reasonable – in short, if you're looking for a seafront spot with friendly service and fantastically fresh fish, this is it. There are three restaurant sections and although the place is huge, it fills up every night so book ahead. The food selection is enormous too, ranging from fish and chips to exquisite sashimi, all served with delicious sides of your liking. If you're not a fan of seafood, you can substitute for chicken or go for the Lebanese salad bar.
Katara Cultural Village Al Gassar **4408 0711**
lwzaar.com
Map **1 K3**

The Lagoon — International

There are many buffet restaurants in Doha but this is certainly up there with the best. Open all day and bursting at the seams with so many choices, the temptation is to try it all and end up being defeated by the never-ending array of delicious creations. With live cooking stations, the talented chefs will prepare certain dishes freshly to order. The Friday brunch is particularly popular, especially with families.
The Ritz-Carlton, Doha Al Gassar **4484 8000**
ritzcarlton.com
Map **1 K1**

Lahore Restaurant — Pakistani

A steady stream of customers at this Pakistani restaurant keeps the food fresh and the service fast. In addition to offering standard Desi fare like curries and biryanis, Lahore Restaurant also whips up various Chinese dishes. Order some chapati for QR 1 apiece to eat with karai chicken, which is spicy, saucy and cheap – a tasty and hearty meal. The mutton haleem is considered the stuff of legend. Lahore's clientele appears to be mostly men hankering for that home-cooked taste, but there is a family seating section.
Musherib St, Nr Le Mirage Musheireb **4432 4165**
Map **2 P8**

Latino — South American

Take a journey to South America at the attractive Latino restaurant. Hidden away on the ground floor, Argentinean Chef Fernando presides over this lively dining venue, while musical duo Chavela add to the ambience with their hot Latin sound. High quality meats and fish are served with traditional chimichurri spicy sauces, vegetarians are also catered for. Open from 18:00 to 02:00, Monday to Saturday.
Sheraton Doha Resort & Convention Hotel Al Dafna **4485 4444**
latinodoha.com
Map **2 R3**

A Bite Of Culture

In addition to theatre, art galleries and a heritage centre, Katara Cultural Village is home to some excellent restaurants and cafes serving regional specialities and more.

Food is an essential part of any culture and nowhere is this more true than in the Middle East, where eating the local way is a must-do for any visitor or expat resident. Although restaurants serving local food are found across Qatar, Katara Cultural Village is among your best bets when looking to gain an insight into the region's varied culinary traditions in an area that's compact enough to explore on foot.

Cultural Dining

Shawarma Albisana (p.368) offers a great introduction to fast food the Middle Eastern way. The choice is not huge, but the authenticity of the dishes on offer can't be faulted: head here for superb shawarmas, including specialities made of wagyu beef on select nights. This really is the all-Arabian experience with a thoroughly modern touch to reflect Qatar's increasingly cosmopolitan stance.

The term 'Middle Eastern' cuisine is loose, covering everything from Turkey to the Gulf. For one end of the spectrum, pop over to Sukar Pasha Ottoman Lounge (p.369). This atmospheric haunt offers a taste of Turkey, inclusive of great mezzes and fragrant shisha (p.22), in a setting that was designed to make you sit back and enjoy an Ottoman-style evening right in the heart of Doha.

Locally sourced ingredients are the star of the show at L'Wzaar Seafood Market (p.361). Fish doesn't get much fresher than this; think shrimp caught off the coast of Bahrain, and Emirati favourites sherri and hammour. While the cooking styles are international – you can opt for anything from fish & chips to sashimi and tom yam – a Lebanese-style bread and vegetable basket served as an appetiser adds a decidedly Middle Eastern touch. A Lebanese-style salad bar is also available.

To finish your dining experience on a sweet note, look no further than Albisana Kunafa (p.352). This cosy dessert joint specialises in two sweet dishes that hail from Palestine and Jordan. Whether you go for the piping hot *kunafa* or opt for *mohalibya*, a chilled pudding, this will be an authentic experience. Middle Eastern desserts can, however, be an acquired taste and for those looking to satisfy a sweet tooth of a different kind, Red Velvet Cupcakery (p.367) is another option.

Smoking a shisha, the Middle Eastern waterpipe, is a popular pastime on these shores and you'll find several shisha lounges and cafes across Katara Cultural Village as well: weave your way around the area and choose one that appeals, then park yourself on a comfortable chair or sofa and get ready to relax over a fragrant smoke.

Generally speaking, dining out the Middle Eastern way is likely to involve several hours spent over shared platters of food, shisha and tea, so it's best to arrive unhurried, hungry and ready for an essential cultural experience. For more detailed information on the regional culinary traditions, Qatari cuisine and dishes not to miss, see *Eating Arabian Style* on p.21.

Varied Attractions

Built in traditional Arabian style, Katara Cultural Village is a massive complex dedicated to history and regional culture. In addition to the numerous restaurants and cafes, the area includes theatres, art galleries and heritage sites, as well as a popular public beach. With such a wide range of attractions, it's no surprise that Katara Cultural Village has established itself as a buzzing lifestyle destination no resident or visitor should miss.

L'Wzaar Seafood Market

Kebabs

Sukar Pasha Ottoman Lounge

Shawarma

Kunafa

Layali Restaurant — Middle Eastern

If you are looking for a truly authentic Lebanese experience, then Layali is a must. Translated, it means 'many nights', and the service and menu here will certainly ensure repeat visits. The food is impeccable and the staff, in their smart black uniforms, are polished and extremely attentive. Many people go for the wide selection of Arabian mezze, either hot or cold, but grilled meats and fish are the real stars.
Souq Najd, Salwa Rd New Al Mirqab **4431 0005**
layalirestaurantqatar.com
Map **2 L10**

Le Central
Restaurant > p.199, 338 — Mediterranean

Bright and airy, with floor-to-ceiling windows and minimalist decor, everything about Le Central gives a delightful sense of lightness. Fitting with the general vibe, the gourmet salad bar is excellent and the Mediterranean-inspired a la carte menu's seafood options – including prawns with citrus sauce – also deserve a special mention. Those looking for a more filling dining experience can opt for weightier meat dishes and some fabulously rich desserts. The business lunch is exceptional value at QR 150 for three courses.
La Cigale Hotel Fereej Bin Mahmoud **4428 8888**
lacigalehotel.com
Map **2 M9**

Le Cigalon
Restaurant > p.199, 338 — International

Le Cigalon's bright, modern feel is accentuated by a giant aquarium and an open kitchen, where talented chefs create culinary delights from all corners of the world. Thanks to a varied international menu, there's something for everyone and the quality of the food is outstanding. A buffet with Lebanese specialities is among the particular highlights: look no further to sample authentic Levantine dishes like kibbeh shishbarak (couscous and meat patties cooked in yoghurt) which can be tricky to find elsewhere in town. Next door, you'll find a fabulous food hall to stock up on gourmet foods for home consumption. It isn't cheap, but the quality and choice is unmatched in Qatar – the cheese counter alone stocks 180 different kinds.
La Cigale Hotel Fereej Bin Mahmoud **4428 8888**
lacigalehotel.com
Map **2 M9**

Liza — Lebanese

Stepping into this sleek Lebanese restaurant is like walking into a lounge in New York. Its modern and metallic feel with the bar situated in the centre of the room, immediately creates a sense of modern style. Even the dishes – though essentially the usual delicious creations that we have come to love about this cuisine – are served uniquely in classy metal

Le Cigalon

platters and terracotta bowls. There is a strong emphasis on seafood dishes which are certainly worth a try and the fish and prawn kibbeh selection is especially tasty.

Porto Arabia The Pearl Qatar **4495 3876**
hdc-global.com
Map **1 M2**

Lobby Lounge > p.201 {Cafe}

The Lobby Lounge serves tea, coffee and light snacks all day long. The well-appointed afternoon tea, available from 14:00 to 18:000, is among the highlights. The items on offer range from classic smoked salmon sandwiches and traditional-style scones to specialities such as gold leaf-plated pastries. Whatever you pick from the tray, the use of high-quality, seasonal ingredients is evident and, as a nod towards regional cuisine, you'll also find specialities such as Ajwa date scones on the menu. Enjoy it all with a glass of champagne or a pot of delicate Jing tea; organic, Fairtrade green tea is also available.

InterContinental Doha The City Onaiza **4015 8888**
intercontinental.com/dohathecity
Map **2 P2**

The Lobby Lounge {Cafe}

A tempting selection of light snacks are available all day, but the real draw card is the divine afternoon tea menu. Choose delectable delicacies such as mini sandwiches, pastries, scones with clotted cream and jam, and petit fours made from the finest ingredients and presented with the flair and finesse that the Ritz-Carlton is famous for. An exquisite range of carefully sourced teas and coffees accompany the gourmet fare, all served in fine china. Relax to live music performances on the harp and piano in the luxurious comfort of grandiose furnishings; an afternoon at Lobby Lounge will leave you feeling like royalty.

The Ritz-Carlton, Doha Al Gassar **4484 8000**
ritzcarlton.com
Map **1 K1**

Market By Jean-Georges {International}

The W Hotel's Market by Jean-Georges has wowed its guests thanks to one particular dish: its black truffle and fontina pizza. Indeed, unusual flavour and texture combos are typical of the creations by this celebrity chef and whether you turn up for a business lunch or an evening with friends, the innovative twists on traditional comfort foods will add a wow-factor. You'll also find perfectly traditional items such as rotisserie chicken with mashed potatoes, while the health-conscious can choose between grilled fish and salads. The Friday Jazz Brunch is popular.

W Doha Hotel & Residences Al Dafna **4453 5000**
marketdoha.com
Map **2 Q1**

Megu {Japanese}

It's abundantly clear that Megu is set to be special as you ride in a private lift to the restaurant's main entrance. Entering the plush surroundings of Megu's bar area, and walking into the huge circular room with private alcoves is a visually stunning experience. The restaurant serves Japanese cuisine but with a modern twist that turns sushi and sashimi dishes into creative masterpieces. Be brave and try the more unusual options. The crispy asparagus served on a skewer and coated in a unique peanut sauce is delightfully light and unique and the kobe beef served on a piping hot black stone will have you salivating for days.

Porto Arabia The Pearl Qatar **4495 3876**
hdc-global.com
Map **1 M2**

Mykonos {Greek}

This is not fine dining, but Mykonos offers something to please everyone. Be prepared to wait for your food while this newcomer establishes itself; you should also leave any preconceptions about traditional Greek food at the door as some of the dishes feature incongruously un-Greek ingredients. Other dishes, such as the crispy courgette balls and the Graviera, stay on the traditional track and are winners. A good place to celebrate a special occasion or to meet friends before heading upstairs for a boogie at Lava (p.372).

InterContinental Doha Al Gassar **4484 4444**
intercontinental.com/doha
Map **1 K3**

Nando's {Portuguese}

This ever popular Portuguese-inspired chain is known for its uniquely flavoured chicken all drenched in mild to spicy sauce, depending on your tastebuds. The chicken is basted and then flame-grilled and served with sides of your choice. You can choose between lemon and herb, mild peri-peri and hot peri-peri, or extra-hot peri-peri for a truly fiery treat. The menu is extensive, including light appetisers, a kids' selection and a few vegetarian options as well. Other branches are located on Al Sadd Street and in City Center Doha (p.331).

Salwa Rd Fereej Al Nasr **4435 6756**
nandos.com
Map **2 L10**

Naurah Bakery {Middle Eastern}

This local eatery offers simple yet satisfying meals of fatayar and manaish – Arabian brick oven-baked bread topped or filled with meat, cheese and zaatar. Perfect for a quick snack or lunch, and priced around QR 4, the fluffy filled bread lends to generous mixing and matching. Pair the salty, juicy spinach cheese fatayar with a creamy, sweet labneh with honey – it's dinner and dessert, done. Naurah is a small establishment,

with only three tables and a handful of chairs, so takeaway is generally a better option than dine-in.
Najma St, Nr Gulf Cinema signal Al Hilal **4435 3532**
Map **2 R12**

Neo Restaurant   International
Although this international restaurant offers Italian, French and Chinese, Neo is best known for its sushi. It's available any night, but Tuesday is the special sushi evening. You pay a set fee and it just keeps coming; it's super-fresh, tender, and undoubtedly the best in Doha. With dark wood, channels of pebbles and subdued lighting, the restaurant has a Japanese feel. Neo prides itself on preparing everything from scratch, from bread to icecream, and you can taste the difference.
Souq Najd, Salwa Rd New Al Mirqab **4432 2508**
neorestaurantqatar.com
Map **2 L10**

The Noodle House   Chinese
A great place for a lip-smackingly good lunch or casual dinner, Noodle House serves up a variety of south-east Asian dishes. Fragrant curries, soups, stir fries and salads are dished up throughout the day to hungry customers seated at bench style tables, elbow to elbow with other diners. Simply tick your choice on the menu pad and grab the attention of one of the serving staff. Two branches have also opened with one on The Pearl offering dine-in and deliveries (4495 3876 ext. 2531) and the other at The Landmark Shopping Mall (6634 2232).
City Center Doha Al Dafna **4411 5063**
thenoodlehouse.com
Map **2 Q2**

The Old Manor   Steakhouse
For those interested in quality food that doesn't cost a fortune, The Old Manor is just right. A cross between a gentlemen's club, an English pub and a steakhouse, the menu offers firm favourites including shepherd's pie, chicken in a basket and, of course, steaks. The cosy little venue is casual and relaxed, with a big-screen TV. The service is quick and efficient but never intrusive. With a great view over the city centre, this is the perfect place to settle down with a pie and a pint.
Mercure Grand Hotel Doha City Centre Al Jasra **4446 2222**
mercuredoha.com
Map **2 Q8**

Opal By Gordon Ramsay   International
This chic bistro by celebrity chef Gordon Ramsay manages to strike the fine balance between upscale and relaxed. The modern dining area is open and lively, while the menu features contemporary

international cuisine. Some unusual combinations help turn the dining experience into a culinary adventure, as do the excellent 'molecular cocktails' created by the inhouse mixologist. The gourmet pizzas are worth a try. Despite offering some fine food in a fun, classy setting, the restaurant's prices remain a notch below most high-end establishments.
St. Regis Doha Al Gassar **4446 0000**
stregisdoha.com
Map **1 K3**

Orangery Cafe Trottoir > p.199, 338   Cafe
With high ceilings, enormous windows and a lovely terrace, this cafe boasts a wonderfully bright and airy feel: in short, it's the perfect venue for a light lunch. The menu ranges from shawarmas to pizza, crepes and waffles, and a good selection of fresh juices and mocktails are available to wash it all down with. However, the dessert selection, including tasty treats from frozen tiramisu to fruit tarts, is not to be missed either. The adjacent gift shop carries gourmet chocolates and unique tea sets.
La Cigale Hotel Fereej Bin Mahmoud **4428 8888**
lacigalehotel.com
Map **2 M9**

Paloma   Tex Mex
The upbeat music, casual atmosphere, and plenty of non-alcoholic drink choices, and a few stronger ones, make this a popular watering hole for those looking for a night out, any day of the week. The restaurant's central feature is a circular bar, adjacent to the dance floor, and this is the most popular spot in the room whether to eat, chat, smoke, or merely people watch. The food is hearty and filling whether you opt for the steak, tacos, burritos, or other Mexican staples. It's busy every night of the week, so be proactive in placing your order.
InterContinental Doha Al Gassar **4484 4444**
intercontinental.com/doha
Map **1 K3**

Pampano   Mexican
Located by the water's edge, Pampano has a beautiful terrace to dine at while watching the luxurious yachts cruise past. The light and airy interior gives the restaurant an effortlessly cool European feel, but the cuisine itself is predominantly Mexican – albeit slightly altered to include local specialties like hammour. For those looking for something more typically Mexican, the Enchiladas Norteñas with braised lamb and corn tortillas with Monterey jack cheese and spices is particularly delicious.
Porto Arabia The Pearl Qatar **4495 3876**
hdc-global.com
Map **1 M2**

Patatas   Lebanese

Patatas is the place to go to indulge without overspending. The answer to every late night junk food craving, this casual-dining Lebanese restaurant offers a tempting array of appetisers, a wide range of hot dogs, burgers and sandwiches and several types of chips. It also boasts a breakfast menu that includes fresh orange juice and pancakes smothered in Nutella and maple syrup. Weather permitting, customers have the option of sitting outside and people-watching while scoffing down their carbs.
The Centre Rawdat Al Khail **4483 3983**
Map **2 M10**

Ponderosa   American

This firmly established restaurant chain offers an enjoyable and energetic dining experience for children and families, as well as being a great place to catch up with large groups of friends. The menu features good quality food with the emphasis on steak, chicken and seafood dishes. The all-you-can-eat buffet is also popular throughout the day, offering American-style fare from the salad bar and self-serve icecream. There are two more branches; one is in West Bay (4483 6206) and the other is located on Salwa Road (4458 3006).
Salwa Rd, Nr Ramada Junction New Al Mirqab
4465 5880
Map **2 M10**

Porcini   Italian

Widely accepted as one of the very best and finest Italian restaurants in Qatar, Porcini delivers an exceptional dining experience. The luxurious, opulent and stylish furnishings radiate the charm and comfort of a cosy lounge room, while warm colours and soft lighting set the mood for privacy. The delectable

menu offers a good selection of fare from across Italy, using the highest quality ingredients and presented with eye-pleasing finesse. The extensive wine selection is sure to impress even the pickiest connoisseur while faultless, attentive service from knowledgeable staff is another of the many reasons why you will be sure to return. Private cooking classes are also available.
The Ritz-Carlton, Doha Al Gassar **4484 8000**
ritzcarlton.com
Map **1 K1**

Ras Al Shawah   Cafe

This food and juice stand is located on the Corniche, Doha's picturesque waterfront. It may look tiny on the outside, but Ras Al Shawah's inexpensive menu, which includes sandwiches, milkshakes and burgers, goes on for several pages. The stand, which is next to a park, also offers plenty of children-friendly options, including popcorn, sweets and a strong, but milky and sugary, tea called 'karak' chai. Ras Al Shawah has indoor seating, but most people order and eat by the water or in their cars.
Nr Sheraton Park Al Dafna
Map **2 Q3**

Red Velvet Cupcakery > p.iv, 186, 353   Cafe

You almost feel as though you've walked into the cupcake section of Willy Wonka's factory when entering Red Velvet: it's bright, it's colourful and everything is designed to take you right back to childhood. That being said, the sweet treats on offer have all the sophistication any grown-up gourmet could wish for. Devil's Food, a rich chocolate buttermilk cake with 24 karat gold leaf garnish, is one of the most popular choices. The Peanut Butter Cup is another must: with its creamy, sweet and salty

Porcini

topping, it's truly mouth-watering and not to be missed. Vegan and gluten-free options are also available.

Katara Cultural Village Al Gassar **4408 0700**
redvelvetdoha.com
Map **1 K3**

Richoux   International

A surprising yet welcome touch of class among City Center Doha's eateries, Richoux's dark woodwork, red leather seats and gold-coloured railings and light fittings are a world away from the shops just outside. One side of the menu features breakfast, drinks, pastries, and a full traditional afternoon tea for two. Flip the menu over and you'll find a comprehensive choice of sandwiches, starters and mains, featuring dishes such as fillet mignon steak and wild mushroom pasta. There's terrace seating at the front, but it may be a little noisy for some.

City Center Doha Al Dafna **4493 1661**
richouxdoha.com
Map **2 Q2**

Rocca   Mediterranean

During the cooler months, dining on the poolside terrace is a pleasure, but for the rest of the year it's equally pleasant to retreat into the cool, calm, white, minimalist cocoon indoors; you'll still get to admire the view through the floor-to-ceiling windows. The succinct but distinctly Mediterranean menu features classics such as king prawns, seafood pasta and wood fired pizzas, as well as lighter fare from grilled halloumi to salads. The soft focaccia bread is delicious, although you may want to go easy on it to save space for a bite of tiramisu to finish your meal on a decadently delicious note.

Grand Hyatt Doha Al Gassar **4448 1234**
doha.grand.hyatt.com
Map **1 K1**

Salsa   Mexican

Serving favourites such as sizzling fajitas, big steaks, and a choice of enchiladas, this lively Mexican restaurant is a great place to come with friends. There are also lighter options of tasty salads on the menu, but portions are generous, and most mains come served with refried beans and Mexican rice. The live band will put anybody in the party mood – and help you dance off your dinner.

Doha Marriott Hotel Al Khulaifat **4429 8464**
marriott-doha.com
Map **2 V8**

Seasons Restaurant   International

This restaurant has a variety of theme nights including French, Swiss, Asian and seafood. The Friday brunch is also popular, where kids are not only welcomed, but

also supervised and well-entertained. The all-you-can-eat buffet may not be as large as some of the other hotels, but the seafood and sushi are outstanding and the cheese is excellent (as you would expect from a Swiss chain). The staff are friendly and eager to please, but not overbearing. This is in the older Mövenpick on the Corniche.

Mövenpick Hotel Doha Slata **4429 1111**
moevenpick-hotels.com
Map **2 S7**

Shawarma

Albisana > p.iv, 186, 353   Middle Eastern

This family-friendly haunt serves genuine Arabian fast food – in a French-style bistro setting. On a regular day you have two choices, chicken or beef shawarma, with optional sides of chopped parsley, onions, potatoes or chilli paste. On a Tuesday, however, you can splash out on a rather unique combination: Japanese Wagyu beef shawarma. There is indoor seating but the most patrons opt for the relaxing alfresco area (which has air-conditioning in the summer). Takeaways are also available.

Katara Cultural Village Al Gassar **4408 1400**
katara.net
Map **1 K3**

Shisha Garden > p.199, 338   Middle Eastern

This is one of the best spots in town for a casual and relaxed evening over some authentic hubbly bubbly. Best enjoyed in the evening, the creatively designed garden cafe is a great spot for a meet-up with colleagues, family and friends. It's also a good choice for sports fans thanks to a number of large television screens that can be viewed from almost every corner of the terrace. When hunger strikes, opt for a selection of mezze and Arabian mains. Tasty fresh juices are also available to order.

La Cigale Hotel Fereej Bin Mahmoud **4428 8888**
lacigalehotel.com
Map **2 M9**

Spice Market   South-East Asian

Echoing the W Hotel's affinity for non-traditional design, Spice Market mixes moody red lighting and Arabian lanterns for local flair, while Oriental-inspired black ash furniture gives a hint of the food on offer. Fans of Asian cuisine will be spoilt for choice, but the good news is that everything comes in 'family style' sharing portions, so turn up with a group of friends for a chance to sample several dishes. The highlights include blackened shrimps with sun-dried pineapple, lobster cake and mango salad. To top it off, there's a selection of innovative cocktails.

W Doha Hotel & Residences Al Dafna **4453 5000**
spicemarketdoha.com
Map **2 Q1**

The Square > *p.201* International

Whether you go a la carte or turn up for the buffet option, the standard of cooking is consistently high at The Square. The choice is broad. The brunch (QR 290 per person including bubbly) offers a tasty selection of international cuisines hailing from Thailand, India, Italy and Japan – to name but a few. In the evening, only half of the cooking stations are open, but the food is no less impressive. Choose between meat and seafood mains, or opt for pizzas and pasta cooked to order. While there's still a fair bit of construction going on in the vicinity, the tables next to the floor-to-ceiling windows allow you to dine while watching the world go by.
InterContinental Doha The City Onaiza **4015 8888**
intercontinental.com/dohathecity
Map **2 P2**

Star Of India Indian

A good range of tasty curries and other culinary treats from the subcontinent have earned this family-oriented haunt a loyal following among local residents. The casual atmosphere is perfect for family outings, while a separate party hall caters for groups of 35 or more. The decor is simple and relaxed, and whether you opt to dine in-house or order takeaway, the food on offer is of excellent value.
Khalifa St, Nr TV & Radio R/A Al Jebailat **4486 4440**
Map **2 K3**

Strata > *p.201* Seafood

Located on the 55th floor, this high-end restaurant has proven itself as one of Qatar's top dining destinations. It's the perfect location for a memorable evening: after admiring the breathtaking city views over a pre-dinner cocktail in the upstairs bar, you can move to the dining area to sample a menu that features delicacies from sashimi to caviar. The set menu offers a five course culinary journey. Whether you opt for this or choose to go a la carte, the food is accompanied with some irresistible bread and an excellent selection of wine. The experience doesn't come cheap, but every riyal is well-spent when the occasion calls for something special.
InterContinental Doha The City Onaiza **4015 8888**
intercontinental.com/dohathecity
Map **2 P2**

Sukar Pasha
Ottoman Lounge > *p.iv, 186, 353* Turkish

At first glance, this relaxing haunt may appear to be a shisha lounge. However, while the hubbly bubbly is certainly top-notch, it's the food that ends up stealing the show. Whether you go for one of the set menus or choose from the a la carte selection, you're in for a treat. Authentic and delicious, even the simple vegetable casserole is good enough to leave you begging for the recipe. The hot and cold mezzes are particularly highly-regarded among those in the know.

After your meal, sit back in one of the comfy armchairs and order a shisha to complete the experience.
Katara Cultural Village Al Gassar **4408 2000**
sukarpasha.qa
Map **1 K3**

T.G.I. Friday's American

This popular American theme restaurant offers a fun dining experience where friends and family can get together and enjoy good food, flowing drinks and a lively atmosphere. While eating is obviously the main focus, the square bar is always busy and a perfect spot to meet for a (non-alcoholic) drink before making for your table. If you're the first to arrive, the uniformed bar staff will keep you entertained, twirling bottles as they serve.
Landmark Mall Umm Lekhba **4488 7008**
tgifridays.com
Map **2 E1**

Taj Rasoi Indian

Serving specialities from around India, Taj Rasoi offers diners traditional dishes cooked with great skill. The mouthwatering menu of tandoori, curries and breads will leave guests impressed and full. The biryanis are slowly cooked and full of taste. Many dishes are also prepared gueridon – at the table – which is an art in itself, plus there is plenty of choice for vegetarians.
Doha Marriott Hotel Al Khulaifat **4429 8470**
marriott-doha.com
Map **2 V8**

Tajine Moroccan

Duck your head through the tiny front door and you'll feel like you're in a lavish 12th century palace in Fez. Dim light shines out of brass lamps and reflects off ornately carved wood trim, making this a perfect spot for a romantic night out or quiet evening with friends. The menu revolves around the traditional tagine – a covered clay pot used for both cooking and serving. Moroccan food tends to rely on spices rather than herbs, and the resulting flavour is earthy and mellow. None of the dishes are spectacular, but the setting is well worth it. Once finished with your meal, take a seat outside, order a shisha and watch the flow of shoppers in the equally traditional souk.
Souk Waqif Al Jasra **4435 5554**
Map **2 Q7**

Tangia Moroccan

Situated in the Wyndham Grand Regency Hotel, Tangia brings a taste of Marrakech to Doha. With only a few local restaurants serving Moroccan food, Tangia attracts diners in search of a spicy tagine or hearty couscous. Occupying a corner section of the hotel's lobby, this restaurant comprises several four-seater booths and tables, adorned with an eclectic

assortment of Moroccan glassware and crockery. Fez-capped waiters serve hit and miss cold vegetable and seafood salads, harissa soup, meaty tangines, vegetarian couscous and lamb kebabs.
Wyndham Grand Regency Doha Al Sadd **4434 3333**
wyndhamgrandregency.com
Map **2 K7**

The Tent   Middle Eastern
As soon as you enter The Tent, the traditional design of the furniture, the soft lighting and the aroma of shisha will awaken your senses to this truly Middle Eastern experience. Here you can sample delicious Arabian fare in real local style. The food is a great example of Arabian cooking, and if you are not familiar with this style of menu, the waiters are more than happy to recommend dishes. It's a good spot for a romantic evening or to relax after a long day, but reservations are recommended if you are planning to arrive after 22:00.
Al Bustan Hotel Slata **4432 8888**
albustanhotel-qa.com
Map **2 T7**

Thai Noodles   Thai
Tucked away in the heart of the souk area, you might need help finding this little piece of Thailand in Doha – but it's worth the effort. As you enter, you are greeted with smiles and the aromas of traditional Thai cooking. Open for breakfast, lunch and dinner, the extensive menu offers a choice of Thai dishes to eat in or take away. The popularity of this place speaks volumes for the deliciously tasting food.
Al Mahmal St, Nr Souq Aseiry Al Souq **4443 4220**
Map **2 R8**

Thai Snack   Thai
Cheap, fast and delicious, this tiny, basic restaurant serves some of the best Thai food in Doha. Though it is always teeming with customers, the staff are incredibly efficient, and meals are on the table within minutes of placing an order. Thai Snack's curries really shine out, as do their soups and sa la pao, delicious steamed buns filled with minced chicken and served with a sweet and sour dipping sauce. This eatery is great for a quick but enjoyable meal and perfect for takeaway (but call ahead!) during the busy work week.
Al Mirghab St, Off C Ring Rd Fereej Al Nasr **4432 9704**
Map **2 K10**

Tse Yang   Chinese
Tse Yang is heady mix of modern chic fused with traditional oriental charm. As you pass by the stylish bar area and through a corridor of mirrors illuminated with a red glow, you arrive into a large dining room with a stunning red chandelier as the focal point. The furniture is opulent and lavish and comparable

to the Forbidden City itself. The extensive menu includes everything from dim sum to Peking duck and the seafood specialities masterfully created by the non-English speaking, Chinese chef in the kitchen is exceptional. Be sure to step out of your comfort zone and ask for recommendations. If in doubt, the honey roasted chicken, deep fried squid and of course the Peking duck are all favourites here.
Porto Arabia The Pearl Qatar **4495 3876**
hdc-global.com
Map **1 M2**

Victoria   International
This tea lounge resembles a classic Victorian library with dark wood panelling and antique English and Arabic books lining one wall of the seating area. The atmosphere is quiet and refined, perfect for a traditional afternoon tea. Individual tea pots and strainers are presented beautifully, and the accompanying stand of treatsranging from mini quiches and sandwiches to dainty pastriessubstantial enough for two people to share. The comfortable sofas invite to while away an entire afternoon over the classy tea service.
Grand Heritage Doha Hotel & Spa Baaya **4445 5555**
grandheritagedoha.com
Map **2 A10**

Wok Mee Noodle House   Asian
Located in the Mövenpick tower in West Bay, this restaurant offers an impressive medley of dishes with origins ranging from Thailand, Vietnam, Japan, China and Malaysia. Modern yet casual, it offers an open view kitchen where you can see the international chef team at work. The menu features many crowd-pleasing dishes from dim sum and pad thai to soups, noodle bowls and savoury main dish specials. Wok Mee also offers unique, Asian-influenced mocktails and speciality dishes ideal for sharing with two people or more. The friendly service is excellent and the prices are on point for quality Asian cuisine.
Movenpick Tower & Suites Doha Al Dafna **4496 6666**
moevenpick-hotels.com
Map **2 R2**

Yen Sushi Bar > p.199, 338   Japanese
Located in La Cigale's traiteur (food hall), this intimate sushi bar can accommodate just 18 people around its rotating belt. Diners can peer over the moving stream of sashimi and watch the masterful chefs prepare some of the best sushi in town underneath fibre optic lighting. Ultra-contemporary bar stools complete the futuristic setting. A few tables line the perimeter of the bar, but sit up close to enjoy the full experience.
La Cigale Hotel Fereej Bin Mahmoud **4428 8888**
lacigalehotel.com
Map **2 M9**

Zaman Restaurant   **Lebanese**

This Lebanese restaurant at the top of the Millennium Hotel doesn't have the views that you might expect from such a lofty address; more fittingly, perhaps it does have a view, but just not the windows for seeing it. This said, the restaurant's style is pleasing with typically Arabian arches and a rustic feel. And as long as you arrive without the expectation of sweeping views, you won't be disappointed: the tasty food selection includes all essential Levantine classics from Lebanese mezze to mixed grills. Everything is served in sizeable portions. Dine on Arabian time and show up late in the evening, or you may find yourself enjoying the entire restaurant and the staff's attentive service all to yourself.

Millennium Hotel Doha Al Sadd **4424 7367**
millenniumhotels.com
Map **2 K8**

BARS, PUBS & CLUBS

Admiral's Club   **Bar**

Set away from the hotel in a separate building by the marina, Admiral's is a popular party spot on Thursdays and Fridays. Things don't really get going until around 22:00, but earlier in the evening it's a popular spot for shisha. During the cooler months, you'll also get to enjoy a wonderful terrace overlooking the yachts moored below in the marina. The dress code is described as 'elegant,' but smart jeans are ok. On Thursday nights, the theme is hip-hop, while Arabian beats take over on Fridays when the whole place fills with Doha's Lebanese party crowd.

The Ritz-Carlton, Doha Al Gassar **4484 8000**
ritzcarlton.com
Map **1 K1**

Cigar Lounge   **Cigar Bar**

Appropriately dark and stately, this classic cigar lounge appeals to both the aficionado and the occasional smoker. After setting up camp in one of the deep leather chairs, choose from an impressive collection of cigars or select one of the in-house options, which are rolled on the spot. Don't miss the uniquely designed ceiling fans that sway gently back and forth. Thankfully for any non-smoking companions, a smoke-free filtration system only leaves the smell of fine leather and rich tobacco.

Sharq Village & Spa Al Khulaifat **4425 6666**
sharqvillage.com
Map **2 U8**

Crystal   **Bar**

A welcome addition to Doha's bar scene, Crystal Lounge is dark and funky. Black Baccarat chandeliers and bold prints in moody colours set the tone, and the capable bar staff serve up a selection of intriguing cocktails. Quiet on nights earlier in the week, the bar's full space is opened up at the weekends and is crammed with Doha's bold and beautiful, mixing and mingling to the DJ's soundtrack. It's a place to be seen, so make sure you dress to impress.

W Doha Hotel & Residences Al Dafna **4453 5000**
crystaldoha.com
Map **2 Q1**

Habanos   **Cigar Bar**

With rich reds and dark mahogany, Habanos has an intimate and cosy feel. The cocktails are divine, and little touches like the complimentary snacks (including possibly the best stuffed olives in Qatar) add to the experience. Given that this is a cigar lounge, smokers are in for a treat, of course. The bar has its very own 'cigar butler' who will make recommendations and even cut and light cigars for you. One of Doha's favourite hangouts for the in-crowd, Habanos makes a good starting point for a party night out or the perfect place to wind up in the wee hours for that one last drink or smoke.

The Ritz-Carlton, Doha Al Gassar **4484 8000**
ritzcarlton.com
Map **1 K1**

Hive *> p.201*   **Bar**

The Hive's chic, relaxed atmosphere and convenient West Bay location make it a perfect choice for after-work drinks with friends. Two televisions screen sports channels so footie fans can also catch a match over a glass or two. The drinks aren't the cheapest in town, but visit on a Wednesday to take advantage of the weekly wine and cheese night, when QR 180 buys you three glasses of grape as well all the French cheese you can eat. On Tuesdays, the ladies enjoy a buy-one-get-one-free deal.

InterContinental Doha The City Onaiza **4015 8888**
intercontinental.com/dohathecity
Map **2 P2**

The Irish Harp   **Bar**

Unlike many Irish bars around the world, the Irish Harp holds back on twee paraphernalia, instead letting the message of good food, good drinks and good company speak for itself. That said, the old-fashioned bar and cabinets full of tat give you the right impression of where you are, but there's not a leprechaun or stolen road sign in sight. One of the few places in Doha where you can come as you are, Irish Harp is a welcome, low key joint, and for this reason, is one of the consistently busiest bars around.

Sheraton Doha Resort & Convention Hotel Al Dafna **4485 4444**
irishharpdoha.com
Map **2 R3**

Jazz Up Bar   **Bar**

Fans of jazz and chilled out vibes will be right at home at the Mövenpick's intimate bar. The cocktail menu features some interesting concoctions to indulge in while humming to the jazzy tunes and if you get a little peckish, a good selection of light bites is also on offer.

Mövenpick Hotel Doha Slata **4429 1111**
moevenpick-hotels.com
Map **2 S7**

Lava   **Bar**

One of the bars that have really managed to heat up Doha's party scene, Lava always pulls a good crowd. Fiery orange lighting sets the scene and whether a live band or a DJ is in charge of the sounds, it won't take long for the bar to fill up. Service can be a bit slow and there's not much room for the table servers to squeeze through if you're lucky enough to have bagged a seat. The best bet is therefore to join the lively crowd on the dancefloor. If you're in need of room to breathe, head outside to the terrace and enjoy a spectacular view of West Bay.

InterContinental Doha Al Gassar **4484 4444**
intercontinental.com/doha
Map **1 K3**

The Library Bar & Cigar Lounge   **Bar**

Cigars, snacks and a whole lot of luxury are what you'll find when you enter the Library Bar. Surrounded by leather buttoned chairs and comfy sofas, you can't help but relax. Abstract art hanging from the dark wood walls adds to the ambience of the gentlemen's club setting. Take your pick from the cigar and food menus while enjoying the splendid sea views and music by the pianist who plays every night from 20:00 until midnight.

Four Seasons Hotel Al Dafna **4494 8888**
fourseasons.com/doha
Map **2 R2**

The Lounge > p.81   **Bar**

This upscale bar's dark walls, minimalist decor and dim lighting create a sophisticated setting for drinks and light bites. Smooth cocktails, savoury nibbles and delectable desserts grace the menu, while the

German Garden

The latest addition to the Doha Marriott, the German Garden (4429 8499) offers the finest Bavarian brews, big screen TVs to catch the latest sporting action and more bratwurst and sauerkraut than you could humanly hope to consume. It's set to be a cracking venue for Oktoberfest later in the year.

Pearl Lounge Club

resident pianist's renditions of George Gershwin and Irving Berlin add to the elegantly moody vibe. The tasting menu is perfect for groups of two or more looking to share some late-night nosh: think tasty mini cheeseburgers, tenderly grilled kebabs and flawlessly roasted eggplants on top of mozzarella. The chocolate fondant deserves a special mention among the many temptations on the Sweet Bites menu.

Kempinski Residences & Suites Al Dafna **4405 3333**
kempinski-residences.com
Map **2 Q1**

Madison Piano Bar > p.199, 338   **Bar**

Still relatively new, Madison is one of the hottest late-night bars in the city. Along with regular live music, the bar/club hosts popular Arabian singers every two months or so. A vaulted, fibre-optic laden ceiling hovers over fashionable media types lounging in red leather chairs – a combination reeking of new money, elite socialites and expensive tastes. Drinks aren't cheap, and tables must be reserved if you are looking to be there on weekend nights, but if you want to be seen and be a part of the in-crowd, then this is the place to be.

La Cigale Hotel Fereej Bin Mahmoud **4428 8888**
lacigalehotel.com
Map **2 M9**

Pearl Lounge Club   **Bar**

This smart club has a reputation for mixing a good cocktail and insiders consider its Cosmopolitan to be second to none. For those that like to nibble while they drink the pink, the Asian influenced bar snacks are loved by all. It is completely separate from the Marriott hotel and so has its own identity, playing ambient music early evening then switching to a variety of styles on different nights, including salsa,

house and Arabian beats. The dress code is more relaxed over the summer, but usually men in jeans can expect to be turned away.
Doha Marriott Hotel Al Khulaifat **4429 8444**
marriott-doha.com
Map **2 V8**

Qube   Nightclub
This cavernous nightclub, buried deep in the Radisson Blu, is the largest club in Doha. It offers a mixture of live music, visiting DJs – including a hook-up with London's Ministry of Sound – and has special nights for hip-hop, UK dance and Indian music. It's got a VIP area and Doha's longest bar. The entry fee usually includes your first drink. Ladies get in free, and there's a ban on shorts, sandals (for men) and under 21s.
Radisson Blu Hotel, Doha Rawdat Al Khail **4428 1555**
radissonblu.com
Map **2 N10**

Seven > p.199, 338   Nightclub
With an all-white decor, smoke machines and thumping beats, this club boasts an unashamedly showy Euro-pop vibe. The resident DJ's house tunes keep the revellers going on the club's sunken dancefloor, as do the tasty (if somewhat pricey) cocktails; free soda is served to those who opt for whole bottles. The price of an annual membership card (QR 100) is offset against the QR 200 entrance fee.
La Cigale Hotel Fereej Bin Mahmoud **4428 8888**
lacigalehotel.com
Map **2 M9**

Sky View Bar > p.199, 338   Bar
This is one of the trendiest bars in Doha. Located on the 15th floor of La Cigale, the aptly name Sky View Bar boasts impressive skyline vistas, and a resident DJ adds to the buzz. Granted, it is a bit cramped, but no one seems to mind – this is where you'll find the beautiful people hanging out. The drinks list includes a good range of cocktails, beers and some fun surprises like jelly shots. Light snacks, including some tasty sushi and sashimi, are also served. It's recommended to book ahead of time if you'd like a table.
La Cigale Hotel Fereej Bin Mahmoud **4428 8888**
lacigalehotel.com
Map **2 M9**

Wahm   Bar
Wahm is advertised around town as the W Hotel's pool bar, but to call it such is to do it a great disservice. True, there is a pool, which at night is lit from below in the W's signature pinks and purples, but it's the indoor and outdoor modern majlis seating and laidback vibe that makes Wahm a venue in itself. The contemporary Arabian theme continues on through to the mezze snacks on offer and to the vibrantly coloured Oriental decor that kits out the venue. Settle down to some shisha, chilled grooves and the company of good friends in an alfresco cabana and you'll more than likely never want to leave.
W Doha Hotel & Residences Al Dafna **4453 5000**
wahmdoha.com
Map **2 Q1**

Sky View Bar

Explorer Products

Residents' Guides

Abu Dhabi — Azerbaijan — Dubai — Oman — Qatar

Mini Visitors' Guides

Abu Dhabi — Baku — Bahrain — Dubai — Qatar — Sharjah

Photography Books & Calendars

IMAGES of ABU DHABI — IMAGES of DUBAI — TELLING TALES — dubai a view from above

Dubai DISCOVERED — dubai a day above the city — IMPRESSIONS DUBAI — IMPRESSIONS ABU DHABI — IMPRESSIONS QATAR

ABU DHABI 2013 — QATAR 2013 — ARABIA 2013 — Dubai 2013 — Dubai 2013 / 2013 Abu Dhabi

Maps

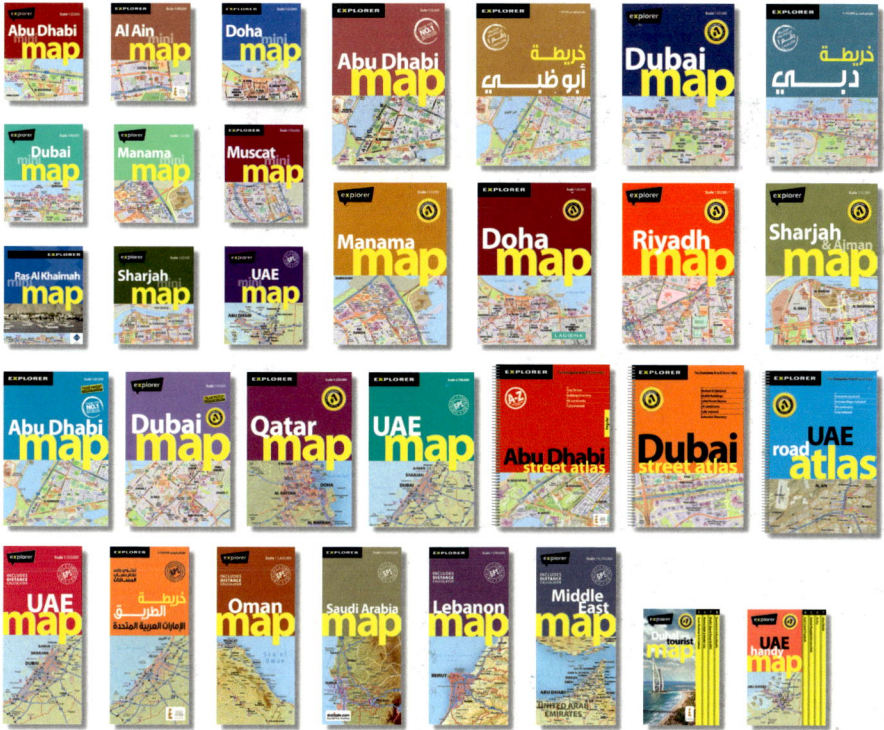

Adventure & Lifestyle Guides

Qatar Country Map

KINGDOM OF BAHRAIN

Ruwais
Madinat Al Shamal
Al Khuwair Hissan
Friendship Bridge (u/c)
Zubarah Fort
AL SHAMAL
Al Ghariyah Resort
Fuwairit
Arabian Gulf

Huwailah
Ras Laffan

Hidd Al Jamal

Al Ghuwairiya
Highland Service Area
AL KHOR
14
Dhakira
Al Khor
1
14
Sultan Beach Resort

QATAR

Hawar Islands (BAHRAIN)

Al Jumailiya
Simaismah

Ras Abruk Peninsula
AL DAAYEN
Jazirat al Mikyar

Jinan Island
UMM SLAL
Gulf of Bahrain
Zekrit
Hole in the Wall
Umm Slal Ali
Lusail Int'l Circuit
Barzan Towers
1A

Camel Race Track
Dukhan
3
Umm Salal Mohammed
Al Jazirah al Aliyah
The Pearl Qatar
Al Nasraniyah
Umm Salal Fort
Al Jazirah as Safiliyah
Al Shihaniyah
Al Wabrah Farm
Shk Faisal Museum
Al Wabrah
Al Wajbah Fort
DOHA
Banana Island

Rawdat Rashed
Umm Bab
AL RAYYAN
39
Drag Racing Track
Al Wakra
Al Udeid Army Camp
Al Wukair
7
5
Satellite Earth Station
55

Al Karaanah
Singing Sand Dune
Mesaieed
Jazirat al Bushayriyah

Jazirat Unaybir
Al Kharrarah
AL WAKRA
Sealine Beach Resort

5
85
Dohat Salwa

Salwa
Abu Samra
QATAR
SAUDI ARABIA
Jazirat al Ashat
Arabian Gulf

KINGDOM OF SAUDI ARABIA
Khor Al Udaid
Al Qaffay Island

© Explorer Group Ltd. 2012

This map is not an authority on international and administrative boundaries

0   20 km   N

388   Qatar Explorer

Qatar Explorer – 5th Edition

Lead editor Jo Iivonen
Editorial team Charlie Scott, Laura Coughlin, Matt Warnock, Rachel McArthur
Freelance contributions by Christine Gerber Rutt, Frances Gillespe, Katy Gillett, Mike Crosby, Shabina Khatri
Proofread by Max Tuttle
Data managed by Amapola Castillo, Derrick Pereira, Ingrid Cupido
Sales by Laura Zuffova
Designed by Ieyad Charaf, Jayde Fernandes, Pete Maloney, Shawn Zuzarte
Maps by Noushad Madathil, Zainudheen Madathil
Photographs by Henry Hilos, Joe Chua Agdeppa, Pamela Grist, Pete Maloney, Victor Romero

Publishing

Publisher Alistair MacKenzie
Associate Publisher Claire England

Editorial

Managing Editor Consumer Publishing Matt Warnock
Editor Jo Iivonen
Corporate Editor Charlie Scott
Digital Projects Editor Rachel McArthur
Web Editor Laura Coughlin
Production Manager Therese Theron
Production Coordinator Kathryn Calderon
Editorial Assistants Amapola Castillo, Ingrid Cupido

Design & Photography

Creative Director Pete Maloney
Art Director Ieyad Charaf
Contract Publishing Manager Chris Goldstraw
Designer Michael Estrada
Junior Designers Didith Hapiz, M. Shakkeer
Layout Manager Jayde Fernandes
Layout Designers Mansoor Ahmed, Shawn Zuzarte
Cartography Manager Zainudheen Madathil
Cartographer Noushad Madathil
Photography Manager Pamela Grist
Image Editor Henry Hilos

Sales & Marketing

Group Media Sales Manager Peter Saxby
Media Sales Area Managers Adam Smith, Bryan Anes, Dominic Keegan, Laura Zuffova, Sabrina Ahmed
Digital Sales Area Manager James Gaubert
Business Development Manager Pouneh Hafizi
Corporate Solutions Account Manager Vibeke Nurberg
Group Marketing & PR Manager Lindsay West
Senior Marketing Executive Stuart L. Cunningham
Sales & Marketing Assistant Shedan Ebona
Group Retail Sales Manager Ivan Rodrigues
Retail Sales Coordinator Michelle Mascarenhas
Retail Sales Area Supervisors Ahmed Mainodin, Firos Khan
Retail Sales Merchandisers Johny Mathew, Shan Kumar
Retail Sales Drivers Shabsir Madathil, Najumudeen K.I., Sujeer Khan
Warehouse Assistant Mohamed Haji

Finance & Administration

Administration Manager Fiona Hepher
Admin Assistant Joy San Buenaventura
Accountant Cherry Enriquez
Accounts Assistants Jeanette Carino Enecillo, Joy Bermejo Belza, Sunil Suvarna
Public Relations Officer Rafi Jamal
Office Assistant Shafeer Ahamed

IT & Digital Solutions

Digital Solutions Manager Derrick Pereira
IT Manager R. Ajay

Contact Us

General Enquiries

We'd love to hear your thoughts and answer any questions you have about this book or any other Explorer product. Contact us at **info@askexplorer.com**

Careers

If you fancy yourself as an Explorer, send your CV (stating the position you're interested in) to **jobs@askexplorer.com**

Contract Publishing

For enquiries about Explorer's Contract Publishing arm and design services contact **contracts@askexplorer.com**

PR & Marketing

For PR and marketing enquiries contact **marketing@askexplorer.com**

Corporate Sales & Licensing

For bulk sales and customisation options, as well as licensing of this book or any Explorer product, contact **leads@askexplorer.com**

Advertising & Sponsorship

For advertising and sponsorship, contact **sales@askexplorer.com**

Explorer Publishing & Distribution
PO Box 34275, Dubai, United Arab Emirates
askexplorer.com

Phone: +971 (0)4 340 8805
Fax: +971 (0)4 340 8806

Useful Numbers

Embassies & Consulates

Bahrain	4483 9362
Brazil	4483 8812
Brunei	4483 1956
China	4493 4203
Cyprus	4493 4390
Egypt	4483 2555
France	4483 2283
Germany	4487 6959
India	4467 2021
Indonesia	4465 7945
Iran	4483 5300
Italy	4483 1828
Japan	4484 0888
Jordan	4483 2202
Kuwait	4483 2111
Lebanon	4493 3330
Libya	4442 1776
Malaysia	4483 6463
Oman	4493 1910
Pakistan	4483 2525
Philippines	4483 1585
Romania	4493 4848
Russia	4483 6231
Saudi Arabia	4483 2030
South Africa	4485 7111
South Korea	4483 2238
Spain	4484 4104
Sri Lanka	4467 7627
Sudan	4483 1508
Syria	4483 1844
Thailand	4493 4426
Tunisia	4483 2645
Turkey	4495 1300
United Arab Emirates	4483 8880
United Kingdom	4442 1991
United States America	4488 4101

24 Hour Pharmacies

Al Bateel Pharmacy	4436 6610
Al Noor Pharmacy	4450 5625
Khulood Pharmacy	4487 7784

Emergency Services

Emergency Services (Police, Fire, Ambulance)	999
Electricity & Water Emergency	991
Vehicle Recovery (Arabian Allied Association)	4413 0970

Airport Information

Doha International Airport

Lost & Found	4462 6531
Enquiries	4465 6666
Airport Immigration/Passport Control	4462 1751

A&E Departments

American Hospital (private)	4442 1999
Al Ahli Hospital (private)	4489 8888
Doha Clinic Hospital (private)	4435 5999
Hamad General Hospital (government)	4439 4444
Women's Hospital (government)	4439 6666
Pediatric Emergency Center	4439 2948

Directory

Directory Assistance	180
Qatar International Dialling Code	+974
Qtel	111
Vodafone	800 7111
Speaking clock (English)	140
Weather Information	4465 6590

Limousine Operators

Doha Limousine	4483 9999
Elite Limousine	4442 6184
Fox Limousines	4462 2777
Qatar Limousine	4486 8688